Stories of Expressionism in Mannheim

Kirchner, Lehmbruck, Nolde.

Geschichten des Expressionismus in Mannheim

Deutscher Kunstverlag

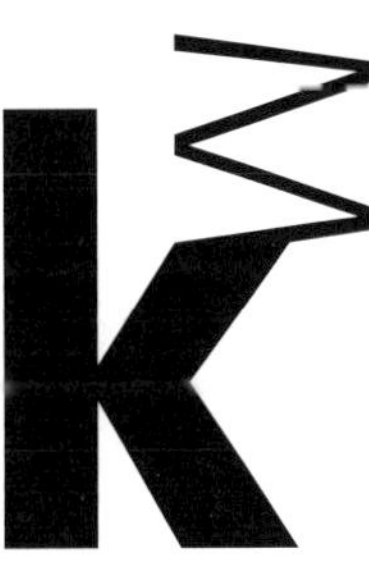

Gefördert von / *Supported by*

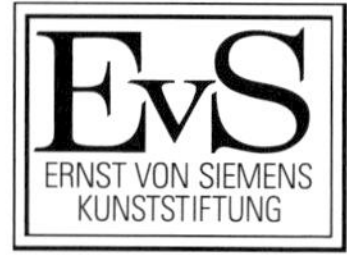

Kirchner, Lehmbruck, Nolde.

Geschichten des Expressionismus in Mannheim

Stories of Expressionism in Mannheim

Herausgegeben von / *edited by*
Luisa Heese und / *and* Johan Holten

6 Foreword
7 **Vorwort**
Johan Holten

10 The Kunsthalle Mannheim and Expressionism:
People, Exhibitions, Collections, Acquisitions, Losses, Compensation
Die Kunsthalle Mannheim und der Expressionismus:
Menschen, Ausstellungen, Sammlungen, Ankäufe, Verluste, Wiedergutmachung
Inge Herold

40 "In Hans Poelzig's Luftreich":
On the Porcelain and Majolica Exhibition at the Kunsthalle Mannheim in 1921
„In Hans Poelzigs Luftreich":
über die Ausstellung Porzellan und Majolika 1921 in der Kunsthalle Mannheim
Mathias Listl

66 Walter Passarge:
Director of the Kunsthalle Mannheim during National Socialism
Walter Passarge:
Direktor der Kunsthalle Mannheim während des Nationalsozialismus
Hannah Krause

78 Catalogue / **Katalog**

80 The Expressive Power of Pure Form:
Expressionist Sculpture
Die Ausdruckskraft der reinen Form:
Skulptur des Expressionismus
Luisa Heese

90 Wilhelm Lehmbruck and Sally Falk:
"a sculptor whose silent majesty this collector loved"
Wilhelm Lehmbruck und Sally Falk:
„ein Bildhauer, dessen schweigsame Hoheit dieser Sammler liebte"
Luisa Heese

104 New Religious Art:
Mannheim's Contribution to Expressionism
Neue religiöse Kunst:
Mannheims Beitrag zum Expressionismus
Ursula Drahoss

114 Alfred Flechtheim, Herbert Tannenbaum, and Rudolf Probst:
Art Dealers for Mannheim
Alfred Flechtheim, Herbert Tannenbaum und Rudolf Probst:
Kunsthändler für Mannheim
Dorotea Lorenz

124 Rosa Schapire:
Promoter of Expressionism
Rosa Schapire:
Förderin des Expressionismus
Dorotea Lorenz

134 Private Collections of Expressionist Art in Mannheim:
The Fuchs-Werle Collection
Privatsammlungen expressionistischer Kunst in Mannheim:
die Sammlung Fuchs-Werle
Luisa Heese

156 The Mannheim Graphic Arts Collection and Its Focus
on Expressionist Woodcuts
**Die Mannheimer Grafiksammlung und ihr Schwerpunkt
auf dem expressionistischen Holzschnitt**
Ursula Drahoss

164 Landscape und Cityscape in Expressionist Art
Landschaft und Großstadt in der Kunst des Expressionismus
Ursula Drahoss

180 Expression and Alienation:
The Portrait
**Ausdruck und Verfremdung:
das Porträt**
Ursula Drahoss

190 Defamation, Confiscation, Resale:
The Expressionism Collection of the Kunsthalle Mannheim under National Socialism
**Diffamierung, Beschlagnahmung, Verwertung:
die Expressionismus-Sammlung der Kunsthalle Mannheim
im Nationalsozialismus**
Luisa Heese

200 "Express your inner experience in the most concise form":
The Sculptor Milly Steger
**„Bringe dein inneres Erleben in knappster Form zum Ausdruck":
die Bildhauerin Milly Steger**
Luisa Heese

208 Depicting the Body:
Nude and Child Models in Brücke Art
**Körperdarstellungen:
Akt- und Kindermodelle in der Brücke-Kunst**
Dorotea Lorenz

220 The Encounter with the "Foreign":
Expressionist Artists between Fascination and Colonial Appropriation
**Die Begegnung mit dem ‚Fremden':
Künstler*innen des Expressionismus zwischen Faszination und
kolonialer Aneignung**
Dorotea Lorenz

232 "An immense gentleness and gravity radiate from her human and animal bodies":
The Artist Maria Uhden
**„Eine ungeheure Sanftmut und Erdschwere strömt aus den Körpern
von Mensch und Tier":
die Künstlerin Maria Uhden**
Dorotea Lorenz

238 The Reception of Expressionism in Mannheim after 1945 up to the Present
Die Rezeption des Expressionismus in Mannheim nach 1945 bis heute
Ursula Drahoss

246 Appendix / **Anhang**
256 Colophon / **Impressum**

Foreword

Johan Holten

With the exhibition *Kirchner, Lehmbruck, Nolde. Stories of Expressionism in Mannheim*, the Kunsthalle Mannheim is dedicating itself to an important chapter in the history of its own collection. Even before World War I, under the direction of Fritz Wichert and Gustav Friedrich Hartlaub, the Kunsthalle was one of the first museums in Germany to acquire and present works by Expressionist artists. They included two of those who have lent their names to the current exhibition—Ernst Ludwig Kirchner and Emil Nolde—but also Erich Heckel, Max Pechstein, Franz Marc, and many others. With their openness to contemporary art, Wichert and Hartlaub set new standards—a decision that was not always uncontroversial. At a time when the public was skeptical about expressive visual language, they defended the artistic radicalness of Expressionism as an intellectual and social project. One expression of this was the well-regarded exhibition *Neue religiöse Kunst* (New Religious Art) of 1918—a milestone in the establishment of Expressionism in German museums.

The current exhibition sheds light not only on the early exhibiting and collecting activities of the Kunsthalle but also their tragic turning point: in 1933, Gustav Friedrich Hartlaub was removed from his office in the face of then-dominant National Socialist cultural policy, and the confiscation of several hundred works followed in 1937. They included numerous major works of Expressionism, only a few of which could be reacquired after 1945. That several of these works are now returning to Mannheim temporarily as loans from museums in Basel, Copenhagen, Berlin, and Duisburg is extremely fortunate.

Another focus of the exhibition is on Expressionist sculpture—with Wilhelm Lehmbruck as a central figure. The Kunsthalle dedicated his first solo exhibition in a museum already in 1916. In 1921, the museum received an outstanding set of modern sculptures as a generous donation from the German Jewish patron of the arts Sally Falk, including Lehmbruck's *Kniende* (Kneeling Woman) as well as important works by Georg Kolbe and Edwin Scharff. Supplemented by additional loans, the exhibition shows the special relationship between Lehmbruck and the Falks. The artist immortalized Adèle and Sally Falk in sculpture, drawing, and printmaking. The exhibition also addresses

Vorwort

Johan Holten

Mit der Ausstellung *Kirchner, Lehmbruck, Nolde. Geschichten des Expressionismus in Mannheim* widmet sich die Kunsthalle Mannheim einem bedeutenden Kapitel ihrer eigenen Sammlungsgeschichte. Bereits in den Jahren vor dem Ersten Weltkrieg gehörte die Kunsthalle unter der Leitung von Fritz Wichert und Gustav Friedrich Hartlaub zu den ersten Museen in Deutschland, die Werke expressionistischer Künstler erwarben und präsentierten. Dazu gehörten die Namensgeber der aktuellen Ausstellung, Ernst Ludwig Kirchner und Emil Nolde, aber auch Erich Heckel, Max Pechstein, Franz Marc und viele andere. Mit dieser Öffnung zur zeitgenössischen Kunst setzten Wichert und Hartlaub Maßstäbe – eine Entscheidung, die nicht immer unumstritten war. In einer Zeit, in der die Öffentlichkeit der expressiven Bildsprache skeptisch gegenüberstand, verteidigten sie die künstlerische Radikalität des Expressionismus als geistiges und gesellschaftliches Projekt. Ausdruck dessen war unter anderem die viel beachtete Ausstellung *Neue religiöse Kunst* von 1918 – ein Meilenstein für die museale Etablierung des Expressionismus in Deutschland.

Die aktuelle Ausstellung beleuchtet nicht nur die frühen Ausstellungs- und Sammlungsaktivitäten der Kunsthalle, sondern auch deren tragischen Einschnitt: 1933 wurde Gustav Friedrich Hartlaub angesichts der nun herrschenden NS-Kulturpolitik seines Amtes enthoben, 1937 folgte die Beschlagnahmung mehrerer hundert Werke. Darunter befanden sich zahlreiche Hauptwerke des Expressionismus, von denen nur wenige nach 1945 zurückerworben werden konnten. Dass einige dieser Werke nun als Leihgaben aus Museen in Basel, Kopenhagen, Berlin und Duisburg temporär nach Mannheim zurückkehren, ist ein großes Glück.

Ein weiterer Schwerpunkt der Ausstellung liegt auf der expressionistischen Skulptur – mit Wilhelm Lehmbruck als zentraler Figur. Ihm widmete die Kunsthalle bereits 1916 eine erste museale Einzelausstellung. 1921 erhielt das Museum durch die großzügige Schenkung des jüdischen Mäzens Sally Falk ein herausragendes Konvolut moderner Skulptur, das Lehmbrucks *Kniende* ebenso umfasste wie bedeutende Werke von Georg Kolbe und Edwin Scharff. Ergänzt um weitere Leihgaben zeigen wir die besondere Beziehung zwischen Lehmbruck und dem Ehepaar Falk. Der Künstler hat Adèle

the importance of the Mannheim entrepreneur Falk for the Kunsthalle, because his donation of this collection of sculptures represented a crucial impulse for its evolution.

In addition to the Kunsthalle's collection, Expressionism shaped important private collections in Mannheim. Fourteen loans from the Fuchs-Werle Collection are being presented equally alongside the Kunsthalle's holdings so that visitors can discover the correspondences in the subject matter and complementary facets of the two collections. It is a great pleasure for me to express here my most sincere gratitude to the Fuchs-Werle family for their extraordinary support of this exhibition and their indefatigable commitment to the Kunsthalle. In addition, Gabriele Graf deserves thanks for loans that supplement significant elements of the Lehmbruck ensemble, as do all the other private collectors in Mannheim.

At the same time, the exhibition is intended to contribute to critical reflection. A hundred years later, our view of central aspects of Expressionist art has changed. The depiction of and fascination with the "foreign" as well as the acquisition of non-European art raises questions from today's perspective that were not yet asked at the time. Furthermore, their approach to female nude models, some of whom were very young, and the closeness of some of the artists to the National Socialist regime—as in Emil Nolde's case—should also be examined critically. The marginalized role of women artists in that era and the epoch that followed deserves particular attention. The extensive holdings of the Kunsthalle's Graphic Arts Collection provide an excellent source for all of these deliberations and for assessing the outstanding graphic qualities of Expressionism.

The exhibition is thus not only a look backward but also a determination of its position now: it tells of collecting and preserving, of pioneering spirit and renewal, of loss, reacquisition, and reevaluation. One year after the *New Objectivity* centennial, the Kunsthalle is once again showing how tightly art, society, and history are interwoven—and how important and enriching it can be to expose these interrelations.

Our special gratitude is owed to the Hector Stiftungen, the circle of donors to the Stiftung Kunsthalle Mannheim; to the Ernst-Ludwig-Seibert-Stiftung; to the Fontana Stiftung; to the Ernst von Siemens Kunststiftung; and to the Kulturstiftung Franz Dieter und Michaela Kaldewei zur Förderung des deutschen Expressionismus, without whose support it would not have been possible to realize this exhibition. In addition, I wish to express my sincere thanks to the curatorial team responsible for the exhibition. Before her departure, Dr. Inge Herold laid the groundwork for the concept, which was then implemented by Luisa Heese, Dr. Ursula Drahoss, and Dorotea Lorenz in collaboration with me. I would also like to thank all the members of the Kunsthalle team who have contributed to the realization of this exhibition. My particular gratitude is due to all the authors of the catalogue, especially to Dr. Mathias Listl and Hannah Krause, as well as the Deutscher Kunstverlag team. Finally, my sincere thanks go to all private and institutional lenders.

Johan Holten
Director, Kunsthalle Mannheim

und Sally Falk in Skulptur, Zeichnung und Druckgrafik verewigt. Darüber hinaus wird die Bedeutung des Mannheimer Unternehmers Falk für die Kunsthalle thematisiert, da seine Schenkung der Skulpturensammlung der Kunsthalle den entscheidenden Impuls für deren Entwicklung gab. Auch außerhalb der Sammlung der Kunsthalle hat der Expressionismus bedeutsame Privatsammlungen in Mannheim geprägt. Vierzehn Leihgaben aus der Sammlung Fuchs-Werle werden gleichberechtigt neben den Beständen der Kunsthalle präsentiert, sodass Besucher*innen die inhaltlichen Korrespondenzen und komplementären Facetten beider Sammlungen entdecken können. Es ist mir eine große Freude, an dieser Stelle der Familie Fuchs-Werle meinen aufrichtigsten Dank für ihre außerordentliche Unterstützung dieser Ausstellung sowie ihr unermüdliches Engagement für die Kunsthalle zum Ausdruck zu bringen. Dank gebührt auch Gabriele Graf für die Leihgaben, die signifikante Elemente des Lehmbruck-Ensembles ergänzen, sowie allen weiteren Mannheimer Privatsammlungen.

Zugleich versteht sich die Ausstellung als Beitrag zur kritischen Reflexion. Hundert Jahre nach ihrer Entstehung hat sich unser Blick auf zentrale Aspekte der expressionistischen Kunst verändert. Die Darstellung und Faszination des ‚Fremden‘ sowie die Aneignung nicht-europäischer Kunst werfen aus heutiger Sicht Fragen auf, die zur damaligen Zeit noch nicht gestellt wurden. Auch ist der Umgang mit zum Teil sehr jungen weiblichen Aktmodellen sowie die Nähe einzelner Kunstschaffender zum NS-Regime – wie im Fall Emil Noldes – kritisch zu betrachten. Die marginalisierte Rolle von Künstlerinnen in der damaligen Zeit sowie in der darauffolgenden Epoche bedarf besonderer Aufmerksamkeit. Die umfangreichen Bestände der Graphischen Sammlung der Kunsthalle bieten einen ausgezeichneten Fundus für all diese Betrachtungen sowie für die Würdigung der herausragenden grafischen Qualitäten des Expressionismus.

Die Ausstellung ist somit nicht nur Rückblick, sondern auch Standortbestimmung: Sie erzählt von Sammeln und Bewahren, von Pioniergeist und Erneuerung, von Verlust, Wiederaneignung und Neubewertung. Ein Jahr nach dem Jahrhundertjubiläum der *Neuen Sachlichkeit* zeigt die Kunsthalle erneut, wie eng Kunst, Gesellschaft und Geschichte miteinander verwoben sind – und wie wichtig und bereichernd es sein kann, diese Verflechtungen offenzulegen.

Unser besonderer Dank gebührt den Hector Stiftungen, dem Stifterkreis der Stiftung Kunsthalle Mannheim, der Ernst-Ludwig-Seibert-Stiftung, der Fontana Stiftung, der Ernst von Siemens Kunststiftung sowie der Kulturstiftung Franz Dieter und Michaela Kaldewei zur Förderung des deutschen Expressionismus, ohne deren Unterstützung die Realisierung dieser Ausstellung nicht möglich gewesen wäre. Zudem gilt es, dem kuratorischen Team, das für die Ausstellung verantwortlich zeichnet, meinen aufrichtigen Dank auszusprechen. Vor ihrem Ausscheiden hat Dr. Inge Herold die Grundlagen des Konzepts gelegt, das in der Folge von Luisa Heese, Dr. Ursula Drahoss und Dorotea Lorenz in Zusammenarbeit mit mir umgesetzt wurde. Bedanken möchte ich mich ebenso bei allen Mitarbeiter*innen des Teams der Kunsthalle, die zur Realisierung dieser Ausstellung beigetragen haben. Mein besonderer Dank gebührt allen Autor*innen des Katalogs, vor allem Dr. Mathias Listl und Hannah Krause, sowie dem Team des Deutschen Kunstverlags. Abschließend gilt mein herzlicher Dank allen privaten und institutionellen Leihgebern.

Johan Holten
Direktor Kunsthalle Mannheim

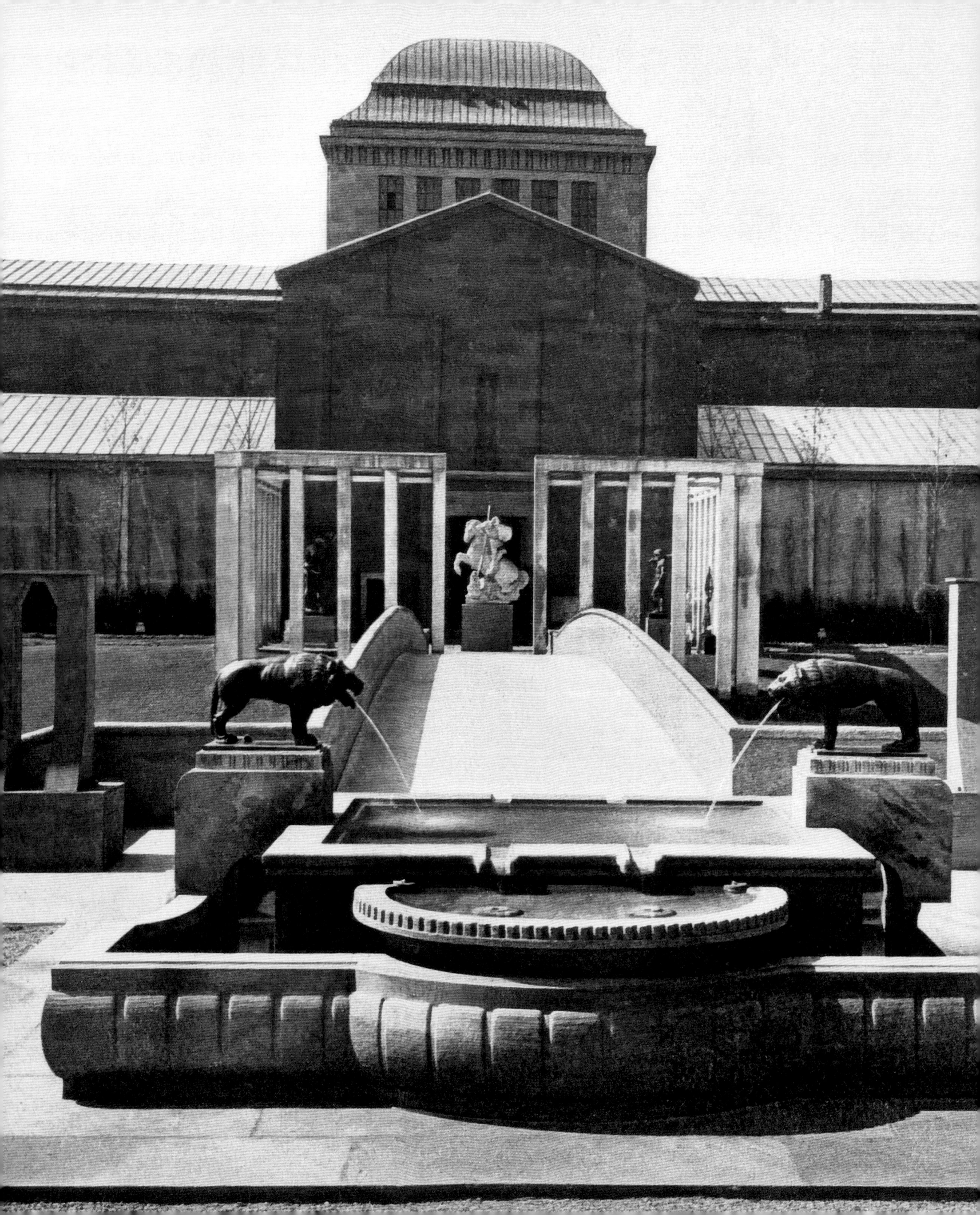

Die Kunsthalle Mannheim und der Expressionismus: Menschen, Ausstellungen, Sammlungen, Ankäufe, Verluste, Wiedergutmachung

The Kunsthalle Mannheim and Expressionism: People, Exhibitions, Collections, Acquisitions, Losses, Compensation

Inge Herold

The Kunsthalle Mannheim and Expressionism

The term "Expressionism" to identify the new artistic movement in Germany in the early twentieth century was first used as it is understood today around 1910. After Impressionism, Symbolism, and Art Nouveau, many young artists—not only in Germany—were searching for a new art in tune with the times. Seeing themselves above all as opposition to the salon painting of the art academies that was supported by the state and the *grande bourgeoisie*, they also turned against the plein air painting of Impressionism with its focus on surface stimuli. At the beginning of the twentieth century, a young generation of painters came together whose will to renew sent them searching for new, modern forms of expression. For all their differences, they had in common an intensification of expressive content and subjective emotion by means of strong, pure color planes and a spontaneous painting style, the disintegration of forms, the distortion of perspective, and a turn away from harmonious balanced composition. Artists such as Ernst Ludwig Kirchner, Erich Heckel, and Karl Schmidt-Rottluff, who had founded the artists' group Die Brücke (The Bridge) in Dresden in 1905, were, alongside Franz Marc, Otto Mueller, Emil Nolde, and Max Pechstein, among its most famous representatives. Only a few women also managed to find their way into the public perception during this period. They included Margarete Moll, Gabriele Münter, Renée Sintenis, Milly Steger, and Marianne von Werefkin. Just a few years after its zenith, not least because of the experience of the war, the movement was already being superseded by Neue Sachlichkeit (New Objectivity). Nevertheless, it would take time before Expressionist art also made it into museum collections. One of the first was the Städtische Kunsthalle Mannheim, which had opened as a museum in 1909, where its first director, Fritz Wichert (1878–1951), initially acquired French and German Impressionist art. Even today, the "French Collection" with Édouard Manet's *The Execution of Emperor Maximilian* (1868–69), is a highlight of the museum, but the Kunsthalle Mannheim is associated above all with the term "Neue Sachlichkeit," which was coined for the legendary exhibition of Gustav Friedrich Hartlaub (1884–1963), the second director of the Kunsthalle, in 1925. The exhibition was subtitled *Deutsche Kunst seit dem Expressionismus* (German Art since Expressionism) and showed the new representational trends of the 1920s. What follows, however, will shed light on just how important Expressionism also was and is for the institution on Friedrichsplatz. It was supported by a wide variety of protagonists and their networks and interests, but also by the political conditions.[1]

First Purchases and Exhibitions from 1913 Onward

In the field of sculpture, the Kunsthalle Mannheim dedicated itself to Expressionist trends as early as 1912 and coined the term "*Ausdrucksplastik*" (expressive sculpture). *Ausstellung von Zeichnungen und Plastiken neuzeitlicher Bildhauer* (Exhibition of Drawings and Sculptures of Modern Sculptors) of 1914, whose catalogue foreword was written by Willy Storck (1889–1927), began with the two antipodes Auguste Rodin and Aristide Maillol and presented the latest developments in German sculpture with works by Karl Albiker and Wilhelm Lehmbruck; Edwin Scharff, Richard Scheibe, Ernst Barlach and Georg Kolbe; Bernhard Hoetger, and Wilhelm Gerstel. Women artists were also represented: Grete (Margarete also Marg) Moll, Renée Sintenis, and Milly Steger. From Sintenis, her portrait of the writer Ernst Toller was acquired later, in 1926, from the Galerie Flechtheim, while a work by Milly Steger, *Frauenbildnis* (Portrait of a Woman) of 1920 (cat. 107), entered the museum in 1973 as a gift from the German-Jewish collector William Landmann, who had emigrated from Mannheim.

"The Kunsthalle's boldest decision is its purchase of a Heckel."

Theodor Däubler, 1916

„Der mutigste Beschluß der Kunsthalle ist ihr Ankauf eines Heckels."

Theodor Däubler, 1916

Die Kunsthalle Mannheim und der Expressionismus

Der Begriff „Expressionismus" als Bezeichnung für die neue künstlerische Bewegung in Deutschland im frühen 20. Jahrhundert wurde, so wie man ihn heute versteht, um 1910 zum ersten Mal verwendet. Nach Impressionismus, Symbolismus und Jugendstil suchten viele junge Künstler*innen – nicht nur in Deutschland – nach einer zeitgemäßen Kunst. Verstanden vor allem als Opposition zu der von Staat und Großbürgertum getragenen „Salon"-Malerei der Kunstakademien, wandten sie sich auch gegen die auf Oberflächenreize ausgerichtete Freilichtmalerei des Impressionismus. So fand sich am Anfang des 20. Jahrhunderts eine junge Generation von Künstler*innen zusammen, die sich mit Erneuerungswillen auf die Suche nach modernen, neuen Ausdrucksformen machte. Bei aller Unterschiedlichkeit war ihnen die Steigerung des Ausdrucksgehaltes und der subjektiven Emotion mittels starker, reiner Farbflächen und einer spontanen Malweise, die Zertrümmerung der Formen sowie die Verzerrung der Perspektive und die Abkehr von der harmonisch ausgewogenen Komposition gemein. Künstler wie Ernst Ludwig Kirchner, Erich Heckel und Karl Schmidt-Rottluff, die 1905 in Dresden die Künstlergruppe Die Brücke gegründet hatten, zählen neben Franz Marc, Otto Mueller, Emil Nolde und Max Pechstein zu den bekanntesten Vertretern. Nur wenigen Frauen gelang es, sich in dieser Zeit ebenfalls einen Platz in der öffentlichen Wahrnehmung zu verschaffen. Zu ihnen gehören Margarete Moll, Gabriele Münter, Renée Sintenis, Milly Steger und Marianne von Werefkin. Bereits wenige Jahre nach ihrem Höhepunkt wurde die Bewegung, nicht zuletzt durch die Erfahrung des Krieges, durch die Neue Sachlichkeit abgelöst. Doch sollte es dauern, bis die Kunst des Expressionismus auch in Museumssammlungen gelangte. Eine der ersten war die der 1909 als Museum eröffneten Städtischen Kunsthalle Mannheim, wo sich der erste Direktor Fritz Wichert (1878–1951) zunächst auf die französische und deutsche Kunst des Impressionismus verlegte. Noch heute ist die „Franzosensammlung" mit Édouard Manets *Erschießung Kaiser Maximilians* (1868/69) ein Highlight des Museums, doch verbindet man mit der Kunsthalle Mannheim vor allem den Begriff der „Neuen Sachlichkeit", der 1925 durch die legendäre Ausstellung Gustav Friedrich Hartlaubs (1884–1963), dem zweiten Direktor der Kunsthalle, geprägt wurde. Die Ausstellung trug den Untertitel „Deutsche Kunst seit dem Expressionismus" und zeigte die neuen gegenständlichen Tendenzen der 1920er-Jahre. Wie wichtig jedoch auch der Expressionismus für das Haus am Friedrichsplatz war und ist, soll im Folgenden beleuchtet werden. Getragen war dies von unterschiedlichsten Protagonist*innen, ihren Netzwerken und Interessen, aber auch von politischen Rahmenbedingungen.[1]

Erste Ankäufe und Ausstellungen ab 1913

Im Bereich der Skulptur widmete man sich in der Kunsthalle Mannheim schon 1912 den expressionistischen Tendenzen und fand die Begrifflichkeit *Ausdrucks-Plastik*. In der 1914 gezeigten *Ausstellung von Zeichnungen und Plastiken neuzeitlicher Bildhauer*, deren Katalogvorwort von Willy Storck (1889–1927) verfasst worden war, wurde ausgehend von den beiden Antipoden Auguste Rodin und Aristide Maillol die aktuelle Entwicklung in der deutschen Skulptur mit Arbeiten von Karl Albiker und Wilhelm Lehmbruck, Edwin Scharff, Richard Scheibe, Ernst Barlach und Georg Kolbe, Bernhard Hoetger und Wilhelm Gerstel vorgestellt. Vertreten waren mit Grete (Margarete oder auch Marg) Moll, Renée Sintenis und Milly Steger auch Künstlerinnen. Von Sintenis wurde später, 1926, über die Galerie Flechtheim das Porträt des Dichters Ernst Toller erworben, während ein Werk von Milly Steger, *Frauenbildnis* von 1920 (Kat. 107) im Jahr 1973 als

In the field of painting, the year 1913 marks the beginning of purchasing activity: from the Galerie Goldschmidt in Frankfurt am Main, Wichert acquired the 1910 portrait *Auguste Forel* by Oskar Kokoschka (cat. 94)—a first emphasis in his collecting strategy was a masterpiece of visionary portraiture by the young artist. For the year 1913, moreover, there was documented contact between Wichert and the young Max Zachmann (1892–1917), who was born in Heidelberg but had been studying at the Kunstakademie Karlsruhe since 1912.[2] The artist was exploring the Expressionist style and turned to Wichert for advice on his artistic work. Wichert was clearly moved by what he saw and arranged a lucrative commission for Zachmann: decorating the dining room in the villa of the Mannheim manufacturer Erich Carl Mayer. As for his work, which unfortunately has not survived, Zachmann chose human existence tied to nature, defined by joie de vivre and harmony. Presumably out of gratitude for Wichert's advocacy and support, Zachmann donated thirty-one graphic works to the Kunsthalle Mannheim in 1915, twenty-nine of which were confiscated as "degenerate" by the National Socialist regime in 1937 (fig. 1). In 1916, the museum purchased four graphic works by Zachmann, which also fell victim to the confiscations. The artist's promising career came to a terrible end already in World War I: he fell in an aerial attack in Flanders in 1917, and his work passed into oblivion. The surviving correspondence between the artist and Wichert demonstrates exemplarily that the Kunsthalle played an important mediating role for both artists and collectors.

Hartlaub and Expressionism

The idea of mediating was extremely important to Wichert. To create a broad basis for it, he founded the Freier Bund zur Einbürgerung der Bildenden Kunst (Free League to Establish Fine Art) in Mannheim in 1911. In 1913, he appointed as its speaker Gustav Friedrich Hartlaub, who had been working as an assistant to the director Gustav Pauli at the Bremer Kunsthalle. Hartlaub's eye soon turned to Expressionism. His first encounter with Expressionist art was at the Sonderbund exhibition in Cologne in 1912. At first, however, he dismissed Expressionism together with abstraction, Cubism, and Futurism as the latest "Quixotism in art."[3] His enthusiasm for Expressionism that began shortly thereafter can surely be traced back to the influence of the poet Theodor Däubler (1876–1934), whom Hartlaub also met personally in the home of the collector Sally Falk (1888–1962) in Mannheim around 1916, as he recalled retrospectively in 1959: "I was often in the home of Mr. Falk . . ., who was a big businessman and earned lots of money but was at the same time a quite ideal friend of the arts, and there I saw a great deal that now led me directly into the center of what was then the most current and modern Expressionist art movement, as it is called. At his home, at Mr. Falk's, no one less than the poet Theodor Däubler socialized."[4] Under the title *Der neue Standpunkt* (The New Standpoint), Däubler published a collection of essays in 1916 that is considered the most important foundation for the art theory of Expressionism. His cosmogony,

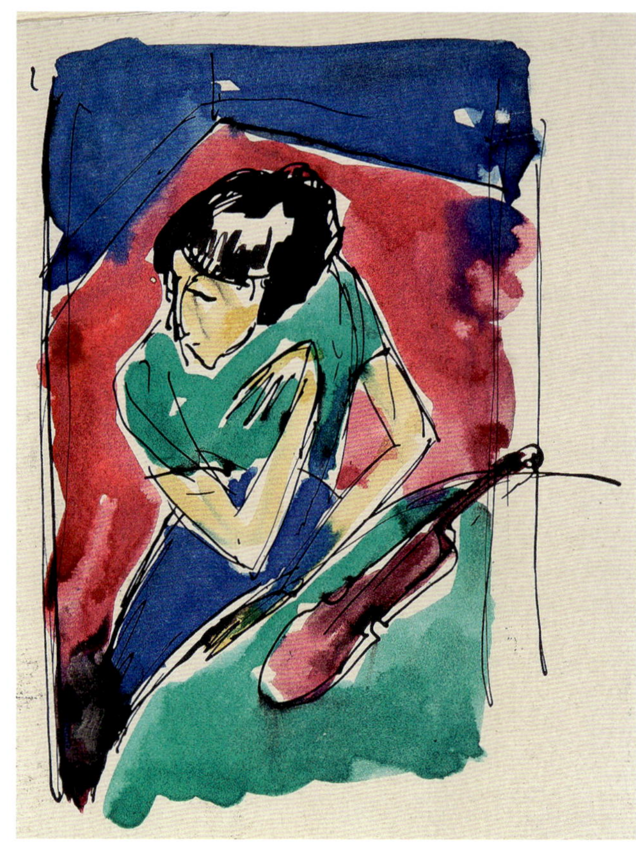

Abb. / Fig. 1
Max Zachmann
Geigerin / Violinist, **vor** / prior to **1915**
Feder in schwarzer Tusche, farbige
Tusche laviert / *Pen in black ink,
colored wash*, 24,3 × 24,6 cm
Kunsthalle Mannheim

THE KUNSTHALLE MANNHEIM AND EXPRESSIONISM

Schenkung des einst aus Mannheim emigrierten jüdischen Sammlers William Landmann ins Museum kam.

Im Bereich der Malerei markiert das Jahr 1913 den Beginn der Ankaufstätigkeit: Wichert erwarb über die Frankfurter Galerie Goldschmidt das 1910 entstandene Bildnis *Auguste Forel* von Oskar Kokoschka (Kat. 94), ein erster sammlungsstrategischer Akzent, ein Meisterwerk visionärer Porträtkunst des jungen Künstlers. Für das Jahr 1913 ist zudem der Kontakt zwischen Wichert und dem jungen, in Heidelberg geborenen und seit 1912 an der Karlsruher Kunstakademie studierenden Max Zachmann (1892–1917) belegt.[2] Der sich im expressionistischen Stil erprobende Künstler wandte sich an Wichert um Rat für sein künstlerisches Schaffen. Offenbar war Wichert angetan von dem, was er sah, und vermittelte Zachmann einen lukrativen Auftrag: die Ausmalung des Speisesaals in der Villa des Mannheimer Fabrikanten Erich Carl Mayer. Als Thema des leider nicht erhaltenen Werkes wählte Zachmann das mit der Natur verbundene Menschsein, bestimmt von Lebensfreude und Harmonie. Wohl als Dank für Wicherts Fürsprache und Unterstützung schenkte Zachmann 1915 der Kunsthalle Mannheim 31 Grafiken, von denen 1937 unter dem NS-Regime 29 als „entartet" beschlagnahmt wurden (Abb. 1). 1916 kaufte das Museum vier Grafiken Zachmanns, die ebenfalls der Beschlagnahmung zum Opfer fielen. Die vielversprechende Karriere des Künstlers erfuhr bereits im Ersten Weltkrieg ein schreckliches Ende: Er fiel 1917 bei einem Luftkampf in Flandern, und sein Werk geriet in Vergessenheit. Der erhaltene Schriftwechsel zwischen dem Künstler und Wichert belegt beispielhaft, dass die Kunsthalle für Kunstschaffende, aber auch für Sammlerinnen und Sammler eine wichtige vermittelnde Rolle spielte.

Hartlaub und der Expressionismus

Wichert war der Gedanke des Vermittelns äußerst wichtig. Um dies auf eine breite Basis zu stellen, gründete er 1911 den Freien Bund zur Einbürgerung der Bildenden Kunst in Mannheim. Als dessen Sprecher berief er 1913 Gustav Friedrich Hartlaub, bislang Assistent des Direktors Gustav Pauli an der Bremer Kunsthalle. Hartlaubs Augenmerk sollte sich bald auf den Expressionismus richten. Seine erste Begegnung mit expressionistischer Kunst fand 1912 auf der Kölner Sonderbund-Ausstellung statt. Hier sollte er aber zunächst den Expressionismus zusammen mit Abstraktion, Kubismus und Futurismus als neueste „Kunst-Donquijoterie" verurteilen.[3] Seine bald darauf einsetzende Begeisterung für den Expressionismus ging sicher auf den Einfluss des Dichters Theodor Däubler (1876–1934) zurück, dem Hartlaub um 1916 im Haus des Mannheimer Sammlers Sally Falk (1888–1962) auch persönlich begegnete, wie er 1959 rückblickend erinnert: „[…] ich war häufig im Hause von Herrn Falk […] und bei ihm, der ein großer Geschäftsmann war und viel Geld verdiente, der aber gleichzeitig ein ganz idealer Kunstfreund war, habe ich sehr viel gesehen, was mich nun mitten in die damals aktuellste und modernste, wie man sagt, expressionistische Kunstbewegung hineinführte. Bei ihm, bei Herrn Falk, verkehrte kein Geringerer als der Dichter Theodor Däubler."[4] Unter dem Titel *Der neue Standpunkt* veröffentlichte Däubler 1916 eine Essaysammlung, die als die bedeutendste kunsttheoretische Begründung des Expressionismus gilt. Seine Kosmogonie, die er schon im 1910 erschienenen Epos *Nordlicht* formulierte, basierte auf der Vorstellung, dass alles Dasein von der Sonne kommt. Die in der ursprünglichen Einheit von Sonne und Erde wirkenden gegensätzlichen Kräfte führten die Trennung herbei, wodurch es zur Schöpfung kam. In der Wiedervereinigung der Erde mit der Sonne sah Däubler das Heil, während das Nordlicht Symbol für die sich im Geist rettende Menschheit war. Hartlaubs Interesse für Magie, Mystik und Okkultes, seine

which he had already formulated in his epic *Nordlicht* (Northern Light), published in 1910, was based on the idea that all existence comes from the sun. The opposing forces active in the original unity of the Sun and the Earth led to the separation that resulted in creation. Däubler saw the reunification of the Earth with the Sun as the salvation, while the northern light was the symbol for the humanity that is being rescued in the spirit. Hartlaub's interest in magic, mysticism, and the occult and his study of theosophy had correspondences and supplements in Däubler's world of ideas. In Berlin's *Börsen-Courier* in 1916, Däubler also praised Hartlaub's first acquisition of an Expressionist painting: *Gewitterlandschaft* (Stormy Landscape) by Erich Heckel (fig. 2), which was purchased from the Kunsthandlung Hans Goltz in Munich: "The Kunsthalle's boldest decision is its purchase of a Heckel."[5]

This initiative by Hartlaub remained isolated, however, because it put him in conflict with Wichert's directives. The latter had been appointed a diplomat at the German embassy in The Hague in 1914. He was to be away from the Kunsthalle until the beginning of 1919, a difficult situation for him but also for Hartlaub, who ran the business of the Kunsthalle together with Willy Storck, director of the Kunsthalle's Kunstwissenschaftliches Institut (Art Historical Institute) since 1911, since differences and competition arose again and again. Inconveniently, coordination processes and strategic issues had to be discussed by letter. To distinguish himself from Wichert's prioritization of French Impressionism, Hartlaub now focused on Expressionism—out of conviction but also to reinforce his own profile. He sought new perspectives and relied, on the one hand, on intense contact with a Mannheim collector and entrepreneur like Sally Falk, who promised an important donation, and, on the other, on his own exhibition project *Neue religiöse Kunst* (New Religious Art), which he initially planned for the autumn of 1917.

The Collector Sally Falk

Sally Falk was a colorful personality.[6] He was an "autocrat" and his wife, Adèle, an extravagant "bird of paradise," George Grosz later recalled in his autobiography.[7] In 1914, Falk had taken over the management of his father's cotton-processing business in Neckarau, which was flourishing during World War I because of the great need for materials for uniforms. Thanks to this boom, the young entrepreneur very quickly came into enormous wealth, which he invested above all in building an important collection of contemporary art. As if possessed, Falk acquired works by Edgar Degas, Auguste Renoir, Paul Cézanne, Paul Gauguin, Pablo Picasso, Marc Chagall, Edvard Munch, Franz Marc, Lyonel Feininger, Wassily Kandinsky, and Oskar Kokoschka. He bought at the best addresses: at Paul Cassirer, Fritz Gurlitt, and Hugo Perls in Berlin; at Heinrich Thannhauser, Georg Caspari, and Hans Goltz in Munich; at Ludwig Schames in Frankfurt am Main. The Kunsthalle Mannheim often served as the place where works were sent for him to view. In George Grosz and Wilhelm Lehmbruck, the entrepreneur was supporting two young artists simultaneously; the work of the

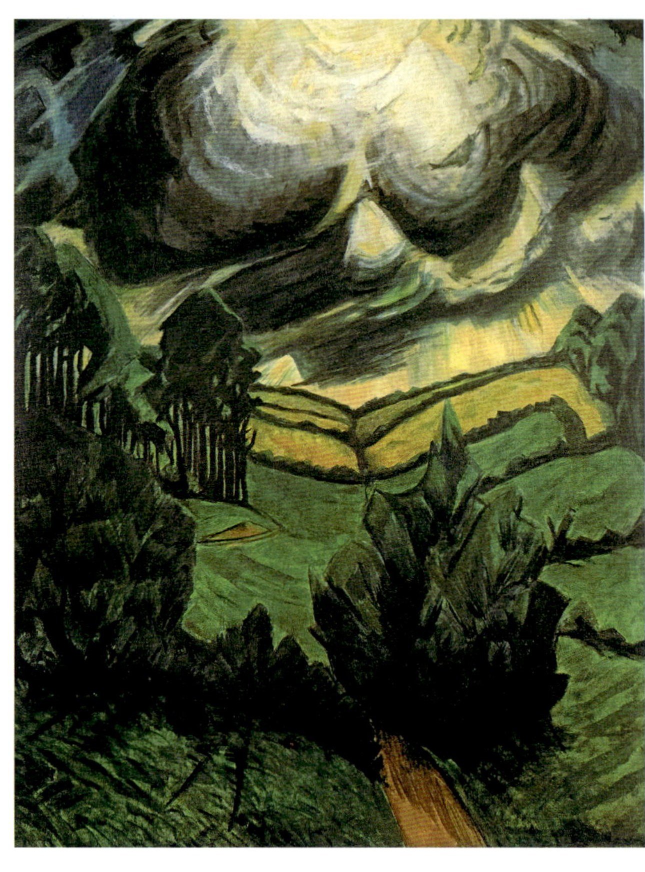

Abb. / Fig. **2**
Erich Heckel, *Gewitterlandschaft* /
Stormy Landscape, **um** / *ca.* **1913/14**
Öl auf Leinwand / *Oil on canvas*, 110 × 145 cm
Tel Aviv Museum of Art

Beschäftigung mit Theosophie fanden in Däublers Ideenwelt Entsprechungen und Ergänzungen. Dieser schrieb dann auch 1916 im Berliner Börsen-Courier lobend über Hartlaubs ersten Ankauf eines expressionistischen Bildes: die um 1913/14 entstandene *Gewitterlandschaft* von Erich Heckel (Abb. 2), erworben über die Kunsthandlung Hans Goltz in München: „Der mutigste Beschluß der Kunsthalle ist ihr Ankauf eines Heckels."[5]

Diese Initiative Hartlaubs blieb jedoch isoliert, stand er damit doch auch in Konflikt mit den Direktiven Wicherts. Dieser war 1914 einem Ruf als Diplomat an die Botschaft in Den Haag gefolgt. Er sollte bis Anfang 1919 der Kunsthalle fern sein, eine schwierige Situation für ihn selbst, aber auch für Hartlaub, der – zusammen mit Willy Storck, seit 1911 Leiter des Kunstwissenschaftlichen Instituts der Kunsthalle – die Geschäfte in der Kunsthalle führte, denn es kam immer wieder zu Differenzen und Konkurrenzsituationen. Abstimmungsprozesse und strategische Fragen mussten umständlich per Brief diskutiert werden. In Abgrenzung zu Wicherts Priorisierung des französischen Impressionismus fokussierte sich Hartlaub aus Überzeugung, aber auch um sein eigenes Profil zu stärken, nun auf den Expressionismus. Er suchte neue Perspektiven und setzte einerseits auf den intensiven Kontakt zu einem Mannheimer Sammler und Unternehmer wie Sally Falk, der eine wichtige Schenkung in Aussicht stellte, andererseits auf sein Ausstellungsvorhaben *Neue religiöse Kunst*, das er zunächst für Herbst 1917 plante.

Der Sammler Sally Falk

Sally Falk war eine schillernde Persönlichkeit.[6] Er sei ein „Autokrat", seine Frau Adèle ein extravaganter „Paradiesvogel" gewesen, erinnerte sich George Grosz später in seiner Autobiografie.[7] 1914 hatte Falk die Leitung des baumwollverarbeitenden Betriebs seines Vaters in Neckarau übernommen, der während des Ersten Weltkrieges aufgrund des großen Bedarfs an Uniformstoffen florierte. Durch diesen Boom gelangte der junge Unternehmer in kurzer Zeit zu enormem Reichtum, den er vor allem in den Aufbau einer bedeutenden Sammlung zeitgenössischer Kunst investierte. Wie besessen erwarb Falk Werke von Edgar Degas, Auguste Renoir, Paul Cézanne, Paul Gauguin, Pablo Picasso, Marc Chagall, Edvard Munch, Franz Marc, Lyonel Feininger, Wassily Kandinsky und Oskar Kokoschka. Er kaufte bei den besten Adressen: bei Paul Cassirer, Fritz Gurlitt und Hugo Perls in Berlin, bei Heinrich Thannhauser, Georg Caspari und Hans Goltz in München, bei Ludwig Schames in Frankfurt. Dabei fungierte die Kunsthalle Mannheim häufig als Ort, wohin Ansichtssendungen für ihn gesandt wurden. Und mit George Grosz und Wilhelm Lehmbruck unterstützte der Unternehmer gleichzeitig zwei junge Künstler, vor allem das Werk des Bildhauers sollte schließlich von großer Bedeutung für Falk und die Kunsthalle werden. Am 2. Mai 1916 berichtete Hartlaub das erste Mal an Wichert von Falk, den er in Berlin getroffen habe, danach tauchte er immer wieder in der Korrespondenz der beiden auf. Am 15. Juni 1916 schrieb Hartlaub: „Augenblicklich ist Lehmbruck mit seiner Frau hier, er modelliert das Ehepaar Falk."[8] Und am 10. Januar 1917: „[...] weil unter den Kriegsgewinnern große Sammlerlust herrscht und weil es gilt, diesen Trieb jetzt auf einigermaßen richtige Bahnen zu lenken", und auch in dem „bescheidenen Ehrgeiz", die Verbindung zu Falk zum Nutzen der Kunsthalle zu gestalten, was „ein dauerndes Zeugnis dafür sein wird, daß auch unsere interimistische Amtsführung nicht ganz ohne Segen für die Kunsthalle gewesen ist."[9] Falk jedoch war eitel, neigte zu schnellen Entscheidungen und reagierte auf Kritik empfindlich, so verweigerte er sich etwa 1916 der *Ausstellung aus Mannheimer Privatbesitz*, weil er in der Presse wegen des Ankaufs eines Cézanne-Gemäldes angegriffen worden war. Hartlaub war es

sculptor in particular would ultimately become very important for Falk and the Kunsthalle. On May 2, 1916, Hartlaub told Wichert about Falk for the first time, after meeting him in Berlin, and thereafter he appears repeatedly in their correspondence. On June 15, 1916, Hartlaub wrote: "At the moment, Lehmbruck is here with his wife; he is modeling Mr. and Mrs. Falk."[8] And on January 10, 1917: "because a great desire to collect is rife among the victors in the war, and because this drive now leads to be directed somewhat to the right paths" and also in the "modest ambition" to make his relationship with Falk useful for the Kunsthalle, which would be "enduring testimony that our interim running of the office has not been entirely without benefits for the Kunsthalle."[9] Falk was, however, vain, inclined to make snap decisions, and sensitive to criticism, so, for example, he rejected the *Ausstellung*

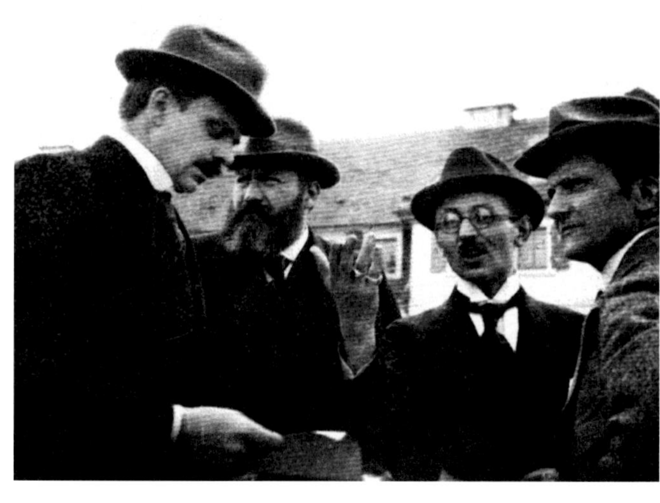

aus Mannheimer Privatbesitz (Exhibition from Private Collections in Mannheim) in 1916, because the purchase of a painting by Paul Cézanne had been attacked in the press. Hartlaub was concerned for his efforts to paint the important collector in the right light; he even called himself the intellectual creator of Falk's collection, which angered the latter so much that he wanted to take back his planned donation. He forbade such presumption in a letter to Wichert in April 1918: "My collection has been formed solely and only from the love that I had for art objects—it needed no custodian."[10]

Wilhelm Lehmbruck and the Sally Falk Donation

In November 1916, the Kunsthalle organized a solo exhibition of the sculptor Wilhelm Lehmbruck (1881–1919) with around twenty-five sculptures, ten paintings, and several graphic works—the first comprehensive museum presentation of his oeuvre in Germany, and the catalogue introduction was written by none other than Däubler. Lehmbruck was not unknown in Mannheim, as he had already exhibited in the exhibition of the Deutscher Künstlerbund (Association of German Artists) at the Kunsthalle in 1913. And in 1914 he had participated in the *Ausstellung von Zeichnungen und Plastiken neuzeitlicher Bildhauer* (Exhibition of Drawings and Sculptures by Modern Sculptors). Finally, a photograph taken on the occasion of his exhibition in 1916 shows him with the architect Hermann Esch, Theodor Däubler, and Willy Storck in Mannheim (fig. 3). In the context of this exhibition, the relatively naturalistic *Große Stehende* (Large Standing Woman) (cat. 17), which Lehmbruck had produced at the beginning of his stay in Paris in 1910, could be acquired as the first of his sculptures for the Kunsthalle. Falk's close connections to the Kunsthalle and to Lehmbruck was manifested in 1917 when he donated the latter's painting *Junges Mädchen (Martha)* (Young Girl [Martha]) (1912; cat. 15) and provided six of the artist's sculptures as loans. Falk tied this loan to the aforementioned promise to transfer these and additional works by other German artists as a donation to the Kunsthalle's collections. In 1921, Falk did indeed make this generous donation even though by then his financial situation had changed completely. For already in July 1917 the businessman, who with his art acquisitions had been living beyond his means and caused the financial ruin of his company, had been forced to sell a large part of his collection. Fortunately, the donation to the Kunsthalle was unaffected by the

Abb./Fig. 3
Hermann Esch, Theodor Däubler, Willy Storck, und/ *and* Wilhelm Lehmbruck, Mannheim, 1916

THE KUNSTHALLE MANNHEIM AND EXPRESSIONISM

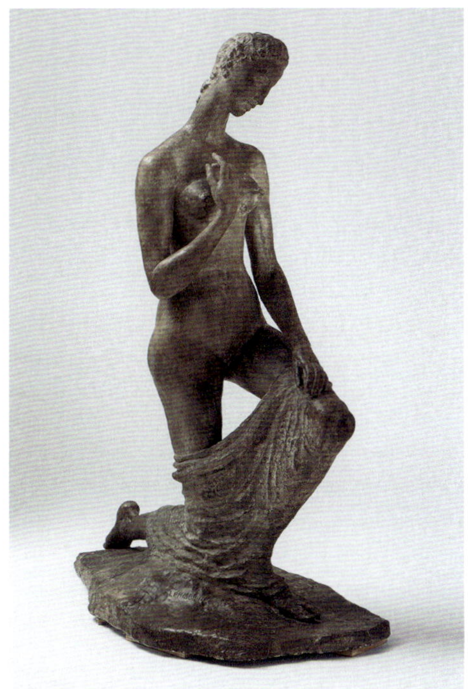

Abb./Fig. 4
Wilhelm Lehmbruck, *Kniende* / Kneeling Woman, 1911
Kunststein / Cast stone, 176,5 × 142,2 × 68,6 cm
Museum of Modern Art, New York

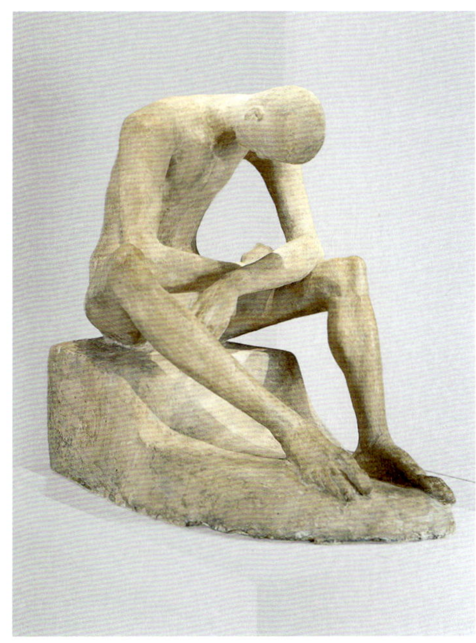

Abb./Fig. 5
Wilhelm Lehmbruck, *Der Gebeugte* /
Seated Youth, **1917**
Kunststein / Composite tinted plaster,
103,2 × 76,2 × 115,5 cm
National Gallery of Art, Washington, DC

angelegen, seine Bemühungen um den wichtigen Sammler ins rechte Licht zu rücken, er bezeichnete sich gar als geistigen Schöpfer von Falks Sammlung, was diesen wiederum derart erboste, dass er seine geplante Stiftung zurückziehen wollte. Solche Anmaßungen verbat er sich in einem Brief vom April 1918 an Wichert: „Meine Sammlung bildete sich einzig und allein aus der Liebe, die ich zu den Kunstdingen hatte – diese brauchte keinen Vormund."[10]

Wilhelm Lehmbruck und die Stiftung Sally Falk

Im November 1916 richtete die Kunsthalle dem Bildhauer Wilhelm Lehmbruck (1881–1919) eine Einzelausstellung mit etwa 25 Skulpturen, zehn Gemälden und mehreren Grafiken aus – die erste umfassende Museumspräsentation seines Œuvres in Deutschland, die Einführung im Katalog verfasste kein anderer als Däubler. In Mannheim war Lehmbruck kein Unbekannter, hatte er doch bereits 1913 bei der Ausstellung des Deutschen Künstlerbundes in der Kunsthalle ausgestellt. Und 1914 war er an der *Ausstellung von Zeichnungen und Plastiken neuzeitlicher Bildhauer* beteiligt gewesen. Ein Foto zeigt ihn schließlich 1916 anlässlich seiner Ausstellung mit dem Architekten Hermann Esch, mit Theodor Däubler und Willy Storck in Mannheim (Abb. 3). Im Kontext dieser Ausstellung konnte mit der verhältnismäßig naturalistischen *Großen Stehenden* (Kat. 17), die zu Beginn von Lehmbrucks Paris-Aufenthalt 1910 entstanden war, auch der erste Ankauf einer seiner Plastiken für die Kunsthalle realisiert werden. Die enge Verbindung Falks zur Kunsthalle und zu Lehmbruck manifestierte sich 1917, als er dessen Gemälde *Junges Mädchen (Martha)* (1912; Kat. 15) zum Geschenk machte und zunächst als Leihgaben sechs Plastiken des Künstlers überließ. An diese Leihgabe knüpfte Falk das schon erwähnte Versprechen, dass diese und weitere Werke anderer deutscher Bildhauer als Stiftung in die Sammlungen der Kunsthalle übergehen sollten. 1921 kam es dann tatsächlich zu dieser umfangreichen Schenkung, auch wenn sich die wirtschaftlichen Verhältnisse Falks zu diesem Zeitpunkt völlig verändert hatten. Denn bereits im Juli 1917 war der Unternehmer, der mit seinen Kunsterwerbungen über die eigenen Verhältnisse gelebt und dadurch auch den finanziellen Ruin seiner Firma verursacht hatte, dazu gezwungen, einen Großteil seiner Sammlung wieder zu verkaufen. Vom finanziellen Zusammenbruch des Unternehmens unberührt blieb glücklicherweise die Stiftung an die Kunsthalle. Sie umfasste sechs Plastiken von Lehmbruck: die *Frauenbüste* (1910; Kat. 21), *Kleine Sinnende* (1910/11; Kat. 19), der *Hagener Torso* (1910/11; Kat. 22), *Kniende* (1911; Abb. 4), *Torso der Großen Sinnenden* (1913/14; Kat. 23) sowie *Der Gebeugte* (1917; Abb. 5). Zudem gelangten von Edwin Scharff *Der Athlet* und von Ernesto de Fiori der lebensgroße *Jüngling (Der Leidende)* (1911/12; Kat. 1) in die Sammlung, von Georg Kolbe die Bronze *Sklavin* (1916; Kat. 2). Diese bedeutende Stiftung, die den Grundstein der Mannheimer Sammlung moderner Plastik legte, wurde 1937 durch die Beschlagnahmungen „entarteter Kunst" zerschlagen: Während ein Teil in der Kunsthalle verblieb und unerklärlicherweise nicht konfisziert wurde, gingen mit den beiden Lehmbruck-Plastiken *Der Gebeugte* und *Kniende* die beiden herausragenden Werke der Stiftung aus der Sammlung verloren, ebenso das Gemälde *Martha* sowie Scharffs *Athlet*.[11] Wie die von ihm gestifteten Kunstwerke war auch Falk selbst von der Gewalt der NS-Diktatur betroffen. Während des Zweiten Weltkrieges lebte er mit seiner Frau zeitweilig in Lyon, dort wurde er von der Gestapo festgenommen, konnte sich aber letztlich durch Flucht befreien. In seiner Wahlheimat Schweiz verschlechterte sich seine finanzielle Lage nach 1945 dann noch einmal. Seinen Lebensunterhalt bestritt Falk jetzt vorwiegend durch den Verkauf ihm noch verbliebener Kunstwerke. 1961 entschloss sich die Stadt Mannheim, dem Stifter aufgrund

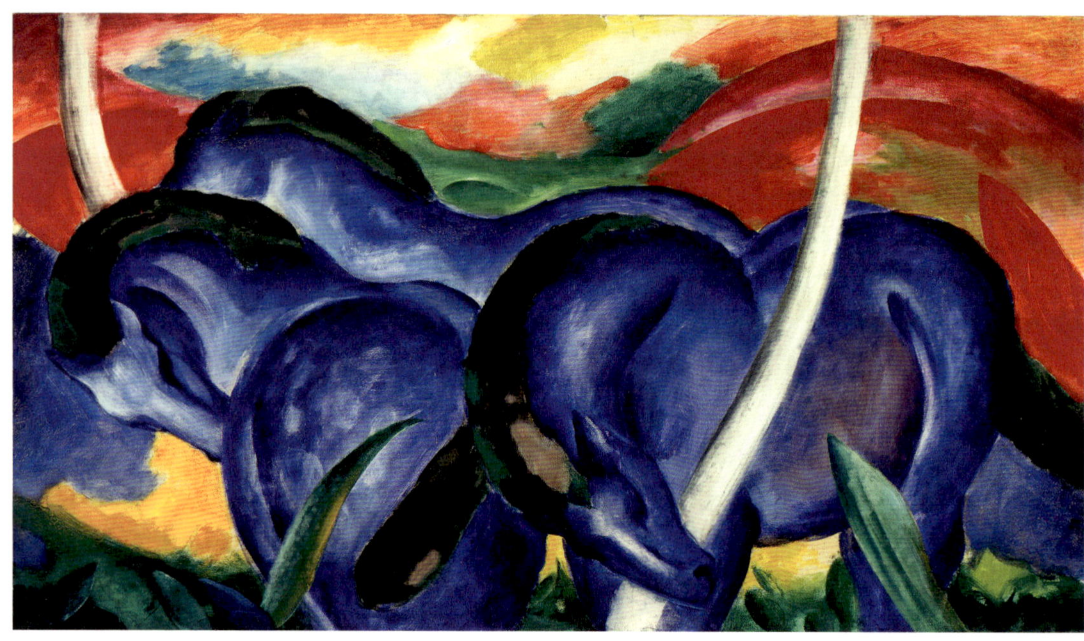

financial collapse of the company. It included six sculptures by Lehmbruck: *Frauenbüste* (Bust of a Woman) (1910; cat. 21), *Kleine Sinnende* (Small Contemplative Woman) (1910/11; cat. 19), the *Hagener Torso* (1910/11; cat. 22), *Kniende* (Kneeling Woman) (1911; fig. 4), *Torso der Großen Sinnenden* (Torso of the Large Contemplative Woman) (1913/14; cat. 23), *Der Gebeugte* (Seated Youth) (1917; fig. 5). In addition, Edwin Scharff's *Der Athlet* (The Athlete), Ernesto de Fiori's life-size *Jüngling (Der Leidende)* (Youth [The Sufferer]) (1911/12; cat. 1), and Georg Kolbe's *Sklavin* (Female Slave) (1916; cat. 2) entered the collection. This important donation, which laid the cornerstone of the Mannheim collection of modern sculpture, was shattered by the confiscations of "degenerate" art in 1937: whereas part of the collection remained in the Kunsthalle and was, inexplicably, not confiscated, with Lehmbruck's sculptures, *Der Gebeugte* and *Kniende*, two outstanding works from the donation were lost from the collection, along with the painting *Martha* and Scharff's *Athlet*.[11] Like the artworks he had donated, Falk himself was affected by the violence of the National Socialist dictatorship. During World War II, he and his wife lived in Lyon for a time, where they were arrested by the Gestapo, but ultimately they were able to escape by fleeing. In his adopted homeland, his financial situation worsened again after 1945. Falk now covered his living expenses primarily by selling his remaining works of art. In 1961, the City of Mannheim decided to award the donor an honorary remuneration for his services to the museum. Today, two plaster busts in the holdings of the Kunsthalle Mannheim are reminders of the businessman and his wife (cat. 11, 12). They came to the Kunsthalle in 1960: Maria Tannenbaum donated them in memory of her husband, the German-Jewish gallerist Herbert Tannenbaum.

Planned and Realized Purchases and the Exhibition
Neue religiöse Kunst in 1918

Returning to the year 1916: in March, the Munich art dealer Caspari sent Franz Marc's painting *Die großen blauen Pferde* (The Large Blue Horses) (1911) to the Kunsthalle on approval (fig. 6). Sally Falk saw it there and initially wanted to donate it to the Kunsthalle but withdrew the proposal

Abb./Fig. 6
Franz Marc, *Die großen blauen Pferde* /
The Large Blue Horses, **1911**
Öl auf Leinwand / *Oil on canvas*, 105 × 181 cm
Walker Art Center, Minneapolis

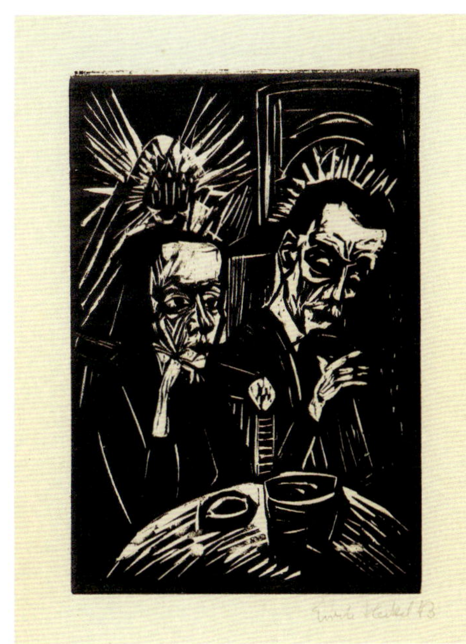

seiner Verdienste für das Museum einen Ehrensold zuzusprechen. Heute erinnern in den Beständen der Kunsthalle Mannheim zwei Gipsbüsten an den Geschäftsmann und seine Frau (Kat. 11, 12). Sie kamen 1960 in die Kunsthalle – Maria Tannenbaum hatte sie dem Haus in Erinnerung an ihren Mann, den jüdischen Galeristen Herbert Tannenbaum, gestiftet.

Geplante sowie realisierte Ankäufe und die Ausstellung *Neue religiöse Kunst* 1918

Zurück in das Jahr 1916: Im März hatte der Münchner Kunsthändler Caspari der Kunsthalle Franz Marcs Gemälde *Die großen blauen Pferde* (1911) zur Ansicht geschickt (Abb. 6). Dort hatte Sally Falk es gesehen und wollte es zunächst der Kunsthalle stiften, trat jedoch von diesem Vorhaben zurück, weil er wie schon erwähnt wegen des Ankaufs eines Gemäldes von Cézanne angefeindet worden war. Falk kaufte das Gemälde dann Ende Mai 1916 für sich selbst, doch musste er es bereits zwei Jahre später wieder an Paul Cassirer veräußern, heute befindet sich das Gemälde im Walker Art Center in Minneapolis. Im Herbst 1916 wiederum bot Reinhard Piper der Kunsthalle Franz Marcs Gemälde *Drei Tiere (Hund, Fuchs und Katze)* (1912; Kat. 102) an. Dort kam es im Januar an, wurde jedoch nicht vom Museum, sondern von Sally Falk erworben. Auch dieses Bild fiel seinem Konkurs zum Opfer, schon im April 1918 verkaufte er es an Cassirer, von dem es wiederum Caspari erwarb, der es schließlich im Oktober 1919 erfolgreich der Kunsthalle anbot. Das Bild, eines der wichtigsten expressionistischen Gemälde der Kunsthalle, wurde 1937 als „entartet" beschlagnahmt und 1939 in der Auktion der Galerie Fischer in Luzern zum Verkauf angeboten. Dort stieß es jedoch auf kein Interesse und wurde am 12. Juli 1940 wieder an die Kunsthalle zurückerstattet.

Von Erich Heckel fand im September/Oktober 1917 eine eigene Werkschau statt, aus der vier Holzschnitte (Abb. 7; Kat. 68), drei Radierungen und eine Lithografie angekauft wurden. Auch in der Ausstellung *Neue religiöse Kunst* sollte er vertreten sein. In diesem Projekt gipfelte schließlich Hartlaubs Beschäftigung mit dem Expressionismus. Er stellte dem immer noch abwesenden Wichert 1917 sein Projekt vor mit dem Hinweis auf das zeitpsychologische Interesse in der gegenwärtigen Kriegszeit. Getragen waren seine Vorstellungen eben von dieser Erfahrung des Krieges, er sah einen idealistischen Ansatz zur Überwindung dieser Krisensituation in einem Rückzug auf das eigene „göttliche Ich". Seine Weltanschauung war dabei weniger geprägt von konfessionellen Vorstellungen als vielmehr von Elementen der theosophischen Gnosis, nach der die Erlösung des Menschen in der Gnosis, d. h. in der Erkenntnis seines kosmischen Geschicks und der Göttlichkeit seines eigenen Selbst, liegt. Bereits für Herbst 1917 geplant, fand die Ausstellung dann erst vom Januar bis März 1918 statt. Sie fasste, wie Hartlaub später schrieb, „dasjenige zusammen, was im Bereiche des deutschen Expressionismus als religiös und metaphysisch erschien."[12] „Mir scheint alle wirkliche expressionistische Kunst setzt, bewußt oder unbewußt eine religiöse Einstellung voraus. Der Expressionist vergeistigt die Natureindrücke, schmilzt sie um."[13] Das Erscheinungsbild der Ausstellung war durch den Krieg bedingt disparat. Und es fehlten wichtige Künstler wie Christian Rohlfs, Adolf Hölzel, Otto Mueller, Oskar Moll, Carl Hofer, da sie, wie sie rückmeldeten, keine religiösen Werke geschaffen hätten. Auch Beckmann sagte ab, da er eine Zeitlang nicht ausstellen wolle, wie er Hartlaub schrieb. Emil Nolde, für Hartlaub „der einsame Fixstern am Expressionistenhimmel"[14], war prominent mit seiner großen Mitteltafel *Kreuzigung* aus dem Zyklus *Das Leben Christi* (um 1912) vertreten. Ernst Ludwig Kirchner, Franz Marc, Karl Schmidt-Rottluff waren mit Grafiken präsent, ebenso Erich Heckel und Ludwig Meidner. Von Oskar Kokoschka

because, as noted above, his acquisition of a painting by Cézanne had been attacked. Falk bought the painting for himself at the end of May 1916, but just two years later, he was forced to sell it to Paul Cassirer; today, the painting is in the Walker Art Center in Minneapolis. In autumn 1916, Reinhard Piper offered Franz Marc's painting *Drei Tiere (Hund, Fuchs und Katze)* (Three Animals [Dog, Fox, and Cat]) (1912; cat. 102) to the Kunsthalle. It arrived in January, but it had been purchased not by the museum but by Sally Falk. This work also fell victim to his bankruptcy, and in April 1918, he was already selling it to Cassirer, from whom Caspari purchased it, ultimately successfully offering it to the Kunsthalle in October 1919. The painting, one of the most important Expressionist paintings in the Kunsthalle, was confiscated as "degenerate" in 1937 and offered for sale in the auction at the Galerie Fischer in Lucerne in 1939. No one showed any interest in it however, and it was returned to the Kunsthalle on July 12, 1940.

Erich Heckel had a first solo show of his works in September and October 1917, from which four woodcuts (fig. 7), three etchings, and a lithograph were purchased. He would also be represented in the exhibition *Neue religiöse Kunst* (New Religious Art). This project was the ultimate culmination of Hartlaub's engagement with Expressionism. In 1917, he presented his project to Wichert, who was still absent, with a reference to current psychological interest in the contemporaneous war. His ideas were supported precisely by this experience of the war; he saw an idealistic approach to overcoming this crisis situation in a retreat to one's own "divine I." His worldview was marked not so much by religious ideas as by elements of theosophic gnosis, according to which humankind would be saved by gnosis, that is, by recognizing their cosmic fate and their own divinity. Originally planned for autumn 1917, the exhibition was not held until January to March 1918. He summarized, as Hartlaub later wrote, "that which seemed religious and metaphysical in the area of German Expressionism."[12] "It seems to me that all true Expressionist art presumes, consciously or unconsciously, a religious attitude. The Expressionist spiritualizes the impressions of nature, recoalescing them."[13] The look of the exhibition was necessarily disparate as a result of the war. And it lacked such important artists as Christian Rohlfs, Adolf Hölzel, Otto Mueller, Oskar Moll, and Carl Hofer, because they had replied that they had not produced any religious works. Beckmann, too, said this now, because he did not want to exhibit for a time, Hartlaub wrote. Emil Nolde, who was for Hartlaub "the lonely fixed star in the Expressionist sky,"[14] was prominently represented with his great central panel *Kreuzigung* (Crucifixion) from the cycle *Das Leben Christi* (The Life of Christ) from around 1912. Ernst Ludwig Kirchner, Franz Marc, and Karl Schmidt-Rottluff were present with graphic works, as were Erich Heckel and Ludwig Meidner. As a stopgap, Oskar Kokoschka's portrait *Auguste Forel* from the museum's collection was shown. At the end of the exhibition, Hartlaub's summary was positive: "The exhibition was attended by more than 10,000 visitors and met with just as much agreement as passionate contradiction. From a certain art-pedagogical viewpoint, it was notable that some visitors who had not previously felt any inner connection to the will of the new art spontaneously gained an understanding of the characteristic forms and colors. Admittedly, they were not so much those of religious inclination but rather those striving in some way for a spiritual, mystical, religious worldview."[15] Hartlaub was one of the first to address a current theme in a museum—an achievement he would repeat in the case of New Objectivity. Hartlaub attributed to Expressionism great significance in terms of the function of art in modern society: he saw in the religious element a common foundation and general tendency that should be introduced into society.

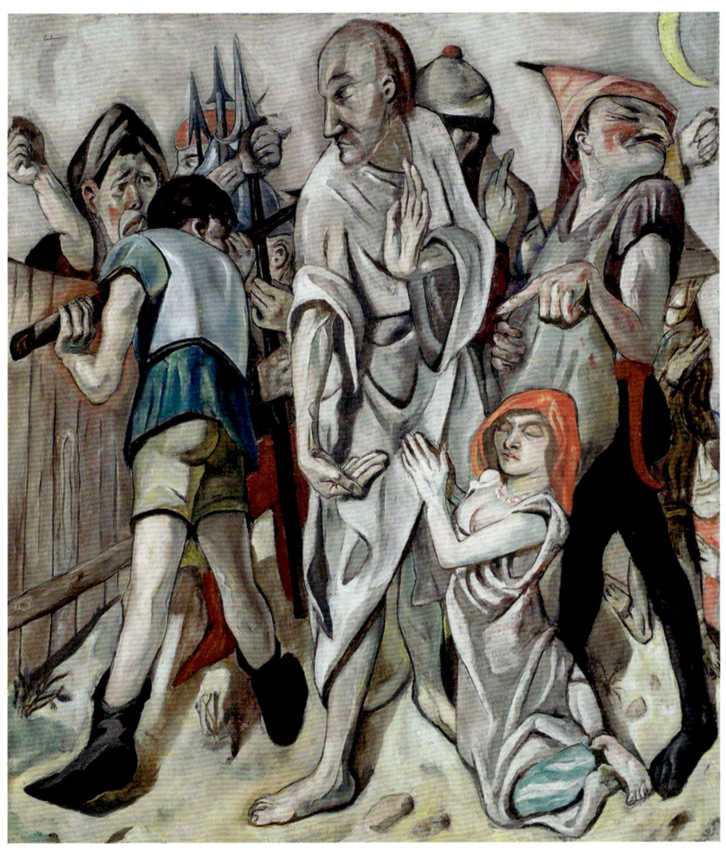

Abb./Fig. 8
Max Beckmann, *Christus und die Sünderin*/
Christ and the Sinner, **1917**
Öl auf Leinwand/*Oil on canvas*, 150 × 128 cm
Saint Louis Art Museum

war als Notlösung das Bildnis *Auguste Forel* aus eigenem Besitz ausgestellt. Hartlaub zog am Ende der Ausstellung ein positives Resümee: „Die Ausstellung wurde von über 10000 Besuchern besucht und fand Zustimmung ebensosehr, wie leidenschaftlichen Widerspruch. Von einem gewissen kunstpädagogischen Gesichtspunkte aus war es bemerkenswert, wie manche Besucher, die bisher in ihrem Inneren keinerlei Beziehung zu dem Wollen der neuen Kunst aufgebracht hatten, von dem religiösen Gegenstande her spontan ein Verständnis für das Eigentümliche der Form und Farbe gewannen. Freilich waren dies weniger die konfessionell Gesinnten, als die irgendwie nach einer geistmäßigen mystisch-religiösen Weltanschauung Strebenden […]".[15] Als einer der Ersten hatte sich Hartlaub museal einem aktuellen Thema gewidmet – eine Leistung, die sich im Fall der Neuen Sachlichkeit wiederholen sollte. Dem Expressionismus wies Hartlaub hinsichtlich der Funktion der Kunst in der modernen Gesellschaft eine große Bedeutung zu: Er erblickte im religiösen Element ein gemeinsames Fundament und eine allgemeine Tendenz, die in die Gesellschaft getragen werden solle.

Das Buch *Kunst und Religion*

Im Januar 1918 erhielt Hartlaub die Anfrage des Verlegers Kurt Wolff aus Leipzig, für die geplante Buchreihe zur Kunst der Gegenwart einen Band zur expressionistischen Kunst zu verfassen. Hartlaub nutzte die Gelegenheit und arbeitete seine Gedanken zum Thema weiter aus, nun frei von allen Beschränkungen, die Ausstellungsvorhaben auferlegten. Das Buch *Kunst und Religion* erschien im Herbst 1918 und ging über den Rahmen der Ausstellung weit hinaus.[16] Nach Hartlaubs Ansicht hatten nur Nolde und Beckmann die vollkommene Umsetzung ihres Inneren durch die Begegnung mit dem christlichen Mythos gefunden: „Von Beckmann zu Nolde führt kein Weg. Sie stehen als

The Book *Kunst und Religion*

In January 1918, Hartlaub was asked by the publisher Kurt Wolff in Leipzig to write a volume on Expressionist art for a planned series of books on contemporary art. Hartlaub took the opportunity and refined his thoughts on the subject, now free of all the restrictions that exhibition projects impose. The book *Kunst und Religion* (Art and Religion) was published in the autumn of 1918 and went far beyond the framework of the exhibition.[16] In Hartlaub's view, only Nolde and Beckmann had fully realized their inner feelings in their encounter with Christian myth: "No path leads from Beckmann to Nolde. They stand as the outermost poles of the will to art in Germany today. May the fact that the work of both was perfected in religious works be a sign for us!"[17] He saw in Beckmann's *Ehebrecherin (Christus und die Sünderin)* (Adulteress [Christ and the Sinner]) (fig. 8) a "certain gnostic, religious view, though that went beyond historical Christianity, . . . a mage-like and yet sublime view of Christ that had never been hazarded before."[18] Wichert purchased this very painting after his return in April 1919. Hartlaub had recommended it to him already in September 1918 after visiting Beckmann in his studio. And, notably, it could also be seen in the exhibition *Die Neue Sachlichkeit*, where it represented the transition from Expressionism to the new style. Nolde functioned as the opposite pole: "Yet the same Nolde, precisely because he is an artist who repeatedly grapples with Christian messages of salvation that he considers a worthy focal point for his production powers, that he paints his doubt, his despair, his presentiment and hope, his hate, his bad dream into them, to take up himself our cross, our sense of decline and transition."[19]

The Nolde exhibition planned for the autumn of 1918—to include sixty-five paintings and around seventy graphic works—could not be held because the war situation was worsening: Mannheim had been the target of severe bombing raids on September 7 and 16. At the same time, Hartlaub's reservations increased; his faith in the mission of Expressionism was shaken. He had associated it with an almost exaggerated hope that it could save the world. The failure of this hope after World War I ultimately led him to his interpretation of New Objectivity. "I do not believe that the cause of the fatigue lies in the matter, he wrote in a letter to Wichert in September 1918, but rather in "human inadequacy" and in the era.[20]

New Beginning after the First World War

The years from 1919 to 1923—after Wichert took up his post as director again in April 1919, and Hartlaub and Storck returned to their previous tasks—were personally challenging. Both Hartlaub and Wichert sought other positions; Storck, in turn, was appointed director of the Staatliche Kunsthalle in Karlsruhe in early 1920. Finally, in 1923, Wichert went to the Schule für freie und angewandte Kunst (School for Fine and Applied Art) in Frankfurt am Main, and Hartlaub became his successor after years of an interim directorship. Irrespective of these human problems, the years from 1919 to 1923 proved to be fruitful with regard to expanding the collection. At a time when Hartlaub was already distancing himself from Expressionism, Wichert continued to build the Expressionism collection. He had already purchased *Stilleben: Figur und Blumen* (Still Life: Figure and Flowers) (1917; cat. 120) by Max Pechstein from Fritz Gurlitt in May 1918. It fell victim to the confiscation actions of the Nazis in 1937 and was bought back in 1948. Wichert had paintings and graphic works sent to him on approval, and visited dealers, galleries, and artists. It is impossible to assess the extent to which Hartlaub was involved in these decisions. Wichert, too, focused on Nolde: in the artist's studio in Berlin in the summer of 1919, he selected *Tulpen* (Tulips) (1915; cat. 103) for purchase.

äußerste Pole des heutigen Kunstwollens in Deutschland sich gegenüber. Daß beider Werk sich in der religiösen Darstellung vollendet hat, sei uns ein Zeichen!"[17] In Beckmanns „Ehebrecherin" (*Christus und die Sünderin*; Abb. 8) sah er eine „gewisse gnostisch-religiöse, über das historische Christentum hinausgehende Auffassung, [...] eine magushafte und doch erhabene Auffassung Christi, wie sie eigentlich noch nie gewagt worden ist."[18] Gerade dieses Bild war es dann, das Wichert nach seiner Rückkehr im April 1919 erwerben sollte. Hartlaub hatte es ihm bereits im September 1918, nach einem Atelierbesuch bei Beckmann, ans Herz gelegt. Und es sollte dann bemerkenswerterweise auch in der Ausstellung *Die Neue Sachlichkeit* zu sehen sein, wo es den Übergang vom Expressionismus zum neuen Stil repräsentierte. Als Gegenpol fungierte Nolde: „Doch derselbe Nolde hat, eben durch die Tatsache, daß er als Künstler immer wieder mit den christlichen Heilsberichten ringt, daß er sie für würdig erachtet, Sammelpunkt seiner produktiven Kräfte zu sein, daß er seinen Zweifel, seine Verzweiflung, seine Ahnung und Hoffnung, seinen Haß, seinen bösen Traum in sie hineinmalt, auch bewiesen, daß diese Stoffe unserer Zeit lebendig, daß sie wie nichts fähig sind, auch unser Kreuz, unsere Untergangs- und Übergangsstimmung auf sich zu nehmen."[19]

Die für den Herbst 1918 geplante Nolde-Ausstellung – vorgesehen waren 65 Gemälde und ca. 70 Grafiken – konnte aufgrund der sich zuspitzenden Kriegslage nicht stattfinden, war Mannheim doch am 7. und 16. September Ziel schwerer Bombenangriffe geworden. Gleichzeitig verstärkten sich Hartlaubs Vorbehalte, sein Glauben an die Mission des Expressionismus war erschüttert. Er hatte mit diesem eine geradezu übersteigerte Welterlösungshoffnung verbunden. Das Scheitern dieser Hoffnung nach dem Ersten Weltkrieg führte letztlich zu seiner Interpretation der Neuen Sachlichkeit. „Ich glaube nicht, dass die Ursache der Ermattung in der Sache liegt", schrieb er in einem Brief vom September 1918 an Wichert, sondern an der „Unzulänglichkeit der Menschen" und an der Zeit.[20]

Neuanfang nach dem Ersten Weltkrieg

Die Jahre von 1919 bis 1923 waren, nachdem Wichert ab April 1919 sein Amt als Direktor wieder wahrnahm und Hartlaub und Storck zu ihren ursprünglichen Aufgaben zurückkehrten, personell herausfordernd. Sowohl Hartlaub als auch Wichert suchten nach anderen Wirkungsstätten, Storck wiederum wurde Anfang 1920 zum Direktor der Staatlichen Kunsthalle in Karlsruhe berufen. Wichert ging 1923 schließlich nach Frankfurt an die Schule für freie und angewandte Kunst und Hartlaub wurde nun nach Jahren des Interimsdirektorats sein Nachfolger. Unabhängig von diesen menschlichen Problemen sollten sich die Jahre zwischen 1919 und 1923 unter dem Aspekt der Sammlungserweiterung als fruchtbar erweisen. Denn zu einem Zeitpunkt, als Hartlaub sich schon vom Expressionismus distanzierte, baute Wichert die Expressionismus-Sammlung weiter aus. Das *Stilleben: Figur und Blumen* (1917; Kat. 120) von Max Pechstein hatte er bereits im Mai 1918 bei Fritz Gurlitt erworben. Es fiel 1937 den Beschlagnahmeaktionen der Nazis zum Opfer und wurde 1948 wieder zurückerworben. Wichert ließ sich Bilder und Grafiken zur Ansicht schicken, besuchte Händler, Galerien und Kunstschaffende. Inwieweit Hartlaub in die Überlegungen einbezogen war, lässt sich nicht beurteilen. Den Fokus legte auch Wichert auf Nolde, im Sommer 1919 wählte er in dessen Berliner Atelier das Gemälde *Tulpen* (1915; Kat. 103) zum Erwerb aus. Auch dieses Bild wurde 1937 beschlagnahmt und befindet sich heute im Museum Ludwig Köln. Ende des Jahres reiste Wichert erneut nach Berlin, um Nolde und seine Frau Ada zu treffen, vermutlich um den 1920 vollzogenen Erwerb von *Vorabend (Marschlandschaft)* (1916, Kat. 106) und

This painting was also confiscated in 1937 and is now in the Museum Ludwig in Cologne. At the end of 1919, Wichert traveled to Berlin again to meet Nolde and his wife, Ada, presumably to make arrangements for the purchase of *Vorabend (Marschlandschaft)* (Twilight [Marsh Landscape]) (1916; cat. 106) and the still life *Figuren und Georginen* (Figures and Dahlias) (1919; cat. 104), which then took place in 1920. These two works were also confiscated in 1937. The former was resold via the Buch- und Kunsthandlung Karl Buchholz in Berlin and acquired by the Kunstmuseum Basel in 1939. The still life, in turn, ended up at the Statens Museum for Kunst in Copenhagen, also via Karl Buchholz. At the end of 1921, the exhibition of works by Nolde that Hartlaub had begun planning was finally held, though somewhat smaller and slightly delayed because damage to the museum building from a large explosion at the Badische Anilin- und Soda-Fabrik (BASF) first had to be repaired.

In 1919, Wichert also purchased two more paintings by Heckel: *Sonnenblumen* (Sunflowers) (1913; cat. 121) from the Kunsthandlung Carl Nicolai in Berlin and *Dorfdom in Flandern* (Village Cathedral in Flanders) (1918; fig. 9) via I. B. Neumann, also in Berlin. The former was on the list of works confiscated as "degenerate," but it remained in the museum. *Dorfdom in Flandern* was confiscated, and its whereabouts today are unknown. In 1922, they were joined by the painting *Drei Frauen* (Three Women) (1921; cat. 105), which was also confiscated in 1937 and is now in the collection of the Brücke-Museum in Berlin. Finally, in February 1922, Heckel's *Gewitterlandschaft*, Hartlaub's first acquisition of an Expressionist work, left the collection when it was sold to the Frankfurt art dealer Ludwig Schames, presumably to generate funds for other purchases—that may have disappointed Hartlaub. In 1920, Wichert purchased Oskar Moll's *Stilleben mit blühender Amaryllis* (Still Life with Blooming Amaryllis) (1917; fig. 10); it was confiscated in 1937 and today it is in a private collection. In 1921, Ernst Ludwig Kirchner's *Rote Häuser, Roter Januar II* (Red Houses, Red January II) (1910; fig. 11) entered the museum, another loss through confiscation, and is now in a private collection. After Wichert's departure, Hartlaub, although he had long since turned away from Expressionism in dis-appointment, nevertheless purchased Kirchner's *Stilleben mit Krug und afrikanischer Schale* (Still Life with Jug and African Bowl) (1912; fig. 12) in 1926, which was also confiscated in 1937 and is now in the Los Angeles County Museum of Art. And in 1925, he acquired Kokoschka's vedute *Amsterdam, Kloveniersburgval I* (cat. 81), painted that same year. That was the last of the acquisitions of Expres-sionist paintings. Solo exhibitions were dedicated to Christian Rohlfs in 1920, Karl Schmidt-Rottluff in 1925, and Oskar Kokoschka in 1931. In retrospect, Wichert's commitment to Expressionism can be linked to his friendship with Georg Swarzenski, the director of the Städel Museum in Frankfurt, who was building an Expressionist collection at the same time. Important works by Max Beckmann were also being acquired in Mannheim and Frankfurt at the same time and in exchange with each other.

From 1933:
The Turning Point of National Socialism

Immediately after the Nazis took power, Hartlaub was suspended from his post in March 1933. Edmund Strübing (1888–1937), curator of the Graphic Arts Collection, took over provisionally as director of the museum. On April 3, 1933, however, Otto Gebele von Waldstein, leader of the local group of the National Socialist Party, was placed alongside him as an advisory consultant. The lat-ter had previously polemicized against Hartlaub many times in the daily newspaper *Das Haken-kreuzbanner* (The Swastika Banner). Almost as soon as he had taken office, he presented a so-called

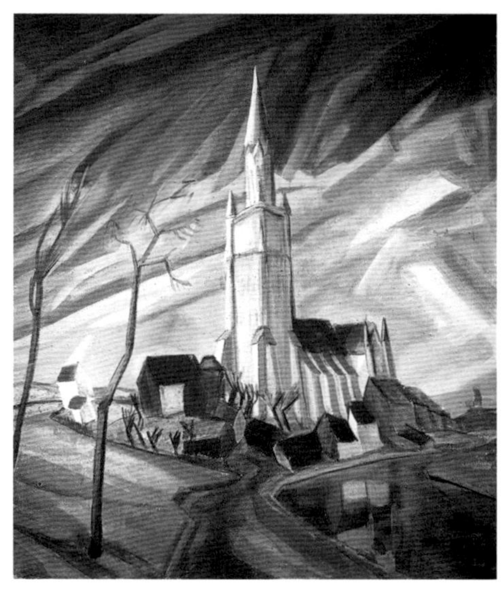

Abb. / Fig. 9
Erich Heckel, *Dorfdom in Flandern* /
Village Cathedral in Flanders, **1918**
Öl auf Leinwand / *Oil on canvas*, 96 × 83 cm
Verbleib unbekannt / *Whereabouts unknown*

THE KUNSTHALLE MANNHEIM AND EXPRESSIONISM

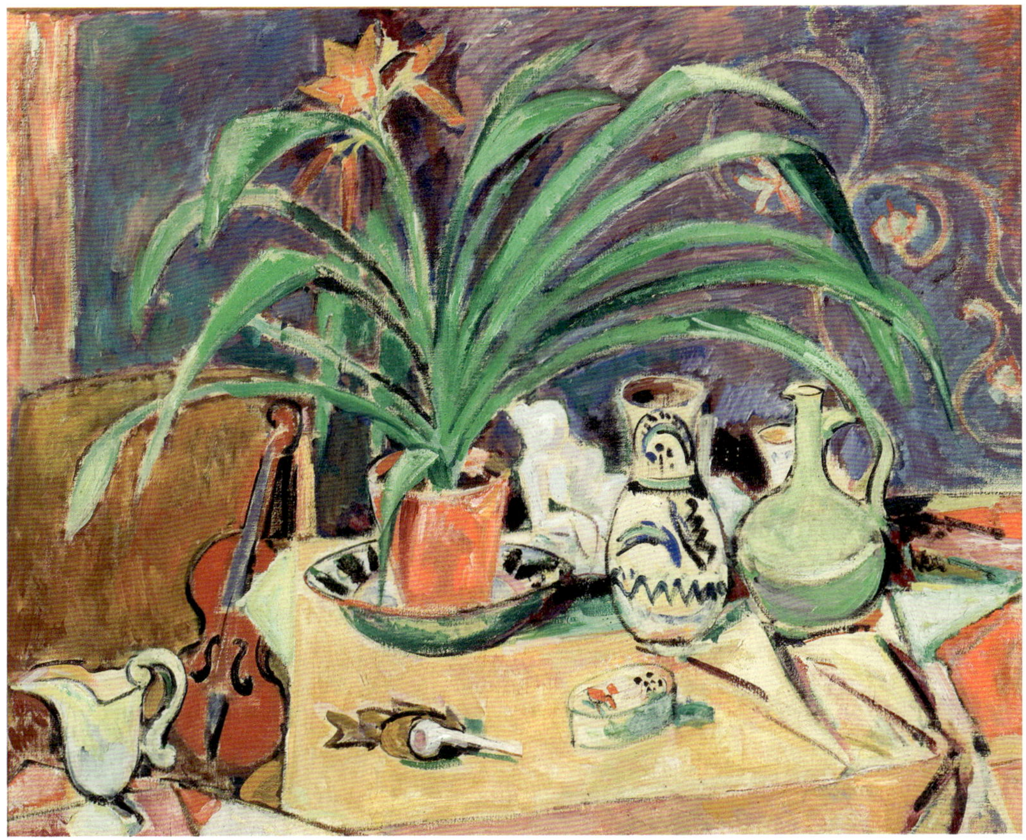

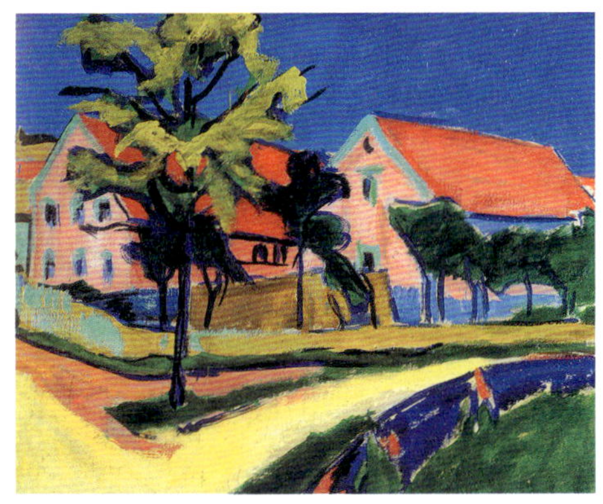

dem Stillleben *Figuren und Georginen* (1919; Kat. 104) vorzubereiten. Auch diese beiden Arbeiten wurden 1937 beschlagnahmt. Ersteres wurde über die Buch- und Kunsthandlung Karl Buchholz in Berlin verwertet und 1939 vom Kunstmuseum Basel erworben. Das Stillleben wiederum gelangte, vermittelt durch Karl Buchholz, ins Statens Museum for Kunst in Kopenhagen. Ende 1921 fand dann schließlich die schon von Hartlaub geplante Ausstellung mit Werken Noldes statt, allerdings etwas weniger umfangreich und leicht verzögert, weil die durch eine große Explosion in der Badischen Anilin- und Soda-Fabrik (BASF) entstandenen Schäden am Museumsgebäude erst behoben werden mussten.

Noch 1919 erwarb Wichert auch zwei weitere Bilder von Heckel: *Sonnenblumen* (1913; Kat. 121) von der Berliner Kunsthandlung Carl Nicolai und *Dorfdom in Flandern* (1918; Abb. 9) über I. B. Neumann, ebenfalls Berlin. Ersteres war auf der Liste der als „entartet" beschlagnahmten Werke, verblieb aber im Museum. Das Bild *Dorfdom in Flandern* wurde beschlagnahmt, der heutige Verbleib ist unbekannt. 1922 kam noch das Gemälde *Drei Frauen* (1921; Kat. 105) hinzu, das ebenfalls 1937 beschlagnahmt wurde und sich heute im Besitz des Brücke-Museums Berlin befindet. Die Sammlung verlassen hat schließlich im Februar 1922 Heckels *Gewitterlandschaft*, Hartlaubs erste Erwerbung eines expressionistischen Werks, verkauft an den Frankfurter Kunsthändler Ludwig Schames, wohl um Mittel für andere Ankäufe zu generieren – Hartlaub mag das enttäuscht haben. 1920 kaufte Wichert Oskar Molls *Stilleben mit blühender Amaryllis* (1917; Abb. 10), es wurde 1937 beschlagnahmt und befindet sich heute in Privatbesitz. 1921 schließlich kam Ernst Ludwig Kirchners *Rote Häuser, Roter Januar II* (1910; Abb. 11) ins Museum, ebenfalls ein Verlust durch Beschlagnahmung, auch dieses befindet sich

exhibition of shame at the Kunsthalle from April to June 1933 under the title *Kulturbolschewistische Bilder* (Cultural Bolshevist Pictures), in which he sought to denounce the directorship of the museum not only for "incompetence" but also for its irresponsible handling of funds from its budget and supposed dependence on Jewish art dealers. It showed works by Max Beckmann, Marc Chagall, Otto Dix, Xaver Fuhr, George Grosz, Paul Klee, Franz Marc, Emil Nolde, and others. The paintings were presented in degrading ways: without frames, hung closely together, and labeled with price tags indicating the "incredible" sums that had been spent on this "inferior art." A so-called *Musterkabinett* (Cabinet of Models) was set up as a contrast to present exemplary works by artists from Mannheim, in this case framed. Despite isolated critical voices, this tendentious show—the first antimodern propaganda show under National Socialism—was a success with the public. Cities such as Munich, Bamberg, Erlangen, Frankfurt, and Cologne wanted to take it. Parts of it were indeed shown at the Kunstverein München from June to July 1933 under the title *Mannheimer Galerieankäufe* (Mannheim Museum Acquisitions). From July to August 1933, it could be seen at the Kunstverein Erlangen as *Mannheimer Schreckenskammer* (Mannheim Chamber of Horrors). With an intent to defame them, the works of art were presented here alongside works by the mentally ill.

1936–1958:
The Kunsthalle under Walter Passarge

In 1936, the art historian Walter Passarge (1898–1958), who had previously been at the Schleswig-Holsteinisches Landesmuseum in Kiel, took over as director of the Kunsthalle. He held that office until his death in 1958, and after 1945 he gave the museum a new direction. His years as director under National Socialism are characterized by the exploration of the possibilities open to him and by working to counter the confiscations of "degenerate" art from the Kunsthalle. Under the direction of Adolf Ziegler, president of the Reichskammer der bildenden Künste (Reich Chamber of the Fine Arts), eighteen paintings, five sculptures, and thirty-five graphic works were confiscated from the Kunsthalle's holdings as examples of "German art of decline" on July 8, 1937.[21] Like many other German art museums, the Kunsthalle was subjected to a second confiscation of "degenerate" art at the end of August. On Augst 28, more than 500 works of art were removed from the collection and transported to Berlin, including numerous works by Expressionists (Erich Heckel, Alexej von Jawlensky, Ernst Ludwig Kirchner, Oskar Kokoschka, Franz Marc, Emil Nolde, Max Pechstein, Christian Rohlfs), some of which were resold by the Galerie Buchholz in Berlin or auctioned in Lucerne in 1939, ending up in international museums and private collections. Only a few works, such as Heckel's *Sonnenblumen*, Kokoschka's *Amsterdam, Kloveniersburgval I*, and Marc's *Drei Tiere (Hund, Fuchs und Katze)* were confiscated but returned to the Kunsthalle during the Nazi era, by means that in some cases can no longer be reconstructed, or had never left it in the first place.

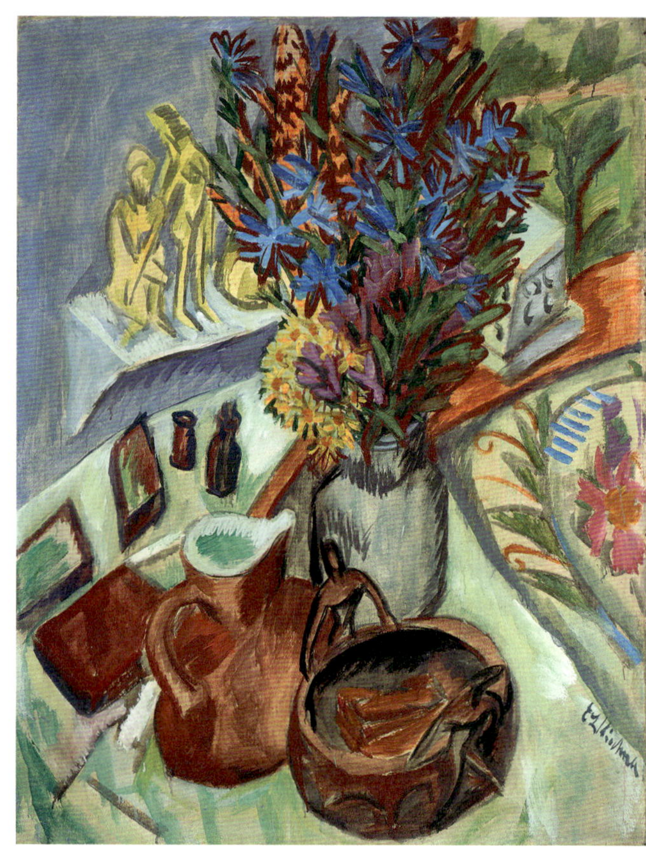

Abb./Fig. **12**
Ernst Ludwig Kirchner, *Stilleben mit Krug und afrikanischer Schale* / *Still Life with Jug and African Bowl,* **1912**
Öl auf Leinwand / *Oil on canvas,* 121 × 91 cm
Los Angeles County Museum of Art

THE KUNSTHALLE MANNHEIM AND EXPRESSIONISM

in Privatbesitz. Nach Wicherts Weggang erwarb Hartlaub schließlich 1926, obwohl er sich vom Expressionismus längst enttäuscht abgewandt hatte, noch Kirchners *Stilleben mit Krug und afrikanischer Schale* (1912; Abb. 12), das ebenfalls 1937 beschlagnahmt wurde und sich heute im Los Angeles County Museum of Art befindet. Und 1925 hatte er Kokoschkas im selben Jahr gemalte Ansicht *Amsterdam, Kloveniersburgval I* erworben (Kat. 81). Damit waren im Bereich der Malerei die Erwerbungen expressionistischer Kunst abgeschlossen, an Ausstellungen widmete man 1920 Christian Rohlfs, 1925 Karl Schmidt-Rottluff und 1931 Oskar Kokoschka Einzelpräsentationen. Rückblickend lässt sich Wicherts Einsatz für den Expressionismus in Verbindung mit seiner Freundschaft zu Georg Swarzenski bringen, dem Leiter des Städel Museums in Frankfurt, der sich zeitgleich um den Aufbau einer Expressionisten-Sammlung bemühte. Auch wichtige Werke von Max Beckmann erwarb man in Mannheim und Frankfurt zeitgleich und im Austausch miteinander.

Ab 1933:
die Zäsur durch den Nationalsozialismus

Sofort nach dem Machtantritt der Nazis wurde Hartlaub im März 1933 vom Dienst suspendiert. Edmund Strübing (1888–1937), Kustos der Graphischen Sammlung, übernahm zunächst kommissarisch die Leitung des Museums. Am 3. April 1933 wurde ihm allerdings Otto Gebele von Waldstein, Leiter der NSDAP-Ortsgruppe, als kommissarischer Hilfsreferent an die Seite gestellt. Dieser hatte schon im Vorfeld in der Tageszeitung *Hakenkreuzbanner* mehrfach gegen Hartlaub polemisiert. Kaum im Amt, präsentierte er von April bis Juni 1933 in der Kunsthalle unter dem Titel *Kulturbolschewistische Bilder* eine sogenannte Schandausstellung, mit der er nicht nur die „Unfähigkeit" der Museumsleitung anprangern wollte, sondern auch deren verantwortungslosen Umgang mit Budgetmitteln sowie die angebliche Abhängigkeit von jüdischen Kunsthändlern. Gezeigt wurden Werke von Max Beckmann, Marc Chagall, Otto Dix, Xaver Fuhr, George Grosz, Paul Klee, Franz Marc, Emil Nolde und anderen. Die Bilder wurden in entwürdigender Weise ohne Rahmen präsentiert, in dichter Hängung und versehen mit Preisschildern, die die „ungeheuren" Summen auflisteten, welche für diese „minderwertige Kunst" ausgegeben worden waren. Als Kontrast wurde ein sogenanntes Musterkabinett eingerichtet, das vorbildliche, nun gerahmte Werke von Mannheimer Künstlern vorstellte. Trotz vereinzelter kritischer Gegenstimmen wurde die tendenziöse Schau, die erste antimoderne Propagandaschau im Nationalsozialismus, ein Publikumserfolg. Städte wie München, Bamberg, Erlangen, Frankfurt und Köln wollten sie übernehmen. Tatsächlich wurden Teile von Juni bis Juli 1933 im Kunstverein München unter dem Titel „Mannheimer Galerieankäufe" gezeigt. Von Juli bis August 1933 war sie als „Mannheimer Schreckenskammer" im Kunstverein Erlangen zu sehen. Hier wurden den Kunstwerken in diffamierender Absicht Arbeiten von psychisch Kranken gegenübergestellt.

1936–1958:
die Kunsthalle unter Walter Passarge

1936 wurde der zuvor am Schleswig-Holsteinischen Landesmuseum in Kiel tätige Kunsthistoriker Walter Passarge (1898–1958) Direktor der Kunsthalle. Er sollte dieses Amt bis zu seinem Tod 1958 innehaben und das Museum nach 1945 wieder neu ausrichten. Seine Jahre als Direktor während des Nationalsozialismus sind geprägt vom Ausloten möglicher Spielräume und vom Einsatz gegen die Beschlagnahmungen „entarteter Kunst" in der Kunsthalle. Unter der Leitung von Adolf Ziegler, Präsident der Reichskammer der bildenden Künste, wurden am 8. Juli 1937 18 Gemälde, fünf

Looking back at Passarge's period in office, the latest research by Hannah Krause has helped provide a more complex picture.[22] The freedom to acquire that his predecessors had enjoyed was not available to him. He turned to the innocuous field of German applied art and thus opened up a new collecting area for the Kunsthalle. As productive as this was, it must also be noted that from 1942 onward he had been hired by the tax office as an "expert" to assess the goods being moved in containers belonging to German-Jewish citizens who had been forced to emigrate. According to Krause, his task was to "secure" valuable art objects for museums or the Reichskammer der bildenden Künste. She concludes that while in office Passarge tried to satisfy the regime's expectations for cultural policy without letting himself be completely controlled ideologically: "His behavior was neither clear resistance nor pure allegiance but rather an expression of a strategic conformity that was characteristic of many cultural figures of that era."[23]

The Network:
The Gallerist Herbert Tannenbaum

The Kunsthalle Mannheim was part of a well-functioning network of galleries, museums, and collectors. Mannheim-born Herbert Tannenbaum (1892–1958) was an influential gallerist in Mannheim in the 1920s.[24] He showed an early enthusiasm for everything artistic, but he began studying law at his father's wish. In addition to grappling with the new medium of film, which made him one of the first German film theorists, Tannenbaum pursued his interests at the Kunsthalle Mannheim in particular. While still a student, he was a member of the Freier Bund from 1911 onward, and immediately after completing his studies he gave several lectures at the Akademie für Jedermann (Academy for Everyone) located there. He continued to pursue this commitment after World War I. In 1920, Tannenbaum founded the Kunsthaus, a store for art and books, located first in A 2, 5 and then from 1921 on the Friedrichsring in Q 7, 17a (fig. 13). The Kunsthaus quickly established itself on the regional art market as the most important gallery for the modern avant-garde. Tannenbaum organized exhibitions of such important artists as Otto Dix, James Ensor, Marc Chagall, and Paul Klee. At the same time, however, he also supported young regional artists, including Willy Oeser, Wilfried Otto, and Georg Scholz. Tannenbaum procured for the Kunsthalle a series of important works, such as Auguste Rodin's *Bust of Gustav Mahler* but also works that were confiscated as "degenerate" art in 1937, including James Ensor's *Death and the Masks* or the two Chagall paintings *La Prise (Rabbin)* (The Pinch of Snuff [Rabbi]) and *La maison bleue à Vitebsk* (Blue House in Vitebsk). Tannenbaum's spectrum was broad; Expressionist art was not necessarily his main emphasis, but he sold graphic works by Heckel, Kirchner, Lehmbruck, Mueller, Nolde, and Schmidt-Rottluff. And he advised the dentist Rudolf Frank and his wife Bertha, collectors in Mannheim who purchased above all Expressionist art from Tannenbaum, such as Otto Mueller's *Mutter und Sohn* (Mother and Son) (fig. 14), created around 1919 and purchased in 1920, or Karl Schmidt-Rottluff's *Roter Blumenstrauß* (Bouquet of Red Flowers) from 1922, acquired in 1928. The Frank Collection, to which works by Heckel, Lehmbruck, and Nolde also belong, has been on permanent loan to the Kunstmuseum Stuttgart since 1992.[25] Already at the beginning of the National Socialist dictatorship, Tannenbaum was a target of those in power. In the exhibition *Kulturbolschewistische Bilder*, which opened at the Kunsthalle in April 1933, numerous paintings and graphic works purchased from him were pilloried. He was accused of having been the driving force behind the acquisition of art described as a waste of public money.

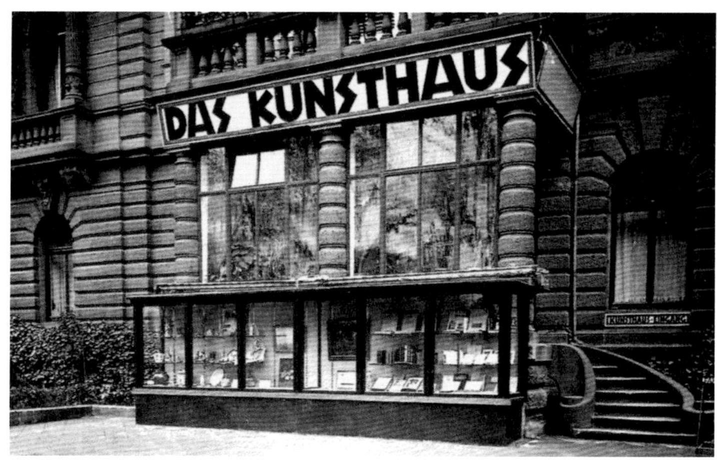

Plastiken und 35 grafische Werke aus dem Bestand der Kunsthalle als Beispiele „deutscher Verfallskunst" beschlagnahmt.[21] Wie zahlreiche andere deutsche Kunstmuseen war auch die Kunsthalle Ende August von einer zweiten Beschlagnahme „entarteter Kunst" betroffen. Am 28. August wurden noch einmal über 500 Kunstwerke aus dem Sammlungsbestand entfernt und nach Berlin abtransportiert, darunter zahlreiche Arbeiten der Expressionisten (Erich Heckel, Alexej von Jawlensky, Ernst Ludwig Kirchner, Oskar Kokoschka, Franz Marc, Emil Nolde, Max Pechstein, Christian Rohlfs), die zum Teil über die Galerie Buchholz in Berlin „verwertet" oder in der Luzerner Aktion im Jahr 1939 versteigert wurden und in internationale Museen oder Privatsammlungen kamen. Nur einzelne Werke wie Heckels *Sonnenblumen*, Kokoschkas *Amsterdam, Kloveniersburgval I* und Marcs *Drei Tiere (Hund, Fuchs und Katze)* waren zwar beschlagnahmt worden, gelangten aber nach zum Teil nicht mehr rekonstruierbaren Vorgängen noch in der Nazi-Zeit wieder in die Kunsthalle zurück oder hatten sie erst gar nicht verlassen.

Im Rückblick auf die Amtszeit von Passarge tragen neueste Forschungen von Hannah Krause zur Differenzierung des bisherigen Bildes bei.[22] Eine freie Ankaufstätigkeit, wie sie seine Vorgänger betrieben hatten, war für ihn nicht möglich. Er wich auf das unverfängliche Feld deutscher Werkkunst aus und erschloss der Kunsthalle ein neues Sammlungsgebiet. So verdienstvoll dies war, bleibt jedoch auch zu konstatieren, dass er seit 1942 als „Sachverständiger" vom Finanzamt beauftragt worden war, das Umzugsgut aus den Containern der in die Emigration gezwungenen Jüdinnen und Juden zu begutachten. Er hatte, so Krause, die Aufgabe, wertvolle Kunstgegenstände für die Museen oder die Reichskammer der bildenden Künste zu „sichern". Sie kommt zu dem Schluss, dass Passarge in seiner Amtszeit die kulturpolitischen Erwartungen des Regimes zu erfüllen suchte, ohne sich vollständig ideologisch vereinnahmen zu lassen. „Sein Verhalten war weder klarer Widerstand noch reine Gefolgschaft – vielmehr Ausdruck einer strategischen Anpassung, wie sie für viele Kulturakteure jener Zeit kennzeichnend war."[23]

Das Netzwerk: der Galerist Herbert Tannenbaum

Die Kunsthalle Mannheim war Teil eines gut funktionierenden Netzwerkes von Galerien, Museen und Sammler*innen. Als Galerist prägend war in den 1920er-Jahren der in Mannheim geborene Herbert Tannenbaum (1892–1958).[24] Er begeisterte sich bereits früh für alles Künstlerische, begann jedoch auf Wunsch des Vaters ein Studium der Rechtswissenschaften. Neben seiner Auseinandersetzung mit dem neuen Medium Film, was ihn zu einem der ersten deutschen Filmtheoretiker machte, ging Tannenbaum seinen Interessen besonders in der Mannheimer Kunsthalle nach. Dort engagierte sich der Student bereits ab 1911 als Mitglied im Freien Bund und übernahm unmittelbar nach dem Studium einige Vorträge in der dort angesiedelten Akademie für Jedermann. Auch nach dem Ersten Weltkrieg setzte er dieses Engagement fort. 1920 gründete Tannenbaum mit dem Kunsthaus eine Kunst- und Buchhandlung, die zunächst in A 2, 5, ab 1921 am Friedrichsring in Q 7, 17a beheimatet war (Abb. 13). Das Kunsthaus etablierte sich schnell auf dem regionalen Kunstmarkt als wichtigste Galerie der modernen Avantgarde. Tannenbaum veranstaltete Ausstellungen so bedeutender

Abb./Fig. 13
Das Kunsthaus von Herbert Tannenbaum /
Herbert Tannenbaum's Kunsthaus, in Q 7, 17a,
Mannheim 1921

Against that backdrop and the increasingly limited opportunities for a Jewish citizen to do business in Mannheim, Tannenbaum decided at the end of 1936 to sell the Kunsthaus to the Dresden art dealer Rudolf Probst (1890–1968). A few months later, he moved to the Netherlands with his wife and daughter and was able to gain a footing in Amsterdam with a small gallery. In 1947, he moved with his family to New York. In that context, shortly before his departure, Max Beckmann painted the portrait *Tannenbaum geht nach New York* (Tannenbaum Goes to New York) (cat. 38). That same year, the artist also emigrated to America from Amsterdam, where he too had been living in exile.

The Gallerist and Art Dealer Rudolf Probst

Rudolf Probst was even more interested in Expressionism than Tannenbaum was; he greatly admired Emil Nolde in particular.[26] Probst had begun working in 1915–16 and then from 1918 at Emil Richter's gallery in Dresden, which had exhibited the art of the Brücke artists as early as 1907 and 1908. With his brother, he visited Nolde in his studio in Berlin in 1917, where he acquired two paintings. In 1919, they began a correspondence that lasted decades. Much like Hartlaub's at the same time, Probst's admiration expressed an almost reverence for Nolde's paintings that was like a substitute religion. He gave lectures on the artist and in

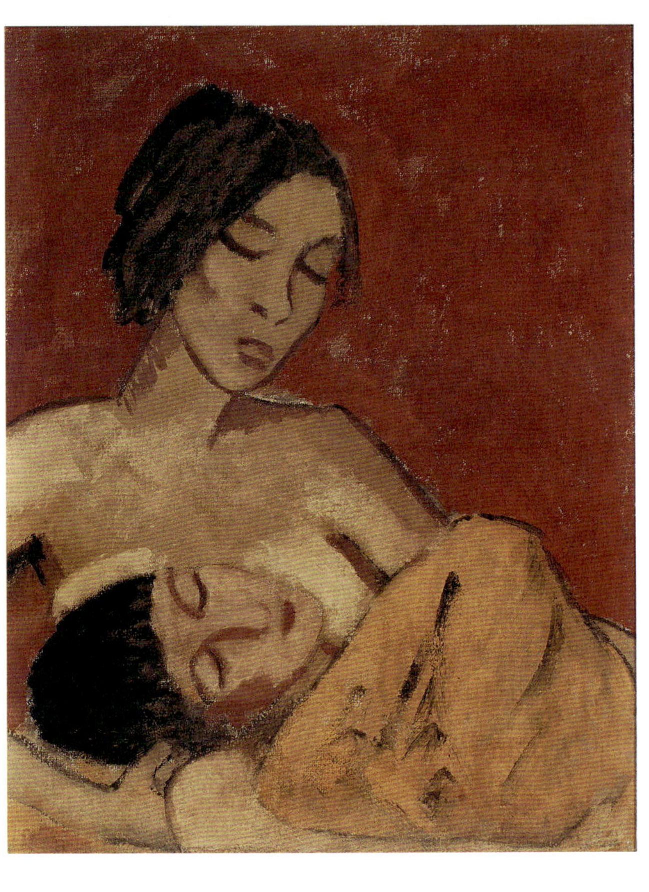

1920 he organized the first exhibition that was a financial success. In 1923, he went independent and opened a gallery in Dresden called Neue Kunst Fides (Fides Modern Art) with a Nolde exhibition. The painting *Pferd und Füllen* (Horse and Filly) (1915) was exhibited there, which from 1927 would be owned by the collector Paula Deetjen of Hagen and later Heidelberg, who sold the work to the Kunsthalle Mannheim in 1949 (cat. 131). Nine more large Nolde shows followed. From the broader circle of Expressionists, Probst showed Heckel and Kirchner often but also Conrad Felixmüller, Schmidt-Rottluff, and Franz Marc, whose widow he had met in 1916–17. The culmination was the large show in 1927 for Emil Nolde's sixtieth birthday, which was presented in the municipal exhibition building. It was the first comprehensive survey of his work and also the largest that the artist had had until then. Julius Meier-Graefe commented ironically: "The speaker [i.e., Probst] compares Nolde to Christus, who was also a magician."[27] And in her review Bettina Feistel-Rohmeder already evoked the disdainful language of the future powers that be when she spoke of "blunders of paint," of the "primitive attempts at art of a people without culture, mirrored in a soul hostile to art."[28] In 1926, Hartlaub had purchased from Probst two graphic works by the Jewish sculptor Jussuf Abbo (fig. 15), which, astonishingly, did not fall victim to the confiscation actions. In 1933, Probst, whose gallery had been in a critical financial situation since 1928, felt compelled to close, in part because of the political conditions. In 1936, he risked a new beginning in Mannheim and took over the Kunsthaus from Tannenbaum, whom he had met in Dresden. The change was announced on January 1, 1937. It was, however, a difficult start: the Emil Nolde exhibition that opened on June 12 was closed early on July 8. Adolf Ziegler, who was

Künstler wie Otto Dix, James Ensor, Marc Chagall oder Paul Klee. Gleichzeitig förderte er aber auch junge regionale Künstler, darunter Willy Oeser, Wilfried Otto oder Georg Scholz. Der Kunsthalle wiederum vermittelte Tannenbaum eine Reihe wichtiger Werke, etwa Auguste Rodins *Büste Gustav Mahler*, aber auch Werke, die 1937 als „entartete Kunst" beschlagnahmt wurden, darunter James Ensors *Der Tod und die Masken* oder die beiden Chagall-Gemälde *Die Prise (Rabbiner)* und *Blaues Haus in Witebsk*. Tannenbaums Spektrum war weit, expressionistische Kunst war nicht unbedingt sein Schwerpunkt, doch verkaufte er Grafiken von Heckel, Kirchner, Lehmbruck, Mueller, Nolde und Schmidt-Rottluff. Und er beriet ein Mannheimer Sammlerpaar, den Zahnarzt Rudolf Frank und dessen Frau Bertha, das bei Tannenbaum vor allem expressionistische Kunst ankaufte, etwa Otto Muellers *Mutter und Sohn* (Abb. 14), um 1919 entstanden und 1920 erworben, oder Karl Schmidt-Rottluffs *Roter Blumenstrauß* aus dem Jahr 1922, erworben 1928. Die Sammlung Frank, zu der auch Arbeiten von Heckel, Lehmbruck und Nolde gehören, befindet sich seit 1992 als Dauerleihgabe im Kunstmuseum Stuttgart.[25] Bereits am Beginn der NS-Diktatur wurde Tannenbaum zur Zielscheibe der neuen Machthaber. In der im April eröffneten Ausstellung *Kulturbolschewistische Bilder* in der Kunsthalle wurden auch zahlreiche von ihm erworbene Gemälde und Grafiken an den Pranger gestellt. Er wurde als treibende Kraft hinter dem als Verschwendung von öffentlichen Mitteln gebrandmarkten Kunsterwerb angeklagt. Vor diesem Hintergrund und den zunehmend eingeschränkten Möglichkeiten für einen jüdischen Bürger, in Mannheim ein Geschäft zu führen, entschied sich Tannenbaum Ende 1936, Das Kunsthaus an den Dresdner Kunsthändler Rudolf Probst (1890–1968) zu verkaufen. Er selbst übersiedelte zusammen mit Frau und Tochter wenige Monate später in die Niederlande und konnte in Amsterdam mit einer kleinen Galerie Fuß fassen. 1947 zog er mit seiner Familie nach New York. In diesem Kontext entstand kurz vor der Abreise Max Beckmanns Porträt *Tannenbaum geht nach New York* (Kat. 38). Auch der Künstler emigrierte im selben Jahr von Amsterdam, wo er im Exil gelebt hatte, nach Amerika.

Der Galerist und Kunsthändler Rudolf Probst

Rudolf Probst war stärker noch als Tannenbaum am Expressionismus interessiert, vor allem Emil Nolde schätzte er sehr.[26] Probst hatte 1915/16 und dann ab 1918 in der Galerie von Emil Richter in Dresden zu arbeiten begonnen, die bereits 1907 und 1908 die Kunst der Brücke-Künstler ausstellte. Mit seinem Bruder besuchte er 1917 Nolde in seinem Berliner Atelier, wo dieser zwei Bilder erwarb. Ab 1919 begann dann ein jahrzehntelanger Briefwechsel. Ähnlich wie bei Hartlaub zeitgleich spricht aus Probsts Bewunderung eine quasi ersatzreligiöse Verehrung der Bilder Noldes, er hielt Vorträge über den Künstler und richtete ihm 1920 eine erste Ausstellung aus, die ein wirtschaftlicher Erfolg werden sollte. 1923 stellte er sich dann auf eigene Füße und eröffnete mit einer Nolde-Ausstellung in Dresden eine Galerie unter dem Namen Neue Kunst Fides. Dort war auch das Gemälde *Pferd und Füllen* (1915) ausgestellt, das sich dann ab 1927 im Besitz der Hagener, später Heidelberger Sammlerin Paula Deetjen befand, die das Werk schließlich 1949 an die Kunsthalle Mannheim verkaufte (Kat. 131). Neun weitere große Nolde-Schauen sollten folgen. Aus dem weiteren Kreis der Expressionisten zeigte Probst neben Heckel häufig Kirchner, auch Conrad Felixmüller, Schmidt-Rottluff und Franz Marc, dessen Witwe er 1916/17 kennengelernt hatte. Höhepunkt war 1927 die große Schau zum 60. Geburtstag von Emil Nolde, die im städtischen Ausstellungsgebäude präsentiert wurde: Es war die erste umfassende Werkschau und auch größte, die der Künstler bis dahin hatte. Julius Meier-Graefe kommentierte ironisch: „Der Festredner (also Probst) vergleicht Nolde mit

in Mannheim at the time in connection with the confiscation action at the Kunsthalle, learned that the Kunsthaus was presenting a Nolde exhibition. He sought it out and forced Probst to close it immediately. Thereafter, Probst had to get permission from Berlin for future exhibitions of contemporary art.

Expressionism at the Kunsthalle after 1945

The rebuilding of a destroyed Mannheim after the war ended, the creation of new infrastructure, and redesigning of cultural life would take years, and it was not until 1948 that Probst decided to start a new art dealership under the name Galerie Rudolf Probst, which he opened in 1949. He had been exchanging with Walter Passarge since the end of the war and supported him in filling the gaps made in 1937: "A duty of honor first to bring to the foreground the artists of rank who were oppressed for twelve years—and in some cases prohibited from working,"[29] Passarge wrote. In 1947, 50,000 Reichsmarks were approved for that purpose. The years after World War II were characterized in art by a general turn to abstraction, which was seen as the new, free, international language. At the same time, the artists who had once been persecuted and had been affected by the confiscations were being rehabilitated throughout Germany. For example, the focus of Documenta 1 of 1955 was not so much the "contemporary art" made after 1945 as the art of the artists that had been defamed as "degenerate" in Germany under National Socialism.

Few of the works that had been confiscated could be reacquired. Probst helped the Kunsthalle regain Pechstein's *Stilleben: Figur und Blumen* (Still Life: Figure and Flowers); he purchased the work from the Galerie Buchholz in Berlin and then placed it with the Kunsthalle. Other works that came to the Kunsthalle via Probst were: from Nolde, *Pferd und Füllen* (1915; cat. 131) in 1949, *Feuerlilien und dunkler Rittersporn* (Tiger Lilies and Dark Larkspur) (1925; cat. 92) in 1951, and *Ferne Mädchen* (Girls from Afar) (1947; cat. 122) in 1952, to replace the three Nolde paintings that had been confiscated. The Kunsthalle purchased from Probst five sculptures by Barlach. From Heckel, the painting *Chinesische Artisten* (Chinese Artistes) (1928) came in 1950; from Carl Hofer, *Gehöft* (Farmstead) (1933) came to the museum in 1950 and *Montagnola* (ca. 1918) in 1954. The lost Kirchner painting *Die roten Häuser* (The Red Houses) was replaced by *Gelbes Engelufer, Berlin* (Yellow Engelufer, Berlin) (1913; cat. 74), which is painted on both sides. The Kunsthalle also purchased from Probst paintings by Willi Baumeister, Lovis Corinth (cat. 128), Oskar Schlemmer, Fritz Winter, August Macke, and Max Ernst—proof of the intense business relationship between the gallery and the museum, which ended in 1959 when Probst closed his gallery. He died on November 19, 1968, but works from his estate by August Macke, Franz Marc, and Emil Nolde were lent to the Kunsthalle for years.

But Probst was not the only dealer to sell to the Kunsthalle: a work by Schmidt-Rottluff, *Sommerliches Fenster* (Window in Summer) (1937; cat. 93), came into the collection from the gallery of Hanna Bekker vom Rath in Frankfurt am Main. Other paintings by artists defamed as "degenerate" were acquired, including Oskar Kokoschka's portrait of a girl *Sonia Dungyersky II* (1912; cat. 132), *Bergbach* (Mountain Brook) (1919/20; cat. 76) by Ernst Ludwig Kirchner, Erich Heckel's *Schlafende Frau* (Sleeping Woman) (1932), Otto Mueller's *Zwei weibliche Akte im Freien* (Two Nude Females in Nature) (ca. 1920; cat. 113), Rudolf Levy's *Landschaft auf Ischia* (Landscape on Ischia) (1938), and finally Karl Schmidt-Rottluff's *Villa mit Turm* (Villa with Tower) (1912; cat. 80) as a loan from the State of Baden-Württemberg. In 1957, a letter drawing and seventeen postcards by Erich Heckel, Ernst Ludwig Kirchner, Max Pechstein, and Karl Schmidt-Rottluff entered the collection of the

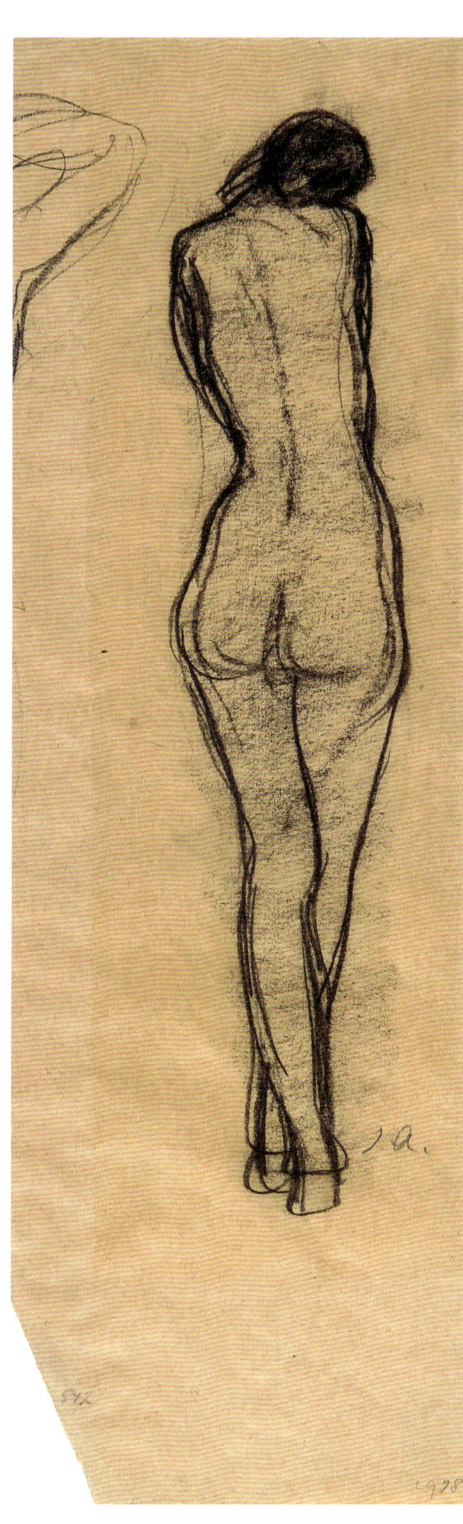

Christus, der auch ein Magier war."[27] Und Bettina Feistel-Rohmeder lässt in ihrer Kritik schon die verächtlich machende Sprache der künftigen Machthaber anklingen, indem sie von „Farbgepatze", „von primitiven Kunstversuchen eines kulturlosen Volkes, widergespiegelt in einer kunstfeindlichen Seele"[28] spricht. Bereits 1926 hatte Hartlaub bei Probst zwei Grafiken des jüdischen Bildhauers Jussuf Abbo (Abb. 15) gekauft, die erstaunlicherweise nicht den Beschlagnahmeaktionen zum Opfer fielen. 1933 sah sich Probst, dessen Galerie sich seit 1928 in wirtschaftlich kritischer Situation befand, auch aufgrund der politischen Rahmenbedingungen gezwungen zu schließen. 1936 wagte er einen Neuanfang in Mannheim und übernahm von Tannenbaum, den er bereits in Dresden kennengelernt hatte, dessen Kunsthaus. Der Wechsel wurde zum 1. Januar 1937 bekannt gegeben. Doch war der Start schwierig: Die am 12. Juni eröffnete Ausstellung zu Emil Nolde wurde am 8. Juli vorzeitig geschlossen. Adolf Ziegler, der im Rahmen der Beschlagnahmeaktion in der Kunsthalle in Mannheim weilte, erfuhr, dass im Kunsthaus eine Nolde-Ausstellung lief. Er suchte diese auf und zwang Probst, sie sofort zu schließen. Weitere Ausstellungen zeitgenössischer Kunst musste dieser künftig in Berlin genehmigen lassen.

Der Expressionismus in der Kunsthalle nach 1945

Der Wiederaufbau des zerstörten Mannheim nach Kriegsende, der Aufbau neuer Infrastrukturen und die Neugestaltung des kulturellen Lebens sollten sich Jahre hinziehen, und erst 1948 entschloss sich Probst zum Neuaufbau einer Kunsthandlung unter dem Namen „Galerie Rudolf Probst", die er 1949 eröffnete. Seit Kriegsende war er in Austausch mit Walter Passarge und unterstützte diesen beim Schließen der 1937 gerissenen Lücken: „Ehrenpflicht, zunächst einmal die seit 12 Jahren unterdrückten – und in einigen Fällen sogar mit Arbeitsverbot belegten – Künstler von Rang in den Vordergrund zu rücken"[29], so Passarge. Dafür bewilligte man ihm 1947 immerhin 50.000 Reichsmark. Die Jahre nach dem Zweiten Weltkrieg waren zwar künstlerisch geprägt von der allgemeinen Hinwendung zur Abstraktion, die als neue freiheitliche Weltsprache betrachtet wurde. Gleichzeitig wurden deutschlandweit aber auch die einst verfolgten und von Beschlagnahmungen betroffenen Künstler*innen rehabilitiert. So war beispielsweise der Schwerpunkt der documenta 1 von 1955 weniger die nach 1945 entstandene „zeitgenössische Kunst" als vielmehr die Kunst derjenigen Künstler*innen, die während der Zeit des Nationalsozialismus unter der Bezeichnung „entartete Kunst" in Deutschland verfemt worden waren.

Wenige der beschlagnahmten Bilder konnten wieder zurückerworben werden. Probst verhalf der Kunsthalle zur Wiederbeschaffung von Pechsteins Gemälde *Stilleben: Figur und Blumen*, er erwarb das Werk von der Berliner Galerie Buchholz und vermittelte es anschließend an die Kunsthalle. Weitere Werke, die über Probst in die Kunsthalle gelangten, waren: von Nolde 1949 *Pferd und Füllen* (1915; Kat. 131), 1951 *Feuerlilien und dunkler Rittersporn* (1925; Kat. 92) und 1952 *Ferne Mädchen* (1947; Kat. 122) als Ersatz für die drei beschlagnahmten Nolde-Bilder. Von Barlach erwarb die Kunsthalle fünf Plastiken bei Probst. Von Heckel kamen 1950 das Gemälde *Chinesische Artisten* (1928), von Carl Hofer *Montagnola* (um 1918) und 1954 *Gehöft* (1933) ins Museum. Das verlorene Kirchner-Bild *Die roten Häuser* wurde durch das doppelseitig bemalte *Gelbes Engelufer, Berlin* (1913; Kat. 74) ersetzt. Weiter kaufte die Kunsthalle bei Probst Gemälde von Willi Baumeister, Lovis Corinth (Kat. 128), Oskar Schlemmer, Fritz Winter, August Macke, Max Ernst – Beleg für die intensive Geschäftsbeziehung zwischen Galerie und Museum, die 1959 endete, als Probst seine Galerie auflöste. Er verstarb am 19. November 1968, doch aus seinem Nachlass waren der

Kunsthalle Mannheim as a gift. They were from their correspondence with Rosa Schapire (1874–1954), who was an important collector, patron, and author who was one of the first women in Germany to receive a doctorate in art history.[30] She supported the Brücke artists, above all Schmidt-Rottluff, and bequeathed some of the postcards in her estate to selected museums. She presumably included the Kunsthalle because she had been in contact with Passarge when he was searching for replacements for lost works after the war ended.

The exhibition activities at the Kunsthalle from 1946 to 1958 also presented Expressionist artists. In the series *Deutsche Kunst des 20. Jahrhunderts* (German Art of the Twentieth Century), paintings and watercolors by Karl Schmidt-Rottluff were shown in 1946. In 1947, an exhibition was dedicated to the art of Franz Marc. In 1949, a Wilhelm Lehmbruck retrospective as shown; in 1950, paintings, watercolors, drawings, and prints by Erich Heckel, followed in 1951 by paintings, watercolors, and drawings by Oskar Kokoschka, as well as other shows with works by Ernst Ludwig Kirchner and Karl Schmidt-Rottluff. In 1952, together with the Galerie Rudolf Probst, Emil Nolde was presented: paintings and watercolors were shown at the Kunsthalle, while prints could be seen at the Galerie Probst; Probst himself spoke at the opening. In 1953, graphic works by Heckel were presented. Finally, in 1954, an exhibition was dedicated to Rudolf Levy's paintings. On the occasion of the exhibition *Die Deutschen Impressionisten und Expressionisten des Saarlandmuseums* (The German Impressionists and Expressionists of the Saarlandmuseum) at the Kunsthalle in 1957, Hartlaub gave the opening speech. Moreover, in 1947 he had again addressed the graphic art of Expressionism in a publication.[31]

From 1959 to the Present

As Walter Passarge's successor, Heinz Fuchs (1917–2001) was the director of the Kunsthalle from 1959 onward, followed by Manfred Fath (b. 1938) from 1983 to 2001. Exhibition activity now focused on the most modern developments, but Expressionism did play a role now and again; there were also occasional acquisitions. In 1961, for example, the exhibition *Gabriele Münter: Gemälde von 1906 bis 1957* (Paintings from 1906 to 1957) was shown. Two important sculptures by Rudolf Belling entered the collection: *Dreiklang* (Triad) (1919; cat. 9) and *Bildnis des Kunsthändlers Alfred Flechtheim* (Portrait of the Art Dealer Alfred Flechtheim) (1927; cat. 36). In 1992, the wood sculpture *Verzückung* (Rapture) (1919; cat. 8) by Oswald Herzog could be purchased with funds from the Wilhelm-Müller-Stiftung. The wood sculpture *Tanzende* (Dancing Couple) (1925; cat. 10) by Hermann Scherer was acquired in 2001 with funds from the Kunsthalle museum shop. With regard to exhibitions, we should mention the *Der doppelte Kirchner* (Kirchner Doubled), shown in 2015, which focused on the phenomenon of canvas that Kirchner painted on both sides, of which the Kunsthalle has *Gelbes Engelufer, Berlin* (verso: fig. 16; cat. 75).

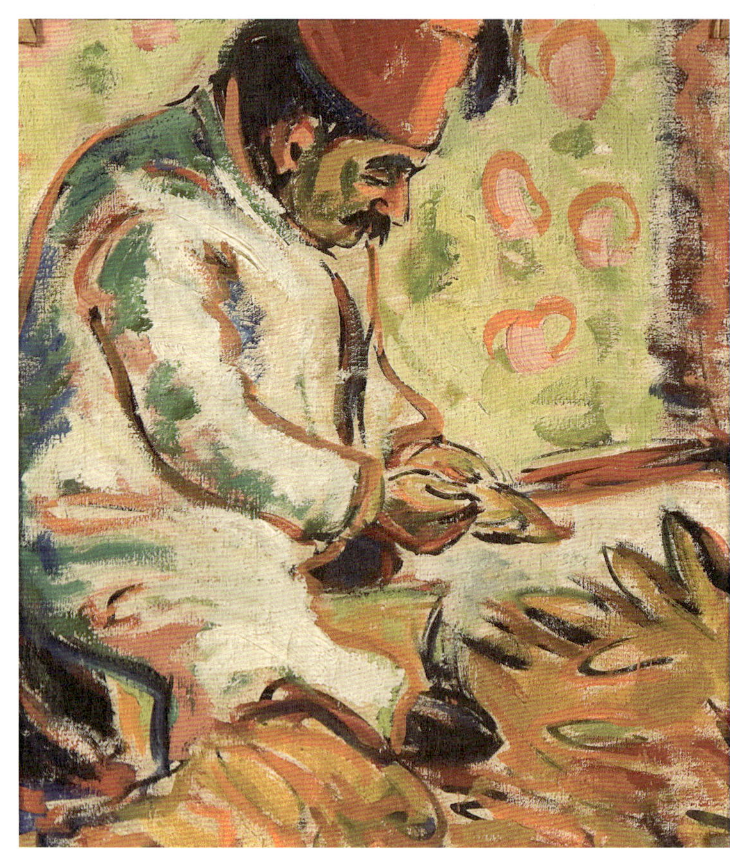

Abb. / Fig. **16**
Ernst Ludwig Kirchner, *Marokkaner*
(Rückseite von *Gelbes Engelufer, Berlin*, 1913) /
Moroccan Man (verso of *Yellow Engelufer, Berlin*, 1913),
um / *ca.* **1909/10**
Öl auf Leinwand / *Oil on canvas*, 71,5 × 80,5 cm
Kunsthalle Mannheim

Kunsthalle noch jahrelang Werke von August Macke, Franz Marc und Emil Nolde als Leihgaben überlassen.

Doch nicht nur Probst verkaufte an die Kunsthalle: Ein Werk von Schmidt-Rottluff, *Sommerliches Fenster* (1937, Kat. 93), kam aus der Galerie von Hanna Bekker vom Rath aus Frankfurt in die Sammlung. Weitere Arbeiten der als „entartet" verfemten Künstler im Bereich Malerei wurden erworben: Dazu gehörten Oskar Kokoschkas Mädchenbildnis *Sonia Dungyersky II* (1912; Kat. 132), und *Bergbach* (1919/20; Kat. 76) von Ernst Ludwig Kirchner, Erich Heckels *Schlafende Frau* (1932), Otto Muellers *Zwei weibliche Akte im Freien* (um 1920; Kat. 113), Rudolf Levys *Landschaft auf Ischia* (1938) und schließlich Karl Schmidt-Rottluffs *Villa mit Turm* (1912; Kat. 80) als Leihgabe des Landes Baden-Württemberg. Als Schenkung kamen 1957 eine Briefzeichnung und 17 Postkarten von Erich Heckel, Ernst Ludwig Kirchner, Max Pechstein und Karl Schmidt-Rottluff in den Besitz der Kunsthalle Mannheim. Sie stammten aus der Korrespondenz von Rosa Schapire (1874–1954), der wichtigen Sammlerin, Mäzenin und Autorin, die als eine der ersten Frauen in Deutschland als Kunsthistorikerin promovierte.[30] Sie förderte neben anderen Brücke-Künstlern vor allem Schmidt-Rottluff und vermachte ausgewählten Museen Teile ihres Nachlasses an Postkarten. Vermutlich wurde die Kunsthalle bedacht, da Schapire mit Passarge in Verbindung gestanden hatte, als dieser nach Kriegsende auf der Suche nach Ersatz für die verlorenen Werke war.

Das Ausstellungsgeschehen in der Kunsthalle von 1946 bis 1958 setzte ebenfalls auf die Präsentation expressionistischer Künstler*innen. In der Reihe *Deutsche Kunst des 20. Jahrhunderts* wurden 1946 Gemälde und Aquarelle von Karl Schmidt-Rottluff gezeigt. 1947 widmete man dem künstlerischen Werk von Franz Marc eine Ausstellung. 1949 wurde eine retrospektive Schau zu Wilhelm Lehmbruck gezeigt sowie 1950 Gemälde, Aquarelle, Zeichnungen und Grafik von Erich Heckel, gefolgt 1951 von Gemälden, Aquarellen und Zeichnungen von Oskar Kokoschka, außerdem weitere Einzelschauen mit Werken von Ernst Ludwig Kirchner und Karl Schmidt-Rottluff. 1952 präsentierte man gemeinsam mit der Galerie Rudolf Probst Emil Nolde: In der Kunsthalle wurden Gemälde und Aquarelle gezeigt, während in der Galerie Probst die Druckgrafik zu sehen waren, zur Eröffnung sprach Probst selbst. 1953 wurden Grafiken von Heckel präsentiert. 1954 widmete man schließlich Rudolf Levy eine Ausstellung seiner Gemälde. Anlässlich der Ausstellung *Die Deutschen Impressionisten und Expressionisten des Saarlandmuseums* 1957 in der Kunsthalle hielt Hartlaub die Eröffnungsrede. Er hatte sich im Übrigen schon 1947 erneut in einer Publikation mit der Grafik des Expressionismus beschäftigt.[31]

Von 1959 bis heute

Als Nachfolger von Walter Passarge leitete seit 1959 Heinz Fuchs (1917–2001) die Kunsthalle, danach 1983 bis 2001 Manfred Fath (*1938). Das Ausstellungsgeschehen stand nun einerseits im Zeichen modernster Entwicklungen, doch auch der Expressionismus spielte immer wieder eine Rolle, auch vereinzelte Ankäufe wurden noch getätigt. 1961 etwa wurde die Ausstellung *Gabriele Münter – Gemälde von 1906 bis 1957* gezeigt. Von Rudolf Belling kamen zwei wichtige Skulpturen in die Sammlung: *Dreiklang* (1919; Kat. 9) und das *Bildnis des Kunsthändlers Alfred Flechtheim* (1927; Kat. 36). Von Oswald Herzog konnte 1993 mit Mitteln der Wilhelm-Müller-Stiftung die Holzskulptur *Verzückung* (1919; Kat. 8) erworben werden. Die Holzskulptur *Tanzende* (1925; Kat. 10) von Hermann Scherer wurde 2001 aus Mitteln des Museumsshops der Kunsthalle angekauft. Im Bereich der Ausstellungen ist die 2015 gezeigte Ausstellung *Der doppelte Kirchner* zu erwähnen,

Expressionist art was also in demand among collectors in Mannheim after 1945 as well. One of them was the Mannheim businessman Hans Werle (1905–2000), who initially collected works from the nineteenth and early twentieth centuries with works by Adolph von Menzel, Carl Schuch, Hans Thoma, Max Liebermann, and Lovis Corinth, among others. From 1961 onward, he focused on the art of Expressionism and put together a high-quality collection with works by Emil Nolde, Ernst Ludwig Kirchner, Karl Schmidt-Rottluff, Erich Heckel, Otto Mueller, and Oskar Kokoschka (cat. 50, 51, 52, 53, 54, 56, 57, 63, 64), supplemented by his son-in-law, Manfred Fuchs, with paintings by Gabriele Münter and Max Pechstein (cat. 55, 60, 61)—today's Fuchs-Werle Collection. Another collection focused on the sculptures of Wilhelm Lehmbruck (cat. 4, 5, 6, 7), thus establishing a connection to the early days of the Kunsthalle.

1 On the history of the Kunsthalle Mannheim, see Inge Herold, ed., *100 Jahre Kunsthalle Mannheim, 1907–2007*, exh. cat. (Mannheim: Kunsthalle Mannheim, 2007).

2 See *Max Zachmann: Entdeckung eines Expressionisten*, exh. cat. (Konstanz: Städtische Wessenberg-Galerie, 2004).

3 See Karoline Hille, "Neue religiöse Kunst. Ausstellung Mannheim 1918: Zur Rezeption des deutschen Expressionismus an der Kunsthalle," in Hille, *Spuren der Moderne: Die Mannheimer Kunsthalle von 1918 bis 1933*, Kunst und Dokumentation 13, Städtische Kunsthalle Mannheim (also PhD diss., Freie Univ. Berlin) (Berlin: Akademie, 1994), p. 30.

4 Quoted in Hille, *Spuren der Moderne* (see note 3), pp. 329–30.

5 Quoted in ibid., p. 37.

6 On Falk, see *Stiftung und Sammlung Sally Falk*, Kunst und Dokumentation 11 (Mannheim: Städtische Kunsthalle, 1994).

7 George Grosz, *A Little Yes and a Big No: The Autobiography of George Grosz*, trans. Nora Hodges (New York: Macmillan, 1983), pp. 105, 103.

8 Quoted in Roland Dorn, "Der Hort in der Mollstraße 18," in *Stiftung und Sammlung Sally Falk* 1994 (see note 6), p. 130.

9 Quoted in ibid., p. 127.

10 Quoted in ibid., p. 128.

11 On this, see Mathias Listl, "The Kunsthalle and Its Jewish Patrons: The Fate of Five Families from Mannheim," in *(Re)Discovery: The Kunsthalle from 1933 to 1945 and the Aftermath*, ed. Mathias Listl and Ulrike Lorenz, exh. cat. (Mannheim: Kunsthalle Mannheim, 2018), pp. 63–85.

12 Quoted in Hille, *Spuren der Moderne* (see note 3), p. 231.

13 Gustav F. Hartlaub to Paul Westheim, late 1917, quoted in ibid., p. 37.

14 Ibid., p. 52.

15 Quoted in ibid., p. 56.

16 Gustav F. Hartlaub, *Kunst und Religion: Ein Versuch über die Möglichkeit neuer religiöser Kunst*, ed. Carl Georg Heise, Das neue Bild: Bücher für die Kunst der Gegenwart 2 (Leipzig: Kurt Wolff, 1919).

17 Ibid., p. 85.

18 Ibid.

19 Ibid., p. 88.

20 Quoted in Hille, *Spuren der Moderne* (see note 3), p 66.

21 *Entartete Kunst: Beschlagnahmeaktionen in der Städtischen Kunsthalle Mannheim 1937*, comp. Hans-Jürgen Buderer, exh. cat. (Mannheim: Kunsthalle Mannheim, 1987); *Beschlagnahmt! Rückkehr der Meisterblätter*, ed. Thomas Köllhofer, Mathias Listl, and Ulrike Lorenz exh. cat. (Mannheim: Kunsthalle Mannheim, 2019); Listl and Lorenz, *(Re)Discovery* (see note 11).

22 See the essay by Hannah Krause, "Walter Passarge: Director of the Kunsthalle Mannheim during National Socialism," in the present volume.

23 Ibid.

24 On Tannenbaum, see *Für die Kunst! Herbert Tannenbaum und sein Kunsthaus*, ed. Karin von Welck, exh. cat. Reiss-Museum der Stadt Mannheim 1994 (Mannheim: Vits & Kehrer, 1994).

25 *Sammlung Rudolf und Bertha Frank*, ed. Wolfgang Beeh, exh. cat. 1986 (Darmstadt: Hessisches Landesmuseum, 1986).

26 On Probst, see Karl-Ludwig Hofmann and Christmut Präger, *Rudolf Probst, Galerist, 1890–1968*, Quellenstudien zur Kunst 11 (Wädenswil: Nimbus, 2021).

27 Quoted in ibid., p. 122.

28 Quoted in ibid., p. 123.

29 Quoted in ibid., p. 326.

30 On this, see Gerd Presler, *"Brücke" an Dr. Rosa Schapire* (Mannheim: Städtische Kunsthalle, 1990).

31 Gustav F. Hartlaub, *Die Graphik des Expressionismus in Deutschland* (Stuttgart: Hatje, 1947).

die das Phänomen der doppelseitig bemalten Leinwände bei Kirchner in den Fokus nahm, verfügt doch die Kunsthalle mit dem Gemälde *Gelbes Engelufer, Berlin* auch über ein solches (Rückseite: Abb. 16; Kat. 75).

Bei Mannheimer Sammler*innen war die Kunst des Expressionismus auch nach 1945 gefragt. So auch bei dem Mannheimer Unternehmer Hans Werle (1905–2000), der zunächst eine Sammlung von Werken des 19. und frühen 20. Jahrhunderts aufbaute, mit unter anderem Werken von Adolph von Menzel, Carl Schuch, Hans Thoma, Max Liebermann und Lovis Corinth. Ab 1961 fokussierte er sich auf die Kunst des Expressionismus und stellte so eine hochkarätige Sammlung mit Werken von Emil Nolde, Ernst Ludwig Kirchner, Karl Schmidt-Rottluff, Erich Heckel, Otto Mueller und Oskar Kokoschka (Kat. 50, 51, 52, 53, 54, 56, 57, 63, 64) zusammen, ergänzt von seinem Schwiegersohn Manfred Fuchs um Gemälde von Gabriele Münter und Max Pechstein (Kat. 55, 60, 61) – heute die Sammlung Fuchs-Werle. Eine andere Sammlung legte den Schwerpunkt auf Skulpturen von Wilhelm Lehmbruck (Kat. 4, 5, 6, 7) und schließt so an die Anfangszeit der Kunsthalle an.

1 Zur Geschichte der Kunsthalle Mannheim siehe: Inge Herold (Hrsg.): 100 Jahre Kunsthalle Mannheim 1907–2007, Mannheim 2007.

2 Siehe: Kat. Ausst. *Max Zachmann. Entdeckung eines Expressionisten*, Städtische Wessenberg-Galerie, Konstanz 2004.

3 Siehe: Karoline Hille, Neue religiöse Kunst. Ausstellung Mannheim 1918. Zur Rezeption des deutschen Expressionismus an der Kunsthalle, in: dies.: *Spuren der Moderne. Die Mannheimer Kunsthalle von 1918 bis 1933*, Kunst und Dokumentation 13, Städtische Kunsthalle Mannheim (zgl. Diss. Freie Univ. Berlin), Berlin 1994, S. 30.

4 Zit. nach: ebd., Anm. 38, S. 329f.

5 Zit. nach: ebd., S. 37.

6 Zu Falk siehe: *Stiftung und Sammlung Sally Falk*, Kunst und Dokumentation 11, hrsg. v. Städtische Kunsthalle Mannheim, Mannheim 1994.

7 George Grosz: *Ein kleines Ja und ein großes Nein*, Reinbek bei Hamburg 1955, S. 107f.

8 Zit. nach: Roland Dorn: Der Hort in der Mollstraße 18, in: *Stiftung und Sammlung Sally Falk* 1994 (wie Anm. 6), S. 130.

9 Zit. nach: ebd., S. 127.

10 Zit. nach: ebd., S. 128.

11 Siehe hierzu: Mathias Listl: Die Kunsthalle und ihre jüdischen Mäzene: Schicksalswege fünf jüdischer Familien aus Mannheim, in: Kat. Ausst. *(Wieder-)Entdecken. Die Kunsthalle 1933 bis 1945 und die Folgen*, Kunsthalle Mannheim 2018, hrsg. v. Mathias Listl u. Ulrike Lorenz, Mannheim 2018, S. 63–82.

12 Zit. nach: Hille 1994 (wie Anm. 3), S. 231.

13 Hartlaub an Paul Westheim, Ende 1917, zit. nach: ebd., S. 37.

14 Ebd., S. 52.

15 Zit. nach: ebd., S. 56.

16 Gustav F. Hartlaub: *Kunst und Religion. Ein Versuch über die Möglichkeit neuer religiöser Kunst*, Leipzig 1919 (Das neue Bild, Bücher für die Kunst der Gegenwart, 2. Bd., hrsg. v. Carl Georg Heise).

17 Ebd., S. 85.

18 Ebd., S. 85.

19 Ebd., S. 88.

20 Zit. nach: Hille 1994 (wie Anm. 3), S. 66.

21 Siehe Kat. Ausst. *Entartete Kunst. Beschlagnahmeaktionen in der Städtischen Kunsthalle Mannheim 1937*, Kunsthalle Mannheim 1987, bearb. v. Hans-Jürgen Buderer, Mannheim 1987; Kat. Ausst. *Beschlagnahmt! Rückkehr der Meisterblätter*, Kunsthalle Mannheim 2019, hrsg. v. Thomas Köllhofer, Mathias Listl u. Ulrike Lorenz, Mannheim 2019; Kat. Ausst. *(Wieder-)Entdecken. Die Kunsthalle 1933 bis 1945 und die Folgen*, Kunsthalle Mannheim 2018, hrsg. v. Mathias Listl u. Ulrike Lorenz, Mannheim 2018.

22 Siehe in diesem Band den Aufsatz von Hannah Krause: Walter Passarge: Direktor der Kunsthalle Mannheim während des Nationalsozialismus.

23 Ebd.

24 Zu Tannenbaum siehe: Kat. Ausst. *Für die Kunst! – Herbert Tannenbaum und sein Kunsthaus*, Reiss-Museum der Stadt Mannheim 1994, hrsg. von Karin von Welck, Mannheim 1994.

25 Kat. Ausst. *Sammlung Rudolf und Bertha Frank*, Hessisches Landesmuseum Darmstadt 1986, hrsg. v. Wolfgang Beeh, Darmstadt 1986.

26 Zu Probst siehe: Karl-Ludwig Hofmann u. Christmut Präger: *Rudolf Probst, Galerist, 1890–1968*, Wädenswil 2021 (Quellenstudien zur Kunst, Bd. 11).

27 Zit. nach: ebd., S. 122.

28 Zit. nach: ebd., S. 123.

29 Zit. nach: ebd., S. 326.

30 Siehe hierzu: Gerd Presler: *„Brücke" an Dr. Rosa Schapire*, Mannheim 1990.

31 Gustav F. Hartlaub: *Die Graphik des Expressionismus in Deutschland*, Stuttgart 1947.

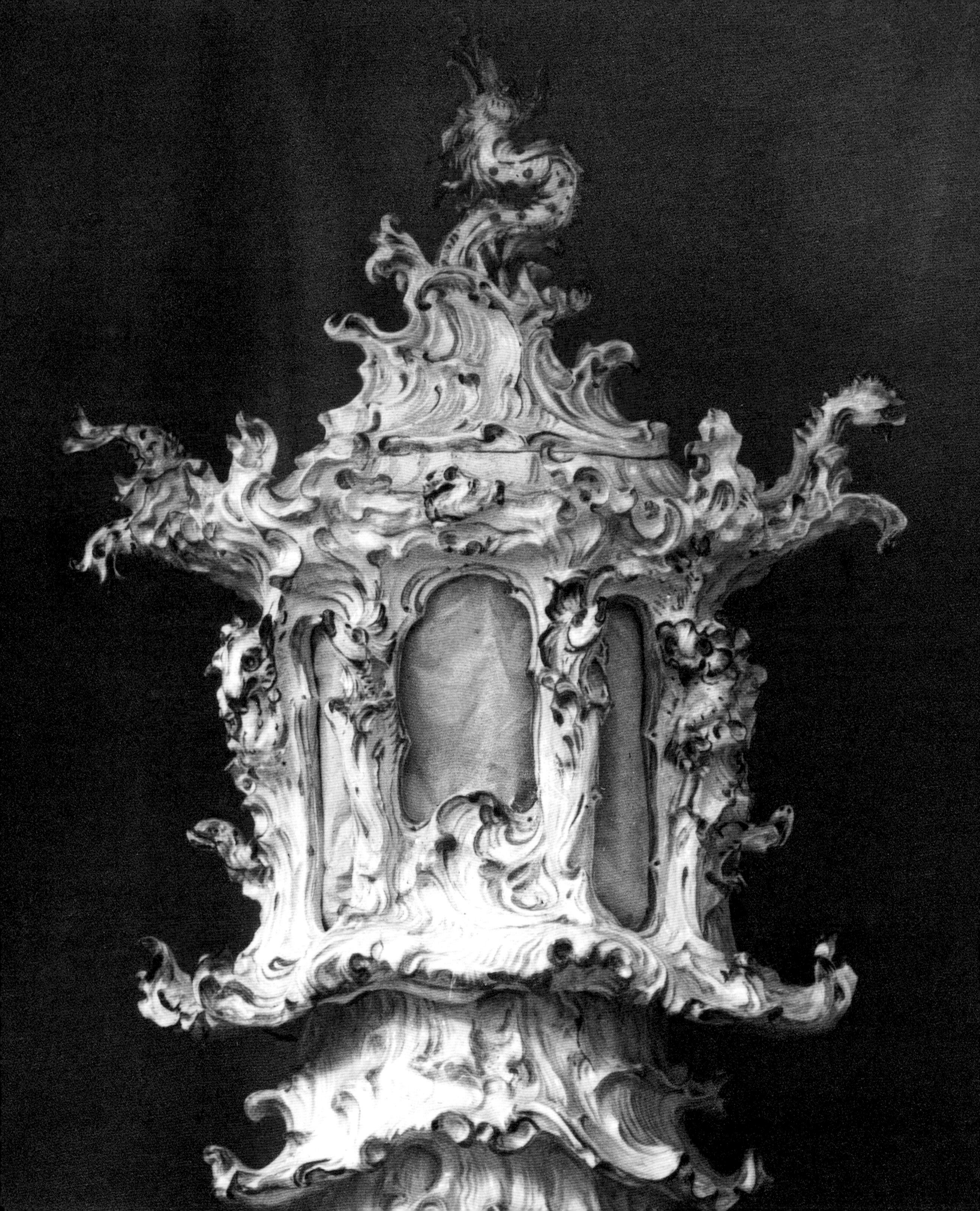

„In Hans Poelzigs *Luftreich*"[1]: über die Ausstellung *Porzellan und Majolika* 1921 in der Kunsthalle Mannheim

"In Hans Poelzig's *Luftreich*"[1]: On the *Porcelain and Majolica* Exhibition at the Kunsthalle Mannheim in 1921

Mathias Listl

The Kunsthalle Mannheim and Expressionism:
Looking at the Museum's Exhibition History up to 1933

Thanks to the numerous acquisitions and gifts, paintings, sculptures, and prints by German and international artists who can be considered Expressionists that found their way into the museum's collections from the early 1910s onward under its first director, Fritz Wichert (1878–1951), the Kunsthalle Mannheim became without a doubt one of the most important early institutional supporters in Germany of that movement in the arts.[2] The same is also true of a whole series of solo and group exhibitions up until 1933 with which the museum, which had been founded in 1909, introduced its public to a number of important representatives and precursors of Expressionism. A list of these artists reads like a who's who of the movement—unfortunately, however, one searches in vain for the names of women.

After Wichert had brought together works by Ernst Barlach, Georg Kolbe, Aristide Maillol, and others in a pioneering exhibition with the very succinct title *Ausdrucks-Plastik* (Expressive Sculpture) in 1912, it was followed toward the end of that decade by presentations of works by Wilhelm Lehmbruck (1916), Erich Heckel (1917), and Emil Nolde (1919). In 1917, the Kunsthalle also showed the collection of Wiesbaden-based Heinrich Kirchhoff, one of the most important German private collections of Expressionist art at the time.

Nor did the museum's focus turn away from Expressionism in the 1920s or under Wichert's successor, Gustav Friedrich Hartlaub (1884–1963), who took over as director in 1923. A list of the shows organized up to 1933 for artists who number among the Expressionists suggests rather the reverse. After works by Christian Rohlfs were shown in the museum's spaces in 1920, the following year there was both a show with paintings and drawings by Alexej von Jawlensky and another exhibition of Emil Nolde. For 1924, one can cite both an exhibition titled *Zwei Künstlerphantasten* (Two Artist-Dreamers) with works by Alfred Kubin and Paul Klee and a show with works by the Austrian graphic artist, painter, and sculptor Georg Ehrlich in the Kunsthalle's Graphisches Kabinett. In 1925, in turn, it presented paintings by Karl Schmidt-Rottluff to its Mannheim audience.

A solo exhibition of paintings and graphic works by Edvard Munch the following year paid homage to a pioneer of the Expressionist movement. Two years later, in 1928, the Kunsthalle focused on James Ensor, another precursor of Expressionism whom German artists in particular saw as an important source of ideas.[3] Vincent van Gogh had a similar effect as a role model, and in 1932 the Kunsthalle was able to show a painting by him that was in a private collection in Mannheim at the time: *Les Alyscamps (Avenue of Tombs)*.[4] The exhibition *Formenwelt der Primitiven* (Form Worlds of the Primitives) in 1923 belonged to this series addressing the precursors and sources of inspiration of Expressionism. Presentations of paintings and graphic works by Max Beckmann (1928), Frans Masereel (1929), Oskar Kokoschka (1931), and Otto Pankok (1932) in the late 1920s and early 1930s focused attention on four important representatives of international Expressionism.

One could cite still more shows at the Kunsthalle in this period under the keyword Expressionism,[5] which would further illustrate the great importance the painting, graphic art, and sculpture of Expressionism had for Kunsthalle Mannheim. What follows, however, will shed light on an exhibition at the Kunsthalle that has not been looked at closely previously: the 1921 exhibition *Porzellan und Majolika* (Porcelain and Majolica) and in particular the contribution to it by Hans Poelzig and Marlene Moeschke. The concept for the exhibition embraced not only very essential stylistic features and artistic persuasions of the Expressionist movement, such as the striving for

Die Kunsthalle Mannheim und der Expressionismus: ein Blick auf die Ausstellungshistorie des Museums bis 1933

Durch zahlreiche Ankäufe und Schenkungen von Gemälden, Skulpturen und Grafiken deutscher wie internationaler, dem Expressionismus zuzurechnender Künstler*innen, die bereits ab den 1910er-Jahren Eingang in die Sammlungen des Museums fanden, gehört die Kunsthalle Mannheim unter ihrem ersten Direktor Fritz Wichert (1878–1951) unzweifelhaft zu den bedeutendsten frühen institutionellen Förderern dieser Kunstrichtung in Deutschland.[2] Gleiches gilt auch für eine ganze Reihe von Einzel- und Gruppenausstellungen, in denen das 1909 gegründete Museum seinem Publikum bis 1933 zahlreiche Vertreter des Expressionismus wie auch wichtige Vorläufer dieser Bewegung vorstellte. Eine Auflistung der bis zu diesem Zeitpunkt in der Kunsthalle präsentierten Künstler – Frauen sucht man auf dieser leider vergeblich – liest sich dabei wie ein *Who's who* dieser Kunstrichtung.

Nachdem Wichert bereits 1912 in einer wegweisenden Ausstellung mit dem sehr prägnanten Titel *Ausdrucks-Plastik* Werke von Ernst Barlach, Georg Kolbe, Aristide Maillol und anderen vereint hatte, folgten bis Ende des Jahrzehnts Präsentationen von Werken Wilhelm Lehmbrucks (1916), Erich Heckels (1917) und Emil Noldes (1919). Mit der Sammlung des in Wiesbaden ansässigen Heinrich Kirchhoff zeigte die Kunsthalle bereits im Jahr 1917 zudem eine der damals bedeutendsten deutschen Privatsammlungen expressionistischer Kunst.

Und auch in den 1920er-Jahren und unter Wicherts Nachfolger Gustav Friedrich Hartlaub (1884–1963), der ab 1923 die Leitung des Hauses übernahm, wendete sich der Fokus des Museums nicht vom Expressionismus ab. Eine Auflistung der bis 1933 durchgeführten Schauen von Künstler*innen, die dem Expressionismus zuzurechnen sind, legt vielmehr das Gegenteil nahe. Nachdem 1920 Arbeiten von Christian Rohlfs in den Räumen des Museums präsentiert wurden, schlossen sich im Folgejahr eine Schau mit Gemälden und Zeichnungen Alexej von Jawlenskys sowie eine weitere Ausstellung Emil Noldes an. Für 1924 ist dann die *Zwei Künstlerphantasten* betitelte Ausstellung mit Werken Alfred Kubins und Paul Klees sowie eine Schau mit Arbeiten des österreichischen Grafikers, Malers und Bildhauers Georg Ehrlich im Graphischen Kabinett der Kunsthalle anzuführen. 1925 wiederum zeigte man dem Mannheimer Publikum Gemälde von Karl Schmidt-Rottluff.

Mit Gemälden und grafischen Werken Edvard Munchs wurde im Folgejahr ein Bahnbrecher der expressionistischen Bewegung mit einer Einzelschau gewürdigt. Wiederum zwei Jahre später, 1928, nahm die Kunsthalle mit James Ensor einen weiteren Vorläufer des Expressionismus in den Fokus, in dem gerade die deutschen Kunstschaffenden einen wichtigen Ideengeber sahen.[3] Diese Vorbildwirkung übte nicht zuletzt auch Vincent van Gogh aus, von dem die Kunsthalle 1932 immerhin das sich damals in Mannheimer Privatbesitz befindende Gemälde *Les Aliscamps (Die Gräberstraße)* zeigen konnte.[4] In dieser Reihe der Beschäftigung mit Vorläufern und Inspirationsquellen des Expressionismus ist schließlich auch die bereits 1923 abgehaltene Ausstellung *Formenwelt der Primitiven* zu nennen. Die Präsentationen von

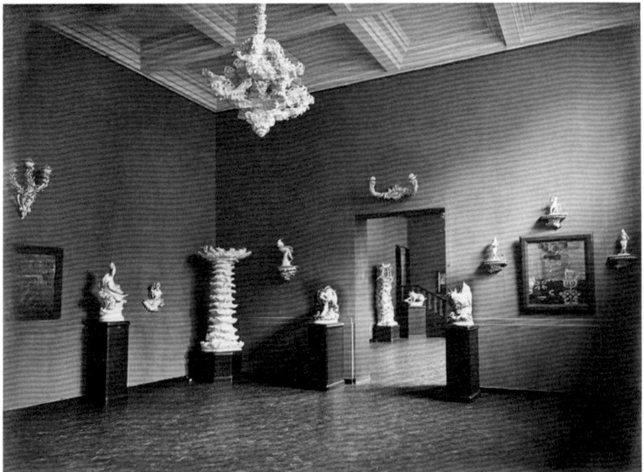

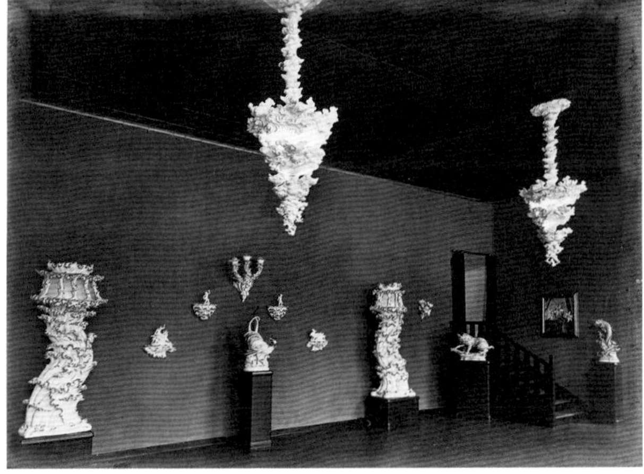

the Gesamtkunstwerk, or "total work of art." Studying this exhibition reveals that many of the early exhibitions at the Kunsthalle were experimental in character and aimed at shaping the taste of a broad public, and its description and reception can make both local and international history immediately after World War I especially palpable.

Porzellan und Majolika:
An Exhibition with a Simple Title and Opulent Art

"I know of course that all we have done to get the decoration of the so-called Porzellan-Palais [Porcelain Palace] in Leipzig underway is not 'permitted.' Because after being intimidated by the failure of Jugendstil, and after every self-respecting manufacturer had bashfully banished the products of that era to the junk pile, they had agreed on a certain well-temperedness—the German style for the crafts, so to speak."[6]

Looking at historical exhibition photographs of the opulent ceramic objects (figs. 17-20, 28) that Hans Poelzig (1869-1936), one of the most important German representatives of modern architecture, is addressing himself here, one does indeed have considerable difficulties categorizing what one sees according to time, style, or function. And even the question of their meaning and purpose—in short, whether something like this is "permitted"—comes up involuntarily. For even after close study, it is not only the specific function of Poelzig's "ecstatic" lamps and lanterns snaking upward or vegetal wall consoles of porcelain that remains largely unclear. The dating of these designs to the early 1920s is anything but obvious given their baroque, expressive formal idiom. The aforementioned Porzellan-Palais and many more of his rousing ceramic designs were first presented at the spring trade fair in Leipzig in 1921,[7] and then just a few months later shown in the exhibition with the simple title *Porzellan und Majolika* at the Kunsthalle Mannheim.[8]

Kunsthalle, Freier Bund, and the *Porzellan und Majolika* Exhibition

The exhibition held at the Kunsthalle Mannheim from June to October 1921 was dedicated primarily to two very traditional materials—porcelain and majolica—that are at home not as much in the fine arts as in the applied arts. Together with the designs by Hans Poelzig, which were presented in two of the seven exhibitions spaces in the western basement of the museum's original building, this show included many other ceramic objects designed by a whole series of renowned artists. In addition to the architect and ceramicist Max Läuger (1864-1952), whose works were a focus of the presentation along with those of Hans Poelzig, there were also designs by the architect and furniture designer Bruno Paul (1874-1968) and by the painter Hans Thoma (1839-1924).[9]

If one looks back at the early days of the Kunsthalle, which was founded as a municipal institution in 1909, one can indeed find explanations for a show like this one that is unusual from today's perspective. For although the Kunsthalle was already focusing clearly on collecting and imparting the genres of painting, sculpture, and graphic arts, the applied arts—that is to say, architecture, industrial and graphic design, the crafts—nevertheless played an important role. As one of the most important protagonists of the German museum reform, it was a major concern of its founding director, Fritz Wichert, that visitors to his institution receive an aesthetic education, and not only through the paintings, sculptures, and graphic works exhibited, such as the top-flight works of French Impressionism acquired during his term. He sought to make his audience sensitive to the design of incomparably more ordinary objects as well, such as furniture design, advertising posters, and industrial buildings.

Gemälden und Grafiken Max Beckmanns (1928), Frans Masereels (1929), Oskar Kokoschkas (1931) sowie Otto Pankoks (1932) richteten Ende der 1920er- bzw. Anfang der 1930er-Jahre die Aufmerksamkeit dann wieder auf vier bedeutende Vertreter des internationalen Expressionismus.

Es könnten noch weitere Schauen der Kunsthalle im genannten Zeitraum unter dem Schlagwort des Expressionismus aufgeführt werden[5], was den hohen Stellenwert von Malerei, Grafik und Skulptur des Expressionismus für die Kunsthalle Mannheim weiter verdeutlichen würde. Im Folgenden soll jedoch nur eine, bis dato nicht näher in den Blick genommene Ausstellung der Kunsthalle näher beleuchtet werden: die 1921 durchgeführte Ausstellung *Porzellan und Majolika*, insbesondere der Beitrag von Hans Poelzig und Marlene Moeschke, der dort zu sehen war. Denn das Konzept dieser Ausstellung umfasste nicht nur sehr wesentliche stilistische Grundzüge und künstlerische Überzeugungen der expressionistischen Bewegung, wie etwa das Streben nach dem Gesamtkunstwerk. Die Beschäftigung mit dieser Ausstellung lässt den experimentellen und auf die Geschmacksbildung der breiten Öffentlichkeit zielenden Charakter vieler früher Ausstellungen der Kunsthalle deutlich werden, zugleich wird aber auch anhand ihrer Beschreibung und Rezeption das lokale bis internationale Zeitgeschehen unmittelbar nach dem Ersten Weltkrieg besonders greifbar.

Porzellan und Majolika: eine Ausstellung mit schlichtem Titel und opulenter Kunst

„Ich weiß selbstverständlich, dass man Alles das, was wir für die Ausgestaltung des sog. Porzellan-Palais in Leipzig auf die Beine gestellt haben, nicht machen ‚darf'. Denn nachdem man durch das Versagen des Jugendstils eingeschüchtert war und jede Manufaktur, die etwas auf sich hält, die Produkte jener Zeit scheu in die Rumpelkammer bannte, hatte man sich auf eine Wohltemperiertheit – den deutschen Werkstil sozusagen – geeinigt."[6]

Betrachtet man auf historischen Ausstellungsfotos die opulenten Keramik-Objekte (Abb. 17–20, 28), die Hans Poelzig (1869–1936), einer der bedeutendsten Vertreter der deutschen Architekturmoderne, hier selbst anspricht, hat man in der Tat zunächst größere Schwierigkeiten, das Gesehene zeitlich, stilistisch oder unter funktionalen Gesichtspunkten einzuordnen. Und ja, auch die Frage, nach deren Sinn und Zweck, also kurz, ob man so etwas „darf", kommt unwillkürlich auf. Denn nicht nur die konkrete Funktion von Poelzigs „rauschenden", sich in Serpentinen nach oben entwickelnden Leuchtern und Laternen oder seiner vegetabilen Wandkonsolen aus Porzellan bleibt auch nach genauerem Studium weitestgehend unklar. Die Datierung dieser Entwürfe auf Anfang der 1920er-Jahre ist ob ihrer barock-expressiven Formensprache alles andere als augenscheinlich. Das erwähnte Porzellan-Palais sowie viele weitere dieser furiosen keramischen Entwürfe wurden 1921 zuerst auf der Leipziger Frühjahrsmesse präsentiert[7], nur wenige Monate später dann innerhalb der Ausstellung mit dem schlichten Titel *Porzellan und Majolika* in der Kunsthalle Mannheim gezeigt.[8]

Kunsthalle, Freier Bund und die Ausstellung *Porzellan und Majolika*

Von Juni bis Oktober 1921 fand in der Kunsthalle Mannheim die Ausstellung statt, welche sich hauptsächlich Objekten aus zwei sehr traditionellen Werkstoffen, Porzellan und Majolika, widmete, die weniger den bildenden als vielmehr den angewandten Künsten zuzurechnen sind. Zusammen mit den Entwürfen von Hans Poelzig, die in zwei der insgesamt sieben Ausstellungsräumen im westlichen Untergeschoss des heutigen Altbaus des Museums präsentiert wurden, umfasste diese Schau eine Vielzahl weiterer keramischer Objekte, die von einer ganzen Reihe namhafter

Around 1900, this city on the Rhine and Neckar Rivers was known outside the immediate region primarily as an industrial city and scarcely as a place of art and culture, so in order to create an "art milieu,"[10] in which ideally all strata of society would show an interest in questions of art and aesthetic design, Wichert founded the Freier Bund zur Einbürgerung der bildenden Kunst (Free League for the Establishment of Fine Art)—or Freier Bund for short.[11] With wide variety of activities, such as lectures, tours, and exhibitions, the association sought to address the general population and create enthusiasm for the aforementioned set of themes—a goal that, measured by the large number of its members and its many events for example,[12] was doubtless achieved. Looking back at the list of exhibitions organized by the Freier Bund, the applied arts in particular occupy a central place. They included such shows as *Moderne Typen (Moderne Druckschriften)* (Modern Typefaces) (1911), *Neues Bauen* (New Building) (1915), *Kleinwohnung und Siedlung* (Small Apartment and Housing Development) (1916), *Spitzen, Glas und Silber* (Lace, Glass, and Silver) (1922), and even themes that seem strange from today's perspective such as *Gute Zigarrenpackungen* (Good Cigar Packaging) (1920) and *Der bunte Stoff und die neue Farbigkeit* (Colorful Material and the New Palette) (1922–23). It took the approach of educating and elevating the taste of the general population, which is also clearly evoked in Wichert's foreword to the *Porzellan und Majolika* exhibition, which was the twenty-sixth Freier Bund show: "We do not wish to explain entirely the essential difference between the two materials [porcelain and majolica]. The viewer should seek it out for himself, be active himself, should ultimately—it is said again and again—look at the things with eyes and nerves and not with a slanting shoulder. And if he wants to do even more, he should acquire. Only by dealing daily with ceramic objects will the sense for what's good, the sense for the wealth of glazes and colors, increase."[13]

The Producers:
The Aelteste Volkstedter Porzellanmanufaktur and the Großherzogliche Majolika-Manufaktur Karlsruhe

To show visitors to his institution the latest developments in the field of porcelain and majolica manufacturing, Wichert won over as partners the Aelteste Volkstedter Porzellanmanufaktur (Oldest Volkstedt Porcelain Manufactory) and the Großherzogliche Majolika-Manufaktur Karlsruhe (Grand Ducal Majolica Manufactory in Karlsruhe), two important German producers of these two materials, who produced all of the works presented with the exception of a few exhibits that Max Läuger made himself. Whereas the majolica maker in Karlsruhe presented works designed by a wide variety of artists, the porcelain manufacturer in Volkstedt showed objects based on designs by just four artists. In addition to Poelzig, they were Gustav Oppel (1891–1978), Hugo Meisel (1887–1966), and Arthur Storch (1870–1947), all three were sculptors and modelers, some of whom had been working closely with the company for decades, and most of whom also made molds for Poelzig's designs.[14] Whereas all the larger objects shown, such as the freestanding and ceiling lamps, the radiator covers, the wall consoles, and the smaller lamps can be traced back to Poelzig and will be examined more closely below, these three artists were responsible for the designs of nearly all the figurines and animals presented on wall consoles.[15]

Whereas in 1921 the majolica producer in Karlsruhe could only point to a relatively brief company history of just over twenty years,[16] the Aelteste Volkstedter Porzellanmanufaktur from Thuringia could already look back on a tradition of more than 150 years.[17] Founded in 1760, it was already enjoying a great heyday at the end of the eighteenth century and was esteemed well beyond its national borders.

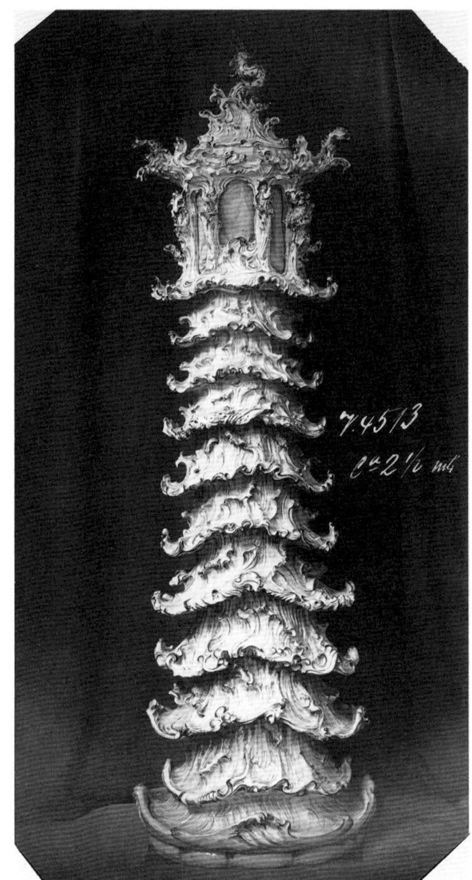

Abb./Fig. **20**
Hans Poelzig und/ and **Marlene Moeschke,** *Großer Wolkenleuchter,* **modelliert von Paul Kramer**/ Large Cloud Chandelier, *molded by* Paul Kramer, **um**/*ca.* **1920/21**

Künstler gestaltet wurden. Neben dem Architekten und Keramiker Max Läuger (1864–1952), dessen Werke wie die Arbeiten von Poelzig ebenfalls einen Schwerpunkt der Präsentation bildeten, finden sich darunter etwa auch Entwürfe des Architekten und Möbeldesigners Bruno Paul (1874–1968) oder des Malers Hans Thoma (1839–1924).[9]

Blickt man auf die Anfänge der 1909 als städtische Institution gegründeten Kunsthalle zurück, finden sich für eine solche, aus heutiger Sicht ungewöhnliche Schau durchaus Erklärungen. Denn obwohl auch bereits damals der Fokus der Kunsthalle eindeutig auf dem Sammeln und Vermitteln der Gattungen Malerei, Skulptur und Grafik lag, spielten ebenso die angewandten Künste, sprich die Architektur, das Industrie- und Grafikdesign, das Kunstgewerbe wie etwa die Textilkunst, von Beginn an eine wichtige Rolle. Denn als einem der wichtigsten Protagonisten der deutschen Museumsreform war es dem Gründungsdirektor Fritz Wichert ein großes Anliegen, die Besucher*innen seines Hauses nicht nur anhand der ausgestellten Gemälde, Skulpturen oder Grafiken, wie etwa der unter seiner Amtszeit erworbenen Spitzenwerke des französischen Impressionismus, ästhetisch weiterzubilden. Auch für die Gestaltung ungleich alltäglicherer Dinge wie Möbelentwürfe, Werbeplakate oder Industriebauten versuchte er sein Publikum zu sensibilisieren.

Um in der um 1900 überregional vor allem als Industriestandort, aber kaum als Ort von Kunst und Kultur wahrgenommenen Stadt an Rhein und Neckar ein „Kunstmilieu"[10] entstehen zu lassen, in dem sich möglichst alle gesellschaftlichen Schichten für Fragen der Kunst und ästhetischen Gestaltung interessieren oder Kenntnisse über sie erlangen können, regte Wichert die Gründung des sogenannten Freien Bundes zur Einbürgerung der bildenden Kunst in Mannheim, kurz Freier Bund, an.[11] Durch verschiedenste Aktivitäten wie Vorträge, Führungen und auch Ausstellungen sollte die Allgemeinbevölkerung durch diesen Verein angesprochen und für den genannten Kreis an Themen begeistert werden, ein Ziel, das – gemessen etwa an der hohen Anzahl seiner Mitglieder und der vielen Veranstaltungen[12] – ohne Zweifel auch erreicht wurde. Sieht man sich im Rückblick die Liste der vom Freien Bund durchgeführten Ausstellungen an, so nehmen dabei vor allem die angewandten Künste eine zentrale Stellung ein. Unter ihnen finden sich Schauen wie *Moderne Typen (Moderne Druckschriften)* (1911), *Neues Bauen* (1915), *Kleinwohnung und Siedlung* (1916), *Spitzen, Glas und Silber* (1922) oder auch aus heutiger Sicht so kuriose Themen wie *Gute Zigarrenpackungen* (1920) oder *Der bunte Stoff und die neue Farbigkeit* (1922/23). Der dabei verfolgte Ansatz, den Geschmack der Allgemeinbevölkerung zu bilden und zu heben, klingt schließlich auch in Wicherts Vorwort der Ausstellung *Porzellan und Majolika*, der insgesamt 26. Schau des Freien Bundes, klar an: „Wir wollen hier nicht den Wesensunterschied beider Stoffe [von Porzellan und Majolika; Anm. d. Verf.] ganz erklären. Der Betrachter soll ihn selber aufspüren, soll selbsttätig sein, soll endlich – es sei immer wieder gesagt – mit Augen und Nerven die Dinge anschauen und nicht mit der schrägen Schulter. Und wenn er noch mehr tun will, soll er kaufen. Nur durch den täglichen Umgang mit keramischen Gegenständen wächst der Sinn für das Gute, wächst das Gefühl für den Reichtum in Glasur und Farbe."[13]

Die Produzenten: die Aelteste Volkstedter Porzellanmanufaktur und die Großherzogliche Majolika-Manufaktur Karlsruhe

Um den Besucher*innen seines Hauses die aktuellsten Entwicklungen auf dem Gebiet der Porzellan- und Majolika-Herstellung zu veranschaulichen, gewann Wichert mit der Aeltesten Volkstedter

The manufactory still had this uninterrupted renown in the early 1920s. But in order to remain at the height of design of its own era, it was increasingly working with contemporary artists from the modern avant-garde. In addition to Hans Poelzig, they included, among others, the Bauhaus artists Otto Lindig (1895–1966) and Theodor Bogler (1897–1968), who had some of their objects produced in Volkstedt. The head of the Aelteste Volkstedter Porzellanmanufaktur in 1921 was Director General Dr. Edmund Troester (1866–1945), who played a crucial role in the company's participation in the exhibition in Mannheim.[18]

The Designers: Hans Poelzig and Marlene Moeschke

Contact between the Thuringian manufactory and Hans Poelzig appears to have been made around 1919. Born in Berlin in 1869, the architect had just become head of municipal planning and building in Dresden after many years teaching at the Kunst- und Kunstgewerbeschule (Art and Applied Art School) in Breslau (now Wrocław), before leaving the city on the Elbe already in 1920 to return to Berlin. Immediately after World War I, Poelzig was, unlike many of his colleagues, able to get several larger commissions, but also found time for small projects separate from his core architecture business.[19] In addition to a cooperation with the manufactory in Volkstedt that lasted at least until 1922, Poelzig also worked on very similar projects with the majolica make in Karlsruhe at the same time, designing for them a majolica chapel that was never built and several majolica fountains.

The reason behind these two cooperations and intense engagement with porcelain and majolica lies not least in Poelzig's approach to work and design.[20] For his buildings, which were usually extremely plastic in form, he used models with an intensity matched by few other colleagues, working with clay or plasticine. By all appearances, these materials were the best and fastest way to lend concrete form to his own architectural ideas for himself as well as to illustrate them for others. The leap from creating entire building complexes to designing incomparably smaller objects of porcelain or majolica was thus not a large one for the architect and was by no means far from the essence of his creative work.

As with nearly all of the projects that Poelzig and his office was able merely to plan on paper actually to or build, in the case of the collaboration with the manufactory in Thuringia too there was no getting around the sculptor and architect Marlene (real name Martha Helene) Moeschke, later Poelzig-Moeschke (1894–1985).[21] With many of these works, it cannot be clearly determined what contribution Poelzig himself made and what should be attributed to his employee and later wife.[22] It should be emphasized that Poelzig himself never held back about that role and—as he did with the other employees in his office—explicitly referred to her creative contribution.[23]

In the spring of 1918, the forty-nine-year-old architect and the Hamburg-born daughter of a merchant of tropical fruit and wine who was born in East Prussia first met at an event at the Preußische Akademie in Berlin and soon began to appreciate each other both professionally and privately. Immediately thereafter, Moeschke began working for the architect, whom she would later marry in 1924–after Poelzig divorced his first wife.

She had arrived in Berlin on a scholarship as a twenty-three-year-old sculptor only shortly before their first meeting. From 1910 to 1916, she had been the first female student to complete an apprenticeship in sculpture at the Kunstgewerbeschule (School of the Applied Arts) in Hamburg. Her teacher, the Viennese Jugendstil artist Richard Luksch (1872–1936), provided important aesthetic inspiration.[24] In particular, his ideas about *Plastik im Raum* (Sculpture in Space), which closely

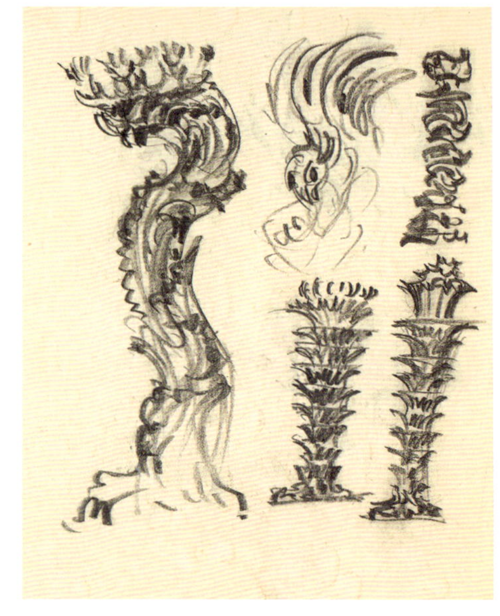

Abb./Figs. **21, 22**
Hans Poelzig, Entwurfszeichnungen für einen *Wolkenleuchter* / Hans Poelzig, Design drawings for a Wolkenleuchter, **um**/*ca.* **1920**

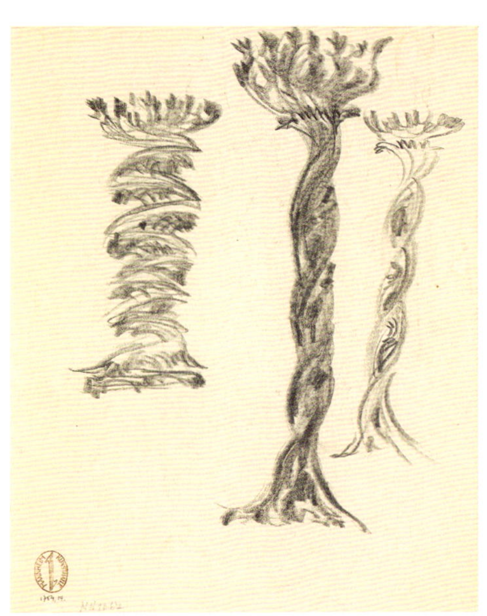

Porzellanmanufaktur und der Großherzoglichen Majolika-Manufaktur Karlsruhe zwei bedeutende deutsche Produzenten beider Werkstoffe als Partner, aus deren Produktion – bis auf einzelne Exponate Max Läugers aus eigener Herstellung – sämtliche präsentierte Objekte stammten. Während die Karlsruher Majolika dabei Arbeiten präsentierte, die von unterschiedlichsten Künstler*innen gestaltet wurden, basierten die von der Volkstedter Porzellanmanufaktur gezeigten Objekte auf Entwürfen von insgesamt nur vier unterschiedlichen Künstlern. Neben Poelzig waren dies Gustav Oppel (1891–1978), Hugo Meisel (1887–1966) und Arthur Storch (1870–1947), alle drei Bildhauer und Modelleure, die zum Teil Jahrzehnte eng mit der Manufaktur zusammenarbeiteten und größtenteils auch die Modellierung der Entwürfe Poelzigs übernahmen.[14] Während alle größeren gezeigten Objekte wie die freistehenden oder von der Decke abgehängten Leuchter, die Heizkörperverkleidungen, die Wandkonsolen und auch die kleineren Leuchter auf Poelzig zurückzuführen sind und im Folgenden noch genauer betrachtet werden, stammen von diesen drei Künstlern die Entwürfe fast aller auf den Wandkonsolen präsentierten Figurinen und Tiere.[15]

Während die Karlsruher Majolika 1921 nur auf eine relativ kurze Firmengeschichte von knapp 20 Jahren verweisen konnte[16], blickte die Aelteste Volkstedter Porzellanmanufaktur aus Thüringen damals bereits auf eine über 150 Jahre andauernde Tradition zurück.[17] Im Jahr 1760 gegründet, erlebte sie bereits Ende des 18. Jahrhunderts eine große Blüte und wurde weit über die eigenen Landesgrenzen hinaus geschätzt. Dieses Renommee hatte die Manufaktur ungebrochen auch Anfang der 1920er-Jahre. Um aber auf der gestalterischen Höhe der eigenen Zeit zu bleiben, arbeitete man in dieser Zeit verstärkt auch mit zeitgenössischen, der modernen Avantgarde zuzurechnenden Künstlern zusammen. Neben Hans Poelzig waren dies unter anderem die beiden Bauhaus-Künstler Otto Lindig (1895–1966) und Theodor Bogler (1897–1968), die einige ihrer Objekte in Volkstedt produzieren ließen. An der Spitze der Aeltesten Volkstedter Porzellanmanufaktur stand 1921 Generaldirektor Dr. Edmund Troester (1866–1945), der entscheidend am Zustandekommen der Beteiligung seiner Firma an der Mannheimer Ausstellung mitwirkte.[18]

Entwurf und Umsetzung: Hans Poelzig und Marlene Moeschke

Der Kontakt zwischen der thüringischen Manufaktur und Hans Poelzig scheint wiederum um 1919 entstanden zu sein. Der 1869 in Berlin geborene Architekt war nach seiner langjährigen Tätigkeit an der Breslauer Kunst- und Kunstgewerbeschule damals gerade Stadtbaurat in Dresden, bevor er die Stadt an der Elbe bereits 1920 in Richtung Berlin wieder verlassen sollte. In der Zeit unmittelbar nach dem Ersten Weltkrieg konnte Poelzig – anders als viele seiner Kollegen – zwar einige größere Aufträge verbuchen, fand gleichzeitig aber auch die Zeit für kleinere Projekte abseits seines architektonischen Kerngeschäfts.[19] Neben der mindestens bis 1922 anhaltenden Kooperation mit der Volkstedter Manufaktur arbeitete Poelzig zeitgleich auch mit der Karlsruher Majolika in ganz ähnlichen Projekten zusammen und entwarf für sie eine letztlich nicht realisierte Majolika-Kapelle sowie mehrere, ebenfalls aus Majolika bestehende Brunnen.

Dass es überhaupt zu diesen beiden Kooperationen und der intensiven Auseinandersetzung mit den Werkstoffen Porzellan und Majolika kam, liegt nicht zuletzt in Poelzigs Arbeits- und Entwurfsprozess begründet.[20] Denn für seine meist stark plastisch durchformten Bauten nutzte er so intensiv wie nur wenige seiner Kollegen Modelle, die er aus Ton oder Plastilin aufbaute. Allem Anschein nach gelang es ihm mit diesen Materialien am besten und schnellsten, die eigenen

linked architecture and sculpture and resulted in an expressive, spatial, architectural sculpture, had a lasting influence on her. She brought these experiences to her joint work with Hans Poelzig, which can be documented especially clearly with the example of the project to convert the Zirkus Schumann in Berlin into Max Reinhardt's *Großes Schauspielhaus* (1919).[25] Just how closely the couple collaborated professionally and the fact that to a large extent Poelzig's designs should always be attributed to Marlene Moeschke as well is demonstrated by their founding an architecture office that they ran together. The couple had opened it in Potsdam only shortly before the exhibition at the Kunsthalle Mannheim under discussion here.

With regard to her participation in the objects shown in Mannheim, the only sentence in which the artist is mentioned in the catalogue to the exhibition is very revealing: "The sculptor Marlene Moeschke contributed artistically to the design and above all the correction of the models cited in what follows, for which Poelzig was responsible himself."[26] As in other cases, this suggests that her principal task was to translate the ideas that her partner had put to paper in an expressive way into detailed plans that could be implemented and to take responsibility for the final check of the finished models. That Poelzig himself provided the first ideas that largely defined the porcelain objects can be considered certain based on twenty-one sketches he made (figs. 21–27). He donated this extremely expressive drawings in graphite and colored pencil to the Kunsthalle. The thank-you letter that Fritz Wichert sent to Marlene Moeschke on September 6, 1921, expresses emphatic praise for her own works, although it remains unclear which precise works the Kunsthalle director was referring to here: "When you visited us here, you were too critical of your own objects. If one lacks the courage to leap past one's own imperfections over and over, in the end one will never finish anything at all."[27]

Consoles, Radiator Covers, Candelabra, and Large Cloud Lamps of Porcelain

"The models displayed in the next rooms here were shown together in the so-called Porzellan-Palais at the Leipzig trade fair; a series of large pieces had originally been intended for a large room designed by Prof. Hans Poelzig but ultimately unbuilt, with a cloud vault, niches, decorative figures, and so on."[28] This explanation in the Mannheim catalogue, according to which the overarching idea for most of the exhibitions shown had been a "cloud room" of porcelain, makes it somewhat easier to approach intellectually Poelzig's exceedingly voluminous objects. For example, on closer inspection one can see that the two *Wolkenleuchter* (Cloud Chandeliers) do indeed consist, as their name suggests, of individual layers of towering, highly animated clouds, and only their interplay results in the classic form of a ceiling chandelier. And the other large-format exhibits, whose size made them extremely complicated to produce, also feature the motif of a puffy, voluminous cloud, not just in the name *(Großer) Wolkenleuchter*. Even more clearly than with the ceiling chandeliers, in the case of one lamp that develops upward out of the floor, this individual form is divided into single layers (fig. 20), and its overall form recalls a pagoda. As with these tower-like buildings, the roof of each of the individual floors projects slightly, with its outer edge turning upward, so that the individual cloud layers here too are slightly curved and taper upward to the projecting edges. The top floor of this miniature porcelain pagoda has a lantern, further underscoring the reference to the forms of Asian traditions in architecture and design. Several dragon-like creatures also adopted from that cultural sphere play around on and crown this element, which is also composed of individual puffy clouds and protects a light source inside. Whereas the outer form derives

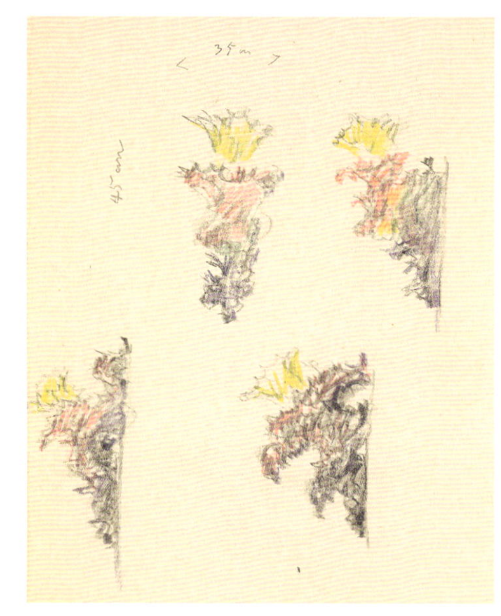

Abb./Fig. **23**
Hans Poelzig, Entwurfszeichnungen für einen mehrarmigen Wandleuchter / *Design drawings for a multi-armed wall lamp,* **um** / *ca.* **1920**

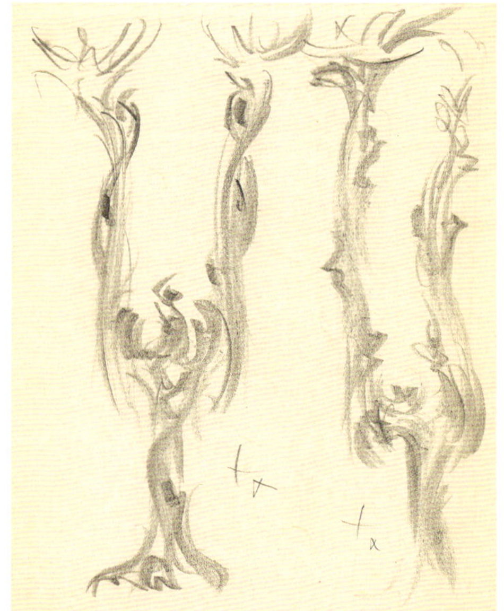

Abb./Fig. **24**
Hans Poelzig, Entwurfszeichnungen für einen Kandelaber / *Design drawings for a candelabra*

baulichen Vorstellungen für sich selbst zu konkretisieren wie auch für andere zu visualisieren. Der Sprung vom Entwerfen ganzer Gebäudekomplexe hin zur Gestaltung ungleich kleinerer Objekte aus Porzellan oder Majolika war für den Architekten demnach also kein allzu großer und lag dem Wesen seines kreativen Arbeitens alles andere als fern.

Wie bei fast allen Projekten, die Poelzig und sein Büro ab 1918 nur auf dem Papier entwarfen oder realisieren konnten, kommt man auch im Falle der Zusammenarbeit mit der Aeltesten Volkstedter Porzellanmanufaktur nicht vorbei an der Bildhauerin und Architektin Marlene (eigentlich Martha Helene) Moeschke, spätere Poelzig-Moeschke (1894–1985).[21] Bei vielen dieser Arbeiten ist nicht eindeutig zu klären, welcher Anteil Poelzig selbst und was seiner Mitarbeiterin und späteren Ehefrau zuzuschreiben ist.[22] Zu betonen ist dabei allerdings, dass der Architekt selbst diesen Anteil nie unterschlug und – wie auch bei den anderen Mitarbeitern seines Büros – auf deren kreative Mitarbeit ausdrücklich hinwies.[23]

Im Frühjahr 1918 hatten sich der damals 49-jährige Architekt und die 1894 in Hamburg geborene Tochter eines aus Ostpreußen stammenden Händlers für Südfrüchte und Wein erstmals bei einer Veranstaltung der Preußischen Akademie in Berlin kennen- und beruflich wie privat schätzen gelernt. Denn unmittelbar darauf wird Moeschke Mitarbeiterin des Architekten, den sie 1924 – nach der Scheidung Poelzigs von seiner ersten Frau – schließlich auch heiraten sollte.

Erst kurz vor ihrem ersten Aufeinandertreffen war die damals 23 Jahre alte Bildhauerin als Stipendiatin nach Berlin gekommen. Zuvor hatte sie von 1910 bis 1916 an der Hamburger Kunstgewerbeschule als erste weibliche Schülerin überhaupt eine Bildhauerlehre absolviert und von ihrem Lehrer, dem Wiener Jugendstilkünstler Richard Luksch (1872–1936), wichtige gestalterische Impulse erhalten.[24] Vor allem dessen Vorstellungen einer „Plastik im Raum", die Architektur und Bildhauerei eng miteinander verbindet und eine expressive, raumgreifende Architekturplastik entstehen lässt, prägten sie nachhaltig. Diese Erfahrungen sollte sie in die gemeinsame Tätigkeit mit Hans Poelzig einbringen, was sich besonders deutlich am Umbauprojekt des Berliner Zirkus Schumann zum Großen Schauspielhaus (1919) Max Reinhardts dokumentieren lässt.[25] Wie eng das Paar beruflich zusammenarbeitete bzw. dass die Entwürfe Poelzigs zu einem guten Teil auch immer Marlene Moeschke zuzuschreiben sind, belegt die Gründung des gemeinsam geführten Bauateliers. Dieses hatte das Paar nur kurz vor der hier besprochenen Ausstellung in der Kunsthalle Mannheim in Potsdam ins Leben gerufen.

Was nun den konkreten Anteil der Künstlerin an den in Mannheim gezeigten Objekten betrifft, so ist der einzige Satz, mit dem sie innerhalb des Katalogs der Mannheimer Ausstellung genannt wird, sehr aufschlussreich. Darin heißt es: „An den im folgenden angeführten eigenen Modellen Poelzigs hat die Bildhauerin Marlene Moeschke entwerfend sowie vor allem durch Korrektur der Modelle künstlerischen Anteil."[26] Wie auch in anderen Fällen dürfte es demnach auch hier ihre vornehmliche Aufgabe gewesen sein, die von ihrem Partner in expressiver Weise zu Papier gebrachten Ideen in ausführbare, detailgenaue Plandarstellungen zu überführen bzw. die finale Kontrolle der realisierten Modelle zu übernehmen. Dass die ersten, die Objekte weitgehend definierenden Ideen dazu Poelzig selbst lieferte, kann wiederum durch insgesamt 21 Skizzen, die der Architekt für die Objekte aus Porzellan anfertigte, als gesichert angesehen werden (Abb. 21–27). Diese in Bleistift oder Buntstift entstandenen, äußerst ausdrucksstarken Zeichnungen machte er der Kunsthalle zum Geschenk. In dem erhaltenen Dankesbrief, den Fritz Wichert am 6. September 1921 an Marlene Moeschke richtete, ist ein entschiedenes Lob für die eigenen Werke der Künstlerin zu finden – auch wenn unklar bleiben

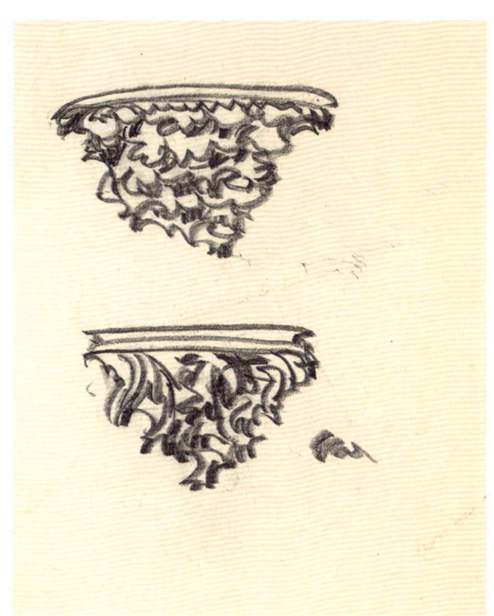

from the Asian tradition as well as the European Baroque, the light fixtures used in this and the other lamps shown employed the latest modern technology: both the ceiling chandeliers and their standing pendants conceal electrical wiring inside to provide the electricity for the lightbulbs they hold or suspend. Poelzig did not always hide this functional form but was also able to play with it and employ it as a design element. This is especially clear in the case of the tree- or bush-like wall lamps (fig. 28), whose stylized branches and twigs terminate in lightbulbs placed like fruit.

Plant forms in porcelain, sometimes more, sometimes less stylized, not only appear in this exhibit but were, along with the motif of a cloud, the second large, overarching theme of the objects presented in Mannheim. Many of them feature an idiom of vegetal forms whose vocabulary consists of stylized calyxes, ramifying branches, and tree trunks and flower stems spiraling upward. This adopting of models from nature can of course be read not only from the exhibits themselves but is sometimes even clearer in Poelzig's preparatory sketches. And finally, the aforementioned citations from the Asian cultural sphere and echoes of Baroque and Rococo forms are other design components that the architect was able to blend into an extremely lively whole that is always intricate

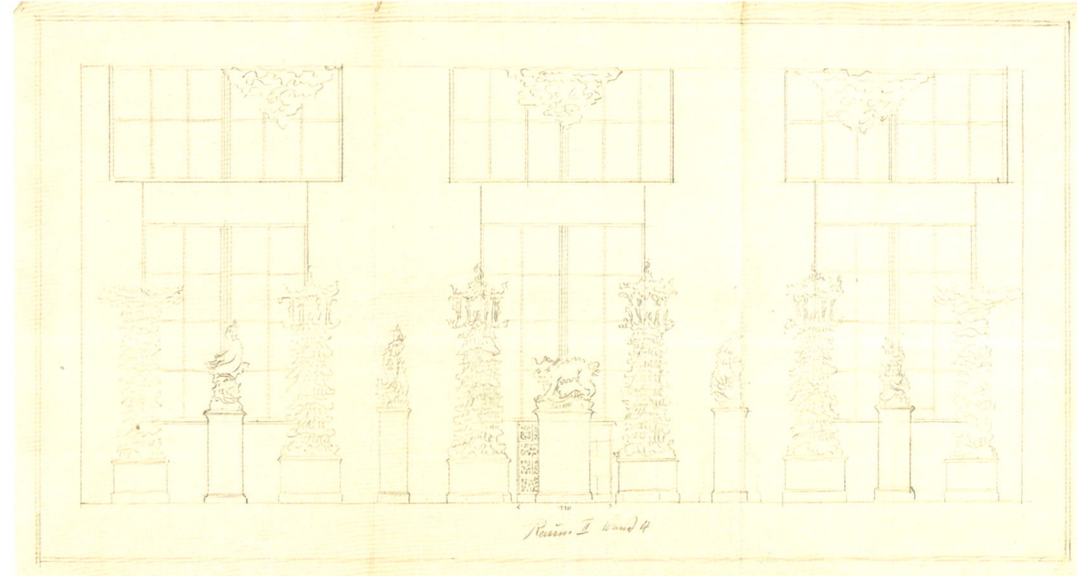

Abb./Figs. 26, 27
Hans Poelzig, Raumpläne für die Ausstellung *Porzellan und Majolika* mit Exponaten der Aeltesten Volkstedter Porzellanmanufaktur /
Plans for the rooms of the Porzellan und Majolika exhibition with the exhibits of the Aelteste Volkstedter Porzellanmanufaktur

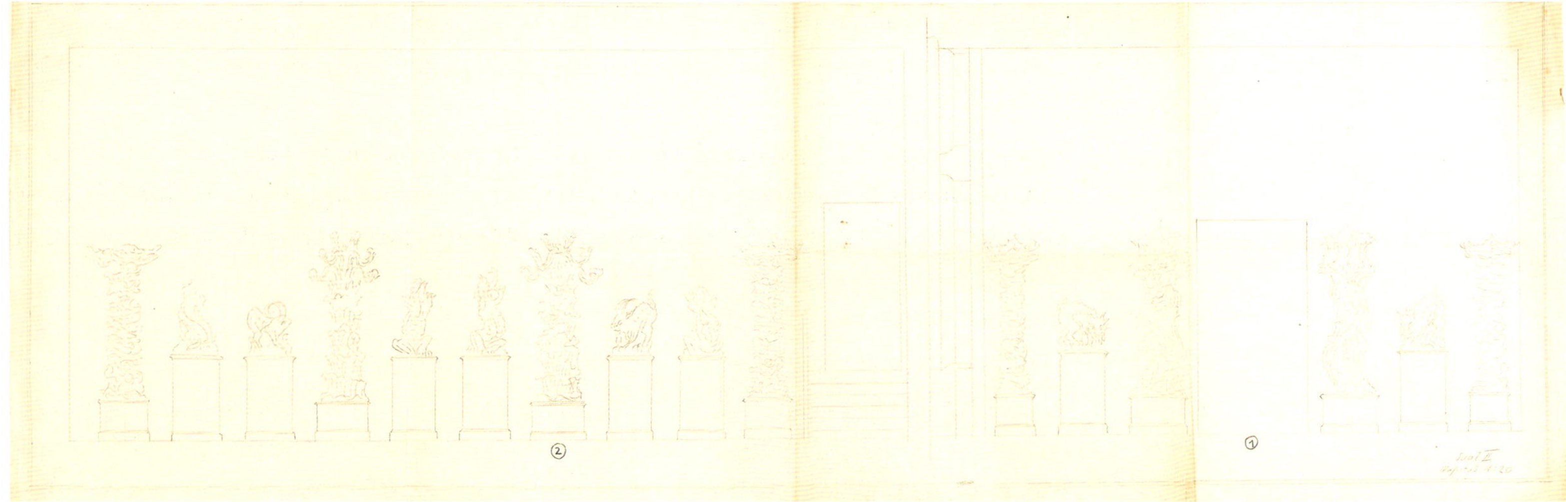

     "IN HANS POELZIG'S *LUFTREICH*": ON THE *PORCELAIN AND MAJOLICA* EXHIBITION AT THE KUNSTHALLE MANNHEIM IN 1921

muss, auf welche Arbeiten genau sich der Direktor der Kunsthalle hier bezog: „Sie waren damals, als Sie uns besuchten, Ihren eigenen Sachen gegenüber zu kritisch eingestellt. Wenn man nicht den Mut hat immer wieder eigene Unvollkommenheiten zu überspringen, bringt man schließlich überhaupt nichts mehr fertig.“[27]

Konsolen, Heizkörperverkleidungen, Kandelaber und große Wolkenleuchter aus Porzellan

„Die hier wie in den nächsten Sälen zur Schau gestellten Modelle waren im sogenannten Porzellan-Palais auf der Leipziger Messe vereinigt; eine Reihe von großen Stücken war ursprünglich für einen großen, von Prof. Hans Poelzig geplanten, jedoch unausgeführt gebliebenen Saal mit Wolkenkuppel, Nischen, dekorativen Figuren usw. bestimmt.“[28] Mit dieser Erläuterung aus dem Mannheimer Ausstellungskatalog, nach der die übergreifende Idee der meisten gezeigten Exponate ein Wolkensaal aus Porzellan gewesen sei, fällt es etwas leichter, sich gedanklich vor allem den äußerst voluminösen Einzelobjekten Poelzigs anzunähern. Denn so erkennt man etwa bei genauerem Betrachten, dass sich die beiden von der Decke herabhängenden *Wolkenleuchter* gemäß ihrem Namen tatsächlich aus einzelnen, sich aufeinandertürmenden, stark bewegten Wolkenschichten aufbauen und erst in ihrem Zusammenspiel die Form klassischer Deckenlüster ergeben. Und auch an weiteren großformatigen, daher herstellungstechnisch äußerst komplizierten Exponaten tritt das Motiv der bauschig-voluminösen Wolke nicht nur in Form der Bezeichnung als *Großer Wolkenleuchter* in Erscheinung. Noch deutlicher als bei den Deckenleuchtern ist diese Einzelform etwa bei einem sich vom Boden aus in die Höhe entwickelnden Leuchter in einzelne Schichten unterteilt (Abb. 20), der in seiner gesamten Gestalt an eine Pagode erinnert. Wie bei diesen turmartigen Gebäuden die Dächer der einzelnen Geschosse jeweils leicht vorspringen und sich an ihren äußeren Enden nach oben hin aufschwingen, so sind auch hier die einzelnen Wolkenebenen jeweils leicht gebogen und an den äußeren, hervorragenden Rändern nach oben hin verjüngend gearbeitet. Das abschließende Stockwerk dieser miniaturisierten Pagode aus Porzellan nimmt dabei eine Laterne ein, in der dieser formbedingte Bezug zur architektonischen wie gestalterischen Tradition Asiens noch zusätzlich unterstrichen wird. Denn mehrere, diesem Kulturkreis entnommene drachenartige Wesen umspielen und bekrönen dieses ebenfalls aus einzelnen Wolkenbauschen gebildete, in seinem Innern die Lichtquelle schützende Element. Während die äußere Gestalt also der asiatischen wie auch der barocken europäischen Tradition entspringt, sind die Art der Beleuchtung dieses wie auch anderer der gezeigten Leuchtkörper auf der Höhe ihrer modernen Entstehungszeit. Denn sowohl die Deckenleuchter als auch ihre aufrecht stehenden Pendants verbergen in ihrem Innern elektrische Leitungen, die die von ihnen getragenen oder gehaltenen Glühbirnen mit dem nötigen Strom versorgen. Dabei versteckt Poelzig diese runde Funktionsform nicht immer, sondern weiß auch mit ihr zu spielen und sie als gestalterisches Element einzusetzen. Besonders deutlich ist dies schließlich im Falle der baum- oder buschartigen Wandleuchter zu beobachten (Abb. 28), deren stilisierte Äste und Zweige ihren Abschluss in den wie Früchte platzierten Glühbirnen finden.

Die aus Porzellan gebildete, einmal mehr, einmal weniger stilisierte Pflanzenform tritt aber nicht nur in diesem Exponat in Erscheinung, sondern ist neben dem Motiv der Wolke das zweite große, übergreifende Thema der in Mannheim präsentierten Objekte. Viele von ihnen kennzeichnet eine vegetabile Formensprache, deren Wortschatz stilisierte Blütenkelche, sich verzweigende Äste oder sich spiralförmig nach oben schraubende Baumstämme und Blumenstängel

despite all the monumentality of the individual pieces. Poelzig's objects subtly reflect the history of their material as well, which as an import from the Far East became a status symbol of European court society in the Baroque era.

In contrast to the functionalist premise of his time, however, according to which the form of the object to be designed should evolve strictly from its function, Poelzig took a decidedly different path here. He wanted instead to produce eloquent objects that would be as expressive as possible, resonating with references to spheres of meaning as diverse as possible. At the same time, their design should not simply have recourse to history but rather reinterpret it and also remain at the artistic apex of their own time. In his review Hildebrand Gurlitt summed up what he had seen of Poelzig's work at the Kunsthalle as follows: "Rocaille forms occur; one thinks of the Baroque, in whose dignity an ardent passion moved, India, China, fairy tales, dreams come to mind, and yet everything is from today and now, and not one form is an old one."[29] Poelzig explored the bounds of porcelain as a material, and in his work it not only has unusual dimensions and massiveness but is also used in new functional contexts. The sometimes-trivial original purpose of his objects—lamp, radiator cover, or console—recedes entirely behind the opulent and expressive outward appearance.

Poelzig's Exhibits in the Mirror of Contemporaneous Criticism

Looking over the response that *Porzellan und Majolika* in general and Poelzig's designs in particular received in the reviews in press at the time, it is precisely this denial of form grounded primarily in the functional that was seen as an essential feature of the exhibits and usually also praised as

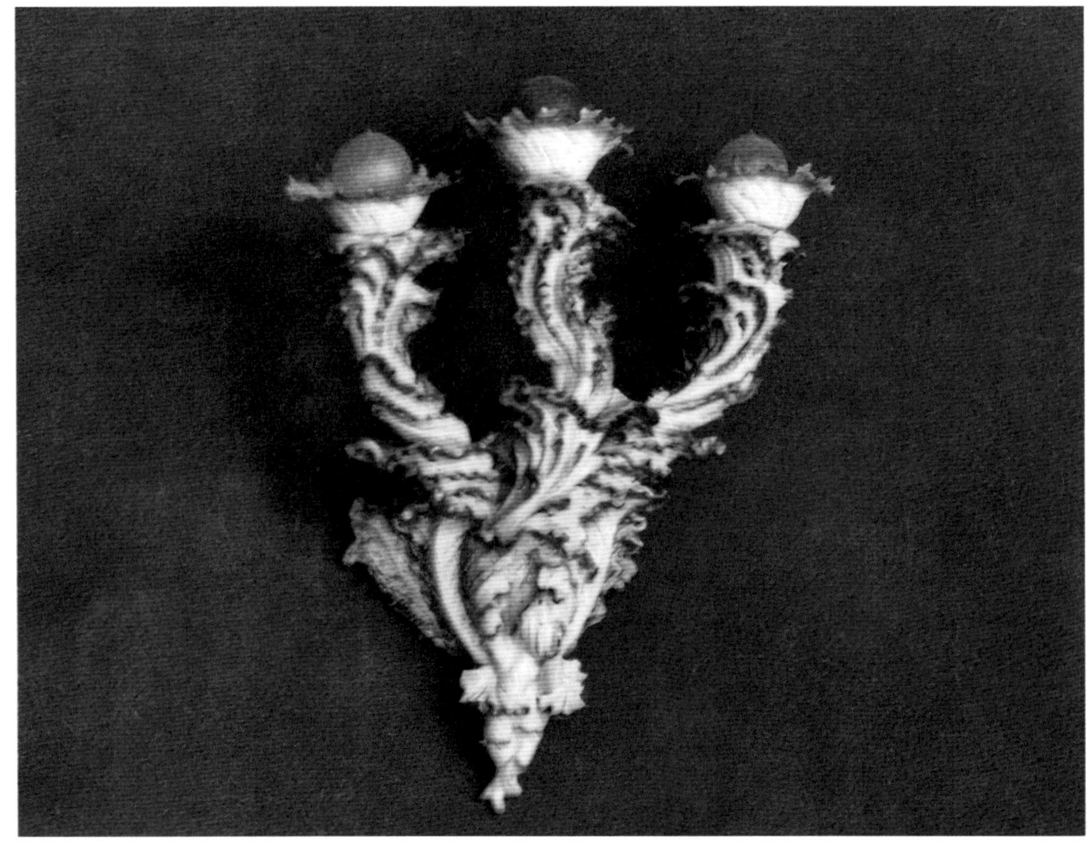

Abb./Fig. **28**
Hans Poelzig und/and **Marlene Moeschke,**
Dreiarmiger Wandleuchter/*Three-armed wall lamp*

bilden. Dieses Aufgreifen von Vorbildern aus der Natur ist dabei natürlich nicht nur den Exponaten abzulesen, sondern zeigt sich mitunter noch deutlicher an den sie vorbereitenden Skizzen Poelzigs. Und schließlich treten mit den bereits erwähnten Zitaten aus dem asiatischen Kulturkreis und den Anklängen an die Formensprache des Barock und Rokoko weitere gestalterische Komponenten hinzu, die der Architekt zu einem jeweils äußerst bewegten, trotz aller Monumentalität einzelner Objekte immer auch feinteiligen Ganzen zu verschmelzen weiß. Auf subtile Weise spiegeln Poelzigs Objekte so auch die Geschichte ihres Materials wider, dass als Import aus dem Fernen Osten im Europa des Barockzeitalters zu einem Statussymbol der höfischen Gesellschaft wurde.

Im Gegensatz zur funktionalistischen Prämisse seiner Zeit aber, nach der sich die Form des zu gestaltenden Objekts strikt aus dessen Funktion entwickeln solle, schlug Poelzig hier also einen entschieden anderen Weg ein. Er wollte vielmehr möglichst ausdrucksstarke, sprechende Objekte hervorbringen, in denen Bezüge zu unterschiedlichsten Bedeutungsfeldern anklingen. Gleichzeitig sollte die Gestaltung kein bloßer Rückgriff auf die Historie, sondern deren Neuinterpretation und künstlerisch auf der Höhe der eigenen Zeit sein. Dieses Vorhaben bringt Hildebrand Gurlitt in seiner Rezension des in der Kunsthalle von Poelzig Gesehenen wie folgt auf den Punkt: „Rocquailleformen kommen vor, man denkt an Barock, in dessen Würde eine glühende Leidenschaft gefahren ist, Indien, China, Märchen, Träume fallen einem ein, und dann ist doch alles von heute und jetzt und keine Form eine alte. Leuchter hängen von der Decke, wie ein Pfeil aus Wolken gebildet; Licht fällt darauf und spiegelt sich klirrend an den harten Flächen oder scheint durch das Porzellan traumhaft gelb wie der Mond."[29] Poelzig lotete die Grenzen des Materials Porzellan aus, das bei ihm nicht nur in ungewöhnlicher Dimensionierung und Massigkeit, sondern auch in neuen funktionalen Zusammenhängen auftritt. Der mitunter triviale ursprüngliche Zweck seiner Objekte als Leuchter, Heizkörperverkleidung oder Konsolen tritt rein äußerlich ganz hinter die opulente und expressive äußere Erscheinung zurück.

Poelzigs Exponate im Spiegel der zeitgenössischen Kritik

Überblickt man das Echo, das die Ausstellung *Porzellan und Majolika* im Allgemeinen und Poelzigs Entwürfe im Besonderen in den Rezensionen der damaligen Berichterstattung hervorrief, so ist es gerade dieses Verneinen der vorrangig funktional begründeten Form, was als wesentliches Merkmal der Exponate erkannt und meist auch als besondere Leistung gewürdigt wurde. So schreibt etwa der Korrespondent des *Freiburger Tagblatts:* „Ein lebendiger Protest gegen den, in bloße geschmackvolle Zweckhaftigkeit geflüchteten, allzu nüchternen Geist des sogenannten modernen Kunstgewerbes."[30] Geradezu hymnisch fällt wiederum das Lob Anton Schacks, eines Berichterstatters der *Vossischen Zeitung,* aus: „Poelzig: ein Name, weht da nicht Wind und Wolke darin? Blitz aus ihm nicht etwas Kühnes, Wildes, Neues? Fürwahr Poelzigs Stücke sind Stücke aus Traumstätten, sind versteinerte Musik, sind auf- und niederwogende Melodien, sind Wolkenhaufen, die über einen phantastischen Himmel ziehend, gedacht sind, sind Gewächse voll geheimnisvollen Lebens und Wucherns."[31] Und an anderer Stelle: „[...] die Sehnsucht nach der Form wurde unter seinen Händen wieder zur wirklichen und großen Form, er allein hat das Zauberlicht einer neuen und wahren Schönheit wieder angezündet und entfacht."[32] Auch der bereits erwähnte Hildebrand Gurlitt kommt in seiner Besprechung der Ausstellung zu einem ganz ähnlichen Schluss: „Diese großen Porzellangebilde sind nicht nur Beleuchtungskörper,

a special achievement. For example, the correspondent of the *Freiburger Tagblatt* wrote: "A living protest against all-too-sober spirit of so-called modern applied art that has fled to merely tasteful functionality."[30] The praise of Anton Schack, who wrote a review in the *Vossische Zeitung*, was almost panegyrical: "Poelzig: Do not wind and cloud waft in the very name? Does not something bold, wild, new flash from it? Poelzig's pieces are truly from the places of dreams, are petrified music, are melodies surging and ebbing, are crowds of clouds passing across a fantastic sky, are forms of mysterious life and luxuriant growth."[31] And elsewhere: "In his hands, yearning for form returned to the genuine and great; he alone has sparked and reignited the magical light of a new and true beauty."[32] The above-cited Hildebrand Gurlitt also comes to a very similar conclusion in his review of the exhibition: "These great porcelain forms are not just lighting fixtures but above all sculptural works of art that are supposed to convey an emotion. What matters to him [Poelzig] is not just purpose but expression. The swing of the lines of these lamps, the flowing of their forms, the whirling of their curves are supposed to pull the viewer along into the elevated emotion that the artist felt when making them."[33] For all the praise of Poelzig's unbridled creativity, however, Gurlitt also addresses the other side of that coin, namely, that his designs could ultimately fall outside their own era: "There are therefore many misgivings about Pölzig's [*sic*] porcelain, but one thing remains certain: They have been created by an artist of rich imagination, incredible passion, and an aspiration to the infinite. These works are an outburst of the old German urge to design the intangible, the moving, the never-ending. In happier times when the architect and client were still more similar in attitude, the same urge produced the great works of the late Gothic and the Baroque. But Pölzig is building for people who do not exist, and hence for all their ecstatic beauty, something of the frantic cry of a desperate man clings to his works."[34]

Poelzig's Designs in the Context of Their Era

Hildebrandt Gurlitt's apt observation inevitably raises the question of how Poelzig's porcelain objects, with their clear reference to historical models, their expressive forms, and their emphasis on the signature style of art in the early 1920s—supposedly the heyday of design ranging from the rational to the functional—could have been made at all and especially by a creative person who was regarded as one of the most important German representatives of modern architecture. But Poelzig's enthusiasm for lively, sculpturally expressive form is a thread running through the architect's entire oeuvre and always remains clearly recognizable even in the clearly more rational-seeming designs of the 1920s and 1930s, such as the famous complex of buildings for I. G. Farben in Frankfurt am Main. On the other hand, this sculptural thinking was rooted in turn in Poelzig's admiration for Baroque and Rococo art, combined with the "will to expression"[35] omnipresent after World War I.[36] For, like so many of his contemporaries after the catastrophe of World War I, Poelzig too was dreaming of a large, shared new dawn in the arts, of the return of its creative powers, and of the emergence of a new formal idiom that both reflected on its own time and its problems and solved them. And like many other artists and art theorists of the time, he was especially looking to the past for guidance. Whereas, say, Walter Gropius in his Bauhaus Manifesto of 1919 declared the idea of building the Gothic cathedral to be the leitmotif not only of a new architecture but also of a new society, for Poelzig—who largely ignored social goals—it was primarily the age of the Baroque and the Rococo or rather its artistic legacies whose spirit he pursued in his own works. In his explanation of the objects shown in Mannheim, Poelzig described what he wanted to probe and translate into new forms in the process using the example of what he felt was missing from contemporaneous design:

sondern vor allem plastische Kunstwerke, die Träger eines Gefühls sein sollen. Nicht auf den Zweck, sondern auf den Ausdruck kommt es ihm [Poelzig; d. Verf.] an. Der Schwung der Linien dieser Lampen, das Strömen ihrer Formen, das Wirbelnde ihrer Kurven sollen dem Beschauer mithineinreißen in das gehobene Gefühl, das der Künstler beim Schaffen hatte."[33] Bei allem Lob für die ungezügelte Kreativität Poelzigs spricht Gurlitt aber auch deren Kehrseite an, die seine Entwürfe letztlich aus der eigenen Zeit fallen lassen würden: „Viele Bedenken gibt es somit gegen Pölzigs [sic!] Porzellan, eins aber bleibt sicher, hier schafft ein Künstler, dem eine reiche Phantasie, eine ungeheure Leidenschaft, ein Drang zum Unendlichen zu eigen ist. Diese Werke sind ein Ausbruch der alten deutschen Sehnsucht, das Unfassbare, Bewegte, nie Endende zu gestalten. Zu glücklicheren Zeiten, als Architekt und Bauherr sich noch in der Gesinnung ähnlicher waren, entstanden aus gleichem Drange die großen Werke der Spätgotik und des Barock. Pölzig baut aber für Menschen, die es nicht gibt, drum bleibt bei aller rauschenden Schönheit an seinen Werken etwas vom rasenden Schrei eines Verzweifelten."[34]

Poelzigs Entwürfe im Kontext ihrer Entstehungszeit

Diese treffende Beobachtung Hildebrandt Gurlitts führt unweigerlich zur Frage, wie Poelzigs Porzellanobjekte mit ihrer deutlichen Referenz an historische Vorbilder, ihrer expressiven Formensprache und ihrer Betonung der künstlerischen Handschrift Anfang der 1920er-Jahre, der vermeintlichen Blütezeit einer rationalen bis funktionalistischen Entwurfshaltung, überhaupt entstehen und darüber hinaus auch von einem Kreativen geschaffen werden konnten, der zu den wichtigsten deutschen Repräsentanten der Architekturmoderne gezählt wird. Poelzigs Begeisterung für die bewegte, plastisch-expressiv gestaltete Form zieht sich jedoch wie ein roter Faden durch das gesamte Schaffen des Architekten und bleibt auch noch in den deutlich rationaler anmutenden Entwürfen der 1920er- und 1930er-Jahre, wie etwa dem bekannten Gebäudekomplex der I. G. Farben in Frankfurt am Main, immer erkennbar. Anderseits wurzelt dieses plastische Denken wiederum in Poelzigs Bewunderung für die Kunst des Barock und Rokoko, die sich nach dem Ersten Weltkrieg mit dem damals omnipräsenten „Willen zum Ausdruck"[35] verbindet.[36] Denn wie so viele seiner Zeitgenoss*innen träumte auch Poelzig nach der Katastrophe des Ersten Weltkrieges vom großen, gemeinsamen Aufbruch in den Künsten, der Wiederkehr ihrer schöpferischen Kräfte und dem Entstehen einer neuen, die eigene Zeit und ihre Probleme reflektierenden wie lösenden Formensprache. Und wie viele andere Künstler*innen und Kunsttheoretiker*innen dieser Zeit suchte dabei gerade auch er Rat in der Vergangenheit. Während etwa Walter Gropius in seinem Bauhausmanifest von 1919 den gotischen Kathedralbaugedanken zum Leitmotiv nicht nur einer neuen Architektur, sondern auch einer neuen Gesellschaft erklärte, ist es bei ihm – unter weitgehender Ausblendung sozialer Zielsetzungen – vorrangig das Zeitalter des Barock und Rokoko bzw. deren künstlerische Hinterlassenschaften, deren Geist er in eigenen Arbeiten nachspürt. Was er dabei ergründen und in neue Formen umsetzen will, beschreibt Poelzig in seiner Erklärung der in Mannheim gezeigten Objekte anhand dessen, was seiner Meinung nach in der damals gerade gegenwärtigen Gestaltung fehlen würde: „Die Tradition ist futsch, der Mut ist futsch, die Form ist futsch, die Schönheit ist futsch! [...] Der deutsche Stil, der sich durchgerungen hat und heilig gesprochen wurde, dem man pflichtschuldig Referenz erweist, ist ohne Musikalität, ohne Form, ohne Schönheit, von einem mehr oder weniger heimlichen Doktrinarismus, wie er dem Deutschen so wohl ansteht."[37] Poelzigs Entwürfe für die Aelteste Volkstedter Porzellanmanufaktur gehören sicherlich

"Tradition is gone, courage is gone, form is gone, beauty is gone! . . . The German style that has prevailed and been declared sacred, to which reference is dutifully made, is without musicality, without form, without beauty and consists of a more or less secret doctrinairism that so befits the Germans."[37] Poelzig's designs for the Aelteste Volkstedter Porzellanmanufaktur most certainly belong to those projects in which this empathy for both the musical and rhythm of Baroque form that he evoked again and again but also for the artistic courage to experiment are most evident and tangible. At the same time, they exemplify a pluralistic modernism in architecture and design that existed for a brief period. They represent just a few years immediately after World War I in which such free artistic experimentation is not only possible but also employed by Hans Poelzig and many other creative people for fantastic projects, though most were only realized on paper. Already by the mid-1920s, the crystalline cathedral buildings of the likes of Hermann Finsterlin (1887–1973) or Walter Gropius (1883–1969), the alpine architecture of the likes of Bruno Taut (1880–1938), and also Poelzig's Baroque indulgences were completely antiquated and inconceivable. Just as the Bauhaus quickly moved from its Expressionist beginnings to a rationalist or functionalist orientation over the further course of that decade, the architectural avant-garde evolved in that direction on an international level as well: no longer the design tradition and the artists' signature but enthusiasm for serial production, economy, and functionality for the primary guidelines for the majority of its protagonists. Fritz Wichert was thus wrong in the end when he predicted that Poelzig's porcelain designs were just the beginning of a larger movement: "Who knows what will yet emerge! . . . It will not take long before others follow in the effort to manufacture bold pieces. What the *Älteste Volkstedter* can do in porcelain, Karlsruhe can perhaps do in majolica as well. Perhaps even better, who knows?"[38]

Striving for the Gesamtkunstwerk: Other Works of Art in the Exhibition

Although we can no longer determine today who was responsible for their hanging,[39] something should be said here for the other works of art in the exhibition. The photographs of the show that have been preserved clearly show that several paintings were hanging among the porcelain and majolica exhibits. Of the four works that can be seen in these photographs, Emil Nolde's painting *Figuren und Georginen* (Figures and Dahlias) of 1919 (fig. 18, cat. 104) is clearly identifiable. This painting, which was acquired by the Kunsthalle the year it was made, was one of the museum's works that was confiscated as "degenerate" by the National Socialists in 1937 and thus seized from Mannheim once and for all. Now it is in the collection of the Statens Museum for Kunst in Copenhagen.

The other three works cannot be clearly attributed to specific artists but are also Expressionist works. They, too, have flower or landscape motifs that were not simply ideally suited to the exhibition thematically. Their interplay with the other exhibits also exemplified the striving for the Gesamtkunstwerk that can be observed in Expressionism in particular, in which the individual artistic genres harmoniously supplement one another.

The Exhibition as a Mirror of Local and International Political Events

It is not just the activities and developments in the history of architecture and design during the transition from a pluralistic modernism to one largely dominated by rational and functional considerations that are made tangible by the exhibits designed by Poelzig and Moeschke. The situation

"Tradition is gone, courage is gone, form is gone, beauty is gone!"

Hans Poelzig, 1921

zu den Projekten, in denen sich dieses Einfühlen in die von ihm immer wieder beschworene Musikalität und Rhythmik barocker Formensprache wie auch der künstlerische Mut zum Experiment am augenscheinlichsten und greifbarsten ausgeprägt sind. Gleichzeitig stehen sie exemplarisch für eine kurze Zeitspanne einer pluralistisch ausgerichteten Architektur- und Designmoderne. Sie repräsentieren nur wenige Jahre unmittelbar nach dem Ersten Weltkrieg, in denen ein derart freies künstlerisches Experimentieren nicht nur möglich, sondern von Hans Poelzig und vielen weiteren Kreativen für fantastische, meist allerdings nur auf dem Papier realisierte Projekte auch genutzt wurde. Bereits Mitte der 1920er-Jahre waren die kristallinen Kathedralbauten eines Hermann Finsterlin (1887–1973) oder Walter Gropius (1883–1969), die alpinen Architekturen eines Bruno Taut (1880–1938) wie auch Poelzigs barocke Schwelgereien schon völlig aus der Zeit gefallen und undenkbar. So wie das Bauhaus nach expressionistischen Anfängen im weiteren Verlauf dieses Jahrzehnts schnell zu einer rationalistischen bis funktionalistischen Ausrichtung fand, so entwickelte sich die Architektur-Avantgarde auch auf internationaler Ebene weiter: Nicht die gestalterische Tradition und die Handschrift der Kunstschaffenden, sondern die Begeisterung für die serielle Produktion, Ökonomie und Zweckmäßigkeit waren für die Mehrheit ihrer Protagonist*innen nun die vorrangigen Leitlinien. So lag letztlich auch Fritz Wichert mit seiner Einschätzung falsch, nach der Poelzigs Entwürfe aus Porzellan nur den Anfang einer größeren Bewegung bilden würden: „Wer weiß, was noch entsteht! [...] Es wird nicht lange dauern bis dem Versuch der einen Manufaktur Wagestücke einer anderen folgen. Was die älteste Volkstedter kann in Porzellan, kann Karlsruhe in Majolika vielleicht auch. Vielleicht noch besser, wer weiß es."[38]

Streben nach dem Gesamtkunstwerk: weitere Kunstwerke der Ausstellung

Auch wenn heute nicht mehr nachzuvollziehen ist, wer für ihre Hängung verantwortlich zeichnete[39], ist an dieser Stelle kurz auf weitere Kunstwerke innerhalb der Ausstellung hinzuweisen. Denn wie auf den von der Schau erhaltenen Fotos deutlich zu erkennen ist, sind einzelne Gemälde zwischen die Exponate aus Porzellan und Majolika gehängt. Von den insgesamt vier auf diesen Aufnahmen zu erkennenden Werken ist Emil Noldes Gemälde *Figuren und Georginen* von 1919 (Abb. 18; Kat.104) eindeutig zu identifizieren. Das bereits in seinem Entstehungsjahr von der Kunsthalle erworbene Gemälde gehörte zu den Werken des Museums, die 1937 von den Nationalsozialisten als „entartet" beschlagnahmt und so Mannheim endgültig entrissen wurden. Heute befindet es sich im Besitz des Statens Museum for Kunst in Kopenhagen.

Die anderen drei Werke können zwar nicht eindeutig bestimmten Künstler*innen zugeordnet werden, sind aber ebenfalls Werke des Expressionismus. Auch sie weisen Blumen- oder landschaftliche Motive auf und fügen sich mit dieser Thematik nicht nur bestens in die Ausstellung ein. Ihr Zusammenspiel mit den übrigen Exponaten steht gleichzeitig exemplarisch für das gerade im Expressionismus zu beobachtende Streben nach dem Gesamtkunstwerk, in dem sich die einzelnen künstlerischen Gattungen harmonisch ergänzen.

Die Ausstellung als Spiegel lokaler bis weltpolitischer Ereignisse

Nicht nur die Vorgänge und Entwicklungen innerhalb der Architektur- und Designgeschichte am Übergang von einer pluralistisch ausgerichteten hin zu einer weitgehend von rationalen bis funktionalen Überlegungen dominierten Moderne werden anhand der von Poelzig und Moeschke

„Die Tradition ist futsch, der Mut ist futsch, die Form ist futsch, die Schönheit ist futsch!"

Hans Poelzig, 1921

of local and world politics in 1921 is also reflected in the form of two events that played out during the show and immediately after its closing, respectively.

One of the greatest catastrophes that the German chemical industry had yet experienced.[40] On the morning of September 21, 1921, the nitrogen plant of the Badische Anilin- und Soda-Fabrik (BASF) in Oppau, very close to Mannheim, exploded. More than 500 people died, and nearly 2,000 were injured. The powerful detonation of the fertilizers stored there—its force was comparable to the explosion of very similar materials in Beirut in 2020—naturally caused great damage within a radius of about seventy-five kilometers as well, including in Mannheim, which was only about ten kilometers away. At the Kunsthalle, windows were broken, and exhibits fell from the walls. From the surviving correspondence on the *Porzellan und Majolika* exhibition, we know that several objects from the Aelteste Volkstedter Porzellanmanufaktur did not survive the enormous blast wave, fell to the floor, and in some cases were irreparably damaged. In his letter to Edmund Troester of September 22, 1921, which listed seven heavily damaged exhibits from the manufactory, including a large lantern, a wall chandelier, and a console by Poelzig— Fritz Wichert wrote of have been lucky under the circumstances: "In view of the powerfulness of the catastrophe, we and you can consider ourselves lucky that much greater damage did not occur. For example, it seems miraculous to me that the large chandelier did not fall from the ceiling. . . . It is inconceivable that the Kunsthalle could reopen within the next ten days, because all of the windows and doors have to be reinstalled first."[41] On the question who was ultimately responsible for the resulting damages and costs, the Kunsthalle ultimately referred to an aid fund established by BASF that would record the resulting damages and hopefully pay them as well. Although the exhibits had been insured by the Kunsthalle, the relevant policies did not cover the case of such a catastrophe.[42]

In addition to the consequences of the explosion in Oppau, which interrupted the exhibition shortly before its planned end[43] the complications did not end when the show was taken down. The news from the Kunsthalle to the Aelteste Volkstedter Porzellanmanufaktur that all of the exhibits that had been provided had been taken down, packed and were ready to be transported back to Thuringia received a reply on October 12 that unfortunately that would be unthinkable at the moment,[44] since all of the group's plants had been on strike for several days. The extremely difficult early years of the Weimar Republic, whose economy struggled with numerous job losses resulting from inflation and deflation in 1921 in particular,[45] are reflected both in this event and in those around the exhibition *Porzellan und Majolika*.

Looking Ahead

Hans Poelzig worked closely with his future wife, Marlene Moeschke, and with the modelers from the Thuringian firm to create objects of great expressivity in which traditional and modern motifs were combined into a new, expressive idiom of forms. Like his designs for the *Großes Schauspielhaus* in Berlin, which was completed in 1919, his very similar but ultimately unrealized plans for the Salzburger Festspielhaus (1922), or his sets for the film *Der Golem—Wie er in die Welt kam* (The Golem—How He Came into the World) (1920), which exemplified on a large scale an experimental and expressive form of modern architecture, these porcelain objects represented on a small scale the new dawn in design immediately after World War I.

Like the overwhelming majority of their professional colleagues, however, the Poelzig-Moeschke duo struck a clearly more sober tone over the remaining course of the 1920s. In a development

"In view of the powerfulness of the catastrophe, we and you can consider ourselves lucky that much greater damage did not occur. For example, it seems miraculous to me that the large chandelier did not fall from the ceiling."

Fritz Wichert, 1921

gestalteten Exponate greifbar. Auch die lokale bis weltpolitische Lage des Jahres 1921 spiegelt sich in Form von zwei Ereignissen wider, die sich während der Schau bzw. unmittelbar nach deren Abbau abspielten.

Dabei war das erste der beiden die größte Katastrophe, die die chemische Industrie in Deutschland bis dato zu verzeichnen hatte.[40] Am Morgen des 21. September 1921 explodierte im in unmittelbarer Nähe zu Mannheim gelegenen Oppau das Stickstoffwerk der Badischen Anilin- und Soda-Fabrik (BASF). Es starben über 500 Menschen, fast 2.000 wurden verletzt. Die gewaltige Detonation der dort gelagerten Düngemittel – in ihrer Wucht mit den ganz ähnlichen, im Jahr 2020 in Beirut explodierten Stoffen zu vergleichen – richtete im Umkreis von etwa 75 Kilometern natürlich auch große Sachschäden an, so auch im nur etwa 10 Kilometer entfernten Mannheim. In der Kunsthalle gingen Scheiben zu Bruch und fielen Exponate von den Wänden. Aus der erhaltenen Korrespondenz zur Ausstellung *Porzellan und Majolika* wissen wir, dass einige Objekte der Aeltesten Volkstedter Porzellanmanufaktur der gewaltigen Druckwelle nicht standhielten, zu Boden fielen und zum Teil irreparable Schäden davontrugen. In seinem Schreiben an Edmund Troester vom 22. September 1921, das sieben stark beschädigte Exponate der Manufaktur – darunter auch eine große Laterne, ein Wandleuchter sowie eine Konsole von Poelzig – auflistet, spricht Fritz Wichert davon, letztlich noch Glück im Unglück gehabt zu haben: „In Anbetracht der Mächtigkeit der Katastrophe können wir und Sie noch von Glück reden, dass nicht viel größerer Schaden eingetreten ist. Z. B. mutet es mir wie ein Wunder an, dass die großen Kronleuchter nicht von der Decke gestürzt sind. […] An eine Wiedereröffnung der Kunsthalle ist für die nächsten 10 Tage kaum zu denken, da ja alle Fenster und Türen erst wieder eingesetzt werden müssen."[41] In der Frage, wer letztlich für die entstandenen Schäden und anfallenden Kosten aufkomme, verwies die Kunsthalle schließlich auf einen von der BASF ins Leben gerufenen Hilfsfonds, der die entstandenen Schäden aufnehmen und hoffentlich auch ausgleichen werde. Zwar seien die Exponate von der Kunsthalle versichert worden, die entsprechenden Policen würden einen derartigen Katastrophenfall aber nicht abdecken.[42]

Neben den Folgen der Oppauer Explosion, die die Ausstellung kurz vor ihrem geplanten Abschluss unterbrach[43], rissen aber auch die Komplikationen nach dem Abbau der Schau nicht ab. Denn auf die Benachrichtigung der Kunsthalle an die Aelteste Volkstedter Porzellanmanufaktur, dass alle zur Verfügung gestellten Exponate abgebaut, verpackt und nun zum Rücktransport nach Thüringen bereit seien, kam von dort am 12. Oktober die Antwort, dass daran aktuell leider nicht zu denken sei.[44] Grund hierfür sei, dass sämtliche Betriebe der Firmengruppe seit einigen Tagen bestreikt würden. Die äußerst schwierigen Anfangsjahre der Weimarer Republik, deren Wirtschaft infolge von Inflation und Deflation gerade im Jahr 1921 mit zahlreichen Arbeitsniederlegungen zu kämpfen hatte[45], spiegeln sich in dieser Begebenheit so auch in den Vorgängen rund um die Ausstellung *Porzellan und Majolika* wider.

Ausblick

Mit den Entwürfen für die Aelteste Volkstedter Porzellanmanufaktur schuf Hans Poelzig in enger Zusammenarbeit mit seiner späteren Ehefrau Marlene Moeschke und den Modelleuren der thüringischen Firma Objekte von starker Ausdruckskraft, in denen sich traditionelle und moderne Motive zu einer neuen expressiven Formensprache verbinden. Wie seine Entwürfe für das 1919 fertiggestellte Große Schauspielhaus in Berlin, seine ganz ähnlichen, letztlich aber nicht verwirklichten Pläne für das Salzburger Festspielhaus (1922) oder seine Kulissen für den Film *Der Golem – Wie er in die Welt kam* (1920) im Großen beispielhaft für eine experimentelle und expressive

Fritz Wichert, 1921

parallel to modern architecture as a whole, the buildings and everyday objects designed by their office focused more on the functional and on economic considerations. Despite largely dispensing with ornaments or obvious historical citations, however, many of the designs in this period—including the I. G. Farben headquarters in Frankfurt am Main (1928–31) and the Haus des Rundfunks (Broadcasting House) in Berlin-Charlottenburg (1929–31)—exude at least at their core the expressive spirit moved by Baroque art that was especially strong around 1920 and that sets the individual form in motion in relation to one another.[46] In the designs for two projects in Ankara from around 1935–36, one again finds the motif of movement that was so fundamental to Poelzig in the form of viewing terraces that are staggered upward. After the National Socialists took power, he was subjected to great hostilities in Germany as one of the most prominent architects of the Weimar Republic, Poelzig made a new beginning in Turkey around 1935. After a third stroke, however, he died in Berlin on June 14, 1936, at the age of sixty-seven. His wife, Marlene Moeschke, closed their joint architecture studio the following year and sold the residence in Berlin-Wilmersdorf she had designed to ensure the family's financial future. Even after 1945, she no longer appeared publicly as an artist, instead dedicating herself above all to perpetuating the memory of her husband and his work. On March 14, 1985, she died in Hamburg at the age of one hundred.

1   Gustav Friedrich Hartlaub, "Läuger," in *Porzellan und Majolika: Aelteste Volkstedter Porzellan-Manufaktur, Grossh. Majolika-Manufaktur Karlsruhe, Max Läuger, 26. Ausstellung des Freien Bundes*, exh. cat. (Mannheim: Kunsthalle Mannheim, 1921), pp. 11–13, esp. p. 11.

2   On this, see the essay by Inge Herold in the present volume.

3   See, for example, Inge Herold, "James Ensor and His Reception in Germany Pre-1945," trans. Lucinda Rennison, in *James Ensor*, ed. Inge Herold and Johan Holten, exh. cat. Kunsthalle Mannheim 2021 (Berlin: Deutscher Kunstverlag, 2021), pp. 30–51.

4   Like Edvard Munch's painting *Anna* immediately before it, Van Gogh's painting was shown as the "Painting of the Month."

5   For example, exhibitions and exhibition participations by artists such as Rudolf Levy (1925) and Willi Oeser (1924 and 1926) and the architect Erich Mendelsohn (1928) could be mentioned.

6   Hans Poelzig, "Der Künstler selbst," in *Porzellan und Majolika* (see note 1), pp. 6–7, esp. p. 6.

7   On the Porzellan-Palais, see esp. Sally Schöne, "Grosse Tiere—grosses Aufsehen! Zur Ausstattung des Porzellan-Palais auf der Leipziger Messe in 1921," in *Porzellanland Thüringen: 250 Jahre Porzellan aus Thüringen*, ed. Museumsverband Thüringen e.V. (Jena: Städtische Museen, 2010), pp. 242–53, and Georg Heinrich Emmerich, *Porzellan-Palais Leipzig* (Munich: Friedrich Bruckmann, 1921). In the Palais, a late Classicist building at Ritterstraße 26, several porcelain manufacturers presented themselves and their wares from that year until 1933. The initiator of this first "trade fair house" of the Leipzig trade fair was the Kommerzienrat (council of commerce) Edmund Troester, who was director general of the Aelteste Volkstedter Porzellanmanufaktur at the time.

Architekturmoderne sind, stehen auch diese Porzellanobjekte im Kleinen für den gestalterischen Aufbruch unmittelbar nach dem Ersten Weltkrieg.

Wie die überwiegende Mehrheit ihrer Berufskolleg*innen schlägt aber auch das Duo Poelzig-Moeschke im weiteren Verlauf der 1920er-Jahre einen deutlich nüchterneren Ton an. In paralleler Entwicklung zur Architekturmoderne insgesamt werden auch die von ihrem Büro geplanten Bauten und Gebrauchsgegenstände sachlicher und sind stärker nach wirtschaftlichen Gesichtspunkten ausgerichtet. Trotz des weitgehenden Verzichts auf Ornamente oder augenscheinliche historische Zitate atmen aber auch viele der in dieser Zeit entstandenen Entwürfe – darunter das Verwaltungsgebäude der I. G. Farben in Frankfurt am Main (1928–1931) oder das Haus des Rundfunks in Berlin-Charlottenburg (1929–1931) – zumindest im Kern jenen um 1920 besonders stark ausgeprägten expressiven, an der Kunst des Barock bewegten Geist, der die Einzelformen zueinander in Bewegung versetzt.[46] Auch in den Entwürfen für zwei Projekte in Ankara, die um 1935/36 entstanden, findet sich dieses für Poelzig so grundlegende Motiv der Bewegung in Form von in der Höhe gestaffelten Aussichtsterrassen wider. Nachdem er in Deutschland mit der Machtübernahme durch das NS-Regime als einer der prominentesten Architekten der Weimarer Republik starken Anfeindungen ausgesetzt war, zeichnete sich für Poelzig um 1936 ein Neuanfang in der Türkei ab. Nach einem dritten Schlaganfall stirbt er allerdings am 14. Juni 1936 im Alter von 67 Jahren in Berlin. Seine Frau Marlene Moeschke löst im folgenden Jahr das gemeinsame Bauatelier auf und verkauft das von ihr gestaltete Wohnhaus in Berlin-Wilmersdorf, um das Fortleben der Familie zu sichern. Auch nach 1945 tritt sie künstlerisch nicht mehr in die Öffentlichkeit, widmet sich stattdessen vor allem dem Andenken ihres Mannes und dessen Werk. Am 14. März 1985 stirbt sie hundertjährig in Hamburg.

1 Gustav Friedrich Hartlaub: Läuger, in: Kat. Ausst. *Porzellan und Majolika. Aelteste Volkstedter Porzellan-Manufaktur, Grossh. Majolika-Manufaktur Karlsruhe, Max Läuger, 26. Ausstellung des Freien Bundes*, Kunsthalle Mannheim 1921, Mannheim 1921, S. 11–13, S. 11.

2 Vgl. hierzu den Beitrag von Inge Herold in diesem Buch.

3 Vgl. etwa Inge Herold: James Ensor und seine Rezeption in Deutschland, in: Kat. Ausst. *James Ensor*, Kunsthalle Mannheim 2021, hrsg. v. Inge Herold u. Johan Holten, Berlin 2021, S. 30–51.

4 Wie unmittelbar vor ihm Edvard Munchs Gemälde *Anna* wurde auch van Goghs Gemälde als „Bild des Monats" gezeigt.

5 Hier sind etwa Ausstellungen oder Ausstellungsbeteiligungen von Künstlern wie Rudolf Levy (1925), Willi Oeser (1924 und 1926) oder dem Architekten Erich Mendelsohn (1928) zu nennen.

6 Hans Poelzig: Der Künstler selbst, in: Kat. Ausst. *Porzellan und Majolika* 1921 (wie Anm. 1), S. 6f., S. 6.

7 Vgl. zum Porzellan-Palais insb. Sally Schöne: Große Tiere – großes Aufsehen! Zur Ausstattung des Porzellan-Palais auf der Leipziger Messe 1921, in: Museumsverband Thüringen e. V. (Hrsg.): *Porzellanland Thüringen. 250 Jahre Porzellan aus Thüringen*, Gera 2010, S. 242–253; sowie Georg Heinrich Emmerich: *Porzellan-Palais Leipzig*, München 1921. In dem 1921 im spätklassizistischen Gebäude Ritterstraße 26 eingerichteten Palais präsentierten sich ab diesem Jahr bis 1933 mehrere Porzellanhersteller mit den von ihnen gefertigten Waren. Initiator dieses ersten „Branchenmessehauses" der Leipziger Messe war Kommerzienrat Edmund Troester, der damalige Generaldirektor der Aeltesten Volkstedter Porzellanmanufaktur.

8 Ein weiterer Ort, an dem Entwürfe Poelzigs für die Aelteste Volkstedter Porzellanmanufaktur

8 Dresden was another place where Poelzig's designs for the Aelteste Volkstedter Porzellanmanufaktur were presented. At the *Jahresschau deutscher Arbeit* (Annual Show of German Crafts) in 1922, the manufactory showed a porcelain pavilion as a separate building designed by Marlene Moeschke. Inside, ampules of porcelain were suspended from a tent-like ceiling construction.

9 Other designers of the objects shown included the painter, graphic artist, and sculptor Paul Scheurich (1883–1945); the sculptor Josef Wackerle (1880–1959); the painter, architect, and craftsman Adalbert Niemeyer (1867–1932); the painter, graphic artist, and ceramicist Willi Münch-Khe (1885–1960); the architect Fritz August Breuhaus de Groot (1883–1960); the painter and sculptor Franz Naager (1870–1942); the sculptor Karl Maximilian Würtenberger (1872–1933); the painter, graphic artist, and ceramicist Emil Pottner (1872–1942); the sculptor and ceramicist Wilhelm Ernst (Willy) Schade (1892–1975); the sculptor Fritz Behn (1878–1970); and the painter and ceramicist Wilhelm Süs (1861–1933). The last named was the only one of the exhibitors who lived in Mannheim. Together with Hans Thoma, he was cofounder of the Großherzogliche Majolika Manufaktur in Karlsruhe. From 1917 until his death in 1933, he was also director of the Gemäldegalerie (Paintings Gallery) in Mannheim Palace.

10 Fritz Wichert, quoted in Jenns Eric Howoldt, *Der Freie Bund zur Einbürgerung der bildenden Kunst in Mannheim: Kommunale Kunstpolitik einer Industriestadt am Beispiel der "Mannheimer Bewegung,"* Europäische Hochschulschriften, Series 28, Kunstgeschichte 18 (Frankfurt am Main: 1982), p. 33.

11 On the Freier Bund, see esp. Howoldt, *Der Freie Bund* (see note 10).

12 See ibid., p. 304. In the year of the exhibition under discussion, membership in the Freier Bund peaked at 11,650 members.

13 Fritz Wichert, "Zur Einführung," *Porzellan und Majolika* (see note 1), pp. 3–5, esp. p. 5.

14 Other modelers who deserve mention were Paul Kramer and Andreas Klötzer as well as Hermann Krannich, who was wrongly identified as "Cranich" in the catalogue of the Mannheim exhibition.

15 Only two vases presented were based on historical models.

16 The manufactory was founded on the initiative of Wilhem Süs and Hans Thoma by Frederick I, Grand Duke of Baden, in 1901.

17 On the history of the manufactory, see esp. Christoph Fritzsche, *Die Aelteste Volkstedter Porzellanmanufaktur: Ihre Geschichte von der Gründung bis heute* (Stuttgart: Arnoldsche, 2013).

18 Troester appears in numerous letters between the Kunsthalle and the Aelteste Volkstedter Porzellanmanufaktur and was very interested in having the exhibition in Mannheim be held.

19 In 1918, he also designed furniture for the Deutsche Werkstätten (German Workshops) in Hellerau, about which no details are known.

20 On this, see Wolfgang Pehnt, "Wille zum Ausdruck: Zu Leben und Werk Hans Poelzigs," in *Hans Poelzig, 1869 bis 1936: Architekt, Lehrer, Künstler,* exh. cat. Akademie der Künste, Berlin, and Deutsches Architekturmuseum, Frankfurt am Main 2008, ed. Wolfgang Pehnt and Matthias Schirren (Munich: Deutsche Verlags-Anstalt, 2007), pp. 10–51, esp. pp. 32–33.

21 On Marlene Moeschke-Poelzig, see esp. Heike Hambrock, *Hans und Marlene Poelzig: Bauen im Geist des Barock; Architekturphantasien, Theaterprojekte und moderner Festbau, 1916–1926* (Delmenhorst: Aschenbeck und Holstein, 2005); Hambrock, "'Also los und Mut! . . . Die Werkstätte, unsere Werkstätte muß eingerichtet werden,'" *Forschung Frankfurt*, no. 2 (2005): pp. 70–76, https://www.forschung-frankfurt.uni-frankfurt.de/36050396/forschung-frankfurt-ausgabe-2-2005-balladen-und-metamorphosen.pdf (accessed June 3, 2025), and Sybille Ehringhaus, "'. . . übrigens im ausgesprochenen Gegensatz zur Auffassung eines Corbusier' . . .: Marlene Moeschke-Poelzig, Bildhauerin und Architektin, 1894–1985," *Frauen Kunst Wissenschaft*, no. 13 (1992): pp. 56–68.

22 See Ehringhaus, "'. . . übrigens im ausgesprochenen Gegensatz . . .'" (see note 21), pp. 58–59. In her essay on Moeschke, Ehringhaus raised this question already in 1992 for Poelzig's oeuvre or rather asked what and how much of Poelzig's work is truly Poelzig and not Moeschke.

23 On this, see Hans Poelzig, "Zur Einführung," in *Poelzig und seine Schule,* exh. cat. Preussische Akademie der Künste zu Berlin 1931 (Berlin: Ernst Wasmuth, 1931), pp. 1–3. On this occasion, the architect listed a total of sixty-one of his own buildings and the contribution of the coworkers involved in each case. Marlene Moeschke was mentioned fourteen times. She is often listed first as the most important collaborator.

24 Finally, in 1916/17, Moeschke also attended the Kunstgewerbeschule (School of the Applied Arts) in Munich.

25 For example, as part of this project she was responsible for drawing the palm-like columns in the building's foyer which both functioned as lighting within the room and provided indirect lighting for the entering visitors.

26 *Porzellan und Majolika* (see note 1), p. 14.

27 Fritz Wichert to Marlene Moeschke, September 6, 1921, in Stadtarchiv Mannheim / MARCHIVUM, Bestand Kunsthalle, Ordner "Ausstellung Porzellan und Majolika I" (= 2012_Ordner 67, pp. 285). It is unclear whether Wichert was speaking here of Moeschke's own sculptures, almost all of which were destroyed in World War II, or whether he also means architectural designs and/or craft works.

28 *Porzellan und Majolika* (see note 1), p. 14.

29 Hildebrand Gurlitt, "Gedichte in Keramik," *Deutsche Allgemeine Zeitung* (Berlin), July 7, 1921.

30 "Eine moderne Keramik-Ausstellung in Mannheim," *Freiburger Tagblatt*, no. 197, July 25, 1921.

31 Anton Schnack, "Majolika und Keramik," *Vossische Zeitung* (Berlin), July 26, 1921.

32 Ibid.

33 Gurlitt, "Gedichte in Keramik" (see note 29).

34 Ibid.

35 Hans Poelzig, "Architekturfragen: Vortrag in der Berliner Sezession, 24. März 1917," *Das Kunstblatt 1* (1917): pp. 129–36, esp. p. 133.

36 On this, see esp. Hambrock 2005 (see note 21), pp. 12ff., and Pehnt 2007 (see note 20), 36ff.

37 Poelzig, "Der Künstler selbst" (see note 6), p. 6.

38 Wichert, "Zur Einführung" (see note 13), p. 4.

39 It is reasonable to assume that the museum was responsible after consultation with the artists involved.

40 On this, see Lisa Sanner, "Als wäre das Ende der Welt da": Die Explosionskatastrophen in der BASF 1921 und 1948, Veröffentlichungen des Stadtarchivs Ludwigshafen am Rhein 42 (Ludwigshafen: Stadtverwaltung Ludwigshafen am Rhein, 2015).

41 Fritz Wichert to Edmund Troester, September 22, 1921, in Stadtarchiv Mannheim / MARCHIVUM, Bestand Kunsthalle, Ordner "Ausstellung Porzellan und Majolika I" (= 2012_Ordner 67, pp. 302–3).

42 See Fritz Wichert to Aelteste Volkstedter Porzellanmanufaktur, October 19, 1921, in Stadtarchiv Mannheim / MARCHIVUM, Bestand Kunsthalle, Ordner "Ausstellung Porzellan und Majolika I" (= 2012_Ordner 67, pp. 319–20).

43 The exhibition was originally planned to run until the end of September 1921. Because it was interrupted by the catastrophe in Oppau, the show was open to the public until October 9.

44 Unknown author at the Aelteste Volkstedter Porzellanmanufaktur to the Kunsthalle Mannheim, October 12, 1921, in Stadtarchiv Mannheim / MARCHIVUM, Bestand Kunsthalle, Ordner "Ausstellung Porzellan und Majolika I" (= 2012_Ordner 67, p. 325).

45 On this, see, for example, Petra Weber, *Gescheiterte Sozialpartnerschaft—Gefährdete Republik? Industrielle Beziehungen, Arbeitskämpfe und der Sozialstaat; Deutschland und Frankreich im Vergleich, 1918–1933–39* (Munich: Oldenbourg, 2010).

46 On the other hand, in the case of the residential home that Poelzig designed with his wife for the Werkbund exhibition at the Weißenhof housing colony in Stuttgarter (1926–27), this motif is at most merely suggested. This rationalist design contrasts starkly with porcelain objects exhibited in Mannheim in 1921.

präsentiert wurden, war Dresden. Auf der *Jahresschau deutscher Arbeit* 1922 zeigte die Manufaktur als eigenständigen Bau einen Porzellanpavillon, der von Marlene Moeschke entworfen wurde. In dessen Innerem hingen Ampeln aus Porzellan von der zeltartigen Deckenkonstruktion herab.

9 Weitere Gestalter der gezeigten Objekte waren der Maler, Grafiker und Kleinplastiker Paul Scheurich (1883–1945), der Bildhauer Josef Wackerle (1880–1959), der Maler, Architekt und Kunstgewerbler Adalbert Niemeyer (1867–1932), der Maler, Grafiker und Keramiker Willi Münch-Khe (1885–1960), der Architekt Fritz August Breuhaus de Groot (1883–1960), der Maler und Bildhauer Franz Naager (1870–1942), der Bildhauer Karl Maximilian Würtenberger (1872–1933), der Maler, Grafiker und Keramiker Emil Pottner (1872–1942), der Bildhauer und Keramiker Wilhelm Ernst (Willy) Schade (1892–1975), der Bildhauer Fritz Behn (1878–1970) sowie der Maler und Keramiker Wilhelm Süs (1861–1933). Letztgenannter war der einzige unter den Ausstellenden aus Mannheim. Zusammen mit Hans Thoma war er nicht nur Begründer der Großherzoglichen Majolika Manufaktur in Karlsruhe. Von 1917 bis zu seinem Tod 1933 war er auch Direktor der im Mannheimer Schloss untergebrachten Gemäldegalerie.

10 Fritz Wichert, zit. nach Jenns Eric Howoldt: *Der Freie Bund zur Einbürgerung der bildenden Kunst in Mannheim. Kommunale Kunstpolitik einer Industriestadt am Beispiel der „Mannheimer Bewegung"* (= Europäische Hochschulschriften, Reihe XXVIII Kunstgeschichte, Bd. 18), Frankfurt am Main 1982, S. 33.

11 Siehe zum Freien Bund insb. Howoldt 1982 (wie Anm. 10).

12 Vgl. ebd., S. 304. Im Jahr der hier besprochenen Ausstellung erreichte die Anzahl der Mitglieder des Freien Bundes mit 11.650 ihren Höchstwert.

13 Fritz Wichert: Zur Einführung, in: Kat. Ausst. *Porzellan und Majolika* 1921 (wie Anm. 1), S. 3–5, S. 5.

14 Zu erwähnen sind als Modelleure zudem Paul Kramer und Andreas Klötzer sowie der im Mannheimer Ausstellungs-Katalog fälschlicherweise als „Cranich" angegebene Hermann Krannich.

15 Nur zwei präsentierte Vasen wurden nach historischen Vorbildern gestaltet.

16 Auf Initiative von Wilhem Süs und Hans Thoma wurde die Manufaktur 1901 vom badischen Großherzog Friedrich I. gegründet.

17 Zur Geschichte der Manufaktur siehe insb. Christoph Fritzsche: *Die Aelteste Volkstedter Porzellanmanufaktur. Ihre Geschichte von der Gründung bis heute*, Stuttgart 2013.

18 Troester tritt in zahlreichen Schreiben zwischen der Kunsthalle und der Aeltesten Volkstedter Porzellanmanufaktur in Erscheinung und war sehr am Zustandekommen der Ausstellung in Mannheim interessiert.

19 1918 kam es auch zu im Detail nicht bekannten Möbelentwürfen für die Deutschen Werkstätten in Hellerau.

20 Siehe dazu Wolfgang Pehnt: Wille zum Ausdruck. Zu Leben und Werk Hans Poelzigs, in: Kat. Ausst. *Hans Poelzig 1869 bis 1936. Architekt, Lehrer, Künstler*, Akademie der Künste, Berlin, und Deutsches Architekturmuseum Frankfurt am Main 2007/2008, hrsg. v. Wolfgang Pehnt u. Matthias Schirren München 2007, S. 10–51, insb. S. 32f.

21 Vgl. zu Marlene Moeschke-Poelzig insb. Heike Hambrock: *Hans und Marlene Poelzig. Bauen im Geist des Barock. Architekturphantasien, Theaterprojekte und moderner Festbau (1916–1926)*, Delmenhorst, Berlin 2005; dies.: „Also los und Mut!… Die Werkstätte, unsere Werkstätte muß eingerichtet werden", in: *Forschung Frankfurt*, H. 2, 2005, S. 70–76 (https://www.forschung-frankfurt.uni-frankfurt.de/36050396/forschung-frankfurt-ausgabe-2-2005-balladen-und-metamorphosen.pdf [abgerufen am 03.06.2025]); sowie Sybille Ehringhaus: „… übrigens im ausgesprochenen Gegensatz zur Auffassung eines Corbusier …". Marlene Moeschke-Poelzig, Bildhauerin und Architektin, 1894–1985, in: *Frauen Kunst Wissenschaft*, Nr. 13, 1992, S. 56–68.

22 Siehe Ehringhaus 1992 (wie Anm. 21), S. 58f. In ihrem Essay über die Künstlerin stellte Ehringhaus diese Frage bereits 1992 für das Gesamtwerk Poelzigs in den Raum bzw. fragte, was und wie viel von Poelzigs Werk auch wirklich Poelzig und nicht Moeschke ist.

23 Vgl. dazu Hans Poelzig: Zur Einführung, in: Kat. Ausst. *Poelzig und seine Schule*, Preußische Akademie der Künste zu Berlin 1931, Berlin 1931, S. 1–3. Bei dieser Gelegenheit führt der Architekt insgesamt 61 eigene Bauten und den jeweiligen Anteil des/der daran beteiligten Mitarbeiter*in auf. Marlene Moeschke wird dabei 14-mal genannt. Oft steht sie dabei als wichtigste Mitarbeiterin an erster Stelle.

24 1916/17 besuchte Moeschke schließlich auch die Kunstgewerbeschule in München.

25 Innerhalb dieses Projekts zeichnete sie etwa für die palmenartigen Säulen im Foyer des Gebäudes verantwortlich, die gleichzeitig auch als Leuchtkörper innerhalb des Raumes fungierten und den eintretenden Besucher*innen ein indirektes Licht spendeten.

26 Kat. Ausst. *Porzellan und Majolika* 1921 (wie Anm. 1), S. 14.

27 Fritz Wichert: Schreiben an Marlene Moeschke vom 6. September 1921, in: Stadtarchiv Mannheim / MARCHIVUM, Bestand Kunsthalle, Ordner „Ausstellung Porzellan und Majolika I" (= 2012_Ordner 67), S. 285. Unklar ist, ob Wichert hier etwa eigenhändige Skulpturen Moeschkes anspricht, die fast alle während des Zweiten Weltkrieges zerstört wurden, oder ob er damit auch architektonische Entwürfe oder kunstgewerbliche Arbeiten meint.

28 Kat. Ausst. *Porzellan und Majolika* 1921 (wie Anm. 1), S. 14.

29 Hildebrand Gurlitt: Gedichte in Keramik, in: *Deutsche Allgemeine Zeitung*, Berlin, 07.07.1921.

30 Anonym: Eine moderne Keramik-Ausstellung in Mannheim, in: *Freiburger Tagblatt*, Nr. 197, 25.07.1921.

31 Anton Schnack: Majolika und Keramik, in: *Vossische Zeitung*, Berlin, 26.07.1921.

32 Ebd.

33 Gurlitt 1921 (wie Anm. 29).

34 Ebd.

35 Hans Poelzig: Architekturfragen. Vortrag in der Berliner Sezession, 24.03.1917, in: *Das Kunstblatt I* (1917), S. 129–136, S. 133.

36 Vgl hierzu insb. Hambrock 2005 (wie Anm. 21), S. 12ff.; sowie Pehnt 2007 (wie Anm. 20), 36ff.

37 Hans Poelzig: Der Künstler selbst, in: Kat. Ausst. *Porzellan und Majolika* 1921 (wie Anm. 1), S. 6.

38 Fritz Wichert: Zur Einführung, in: Kat. Ausst. *Porzellan und Majolika* 1921 (wie Anm. 1), S. 4.

39 Anzunehmen ist, dass dies in Rücksprache mit den beteiligten Künstlern dem Museum oblag.

40 Vgl. dazu Lisa Sanner: *„Als wäre das Ende der Welt da". Die Explosionskatastrophen in der BASF 1921 und 1948*, hrsg. v. d. Stadtverwaltung Ludwigshafen am Rhein (= Veröffentlichungen des Stadtarchivs Ludwigshafen am Rhein, Bd. 42), Ludwigshafen 2015.

41 Fritz Wichert: Schreiben an Edmund Troester vom 22. September 1921, in: Stadtarchiv Mannheim /MARCHIVUM, Bestand Kunsthalle, Ordner „Ausstellung Porzellan und Majolika I" (= 2012_Ordner 67), S. 302f.

42 Siehe Fritz Wichert: Schreiben an die Aelteste Volkstedter Porzellanmanufaktur vom 19. Oktober 1921, in: Stadtarchiv Mannheim / MARCHIVUM, Bestand Kunsthalle, Ordner „Ausstellung Porzellan und Majolika I" (= 2012_Ordner 67), S. 319f.

43 Ursprünglich war die Laufzeit der Ausstellung bis Ende September 1921 geplant. Durch die Unterbrechung infolge der Oppauer Katastrophe war die Schau für das Publikum schließlich bis zum 9. Oktober zugänglich.

44 Unbekannt, Schreiben der Aeltesten Volkstedter Porzellanmanufaktur an die Kunsthalle Mannheim vom 12. Oktober 1921, in: Stadtarchiv Mannheim /MARCHIVUM, Bestand Kunsthalle, Ordner „Ausstellung Porzellan und Majolika I" (= 2012_Ordner 67), S. 325.

45 Vgl. hierzu etwa Petra Weber: *Gescheiterte Sozialpartnerschaft – Gefährdete Republik? Industrielle Beziehungen, Arbeitskämpfe und der Sozialstaat. Deutschland und Frankreich im Vergleich (1918–1933/39)*, München 2010.

46 Wenn überhaupt nur zu erahnen ist dieses Motiv dagegen im Falle des Wohnhauses für die Werkbundausstellung am Stuttgarter Weißenhof (1926/27), das Poelzig zusammen mit seiner Frau entwarf. Dieser rationalistische Entwurf steht im starken Gegensatz zu den 1921 in Mannheim ausgestellten Porzellanobjekten.

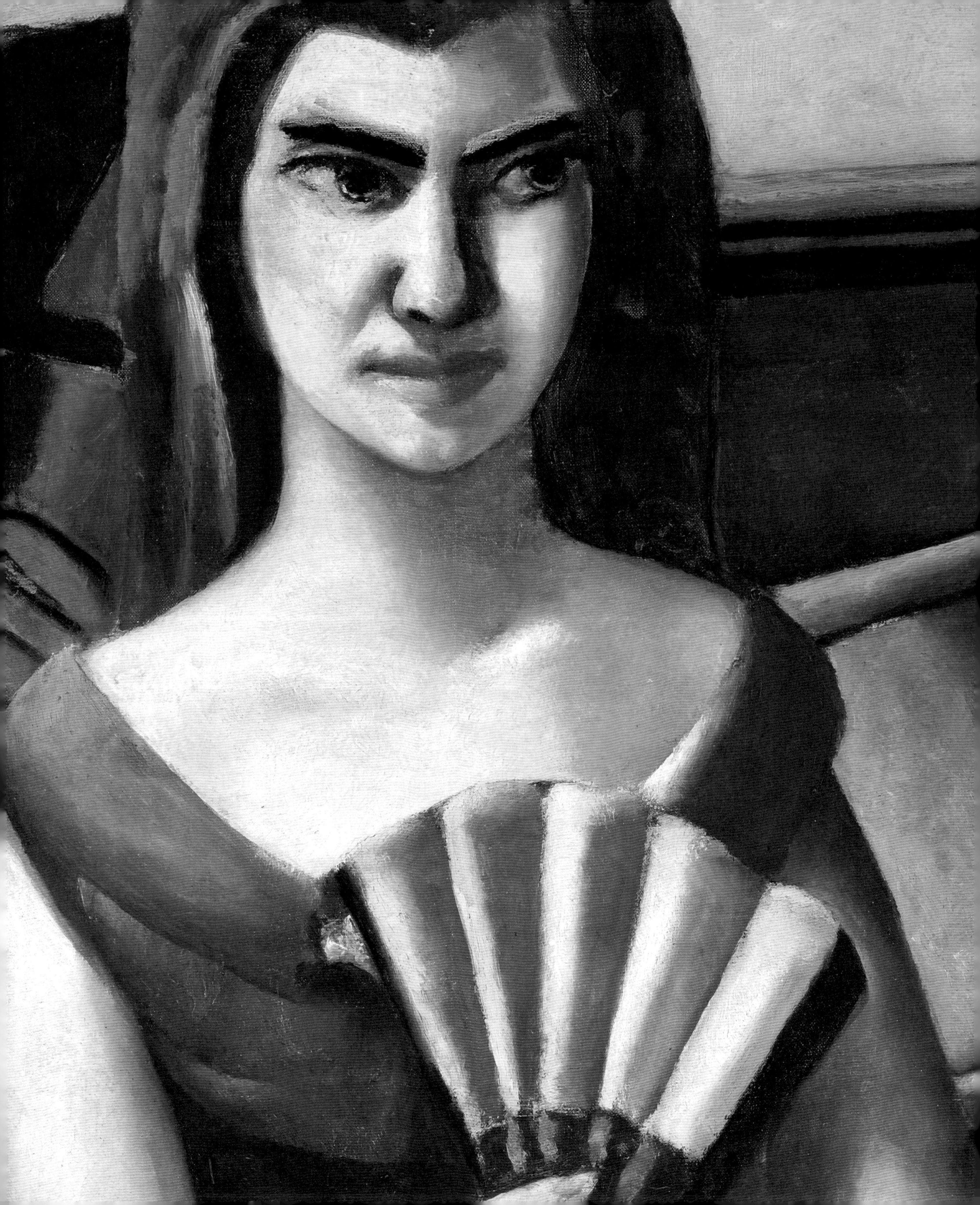

Walter Passarge: Direktor der Kunsthalle Mannheim während des Nationalsozialismus

Walter Passarge: Director of the Kunsthalle Mannheim during National Socialism

Hannah Krause

Walter Passarge (1898–1958) was the director of the Kunsthalle Mannheim from 1936 until his death in 1958. Soon after World War II ended, he opened the first room in the damaged Kunsthalle Mannheim with an exhibition of Expressionist works—including works by artists who only shortly before had still been defamed as "degenerate" by the National Socialist regime. But was this truly a symbol of cultural renewal? How had the Kunsthalle under the same leadership managed to position itself successfully during the National Socialist period?

The recourse to Expressionism under the cover of rehabilitating it served, not only in Mannheim, as a form of strategic self-exoneration, a phenomenon typical of the postwar era, but the reference to the period before 1933 also pushed the intervening years into the background. Only museums' "loss" as a result of the confiscation of "degenerate" works in 1937 was singled out and addressed publicly—as a victim's story.

But many museums, including the Kunsthalle Mannheim, had not been simply victims of the regime. They also operated as tacit supporters or profiteers, cooperating or making arrangements with the Nazi system. Who was Walter Passarge, and what room to maneuver did he actually have during National Socialism?[1]

Walter Passarge as a Person

Walter Kurt Adolf Passarge was born in Erfurt in 1898 and in 1919 was a cofounder of a group of local Expressionist artists called "Jung-Erfurt" (Young Erfurt), which was supported by the progressive museum directors Edwin Redslob and Walter Kaesbach, who turned Erfurt into a center of the avant-garde.[2]

Passarge studied art history, history, and philosophy in Greifswald, Berlin, and Leipzig and received his PhD in 1923 under Wilhelm Pinder with a dissertation on the art of the Middle Ages.[3] Initially, he moved in modernist circles and was also exchanging correspondence with Bauhaus protagonists,[4] when he took over as interim director of the Anger-Museum in Erfurt in 1924.[5] During later stages of his career in Kassel and Kiel, he worked as a university lecturer and as assistant director of the Thaulow-Museum in Kiel and engaged in patriotic, national discourses concerning folk art in a way that was typical of the time and place—and in particular with the construction of the "Nordisch" (Nordic/Northern) as an artistic leitmotif. Such discourses were compatible with National Socialist ideology and demonstrates that they existed even prior to 1933.

In 1936, Passarge was appointed director of the Kunsthalle Mannheim at the instigation of Carl Renninger, the city's National Socialist mayor. Although Passarge was not a member of the National Socialist Party, he was given the post because one of its focuses was at center of his own interests: the crafts.

Passarge's Program:
Modern Crafts and German and Contemporary Art

Walter Passarge's appointing to the Kunsthalle Mannheim was part of an extensive National Socialist reorientation of the city's cultural policies. Mayor Renninger wanted "fresh channels" for the city's future cultural policy, calling for "making art . . . a matter for the whole population . . . and anchor it . . . in the awareness of ordinary people unprejudiced by any 'education' at all as a strong tie between the arts and the crafts," as was reported by the *Neue Mannheimer Zeitung* when he took office.[6]

Walter Passarge (1898–1958) war von 1936 bis zu seinem Tod im Jahr 1958 Direktor der Kunsthalle Mannheim. Bereits kurz nach Kriegsende eröffnete er den ersten Raum in der beschädigten Kunsthalle Mannheim mit einer Ausstellung expressionistischer Werke – darunter Arbeiten von Künstlern, die noch kurz zuvor vom NS-Regime als „entartet" diffamiert worden waren. Doch war dies wirklich ein Symbol kultureller Erneuerung? Wie war es möglich, dass sich unter derselben Leitung die Kunsthalle während der NS-Zeit durchaus erfolgreich positionierte?

Der Rückgriff auf den Expressionismus unter dem Deckmantel der Rehabilitierung diente nicht nur in Mannheim oft einer strategischen Selbstentlastung, ein Phänomen der Nachkriegszeit: Der Bezug zur Zeit vor 1933 ließ die Jahre dazwischen in den Hintergrund treten. Einzig der „Verlust" der Museen durch die Beschlagnahmung „entarteter" Werke 1937 wurde herausgegriffen und öffentlich thematisiert – als Opfergeschichte.

Doch viele Museen – so auch die Kunsthalle Mannheim – waren keine reinen Opfer des Regimes. Sie agierten ebenso als Mitläufer oder Profiteure, kooperierten oder arrangierten sich mit dem NS-System. Doch wer war Walter Passarge und über welche Handlungsspielräume verfügte er tatsächlich während des Nationalsozialismus?[1]

Die Person Walter Passarge

Walter Kurt Adolf Passarge wurde 1898 in Erfurt geboren und war 1919 Mitbegründer einer lokalen expressionistischen Künstlergruppe mit dem Namen „Jung-Erfurt", gefördert durch die progressiven Museumsdirektoren Edwin Redslob und Walter Kaesbach, die Erfurt zu einem Zentrum der Avantgarde machten.[2]

Passarge studierte Kunstgeschichte, Geschichte und Philosophie in Greifswald, Berlin und Leipzig und wurde 1923 bei Wilhelm Pinder mit einer Dissertation zur Kunst des Mittelalters promoviert.[3] Er bewegte sich zunächst in einem modernen Umfeld und stand unter anderem im Austausch mit Bauhaus-Protagonisten[4], als er 1924 kommissarisch die Museumsleitung des Anger-Museums in Erfurt übernahm.[5] Während seiner weiteren beruflichen Stationen in Kassel und Kiel war er als Dozent tätig und setzte sich ab 1927 als Direktionsassistent am Thaulow-Museum zeit- und ortstypisch mit patriotischen, nationalistischen und auf Volkskunst bezogenen Diskursen auseinander – insbesondere dem Konstrukt des „Nordischen" als künstlerischem Leitmotiv. Dies waren NS-anschlussfähige Diskurse und zeigt, dass diese schon vor 1933 existierten.

1936 wurde Passarge auf Betreiben des NS-Oberbürgermeisters Carl Renninger zum Direktor der Kunsthalle Mannheim ernannt. Obwohl er kein NSDAP-Mitglied war, erhielt er diesen Posten, denn ein anderer Schwerpunkt stand im Mittelpunkt des Interesses: das Kunsthandwerk.

Passarges Programm:
modernes Kunsthandwerk – deutsch – zeitgenössisch

Walter Passarges Berufung an die Kunsthalle Mannheim war Teil einer umfassenden NS-kulturpolitischen Neuausrichtung der Stadt. Oberbürgermeister Renninger wollte „frisches Fahrwasser" für die künftige städtische Kulturpolitik, „die Kunst [...] zu einer Sache des ganzen Volkes [...] machen und sie [...] im Bewußtsein des einfachen, durch keinerlei ‚Bildung' vorbelasteten Menschen als wesentlichen Bestandteil seines Daseins verankern, [...] mit allem Nachdruck [... eine] stärkere Bindung zwischen bildender Kunst und Kunsthandwerk" fördern, so berichtet es die Neue Mannheimer Zeitung zur Amtseinführung.[6]

Accordingly, Passarge adopted the focus on the new collecting emphasis of *Werkkunst der Gegenwart* (contemporary crafts) not of his own motivation or as a supposed nonpolitical terrain, as often been assumed, but was rather addressing a specific political task: the crafts should function as a form of expression that was close to the people and established identity. In his inaugural speech, Passarge announced his intention not only to build a collection of "exemplary craft works" but also to cultivate "Northern" and "folkish"[7] art—concepts that were clearly ideologically charged in the National Socialist discourse on culture at the time.

Passarge immediately positioned himself with his first exhibition, *Deutsche Werkkunst der Gegenwart* (German Applied Art of the Present) in 1936, and with the eponymous book (1937), because he showed a selection of what he considered the best applied artists of the time. Modern craft art was thus presented as compatible with the National Socialist system as long as it was "close to the people" and formally lucid. Passarge's defining criteria were simplicity, truth to materials, and purity of form. These are echoes of the design ideals of the German Werkbund and of the Bauhaus—which shows that specific elements of modernism could be united with the aesthetic and ideological demands of the National Socialist system.

Research into biographical ambivalences and institutional continuities has been growing constantly and has shown how several modern artists from the circles around the Bauhaus,[8] Neue Sachlichkeit (New Objectivity),[9] and Expressionism[10] came to terms with the regime. The result was an ideological-compatible modernism during National Socialism that was supported by, among others, networks that included those of museum directors that existed prior to 1933.

Passarge's concept for his exhibitions of the following years originally sought to systematically treat the crafts, painting, graphic arts, and sculpture as equals, always emphasizing the "German" and the contemporary: for example, his exhibition titles included *Junge deutsche Bildhauer* (Young German Sculptors), *Neue Deutsche Malerei* (New German Painting), *Deutsche Aquarellisten der Gegenwart* (German Watercolorists of the Present), and *Deutsche Textilkunst der Gegenwart* (German Textile Art of the Present). One striking feature of his exhibition catalogues and presentations was a consistent emphasis on regional qualities in the production of art from a given *Gau* ("region" in the National Socialist terminology). But this apparent focus on regionality should not be understood as apolitical either, because it could be integrated with the National Socialist concept of art that was "rooted in the popular folkish traditions." The press supported this reading by interpreting works of art as the expression of a supposedly uniform "German being."

Although Passarge did not openly engage in propaganda or explicitly adopt the racist ideology of the National Socialists, he operated within a system in which curatorial decisions had political significance. Passarge conformed by emphasizing German "roots" and typical regional traditions as well as seemingly apolitical applied arts as a component to establish the identity of the *Volksgemeinschaft* (racial community). Passarge's willingness to conform also contributed to making it possible to ideologically recode certain forms of modernism and integrate them into the National Socialist cultural scene.

The Confiscation Actions in 1937 and Their Consequences for Passarge

Passarge was initially able to feel confident about the orientation of his exhibition program—not least because he had Mayor Renninger's backing. But in July and August 1937, just a year after taking office, the *Entartete Kunst* (degenerate art) action resulted in about 570 works being confiscated

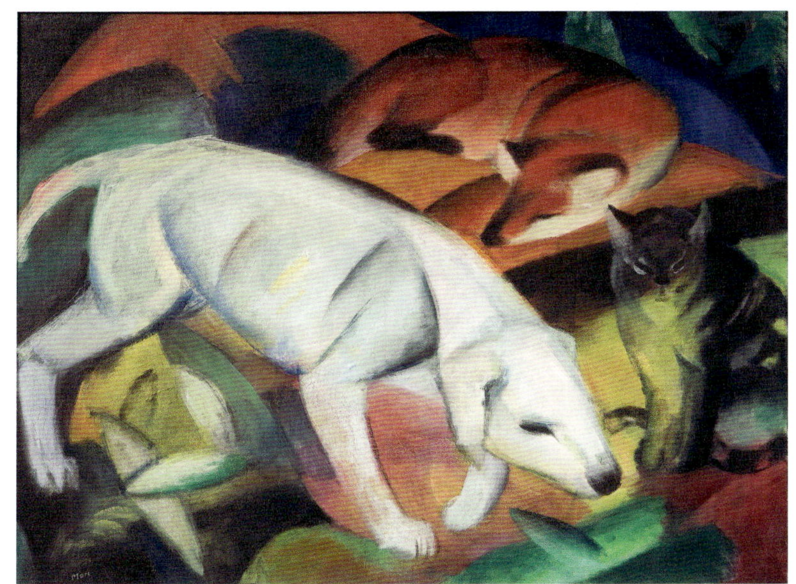

Passarge übernahm die Ausrichtung auf den neuen Sammlungsschwerpunkt der „Werkkunst der Gegenwart" demnach nicht aus eigenem Antrieb oder als vermeintlich unpolitisches Terrain, wie bisher oft angenommen, sondern erfüllte damit einen konkreten politischen Auftrag: Kunsthandwerk sollte als identitätsstiftende, volksnahe Ausdrucksform fungieren. Auch in seiner Antrittsrede kündigte Passarge neben dem Aufbau einer Sammlung „vorbildlicher kunsthandwerklicher Arbeiten" auch die Pflege „nordischer" und „volkstümlicher"[7] Kunst an – Begriffe, die im NS-Kulturdiskurs eindeutig ideologisch aufgeladen waren.

Mit seiner ersten Ausstellung *Deutsche Werkkunst der Gegenwart* im Jahr 1936 und dem gleichnamigen Buch (1937) positionierte sich Passarge sogleich: Er zeigte eine Auswahl der seiner Meinung nach besten Kunsthandwerker*innen der Gegenwart. Moderne Stile wurden dabei als mit dem NS-System vereinbar dargestellt, solange sie „volksnah" und formklar waren. Passarges bestimmende Kriterien waren Einfachheit, Materialgerechtigkeit und Reinheit der Form. Hier klingen Gestaltungsideale des Deutschen Werkbundes und des Bauhauses an – dies zeigt, dass bestimmte Elemente der Moderne durchaus mit den ästhetischen und ideologischen Anforderungen des NS-Systems vereinbar waren.

Die Forschung zu biografischen Ambivalenzen und institutionellen Kontinuitäten nimmt stetig zu und offenbart, wie auch einige Künstler*innen der Moderne, aus dem Bauhaus[8], der Neuen Sachlichkeit[9] oder expressionistischen Kreisen[10], sich mit dem Regime arrangierten. Es entstand eine ideologisch anschlussfähige Moderne während der Zeit des Nationalsozialismus, welche unter anderem getragen wurde von Netzwerken, auch von Museumsdirektoren, die bereits vor 1933 bestanden.

Passarges Ausstellungskonzept für die folgenden Jahre sah ursprünglich eine systematische Gleichbehandlung von Kunsthandwerk, Malerei, Grafik und Skulptur vor, immer mit Betonung des „Deutschen" und des Zeitgenössischen: Die Ausstellungstitel lauteten zum Beispiel *Junge deutsche Bildhauer, Neue Deutsche Malerei, Deutsche Aquarellisten der Gegenwart* oder *Deutsche Textilkunst der Gegenwart*. Auffällig ist dabei in den Ausstellungskatalogen und der Darbietung die konsequente Betonung des Regionaltypischen in der Kunstproduktion der einzelnen „Gaue". Diese scheinbar auf Regionalität zielende Fokussierung ist ebenfalls nicht als unpolitisch zu verstehen, denn sie ließ sich in das nationalsozialistische Konzept einer „volkstümlich verwurzelten" Kunst integrieren. Die Presse unterstützte diese Lesart, indem sie Kunstwerke als Ausdruck eines angeblich einheitlichen „deutschen Wesens" deutete.

Auch wenn Passarge keine offene Propaganda betrieb und die NS-Rassenideologie nicht explizit aufgriff, bewegte er sich innerhalb eines Systems, in dem kuratorische Entscheidungen politisch aufgeladen waren. Passarge passte sich an, indem er deutsche Wurzeln und regionaltypische Traditionen sowie das scheinbar Unpolitische des Kunsthandwerks als identitätsstiftender Teil für die „Volksgemeinschaft" unterstrich. Passarges Bereitschaft zur Anpassung trug auch dazu bei, dass bestimmte Formen der Moderne ideologisch neu codiert und in den NS-Kulturbetrieb integriert werden konnten.

Abb./Fig. **29**
Franz Marc, *Drei Tiere (Hund, Fuchs und Katze)*/
Three Animals (Dog, Fox, and Cat), **1912**
Öl und Tempera auf Leinwand / *Oil and tempera on canvas*, 80 × 105 cm
Kunsthalle Mannheim

from the Kunsthalle's holdings with state sanction, including pieces from the *Junge deutsche Bildhauer* exhibition that Passarge had curated. This made Passarge considerably uncertain about his curatorial decisions.[11] It seemed that nearly an entire artistic movement was being denounced and wiped out from all of Germany's museums, and it affected artists whom Passarge admired, such as Gerhard Marcks, Wilhelm Lehmbruck, and Lovis Corinth.

In the second confiscation action in August 1937, it seems that Passarge kept works and did not send them to Berlin. Several modern works thus remained in Mannheim,[12] something that Passarge himself later described as "resistance,"[13] thus helping to shape his own narrative.

From August 1937 onward, Passarge could no longer exhibit the works that he personally considered forward-looking. There was now a list of artists he had to forgo. Passarge then placed in storage many works that until then had apparently been part of the collection on display, and he checked with the authorities that he reported to and with his network of museum professionals and academy professors about which artists could and should still be exhibited. He canceled planned exhibitions and lectures by the artists affected, such as Walter Dexel.

There were, however, several "cases of doubt"[14] whose defamation Passarge did not approve of, and he dared to advocate for them, as he did for James Ensor and Edvard Munch, for example. In the case of Munch, Passarge referred to birthday telegrams with words of praise that Joseph Goebbels had personally sent to the artist.[15] In the case of Ensor, he urged considering the negative effect abroad politically. He was not arguing against defamation or confiscation on principle but using tactics to extricate a few "cases of doubt."

With the support of Mayor Renninger, Passarge asked the Reichskammer der bildenden Künste (Reich Chamber of Fine Arts) to return works that had been confiscated and appealed to questions of ownership. It was an astonishing act, and together with his refusal to approve exhibitions by the state administration it suggests a communal self-image that wanted to preserve the Kunsthalle as a place with artistic freedom. At the same time, it also makes clear the limits on its maneuverability since both efforts were unsuccessful and no further negative consequences happened.

Another turning point for Passarge came with new guidelines from the Ministry of Education that had been announced by Graf von Baudissin at the conference of German museum directors in November 1937: museums were no longer to concern themselves with the painting or sculpture of living artists and were to leave that to the arts societies.[16] Museums were to restrict themselves to officially approved positions and retrospectives that gave preference to graphic arts and the applied arts or showed recognized living figures on special occasions. Passarge responded with annoyance—this represented a great incision for his program.

He continued to show contemporary art during the war but now almost exclusively in the form of drawings, watercolors, and prints—a retreat imposed from above but not the abandonment of his goal to anchor contemporary art in the museum.

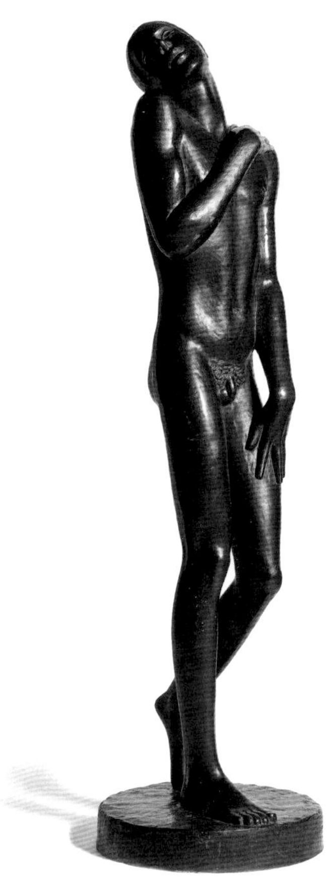

Abb. / Fig. 30
Ernesto de Fiori, *Jüngling (Der Leidende)* /
Youth (The Sufferer), **1911/12**
Bronze, 183 × 49,5 × 49,5 cm
Kunsthalle Mannheim

Beschlagnahmeaktionen 1937 und ihre Konsequenzen für Passarge

Passarge konnte sich bei der Ausrichtung seines Ausstellungsprogramms zunächst sicher fühlen – nicht zuletzt dank der Rückendeckung durch Oberbürgermeister Renninger. Als aber ein Jahr nach seinem Amtsantritt durch die Aktion „Entartete Kunst" im Juli/August 1937 rund 570 Werke aus dem Bestand der Kunsthalle staatlich sanktioniert beschlagnahmt wurden, darunter auch Werke aus der von Passarge kuratierten Ausstellung *Junge deutsche Bildhauer*, verunsicherte dies Passarge erheblich in seinen kuratorischen Entscheidungen.[11] Fast eine gesamte künstlerische Bewegung schien aus allen Museen Deutschlands angeprangert und ausgelöscht worden zu sein und es betraf Künstler, welche Passarge schätzte, wie Gerhard Marcks, Wilhelm Lehmbruck und Lovis Corinth.

Bei der zweiten Beschlagnahmeaktion im August 1937 hielt Passarge allem Anschein nach Werke zurück und sendete sie nicht nach Berlin. So verblieben einige moderne Werke in Mannheim,[12] was Passarge später selbst als „Widerstand"[13] bezeichnete und damit sein eigenes Narrativ mitgestaltete.

Ab August 1937 konnte Passarge nicht mehr ausstellen, wen er persönlich für richtungsweisend hielt. Nun gab es eine Liste von Künstler*innen, auf die er verzichten musste. Passarge magazinierte daraufhin viele Werke, die offensichtlich bis dahin noch in der Schausammlung hingen, und vergewisserte sich bei seinen vorgesetzten Behörden und in seinem Netzwerk an Museumsleuten und Akademieprofessoren, welche Kunstschaffenden man noch ausstellen könne und weiterhin ausstellen solle. Er sagte betroffenen Künstlern, wie Walter Dexel, bereits vereinbarte Ausstellungen oder Vorträge ab.

Es gab jedoch einige „Zweifelsfälle",[14] mit deren Diffamierung Passarge nicht einverstanden war, und er wagte es, sich für sie einzusetzen, wie etwa für James Ensor oder Edvard Munch. Bei Munch verwies Passarge auf ein Geburtstagstelegramm, welches Joseph Goebbels persönlich an den Künstler mit lobenden Worten versandt hatte.[15] Bei Ensor mahnte er, auf die schlechte außenpolitische Wirkung zu achten. Er argumentierte also nicht grundsätzlich gegen eine Diffamierung oder Beschlagnahme, sondern versuchte, taktisch einige „Zweifelsfälle" wieder herauszulösen.

Mit der Unterstützung des Oberbürgermeisters Renninger forderte Passarge von der Reichskammer der bildenden Künste die Rückgabe der beschlagnahmten Werke und berief sich dabei auf die Eigentumsverhältnisse. Ein erstaunlicher Akt, der zusammen mit der Weigerung, Ausstellungen der Landesleitung zur Genehmigung vorzulegen, auf ein kommunales Selbstverständnis hindeutet, welches die Kunsthalle als ein Ort mit Gestaltungsfreiheit bewahren wollte. Gleichzeitig werden hier auch die Grenzen ihres Handlungsspielraums deutlich, denn beides war nicht erfolgreich und hatte keine weiteren negativen Konsequenzen.

Eine weitere Zäsur für Passarge kam mit neuen Richtlinien des Erziehungsministeriums, welche auf der Tagung deutscher Museumsleiter im November 1937 von Graf von Baudissin verkündet wurden: Museen sollten sich nicht länger mit Malerei oder Skulptur lebender Künstler*innen befassen und diese Aufgabe fortan den Kunstvereinen überlassen.[16] Museen sollten sich auf offiziell bewährte Positionen beschränken und Retrospektiven zeigen, die Gattungen der Grafik und des Kunsthandwerks bevorzugt ausstellten oder zu besonderen Anlässen auch anerkannte lebende Persönlichkeiten zeigten. Passarge reagierte verärgert – dies war ein großer Einschnitt in sein Programm.

Auch während des Krieges zeigte er weiterhin zeitgenössische Kunst, allerdings nun fast ausschließlich in Form von Zeichnungen, Aquarellen oder Druckgrafiken – ein verordneter Rückzug, nicht aber die Aufgabe seines Anspruchs, zeitgenössische Kunst museal zu verankern.

Returns during the National Socialist Period

Although not an immediate reaction to Passarge's and Renninger's requests that words that had been confiscated as "degenerate" be returned, one indication of some room for maneuver in the ministries came when the Ministry of Propaganda returned works. In February 1938, three prints were returned to the Kunsthalle; in 1939, the sculpture *Der Jüngling (Der Leidende)* (Youth [The Sufferer]) by Ernesto de Fiori (fig. 30; cat. 1); and finally the painting *Drei Tiere (Hund, Fuchs und Katze)* (Three Animals [Dog, Fox, and Cat]) by Franz Marc (fig. 29; cat. 102) was returned to the Kunsthalle Mannheim with the stipulation that it be neither sold nor exhibited.

Passarge's Acquisitions

As a rule, Passarge purchased works for the Kunsthalle collection directly from the artists, from workshops, and preferably from exhibitions. Nevertheless, there are a few works that he acquired "by order of the mayor" as was noted in the inventory to distance himself from them. Moreover, in 1942 he was asked by the tax office to serve as an "expert" to appraise moving containers with the possessions of people who were being forced to emigrate.[17] A total of around 670 containers were brought to Mannheim, opened by the Verwertungsstelle volksfremden Vermögens (Office for the Liquidation of Alien Property), sorted, assessed, and finally sold for profit to be distributed to victims of air raids. Passarge had the task of "securing" valuable art objects for museums or the Reichskammer der bildenden Künste. All of this was done openly, and everyone involved—including Walter Passarge—was aware of the origin of the works.

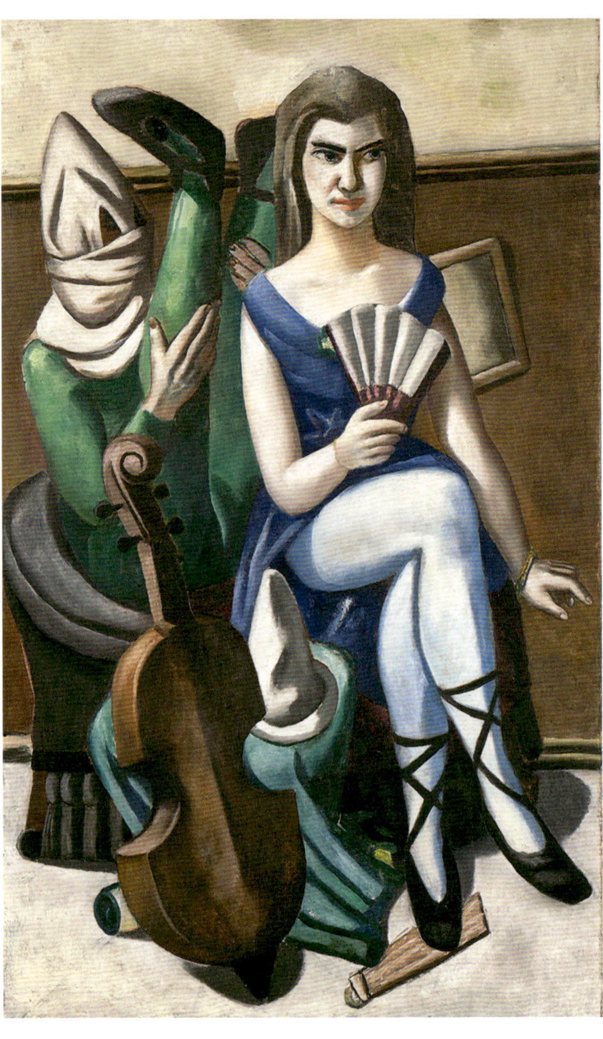

Passarge's Stance (or Gaps in His Memory?) after 1945

Passarge apparently got through de-Nazification without a problem and soon resumed his work as director of the Kunsthalle Mannheim. It is, however, striking that he was uncooperative in the search for the whereabouts of the art collections of Jewish Germans from Mannheim. He could "not recall"[18] and said nothing about his role as an expert for the Verwertungsstelle volksfremden Vermögens or as lecturer at Heidelberg University under National Socialism. This points to a strategy that was widespread in the postwar era: self-protection and the wish to look ahead not back.

Against this backdrop, Passarge's efforts to rehabilitate Expressionism seem like a good opportunity to turn attention away from himself. As the art business recovered gradually, more and more works that had been confiscated as "degenerate" found their way to the market. The question of returning such works to the museums led to contentious debates among museum professionals. I mention here only the first request for return from the Kunsthalle Mannheim, which concerned the art dealer Günther Franke and ultimately led to the return of *Fastnacht (Pierrette und Clown)* (Carnival [Pierrette and Clown]) by Max Beckmann (fig. 31).

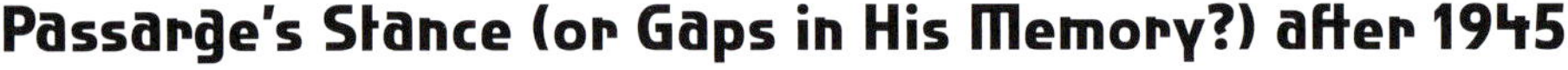

Abb./Fig. 31
Max Beckmann, *Fastnacht (Pierrette und Clown)* / Carnival (Pierrette and Clown), 1925
Öl auf Leinwand / *Oil on canvas*, 160 × 100 cm
Kunsthalle Mannheim

Rückgaben während der NS-Zeit

Nicht unmittelbar als Reaktion auf Passarges und Renningers Rückforderungen der als „entartet" beschlagnahmten Werke, aber als Indiz für gewisse ministeriale Handlungsspielräume können die Rückgaben seitens des Propaganda-Ministeriums gesehen werden. Im Februar 1938 erhielt die Kunsthalle drei Grafiken zurück, 1939 die Skulptur *Der Jüngling (Der Leidende)* von Ernesto de Fiori (Abb. 30; Kat. 1) und schließlich gelangte das Gemälde *Drei Tiere (Hund, Fuchs und Katze)* von Franz Marc (Abb. 29; Kat. 102) im Jahr 1940 in die Kunsthalle Mannheim mit der Auflage zurück, es weder zu veräußern noch auszustellen.

Passarges Erwerbungen

Passarge kaufte in der Regel direkt von den Künstler*innen Werke für die Sammlung der Kunsthalle an, aus den Werkstätten und bevorzugt aus den Ausstellungen heraus. Dennoch gab es einige wenige Werke, welche er „auf Anordnung des OB" ankaufte, wie es distanzierend im Inventarbuch vermerkt ist. Zudem war er 1942 als „Sachverständiger" vom Finanzamt beauftragt worden, das Umzugsgut aus den Containern der in die Emigration gezwungenen Menschen zu begutachten.[17] Es wurden insgesamt circa 670 Container nach Mannheim zurückgeholt, von der „Verwertungsstelle volksfremden Vermögens" geöffnet, sortiert, geschätzt und schließlich gewinnbringend verkauft sowie an Fliegergeschädigte verteilt. Passarge hatte die Aufgabe, wertvolle Kunstgegenstände für die Museen oder die Reichskammer der bildenden Künste zu „sichern". Dies alles geschah öffentlich und alle, die sich beteiligten, wussten um die Herkunft – auch Walter Passarge.

Passarges Haltung (oder Erinnerungslücken?) nach 1945

Passarge durchlief die Entnazifizierung offenbar problemlos und nahm seine Arbeit als Direktor der Kunsthalle Mannheim umgehend wieder auf. Auffällig bleibt jedoch seine fehlende Kooperationsbereitschaft bei der Suche nach dem Verbleib jüdischer Mannheimer Kunstsammlungen. Er konnte sich „nicht erinnern"[18] und verschwieg seine Rolle als Gutachter bei der „Verwertungsstelle volksfremden Vermögens" sowie als Dozent an der Heidelberger Universität in der NS-Zeit. Dies deutet auf eine Strategie hin, wie sie in der Nachkriegszeit verbreitet war: Selbstschutz und der Wunsch, nach vorn zu schauen.

Vor diesem Hintergrund wirkt Passarges Engagement für die Rehabilitierung des Expressionismus wie eine gute Gelegenheit, von sich selbst abzulenken. Mit der allmählichen Rückkehr zum Kunstbetrieb traten zunehmend Werke, die zuvor als „entartet" beschlagnahmt worden waren, auf dem Kunstmarkt wieder in Erscheinung. Die Frage nach der Rückführung solcher Werke in die jeweiligen Museen führte unter Museumsleuten zu kontrovers geführten Debatten. Hier sei nur auf die erste Rückforderung der Kunsthalle Mannheim verwiesen, welche den Kunsthändler Günther Franke betraf und schließlich die Rückkehr des Werkes *Fastnacht (Pierrette und Clown)* von Max Beckmann (Abb. 31) ermöglichte.

Passarge konzentrierte sich zunehmend auf Ersatz-Ankäufe, als er resigniert feststellen musste, dass selbst mit juristischen Mitteln die beschlagnahmten Werke nicht in die Kunsthalle zurückzufordern seien. Nun erwarb er gezielt formal verwandte Arbeiten, um die Verluste auszugleichen und das Sammlungsprofil zu rekonstruieren.[19] Er begründete seine Erwerbungen mit der bildungspolitischen Verpflichtung, der Jugend jene Kunst nahezubringen, die aus der öffentlichen Wahrnehmung verdrängt worden war.

Passarge concentrated increasingly on acquisitions to replace works when he was forced to acknowledge with resignation that the works that had been confiscated could not be brought back to the Kunsthalle even by legal means. He began to acquire formally similar works to compensate for the loses and to reconstruct the collection's former profile.[19] He justified his acquisitions with the educational duty to introduce young people to the art that had been forced out of public viewing. These were great, blameless objectives, and no one asked about the other museum-policy, curatorial, or moral decisions Passarge had made under National Socialism.

During his term in office, Walter Passarge fulfilled the cultural-policy expectations of the National Socialist regime without being compromised ideologically. His emphasis on the "German" and the "popular" was in keeping with official orders but he preserved his curatorial maneuverability in which modern forms of expression could live on. His behavior was neither clear resistance nor pure allegiance but rather an expression of a strategic conformity that was characteristic of many cultural figures of that era.

1   Walter Passarge's biographical stations, his term in office at the Kunsthalle Mannheim, his institutional room to manoeuvre, and his network form the central fields of investigation of the present author's dissertation. The analysis is based on the fundamental preliminary work by Thomas Köllhofer, "Walter Passarge (1936–1958): Von der Diktatur zum Aufbruch in die Moderne," in exh. cat. *100 Jahre Kunsthalle Mannheim 1907–2007*, Kunsthalle Mannheim 2007, ed. Inge Herold (Mannheim 2007), pp. 56–81.

2   Cornelia Nowak, "'An die Freunde der Kommenden': Die expressionistische Künstlergruppe 'Jung-Erfurt,'" in *Expressionismus in Thüringen: Facetten eines kulturellen Aufbruchs*, ed. Cornelia Nowak, Kai Uwe Schierz, and Justus H. Ulbricht, exh. cat. Galerie am Fischmarkt, Angermuseum, and Barfüsserkirche, Erfurt (Jena 1999), pp. 34–43.

3   Walter Passarge, "Das Vesperbild in der deutschen Plastik vom Beginn des 14. bis zum Anfang des 16. Jahrhunderts," PhD diss. (University of Leipzig, 1923).

4   Correspondence between Passarge, Walter Gropius, and László Moholy-Nagy has been preserved in the Bauhaus-Archiv in Berlin: Teilnachlass Walter Gropius, Papers II, portfolio 619.

5   Angermuseum Erfurt, *Jahresberichte, 1881–1940*, in this case for 1924, Stadtarchiv Erfurt, 1-2/322-22574.

6   C. O. E., "Mannheims kulturpolitische Aufgaben," *Neue Mannheimer Zeitung*, July 11, 1936.

7   Ibid.

8   *Bauhaus-Moderne im Nationalsozialismus: Zwischen Anbiederung und Verfolgung*, ed. Winfried Nerdinger (Munich 1993); *Bauhaus und Nationalsozialismus*, ed. Anke Blümm, Elisabeth Otto, and Patrick Rössler, exh. cat. Museum Neues Weimar, Bauhaus-Museum Weimar, and Schiller-Museum 2024 (Weimar; Munich 2024).

9   *Die Neue Sachlichkeit: Ein Jahrhundertjubiläum / The New Objectivity: A Centennial Anniversary*, exh. cat. Kunsthalle Mannheim 2024–25, ed. Inge Herold and Johan Holten (Berlin 2025).

10 See, among others, *Emil Nolde—eine deutsche Legende: Der Künstler im Nationalsozialismus*, ed. Bernhard Fulda, Christan Ring, and Aya Soika (Munich 2019); *Flucht in die Bilder? Die Künstler der Brücke im Nationalsozialismus*, ed. Meike Hoffmann, Aya Soika, and Lisa M. Schmidt (Munich 2019); Isgard Kracht, *Inszeniert und Instrumentalisiert: Expressionismus im Nationalsozialismus: Ernst Barlach, Franz Marc, Emil Nolde*, (Berlin 2023).

11 The *Entartete Kunst* (Degenerate Art) action for Mannheim is described in detail in *Entartete Kunst: Beschlagnahmeaktionen in der Städtischen Kunsthalle Mannheim 1937*, ed. Hans-Jürgen Buderer, exh. cat. (Mannheim 1987); *Beschlagnahmt! Rückkehr der Meisterblätter*, Kunsthalle Mannheim 2019, ed. Thomas Köllhofer, Mathias Listl, and Ulrike Lorenz, exh. cat. (Mannheim 2019); *(Re)Discovery: The Kunsthalle from 1933 to 1945 and the Aftermath*, ed. Mathias Listl and Ulrike Lorenz, exh. cat. (Mannheim 2018).

12 It is described in most detail by Mathias Listl, "Zerstört oder über die ganze Welt verstreut: Über das Schicksal 'Entarteter Kunst' aus der Graphischen Sammlung der Kunsthalle Mannheim," in *Beschlagnahmt!* 2019 (see note 11), pp. 77–91.

13 For example, in Stadtarchiv Mannheim / MARCHIVUM, Bestand Kunsthalle, Zug. 02/2012, no. 652, fols. 323–24, and Generallandesarchiv Karlsruhe, 276-1 no. 23082, fols. 141–42.

14 Stadtarchiv Mannheim / MARCHIVUM, Bestand Kunsthalle, Zug. 02/2012, no. 651, fols. 180-182.

15 Heinz Fuchs cites the telegram in an essay from 1949: Heinz Fuchs, "'Reinigung' und 'Wiedergutmachung,'" *mannheim heute: Zweimonatsschrift für Arbeit und Kultur* 1, no. 2 (1949): pp. 4–8.

16 Stadtarchiv Mannheim / MARCHIVUM, Bestand Kunsthalle, Zug. 02/2012, no. 651, fol. 148, and no. 156, fols. 354 and 393.

17 The first research on the subject came in 2005 from the Arbeitskreis Justiz und Geschichte des Nationalsozialismus in Mannheim e.V.: *Betrifft: "Aktion 3": Die Verwertung jüdischen Eigentums in Mannheim "Arisierung" von Gegenständen des täglichen Gebrauchs*. They were followed by the study by Christiane Fritsche, *Ausgeplündert, zurückerstattet und entschädigt: Arisierung und Wiedergutmachung in Mannheim* (Ubstadt-Weiher 2013). Many details are also provided in Cassandra Louise Ihle, "Der Hausrat Mannheimer Juden und seine Verwertung: Der Weg jüdischen Umzugsguts von Mannheim nach Rotterdam und wieder zurück," bachelor's thesis, Univ. Mannheim, 2018. Important new clues have emerged recently: *Unrecht & Profit: Das Badische Landesmuseum im Nationalsozialismus*, ed. Katharina Siefert, exh. cat. Badisches Landesmuseum Karlsruhe 2025 (Oppenheim am Rhein 2025), pp. 65–72.

18 Stadtarchiv Mannheim / MARCHIVUM, Bestand Kunsthalle, Zug. 02/2012, no. 650, and Generallandesarchiv Karlsruhe, 480 no. 12053, files 1–3.

19 See Jochen Kronjäger, "Die Ausstellungs- und Sammlungsaktivitäten der Kunsthalle Mannheim von 1945 bis 1955. Versuch einer Bilanz," in *Menschenbilder: Figur in Zeiten der Abstraktion, 1945–1955*, ed. Manfred Fath, Inge Herold, and Thomas Köllhofer, exh. cat. Kunsthalle Mannheim, 1998–99 (Ostfildern-Ruit 1998), pp. 286–300. Hannah Krause, "Die Kunsthalle Mannheim zwischen 1945 und 1955," in *"So fing man einfach an, ohne viele Worte": Ausstellungswesen und Sammlungspolitik in den ersten Jahren nach dem Zweiten Weltkrieg*, ed. Julia Friedrich and Andreas Prinzing (Berlin 2013), pp. 147–56.

Hohe einwandfreie Ziele und niemand fragte nach anderen museumspolitischen, kuratorischen und moralischen Entscheidungen, die Passarge während der NS-Zeit getroffen hatte.

Walter Passarge erfüllte in seiner Amtszeit die kulturpolitischen Erwartungen des NS-Regimes, ohne sich vollständig ideologisch vereinnahmen zu lassen. Seine Betonung des „Deutschen" und des „Volkstümlichen" entsprach dem offiziellen Auftrag, doch zugleich bewahrte er sich kuratorische Freiräume, in denen moderne Ausdrucksformen fortbestehen konnten. Sein Verhalten war weder klarer Widerstand noch reine Gefolgschaft – vielmehr Ausdruck einer strategischen Anpassung, wie sie für viele Kulturakteure jener Zeit kennzeichnend war.

1 Walter Passarges biografische Stationen, seine Amtsführung an der Kunsthalle Mannheim, seine institutionellen Handlungsspielräume sowie sein Netzwerk bilden zentrale Untersuchungsfelder der aktuellen Dissertation der Autorin. Eine zentrale Grundlage für die vorliegende Analyse bilden die fundierten Vorarbeiten von Thomas Köllhofer, die hier kritisch aufgegriffen und durch neue Perspektiven ergänzt werden: Thomas Köllhofer: Walter Passarge (1936–1958). Von der Diktatur zum Aufbruch in die Moderne, in: Kat. Ausst. *100 Jahre Kunsthalle Mannheim 1907–2007*, Kunsthalle Mannheim 2007, hrsg. v. Inge Herold, Mannheim 2007, S. 56–81.

2 Cornelia Nowak: „An die Freunde der Kommenden" – Die expressionistische Künstlergruppe „Jung-Erfurt", in: Kat. Ausst. Expressionismus in *Thüringen. Facetten eines kulturellen Aufbruchs*, Galerie am Fischmarkt, Angermuseum, Barfüßerkirche Erfurt, hrsg. von Cornelia Nowak, Kai Uwe Schierz u. Justus H. Ulbricht, Jena 1999, S. 34-43.

3 Walter Passarge: *Das Vesperbild in der deutschen Plastik vom Beginn des 14. bis zum Anfang des 16. Jahrhunderts*, Diss. Univ. Leipzig 1923.

4 Korrespondenz zwischen Passarge, Walter Gropius und László Moholy-Nagy hat sich im Bauhaus-Archiv in Berlin erhalten: Teilnachlass Walter Gropius, Papers II, Mappe 619.

5 Angermuseum Erfurt: *Jahresberichte 1881-1940*, hier 1924, Stadtarchiv Erfurt, 1-2/322-22574.

6 C. O. E.: Mannheims kulturpolitische Aufgaben, in: *Neue Mannheimer Zeitung*, 11.07.1936.

7 Ebd.

8 Winfried Nerdinger (Hrsg.): *Bauhaus-Moderne im Nationalsozialismus. Zwischen Anbiederung und Verfolgung*, München 1993; Kat. Ausst. *Bauhaus und Nationalsozialismus*, Museum Neues Weimar, Bauhaus-Museum Weimar und Schiller-Museum 2024, hrsg. v. Anke Blümm, Elisabeth Otto u. Patrick Rössler, München/Weimar 2024.

9 Kat. Ausst. *Die Neue Sachlichkeit. Ein Jahrhundertjubiläum*, Kunsthalle Mannheim 2024/25, hrsg. v. Inge Herold u. Johan Holten, Berlin 2025.

10 Vgl. u. a. Bernhard Fulda, Christan Ring u. Aya Soika (Hrsg.): *Emil Nolde – eine deutsche Legende. Der Künstler im Nationalsozialismus*, München 2019; Meike Hoffmann, Aya Soika u. Lisa M. Schmidt (Hrsg.): *Flucht in die Bilder? Die Künstler der Brücke im Nationalsozialismus*, München 2019; Isgard Kracht: *Inszeniert und instrumentalisiert. Expressionismus im Nationalsozialismus: Ernst Barlach, Franz Marc, Emil Nolde*, Berlin/Boston 2023.

11 Detailliert ist die Aktion „Entartete Kunst" für Mannheim geschildert in: Kat. Ausst. *Entartete Kunst. Beschlagnahmeaktionen in der Städtischen Kunsthalle Mannheim 1937*, Kunsthalle Mannheim 1987/88, hrsg. v. Hans-Jürgen Buderer, Mannheim 1987; Kat. Ausst. *Beschlagnahmt! Rückkehr der Meisterblätter*, Kunsthalle Mannheim 2019, hrsg. v. Thomas Köllhofer, Mathias Listl u. Ulrike Lorenz, Mannheim 2019; Kat. Ausst. *(Wieder-) Entdecken. Die Kunsthalle 1933 bis 1945 und die Folgen*, Kunsthalle Mannheim 2018, hrsg. v. Mathias Listl u. Ulrike Lorenz, Mannheim 2018.

12 Am detailliertesten schildert es Mathias Listl: Zerstört oder über die ganze Welt verstreut: Über das Schicksal „Entarteter Kunst" aus der Graphischen Sammlung der Kunsthalle Mannheim, in: Kat. Ausst. *Beschlagnahmt! Rückkehr der Meisterblätter*, Kunsthalle Mannheim 2019, hrsg. v. Thomas Köllhofer, Mathias Listl u. Ulrike Lorenz, Mannheim 2019, S. 77–91.

13 Bspw. in: Stadtarchiv Mannheim/MARCHIVUM, Bestand Kunsthalle, Zug. 02/2012, Nr. 652, Bl. 323/324; oder Generallandesarchiv Karlsruhe, 276-1 Nr. 23082, Bl. 141/142.

14 Stadtarchiv Mannheim / MARCHIVUM, Bestand Kunsthalle, Zug. 02/2012, Nr. 651, Bl. 180-182.

15 Heinz Fuchs gibt 1949 den Wortlaut des Telegramms in seinem Aufsatz wieder: Heinz Fuchs: „Reinigung" und „Wiedergutmachung", in: *mannheim heute. Zweimonatsschrift für Arbeit und Kultur*, 1 (1949), Heft 2, S. 4–8.

16 Stadtarchiv Mannheim / MARCHIVUM, Bestand Kunsthalle, Zug. 02/2012, Nr. 651, Bl. 148, sowie Nr. 156, Bl. 354 u. 393.

17 Die ersten Recherchen hierzu kamen 2005 vom Arbeitskreis Justiz und Geschichte des Nationalsozialismus in Mannheim e. V.: *Betrifft: „Aktion 3". Die Verwertung jüdischen Eigentums in Mannheim. „Arisierung" von Gegenständen des täglichen Gebrauchs*. Ergebnisse lokalhistorischer Erkundungen vorgetragen auf der Veranstaltung am 13.01.2005, https://www.akjustiz-mannheim.de/index.php/arisierung/recherchen [abgerufen am 24.06.2025]. Es folgte die große Studie von Christiane Fritsche: *Ausgeplündert, zurückerstattet und entschädigt. Arisierung und Wiedergutmachung in Mannheim*, Ubstadt-Weiher u. a. 2013. Viele Details liefert auch: Cassandra Louise Ihle: *Der Hausrat Mannheimer Juden und seine Verwertung. Der Weg jüdischen Umzugsguts von Mannheim nach Rotterdam und wieder zurück*, Bachelorarbeit Univ. Mannheim 2018. Aktuell gibt es neue wichtige Hinweise: Kat. Ausst. *Unrecht & Profit. Das Badische Landesmuseum im Nationalsozialismus*, Badisches Landesmuseum Karlsruhe 2025, hrsg. v. Katharina Siefert, Oppenheim am Rhein 2025, S. 65–72.

18 Stadtarchiv Mannheim / MARCHIVUM, Bestand Kunsthalle, Zug. 02/2012, Nr. 650; sowie Generallandesarchiv Karlsruhe, 480 Nr. 12053, Akte 1-3.

19 Vgl. Jochen Kronjäger: Die Ausstellungs- und Sammlungsaktivitäten der Kunsthalle Mannheim von 1945 bis 1955. Versuch einer Bilanz, in: Kat. Ausst. *Menschenbilder. Figur in Zeiten der Abstraktion (1945–1955)*, Kunsthalle Mannheim 1998/99, hrsg. v. Manfred Fath, Inge Herold u. Thomas Köllhofer, Ostfildern-Ruit 1998, S. 286–300. Hannah Krause: Die Kunsthalle Mannheim zwischen 1945 und 1955, in: Julia Friedrich u. Andreas Prinzing (Hrsg.): *„So fing man einfach an, ohne viele Worte". Ausstellungswesen und Sammlungspolitik in den ersten Jahren nach dem Zweiten Weltkrieg*, Berlin 2013, S. 147-156.

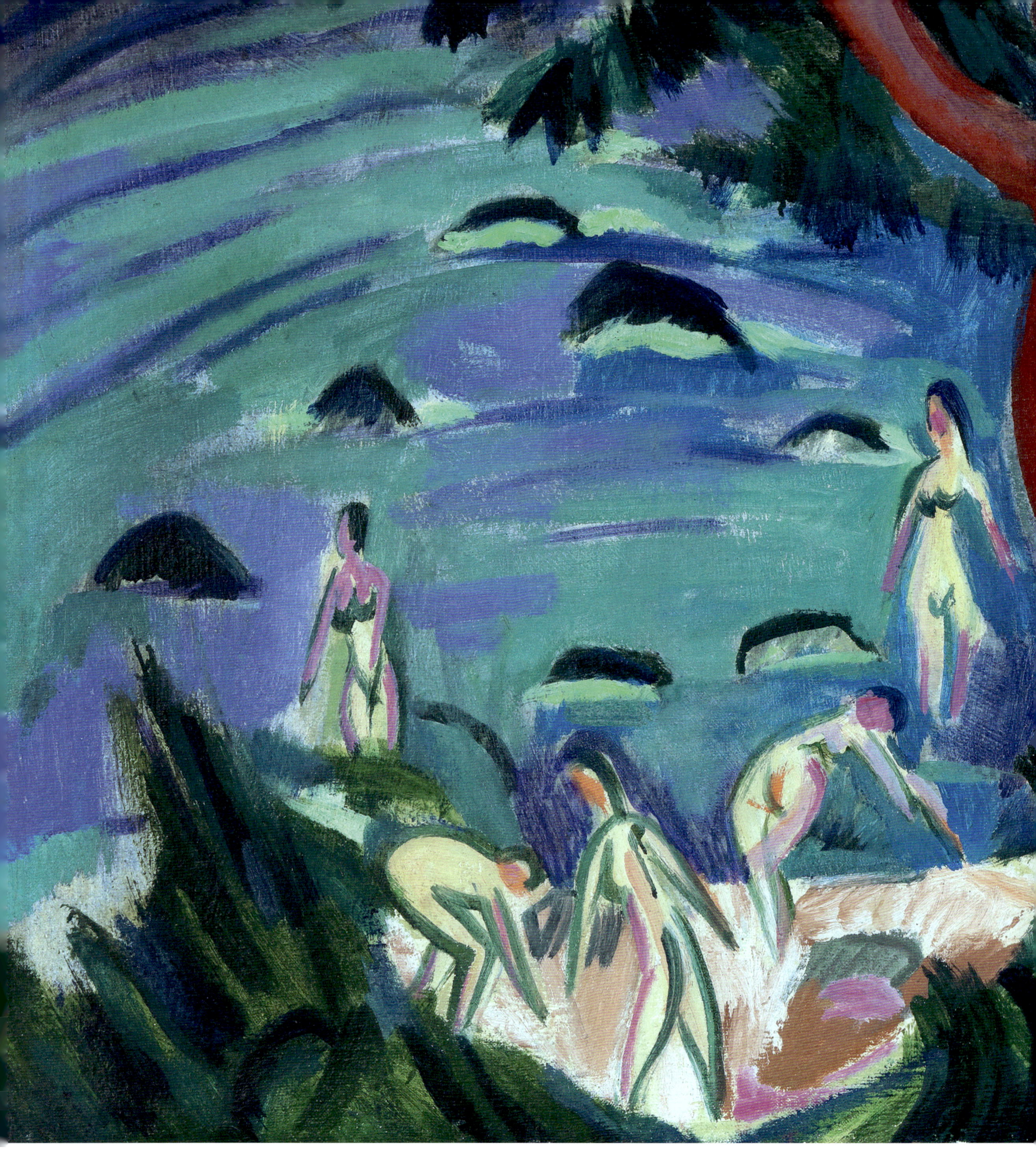

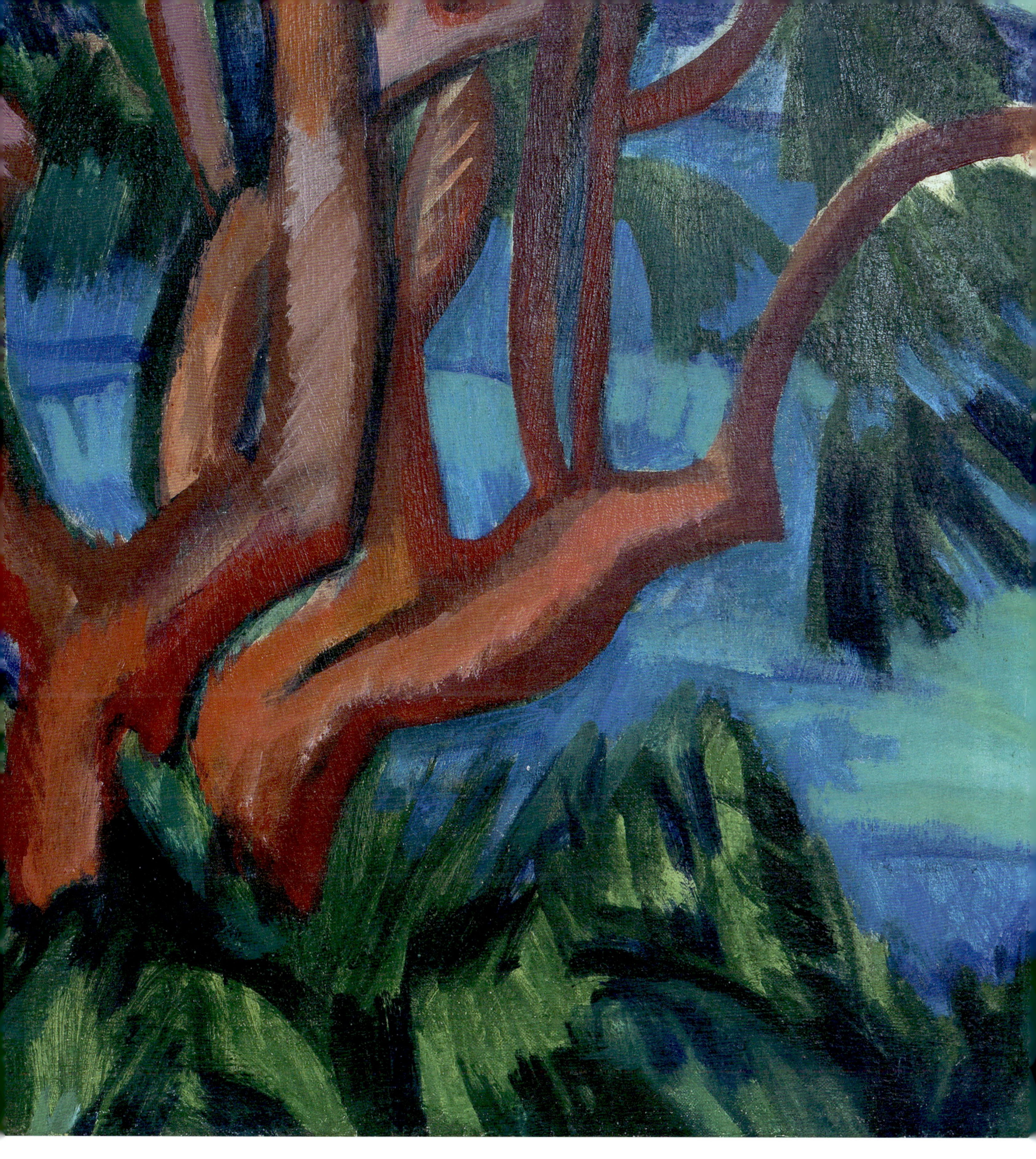

The Expressive Power of Pure Form: Expressionist Sculpture

Luisa Heese

An exhibition titled *Ausdrucks-Plastik* (Expressive Sculpture) opened in February 1912 at the Kunsthalle Mannheim that offered the first survey of the contemporary sculpture of its day and its expressive tendencies. It may even have been the first show ever to present cast sculpture exclusively.[1] In addition to Aristide Maillol and George Minne, who were considered important inspiration for the development of Expressionist sculpture, it presented works by Karl Albiker, Ernst Barlach, Bernhard Hoetger, and Georg Kolbe, among others. The text in the accompanying catalogue reads: "The new sculptors set out, consciously or unconsciously, from the idea that sculpture must above all regain its soul."[2] The positions presented were characterized by work with the human figure. To distinguish themselves from the classical academic sculpture of the nineteenth century, in which the human image was above all part of an allegorical narrative, these sculptors of the early twentieth century elevated the figure to an autonomous work of art that was based on the expression of states of mind and inner emotions. In the foreword of the catalogue, Georg Kolbe wrote about the artists participating: "despite the differences in their penchants for the art of antiquity, of the

Gothic, of the Renaissance, and so on, all of them are creating directly from life, seeking to express life today and using the proper means to reproduce it: pure form."[3] Two years later, in May 1914, it was followed by the even larger *Ausstellung von Zeichnungen und Plastiken neuzeitlicher Bildhauer* (Exhibition of Drawings and Sculptures by Modern Sculptors) at the Kunsthalle Mannheim, which included works by forty-four artists, including, in addition to the artists already presented in 1912, Ernesto de Fiori, Wilhelm Lehmbruck, Max Pechstein, Edwin Scharff, Renée Sintenis, and Milly Steger. Many of these artists (just as much as contemporaneous art critics) found that the term Expressionism was suited to their efforts. In 1918, Wilhelm Lehmbruck wrote to his friend, the writer Fritz von Unruh, for example: "We Expressionists—for, my dear Unruh, we are mocked with this name as well—what we Expressionists are seeking is: to extract from our material precisely the spiritual content. Its utmost expression, and that is precisely why we are being crushed in a world that is so deeply stuck in materialism."[4]

Although the sculptures of Expressionism did not so much follow a common style, several shared features can nevertheless be noted, as the influential Berlin publisher and art dealer Herwarth Walden did in *Der Sturm: Eine Einführung* in 1918: "Expressionist sculpture also no longer strives to imitate natural forms but rather to create absolute forms. Just as painting demands the plane as the material for artistic design, the corporeal form is the prerequisite for sculpture. But its design lies not in imitating nature but rather in the relationships of the individual three-dimensional forms."[5] The sculptors were concerned with expressing the inner experiences of human beings and achieving this by using means such as reduction, deformation, elongated proportions, and often coarse materials such as cast stone or wood. The sculpture of Expressionism thus including such divergent positions as those seeing "metaphysical" expression, such as Lehmbruck, Barlach, and Steger, but also "vitalist" artists oriented entirely around the "experience of transcendental matters in the worldly,"[6] such as the Brücke artists with their exotic, primitivist wood sculptures, as well as positions moving even further in the direction of formal abstraction, such as Alexander Archipenko, Oswald Herzog, William Wauer, and Rudolf Belling.[7]

After the exhibition *Ausdrucks-Plastik*, sculptural works of Expressionism were acquired gradually for the collection of the Kunsthalle Mannheim: *Chinese* (Chinese Man) by Georg Kolbe of 1911 could be purchased directly from the artist already in 1913.

Die Ausdruckskraft der reinen Form: Skulptur des Expressionismus

Luisa Heese

Mit dem Titel *Ausdrucks-Plastik* eröffnete im Februar 1912 in der Kunsthalle Mannheim eine Ausstellung, die erstmalig einen Überblick über die damals zeitgenössische Bildhauerei mit ihren expressiven Tendenzen gab – und möglicherweise sogar die erste Schau überhaupt war, die ausschließlich Plastiken präsentierte.[1] Neben Aristide Maillol und George Minne, die als wichtige Inspiration für die Entwicklung der expressionistischen Plastik galten, wurden unter anderem Werke von Karl Albiker, Ernst Barlach, Bernhard Hoetger und Georg Kolbe präsentiert. Im Begleittext des Katalogs heißt es: „Die neuen Plastiker gehen bewußt oder unbewußt von dem Gedanken aus, daß in der Bildhauerei vor allem einmal die Beseelung wieder gewonnen werden müsse."[2] Die präsentierten Positionen waren geprägt von der Auseinandersetzung mit der menschlichen Figur. In Abgrenzung zur klassischen akademischen Bildhauerei des 19. Jahrhunderts, in der das Menschenbild vor allem Teil allegorischer Narrative war, erhoben diese Bildhauer*innen des frühen 20. Jahrhunderts die Figur zum autonomen Kunstwerk, den Ausdruck seelischer Zustände und innerer Empfindungen zur gestalterischen Grundlage. So schrieb Georg Kolbe im Vorwort des Katalogs über die teilnehmenden Künstler: „[...] trotz ihren verschiedentlichen Neigungen zur Kunst der Antike, der Gotik, der Renaissance usw., schöpfen alle unmittelbar aus dem Leben, suchen den Ausdruck des heutigen Lebens und verwenden zur Wiedergabe das rechte Mittel: die reine Form."[3] Zwei Jahre später folgte im Mai 1914 die noch umfangreichere *Ausstellung von Zeichnungen und Plastiken neuzeitlicher Bildhauer* in der Kunsthalle Mannheim, die Werke von 44 Künstler*innen umfasste, darunter neben den bereits 1912 präsentierten Positionen auch Ernesto de Fiori, Wilhelm Lehmbruck, Max Pechstein, Edwin Scharff, Renée Sintenis und Milly Steger. Viele dieser Künstler*innen (ebenso wie die zeitgenössische Kunstkritik) fanden im Begriff des Expressionismus die namentliche Entsprechung ihrer Bestrebungen. Wilhelm Lehmbruck etwa schrieb 1918 an seinen Freund, den Schriftsteller Fritz von Unruh: „Wir Expressionisten, mein lieber Unruh, man verspottet uns mit diesem Namen auch, was wir Expressionisten suchen, ist: präzis aus unserem Material den geistigen Gehalt herauszuziehen. Seinen äußersten Ausdruck, und das ist's gerade, warum man zerquetscht wird in einer Welt, die so tief im Materialismus steckt."[4]

Obwohl die Skulpturen des Expressionismus weniger einem gemeinsamen plastischen Stil folgten, lassen sich dennoch einige gemeinsame Merkmale festhalten, die der einflussreiche Berliner Verleger und Kunsthändler Herwarth Walden 1918 in der Schrift *Der Sturm: Eine Einführung* festhielt: „Auch die expressionistische Plastik hat das Streben, nicht mehr die Naturformen nachzuahmen, sondern absolute Gebilde zu schaffen. Wie die Malerei die Fläche als Material der künstlerischen Gestaltung fordert, so hat die Bildhauerei die körperliche Form zur Voraussetzung. Ihre Gestaltung liegt aber nicht in der Nachahmung der Natur, sondern in den Beziehungen der einzelnen plastischen Formen."[5] Es ging den Bildhauer*innen darum, innere Erfahrungen des Menschlichen zum Ausdruck zu bringen und dies durch Mittel wie Reduktion, Deformation, gelängte Proportionen und oft auch derbe Materialien wie Steinguss oder Holz zu erreichen. Die Skulptur des Expressionismus umfasste damit so divergente Positionen wie die nach dem „metaphysischen" Ausdruck suchenden, beispielsweise Lehmbruck, Barlach oder Steger, aber auch die „vitalistischen", ganz auf das „Erleben transzendentaler Dinge im Irdischen"[6] ausgerichteten Künstler, wie die Brücke-Mitglieder mit ihren exotistisch-primitivistischen Holzskulpturen, und die noch stärker in die formale Abstraktion strebenden Positionen von Archipenko, Oswald Herzog, William Wauer und Rudolf Belling.[7]

The most important step in building the collection of contemporary art, however, followed in 1921 when works by Lehmbruck, de Fiori, and Kolbe were donated by the Mannheim art patron Sally Falk.[8] Several key works entered the collection only much later, such as, in 1964, William Wauer's *Lebendiges Eisen* (Vivid Iron) of 1916, in which he was already experimenting with hollow forms; *Dreiklang* (Triad) by Rudolf Belling (1919; cat. 9) was not received into the collection until the 1980s. Conceived as a set design, the dynamic form of three abstracted dancers was intended to unite symbolically the three arts of painting, sculpture, and architecture. Belling had originally planned for *Dreiklang* to be six meters tall, walled in with bricks, and covered with colored plaster,[9] as a "podium for a musical chapel for performances of [Paul] Hindemith, [Arnold] Schönberg, and [Igor] Stravinsky,"[10] but that did not come to pass. The bronze model is now considered one of the earliest works of sculptural abstraction, and it testifies to the atmosphere after World War I.

After 1945, the art of sculpture was initially overlooked in the reception of Expressionism: from the 1950s to the 1970s, numerous exhibitions paid homage to the movement, but they largely ignored Expressionist sculpture and concentrated on painting and graphic art. Indeed, until the 1980s, there was a debate whether sculpture positions like those of Barlach and Lehmbruck could be considered Expressionist at all.[11] It had, however, already been noted in writings of the time that "sculpture by nature comes much closer to the lines of thought of Expressionism than painting does, since its essential feature is already abstraction."[12] The reception changed only after 1983 thanks to the exhibition and publication *German Expressionist Sculpture* by the American art historian Stephanie Barron, though she focused heavily on the sculpture of the Brücke artists and left out other important positions. The exhibition was presented first at the Los Angeles County Museum of Art and then, under the title *Skulptur des Expressionismus*, at the Josef-Haubrich-Kunsthalle in Cologne.

1   See Ursel Berger, "Einführung," in Berger, ed., *Ausdrucksplastik, Bildhauerei im 20. Jahrhundert 1* (Berlin: Georg Kolbe Museum, 2002), pp. 7–9, esp. p. 8.
2   *Ausdrucks-Plastik*, exh. cat. 1912 (Mannheim: Kunsthalle Mannheim, 1912), p. 3.
3   Georg Kolbe, "Moderne Plastik," in *Ausdrucks-Plastik* (see note 2), p. 1.
4   Fritz von Unruh, "Begegnung mit Wilhelm Lehmbruck," in *Wilhelm Lehmbruck: Sieben Beiträge zum Gedenken seines 50. Todestages*, ed. Günter von Roden and Siegfried Salzmann, Duisburger Forschungen 13 (Duisburg, 1969), pp. 15–18, esp. p. 17.
5   Herwarth Walden, *Der Sturm: Eine Einführung* (Berlin: Der Sturm, 1918), n.p.
6   Karl Schmidt-Rottluff to Gustav Schiefler, 1913, quoted in *Karl Schmidt-Rottluff: Retrospektive*, exh. cat. Kunsthalle Bremen 1989, ed. Gunther Thiem and Armin Zweite (Munich: Prestel, 1989), p. 37. And quoted in Anita Beloubek-Hammer, "'Was wir Expressionisten suchen …': Wilhelm Lehmbruck und der Expressionismus," in *Wilhelm Lehmbruck*, exh. cat. Gerhard-Marcks-Haus Bremen; Georg-Kolbe-Museum Berlin; Lehmbruck-Museum Duisburg; Kunsthalle Mannheim (2000/2001), pp. 133–56, esp. p. 135.
7   See Anita Beloubek-Hammer, *Die schönen Gestalten der besseren Zukunft: Die Bildhauerkunst des Expressionismus und ihr geistiges Umfeld*, vol. 1 (Cologne: LETTER-Stiftung, 2007), p. 14.
8   On Sally Falk, see also Luisa Heese, "Wilhelm Lehmbruck and Sally Falk: 'The Sculptor Whose Silent Majesty This Collector Loved,'" in the present volume.
9   See *Kunstausstellung Berlin 1920 im Landesausstellungsgebäude*, exh. cat. (Berlin: Kunstausstellung Berlin, 1920), p. 69, https://doi.org/10.11588/diglit.47569#0071 (accessed July 31, 2025).
10   *H. M. Pechstein und Rudolf Belling*, exh. cat. (Cologne: Galerie Goyert, 1921).
11   See Beloubek-Hammer, *Die schönen Gestalten der besseren Zukunft* (see note 7), p. 9.
12   Max Osborn, "Berliner Sezessionsplastik," *Deutsche Kunst und Dekoration* 45, no. 5 (February 1920), pp. 293–94, esp. p. 293. See also Beloubek-Hammer, *Die schönen Gestalten der besseren Zukunft* (see note 7), p. 13.

Nach der Ausstellung *Ausdrucks-Plastik* wurden schrittweise plastische Werke des Expressionismus für die Sammlung der Kunsthalle Mannheim erworben: Das 1911 entstandene Werk *Chinese* von Georg Kolbe konnte bereits 1913 direkt vom Künstler erstanden werden. Der wichtigste Schritt zum Aufbau der zeitgenössischen Skulpturensammlung erfolgte jedoch 1921 durch die Stiftung von Werken Lehmbrucks, de Fioris und Kolbes durch den Mannheimer Mäzen Sally Falk.[8] Einige Schlüsselwerke kamen auch erst deutlich später in die Sammlung, so beispielsweise 1964 William Wauers Werk *Lebendiges Eisen* von 1916, in dem er bereits mit Hohlräumen experimentierte; auch das Werk *Dreiklang* von Rudolf Belling (1919; Kat. 9) wurde erst in den 1980er-Jahren in die Sammlung aufgenommen. Zunächst als Bühnenbild konzipiert, sollte die dynamische Form dreier abstrahierter Tänzerinnen symbolisch die drei Künste Malerei, Plastik, Architektur vereinen. Ursprünglich hatte Belling geplant, den *Dreiklang* sechs Meter hoch, in Ziegeln gemauert und farbig verputzt[9] umzusetzen, als „Podium für eine Musikkapelle für Aufführungen von Hindemith, Schönberg und Strawinsky"[10], wozu es jedoch nie kam. Das in Bronze umgesetzte Modell gilt heute als eines der wichtigsten frühen Werke der bildhauerischen Abstraktion und zeugt von der Atmosphäre nach dem Ersten Weltkrieg.

Nach 1945 wurde die Bildhauerkunst in der Rezeption des Expressionismus zunächst vernachlässigt: in den 1950ern bis in die 1970er-Jahre hinein fanden zahleiche würdigende Ausstellungen statt, die jedoch die expressionistische Plastik weitgehend ignorierten und sich auf Malerei und Grafik konzentrierten. Vielmehr wurde bis in die 1980er-Jahre diskutiert, ob bildhauerische Positionen wie jene von Barlach und Lehmbruck überhaupt als expressionistisch gelten konnten.[11] Dabei war bereits in zeitgenössischen Schriften festgehalten worden, dass „die Plastik den Gedankengängen des Expressionismus von Hause aus viel weiter entgegen[kämel als die Malerei; denn der Grundzug ihres Wesens ist bereits Abstraktion."[12] Die Rezeption änderte sich erst ab 1983 durch die Ausstellung sowie die Publikation *German Expressionist Sculpture* der US-amerikanischen Kunsthistorikerin Stephanie Barron, die allerdings stark auf die plastischen Werke der Brücke-Mitglieder fokussierte und andere wichtige Positionen wiederum ausließ. Die Ausstellung wurde zunächst im Los Angeles County Museum of Art und danach auch mit dem Titel *Skulptur des Expressionismus* in der Josef-Haubrich-Kunsthalle in Köln präsentiert.

1 Vgl. Ursel Berger: Einführung, in: dies. (Hrsg.): *Ausdrucksplastik* (Bildhauerei im 20. Jahrhundert, Bd. 1), hrsg. v. Georg Kolbe Museum, Berlin 2002, S. 7–9, S. 8.
2 Kat. Ausst. *Ausdrucks-Plastik*, Kunsthalle Mannheim 1912, Mannheim 1912, S. 3.
3 Georg Kolbe: Moderne Plastik, in: Kat. Ausst. *Ausdrucks-Plastik* 1912 (wie Anm. 2), S. 1.
4 Fritz von Unruh: Begegnung mit Wilhelm Lehmbruck, in: Günter von Roden u. Siegfried Salzmann (Hrsg.): *Wilhelm Lehmbruck: Sieben Beiträge zum Gedenken seines 50. Todestages*, Duisburger Forschungen, 13, 1969, Duisburg 1969, S. 15–18, S. 17.
5 Herwarth Walden: *Der Sturm: Eine Einführung*, Berlin 1918, o. S.
6 Karl Schmidt-Rottluff: Brief an Gustav Schiefler, 1913, zit. nach: Kat. Ausst. *Karl Schmidt-Rottluff, Retrospektive*, Kunsthalle Bremen 1989, hrsg. v. Gunther Thiem u. Armin Zweite, München 1989, S. 37. Und zit. nach: Anita Beloubek-Hammer: „Was wir Expressionisten suchen …". Wilhelm Lehmbruck und der Expressionismus, in: Kat. Ausst. *Wilhelm Lehmbruck*, Gerhard-Marcks-Haus Bremen; Georg-Kolbe-Museum Berlin; Lehmbruck-Museum Duisburg; Kunsthalle Mannheim 2000/2001, S. 133–156, S. 135.
7 Vgl. Anita Beloubek-Hammer: *Die schönen Gestalten der besseren Zukunft. Die Bildhauerkunst des Expressionismus und ihr geistiges Umfeld*, Bd. 1, Köln 2007, S. 14.
8 Zu Sally Falk siehe auch in diesem Katalog den Text *Wilhelm Lehmbruck und Sally Falk: „ein Bildhauer, dessen schweigsame Hoheit dieser Sammler liebte".
9 Vgl. Kat. Ausst. *Kunstausstellung Berlin 1920 im Landesausstellungsgebäude*, hrsg. v. Grosse Berliner Kunstausstellung, Berlin 1920, S. 69, https://doi.org/10.11588/diglit.47569#0071 [abgerufen am 31.07.2025].
10 Kat. Ausst. *H. M. Pechstein und Rudolf Belling*, Galerie Goyert, Köln 1921.
11 Vgl. Beloubek-Hammer 2007 (wie Anm. 7), S. 9.
12 Max Osborn: Berliner Sezessionsplastik, in: *Deutsche Kunst und Dekoration*, Bd. 45, 10/1919–3/1920, H. 5 (2/1920), 1920, S. 293f., S. 293. Vgl. auch Beloubek-Hammer 2007 (wie Anm. 7), S. 13.

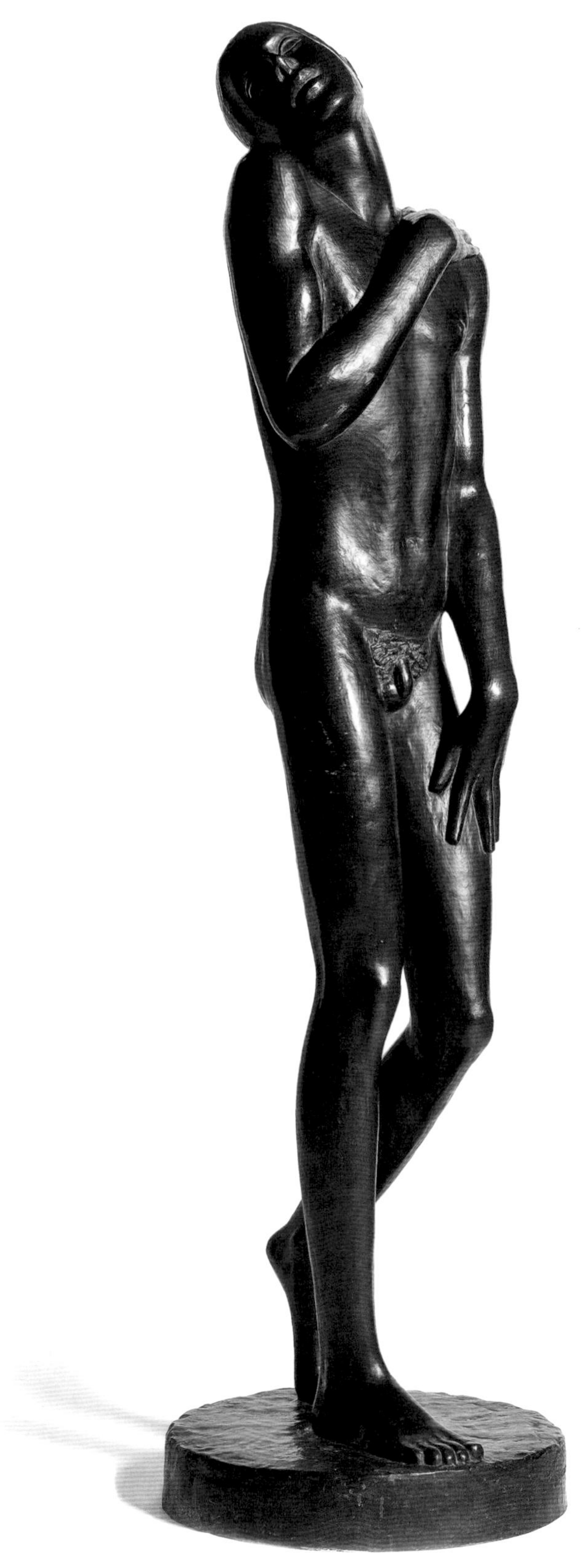

1 | **Ernesto de Fiori**, *Jüngling (Der Leidende)* / *Youth (The Sufferer)*, **1911/12,** Kunsthalle Mannheim

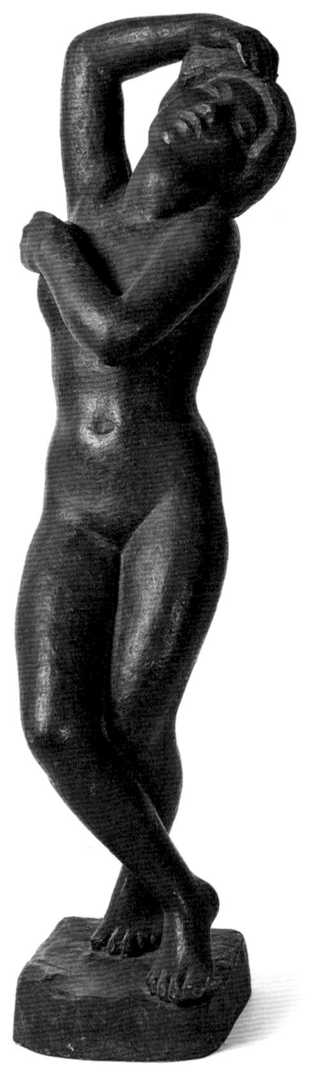

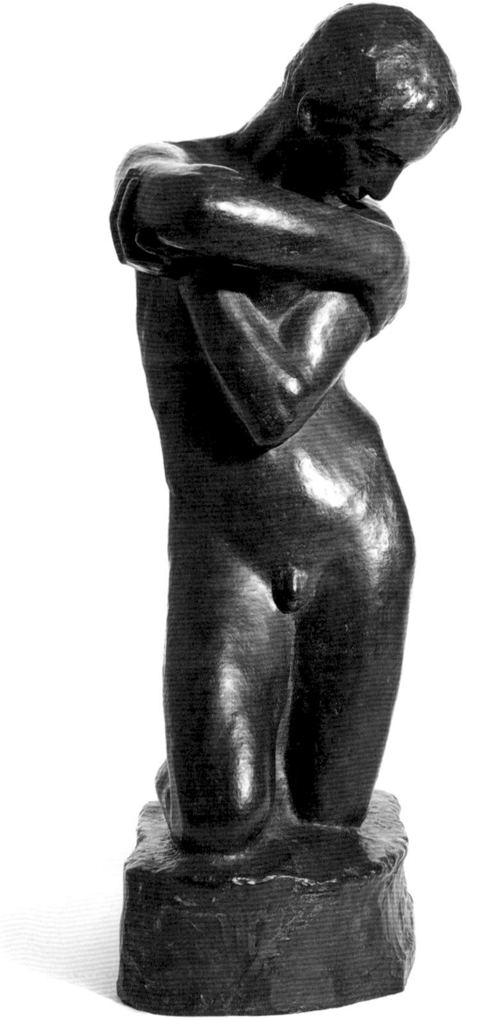

2 | **Georg Kolbe,** *Sklavin* / *Female Slave,* **1916,** Kunsthalle Mannheim

3 | **George Minne,** *Adolescent à genoux, I.*
(Kniender Jüngling I.) / *Kneeling Youth I.,* **1925,** Kunsthalle Mannheim

85

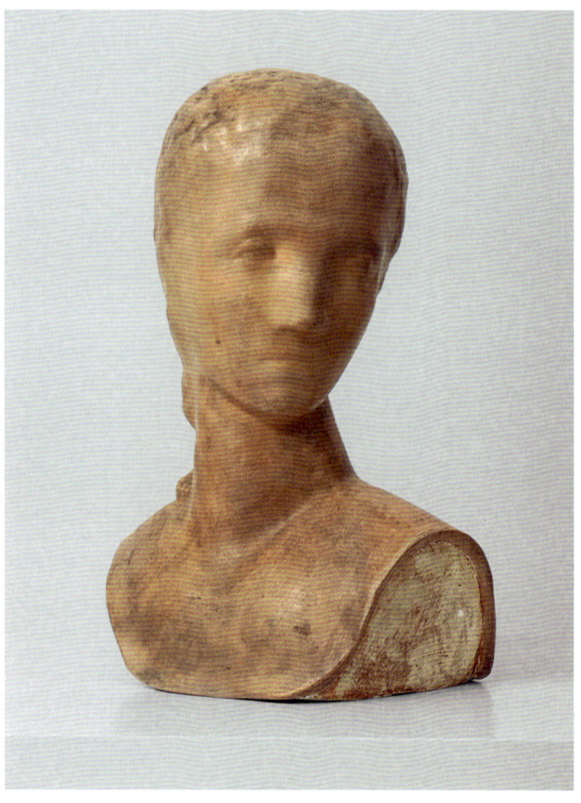

4 | **Wilhelm Lehmbruck,** *Kopf der Schreitenden* / Head of Striding Woman, **nach** / after **1914,**
Privatbesitz / *Private collection*, Mannheim

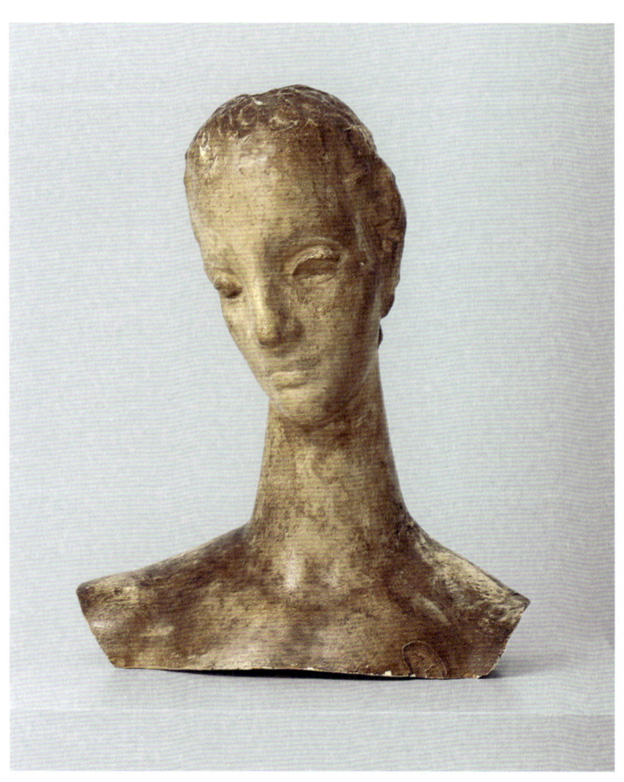

5 | **Wilhelm Lehmbruck,** *Büste der Großen Sinnenden* /
Bust of Large Contemplative Woman, **nach** / after **1914,**
Privatbesitz / *Private collection*, Mannheim

6 | **Wilhelm Lehmbruck,** *Büste der Knienden* /
Bust of Kneeling Woman, **1911,**
Privatbesitz / *Private collection*, Mannheim

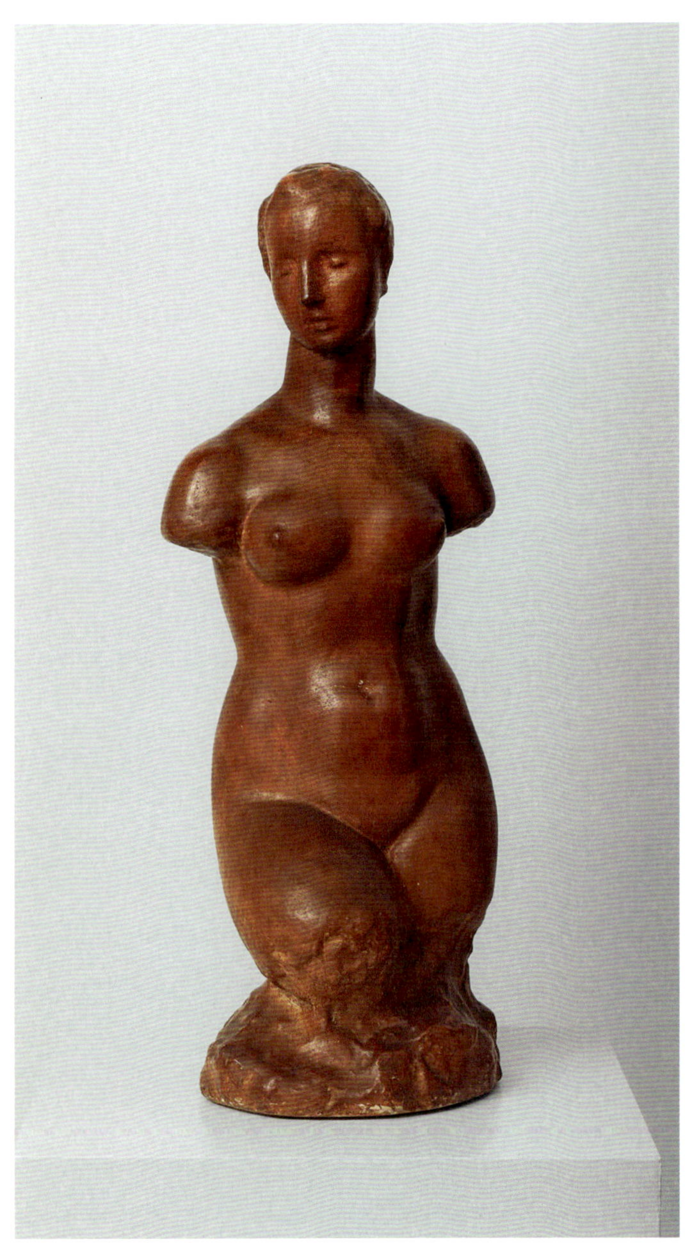

7 | **Wilhelm Lehmbruck,** *Hagener Torso* / *Hagen Torso,* **1910/11,** Privatbesitz / *Private collection,* Mannheim

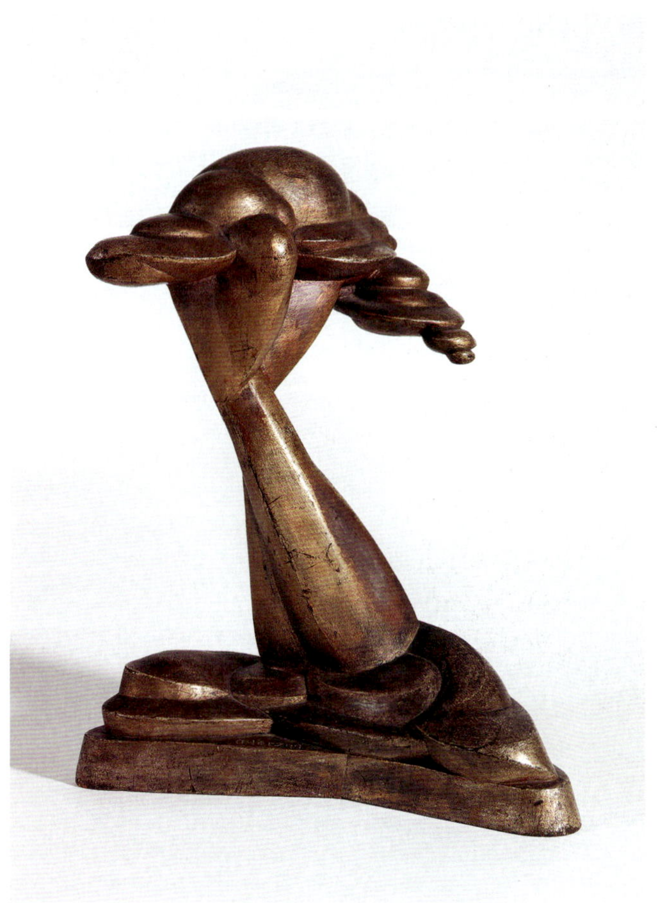

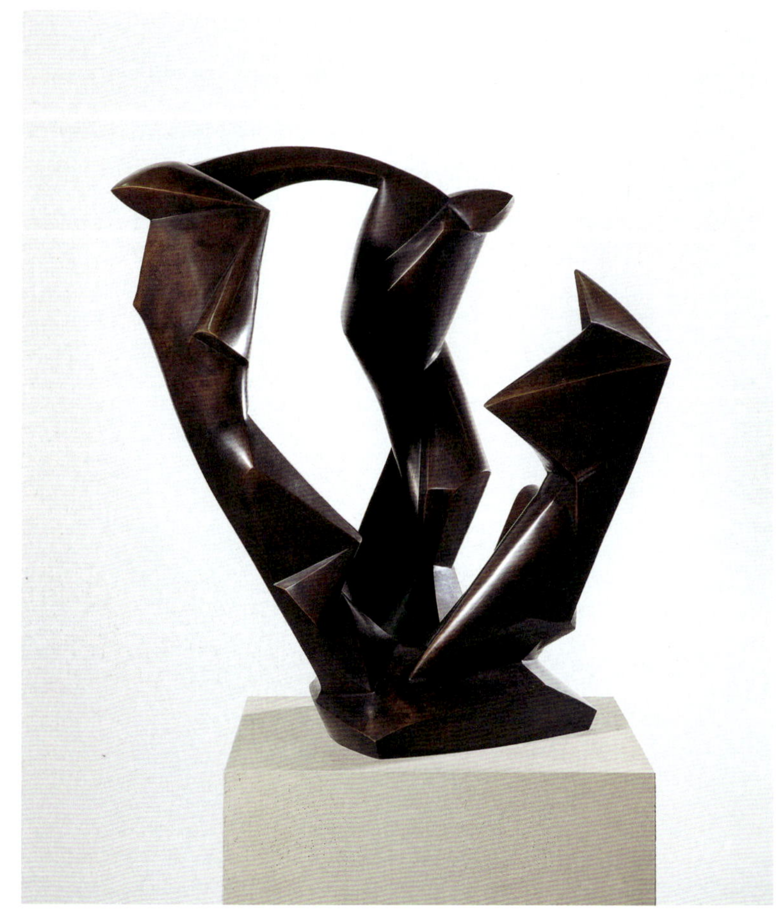

8 | **Oswald Herzog,** *Verzückung* / *Rapture,* **1919,** Kunsthalle Mannheim

9 | **Rudolf Belling,** *Dreiklang* / *Triad,* **1919,** Kunsthalle Mannheim

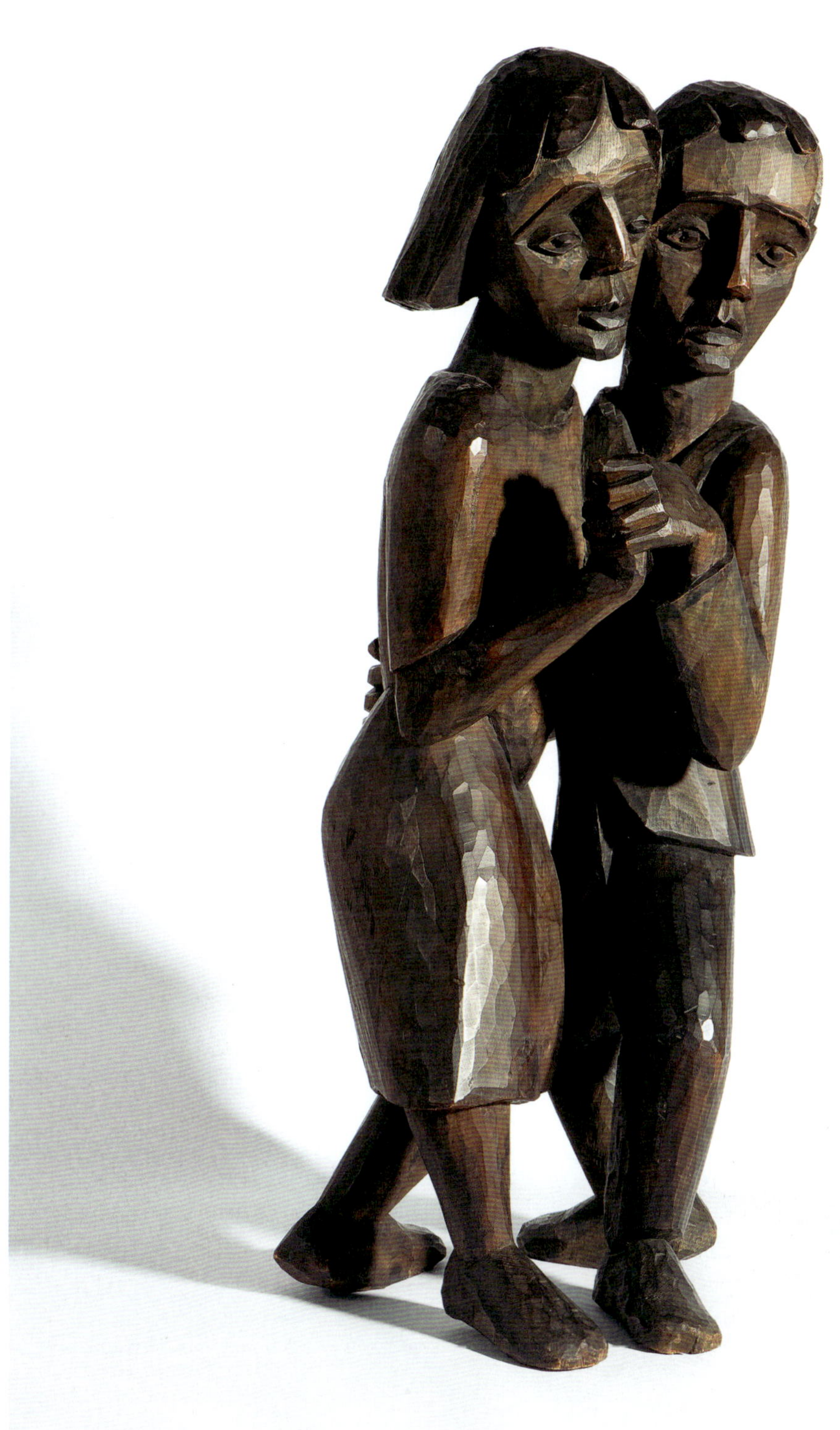

10 | **Hermann Scherer,** *Tanzende* / *Dancing Couple*, **1925,** Kunsthalle Mannheim

Wilhelm Lehmbruck and Sally Falk: "a sculptor whose silent majesty this collector loved"[1]

Luisa Heese

In a creative period of just a few years, Wilhelm Lehmbruck (1881–1919) developed his sculptural oeuvre from "Wilhelmine ideology to the Expressionist design of symbolic figures."[2] Born in Duisburg-Meiderich to working-class parents, he studied with Karl Janssen in Düsseldorf and then moved to Paris where he quickly broke with classical design principles. Focus on the individual figure that expressed both inner emotional worlds and worldviews as well as elongation, reduction of forms, and deformation of the body became central elements of his artistic work. He soon received international attention by appearing in important exhibitions. For example, he participated in the Armory Show in New York in 1913 and in the Werkbund exhibition in Cologne in 1914; that same year the Galerie Levesque in Paris organized a large solo exhibition; his works were also shown in Mannheim in these years. Lehmbruck was not yet represented here in the pioneering exhibition *Ausdrucks-Plastik* (Expressive Sculpture) of 1912, but already in 1913 he was participating with three works in the exhibition of the Deutscher Künstlerbund (Association of German Artists) at the Kunsthalle, including *Kniende* (Kneeling Woman) (fig. 4, p.19)—the work that the Expressionist poet Theodor

Däubler would somewhat later call "the preface to Expressionism in sculpture."[3] Lehmbruck was also represented by two works in the exhibition *Ausstellung von Zeichnungen und Plastiken neuzeitlicher Bildhauer* (Exhibition of Drawings and Sculptures by Modern Sculptors), held at the Kunsthalle in 1914. Lehmbruck was no longer living in Paris at the time: when World War I began, he had to leave France and initially moved to Berlin.

In 1915, Willy Storck, a research associate at the Kunsthalle Mannheim, and Gustav Friedrich Hartlaub, the deputy of Director Fritz Wichert since 1914, put Lehmbruck in contact with the textile manufacturer Sally Falk (Salomon Falk, 1888–1962), who after the death of his father took over the latter's cotton-processing business in Mannheim-Neckarau. Falk, a passionate art collector, immediately began to acquire the artist's works. This was followed by numerous visits to the artist's studio, invitations for Lehmbruck and his family to come to Mannheim, the Black Forest, and later to Arosa, Switzerland. They even agreed on a "monthly annuity"[4] that provided Falk with delivered works as well as a right of first refusal and made him the artist's most important supporter.

In 1916, Lehmbruck was commissioned to make portrait busts of Falk and his wife, Adèle, who was from Geneva—his biggest commission during the war years. He made the busts on a stay in Mannheim in June 1916 that lasted at least four weeks, though presumably Lehmbruck merely made plaster casts of the clay models there, because problems arose when Franz Gelb was casting them in his studio in Mannheim Palace. Anita Lehmbruck later recalled "my husband was quite dissatisfied back then with the casting of the busts by F."[5] Later the models were realized in more precious materials: the bust of Sally Falk in bronze and that of Adèle Falk in marble.[6]

The portrait busts in plaster (cat. 11, 12)—in the Kunsthalle collection since 1960 as a gift from Maria Tannenbaum in memory of her husband—clearly show how the individual features of the people portrayed recede in favor of the profoundly felt inner expression: the long heads and necks are rendered planar, the forms reduced to the essential, and the facial features idealized. The large eyes under heavy lids are looking into the distance in an undirected way. It is no longer about a likeness to the physical appearance that is faithful to the details but rather about the "*ethos* of the person."[7]

In 1916, the work *Large Standing Woman* (cat. 17) could be purchased for the Kunsthalle, then that winter the exhibition

Wilhelm Lehmbruck und Sally Falk: „ein Bildhauer, dessen schweigsame Hoheit dieser Sammler liebte"[1]

Luisa Heese

In nur wenigen Schaffensjahren entwickelte Wilhelm Lehmbruck (1881–1919) sein bildhauerisches Werk von „wilhelminischer Ideologie zu expressionistischer Gestaltung von Symbolfiguren"[2]. Als Arbeitersohn in Duisburg-Meiderich geboren, zog er nach seinem Studium bei Karl Janssen in Düsseldorf nach Paris und brach dort schnell mit den klassischen Gestaltungsprinzipien. Der Fokus auf die Einzelfigur, die als Ausdrucksträgerin innerer Gefühlswelten ebenso wie weltanschaulicher Ideen fungierte, sowie die Längung, formale Reduktion und Deformation des Körpers wurden zu zentralen Elementen seines künstlerischen Schaffens. Internationale Aufmerksamkeit erhielt er bald durch die Beteiligung an großen Ausstellungen. So nahm er 1913 an der Armory Show in New York teil sowie 1914 an der Werkbund-Ausstellung in Köln, im selben Jahr noch veranstaltete in Paris die Galerie Levesque eine große Einzelschau; auch in Mannheim wurden seine Werke in diesen Jahren gezeigt. Lehmbruck war hier zwar noch nicht in der bahnbrechenden Ausstellung *Ausdrucks-Plastik* von 1912 vertreten, aber bereits 1913 nahm er mit drei Werken an der Ausstellung des Deutschen Künstlerbundes in der Kunsthalle teil, darunter die *Kniende* (S. 19, Abb. 4) – jenes Werk, das etwas später von dem expressionistischen Dichter Theodor Däubler als „das Vorwort zum Expressionismus in der Skulptur"[3] bezeichnet wurde. Auch in der *Ausstellung von Zeichnungen und Plastiken neuzeitlicher Bildhauer,* die 1914 in der Kunsthalle stattfand, war Lehmbruck mit zwei Werken vertreten. Zu dieser Zeit lebte Lehmbruck bereits nicht mehr in Paris – mit Beginn des Ersten Weltkrieges musste er Frankreich verlassen und zog zunächst nach Berlin.

Durch Vermittlung von Willy Storck, wissenschaftlicher Mitarbeiter der Kunsthalle Mannheim, und Gustav Friedrich Hartlaub, seit 1914 Stellvertreter des Direktors Fritz Wichert, kam Lehmbruck 1915 in Kontakt mit dem Textilfabrikanten Sally Falk (Salomon Falk, 1888–1962), der nach dem Tod seines Vaters den baumwoll-verarbeitenden Betrieb in Mannheim-Neckarau übernommen hatte. Falk, ein leidenschaftlicher Kunstsammler, begann sogleich, Werke des Künstlers zu erwerben. Es folgten zahlreiche Besuche in dessen Atelier, Einladungen für Lehmbruck mit Familie nach Mannheim, in den Schwarzwald und später nach Arosa in der Schweiz. Man einigte sich sogar auf eine „monatliche Rente"[4], die Falk Werklieferungen sowie ein Vorkaufsrecht einräumte und ihn zum wichtigsten Förderer des Künstlers machte.

1916 erhielt Lehmbruck den Auftrag, Porträtbüsten von Falk und seiner aus Genf stammenden Frau Adèle anzufertigen – sein größter Auftrag während der Kriegsjahre. Die Büsten entstanden bei einem mindestens vierwöchigen Aufenthalt in Mannheim im Juni 1916, wobei Lehmbruck hier wohl nur die Abformungen der Tonmodelle in Gips anfertigte, da sich beim Abgießen im Atelier von Franz Gelb im Mannheimer Schloss Probleme ergaben. Anita Lehmbruck erinnerte sich später, „daß damals beim Gießen der Büsten von F. mein Mann schon recht unzufrieden war."[5] Später wurden die Modelle in edlere Materialien umgesetzt: die Büste von Sally Falk in Bronze, jene von Adèle Falk in Marmor.[6]

An den Bildnisbüsten in Gips (Kat. 11, 12), die sich – als Schenkung von Maria Tannenbaum in Gedenken an ihren Mann, Dr. Herbert Tannenbaum – seit 1960 in der Sammlung der Kunsthalle befinden, zeigt sich deutlich, wie die individuellen Züge der dargestellten Personen zugunsten eines tief empfundenen inneren Ausdrucks zurücktreten: Die langen Köpfe und Hälse sind flächig gestaltet, die Formen reduziert auf das Wesentliche, die Gesichtszüge idealisiert. Die großen Augen schauen jeweils unter schweren Lidern ohne gerichteten Blick in die Ferne. Es geht nicht mehr um die detailgetreue Ähnlichkeit der körperlichen Erscheinung, sondern um das „Ethos der Person".[7]

Kollektiv-Ausstellung Wilhelm Lehmbruck was held at the Kunsthalle Mannheim with Falk's support. It was the first and only comprehensive exhibition of the artist's works during his lifetime. Both the introduction to the catalogue and a lecture at the exhibition opening were written by Theodor Däubler, who had a close friendship with Sally Falk and whom Hartlaub also admired greatly.[8] Falk's plans to donate sculptures by Lehmbruck to the Kunsthalle were taking shape during the preparations for this exhibition. He had already given the painting *Junges Mädchen (Martha)* (Young Girl [Martha]) (cat. 15) to the Kunsthalle in 1917, the donation was to include the works *Der Gebeugte* (Seated Youth) (p. 19, fig. 5), *Kniende* (Kneeling Woman) (p. 19, fig. 4), *Badende* (Bathing Woman) (cat. 20), *Frauenbüste* (Female Bust) (cat. 21), *Kleine Sinnende* (Small Contemplative Woman) (cat. 19), *Hagener Torso* (Hagen Torso) (cat. 22), and *Torso der Großen Sinnenden* (Torso of Large Contemplative Woman) (cat. 23)— in addition to works by Edwin Scharff, Georg Kolbe (cat. 2), and Ernesto de Fiori (cat. 1). In March 1917, the notarized deed for the donation was signed; it came into force in August 1921.[9] Lehmbruck did not live to experience it: he had taken his own life in 1919.

Sally Falk's donation to the Kunsthalle Mannheim established the collection's emphasis on modern sculpture with a particular focus on the genesis of Expressionism. Parts of this important donation fell victim to the confiscations by the National Socialist regime in 1937. They were resold abroad by, among others, Karl Buchholz's art and book dealership in Berlin: *Der Gebeugte* is now in the National Gallery of Art in Washington, DC, and *Kniende* in the Museum of Modern Art in New York. The painting *Junges Mädchen (Martha)*, which is now in the Lehmbruck Museum in Duisburg, was sold in the auction *Gemälde und Plastiken moderner Meister aus deutschen Museen* (Paintings and Sculptures by Modern Masters from German Museums) in Lucerne, Switzerland, in 1939. Astonishingly, Lehmbruck's other works were not confiscated and remained at the Kunsthalle. They now form the core of the Sculpture Collection in Mannheim.

1 Paul Westheim, "Erinnerung an eine Sammlung," *Das Kunstblatt* 2, no. 8 (August 1918), pp. 233–41, esp. p. 240.
2 Dietrich Schubert, "Wilhelm Lehmbruck," in *Skulptur des Expressionismus*, ed. Stephanie Barron, exh. cat. (Munich: Prestel, 1984), pp. 133–41, esp. p. 133.
3 Theodor Däubler, "Expressionismus," *Die neue Rundschau* 17, no. 2 (1916), pp. 1136–37.
4 Susanne Schiller, "Die Stiftung Sally Falk: Ein Sammler und seine Bedeutung für die Mannheimer Kunsthalle," *Stiftung und Sammlung Sally Falk*, ed. Städtische Kunsthalle Mannheim, Kunst und Dokumentation 11 (Mannheim 1994), pp. 11–74, esp. p. 16.
5 Almut Eckell, Karoline Hille, and Roland Dorn, "Die Skulpturen der Stiftung Falk einschließlich der Falk-Porträts der Stiftung Tannenbaum", in *Stiftung und Sammlung Sally Falk* (see note 4), pp. 75–106, esp. p. 100.
6 Both are now in the Tel Aviv Museum of Art, see ibid., pp. 96ff.
7 Dietrich Schubert, *Die Kunst Lehmbrucks*, 2nd ed. (Dresden: Verlag der Kunst, 1990), p. 233.
8 See Karoline Hille, *Spuren der Moderne: Die Mannheimer Kunsthalle von 1918 bis 1933,* Kunst und Dokumentation 13, Städtische Kunsthalle Mannheim (also PhD diss. Freie Univ. Berlin) (Berlin: Akademie, 1994), p. 34.
9 This same year, Falk was forced to liquidate his company; on this and on the further course of the Falks' lives, see the text by Inge Herold in the present volume.

1916 konnte das Werk *Große Stehende* (Kat. 17) für die Kunsthalle
erworben werden; im Winter fand dann, mit Unterstützung Falks,
die *Kollektiv-Ausstellung Wilhelm Lehmbruck* in der Kunsthalle
Mannheim statt. Sie blieb die erste und einzige umfassende
Ausstellung seiner Werke zu Lebzeiten. Sowohl die Einleitung
des Katalogs als auch einen Vortrag zur Ausstellungseröffnung
verfasste Theodor Däubler, der mit Sally Falk eine enge Freundschaft pflegte und auch von Hartlaub sehr verehrt wurde.[8] Bereits
im Zuge der Vorbereitungen zu dieser Ausstellung reiften die
Pläne Falks zu einer Stiftung von Plastiken von Lehmbruck an die
Kunsthalle. Nachdem er das Gemälde *Junges Mädchen (Martha)*
(Kat. 15) bereits 1917 der Kunsthalle geschenkt hatte, waren für
die Stiftung die Werke *Der Gebeugte* (S. 19, Abb. 5), *Kniende*
(S. 19, Abb. 4), *Badende* (Kat. 20), *Frauenbüste* (Kat. 21), *Kleine
Sinnende* (Kat. 19), *Hagener Torso* (Kat. 22) und *Torso der Großen
Sinnenden* (Kat. 23) vorgesehen – außerdem kamen schließlich
noch Werke von Edwin Scharff, Georg Kolbe (Kat. 2) und Ernesto
de Fiori (Kat. 1) dazu. Im März 1917 unterzeichnete man die
notarielle Stiftungsurkunde, im August 1921 wurde sie dann
rechtskräftig.[9] Lehmbruck erlebte dies nicht mehr – er nahm sich
1919 das Leben.

Durch die Stiftung Sally Falks an die Kunsthalle Mannheim konnte
der Sammlungsschwerpunkt auf moderne Skulptur mit beson-
derem Hinblick auf die Genese des Expressionismus etabliert
werden. Teile dieser bedeutenden Stiftung fielen jedoch 1937
den Beschlagnahmungen durch das NS-Regime zum Opfer. Sie
wurden unter anderem über die Buch- und Kunsthandlung Karl
Buchholz in Berlin ins Ausland „weiterverwertet": *Der Gebeugte*
befindet sich heute in der National Gallery in Washington, die
Kniende im Museum of Modern Art in New York. Das Gemälde
Junges Mädchen (Martha), das sich heute im Lehmbruck Museum
in Duisburg befindet, wurde über die Luzerner Auktion *Gemälde
und Plastiken moderner Meister aus deutschen Museen* versteigert. Die restlichen Werke Lehmbrucks waren von den Beschlagnahmungen erstaunlicherweise nicht betroffen und verblieben
in der Kunsthalle. Sie bilden bis heute den Kern der Mannheimer
Skulpturensammlung.

1   Paul Westheim: Erinnerung an eine Sammlung, in: *Das Kunstblatt*, 2. Jg, Heft
    8, August 1918, S. 233–241, S. 240.
2   Dietrich Schubert: Wilhelm Lehmbruck, in: Stephanie Barron (Hrsg.): *Skulptur
    des Expressionismus*, München 1984, S. 133–141, S. 133.
3   Theodor Däubler: Expressionismus, in: *Die neue Rundschau*, 17. Jg., Heft 2,
    Frankfurt am Main 1916, S. 1136f.
4   Susanne Schiller: Die Stiftung Sally Falk. Ein Sammler und seine Bedeutung
    für die Mannheimer Kunsthalle, in: *Stiftung und Sammlung Sally Falk*, Kunst
    und Dokumentation 11, hrsg. v. Städtische Kunsthalle Mannheim, Mannheim
    1994, S. 11–74, S. 16.
5   Almut Eckell, Karoline Hille und Roland Dorn: Die Skulpturen der Stiftung
    Falk einschließlich der Falk-Porträts der Stiftung Tannenbaum", in: *Stiftung
    und Sammlung Sally Falk* 1994 (wie Anm. 4), S. 75–106, S. 100.
6   Beide befinden sich heute im Tel Aviv Museum of Art, vgl. ebd., S. 96ff.
7   Dietrich Schubert: *Die Kunst Lehmbrucks*, 2. Aufl., Dresden 1990, S. 233.
8   Vgl. Karoline Hille: *Spuren der Moderne. Die Mannheimer Kunsthalle von
    1918 bis 1933*, Kunst und Dokumentation 13, Städtische Kunsthalle Mann-
    heim (zgl. Diss. Freie Univ. Berlin), Berlin 1994, S. 34.
9   Im selben Jahr musste Falk die Liquidation seiner Firma betreiben – siehe
    den Text von Inge Herold in diesem Buch, auch zum weiteren Lebensverlauf
    des Ehepaares Falk.

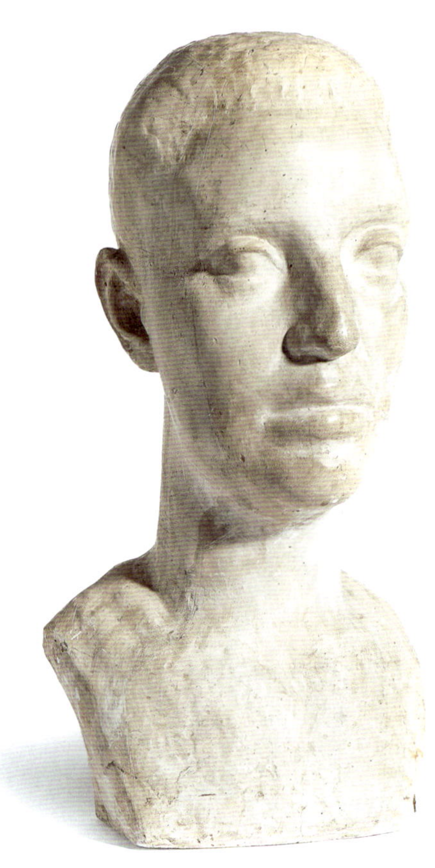

11 | **Wilhelm Lehmbruck,** *Bildnisbüste Sally Falk /*
Portrait Bust of Sally Falk, **1916,** Kunsthalle Mannheim

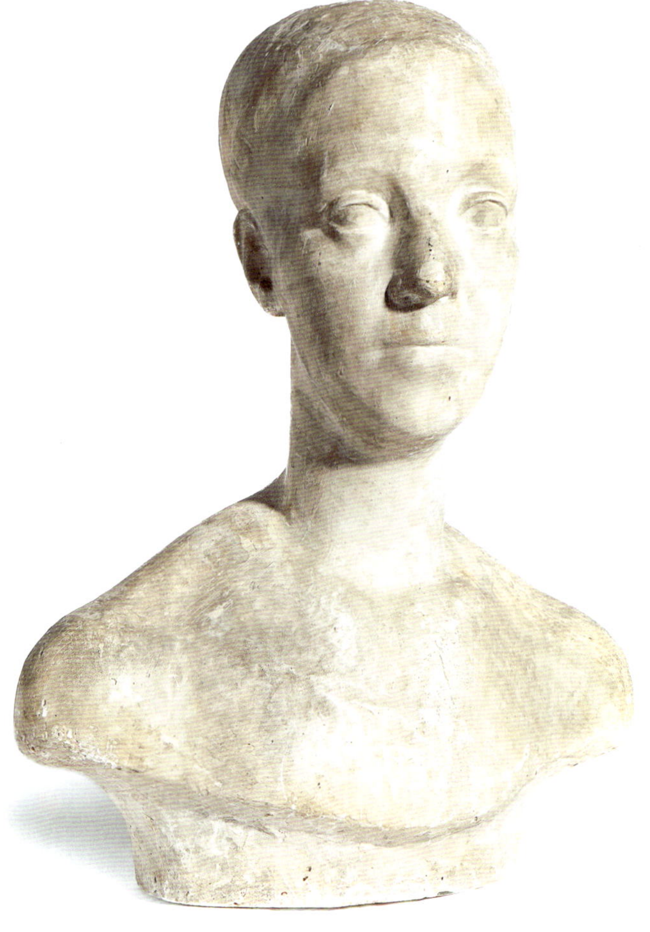

12 | **Wilhelm Lehmbruck,** *Bildnisbüste Frau Adèle Falk /*
Portrait Bust of Adèle Falk, **1916,** Kunsthalle Mannheim

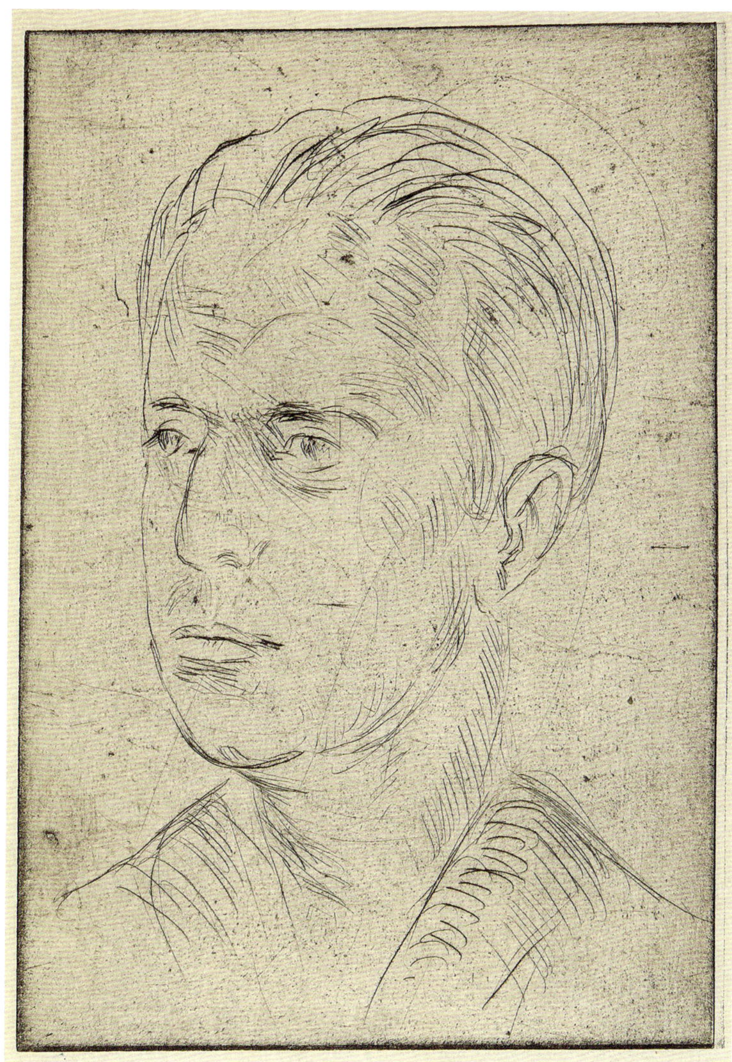 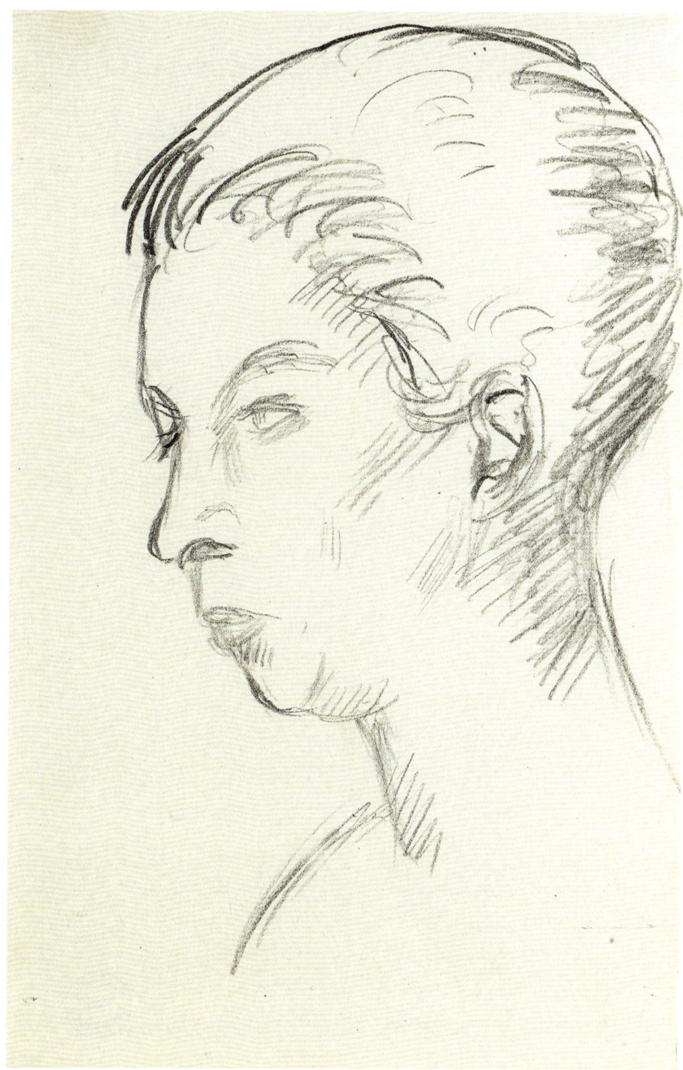

13 | **Wilhelm Lehmbruck,** *Porträt Sally Falk* /
Portrait of Sally Falk, **1916,** Kunsthalle Mannheim

14 | **Wilhelm Lehmbruck,** *Porträtkopf Frau F.* /
Portrait Head of Mrs. F., **1916,** Staatsgalerie Stuttgart

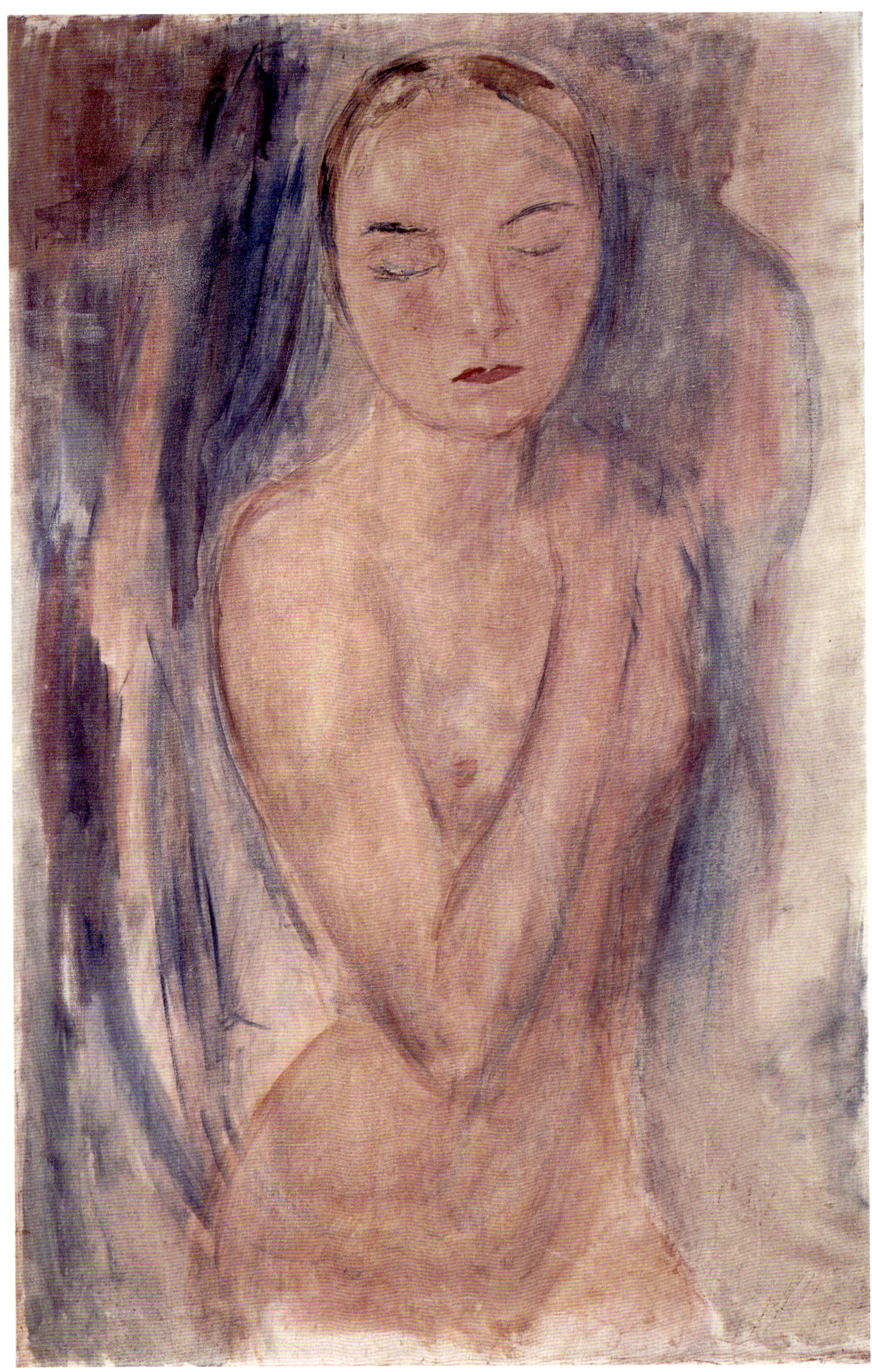

15 | **Wilhelm Lehmbruck, _Junges Mädchen (Martha)_** / _Young Girl (Martha)_, **1912,** Lehmbruck Museum, Duisburg

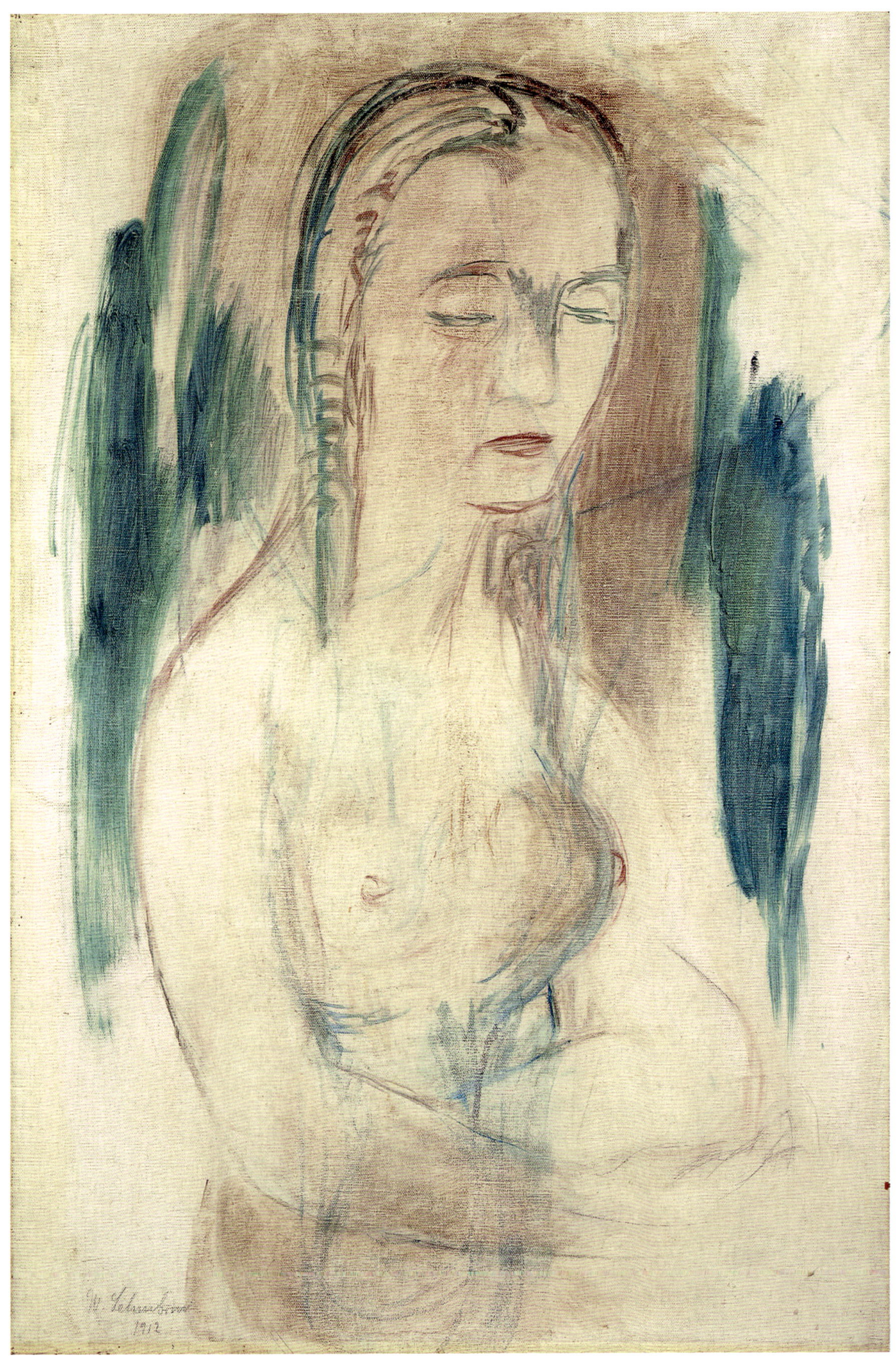

16 | **Wilhelm Lehmbruck,** *Brustbild eines weiblichen Aktes* / *Head and Shoulders of a Female Nude,* **1912,** Lehmbruck Museum, Duisburg

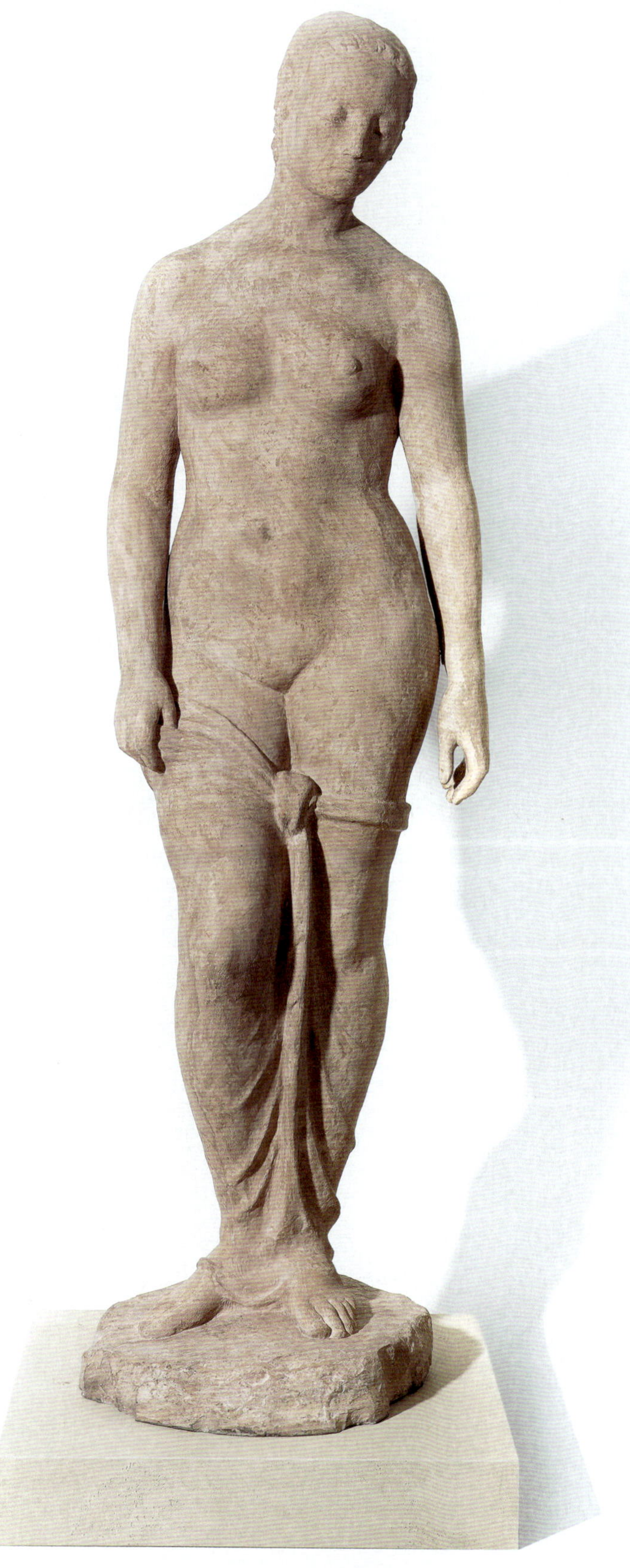

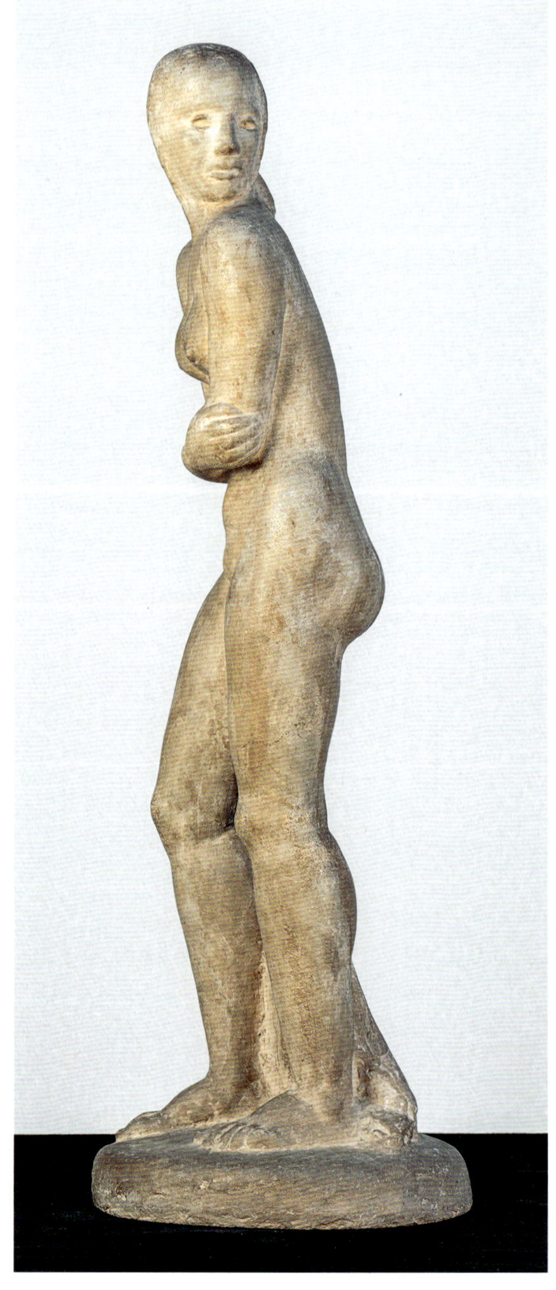

17 | **Wilhelm Lehmbruck,** *Große Stehende* /
Tall Standing Woman, **1910,** Kunsthalle Mannheim

18 | **Wilhelm Lehmbruck,** *Rückblickende* /
Woman Looking Back, **1914,** Kurpfälzisches Museum, Heidelberg

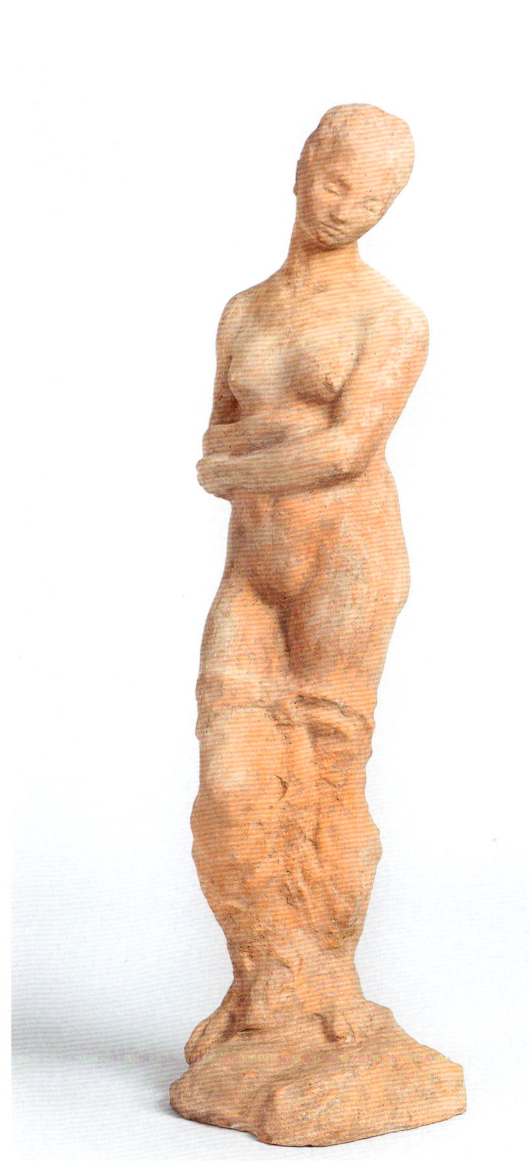

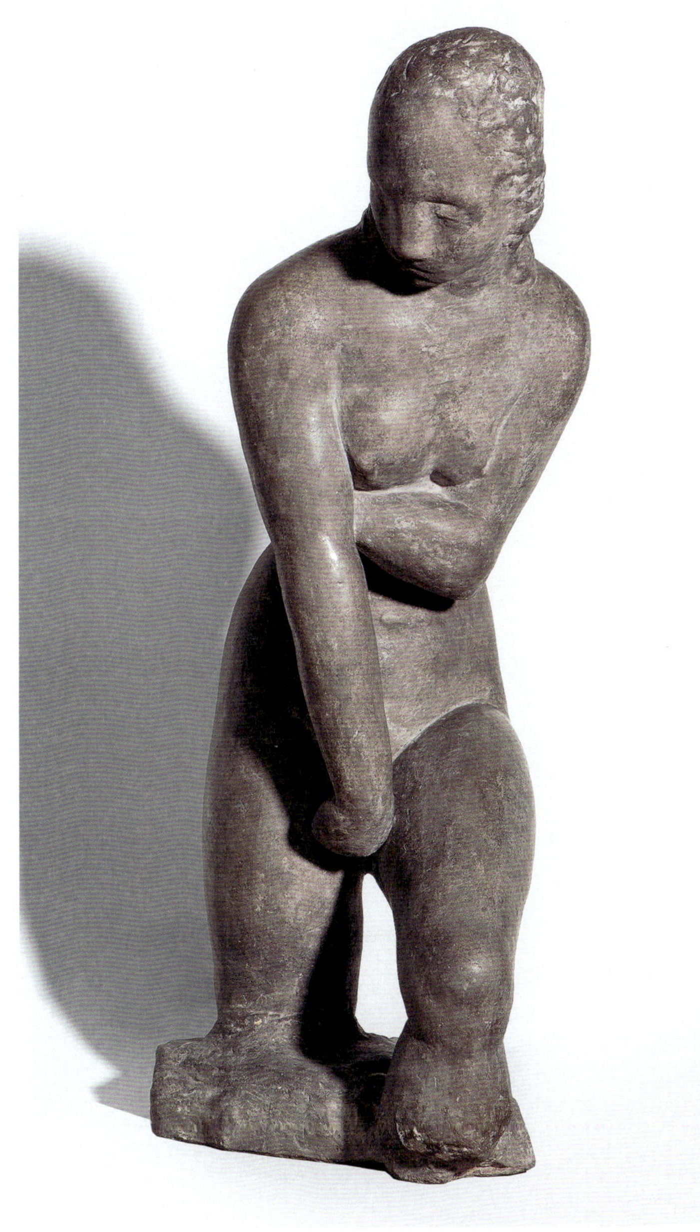

19 | Wilhelm Lehmbruck, *Kleine Sinnende* /
Small Contemplative Woman, **1910/11,** Kunsthalle Mannheim

20 | Wilhelm Lehmbruck, *Badende* /
Bathing Woman, **1913,** Kunsthalle Mannheim

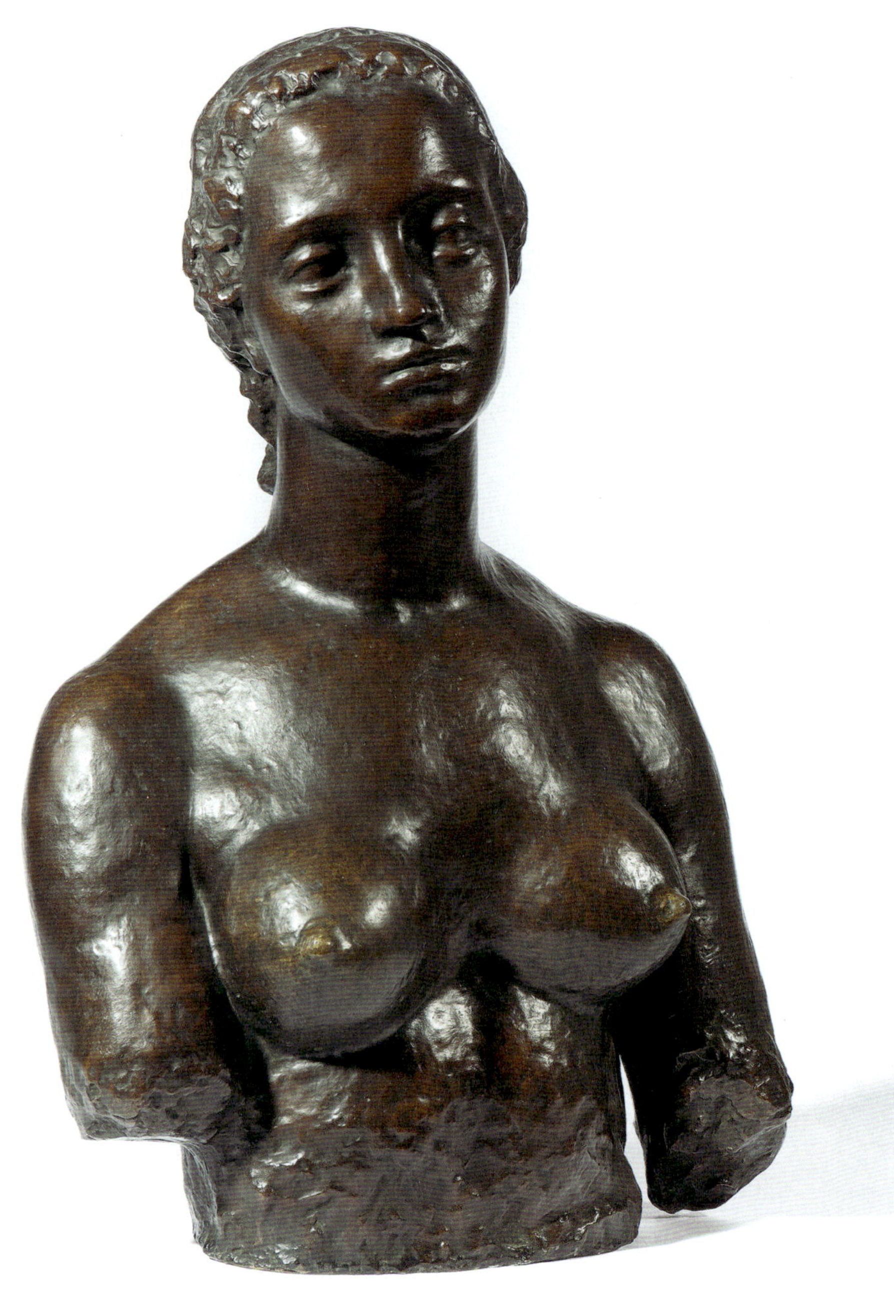

21 | **Wilhelm Lehmbruck, *Frauenbüste (Büste Frau L.)* /**
Bust of Woman (Bust Mrs L.), **1910,** Kunsthalle Mannheim

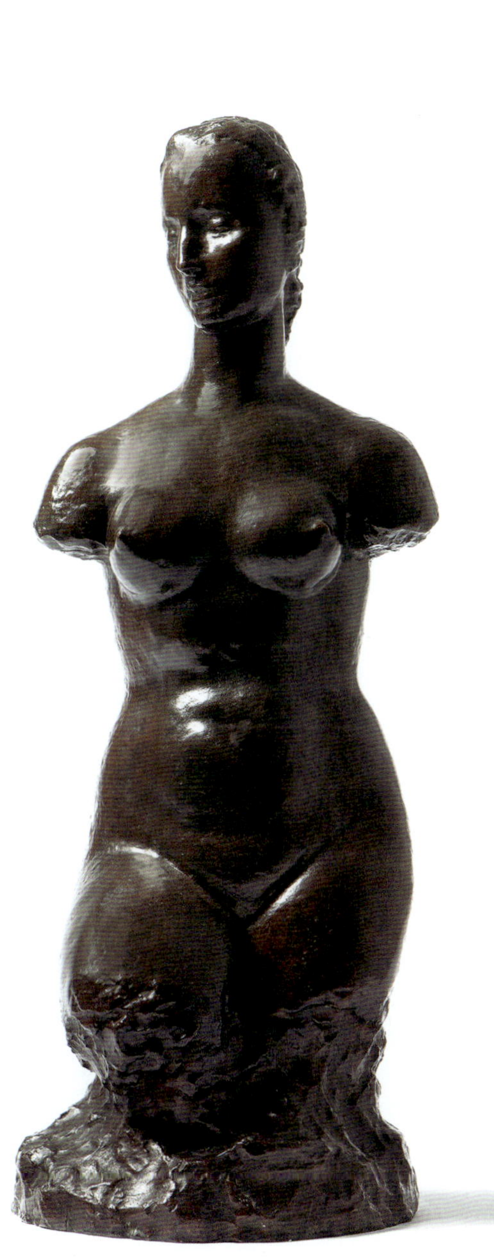

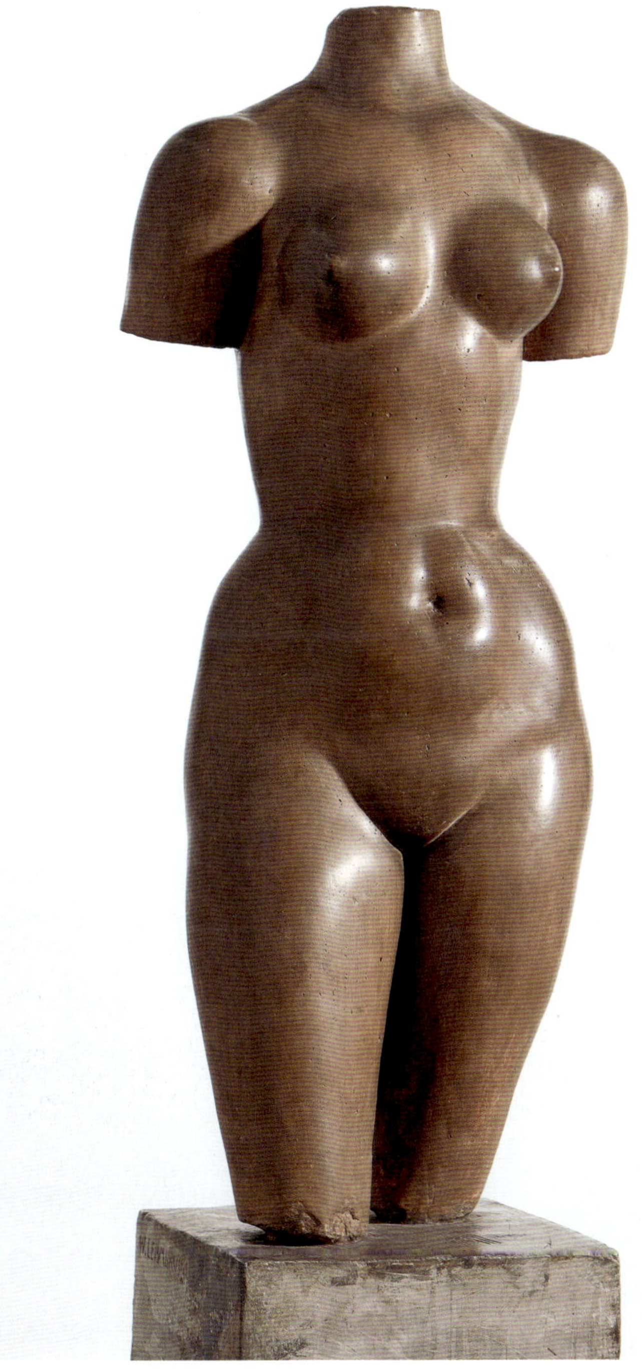

22 | **Wilhelm Lehmbruck,** *Kleiner weiblicher Torso, sog. Hagener Torso* /
Small Female Torso, "Torso From Hagen", **1910/11,** Kunsthalle Mannheim

23 | **Wilhelm Lehmbruck,** *Torso der Großen Sinnenden* /
Torso of the Tall Contemplative Woman, **1913/14,** Kunsthalle Mannheim

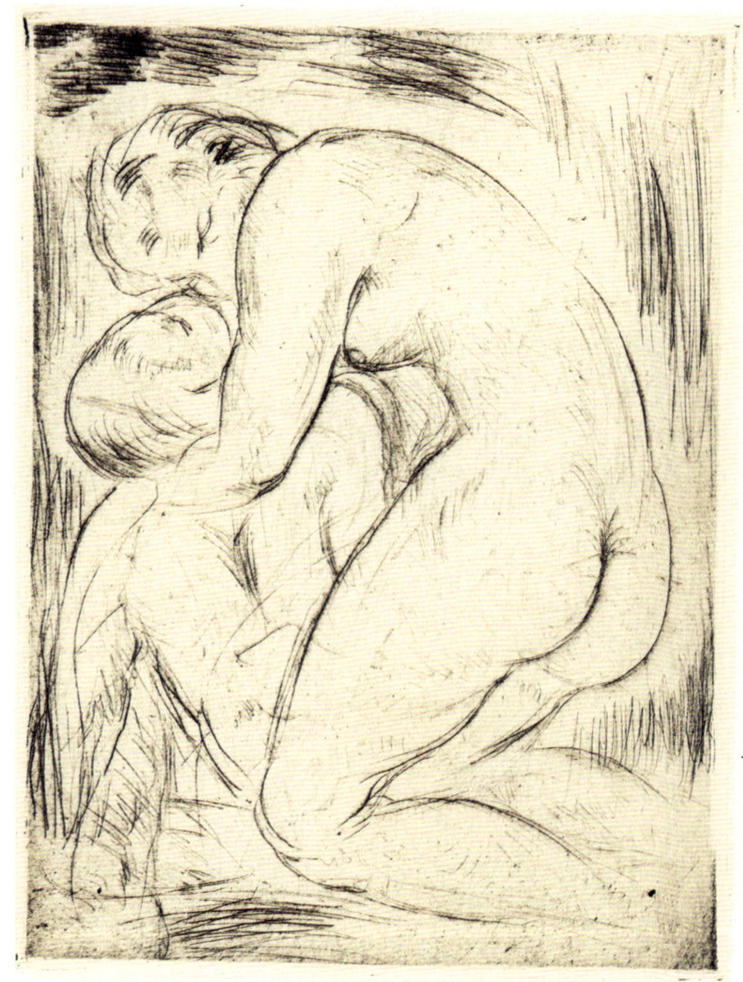

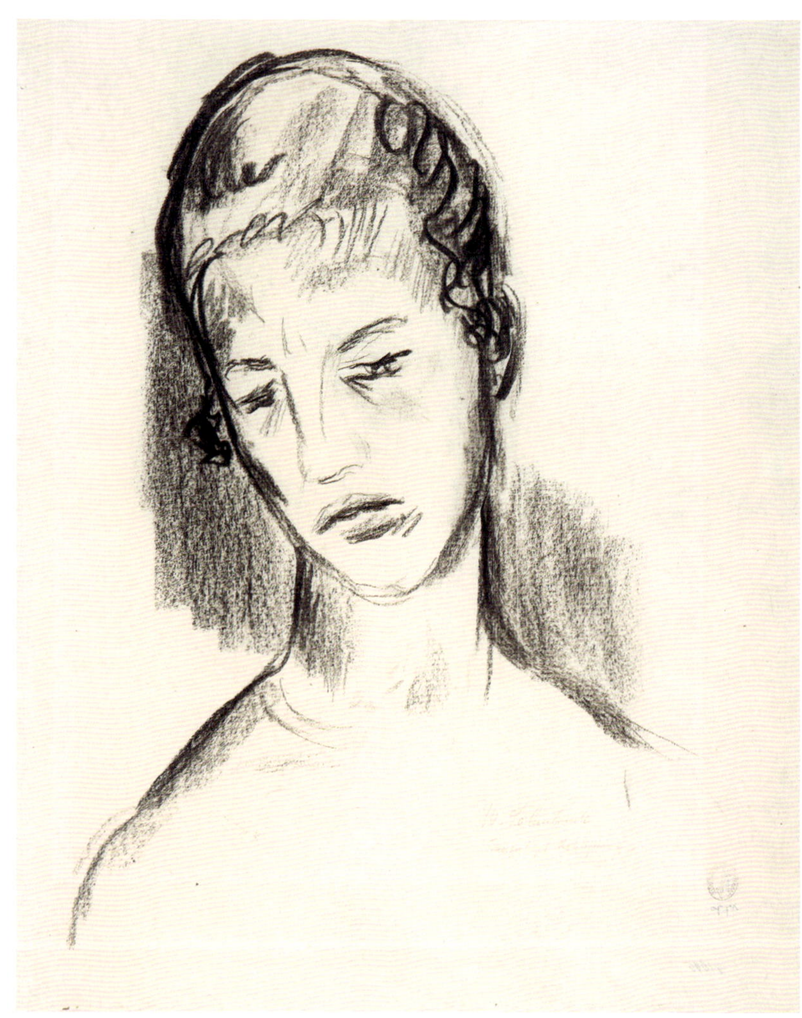

24 | **Wilhelm Lehmbruck, *Der tote Mann* /**
The Dead Man, **1914,** Kunsthalle Mannheim

25 | **Wilhelm Lehmbruck, *Frauenkopf* /**
Head of a Woman, **1916,** Kunsthalle Mannheim

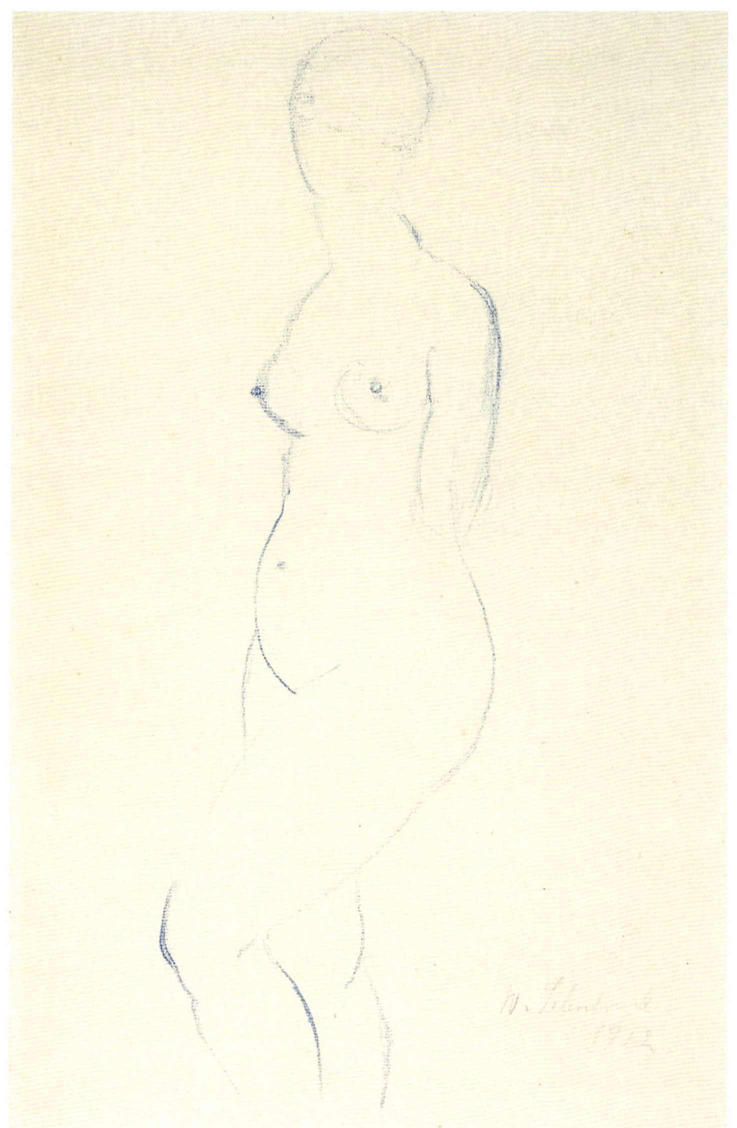

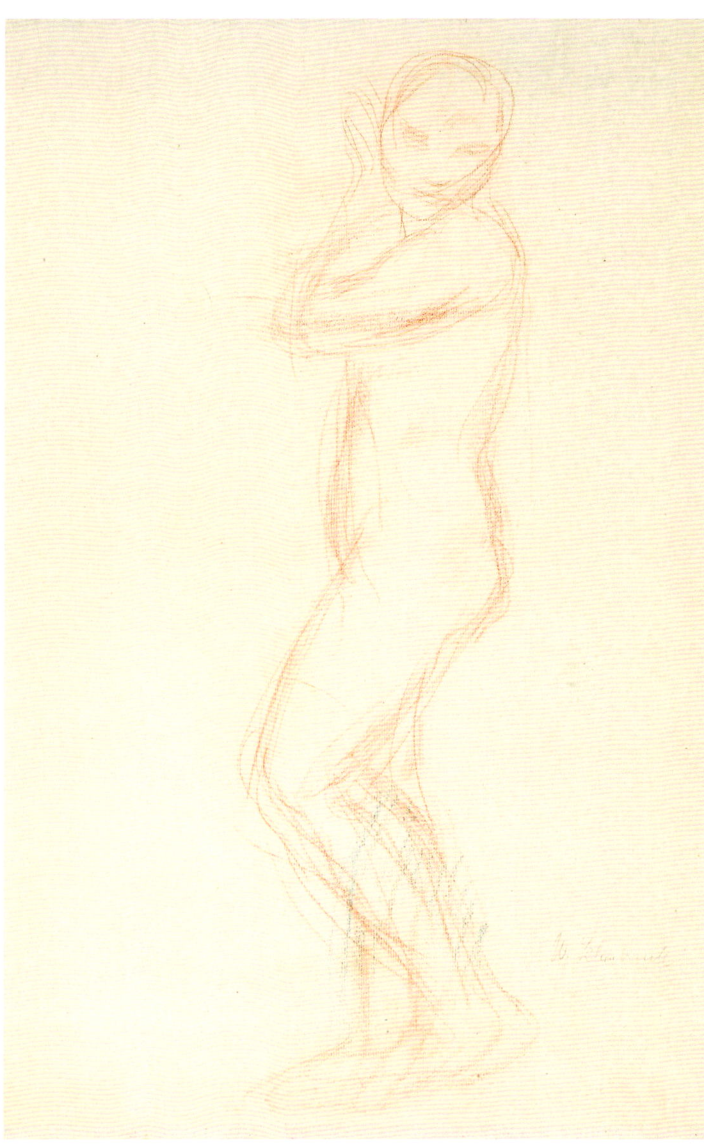

New Religious Art: Mannheim's Contribution to Expressionism

Ursula Drahoss

In 1918, Gustav Friedrich Hartlaub opened the exhibition *Neue religiöse Kunst* (New Religious Art) at the Kunsthalle Mannheim with the intention of showing how much artists of Expressionism emphasized the expression of a deeper religious feeling in their art against the backdrop of World War I and without any connections to church or denomination. Dissatisfaction with the religious art of the recent past had been summed up by Ludwig Meidner in his letter in response to Hartlaub's invitation to participate in the exhibition, saying that "everything religious that art of the past decades has produced [is] purely artistic and remote from God."[1] (p. 106, fig. 32)

The break with the art of Impressionism, which was based on external optical stimuli, and the embrace of "the perceived internal value"[2] had already begun in 1909 when Emil Nolde submitted religious paintings with his application to participate in an exhibition of the Berlin Secession that were rejected by the jury chaired by Max Liebermann. The subsequent dispute between Nolde and Liebermann peaked in the dividing conflict between the artists who saw themselves as the Expressionist avant-garde and the defenders of Impressionism based on the French model.

A few years later, the exhibition in Mannheim in 1918 conceived by Hartlaub was intended to show how a new, deeper, spiritual meaning was expressed in contemporary art. This was also clearly reflected in the overall selection of works for the exhibition, which nevertheless had no closed, strict program and whose themes emphasized not so much Biblical stories as the Christian mystery with examples of more artists once again taking up depictions of the Crucifixion, the Lord's Supper and Pentecost, Baptism and Madonnas.

Like his superior Fritz Wichert, who as the first director of the Kunsthalle Mannheim had until now been very open to Impressionism and modern art, Hartlaub, too, initially had reservations about Expressionism. Only making the acquaintance of the poet Theodor Däubler in 1916 caused Hartlaub to warm up to this new art.[3] He began planning the acquisition of Expressionist art and thinking about pertinent exhibitions. In order to realize his exhibition project, Hartlaub wrote to artists and collections to ask for works. In 1918, visitors then had two months to familiarize themselves with the new significance of religion in Expressionist art in a presentation of more than 200 paintings, drawings, and prints.[4] After Mannheim, parts of the exhibition were also shown at the Galerie Ernst Arnold in Dresden.

A slender exhibition catalogue (p. 107, fig. 33) names all of the artists who participated in Hartlaub's project and their works on view,[5] but the later fate of these exhibits permits only a very fragmentary reconstruction of the show . Many of the works exhibited fell victim to the confiscations by the National Socialists in 1937, ended up in other collections, or are considered lost.[6]

Emil Nolde occupied the most important place in the exhibition. He was a pioneer of the revival of the religious image in Expressionism and for Hartlaub the "lonely fixed star in the Expressionist sky."[7] The paintings that had been rejected by the jury of the Berlin Secession in 1909 could also be seen. These works had been considered expressing religious subject matter inappropriately in the form of figures resembling peasants and grotesquely exaggerated characters in contrasting colors and simplified forms.

Among other works, Karl Schmidt-Rottluff contributed to the *Neue religiöse Kunst* exhibition colorfully painted masks of chased metal that Hartlaub felt conveyed a sense of the Egyptian/ Ethiopian and, in his view, adopted the primal visage of an archaic religiousness in the broadest sense that was devoid of Eurocentric or Hellenist ideas.[8]

Neue religiöse Kunst: Mannheims Beitrag zum Expressionismus

Ursula Drahoss

1918 eröffnete Gustav Friedrich Hartlaub in der Kunsthalle Mannheim die Ausstellung *Neue religiöse Kunst* mit der Absicht zu zeigen, wie sehr die Künstler*innen des Expressionismus vor dem Hintergrund des Ersten Weltkrieges jenseits kirchlicher und konfessioneller Bindungen den Ausdruck eines tieferen religiösen Empfindens in den Vordergrund ihrer Kunst rückten. Die Unzufriedenheit mit der religiösen Kunst der jüngeren Vergangenheit brachte Ludwig Meidner in seinem Antwortschreiben auf Hartlaubs Einladung zur Teilnahme an der Ausstellung auf den Punkt, wenn er meinte, dass „[…] alles, was die Kunst der letzten Jahrzehnte an Religiösem hervorgebracht hat […] artistisch und fern von Gott"[1], sei (S. 106, Abb. 32). Der Bruch mit einer an äußeren optischen Reizen orientierten Kunst des Impressionismus und die Hinwendung „zum empfundenen inneren Wert"[2] hatte bereits 1909 begonnen, als Emil Nolde sich mit religiösen Bildern um die Teilnahme an einer Ausstellung der Berliner Secession beworben hatte, von der Jury unter dem Vorsitz von Max Liebermann aber abgelehnt worden war. Der nachfolgende Streit zwischen Nolde und Liebermann gipfelte in der spaltenden Auseinandersetzung jener Künstler, die sich als expressionistische Avantgarde verstanden, mit den Verfechtern des Impressionismus nach französischem Vorbild.

Die von Hartlaub 1918 in Mannheim konzipierte Ausstellung sollte ein paar Jahre später aufzeigen, wie sich in der zeitgenössischen Kunst ein neuer, tieferer, spiritueller Sinn ausdrückte. Dies spiegelte sich in der Gesamtauswahl der Werke für die Ausstellung deutlich wider, dennoch hatte sie kein in sich abgeschlossenes und stringentes Programm. Es ging thematisch weniger um die biblischen Geschichten an sich als vielmehr um das christliche Mysterium, wie die Künstler*innen es neu formulierten in den nun wieder vermehrt aufgegriffenen Darstellungen von Kreuzigung, Abendmahl und Pfingsten, Taufe und Madonnen.

Wie sein Vorgesetzter Fritz Wichert, der als erster Direktor der Mannheimer Kunsthalle dem Impressionismus und der Kunst der Moderne bis hierhin sehr aufgeschlossen gegenüberstand, hatte auch Hartlaub zunächst Vorbehalte gegenüber dem Expressionismus. Erst die Bekanntschaft mit dem Dichter Theodor Däubler 1916 brachte Hartlaub dazu, sich mit dieser neuen Kunst anzufreunden.[3] Er begann, Ankäufe expressionistischer Kunst zu planen und über entsprechende Ausstellungen nachzudenken. Um sein Ausstellungsprojekt zu realisieren, schrieb Hartlaub Künstler*innen und Kunstsammler*innen an und bat um Werke. Im Jahr 1918 konnten sich die Besucher*innen schließlich zwei Monate lang anhand von über 200 Gemälden, Zeichnungen und Grafiken mit der neuen Bedeutung des Religiösen in der Kunst des Expressionismus vertraut machen.[4] Nach Mannheim wurden Teile der Ausstellung auch in der Galerie Ernst Arnold in Dresden gezeigt.

Ein schmaler Ausstellungskatalog (S. 107, Abb. 33) nennt zwar sämtliche an Hartlaubs Projekt beteiligten Künstler*innen und ihre ausgestellten Werke,[5] doch lässt das weitere Schicksal der Exponate nur eine sehr lückenhafte Rekonstruktion der Ausstellung zu. Viele der ausgestellten Werke fielen 1937 den Beschlagnahmungen unter der NS-Kulturpolitik zum Opfer, gelangten in andere Sammlungen oder gelten als verschollen.[6]

Emil Nolde nahm in der Ausstellung den wichtigsten Platz ein. Er war der Wegbereiter der Wiederbelebung des religiösen Bildes im Expressionismus und für Hartlaub der „einsame Fixstern am Expressionisten-Himmel"[7]. Von ihm waren in der Ausstellung auch die 1909 von der Jury der Berliner Secession abgelehnten Bilder zu sehen, denen man vorgeworfen hatte, mit bäuerlich anmutenden Figuren sowie ins Groteske übersteigerten

Other artists referred explicitly to the art of the Middle Ages when asked by Hartlaub to submit contributions for this exhibition. In their effort to break with the artistic tradition of modernism, they went back to anticlassical and antinaturalistic eras in art, such as Josef Weisz, who modeled his work on a fifteenth-century painting (cat. 28).

1 Ludwig Meidner to Hartlaub, September 12, 1917, Archive Kunsthalle Mannheim / MARCHIVUM.
2 Emil Nolde, *Jahre der Kämpfe*, 2nd ed. (Flensburg: C. Wolff, 1957), p. 109.
3 Karoline Hille, *Spuren der Moderne: Die Mannheimer Kunsthalle von 1918 bis 1933*, Kunst und Dokumentation 13, Städtische Kunsthalle Mannheim (also PhD diss. Freie Univ. Berlin) (Berlin: Akademie, 1994), p. 34.
4 *Neue religiöse Kunst (Malerei, Graphik, Zeichnung)*, ed. Gustav Hartlaub, exh. cat. (Mannheim: Kunsthalle Mannheim, 1918).
5 Ibid., pp. 5–17.
6 *Beschlagnahmt! Rückkehr der Meisterblätter*, ed. Thomas Köllhofer, Mathias Listl, and Ulrike Lorenz, exh. cat. (Mannheim: Kunsthalle Mannheim, 2019).
7 Hille, *Spuren der Moderne* (see note 3), p. 52.
8 Ibid., p. 48.

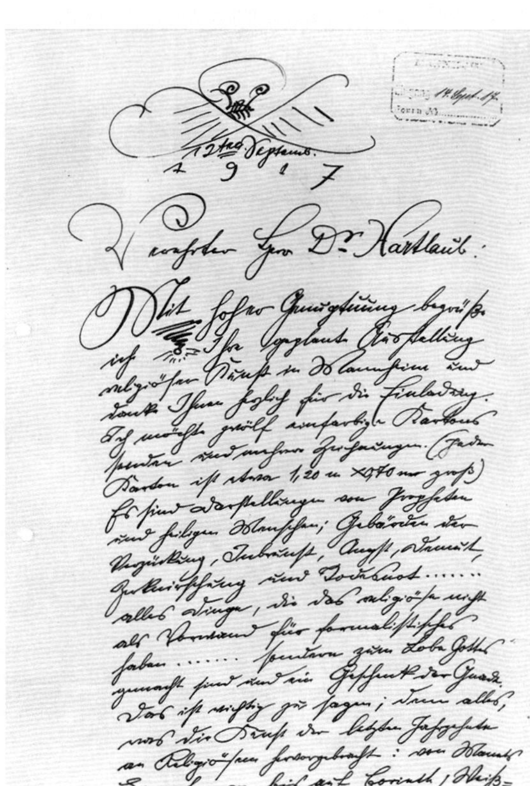

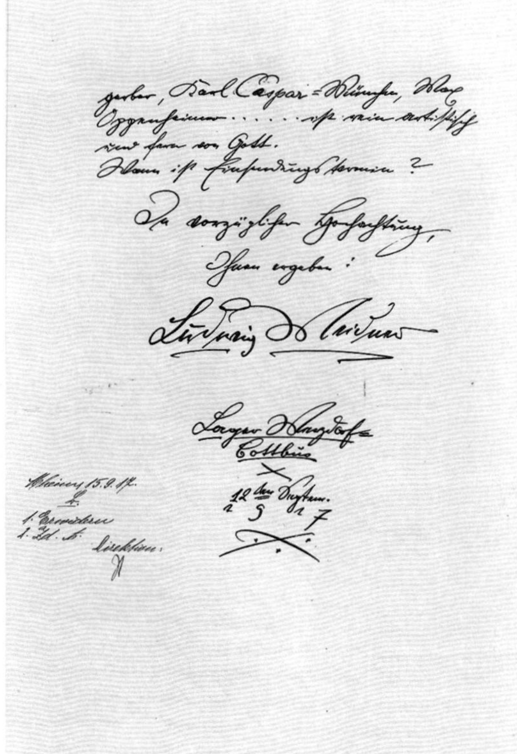

Abb./Fig. 32
Brief von / *Letter from* Ludwig Meidner an / *to* Gustav F. Hartlaub, 12. September 1917,
Archiv Kunsthalle Mannheim / MARCHIVUM

Charakteren in kontrastreichen Farben und vereinfachten Formen religiöse Inhalte unangemessen wiederzugeben.

Karl Schmidt-Rottluff trug für die Ausstellung *Neue religiöse Kunst* unter anderem mit in Metall getriebenen und farbig gefassten Masken bei, in denen Hartlaub eine ägyptisch-äthiopische Anmutung sah, die für ihn das Urgesicht einer im weitesten Sinn archaischen Religiosität aufgriff und nicht von eurozentristischen oder hellenistischen Vorstellungen geprägt war.[8]

Andere Künstler*innen wiederum bezogen sich explizit auf die Kunst des Mittelalters, als sie von Hartlaub aufgefordert wurden, Beiträge für diese Ausstellung einzureichen. In ihrem Bestreben, mit der Kunsttradition der Moderne zu brechen, griffen sie auf antiklassische und antinaturalistische Kunstepochen zurück und orientierten sich, wie zum Beispiel Josef Weisz, unter anderem am Vorbild der Malerei des 15. Jahrhunderts (Kat. 28).

1 Brief von Ludwig Meidner an Gustav F. Hartlaub vom 12. September 1917, Archiv der Kunsthalle Mannheim / MARCHIVUM.
2 Emil Nolde: *Jahre der Kämpfe,* Flensburg 1957, S. 109.
3 Karoline Hille: *Spuren der Moderne. Die Mannheimer Kunsthalle von 1918 bis 1933,* Kunst und Dokumentation 13, Städtische Kunsthalle Mannheim, (zgl. Diss. Freie Univ. Berlin), Berlin 1994, S. 34.
4 Kat. Ausst. *Neue religiöse Kunst (Malerei, Graphik, Zeichnung),* Städtische Kunsthalle Mannheim 1918, hrsg. v. Direktion i. V.: Dr. Hartlaub, Mannheim 1918.
5 Ebd., S. 5–17.
6 Kat. Ausst. *Beschlagnahmt! Rückkehr der Meisterblätter,* Kunsthalle Mannheim 2019, hrsg. v. Thomas Köllhofer, Mathias Listl, Ulrike Lorenz, Mannheim 2019.
7 Hille 1994 (wie Anm. 3), S. 52.
8 Ebd., S. 48.

Abb./Fig. 33
Städtische Kunsthalle Mannheim, Ausstellungskatalog/ *Exhibition catalogue* **Neue religiöse Kunst** *(New Religious Art),* **1918,** Archiv Kunsthalle Mannheim

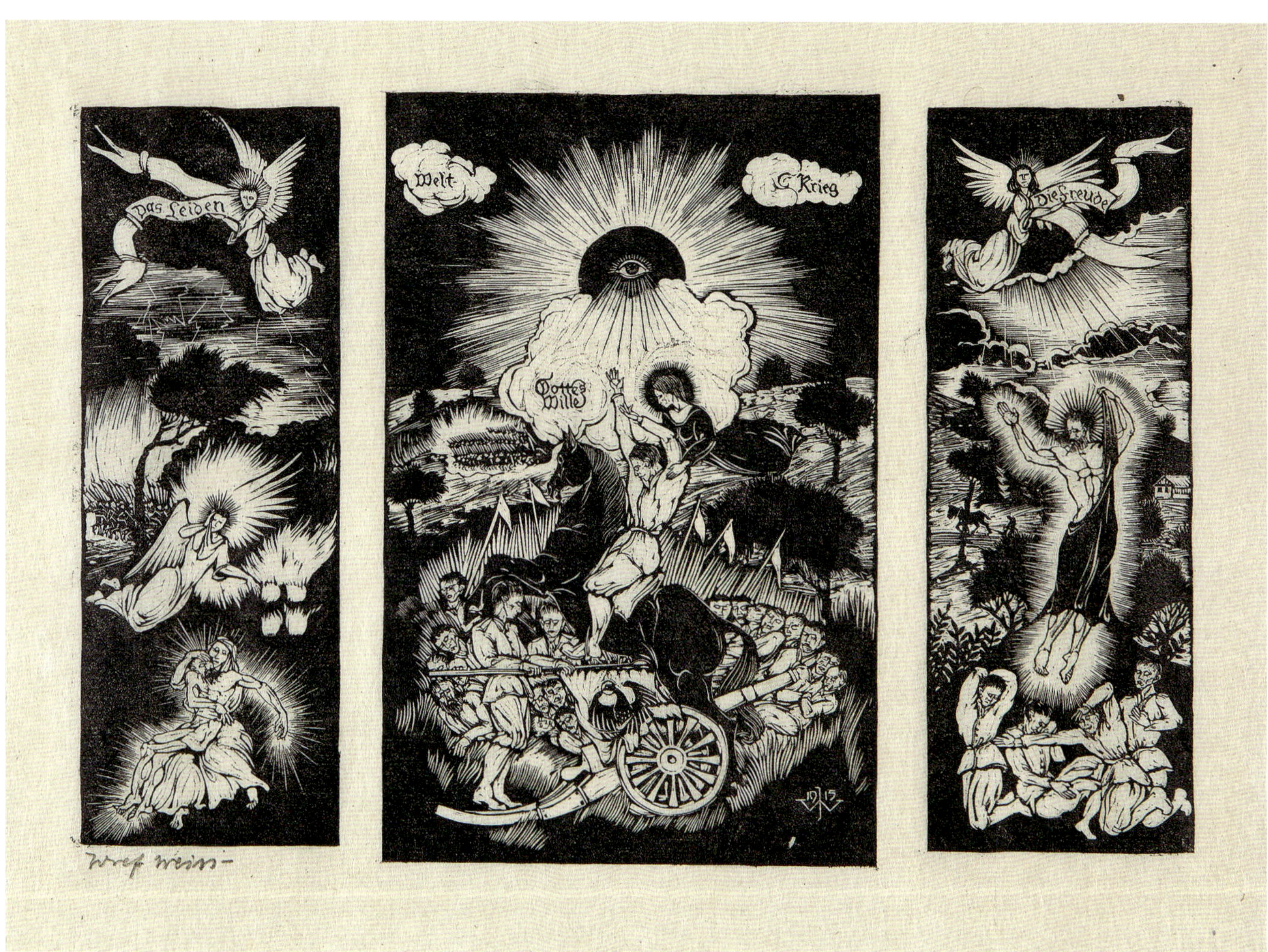

28 | **Josef Weisz,** *Altarbild* **(Triptychon)** / *Altarpiece* (Triptych), **1915,** Kunsthalle Mannheim

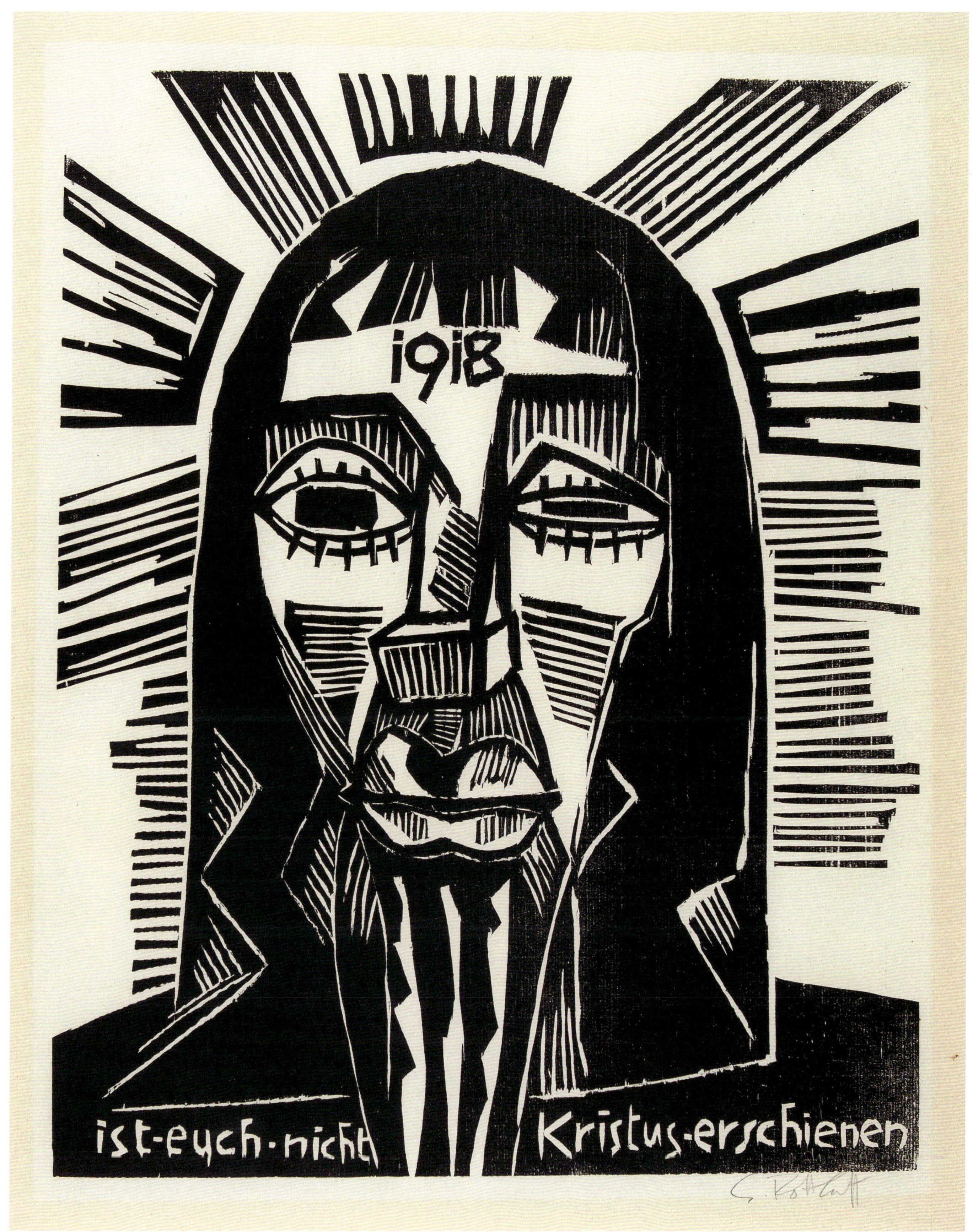

29 | Karl Schmidt-Rottluff, *Kristus* / *Christ*, **1918,** Kunsthalle Mannheim

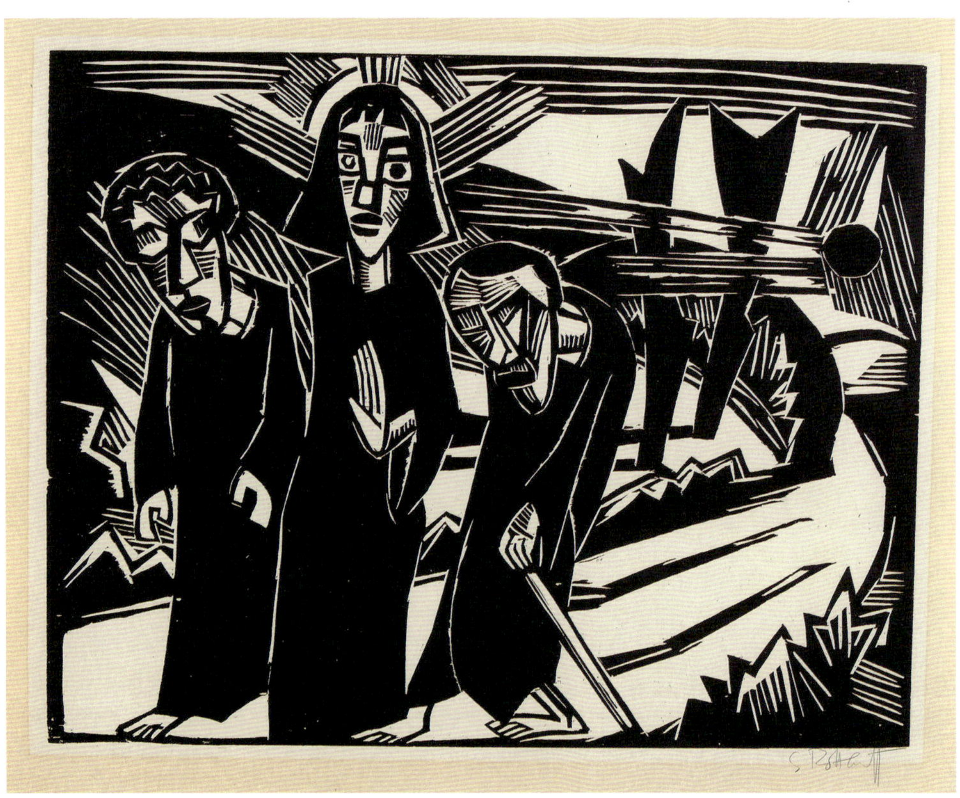

30 | **Karl Schmidt-Rottluff,** *Gang nach Emmaus* / *Road to Emmaus,* **1918,** Kunsthalle Mannheim

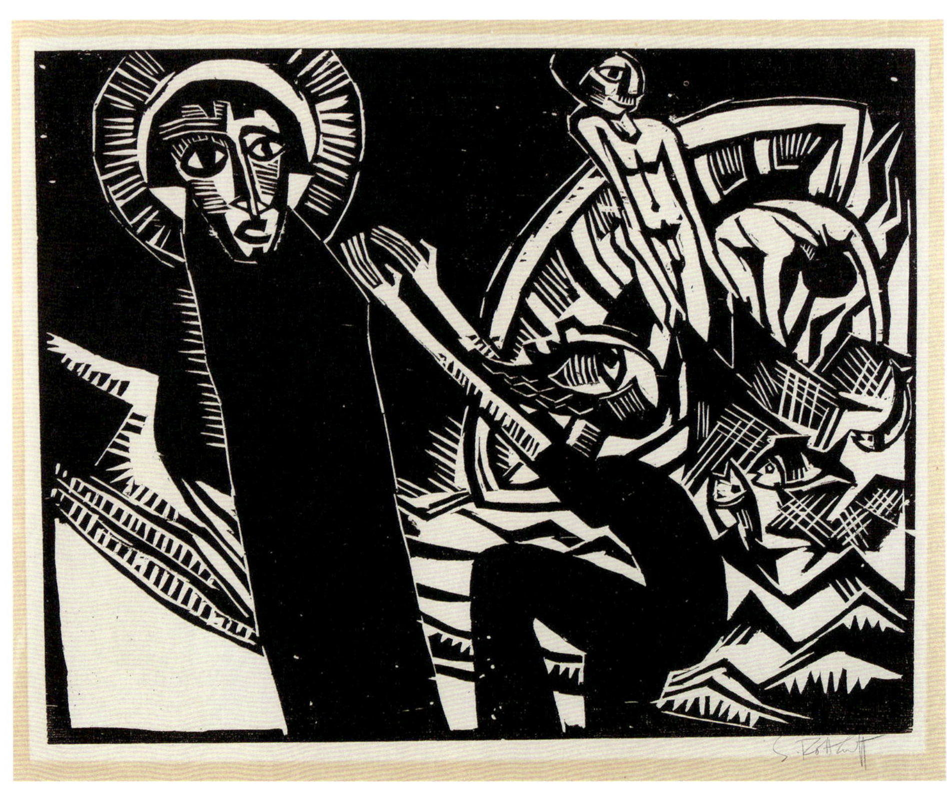

31 | **Karl Schmidt-Rottluff,** *Petri Fischzug* / *Miraculous Catch of Fishes,* **1918,** Kunsthalle Mannheim

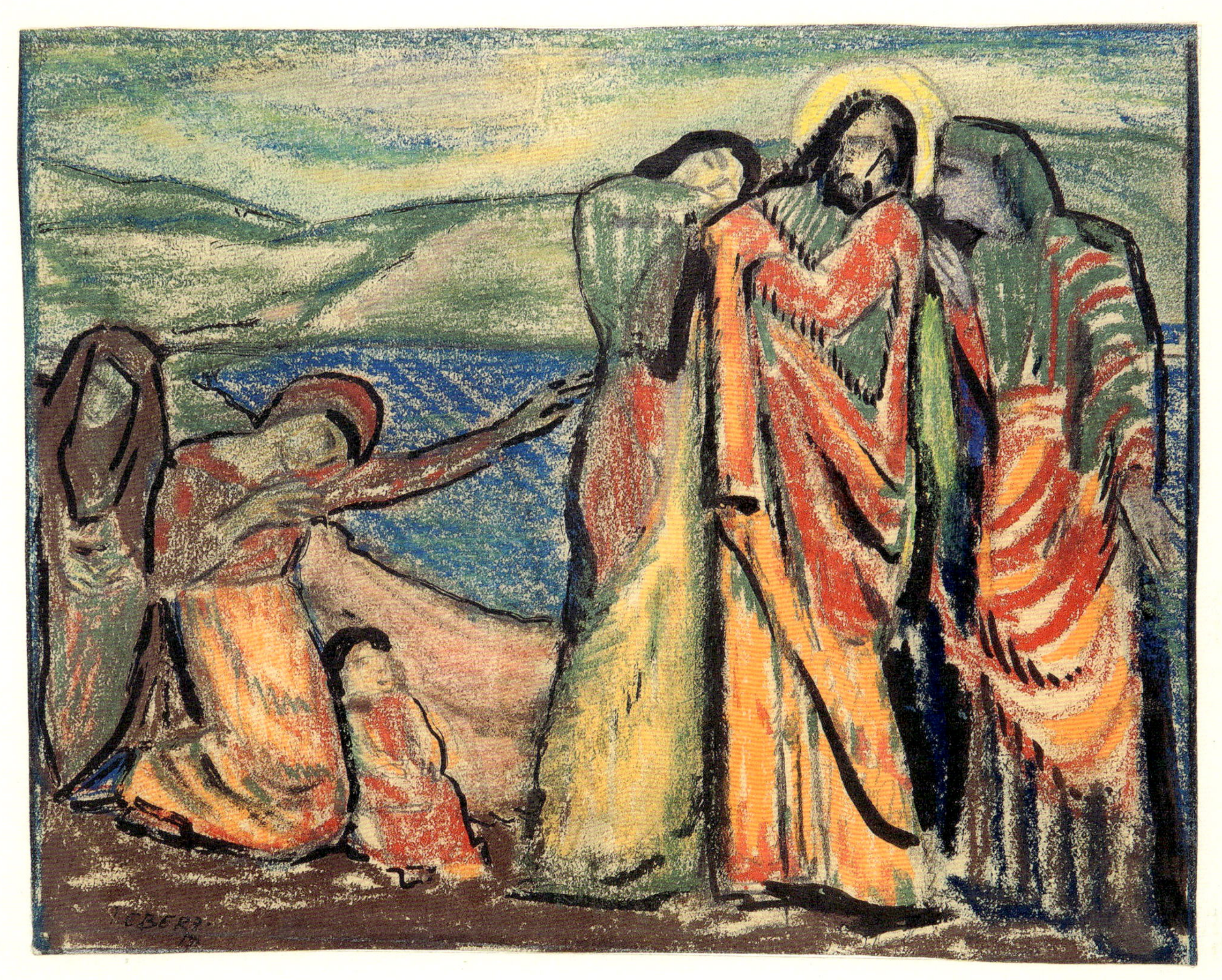

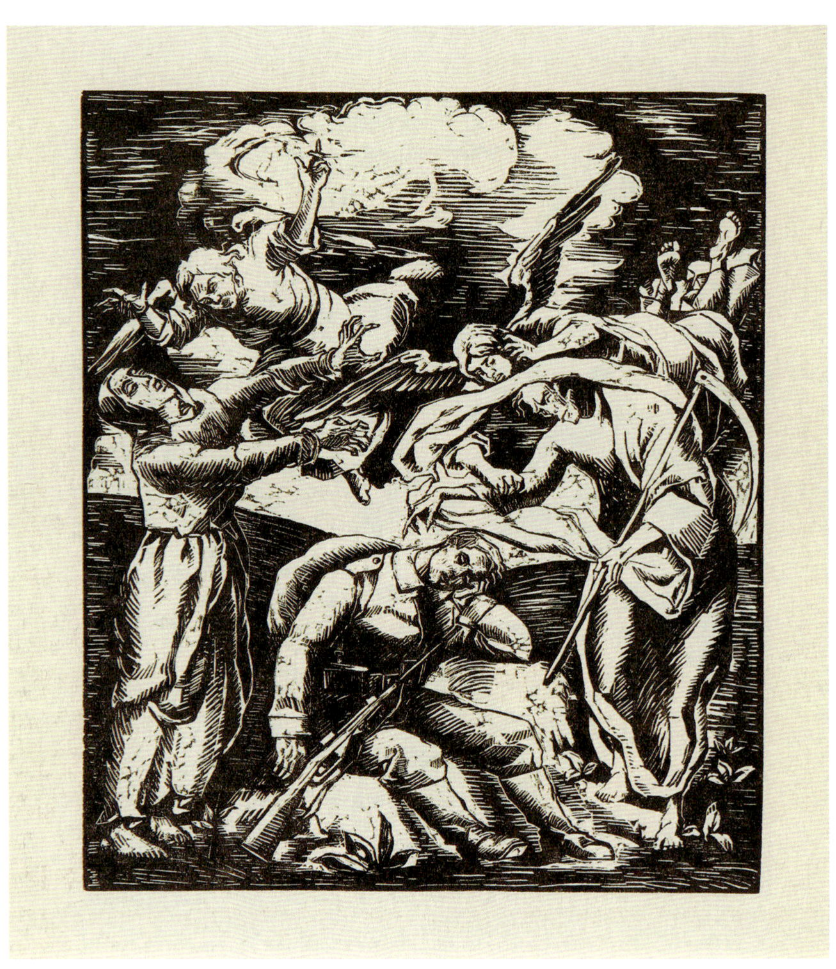

ⴲ | **Hilde Schindler,** *Der Krieg* / *The War,* **1915,** Kunsthalle Mannheim

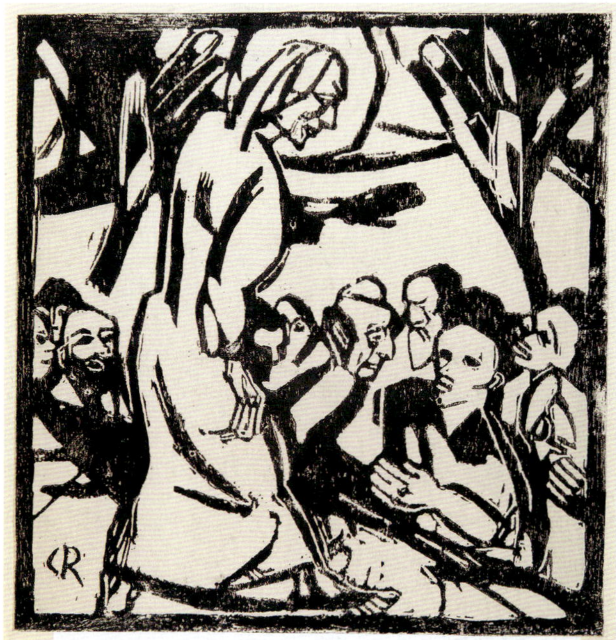

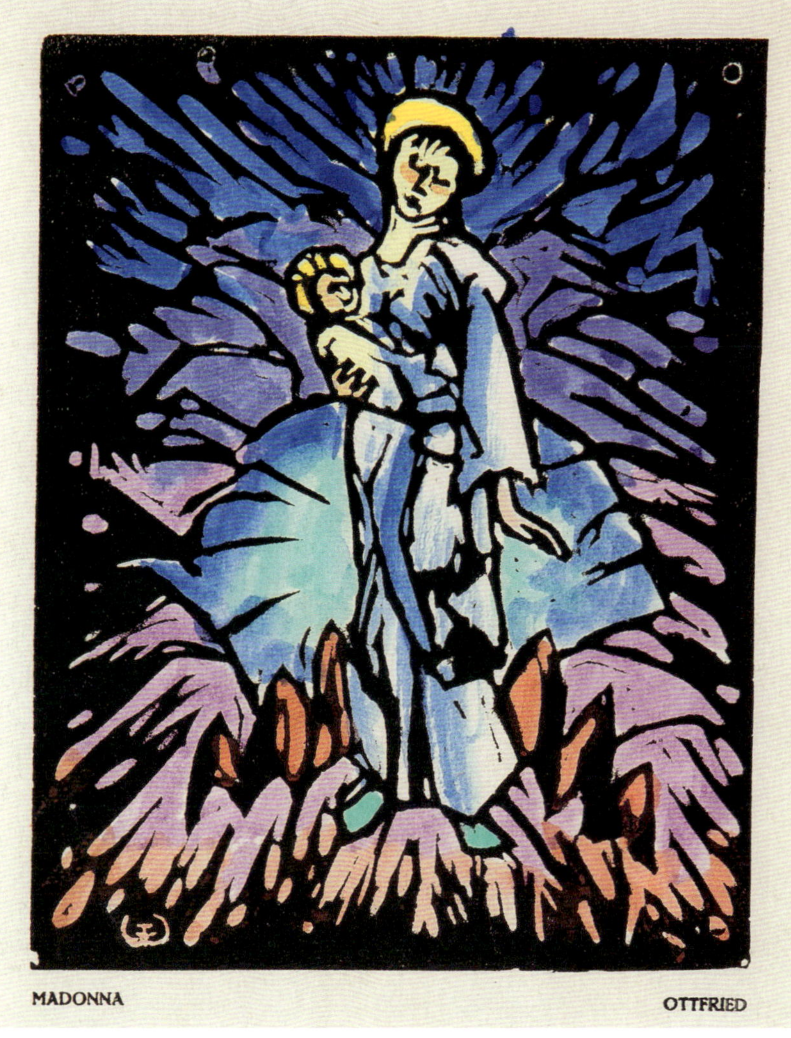

34 | **Christian Rohlfs,** *Bergpredigt* / *Sermon on the Mount,* **1916,** Kunsthalle Mannheim

35 | **Wilfried Otto,** *Madonna* / *Virgin,* **1918,** Kunsthalle Mannheim

Alfred Flechtheim, Herbert Tannenbaum, and Rudolf Probst: Art Dealers for Mannheim

Dorotea Lorenz

Art dealers played a very important role in the spread of modern art in the early twentieth century: one need only think of such prominent names as Daniel-Henry Kahnweiler, who was born in Mannheim and was a pioneer of Cubism in Paris, or Herwarth Walden and Paul Cassirer as promoters of the avant-garde in Berlin.

As mediators between artists and collectors in Mannheim, Herbert Tannenbaum and later Rudolf Probst in particular contributed crucially to supporting art movements and the people that would come to be considered major figures of classical modernism. Alfred Flechtheim's activity had a national effect on the perception of contemporary art. In addition, all three were essential figures before and after World War II in getting works to the Kunsthalle Mannheim and building its collection.

Alfred Flechtheim

Alfred Flechtheim (1878–1937) was perhaps the most colorful figure among the gallerists of the early twentieth century. He was from a family of wealthy German-Jewish merchants from Westphalia. Instead of pursuing a career as a grain dealer in his father's business, he became an art dealer with support from Paul Cassirer. His paths took him to Paris, Berlin, and London before he opened the Galerie für alte und neue Kunst (Gallery for Old and New Art) in Düsseldorf in 1913. Branches in Berlin, Frankfurt am Main, Cologne, and Vienna followed. He soon became a key figure on the international art market, representing artists such as George Grosz, Pablo Picasso, Paul Gauguin, Paul Cézanne, and many others who would later enter the canon of modern art. Flechtheim was famous for the high quality of his exhibitions, which altered awareness of contemporary art. In his Berlin gallery in the spring of 1928, he organized a large Max Beckmann exhibition that was then shown at the Städtische Kunsthalle Mannheim as well. The director of the Kunsthalle Mannheim at the time, Gustav Friedrich Hartlaub, acquired Beckmann's *Stilleben mit Holzscheiten* (Still Life with Firewood) through Alfred Flechtheim's gallery in Düsseldorf.[1] Moreover, the gallerist and the director always maintained a lively interchange.[2]

Already by 1929, the art dealer was faced with a sharp financial decline caused by the Great Depression. The systematic defamation of Flechtheim and the condemnation of the art he was selling forced him to emigrate via Switzerland and France to London, where he died impoverished in 1937. The artworks preserved in his gallery were lost, as was his private art collection, which was confiscated by the Gestapo after the death of his widow, Betty, in 1941. Numerous works handled by Flechtheim are now in museums in Germany and abroad.[3]

Rudolf Belling created an impressive bronze portrait sculpture of Alfred Flechtheim in 1927 (cat. 36). The art dealer's head is not rendered in its complete form but rather almost entirely diffused. Only a few lines that lead from the eyes by way of the nose to the mouth and finally the pedestal come together into an unconventional likeness of Flechtheim.

Herbert Tannenbaum

Herbert Tannenbaum (1892–1958), the son of German-Jewish parents, attended secondary school in Mannheim and at the urging of his father studied law in Heidelberg and Munich from 1910 onward. His interests, however, were in film, art, and theater. Already from 1911, he was a member of the Freier Bund zur Einbürgerung der bildenden Kunst (Free League to Establish Fine Art) that Fritz Wichert had founded in Mannheim, and he gave his first lectures there. In World War I, he was deployed on the Western Front, which foiled his plan to begin studying art history in Berlin.[4]

In 1920, he opened his own art and bookstore in Mannheim: Das Kunsthaus (p. 31, fig. 13), where he sold books, journals, and

Alfred Flechtheim, Herbert Tannenbaum und Rudolf Probst: Kunsthändler für Mannheim

Dorotea Lorenz

Die Rolle von Kunsthändler*innen bei der Verbreitung moderner Kunst im frühen 20. Jahrhundert war von großer Bedeutung: Man denkt an prominente Namen wie den in Mannheim geborenen Daniel-Henry Kahnweiler, Wegbereiter des Kubismus in Paris, an Herwarth Walden oder Paul Cassirer als Förderer der Avantgarde in Berlin.

Als Vermittler zwischen Künstler*innen und Sammler*innen trugen in Mannheim insbesondere Herbert Tannenbaum und später Rudolf Probst maßgeblich dazu bei, Kunstströmungen und jene Werke zu fördern, die später als die Hauptwerke der klassischen Moderne gelten sollten. Alfred Flechtheims Tätigkeit wirkte sich deutschlandweit auf die Wahrnehmung zeitgenössischer Kunst aus. Darüber hinaus waren alle drei vor und nach dem Zweiten Weltkrieg entscheidende Akteure bei der Vermittlung von Werken an die Kunsthalle Mannheim und beim Aufbau ihrer Sammlung.

Alfred Flechtheim

Alfred Flechtheim (1878–1937) war die vielleicht schillerndste Figur unter den Galeristen im frühen 20. Jahrhundert. Er stammte aus einer wohlhabenden jüdischen Kaufmannsfamilie aus Westfalen. Anstatt eine Karriere als Getreidehändler im väterlichen Betrieb zu verfolgen, wurde er mit Unterstützung von Paul Cassirer Kunsthändler. Seine Wege führten ihn nach Paris, Berlin und London, bevor er in Düsseldorf 1913 die Galerie für alte und neue Kunst eröffnete. Dependancen in Berlin, Frankfurt am Main, Köln und Wien folgten. Bald wurde er zu einer Schlüsselfigur im internationalen Kunstmarkt, vertrat Künstler wie George Grosz, Pablo Picasso, Paul Gauguin, Paul Cézanne und viele andere, die später in den Kanon der klassischen Moderne eingehen sollten. Flechtheim war bekannt für seine hochwertigen Ausstellungen, die das Bewusstsein für die zeitgenössische Kunst veränderten. In seiner Berliner Galerie organisierte er im Frühjahr 1928 eine große Max-Beckmann-Ausstellung, die anschließend auch in der Städtischen Kunsthalle Mannheim gezeigt wurde. Der damalige Direktor der Kunsthalle Mannheim, Gustav Friedrich Hartlaub, erwarb das *Stilleben mit Holzscheiten* Beckmanns über die Düsseldorfer Galerie von Alfred Flechtheim.[1] Darüber hinaus standen der Galerist und der Direktor stets in regem Austausch.[2]

Bereits im Jahr 1929 musste der Kunsthändler durch die Weltwirtschaftskrise einen finanziellen Einbruch verkraften. Die systematischen Diffamierungen gegenüber Flechtheim und die Verfemung der von ihm vertriebenen Kunst, zwangen ihn bereits im Jahr 1933 über die Schweiz und Paris zur Flucht nach London, wo er 1937 verarmt starb. Die in seiner Galerie verwahrten Kunstwerke gingen verloren, ebenso seine private Kunstsammlung, die nach dem Tod der Witwe Betty 1941 von der Gestapo beschlagnahmt wurde. Zahlreiche der von Flechtheim gehandelten Werke befinden sich heute in Museen im In- und Ausland.[3]

Rudolf Belling schuf 1927 ein beeindruckendes plastisches Bronzeporträt von Alfred Flechtheim (Kat. 36). Der Kopf des Kunsthändlers wird dabei nicht in seiner vollen Form wiedergegeben, sondern beinahe vollständig aufgelöst. Nur wenige Linien, die von den Augen, über die Nase zum Mund und schließlich dem Sockel führen, fügen sich zu einem eigenwilligen Abbild Flechtheims zusammen.

Herbert Tannenbaum

Herbert Tannenbaum (1892–1958), Sohn jüdischer Eltern, besuchte das Gymnasium in Mannheim und studierte auf Drängen des Vaters ab 1910 Jura in Heidelberg und München. Sein Interesse galt jedoch dem Film, der Kunst und dem Theater. Bereits ab 1911 war er Mitglied in dem von Fritz Wichert gegründeten Freien Bund zur Einbürgerung der bildenden Kunst in Mannheim, wo er erste Vorträge hielt. Im Ersten Weltkrieg wurde er an der Westfront eingesetzt, weshalb er das geplante Kunstgeschichte-Studium in Berlin nicht aufnehmen konnte.[4]

works of art and offered advice on all artistic issues. He actively promoted avant-garde artists such as Marc Chagall, Paul Klee, and Otto Dix but also regional artists such as Wilfried Otto, Xaver Fuhr, Will Sohl, and Georg Scholz.[5]

Tannenbaum was a central figure in the development of the collection of the Kunsthalle Mannheim: Numerous important works entered the Kunsthalle by way of his gallery—many of them were then confiscated as "degenerate" in 1937. Even earlier, in 1933, a series of works he had procured for the Kunsthalle Mannheim had been condemned in an exhibition there: *Kulturbolschewistische Bilder* (Cultural Bolshevist Pictures). Tannenbaum also ended up in the sights of National Socialist cultural policy, which considered him abhorrent as a Jew and supporter of "degenerate" art. In 1936, he had to sell his gallery to the Dresden art dealer Rudolf Probst who continued to run it with an altered program.

Tannenbaum fled into exile in Amsterdam and opened a small gallery there again. He survived the way and the German occupation but had to withdraw from the public entirely during this period. While in exile, he established new friendships with artists such as Max Beckmann und Heinrich Campendonk.[6] In 1947, Tannenbaum decided to make a fresh start in New York. On this occasion Max Beckmann dedicated to him the portrait *Tannenbaum geht nach New York* (Tannenbaum Goes to New York), which the Kunsthalle Mannheim was able to acquire in 2004 (cat. 38). With his entrepreneurial talent, Tannenbaum successfully built up a new art dealership near New York and traveled repeatedly to Germany. He died unexpectedly in Frankfurt am Main in 1958, shortly before his return flight.[7]

In 1960, his widow, Maria Tannenbaum, bequeathed to the Kunsthalle Mannheim Wilhelm Lehmbruck's busts of the collectors Adèle and Sally Falk (cat. 11, 12). Finally, Wladimir von Zabotin's *Porträt Maria und Herbert Tannenbaum* (Portrait of Maria and Herbert Tannenbaum) (cat. 37) entered the collection of the Kunsthalle Mannheim in 2001 as a gift from their daughter Beatrice Newman.

Rudolf Probst

Rudolf Probst (1890–1968) first studied law, then art history in Munich and Würzburg. After World War I, in which he served as an orderly in a military hospital Würzburg,[8] he began to work at the Galerie Emil Richter in Dresden, which had an essential influence on cultural developments in the Saxon city. In 1923, he founded the Galerie Neue Kunst Fides there, which showed works by Emil Nolde, Lyonel Feininger, Paul Klee, Wassily Kandinsky, and others.[9]

Under pressure from the National Socialists, Probst had to close his gallery in 1933. In 1936, he acquired Herbert Tannenbaum's Kunsthaus in Mannheim, but there he was confronted with massive restrictions and, after a Nolde exhibition in 1937, had to cease showing any works classified as "degenerate."[10] The Kunsthaus was destroyed in a bombing raid on the city in 1943. In 1949, he opened the Galerie Rudolf Probst in the Mannheim Palace, which was an important place for museums and collectors rebuilding their collections in the postwar period.

After World War II, Probst played a crucial role in helping the Kunsthalle Mannheim and its director, Walter Passarge, compensate for its losses from confiscated works. With his assistance, a series of works returned to the Kunsthalle collection. For example, Max Pechstein's *Stilleben: Figur und Blumen* (Still Life: Figure and Flowers) of 1917 (cat. 120), which had been purchased in 1938 and confiscated in 1937, reentered the collection. In addition, Nolde's *Pferd und Füllen* (Horse and Filly) (1915; cat. 131), *Feuerlilien und dunkler Rittersporn* (Tiger Lilies and Dark Larkspur) (1925; cat. 92), and *Ferne Mädchen* (Girls from Afar) (1947; cat. 122), which were intended to replace the confiscated works *Tulpen* (Tulips) (1915; cat. 103), *Vorabend (Marschlandschaft)* (Twilight [Marshy Landscape]) (1916; cat. 106), and *Figuren und Georginen* (Figures and Dahlias) (1919; cat. 104).[11]

After the gallery closed in 1959, Probst auctioned many of the works still in his possession. He died in Heidelberg in 1968.

1 Karoline Hille, *Spuren der Moderne: Die Mannheimer Kunsthalle von 1918 bis 1933*, Kunst und Dokumentation 13, Städtische Kunsthalle Mannheim (also PhD diss. Freie Univ. Berlin) (Berlin: Akademie, 1994), p. 264
2 See, for example, ibid., pp. 264–68.
3 See the Koordinationsstelle für Provenienzforschung in Nordrhein-Westfalen, http://alfredflechtheim.com/ (accessed May 21, 2025).
4 Mathias Listl, "The Kunsthalle and Its Jewish Patrons: The Fate of Five Families from Mannheim," in *(Re)Discovery: The Kunsthalle from 1933 to 1945 and the Aftermath*, ed. Mathias Listl and Ulrike Lorenz, exh. cat. (Mannheim: Kunsthalle Mannheim, 2018), pp. 63–85, esp. p. 74.
5 Ibid., p. 77; Karl-Ludwig Hofmann and Christmut Präger, "Herbert Tannenbaum als Kunsthändler," in *Für die Kunst! Herbert Tannenbaum und sein Kunsthaus*, ed. Karl-Ludwig Hofmann, exh. cat. Reiss-Museum der Stadt Mannheim (Mannheim: Vits & Kehrer, 1994), pp. 37–71, esp. p. 54.
6 Listl, "The Kunsthalle and Its Jewish Patrons" (see note 4), p. 77.
7 Ibid., p. 80.
8 Karl-Ludwig Hofmann and Christmut Präger, *Rudolf Probst, Galerist, 1890–1968*, Quellenstudien zur Kunst 11 (Wädenswil: Nimbus, 2021), pp. 32–33.
9 See ibid., pp. 9–10.
10 See ibid., p. 197.
11 See ibid., pp. 326–32.

Im Jahr 1920 eröffnete Tannenbaum in Mannheim seine eigene Kunst- und Buchhandlung Das Kunsthaus (S. 31, Abb. 13), in der er Bücher, Zeitschriften und Kunstwerke verkaufte und Beratung in allen künstlerischen Fragen anbot. Er setzte sich aktiv für die Förderung avantgardistischer Künstler wie Marc Chagall, Paul Klee und Otto Dix ein, aber auch für regionale Künstler wie Wilfried Otto, Xaver Fuhr, Will Sohl und Georg Scholz.[5]

Für den Aufbau der Sammlung der Kunsthalle Mannheim war Tannenbaum eine zentrale Figur: Zahlreiche bedeutende Werke gelangten über seine Galerie in die Kunsthalle – viele von ihnen wurden wiederum im Jahr 1937 als „entartet" beschlagnahmt. Zuvor, im Jahr 1933, waren eine Reihe der von ihm vermittelten Werke im Rahmen der Ausstellung *Kulturbolschewistische Bilder* in der Kunsthalle Mannheim verfemt worden. Auch Tannenbaum geriet ins Visier der Kulturpolitik des NS-Regimes, für die er als Jude und Förderer „entarteter" Kunst als verabscheuenswürdig galt. Im Jahr 1936 musste er seine Galerie an den Dresdner Kunsthändler Rudolf Probst verkaufen, der sie mit verändertem Programm weiterführte.

Tannenbaum floh ins Exil nach Amsterdam und eröffnete dort erneut eine kleine Galerie. Er überlebte den Krieg sowie die deutsche Besatzung, musste sich aber in dieser Zeit vollständig aus der Öffentlichkeit zurückziehen. Mit Künstlern wie Max Beckmann und Heinrich Campendonk entstanden im Exil neue Freundschaften.[6] Im Jahr 1947 entschied sich Tannenbaum zu einem Neuanfang in New York. Max Beckmann widmete ihm bei dieser Gelegenheit das Porträt *Tannenbaum geht nach New York,* welches die Kunsthalle Mannheim im Jahr 2004 ankaufen konnte (Kat. 38). Mit unternehmerischem Geschick baute Tannenbaum in der Nähe von New York erfolgreich eine neue Kunsthandlung auf und reiste wiederholt nach Deutschland. Er starb im Jahr 1958 unerwartet in Frankfurt am Main kurz vor dem Rückflug.[7]

Seine Witwe, Maria Tannenbaum, vermachte der Kunsthalle Mannheim im Jahr 1960 Wilhelm Lehmbrucks Büsten des Sammlerpaares Adèle und Sally Falk (Kat. 11, 12). Wladimir von Zabotins *Porträt Maria und Herbert Tannenbaum* (Kat. 37) gelangte schließlich 2001 durch eine Schenkung ihrer Tochter Beatrice Newman in die Sammlung der Kunsthalle Mannheim.

Rudolf Probst

Rudolf Probst (1890–1968) studierte zunächst Jura, dann Kunstgeschichte in München und Würzburg. Nach dem Ersten Weltkrieg, in dem er als Krankenpfleger im Lazarett in Würzburg diente[8], fing er an, in der Galerie Emil Richter in Dresden zu arbeiten, die wesentlichen Einfluss auf die kulturelle Entwicklung der sächsischen Stadt hatte. Im Jahr 1923 gründete er dort die Galerie Neue Kunst Fides, die Werke von Emil Nolde, Lyonel Feininger, Paul Klee, Wassily Kandinsky und anderen zeigte.[9]

Unter dem Druck der Nationalsozialisten musste Probst seine Galerie im Jahr 1933 schließen. 1936 erwarb er Das Kunsthaus von Herbert Tannenbaum in Mannheim, traf aber auch hier auf massive Restriktionen und musste nach einer Nolde-Ausstellung 1937 auf alle als „entartet" eingestuften Werke verzichten.[10] Das Kunsthaus wurde bei einem Bombenangriff auf die Stadt im Jahr 1943 zerstört. Im Jahr 1949 eröffnete er im Mannheimer Schloss die Galerie Rudolf Probst, die in der Nachkriegszeit eine wichtige Anlaufstelle für Museen und Sammler*innen beim Wiederaufbau ihrer Sammlung war.

Außerdem half Probst nach dem Zweiten Weltkrieg der Kunsthalle Mannheim und Direktor Walter Passarge maßgeblich dabei, die Verluste der Beschlagnahmungen wieder auszugleichen. Durch seine Vermittlung gelangte eine Reihe an Werken wieder in die Sammlung der Kunsthalle. So konnte beispielsweise Max Pechsteins *Stilleben: Figur und Blumen* von 1917 (Kat. 120), das 1918 angekauft und 1937 beschlagnahmt wurde, wieder in die Sammlung gelangen. Außerdem auch Noldes *Pferd und Füllen* (1915; Kat. 131), *Feuerlilien und dunkler Rittersporn* (1925; Kat. 92) sowie *Ferne Mädchen* (1947; Kat. 122), welche die beschlagnahmten Werke *Tulpen* (1915; Kat. 103), *Vorabend (Marschlandschaft)* (1916; Kat. 106) und *Figuren und Georginen* (1919; Kat. 104) ersetzen sollten.[11]

Nach Schließung der Galerie im Jahr 1959 versteigerte Probst viele der Werke, die noch in seinem Besitz geblieben waren. Er starb im Jahr 1968 in Heidelberg.

1 Karoline Hille: *Spuren der Moderne. Die Mannheimer Kunsthalle von 1918 bis 1933,* Kunst und Dokumentation 13, Städtische Kunsthalle Mannheim (zgl. Diss. Freie Univ. Berlin), Berlin 1994, S. 264.
2 Vgl. beispielsweise ebd., S. 264–268.
3 Vgl. Koordinationsstelle für Provenienzforschung in Nordrhein-Westfalen: http://alfredflechtheim.com/projekt [abgerufen am 21.05.2025].
4 Mathias Listl: Die Kunsthalle und ihre jüdischen Mäzene: Schicksalswege fünf jüdischer Familien aus Mannheim, in: Kat. Ausst. *(Wieder-)Entdecken. Die Kunsthalle 1933 bis 1945 und die Folgen,* Kunsthalle Mannheim 2018, hrsg. v. Mathias Listl u. Ulrike Lorenz, Mannheim 2018, S. 63–85, S. 74f.
5 Ebd., S. 77; Karl-Ludwig Hofmann u. Christmut Präger: Herbert Tannenbaum als Kunsthändler, in: Kat. Ausst. *Für die Kunst! Herbert Tannenbaum und sein Kunsthaus,* Reiss-Museum der Stadt Mannheim, hrsg. v. Karl-Ludwig Hofmann, Mannheim 1994, S. 37–71, S. 54.
6 Listl 2018 (wie Anm. 4), S. 80.
7 Ebd., S. 80.
8 Karl-Ludwig Hofmann u. Christmut Präger: *Rudolf Probst, Galerist, 1890–1968,* Wädenswil 2021 (Quellenstudien zur Kunst, Bd. 11), S. 32f.
9 Vgl. ebd., S. 9f.
10 Vgl. ebd., S. 197.
11 Vgl. ebd., S. 326–332.

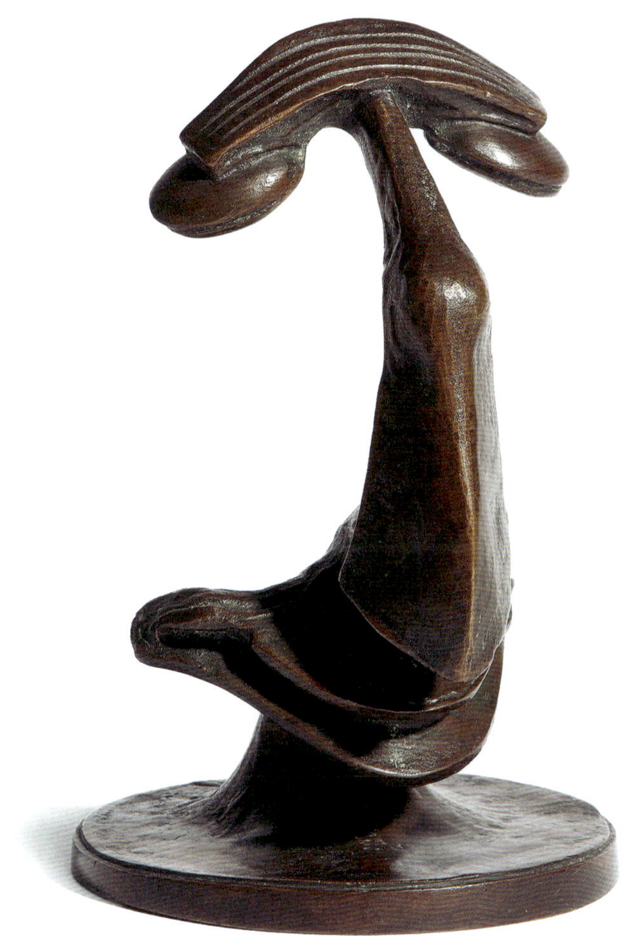

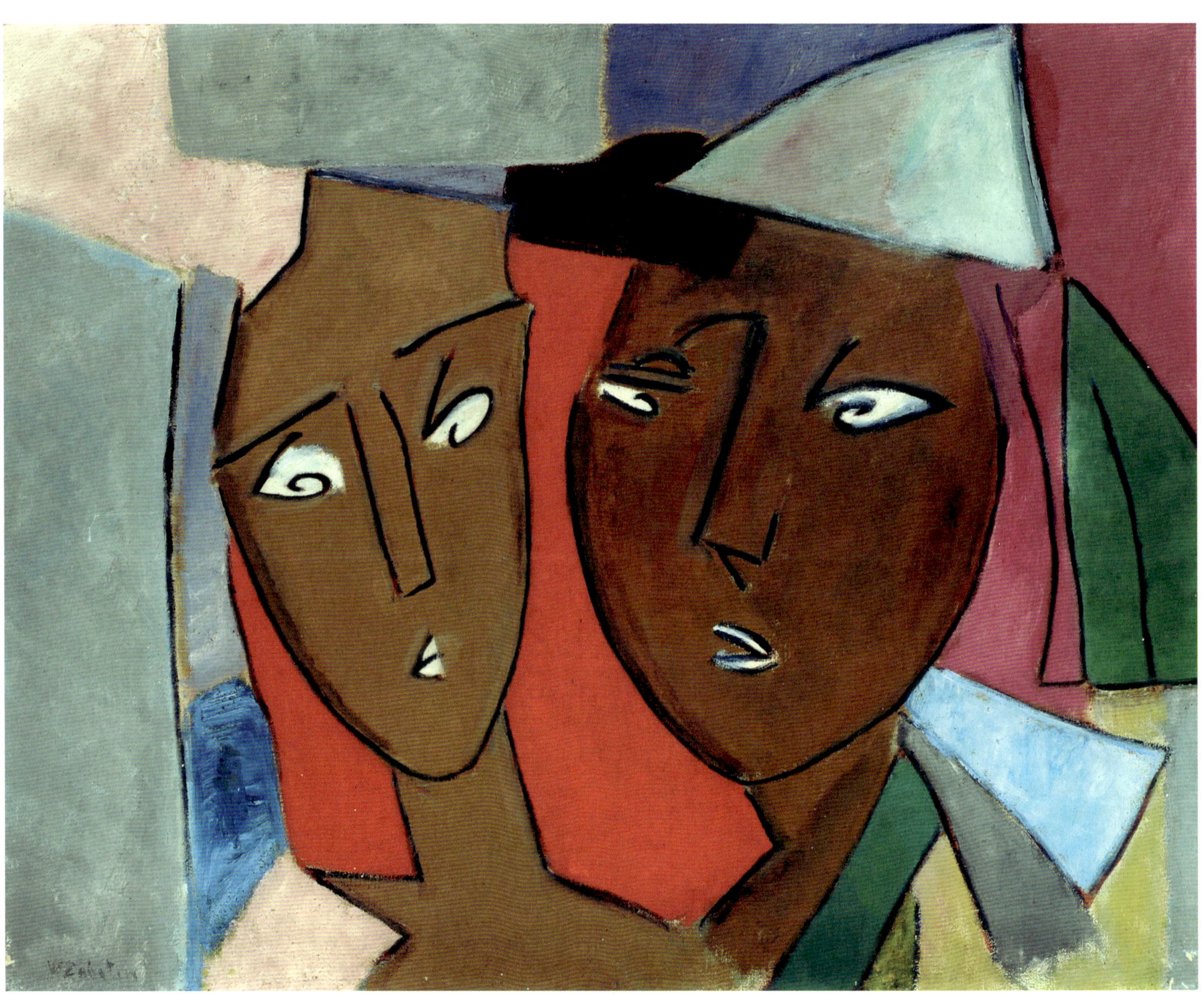

37 | **Wladimir von Zabotin,** *Porträt Maria und Herbert Tannenbaum* / *Portrait of Maria and Herbert Tannenbaum,* **1920/21,** Kunsthalle Mannheim

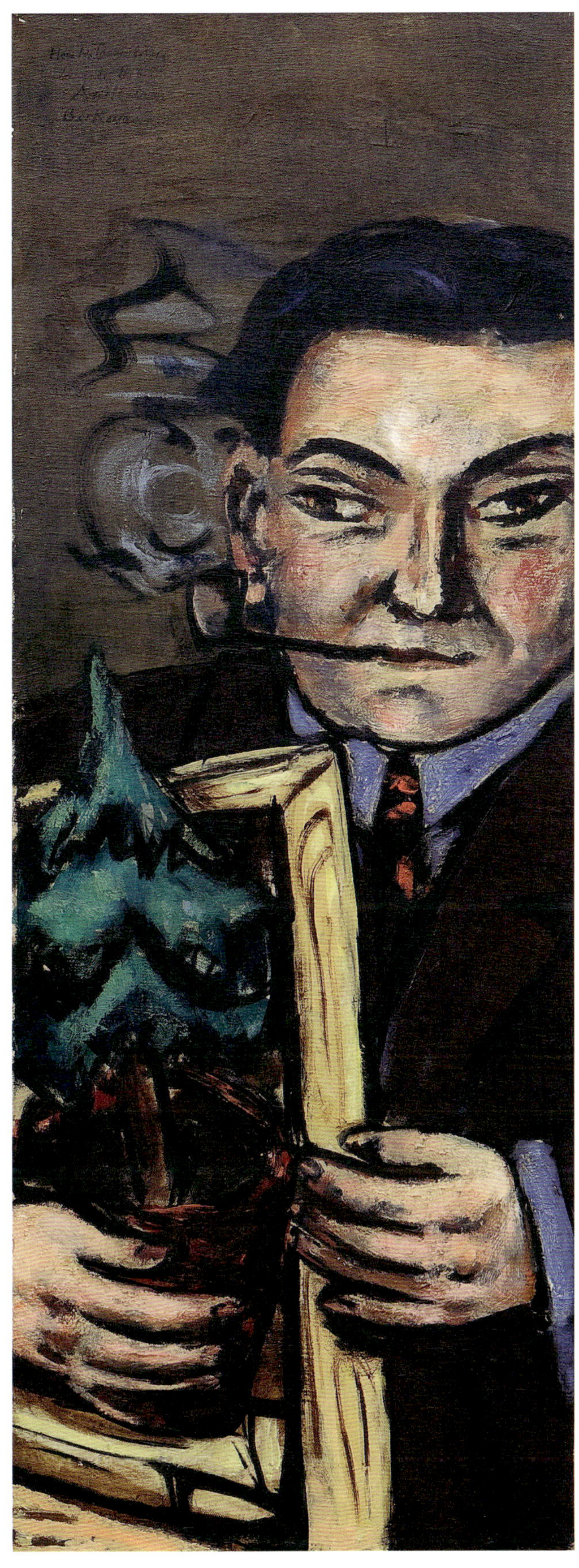

38 | **Max Beckmann,** *Tannenbaum geht nach New York* / *Tannenbaum Goes to New York,* **1947,** Kunsthalle Mannheim

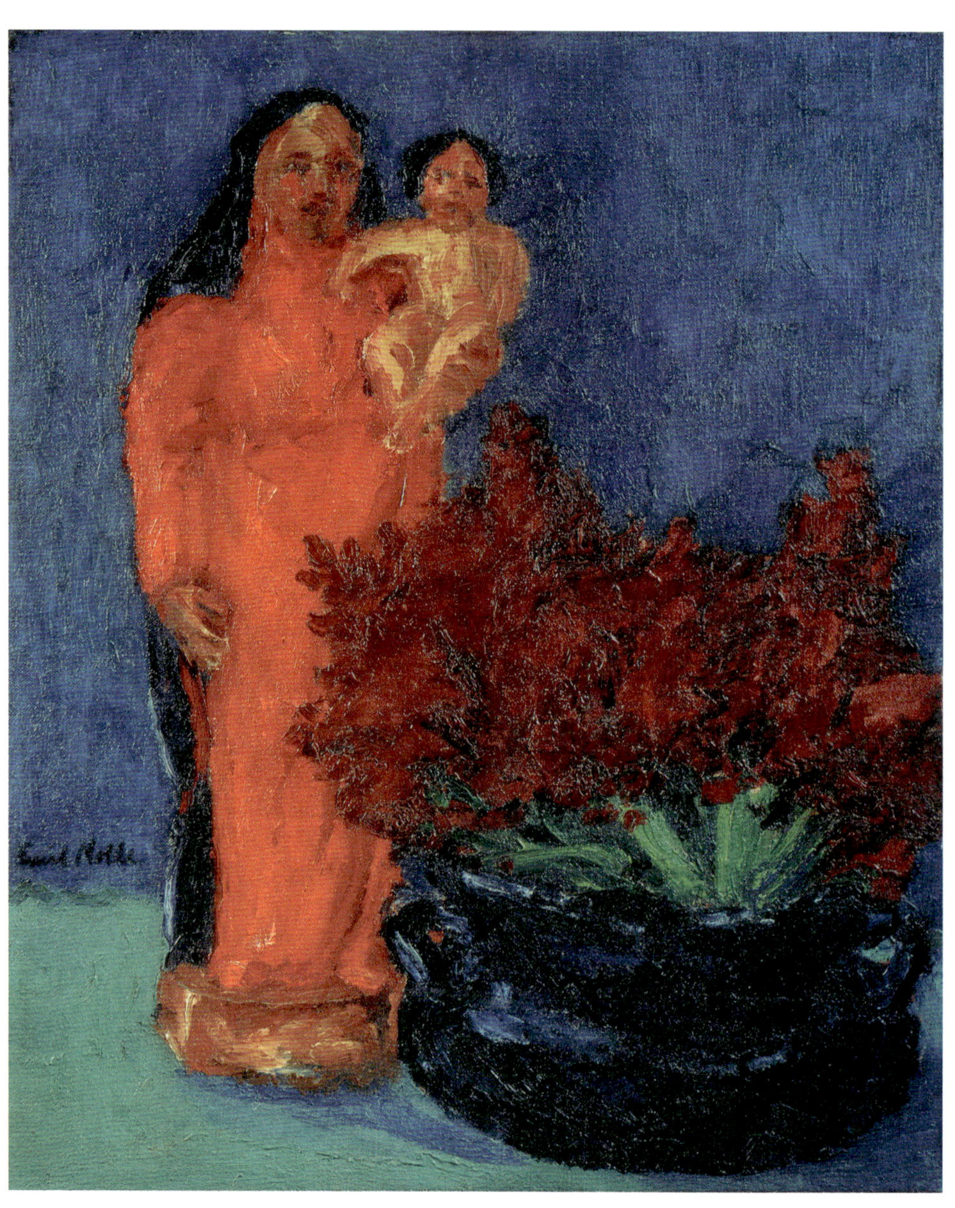

39 | **Emil Nolde,** *Madonna mit Blumen* / *Virgin with Flowers,* **1915,** Simu Stiftung / *Simu Foundation*

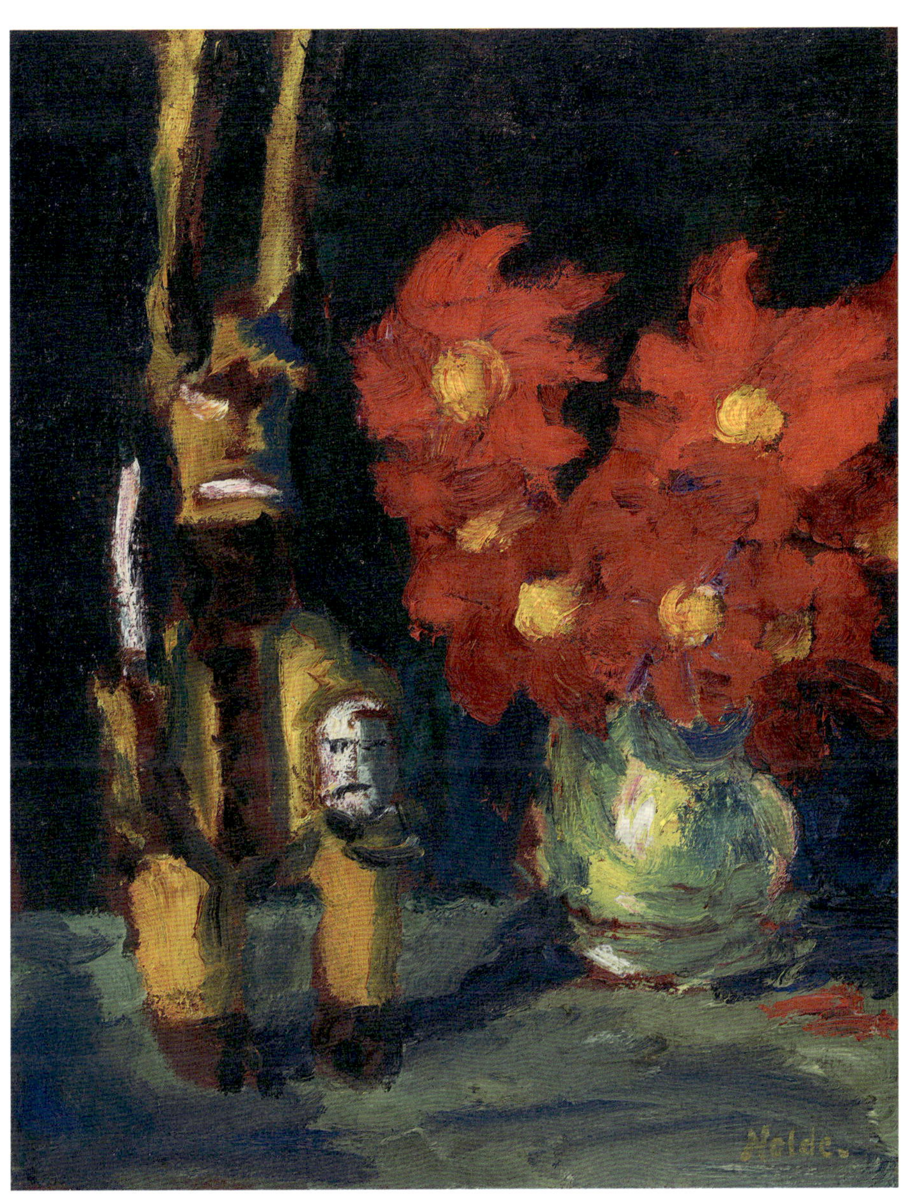

Rosa Schapire: Promoter of Expressionism

Dorotea Lorenz

Art historian, collector, patron of the arts, art critic, author: Rosa Schapire (1874–1954) occupied a central position in the promotion of Expressionist art and the Brücke (Bridge) artists' group at the beginning of the twentieth century. She tirelessly advocated for the Brücke artists in particular, by organizing exhibitions, writing essays and reviews, and procuring artworks for museums and collectors.[1] As signs of gratitude for her commitment, the artists gave her a number of portraits, art postcards, handmade jewelry, and even furniture. These gifts mark the beginning of her collection, which by 1939 included more than 600 works.[2]

Born to a Jewish family in Brody (then Austria-Hungary, now Ukraine) in 1874, Rosa Schapire moved to Hamburg in 1893. From 1901 onward, she studied art history in Zurich, Leipzig, Berlin, and Heidelberg, where she was one of the first women to receive a doctorate, with a dissertation on the Frankfurt painter Johann Ludwig Ernst Morgenstern. But because an academic or university career was not open to her as a woman, she pursued a career as a freelance art historian. In 1907, she joined the Brücke artists' group as a passive member. She soon met Karl Schmidt-Rottluff; their decades-long, close friendship is documented in numerous

portraits that the artist made of her over the years. Schmidt-Rottluff even transformed Schapire's living room into an "Expressionist Gesamtkunstwerk" with painted furniture and textiles.[3] In 1915, Schmidt-Rottluff produced a woodcut portrait of Rosa Schapire (cat. 41). Striking horizontal and vertical lines, stark black-and-white contrast, and expressive facial features come together into a masklike portrait. Although Schapire's upward gaze looks reflective and serious, at the same time Schmidt-Rottluff created a portrait of the art historian that characterizes her as an energetic and strong personality. The portrait also testifies to the fascination Schmidt-Rottluff and the other Brücke artists had for the woodcut as medium, which in contrast to other art forms they regarded as authentic and original.[4] The reception of African and other non-European art, which Schmidt-Rottluff collected all his life and repeatedly integrated into his works, is also unmistakable. In 1924, Schapire published a catalogue raisonné of Schmidt-Rottluff's prints up to 1923. Her publishing activity was not limited to art-historical themes. Her sociopolitical commitment became evident early on, which was focused above all on women's rights. With the writer Ida Dehmel, she cofounded the Frauenbund zur Förderung deutscher bildender Kunst (Women's League for the Promotion of German Fine Arts); together, they dedicated themselves to the support of Expressionism.[5]

The takeover of power by the National Socialist regime in 1933 and later the beginning of World War II caused rifts in Schapire's life and work as well. After she was defamed as a "critic in the time of the System [*Systemzeit*],"[6] in the *Entartete Kunst* (Degenerate Art) exhibition in Munich in 1937, where a portrait of her by Schmidt-Rottluff from 1915 was also shown, she felt compelled to emigrate to London two years later. Despite more difficult living and working conditions, there too she continued to work to make Expressionist art better known. A significant part of her collection and her correspondence with Karl Schmidt-Rottluff was destroyed when she emigrated.[7] Nevertheless, thanks to Schapire's indefatigable commitment and with works from her own collection as well, the Karl Schmidt-Rottluff's first exhibition in the United Kingdom could be held at the Leicester Museum in 1953.

After Schapire's death in London in 1954, her collection went to museums to which she felt especially strong ties.[8] A drawing in a letter and seventeen postcards entered the Kunsthalle Mannheim in 1957. Schapire had been sent them by Erich Heckel,

Rosa Schapire: Förderin des Expressionismus

Dorotea Lorenz

Kunsthistorikerin, Sammlerin, Mäzenin, Kunstkritikerin, Autorin: Rosa Schapire (1874–1954) kam in der Förderung expressionistischer Kunst und der Künstlergruppe Brücke Anfang des 20. Jahrhunderts eine zentrale Position zu. Unermüdlich setzte sie sich vor allem für die Brücke-Künstler ein, indem sie Ausstellungen organisierte, Aufsätze und Rezensionen verfasste oder Kunstwerke an Museen und Sammler*innen vermittelte.[1] Als Zeichen der Dankbarkeit für ihren Einsatz schenkten die Kunstschaffenden ihr eine Vielzahl an Porträts, Kunstpostkarten, handgefertigten Schmuck und sogar Möbel. Diese Schenkungen markierten den Beginn ihrer Sammlung, die bis zum Jahr 1939 mehr als 600 Werke umfasste.[2]

Im Jahr 1874 in eine jüdische Familie in Brody (damals Österreich-Ungarn, heute Ukraine) geboren, zog Rosa Schapire im Jahr 1893 nach Hamburg. Ab 1901 studierte sie Kunstgeschichte in Zürich, Leipzig, Berlin und Heidelberg, wo sie als eine der ersten Frauen über den Frankfurter Maler Johann Ludwig Ernst Morgenstern promoviert wurde. Da ihr als Frau eine Karriere im akademischen und universitären Bereich nicht offenstand, setzte sie ihre Laufbahn als freischaffende Kunsthistorikerin fort. Sie trat im Jahr 1907 als passives Mitglied in die Künstlergruppe Brücke ein. Schon bald lernte sie Karl Schmidt-Rottluff kennen – von ihrer jahrzehntelangen, engen Freundschaft zeugen zahlreiche Porträts, die der Künstler über Jahre hinweg von ihr anfertigte. Sogar das Wohnzimmer Schapires verwandelte Schmidt-Rottluff mit bemalten Möbeln und Textilien in ein „expressionistisches Gesamtkunstwerk".[3] Im Jahr 1915 fertigte Schmidt-Rottluff ein Holzschnitt-Porträt Rosa Schapires an (Kat. 41). Markante horizontale und vertikale Linien, ein starker Schwarz-Weiß-Kontrast und die kantigen, expressiven Gesichtszüge fügen sich zu einem maskenhaften Bildnis zusammen. Wirkt der nach oben gerichtete Blick Schapires nachdenklich und ernst, so schafft Schmidt-Rottluff zugleich ein Porträt der Kunsthistorikerin, das sie als energische und kraftvolle Persönlichkeit charakterisiert. Das Bildnis zeugt auch von der Faszination Schmidt-Rottluffs und der Brücke-Künstler für das Medium Holzschnitt, das im Gegensatz zu anderen Kunstformen als authentisch und ursprünglich galt.[4] Unverkennbar ist außerdem die Rezeption afrikanischer und nicht-europäischer Kunst, die Schmidt-Rottluff zeitlebens sammelte und immer wieder in seinen Werken einbaute. Im Jahr 1924 veröffentlichte Schapire ein Werkverzeichnis der Druckgrafik Schmidt-Rottluffs bis zum Jahr 1923. Ihre publizistische Tätigkeit beschränkte sich jedoch nicht nur auf kunsthistorische Themen. Schon früh zeigte sich ihr gesellschaftspolitisches Engagement, das vor allem den Rechten der Frau galt. Mit der Literatin Ida Dehmel gründete sie den Verein Frauenbund zur Förderung deutscher bildender Kunst; gemeinsam widmeten sie sich der Förderung des Expressionismus.[5]

Die Machtübernahme durch das NS-Regime im Jahr 1933 und später der Beginn des Zweiten Weltkrieges markierten Brüche auch im Leben und Wirken Schapires. Nach ihrer Diffamierung bei der 1937 in München stattfindenden Ausstellung *Entartete Kunst* als „Kritiker[in] der Systemzeit"[6], wo auch ihr Porträt von Schmidt-Rottluff aus dem Jahr 1915 gezeigt wurde, sah sie sich zwei Jahre später gezwungen, nach London zu emigrieren. Trotz erschwerter Arbeits- und Lebensbedingungen engagierte sie sich auch hier weiterhin für die Bekanntheit der Kunst des Expressionismus. Ein bedeutender Teil ihrer Sammlung sowie der Korrespondenz mit Karl Schmidt-Rottluff wurde vor ihrer Emigration vernichtet.[7] Dennoch konnte durch Schapires unermüdlichen Einsatz und bestückt mit Werken auch aus ihrer eigenen Sammlung im Jahr 1953 im Leicester Museum die erste Ausstellung Karl Schmidt-Rottluffs in England stattfinden.

Ernst Ludwig Kirchner, Max Pechstein, and Karl Schmidt-Rottluff between 1909 and 1931. It is no longer possible to reconstruct entirely why the Kunsthalle received part of her collection. Surely the Kunsthalle's early interest in Expressionist art played a role in her making this bequest. Moreover, Walter Passarge, the director of the Kunsthalle from 1936 to 1958, was presumably in contact with the art historian after the war's end when he was trying to compensate for the losses of the National Socialist confiscation of works.[9] On the occasion of a Schmidt-Rottluff exhibition in 1951, Passarge wrote a foreword about which Schapire expressed her enthusiasm.[10] In these artists' postcards, the Kunsthalle Mannheim has a unique documentation of the professional and in some cases also friendly relationships between Schapire and the artists. The motifs—largely landscapes, a portrait of Schapire, and portraits of others—express not only the artists' bond with and acknowledgment of the art historian but also, in combination with the texts, "not infrequently [offer] insights into the history behind the paintings."[11]

Although her commitment to Expressionist art made a crucial contribution to that movement becoming established, Rosa Schapire has since fallen into oblivion. Scholars today are increasingly recognizing her role as an emissary of contemporary art and supporter of young artists who was comparable to figures such as Gustav Friedrich Hartlaub. Nevertheless, it remains an important task to continue to draw attention to her contribution to art history and assess it adequately.

1 Leonie Beiersdorf, "Einführung," in *Rosa: Eigenartig grün: Rosa Schapire und die Expressionisten,* Museum für Kunst und Gewerbe Hamburg 2009, ed. Silke Schulze (Ostfildern: Hatje Cantz, 2009), pp. 20–27, esp. p. 20.
2 Sabine Schulze, "Rosa: Eigenartig grün," in Schulze, *Rosa: Eigenartig grün* (see note 1), pp. 8–19, esp. p. 11.
3 Ibid., p. 10.
4 See Christian Weikop, "Karl Schmidt-Rottluffs arborealer Expressionismus," in Schulze, *Rosa: Eigenartig grün* (see note 1), pp. 186–215.
5 Parvati Vasanta, "'Aber unsere Ziele haben wir höher gesteckt': Rosa Schapire und der Frauenbund zur Förderung deutscher bildender Kunst," in *Rosa und Anna Schapire: Sozialwissenschaft, Kunstgeschichte und Feminismus um 1900,* ed. Burcu Dogramaci and Gabriele Sandner (Berlin: AvivA, 2017), pp. 161–74, esp. p. 161.
6 Burcu Dogramaci, "Still Fighting for Modern Art: Rosa Schapire in England," in Dogramaci and Sandner, *Rosa und Anna Schapire* (see note 5), pp. 229–56, esp. p. 229.
7 Schulze, "Rosa: Eigenartig grün" (see note 2), p. 14.
8 Gerd Presler, *"Brücke" an Dr. Rosa Schapire* (Mannheim: Kunsthalle, 1990), p. 7.
9 Ibid.
10 Susanne Wittek, *"Es gibt keinen direkteren Weg zu mir als über Deine Kunst": Rosa Schapire im Spiegel ihrer Briefe an Karl Schmidt-Rottluff, 1950–1954,* Künstler in Hamburg 2 (Göttingen: Wallstein, 2022), p. 147.
11 Presler, *"Brücke" an Dr. Rosa Schapire* (see note 8), p. 7.

Nach dem Tod Schapires in London im Jahr 1954 ging ihre Sammlung an Museen, denen sie sich besonders verbunden fühlte.[8] In den Besitz der Kunsthalle Mannheim gelangten im Jahr 1957 eine Briefzeichnung und 17 Postkarten. Diese hatte Schapire zwischen 1909 und 1931 von Erich Heckel, Ernst Ludwig Kirchner, Max Pechstein und Karl Schmidt-Rottluff zugesandt bekommen. Warum gerade die Kunsthalle Mannheim einen Teil ihrer Sammlung erhielt, lässt sich nicht mehr vollständig rekonstruieren. Sicherlich spielte das frühe Interesse der Kunsthalle an expressionistischer Kunst eine Rolle bei der Zuweisung dieses Vermächtnisses. Zudem stand Walter Passarge, Direktor der Kunsthalle von 1936 bis 1958, vermutlich in Kontakt mit der Kunsthistorikerin, als es nach Kriegsende darum ging, die Verluste der nationalsozialistischen Beschlagnahmung wieder auszugleichen.[9] Passarge verfasste anlässlich einer Schmidt-Rottluff-Ausstellung im Jahr 1951 ein Vorwort, zu dem sich Schapire begeistert äußerte.[10] Mit den Künstlerpostkarten liegt der Kunsthalle Mannheim eine einzigartige Dokumentation über das berufliche und teilweise auch freundschaftliche Verhältnis zwischen Schapire und den Künstlern vor. Die Motive, zum Großteil Landschaften, ein Porträt Schapires und Personenbildnisse drücken nicht nur die Verbundenheit und Anerkennung gegenüber der Kunsthistorikerin aus, sondern ergeben in Verbindung mit den Texten „nicht selten Aufschlüsse über die Entstehungsgeschichte von Gemälden"[11].

Obwohl ihr Engagement für die Kunst des Expressionismus maßgeblich zur Etablierung dieser Kunstrichtung beigetragen hat, ist Rosa Schapire zwischenzeitlich in Vergessenheit geraten. Ihre Rolle als Vermittlerin zeitgenössischer Kunst und Förderin junger Kunstschaffender, vergleichbar mit Persönlichkeiten wie Gustav Friedrich Hartlaub, ist heute in Fachkreisen zwar zunehmend anerkannt. Dennoch bleibt es eine wichtige Aufgabe, ihren Beitrag zur Kunstgeschichte weiter sichtbar zu machen und angemessen zu würdigen.

1 Leonie Beiersdorf: Einführung, in: Kat. Ausst. *Rosa. Eigenartig grün. Rosa Schapire und die Expressionisten*, Museum für Kunst und Gewerbe Hamburg 2009, hrsg. v. Silke Schulze, Ostfildern 2009, S. 20–27, S. 20.

2 Sabine Schulze: Rosa. Eigenartig grün, in: Kat. Ausst. *Rosa. Eigenartig grün. Rosa Schapire und die Expressionisten*, Museum für Kunst und Gewerbe Hamburg 2009, hrsg. v. Silke Schulze, Ostfildern 2009, S. 8–19, S. 11.

3 Ebd., S. 10.

4 Vgl. Christian Weikop: Karl Schmidt-Rottluffs arborealer Expressionismus, in: Kat. Ausst. *Rosa. Eigenartig grün. Rosa Schapire und die Expressionisten*, Museum für Kunst und Gewerbe Hamburg 2009, hrsg. v. Silke Schulze, Ostfildern 2009, S. 186–215.

5 Parvati Vasanta: „Aber unsere Ziele haben wir höher gesteckt" – Rosa Schapire und der *Frauenbund zur Förderung deutscher bildender Kunst*, in: Burcu Dogramaci u. Gabriele Sandner (Hrsg.): *Rosa und Anna Schapire. Sozialwissenschaft, Kunstgeschichte und Feminismus um 1900*, Berlin 2017, S. 161–174, S. 161.

6 Burcu Dogramaci: Still Fighting for Modern Art. Rosa Schapire in England, in: Burcu Dogramaci u. Gabriele Sandner (Hrsg.): *Rosa und Anna Schapire. Sozialwissenschaft, Kunstgeschichte und Feminismus um 1900*, Berlin 2017, S. 229–256, S. 229.

7 Schulze 2009 (wie Anm. 2), S. 14.

8 Gerd Presler: „*Brücke*" *an Dr. Rosa Schapire*, Mannheim 1990, S. 7.

9 Ebd., S. 7.

10 Susanne Wittek: „*Es gibt keinen direkteren Weg zu mir als über Deine Kunst*". Rosa Schapire im Spiegel ihrer Briefe an Karl Schmidt-Rottluff *1950–1954*, Göttingen 2022 (Künstler in Hamburg, Bd. 2), S. 147.

11 Presler 1990 (wie Anm. 8), S. 7.

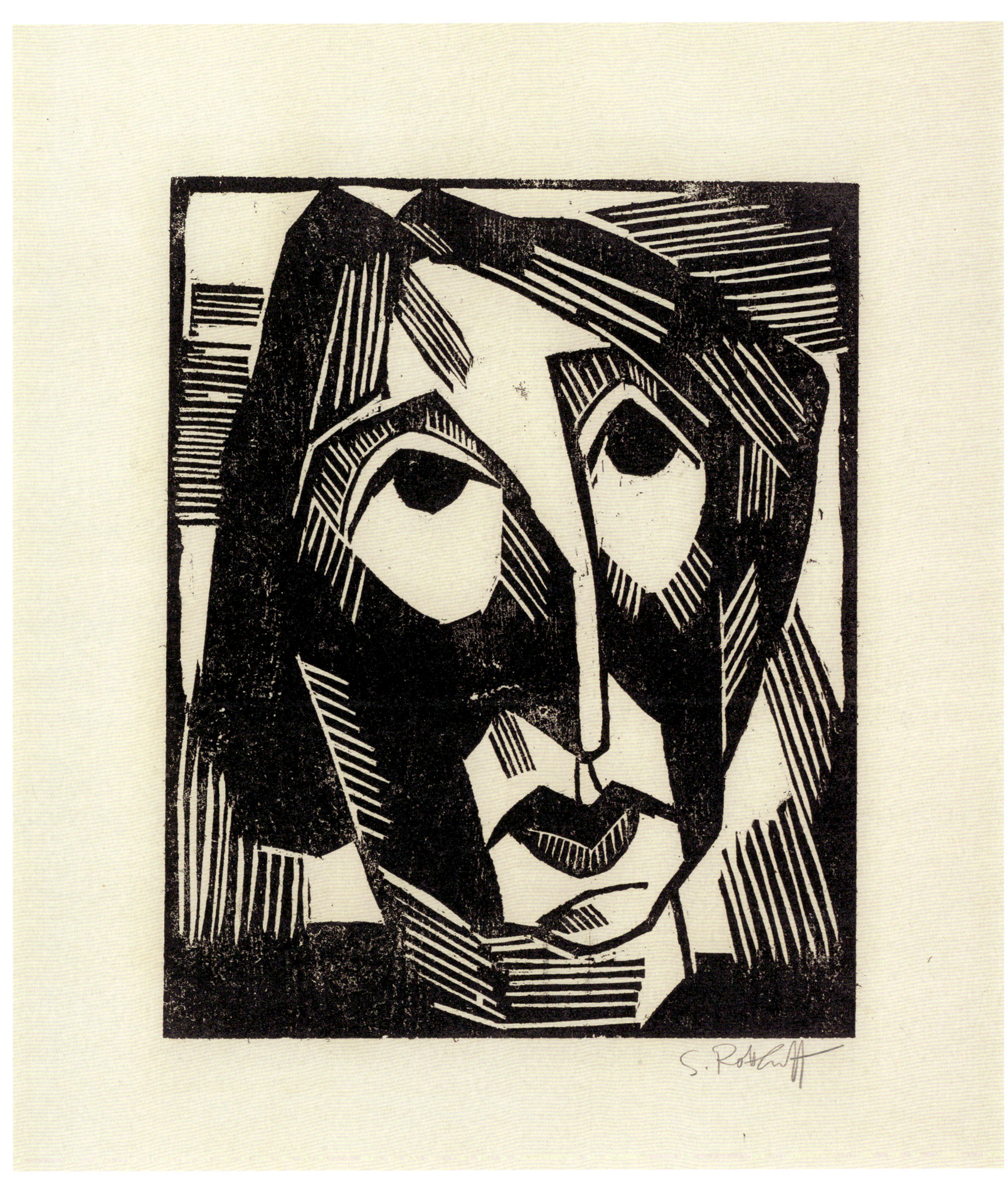

41 | **Karl Schmidt-Rottluff,** *Bildnis R. S. (Rosa Schapire)* / *Portrait R. S. (Rosa Schapire),* **1915,** Städel Museum, Frankfurt am Main

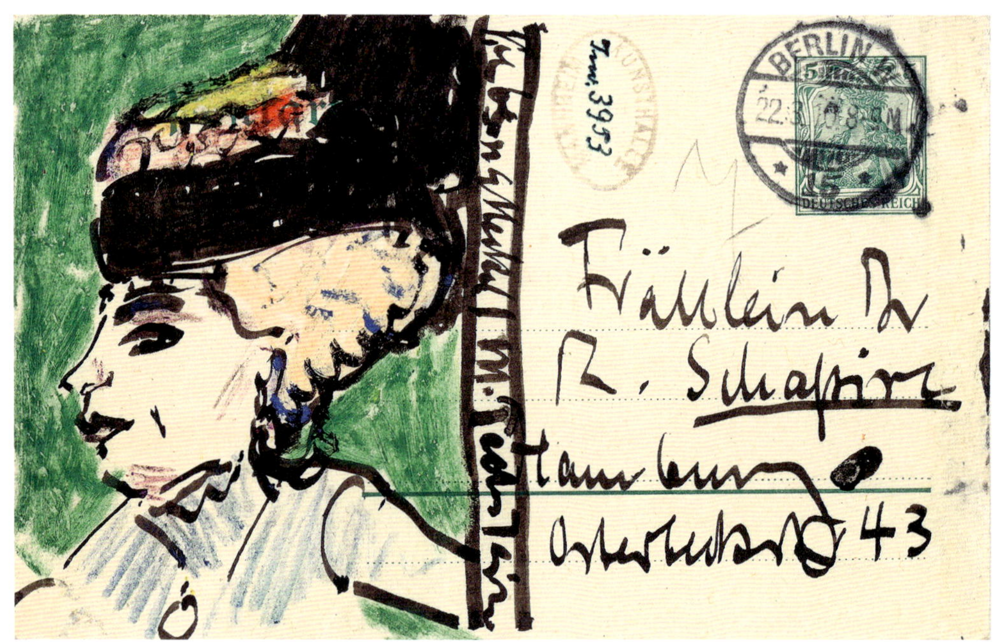

42 | **Max Pechstein,** *Dame mit Hut* / *Lady with Hat*, **1910,** Kunsthalle Mannheim

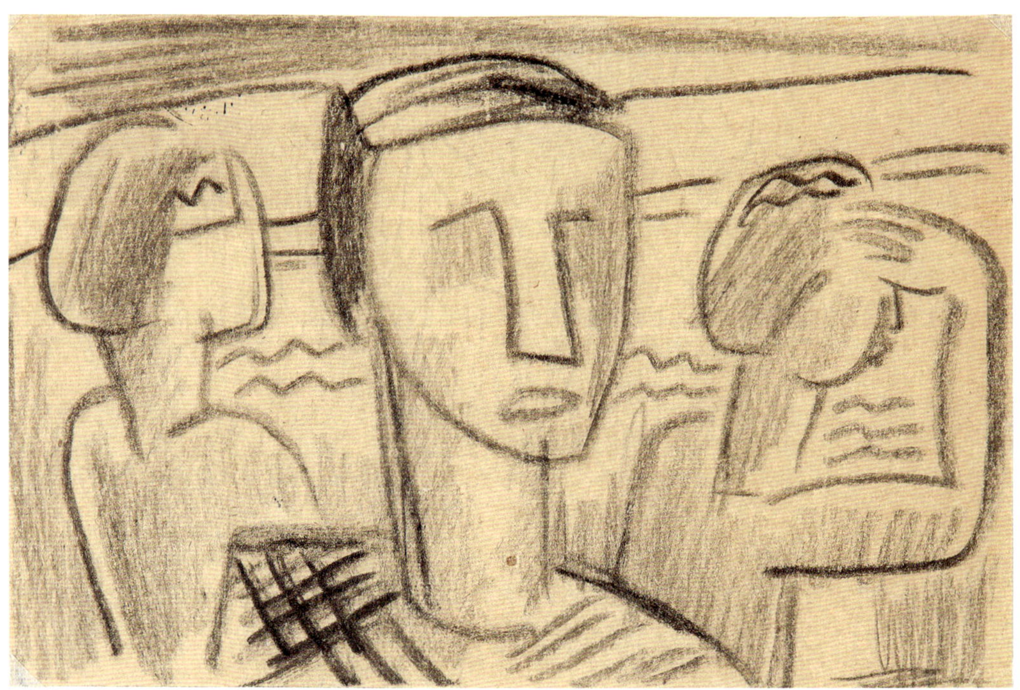

43 | **Karl Schmidt-Rottluff,** *Drei am Meer* / *Three Figures by the Sea*, **1920,** Kunsthalle Mannheim

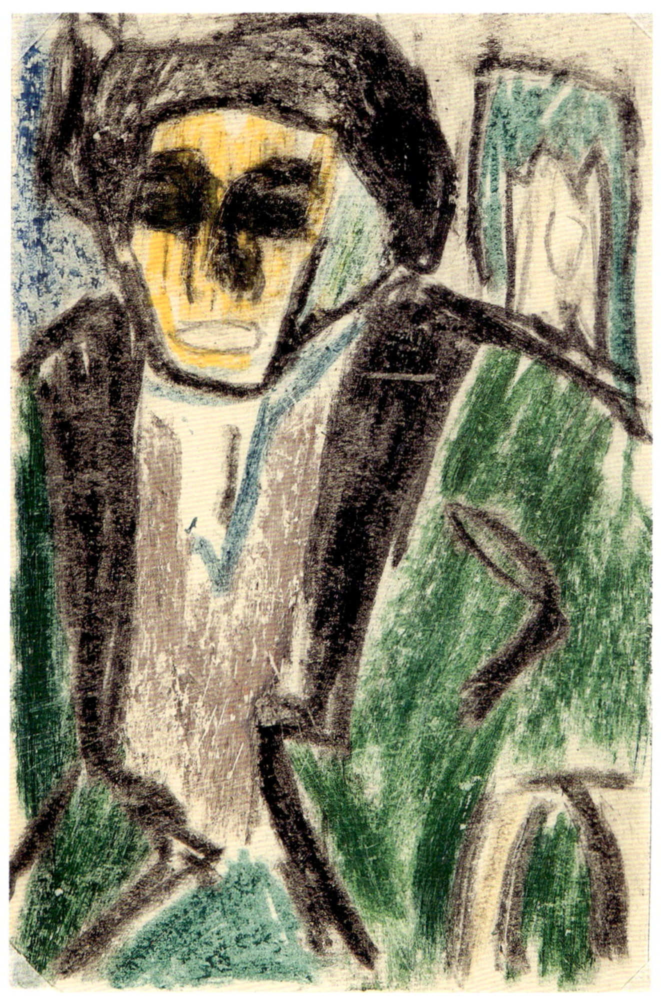

44 | **Karl Schmidt-Rottluff,** *Bildnis (vermutlich Rosa Schapire)* /
Portrait (presumably Rosa Schapire), **1911,** Kunsthalle Mannheim

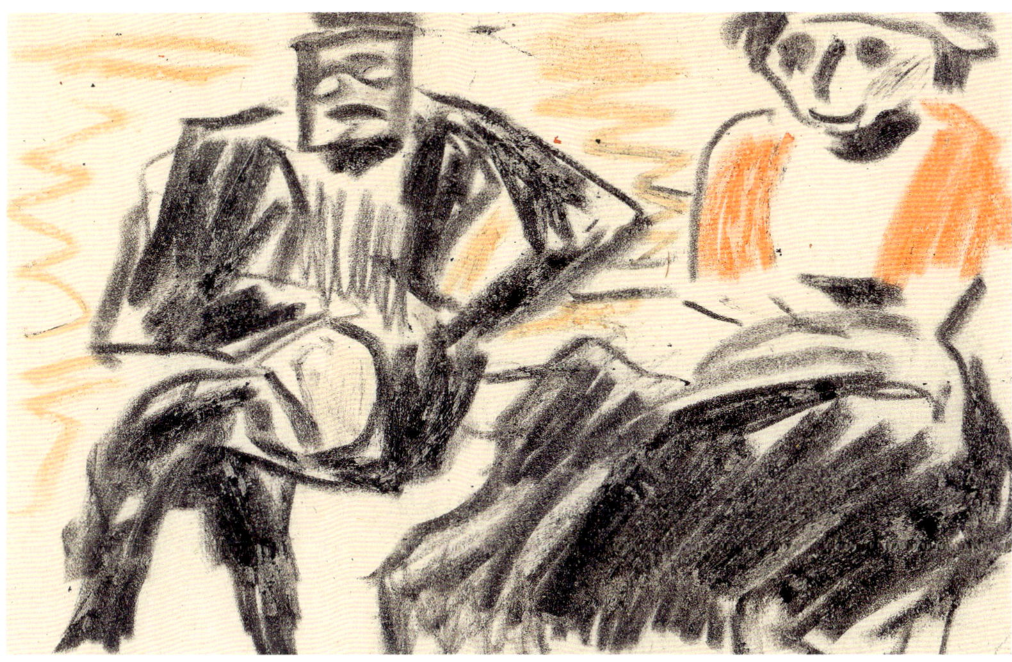

45 | **Erich Heckel,** *Sitzendes Paar* / *Seated Couple*, **1909,** Kunsthalle Mannheim

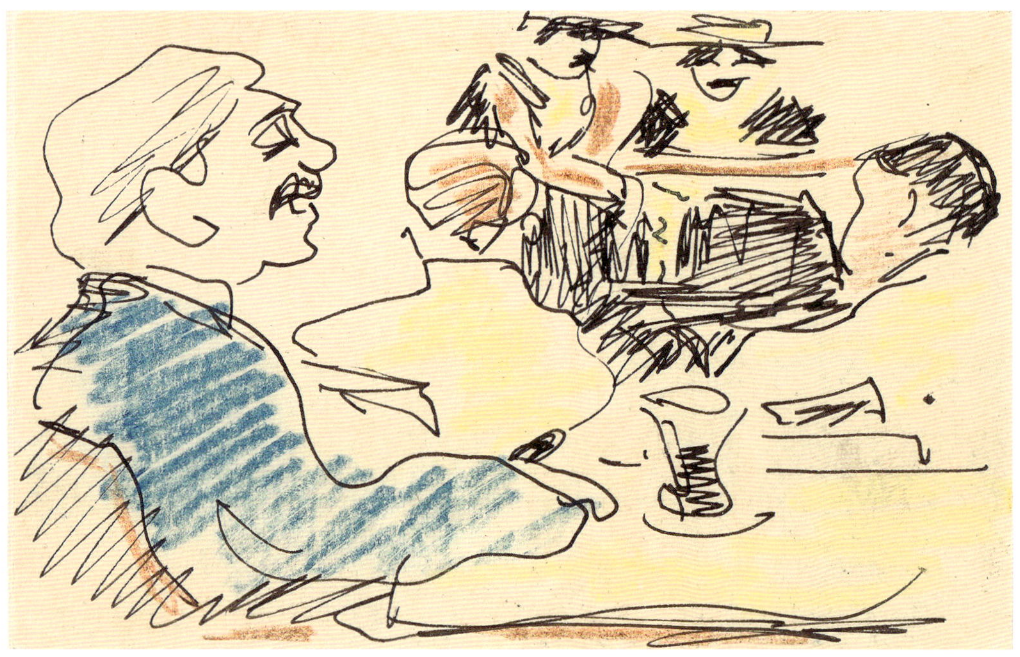

46 | **Max Pechstein,** *Im Restaurant /*
In the Restaurant, **1909,** Kunsthalle Mannheim

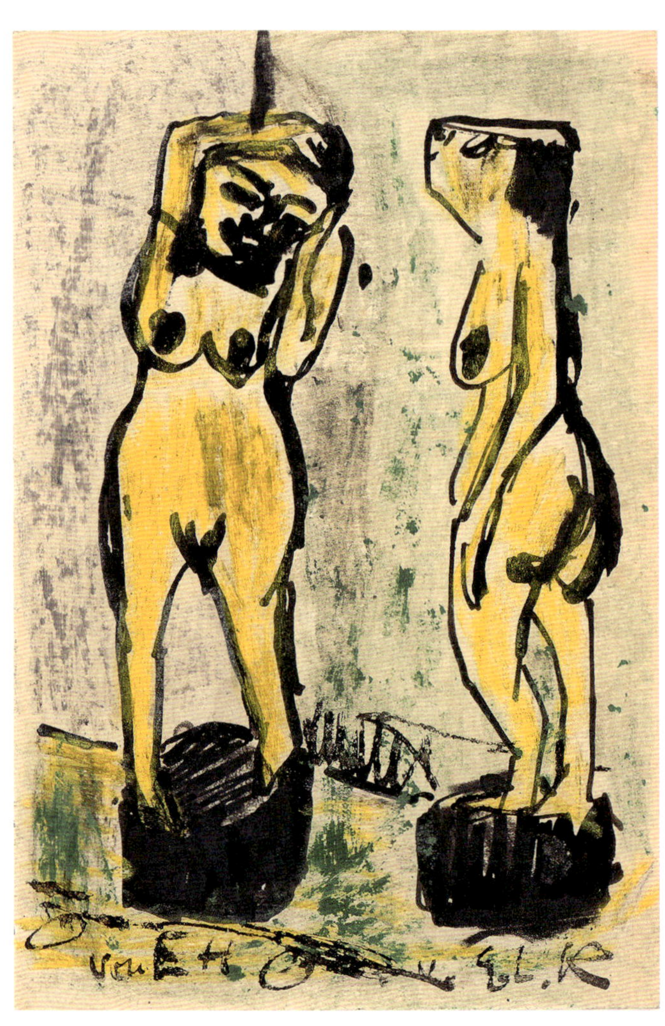

47 | **Ernst Ludwig Kirchner, Erich Heckel,** *Zwei Plastiken* / *Two Sculptures,* **1910,** Kunsthalle Mannheim

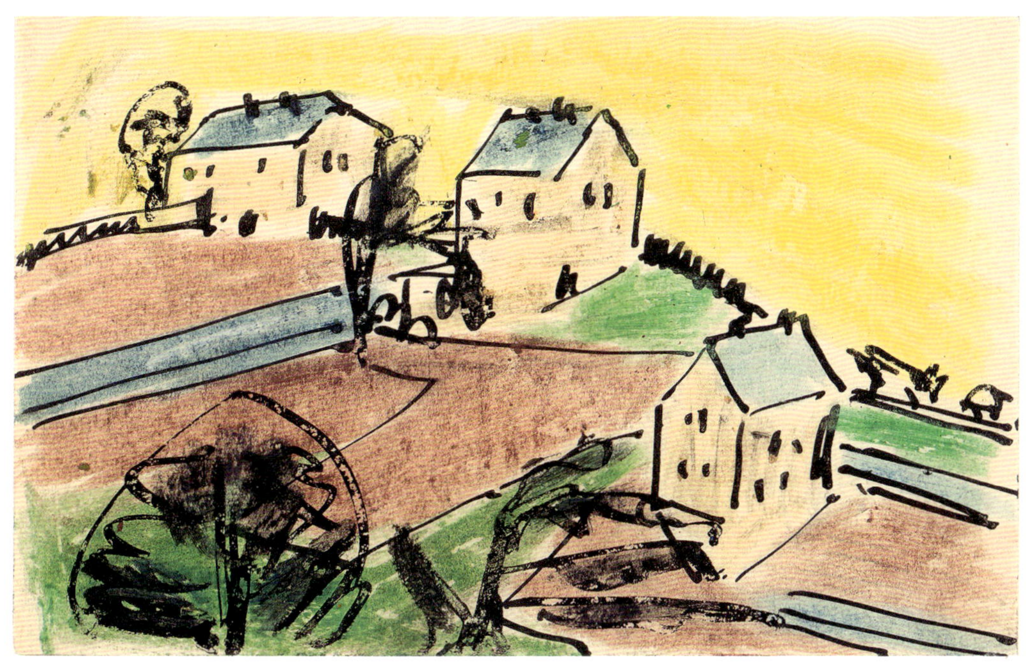

48 | **Ernst Ludwig Kirchner,** *Landschaft: Hügel mit Feldern und drei Häuser /*
Landscape: Hill with Fields and Three Houses, **1911,** Kunsthalle Mannheim

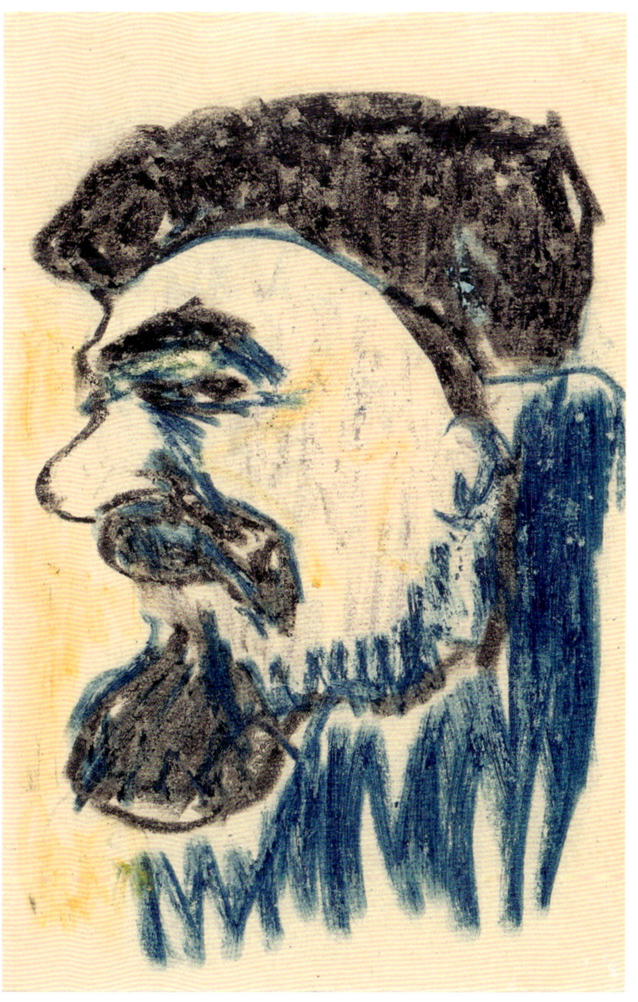

49 | **Erich Heckel,** *Bärtiger Mann /Bearded Man,* **1909,** Kunsthalle Mannheim

Private Collections of Expressionist Art in Mannheim: The Fuchs-Werle Collection

Luisa Heese

"Dear Mr. Probst," wrote the businessman and passionate art collector Hans Werle (1905–2000) on February 17, 1961, to the art dealer,[1] who was in the meantime living Starnberg, "I take the liberty of making a big request of you today. Perhaps you still recall our last talk a few years ago in your apartment on Richard Wagner-Strasse in Mannheim, about modern art and especially Expressionism. At the time I could not yet agree with your view of art but today I must 'penitently' concede that you were right—I too have learned to appreciate and love modern art. My greatest wish would be to purchase a beautiful oil painting by Nolde."[2]

In 1948, in the wake of the currency reform, Hans Werle founded an import-export business for wheat and flour that flourished to such an extent that he was able to invest his wealth in building an art collection. Initially, the collection concentrated on works of the nineteenth century and the early twentieth by Adolph von Menzel, Hans Thoma, and Max Liebermann. In Mannheim at the time, a loose circle of art enthusiasts formed who met regularly to discuss artistic subjects and to visit galleries and art fairs together. In addition to Hans Werle, they included the gallerist Friedrich Kaltreuther, the collector Wolfgang Burger, and the art historian Karl Ludwig Hofmann. In the early 1960s, as is clear from his letter to Probst, Werle increasingly turned to Expressionism. This reorientation of the focus of his collection went hand in hand with gradual separation from works he had acquired earlier so that the profile of his collection could get continuously honed. His first purchase of Expressionist art was indeed a work by Emil Nolde: in 1961, he bought the painting *Landschaft am Nachmittag* (Landscape in the Afternoon) of 1920 (cat. 57). Until 1975, this was followed by paintings by Alexej von Jawlensky, Ernst Ludwig Kirchner, David Davidovich Burliuk, Erich Heckel, Karl Schmidt-Rottluff, Otto Mueller, and Oskar Kokoschka. Werle was in direct contact with Kokoschka to commission a view of Heidelberg from the Philosophenweg (Philosopher's Path) across the Neckar, but it did not come to pass. In the mid-1970s, Hans Werle ceased collecting.

Fortunately, his passion for collection was inherited by the next generation: a large part of his Expressionism went to his daughter Lilo Fuchs (née Werle), who together with her husband, Manfred Fuchs, not only kept it together but also expanded it. Manfred Fuchs, who had himself been active as an artist in his youth (he regularly visited the Kunsthalle with his art teacher at the Karl-Friedrich-Gymnasium to make copy drawings of originals; he also joined a group for plein air drawing on the Neckar meadows in Seckenheim and attended courses at the local art school), abandoned his career as an artist to take over his father's business. He acquired his first works in the mid-1950s at the Antiquariat Tenner in Heidelberg: graphic works by Henry Moore, Marc Chagall, and George Rouault. In 1967, he attended a Gabriele Münter exhibition at the Heidelberger Kunstverein, which left a lasting impression. In 1970, finally, he acquired for their joint collection Gabriele Münter's *Gebirgslandschaft* (Mountain Landscape) of 1910 (cat. 60)—an important work that

Privatsammlungen expressionistischer Kunst in Mannheim: die Sammlung Fuchs-Werle

Luisa Heese

„Sehr geehrter Herr Probst", schrieb der Kaufmann und leidenschaftliche Kunstsammler Hans Werle (1905–2000) am 17. Februar 1961 an den Kunsthändler Rudolf Probst[1], der inzwischen in Starnberg residierte, „ich erlaube mir, Sie heute mit einer grossen Bitte in Anspruch zu nehmen. Vielleicht erinnern Sie sich noch unserer letzten Unterredung vor ein paar Jahren in Ihrer Wohnung Richard Wagner-Strasse Mannheim über moderne Kunst insbesondere den Expressionismus. Ich konnte damals Ihrer Kunstauffassung noch nicht folgen, heute muss ich Ihnen ‚reumütig' Recht geben – auch ich habe die moderne Kunst schätzen und lieben lernen. Mein grösster Wunsch wäre, ein schönes Oelgemälde von Nolde zu kaufen."[2]

Hans Werle hatte 1948 im Zuge der Währungsreform ein Handelsunternehmen für den Im- und Export von Weizen und Mehl gegründet, das so florierte, dass er sein Vermögen in den Aufbau einer Kunstsammlung investieren konnte. Zunächst waren es Werke des 19. und frühen 20. Jahrhunderts von Adolph von Menzel, Hans Thoma oder Max Liebermann, auf die sich der Sammler konzentrierte. In Mannheim entwickelte sich in dieser Zeit ein loser Bekanntenkreis von Kunstbegeisterten, die sich bei den regelmäßigen Treffen zu Kunstthemen austauschten und gemeinsam Galerien und Messen besuchten. Hierzu zählten neben Hans Werle auch der Galerist Friedrich Kaltreuther, der Sammler Wolfgang Burger und der Kunsthistoriker Karl Ludwig Hofmann. Anfang der 1960er-Jahre, wie in seinem Schreiben an Probst deutlich wird, wendete Werle sich verstärkt dem Expressionismus zu. Diese Neuausrichtung seines Sammlungsschwerpunktes ging mit der schrittweisen Trennung von vormals erstandenen Werken einher, sodass sich das Sammlungsprofil kontinuierlich schärfen konnte. Seine erste Erwerbung der expressionistischen Kunst sollte dann tatsächlich ein Werk von Emil Nolde sein: 1961 erstand er das Gemälde *Landschaft am Nachmittag* aus dem Jahr 1920 (Kat. 57). Bis 1975 folgten weitere Gemälde von Alexej von Jawlensky, Ernst Ludwig Kirchner, Erich Heckel, Karl Schmidt-Rottluff, Otto Mueller und Oskar Kokoschka. Mit Letzterem stand Werle noch in direktem Kontakt, um über eine Auftragsarbeit für eine Heidelberger Stadtansicht vom Philosophenweg aus über den Neckar zu verhandeln, die allerdings nicht mehr zustande kam. Mitte der 1970er-Jahre stellte Hans Werle seine Sammeltätigkeit ein.

Die Leidenschaft des Sammelns vererbte sich glücklicherweise an die nächste Generation: Ein Großteil der Expressionismus-Sammlung ging an seine Tochter Lilo Fuchs (geb. Werle) über, die gemeinsam mit ihrem Ehemann Manfred Fuchs diese nicht nur zusammenhielt, sondern noch erweiterte. Manfred Fuchs, der sich selbst als Jugendlicher künstlerisch betätigt hatte (mit seinem Kunstlehrer am Karl-Friedrich-Gymnasium besuchte er regelmäßig die Kunsthalle, um Originale abzuzeichnen; ebenso schloss er sich einer Gruppe zum Freizeichnen auf den Seckenheimer Neckarwiesen an und belegte Kurse an der örtlichen Kunstschule), stellte eine Laufbahn als Künstler zugunsten der Übernahme des väterlichen Betriebs hintan. Er erwarb die ersten Werke bereits Mitte der 1950er-Jahre im Heidelberger Antiquariat Tenner, grafische Arbeiten von Henry Moore, Marc Chagall und George Rouault. 1967 besuchte er eine Ausstellung von Gabriele Münter

had remained in the artist's possession until her death. More acquisitions followed in the succeeding decades, so that the Fuchs-Werle Collection is still today the most important private collection in Mannheim with a focus on Expressionism. Now it is being presented to the public this extensively for the first time.

Expressionism left behind other important traces in private collections in Mannheim: works by Wilhelm Lehmbruck, Max Pechstein, and Karl Hofer. Happily, they too can be presented in the current exhibition and hence be made accessible to the public for a time in order to continue telling the stories of Expressionism in Mannheim.

1   On Probst, see also the text by Dorotea Lorenz on art dealers and gallerists for Mannheim in the present volume.
2   Hans Werle to Rudolf Probst, February 17, 1961, private archive of the Fuchs-Werle Collection, Mannheim.

im Heidelberger Kunstverein, die ihn nachhaltig beeindruckte.
1970 erwarb er schließlich für die gemeinsame Sammlung Gabriele Münters *Gebirgslandschaft* von 1910 (Kat. 60) – ein bedeut-
sames Werk, das bis zu ihrem Tode im Besitz der Künstlerin
gewesen war. In den nachfolgenden Jahrzehnten folgten weitere
Ankäufe, die die Sammlung Fuchs-Werle bis heute zur wichtigsten Privatsammlung mit dem Schwerpunkt Expressionismus
in Mannheim machen – sie wird nun zum ersten Mal in diesem
Umfang öffentlich präsentiert.
Der Expressionismus hat noch weitere bedeutende Spuren
in Mannheimer Privatsammlungen mit Werken von Wilhelm
Lehmbruck, Max Pechstein und Karl Hofer hinterlassen. Auch
diese können erfreulicherweise in der aktuellen Ausstellung
präsentiert und damit zeitweise der Öffentlichkeit zugänglich
gemacht werden, um somit die Geschichten des Expressionismus in Mannheim weiterzuerzählen.

1   Zu Probst siehe in diesem Buch auch den Text von Dorotea Lorenz zu Kunst-
    händlern und Galeristen für Mannheim.
2   Hans Werle: Brief an Rudolf Probst vom 17. Februar 1961, Privatarchiv
    Sammlung Fuchs-Werle, Mannheim.

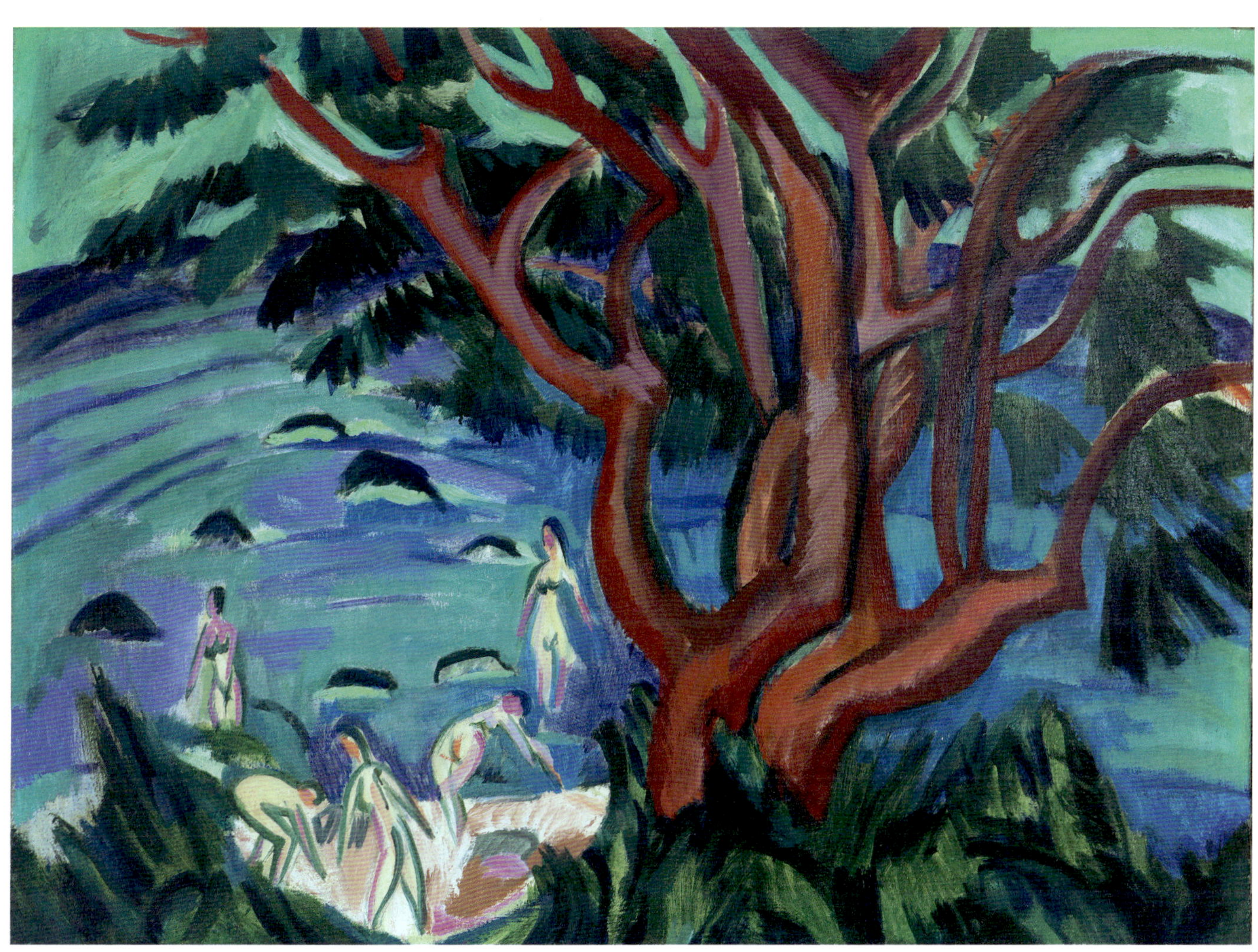

50 | **Ernst Ludwig Kirchner,** *Roter Baum am Strand* / *Red Tree at the Beach,* **1913,** Sammlung Fuchs-Werle / *Fuchs-Werle Collection*

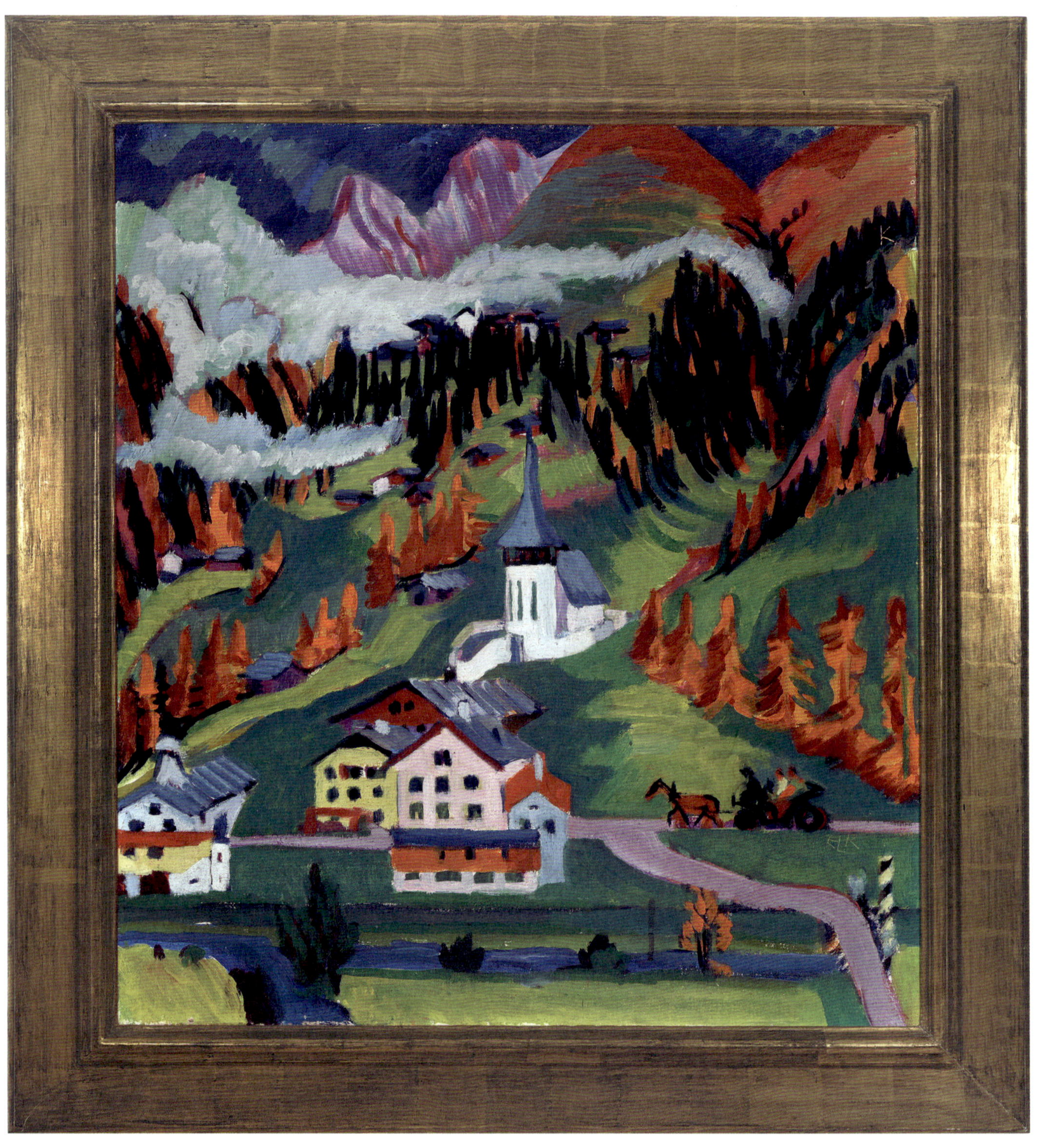

51 | **Ernst Ludwig Kirchner, *Frauenkirch im Herbst*** / *Frauenkirch in the Autumn*, **1920,**
Sammlung Fuchs-Werle / *Fuchs-Werle Collection*

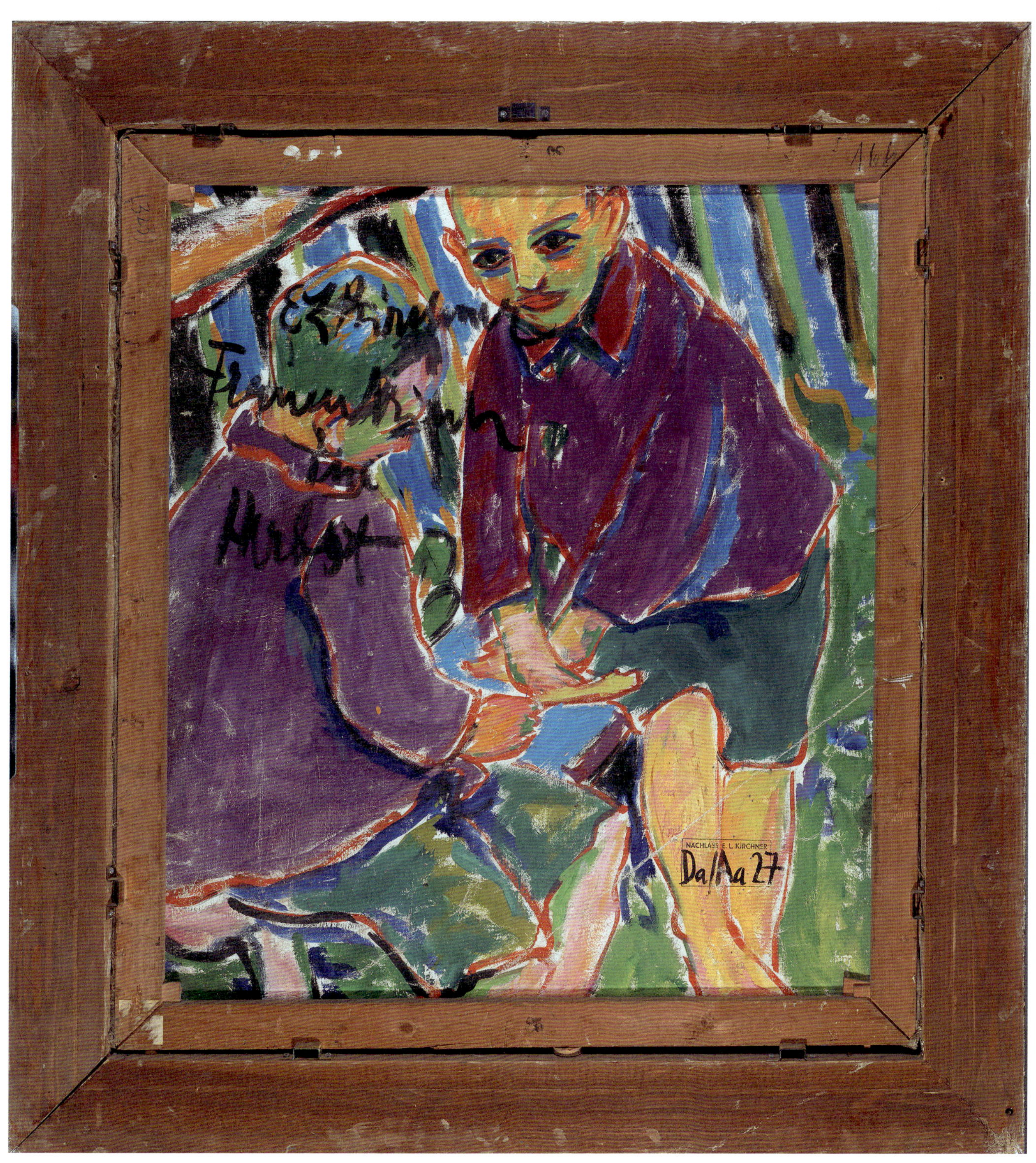

52 | **Ernst Ludwig Kirchner, *Zwei spielende Kinder* (Rückseite von *Frauenkirch im Herbst*)** / *Two Children Playing* (verso of Frauenkirch in the Autumn), **1909,**
Sammlung Fuchs-Werle / *Fuchs-Werle Collection*

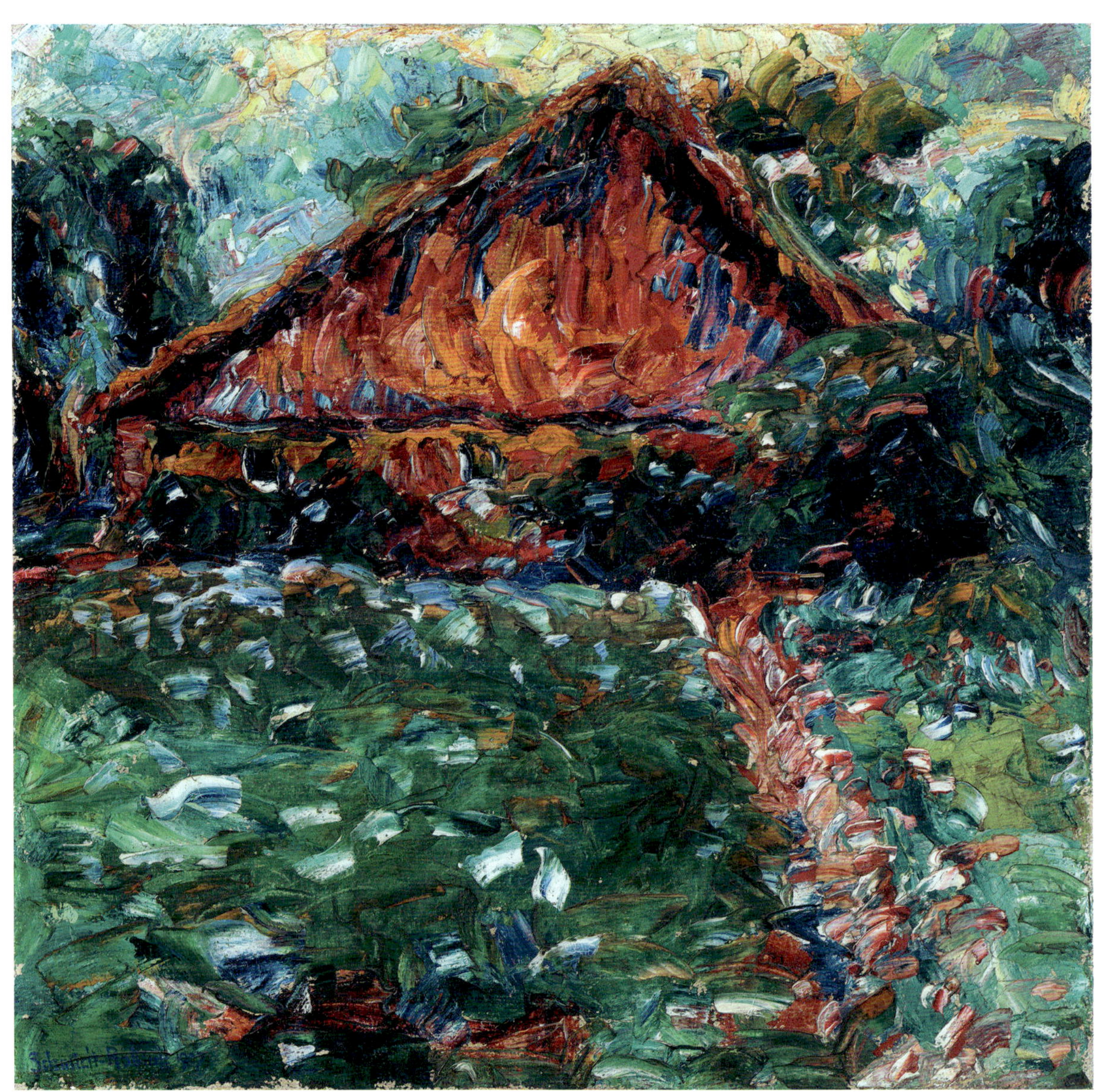

53 | **Karl Schmidt-Rottluff, *Der rote Weg* /** *The Red Road,* **1907,** Sammlung Fuchs-Werle / *Fuchs-Werle Collection*

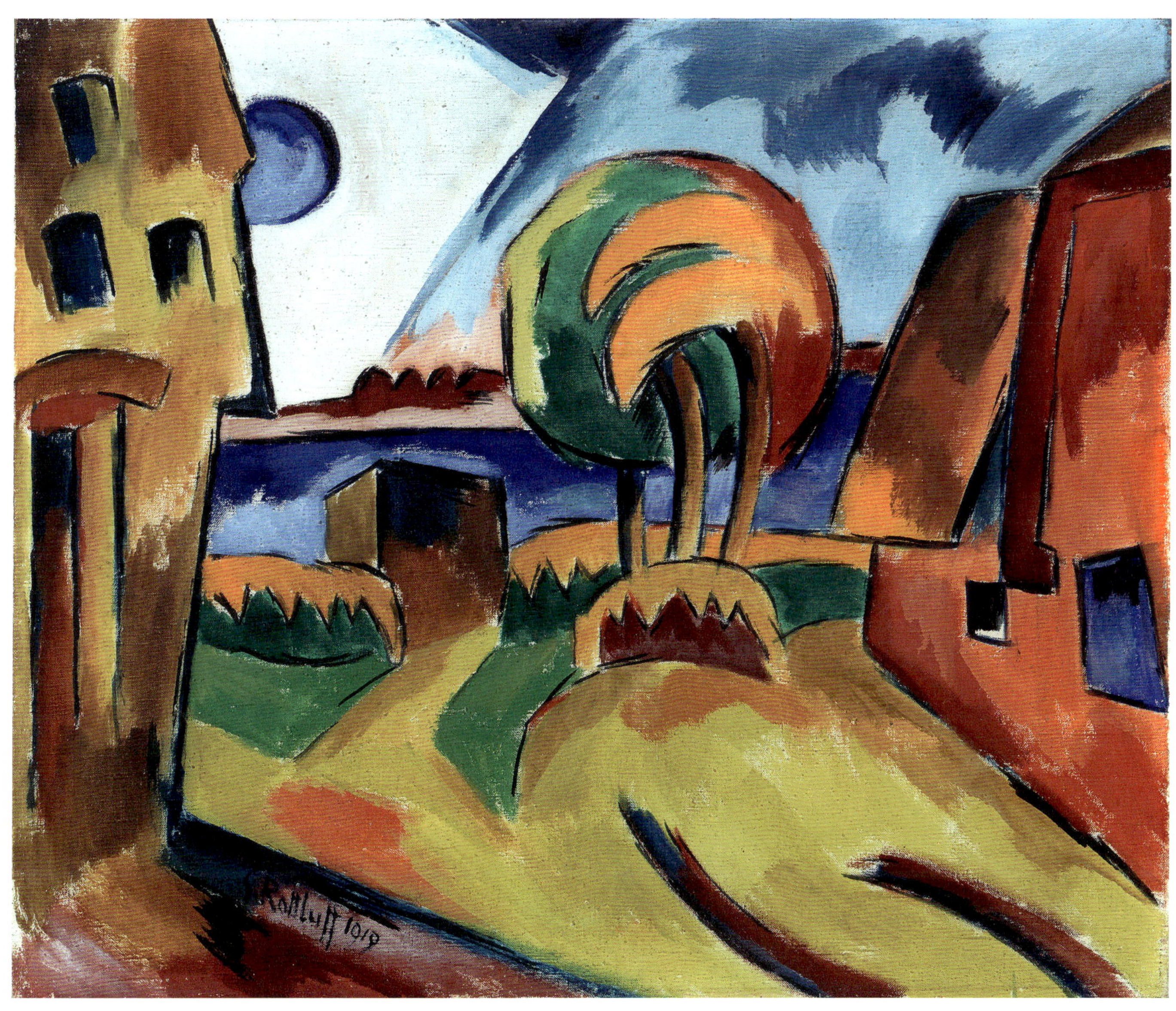

54 | Karl Schmidt-Rottluff, *Landschaft mit früher Sonne* / Landscape with Early Sun, 1919, Sammlung Fuchs-Werle / Fuchs-Werle Collection

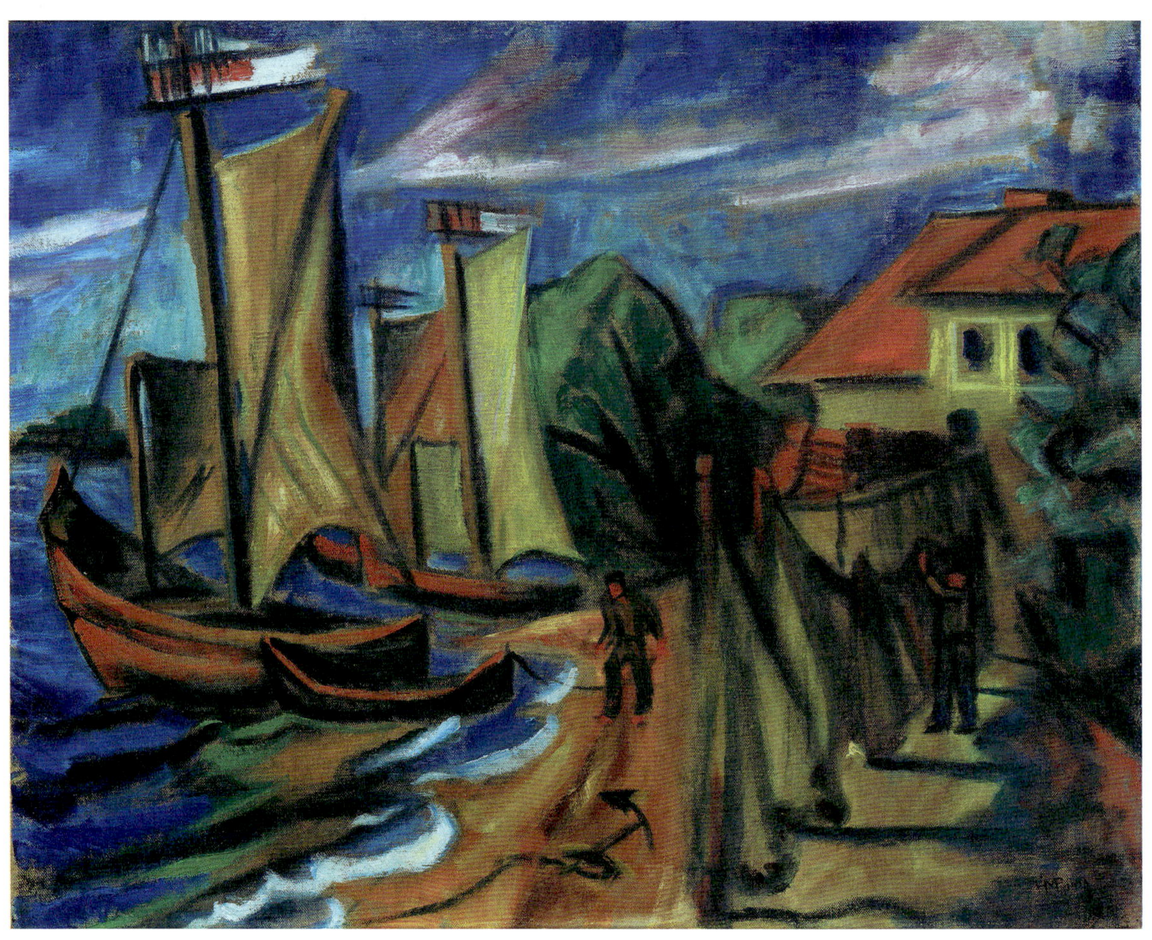

55 | **Max Pechstein, *Sommermorgen*** / *Summer Morning,* **1919,** Sammlung Fuchs-Werle / *Fuchs-Werle Collection*

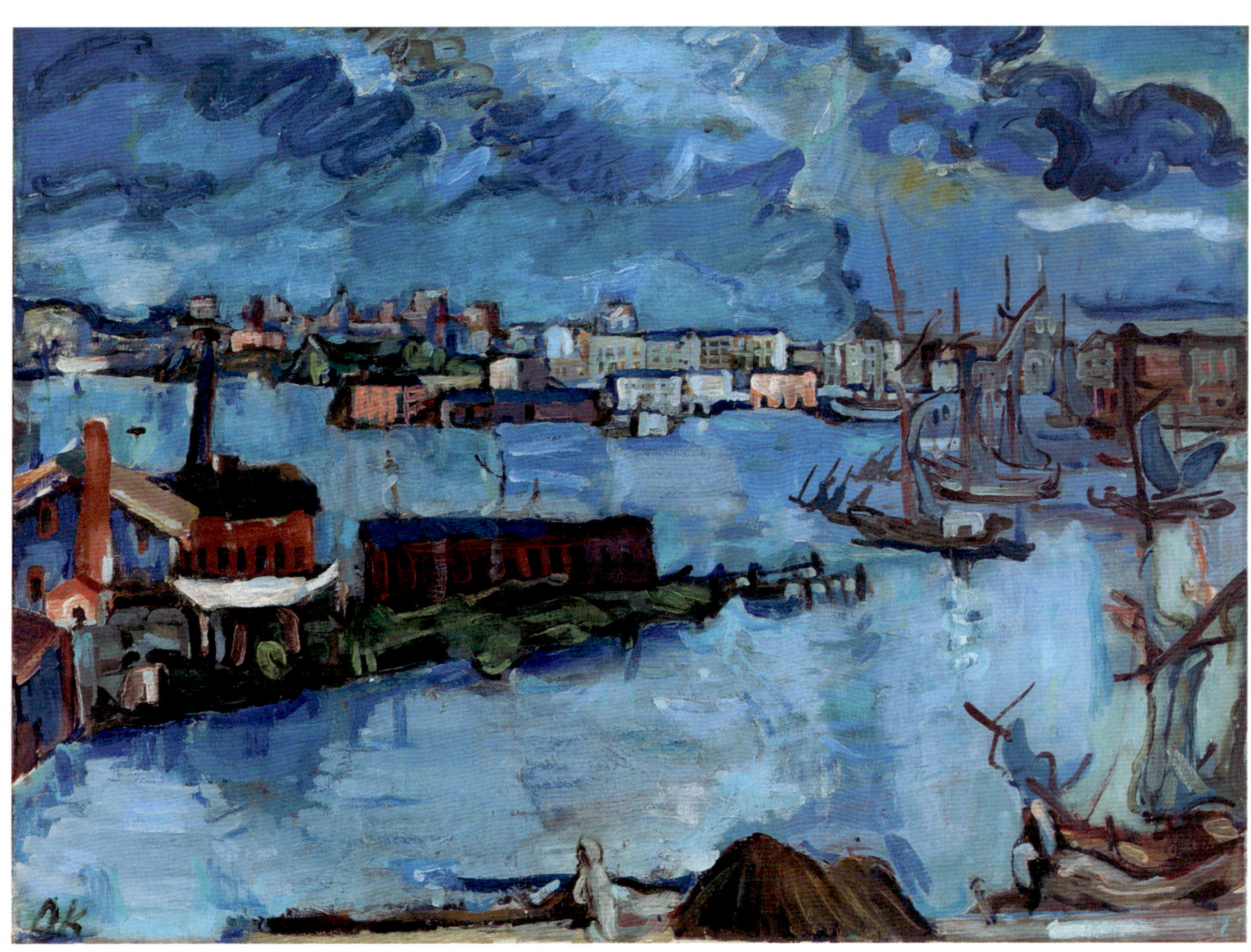

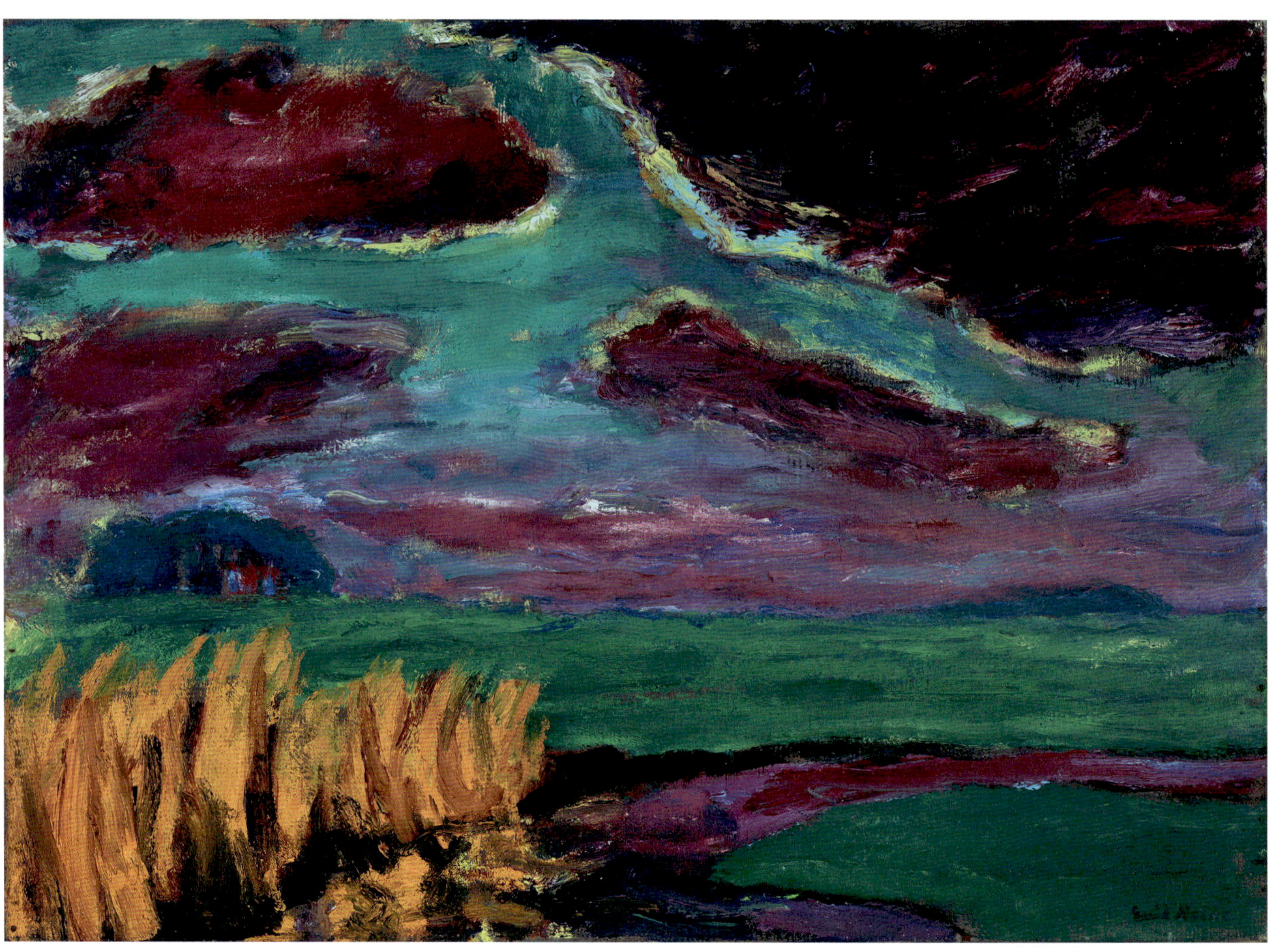

57 | **Emil Nolde, *Landschaft am Nachmittag* /** *Landscape in the Afternoon,* **1920,** Sammlung Fuchs-Werle / *Fuchs-Werle Collection*

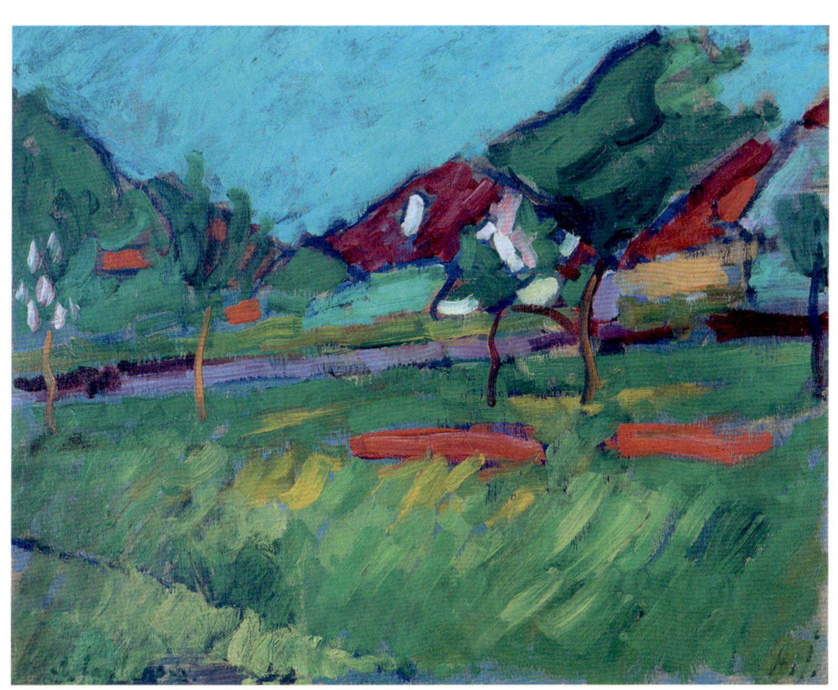

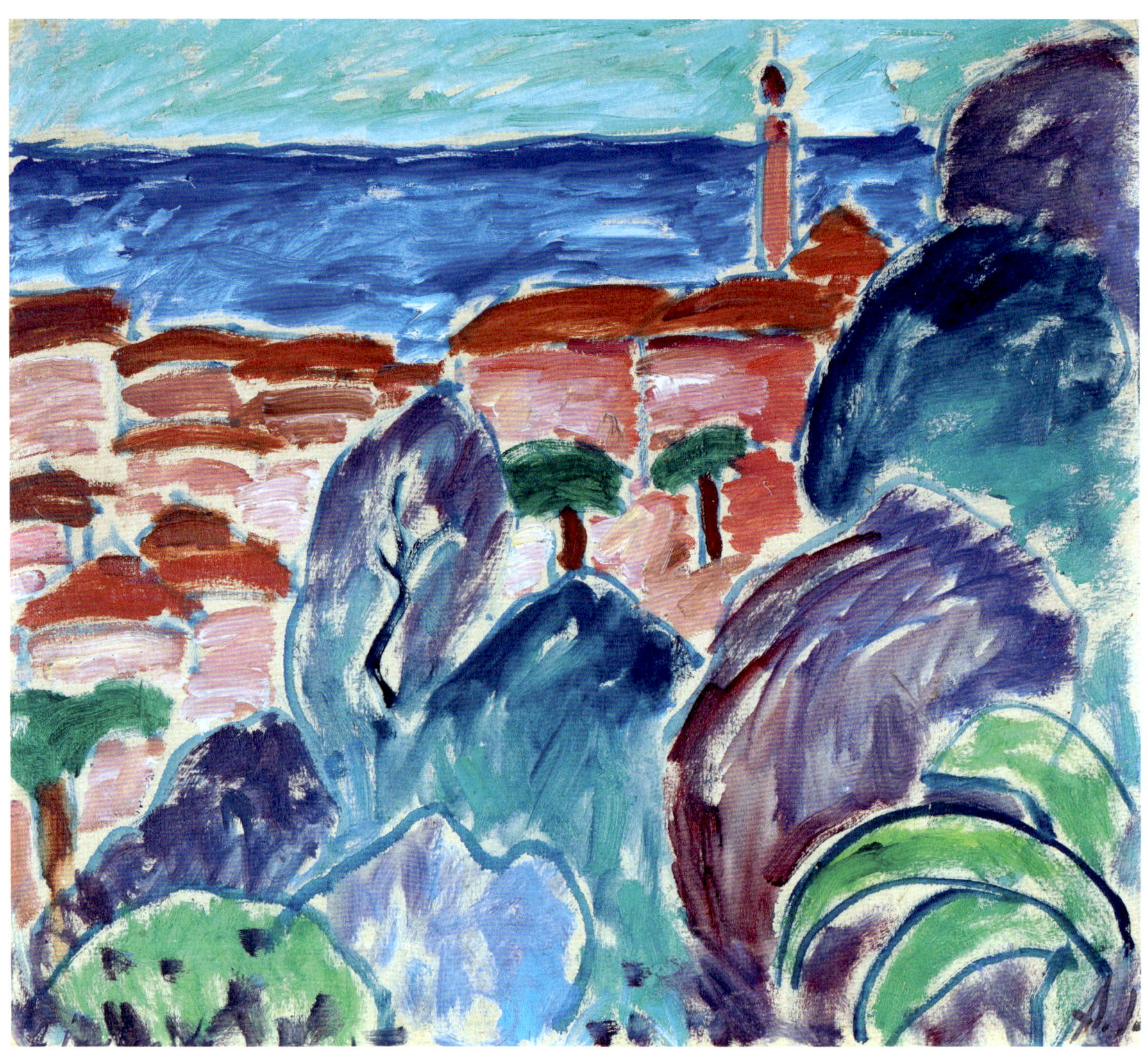

59 | **Alexej von Jawlensky,** *Küstenstadt* / *Coastal City,* **1914,** Sammlung Fuchs-Werle / *Fuchs-Werle Collection*

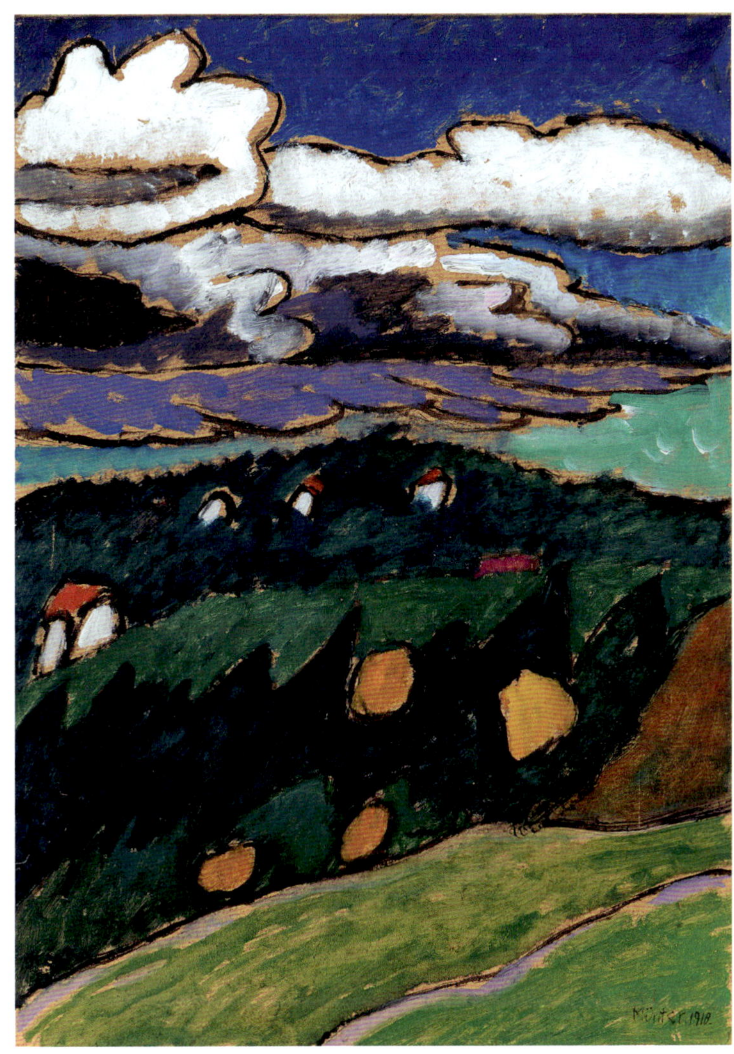

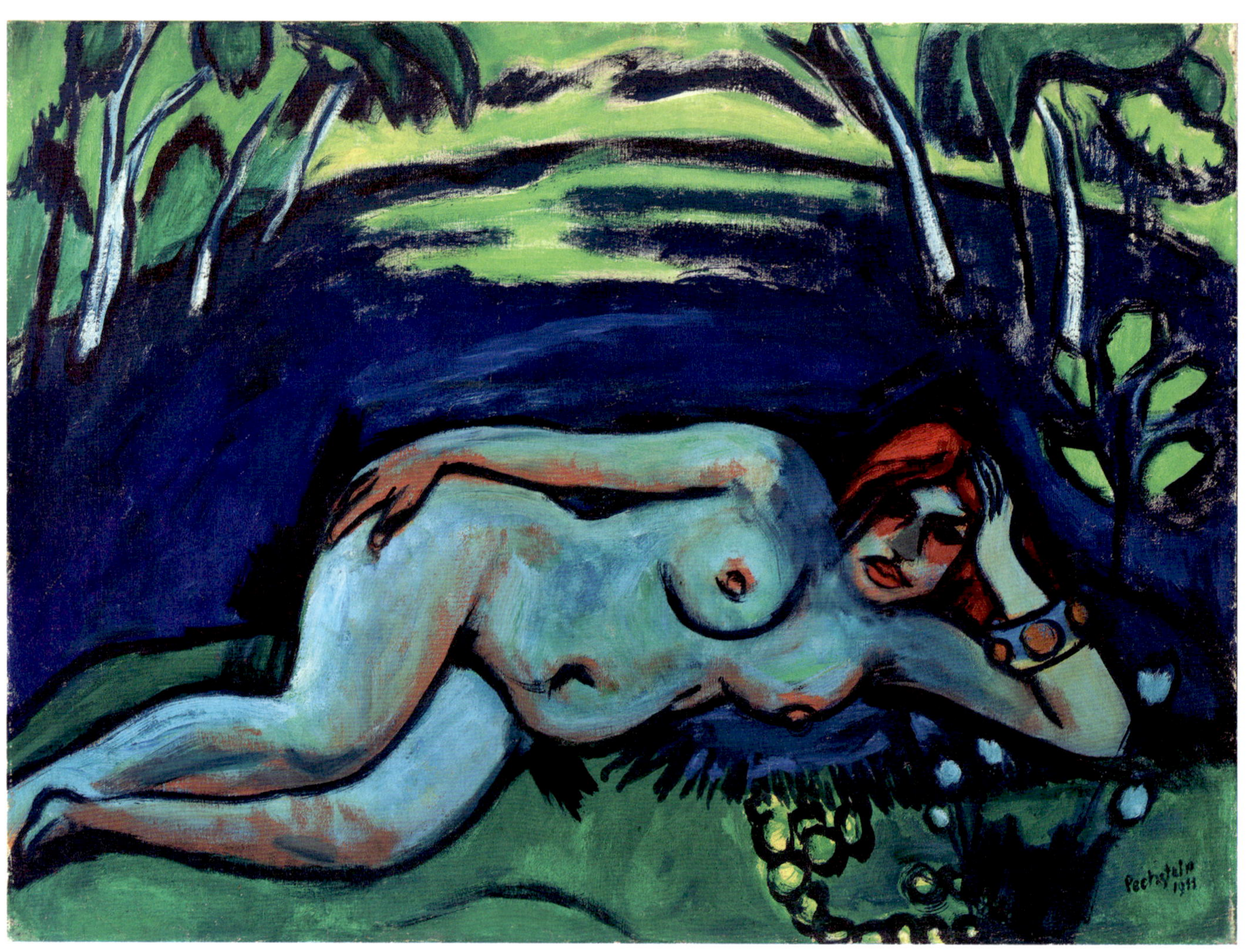

61 | **Max Pechstein,** *Früher Morgen* / *Early Morning,* **1911,** Sammlung Fuchs-Werle / *Fuchs-Werle Collection*

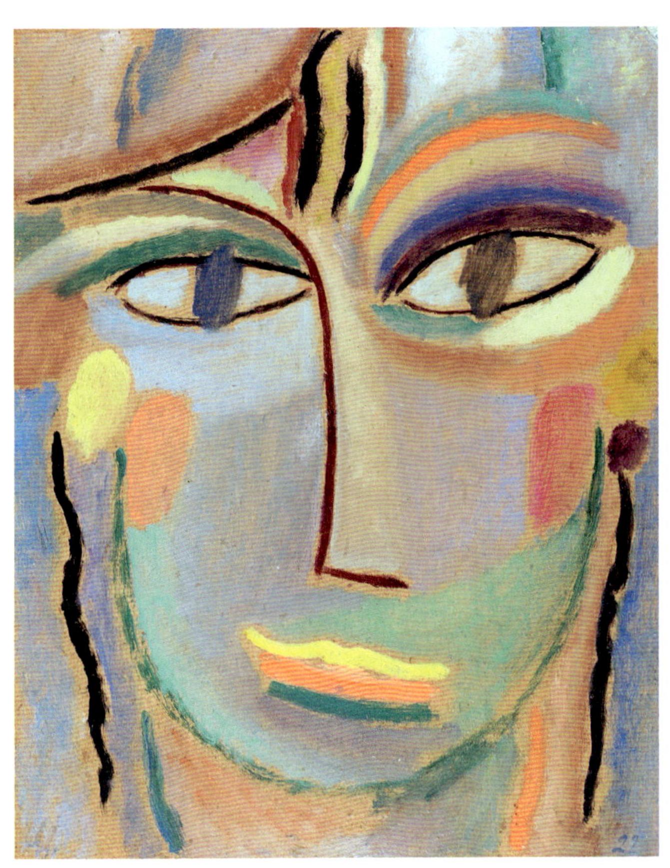

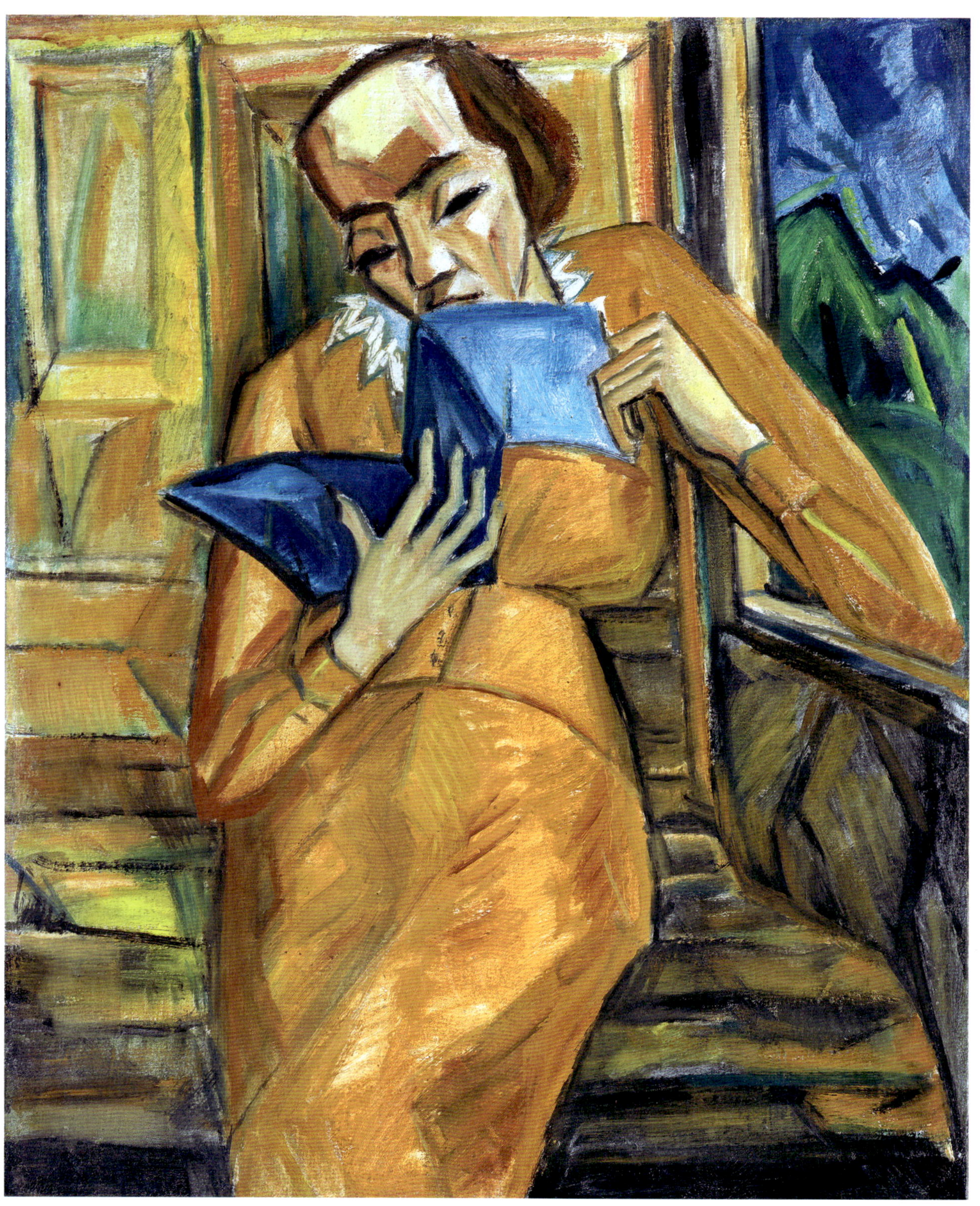

63 | **Erich Heckel,** *Lesendes Mädchen* / *Girl Reading,* **1913,** Sammlung Fuchs-Werle / *Fuchs-Werle Collection*

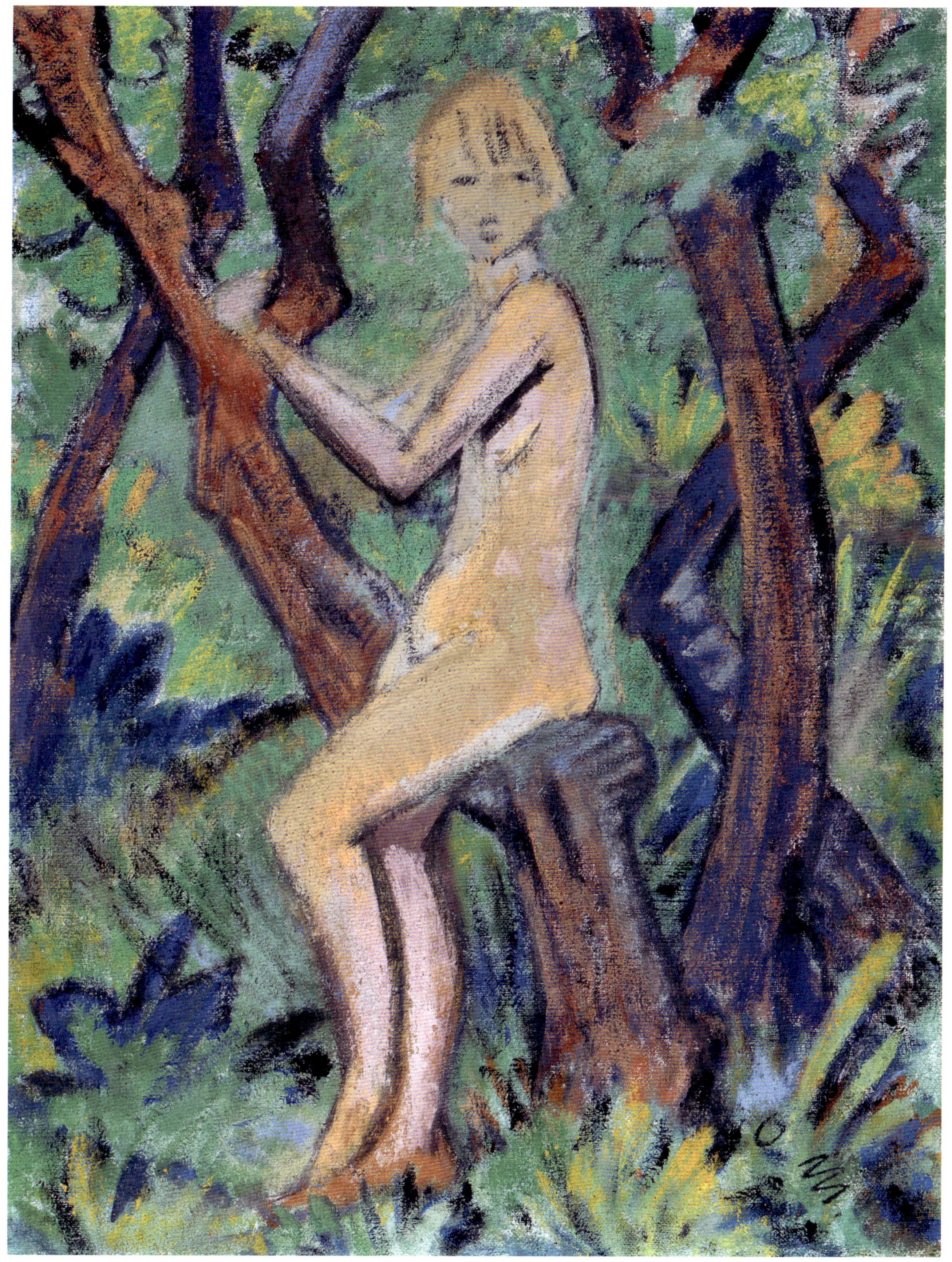

64 | **Otto Mueller, *Nacktes Mädchen auf Baum* / *Naked Girl on Tree*, 1910,** Sammlung Fuchs-Werle / *Fuchs-Werle Collection*

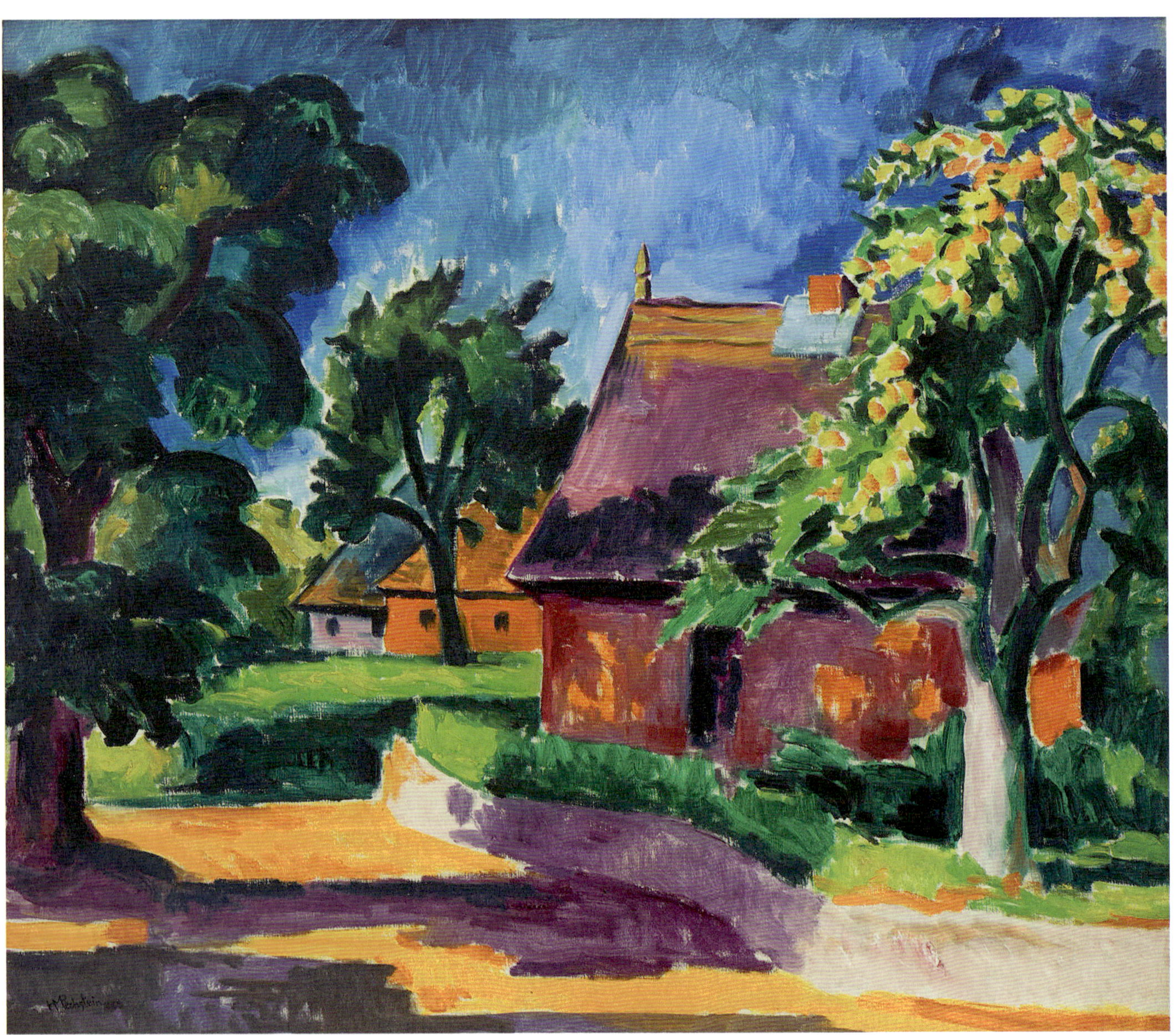

65 | **Max Pechstein,** *Bauerngehöft – Spätsommer* / *Farmstead – Late Summer,* **o. J.** / *n. d.,* Privatbesitz / *Private collection,* Mannheim

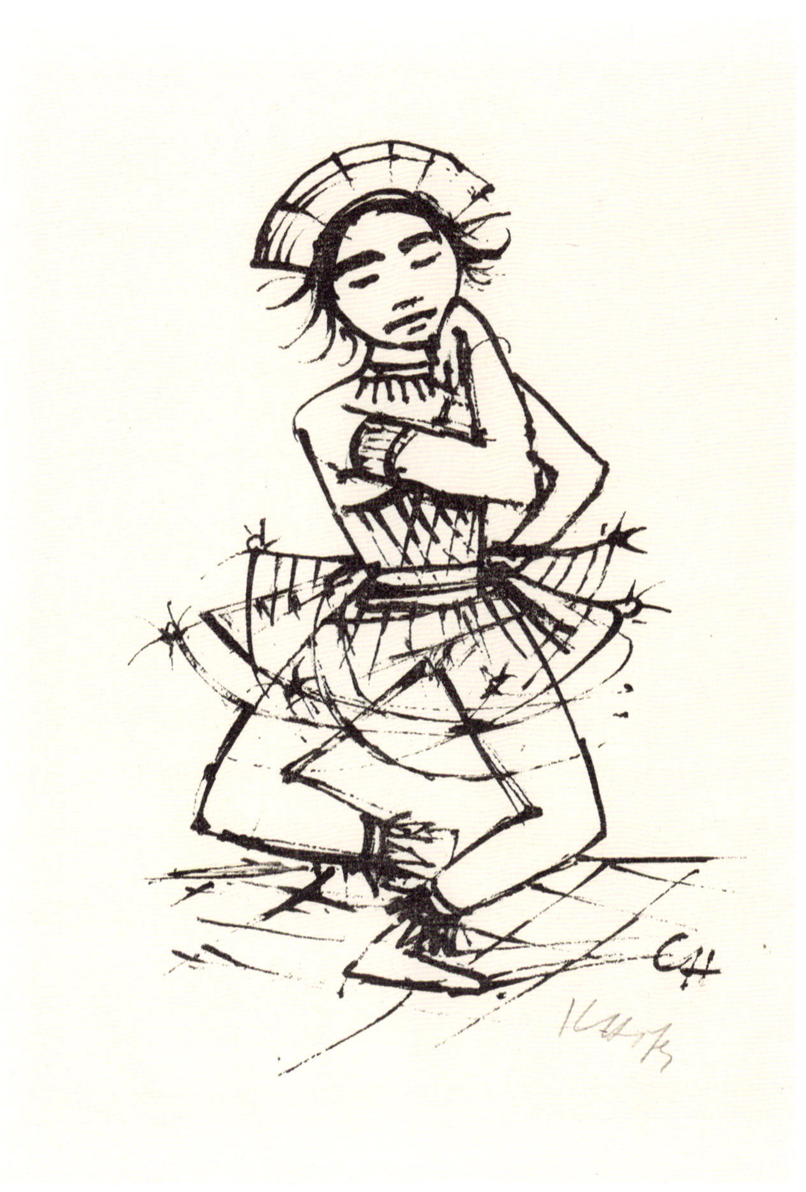

66 | **Karl Hofer,** *Javanische Tänzerin* / *Javanese Dancer,* **1921,** Sammlung Geber / *Geber Collection*

155

The Mannheim Graphic Arts Collection and Its Focus on Expressionist Woodcuts

Ursula Drahoss

The Graphic Arts Collection of the Kunsthalle Mannheim opened in 1910–11 to supplement the Painting and Sculpture Gallery and in so doing served above all a didactic function: it was part of a concept initiated by Fritz Wichert and continued by Gustav Friedrich Hartlaub to establish an academy for everyone in Mannheim. Hence the Graphic Arts Collection had an art historical institute with a reading room and library attached to it (p. 158, fig. 34). With lectures on popular scholarship, it was intended to make the public in Mannheim enthusiastic about the Kunsthalle. Targeted acquisition of graphic arts was also part of this museum strategy. From the founding of the Graphic Arts Collection on, Expressionist works were acquired continuously.[1]

Works were purchased from booksellers and art dealers as well as galleries, which at the time were among the most important addresses for Expressionist art, such as the Graphisches Kabinett of Israel Ber Neumann in Berlin (p. 159, fig. 35) the Galerie Ernst Arnold in Dresden, and the Kunsthandlung Ludwig Schames in Frankfurt am Main. In addition, works were acquired directly from artists such as Max Pechstein, Walther Bötticher, Emil Nolde, Karl Friedrich Zähringer, and Heinrich Campendonk. With this acquisition policy, the still young Graphic Arts Collection focused on Expressionist graphic art.

Building the collection was not free of tensions, however. The director at the time, Fritz Wichert, and his deputy, Gustav Friedrich Hartlaub, had divergent views about the orientation of the collection. When Wichert was appointed to serve in the diplomatic service in The Hague during World War I, Hartlaub took over as interim director of the Kunsthalle from 1914 to 1919 and during that time intensely championed Expressionism. In his book *Neue deutsche Grafik* (New German Graphic Art), published in 1920,[2] (p. 159, fig. 36) Hartlaub devoted great attention to the woodcut along with the etching and the lithograph. After a heyday with Albrecht Dürer, centuries of neglect, and a revival by the Romantics as *Faksimileschnitt* (facsimile engraving), this technique had fallen victim to the industrialization of art in the nineteenth century and mutated into the soulless wood engraving. In contrast to the wood engraving, which served to reproduce art and was usually executed by professional xylographers and was thought of more as a craft than as an art, in the medium of the woodcut the graphic artist worked the printing block himself and was usually also responsible for the printing process.[3] The Expressionists were following the lead of the Symbolists, but especially Paul Gauguin and Edvard Munch, and contributed to a revival of the woodcut, which Hartlaub called "second" or "new" Romanticism.[4] In his publications, Hartlaub could not help but use a Biblical metaphor to emphasize the new significance of the woodcut in Expressionism.[5] Expressionist artists appreciated this laborious process of form creation and hence the elemental expressive power that resulted from the resistance that the hardness of the material offered the cutting hand. The woodcarver drew the motif on a primed woodblock and cut along the contours to create the printing block. Then the nonrecessed surfaces were inked and the paper printed—using either a hand press or the ball of the hand. The grain of the wood and the cracks and fissures in the plate lend the print a raw, primal expressive power. The woodcuts of artists such as Ernst Ludwig Kirchner, Erich Heckel, Karl Schmidt-Rottluff, Nolde, Pechstein, and August Macke reveal this impetus of creation—inspired by, among other things, their knowledge of non-European works, travels to the South Seas or North Africa, and also influenced by Paul Gauguin's depictions of so-called exotic cultures. The associated idealization and appropriation of non-European art forms, which the Expressionists often venerated as "primitive" or unspoiled,

Die Mannheimer Grafiksammlung und ihr Schwerpunkt auf dem expressionistischen Holzschnitt

Ursula Drahoss

Die Graphische Sammlung der Kunsthalle Mannheim wurde 1910/11 als Ergänzung zur Gemälde- und Skulpturengalerie eröffnet und erfüllte hier vor allem eine didaktische Funktion: Sie war Teil des von Fritz Wichert initiierten und von Gustav Friedrich Hartlaub weiterentwickelten Konzepts, in Mannheim eine Akademie für Jedermann einzurichten. So war dem Graphischen Kabinett ein Kunstwissenschaftliches Institut mit Lesesaal und Bibliothek angegliedert (S. 158, Abb. 34). Mit populärwissenschaftlichen Vorträgen sollte das Mannheimer Publikum für die Kunsthalle begeistert werden. Teil dieser neuen Museumsstrategie war auch der gezielte Ankauf von Grafik. Seit der Gründung der Graphischen Sammlung wurden kontinuierlich Werke des Expressionismus erworben.[1]

Man kaufte Werke bei Buch- und Kunsthandlungen sowie Galerien, die damals zu den bedeutendsten Adressen für expressionistische Kunst zählten, wie etwa das Graphische Kabinett von Israel Ber Neumann in Berlin (S. 159, Abb. 35), die Galerie Ernst Arnold in Dresden und die Kunsthandlung Ludwig Schames in Frankfurt am Main. Darüber hinaus wurden Werke direkt bei Künstlern wie Max Pechstein, Walther Bötticher, Emil Nolde, Karl Friedrich Zähringer

und Heinrich Campendonk erworben. Mit dieser Ankaufspolitik legte die noch junge Graphische Sammlung den Grundstein für ihren Schwerpunkt auf expressionistischer Grafik.

Der Aufbau der Sammlung war jedoch nicht frei von Spannungen. Zwischen dem damaligen Direktor Fritz Wichert und seinem Stellvertreter Gustav Friedrich Hartlaub kam es zu unterschiedlichen Auffassungen über die Ausrichtung der Sammlung. Als Wichert im Ersten Weltkrieg in diplomatischem Dienst nach Den Haag berufen wurde, übernahm Hartlaub von 1914 bis 1919 kommissarisch die Leitung der Kunsthalle und setzte sich in dieser Zeit intensiv für den Expressionismus ein. In seinem 1920 erschienenen Buch *Neue deutsche Graphik*[2] (S. 159, Abb. 36) widmete Hartlaub dem Holzschnitt neben Radierung und Lithografie die größte Aufmerksamkeit. Nach einer Blütezeit bei Dürer, einer jahrhundertelangen Vernachlässigung und einer Wiederbelebung als „Faksimileschnitt" durch die Romantiker war diese Technik im 19. Jahrhundert der Industrialisierung der Kunst zum Opfer gefallen und zum seelenlosen Holzstich mutiert. Im Gegensatz zum Holzstich, der zur Reproduktion künstlerischer Vorlagen herangezogen, meist von professionellen Xylografen ausgeführt und eher als handwerkliche denn als künstlerische Technik verstanden wurde, bearbeiteten Künstlergrafiker*innen im Holzschnitt den Druckstock selbst und führten auch den Druck zumeist selbst aus.[3] Die Expressionist*innen knüpften dabei an die Symbolist*innen, vor allem aber an Paul Gauguin und Edvard Munch an und verhalfen dem Holzschnitt zu einer Wiederbelebung, die Hartlaub als „zweite" oder „Neuromantik" bezeichnete.[4] Hartlaub konnte sogar nicht umhin, in seinen Publikationen die neue Bedeutung des Holzschnitts im Expressionismus mit einer biblischen Metapher hervorzuheben.[5] Die Künstler*innen des Expressionismus schätzten den mühsamen Prozess der Formgebung und damit die elementare Ausdruckskraft, die aus dem Widerstand entsteht, den die Härte des Materials der schneidenden Hand entgegensetzt. Die Holzschneider*innen zeichnen das Motiv auf eine grundierte Holzplatte und schneiden es entlang der Konturen in den so entstehenden Druckstock. Anschließend werden die erhabenen Flächen eingefärbt und auf Papier gedruckt – entweder per Handpresse oder mit dem Handballen. Durch die Holzmaserung sowie Risse und Sprünge in der Holzplatte erhält der Druck eine rohe, ursprüngliche Ausdruckskraft. Besonders in den Holzschnitten von Künstlern wie Ernst Ludwig Kirchner, Erich Heckel, Karl Schmidt-Rottluff, Emil Nolde, Max Pechstein oder auch August Macke

is a view shaped by colonialism that must be regarded critically today. For example, Gustav Friedrich Hartlaub described the woodcuts of Karl Schmidt-Rottluff as "jagged, cuneiform, radial script," which in his opinion recalled non-European art forms; he praised its "overpowering force" and emphasized that its manner of expression was unique and could not be imitated.[6]

1 Thomas Köllhofer, "Die Graphische Sammlung in der Kunsthalle Mannheim bis zur Mitte des 20. Jahrhunderts," in *Streifzüge durch die Moderne: Die Graphische Sammlung der Kunsthalle Mannheim*, ed. Christine Hopfengart and Ulrike Lorenz (Cologne: Wienand, 2015), pp. 11–17, esp. p. 14.
2 Gustav F. Hartlaub, *Neue deutsche Graphik* (Berlin: Reiß, 1920).
3 Theresa Nisters, "Zurück zum Ursprung, zu den Quellen, zur Natur und zum Material": Holz—Material mit Geschichte," in *Geheimnis der Materie: Kirchner, Heckel, Schmidt-Rottluff*, ed. Regina Freyberger, exh. cat. Städel Museum Frankfurt am Main 2019 (Dresden: Sandstein, 2019), pp. 30–47, esp. p. 34.
4 Hartlaub, *Neue deutsche Graphik* (see note 2), p. 18.
5 Hartlaub, *Neue deutsche Graphik* (see note 2), "Im Anfang war der Holzschnitt," p. 7; Gustav F. Hartlaub, *Die Graphik des Expressionismus in Deutschland* (Stuttgart and Calw: Hatje, 1947), p. 11.
6 Hartlaub, *Die Graphik des Expressionismus* (see note 5), pp. 35–36.

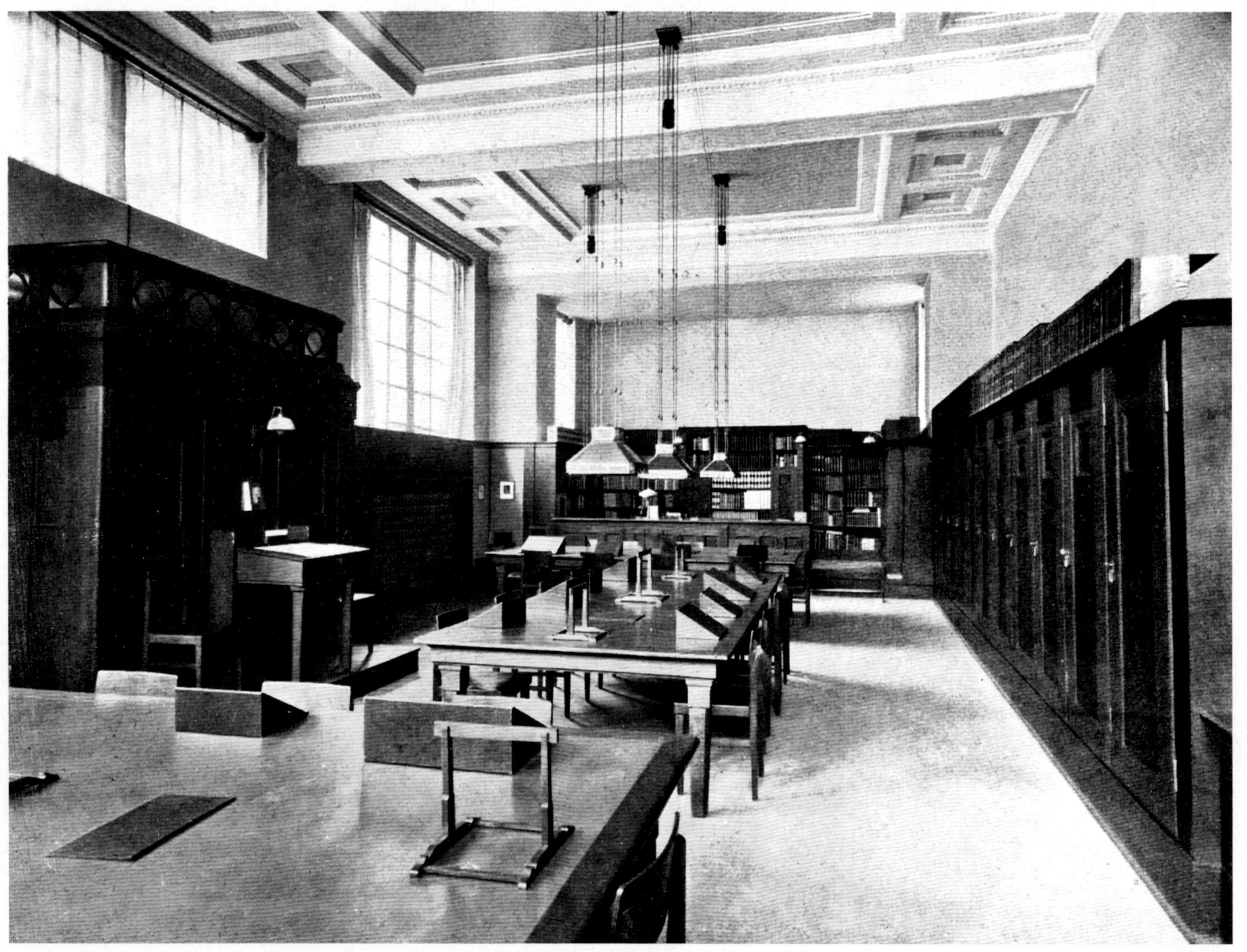

Abb./Fig. 34
Kunstwissenschaftliches Institut / *Art Historical Institute,*
Archiv Kunsthalle Mannheim

lässt sich dieser Gestaltungsimpuls erkennen – inspiriert unter anderem durch ihre Kenntnis nicht-europäischer Kunstwerke, Reisen in die Südsee oder nach Nordafrika und auch beeinflusst von Paul Gauguins Darstellungen sogenannter exotischer Kulturen. Kunsthistorisch problematisch sind jedoch die damit verbundene Aneignung und idealisierende Projektion nicht-europäischer Kunstformen, die von den Expressionist*innen häufig als ursprünglich oder ‚primitiv' verklärt wurden – ein kolonial geprägter Blick, der heute kritisch hinterfragt werden muss. So beschrieb Gustav Friedrich Hartlaub die Holzschnitte von Karl Schmidt-Rottluff als „Zacken-, Keil- und Strahlenschrift", die seiner Meinung nach an nicht-europäische Kunstformen erinnere; er lobte ihre „überwältigende Kraft" und betonte, dass ihre Ausdrucksweise einzigartig und nicht imitierbar sei.[6]

1 Thomas Köllhofer: Die Graphische Sammlung in der Kunsthalle Mannheim bis zur Mitte des 20. Jahrhunderts, in: Christine Hopfengart u. Ulrike Lorenz (Hrsg.): *Streifzüge durch die Moderne. Die Graphische Sammlung der Kunsthalle Mannheim*, Köln 2015, S. 11–17, S. 14.
2 Gustav F. Hartlaub: *Neue deutsche Graphik*, Berlin 1920.
3 Theresa Nisters: „Zurück zum Ursprung, zu den Quellen, zur Natur und zum Material" Holz – Material mit Geschichte, in: Kat. Ausst. *Geheimnis der Materie. Kirchner Heckel Schmidt-Rottluff*, Städel Museum Frankfurt am Main 2019, hrsg. v. Regina Freyberger, Dresden 2019, S. 30–47, S. 34.
4 Hartlaub 1920 (wie Anm. 2), S. 18.
5 Ebd., „Im Anfang war der Holzschnitt", S. 7; Gustav F. Hartlaub: *Die Graphik des Expressionismus in Deutschland*, Stuttgart/Calw 1947, S. 11.
6 Hartlaub 1947 (wie Anm. 5), S. 35f.

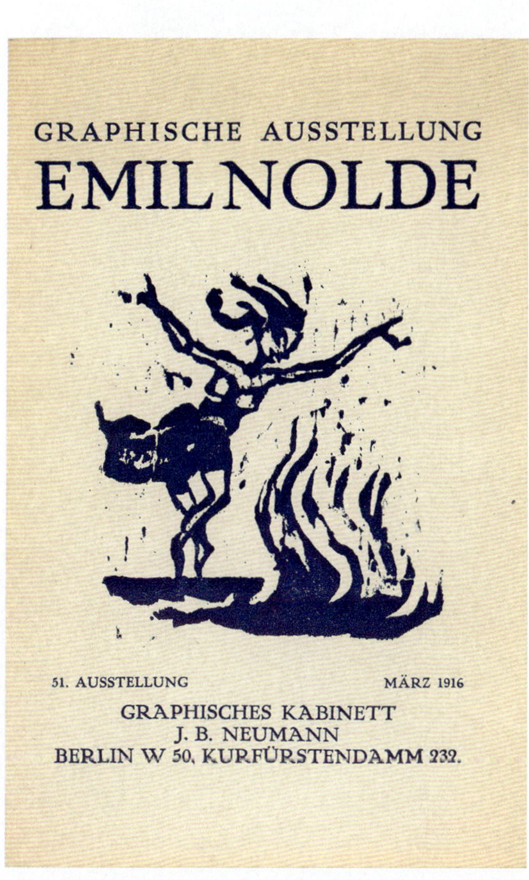

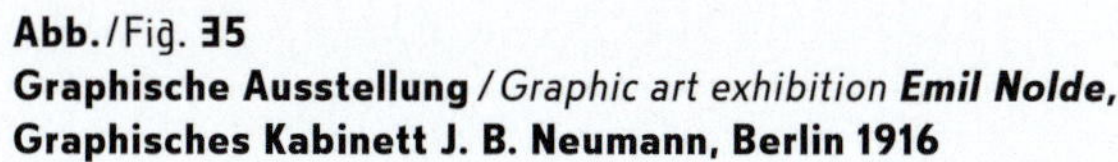
Abb. / Fig. 35
Graphische Ausstellung / *Graphic art exhibition* **Emil Nolde**,
Graphisches Kabinett J. B. Neumann, Berlin 1916

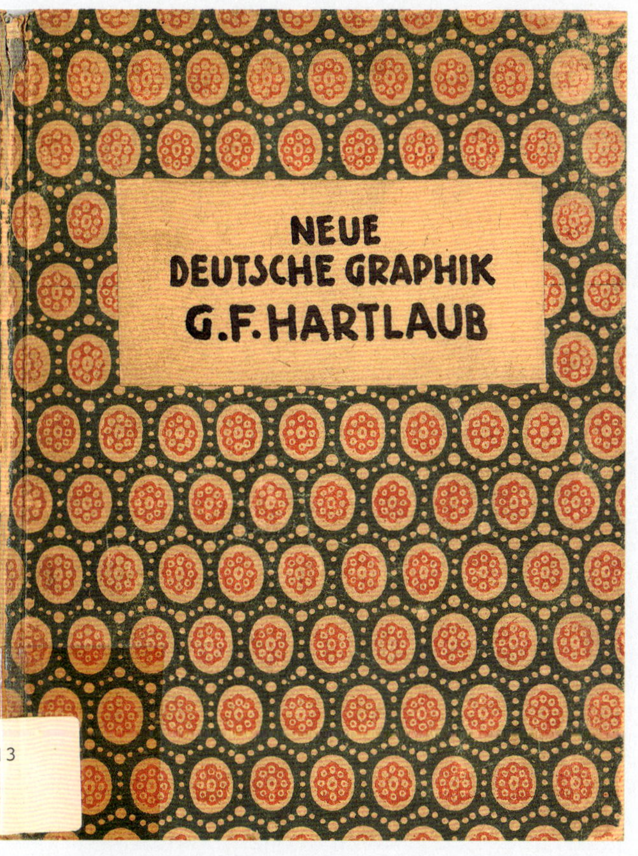

Abb. / Fig. 36
Gustav F. Hartlaub, *Neue deutsche Graphik* /
New German Graphic Art, **Berlin 1920**

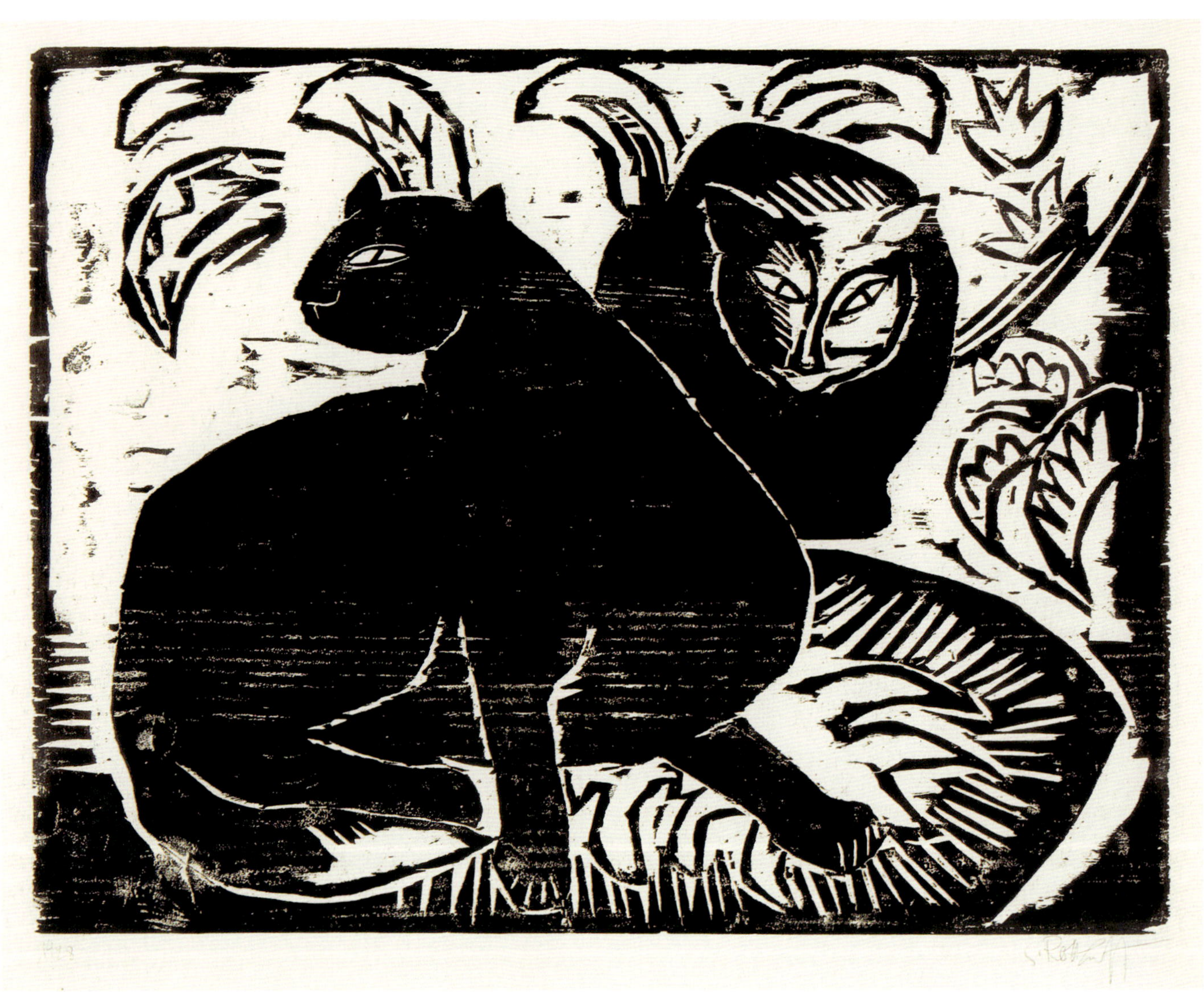

67 | **Karl Schmidt-Rottluff,** *Katzen II* / *Cats II,* **1914,** Kunsthalle Mannheim

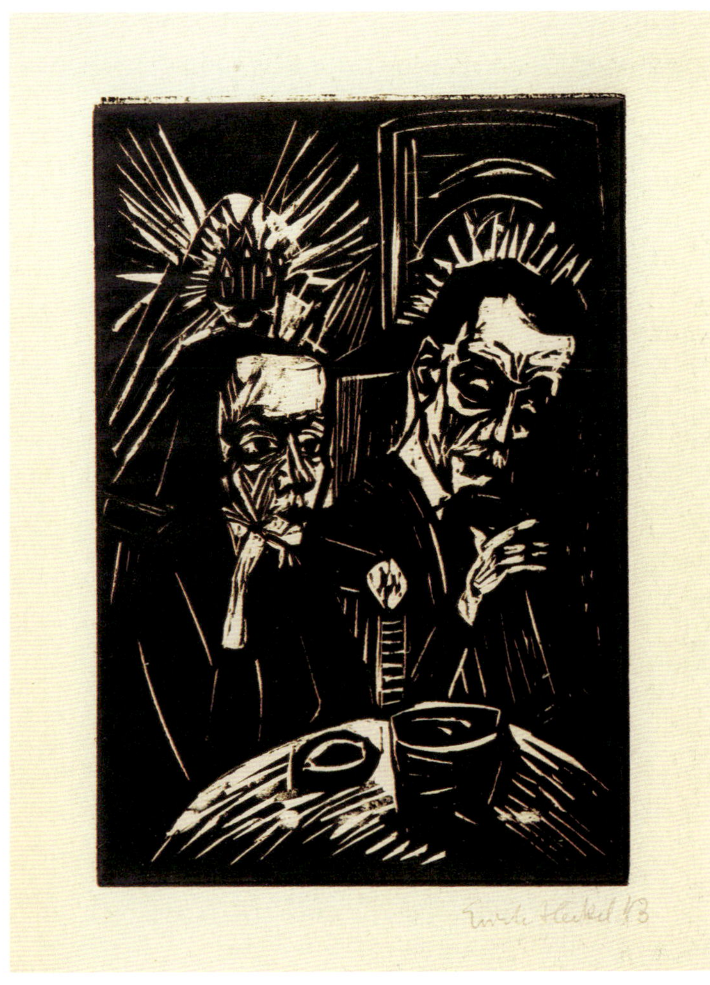

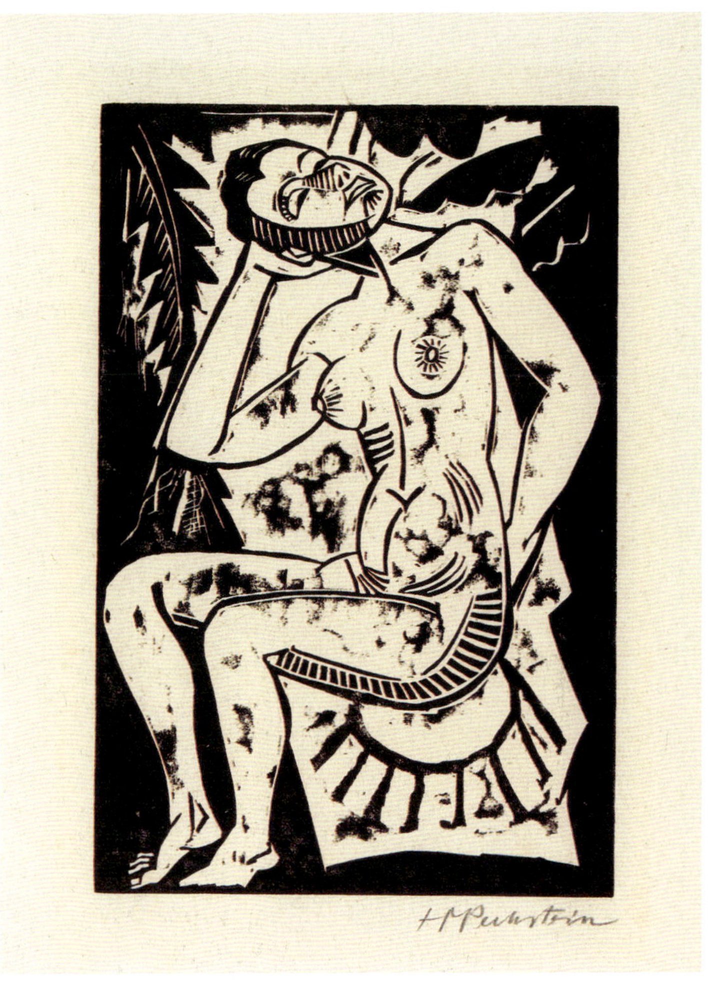

68 | **Erich Heckel,** *Beim Vorlesen* / *Reading Aloud,* **1914,** Kunsthalle Mannheim

69 | **Max Pechstein,** *Sitzender Akt* / *Seated Nude,* **1918,** Kunsthalle Mannheim

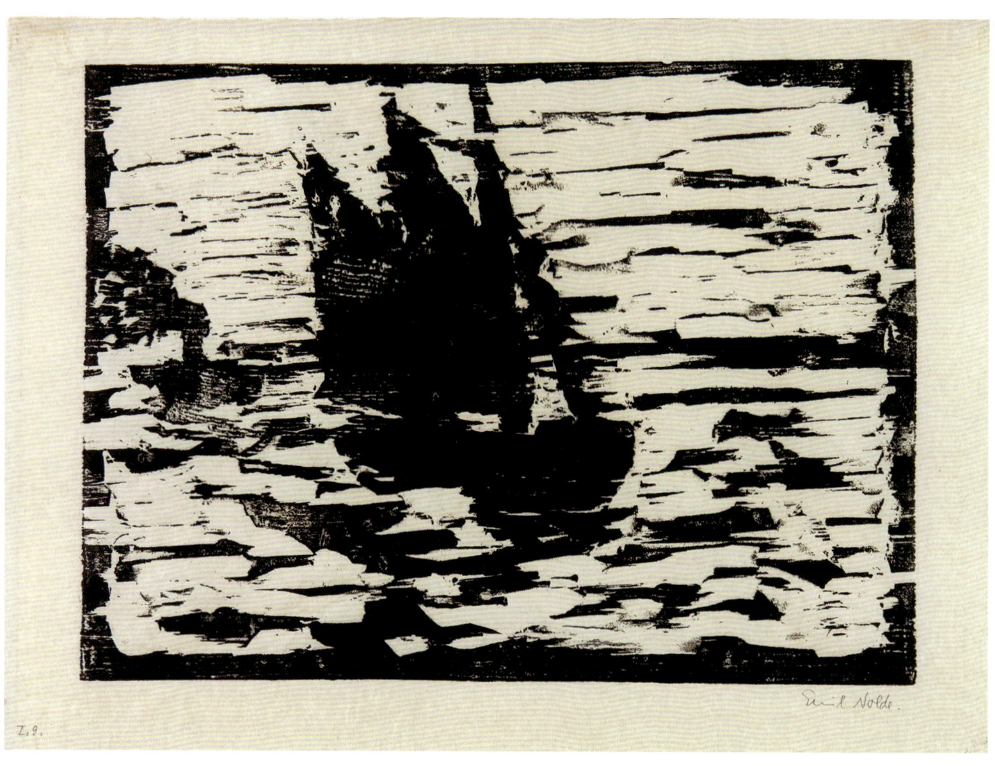

70 | **Emil Nolde,** *Segelboot* / *Sailing Boat,* **1910,** Kunsthalle Mannheim

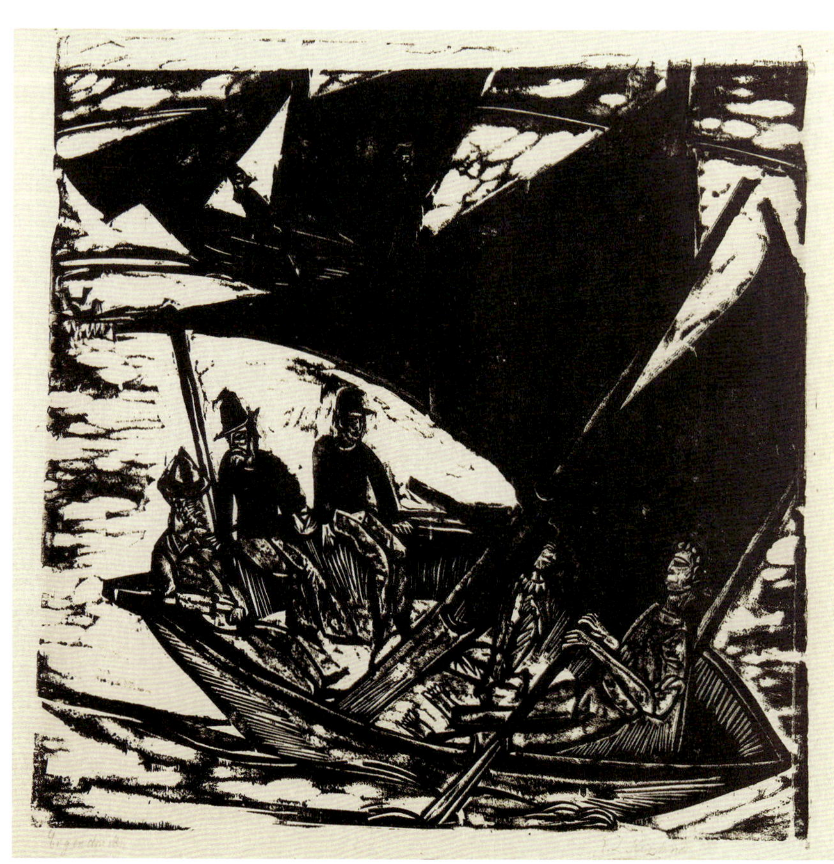

71 | **Ernst Ludwig Kirchner,** *Segelboote bei Fehmarn* / *Sailboats near Fehmarn,* **1914,** Kunsthalle Mannheim

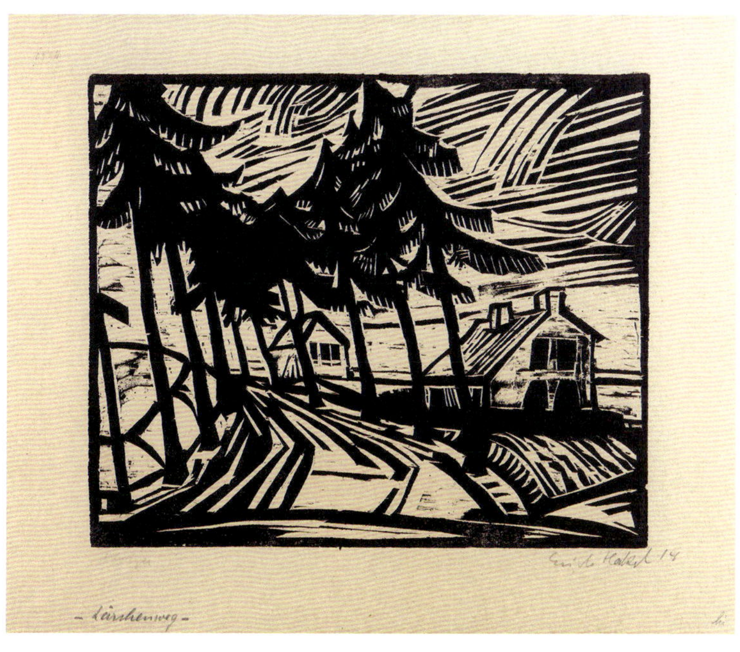

72 | **Erich Heckel,** *Lärchenweg* / *Road with Larches,* **1914,** Kunsthalle Mannheim

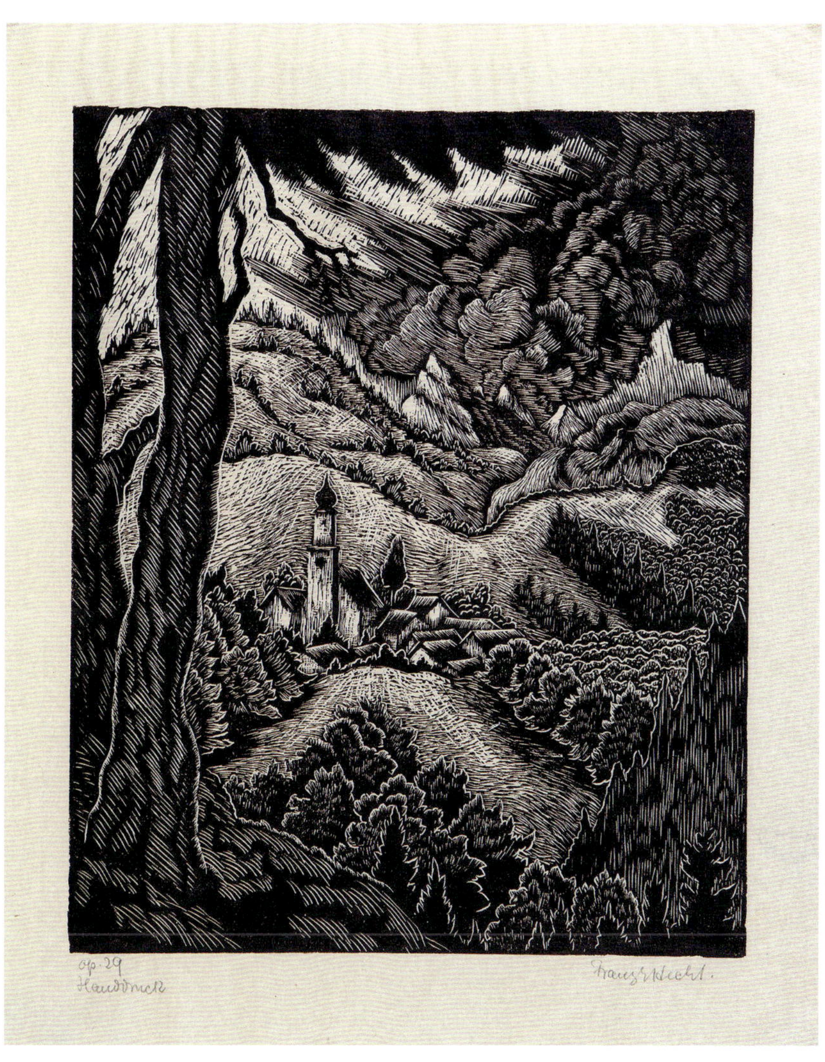

73 | **Franz Emanuel Hecht,** *Kirche* / *Church,* **um** / *ca.* **1918,** Kunsthalle Mannheim   **163**

Landscape and Cityscape in Expressionist Art

Ursula Drahoss

In Expressionism, the landscape and cityscape became fields for experimenting with color and form. The genre underwent a revival that dispensed with traditional and academic rules of composition. Nature is no longer reproduced as a likeness but rather transformed by artistic means. The landscape became a mirror of the inner experiences of artists. At the same time, the metropolis moves into focus: urban subjects influence a new mode of expression.

Between 1908 and 1910, Alexej von Jawlensky made regular visits to Murnau on the Staffelsee. There, working closely with husband-and-wife artists Wassily Kandinsky and Gabriele Münter and his own life partner Marianne von Werefkin, he developed a new, expressive visual idiom, which is particularly evident in the painting *Sommer in Murnau* (Summer in Murnau) of 1908 (cat. 58). With powerful, luminous colors and a reduction to the essential, Jawlensky offered new impulses that pointed the way forward for the art of Kandinsky and Franz Marc as well. Whereas the artists of the Blauer Reiter (Blue Rider) tended to a visual language closer to abstraction, the Brücke association of artists, which had been founded in

Dresden in 1905, was oriented more toward representationalism. Max Pechstein, the only painter in the group with an academic education, lived in Berlin from 1908 onward. In 1911, Erich Heckel, Karl Schmidt-Rottluff, and Ernst Ludwig Kirchner followed him there. In his Berlin years, Kirchner grappled especially intensely with life in the big city. The painting *Gelbes Engelufer, Berlin* (Yellow Engelufer, Berlin) of 1913 (cat. 74) directs the eye to the Luisenkanal and in the background the towers of the Melanchthonkirche, which was later destroyed in World War II. Its radical style is characteristic of Kirchner: distorted perspective and oblique perspectives reflect the dynamics and disjointedness of modern urban life. Today, the painting is regarded as one of the most important examples of Expressionist depictions of the city, and it is also noteworthy that it was painted on two sides. The painting on the verso, which had been painted in 1909–10, depicts a Moroccan man sitting on the ground in bright, expressive colors[1] (cat. 75).

Whereas many Expressionist artists used the city as a motif to express inner tensions, stimulation, and dynamism, the country-side for them was above all a place of yearning and retreat. For Ernst Ludwig Kirchner, the country sometimes meant both quiet and disquiet. Between 1908 and 1914, he spent the summer months relaxedly painting nature on the Baltic Sea island of Fehmarn. Because of a psychological crisis caused by the war, he spent time in the sanatorium Dr. Kohnstamm in Königstein im Taunus in 1915–16, where he produced the woodcut *Taunuslandschaft* (Taunus Landscape) in 1916 (cat. 77). He interrupted his cure several times because the regulated course of the day at the sanatorium stifled his creative drive.[2] For *Taunuslandschaft*, Kirchner chose a panorama format that unites the picturesquely located buildings, a steaming train, and extended forests. This print is not only the topographical reproduction of a landscape but a mirror of his inner turmoil.

Emil Nolde created landscapes as meditations on the elemental forces of nature and lent them an atmospheric charge. The artist was born near the German-Danish border and felt a close connection to the broad, marshy landscapes between the North and Baltic Seas. His painting *Vorabend (Marschlandschaft)* (Twilight [Marsh Landscape]) of 1916 fuses the sky and earth into a unity. Warm shades of yellow of the setting sun contrast with heavy, bluish-violet clouds (cat. 106). The painting was acquired directly from the artist for the Kunsthalle Mannheim in 1920. Already in 1933, however, it was defamed in the National Socialist

Landschaft und Großstadt in der Kunst des Expressionismus

Ursula Drahoss

Im Expressionismus werden auch das Landschafts- und Stadtbild zum Experimentierfeld für Farbe und Form. Das Genre erfährt eine Erneuerung, indem auf traditionelle und akademische Kompositionsregeln verzichtet wird. Die Natur wird nicht mehr abbildend dargestellt, sondern mit künstlerischen Mitteln transformiert. Die Landschaft wird zum Spiegel innerer Erlebnisse der Künstler*innen. Zugleich rückt die Großstadt ins Zentrum: Urbane Sujets prägen eine neue Ausdrucksweise.

Zwischen 1908 und 1910 hielt sich Alexej von Jawlensky regelmäßig in Murnau am Staffelsee auf. Dort entwickelte er im engen Umgang mit dem Künstlerpaar Wassily Kandinsky und Gabriele Münter wie auch mit seiner Lebensgefährtin Marianne von Werefkin eine neue, expressive Bildsprache, was besonders anschaulich etwa im Gemälde *Sommer in Murnau* von 1908 (Kat. 58) wird. Mit kräftigen, leuchtenden Farben und der Reduktion auf das Wesentliche setzte Jawlensky neue Impulse, die wegweisend auch für die Kunst von Kandinsky und Franz Marc wurden. Während die Künstler*innen des Blauen Reiter eher einer der Abstraktion nahestehenden Formensprache zuneigten, war die bereits 1905 in Dresden gegründete Künstlergruppe Brücke stärker gegenständlich orientiert. Max Pechstein, der einzige akademisch ausgebildete Maler der Gruppe, lebte seit 1908 in Berlin. Ihm folgten 1911 Erich Heckel, Karl Schmidt-Rottluff und Ernst Ludwig Kirchner. In seinen Berliner Jahren setzte sich Kirchner besonders intensiv mit dem Großstadtleben auseinander. Das Gemälde *Gelbes Engelufer, Berlin* von 1913 (Kat. 74) lenkt den Blick auf den Luisenkanal und im Hintergrund auf die Türme der später im Krieg zerstörten Melanchthonkirche. Charakteristisch für Kirchner ist seine stilistische Radikalität: Perspektivische Verzerrungen und schräge Blickwinkel spiegeln die Dynamik und Zerrissenheit des modernen Großstadtlebens wider. Das Gemälde zählt heute zu den bedeutendsten Beispielen expressionistischer Stadtdarstellungen und auch seine doppelseitige Bemalung ist bemerkenswert. Auf dem bereits 1909/10 entstandenen Gemälde der Rückseite ist ein am Boden sitzender Marokkaner in leuchtenden, expressiven Farben dargestellt[1] (Kat. 75).

War die Stadt für die Künstler*innen des Expressionismus ein Motiv, um innere Spannungen, Erregung und Dynamik auszudrücken, so galt ihnen die Landschaft überwiegend als Ort der Sehnsucht und des Rückzugs. Für Ernst Ludwig Kirchner bedeutete die Landschaft zeitweise beides: Ruhe und Unruhe. Zwischen 1908 und 1914 malte er in den Sommermonaten auf der Ostseeinsel Fehmarn ungezwungen die Natur. Wegen einer kriegsbedingten seelischen Krise hielt er sich 1915/16 im Sanatorium Dr. Kohnstamm in Königstein im Taunus auf, wo 1916 der Holzschnitt *Taunuslandschaft* entstand (Kat. 77). Mehrmals brach er die Kur ab, da ihn der reglementierte Tagesablauf im Sanatorium in seinem Schaffensdrang hemmte.[2] Rastlos pendelte er zwischen Stadt und Land. Für seine *Taunuslandschaft* wählte Kirchner ein Panoramaformat, das malerisch gelegene Häuser, eine dampfende Eisenbahn und ausgedehnte Wälder vereint. Das Blatt ist nicht nur topografische Wiedergabe einer Landschaft, sondern auch Spiegel eines inneren Aufgewühltseins.

Emil Nolde schuf Landschaften als Meditationen über die elementaren Kräfte der Natur und lud sie atmosphärisch auf. Der nahe der deutsch-dänischen Grenze geborene Künstler war den weiten Marschlandschaften zwischen Nord- und Ostsee eng verbunden. In seinem Gemälde *Vorabend (Marschlandschaft)* von 1916 verschmelzen Himmel und Erde zu einer Einheit: Warme Gelbtöne der untergehenden Sonne kontrastieren mit schweren, blauvioletten Wolken (Kat. 106). Das Gemälde wurde im Jahr 1920 direkt vom Künstler für die Kunsthalle Mannheim

propaganda exhibition *Kulturbolschewistische Bilder* (Cultural Bolshevist Pictures) in Mannheim—which was also an attack on then-director Gustav Friedrich Hartlaub's acquisition policy. After the painting had been confiscated from the Kunsthalle as part of the *Entartete Kunst* (Degenerate Art) action in 1937, shown in the eponymous exhibition in Munich, and then sold, the Kunstmuseum Basel purchased it in 1939 through the Galerie Karl Buchholz. In 1941, Nolde was prohibited from practicing his profession, but he nevertheless remained faithful to the regime.[3] The discussion of Nolde's artistic oeuvre against the background of his political stance continues today.[4]

1   Inge Herold, "Kirchners Rückseitenbild 'Der Marokkaner' in der Kunsthalle Mannheim," *Der doppelte Kirchner: Die zwei Seiten der Leinwand*, exh. cat. Kunsthalle Mannheim; Kirchner Museum Davos 2015 (Cologne: Wienand, 2015), pp. 114–24, esp. p. 118.
2   Hanna Strzoda, "Ernst Ludwig Kirchner in Königstein und Frankfurt," in *Expressionismus im Rhein-Main-Gebiet. Künstler, Händler, Sammler*, exh. cat. Museum Giersch, Frankfurt am Main 2011 (Petersberg: Imhof 2011), pp. 20–32, esp. p. 21.
3   In the early 1930s, Emil Nolde and his wife welcomed the National Socialists' seizure of power, hoping that Nolde's art would receive greater recognition under the new regime. Nolde joined the Nationalsozialistische Arbeitsgemeinschaft Nordschleswig (NSAN; National Socialist Working Community of North Schleswig), which he hoped would result in more support for his work as an artist. See Denise Daum, "Nolde in der Südsee: Primitivismus, Kolonialismus und Reiseerfahrung," in *Begegnung und Verhandlung: Möglichkeiten eines Kulturwandels durch Reise*, ed. Christian Berkemeier et al. (Münster: Lit, 2004), pp. 33–49, esp. p. 42.
4   Although Nolde had antisemitic views and offered his services to the National Socialists, his art was banned by them, and he was prohibited from practicing his profession from 1941 as well. After 1945, he presented himself as a victim of National Socialism, without revealing his antisemitic convictions; for a long time, this narrative was accepted uncritically. See Christian Ring, ed., *Emil Nolde in seiner Zeit: Im Nationalsozialismus*, conference volume for a symposium organized by the Stiftung Seebüll Ada und Emil Nolde in cooperation with the *Frankfurter Allgemeine Zeitung*, Hamburg Freie Akademie der Künste 2017 (Munich: Prestel; Neukirchen: Nolde Stiftung Seebüll, 2019).

erworben. Doch bereits 1933 war es in der nationalsozialistischen Propagandaschau *Kulturbolschewistische Bilder* in Mannheim diffamierend zu sehen – auch, um die Ankaufspolitik des damaligen Direktors Gustav Friedrich Hartlaub anzugreifen. Nachdem das Bild 1937 im Rahmen der Aktion *Entartete Kunst* aus der Kunsthalle beschlagnahmt, in der Münchner Ausstellung gezeigt und dann veräußert wurde, konnte es 1939 das Kunstmuseum Basel über die Galerie Karl Buchholz erwerben. 1941 erhielt Nolde ein Berufsverbot, er blieb dem Regime dennoch weiterhin treu.[3] Die Diskussion um Noldes künstlerisches Werk vor dem Hintergrund seiner politischen Haltung ist bis heute nicht verstummt.[4]

1 Inge Herold: Kirchners Rückseitenbild „Der Marokkaner" in der Kunsthalle Mannheim, in: Kat. Ausst. *Der doppelte Kirchner. Die zwei Seiten der Leinwand*, Kunsthalle Mannheim / Kirchner Museum Davos 2015, hrsg. v. Inge Herold, Köln 2015, S. 114–124, S. 118.
2 Hanna Strzoda: Ernst Ludwig Kirchner in Königstein und Frankfurt, in: Kat. Ausst. *Expressionismus im Rhein-Main-Gebiet. Künstler, Händler, Sammler*, Museum Giersch 2011, hrsg. v. Museum Giersch, Frankfurt am Main 2011, S. 20–32, S. 21.
3 Anfang der 1930er-Jahre begrüßten Emil Nolde und seine Frau die Machtergreifung der Nationalsozialisten in der Hoffnung, dass Noldes Kunst unter dem neuen Regime mehr Anerkennung finden würde. Nolde trat der Nationalsozialistischen Arbeitsgemeinschaft Nordschleswig (NSAN) bei und erhoffte sich dadurch eine stärkere Unterstützung seiner künstlerischen Arbeit. Vgl. Denise Daum: *Nolde in der Südsee. Primitivismus, Kolonialismus und Reiseerfahrung*, in: Christian Berkemeier u. a. (Hrsg.): *Begegnung und Verhandlung. Möglichkeiten eines Kulturwandels durch Reise*, Münster 2004, S. 33–49, S. 42.
4 Obwohl Nolde antisemitisch eingestellt war und sich den Nationalsozialisten andiente, wurde seine Kunst von diesen geächtet und 1941 erhielt auch er ein Berufsverbot. Nach 1945 stellte er sich – ohne seine antisemitischen Überzeugungen offenzulegen – als Opfer des Nationalsozialismus dar; dieses Narrativ wurde lange Zeit unkritisch übernommen. Vgl. Christian Ring u. a. (Hrsg.): *Emil Nolde in seiner Zeit: im Nationalsozialismus* (Tagungsband zum Symposium, veranstaltet von der Stiftung Seebüll Ada und Emil Nolde in Kooperation mit der Frankfurter Allgemeinen Zeitung, Hamburg Freie Akademie der Künste 2017), München/London/New York/Neukirchen/Nolde Stiftung Seebüll 2019.

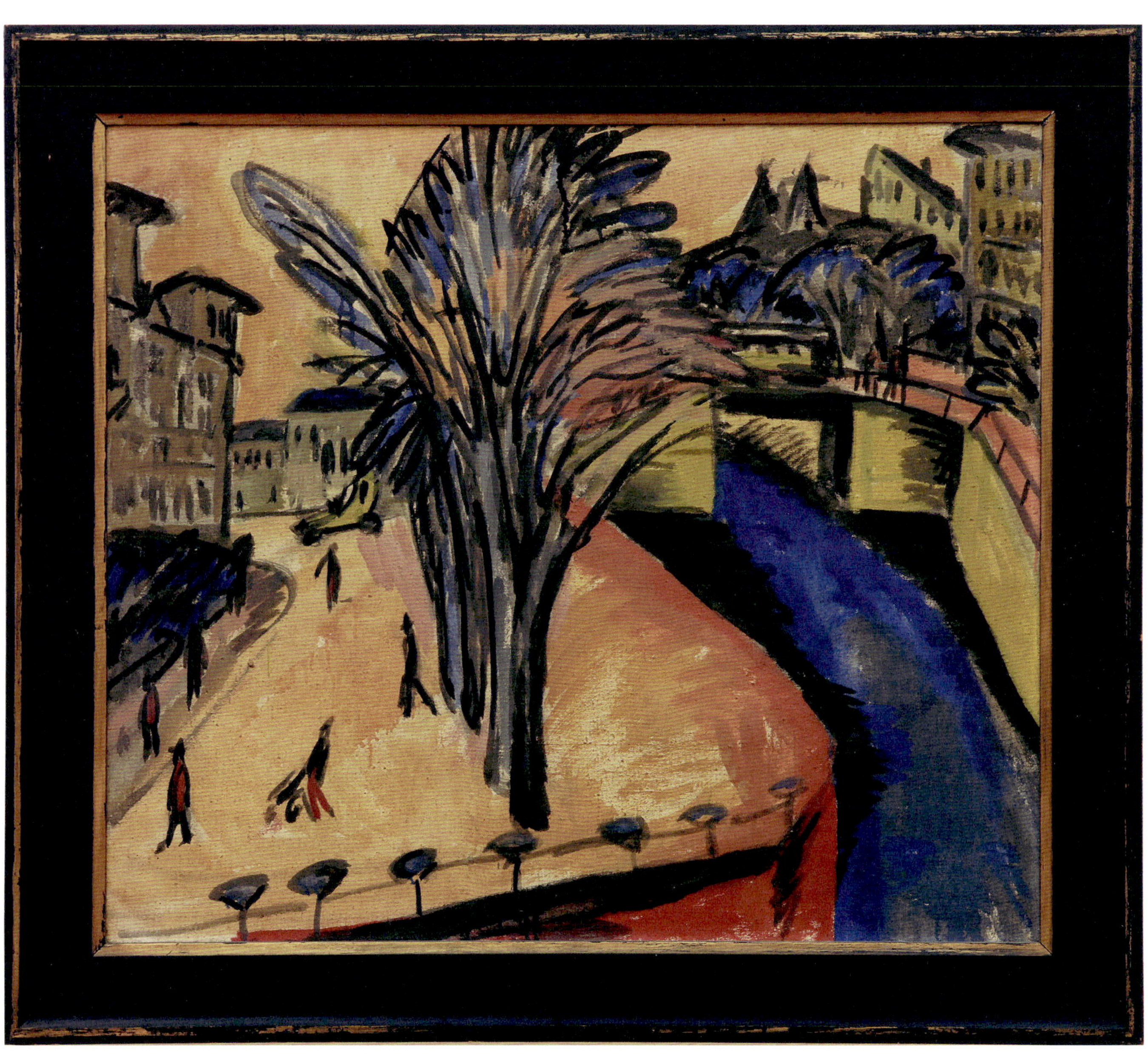

74 | **Ernst Ludwig Kirchner,** *Gelbes Engelufer, Berlin* / *Yellow Engelufer, Berlin,* **1913,** Kunsthalle Mannheim

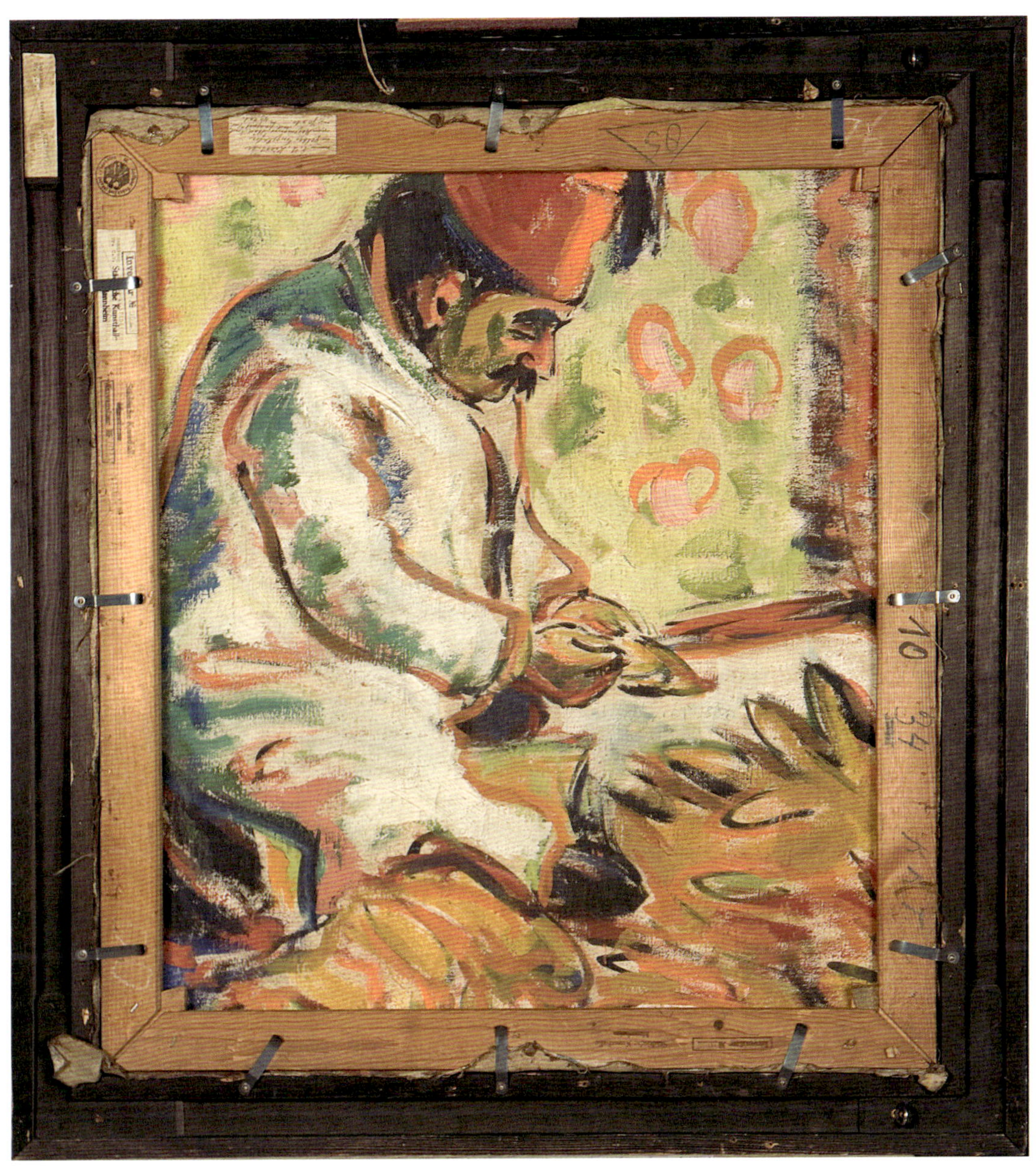

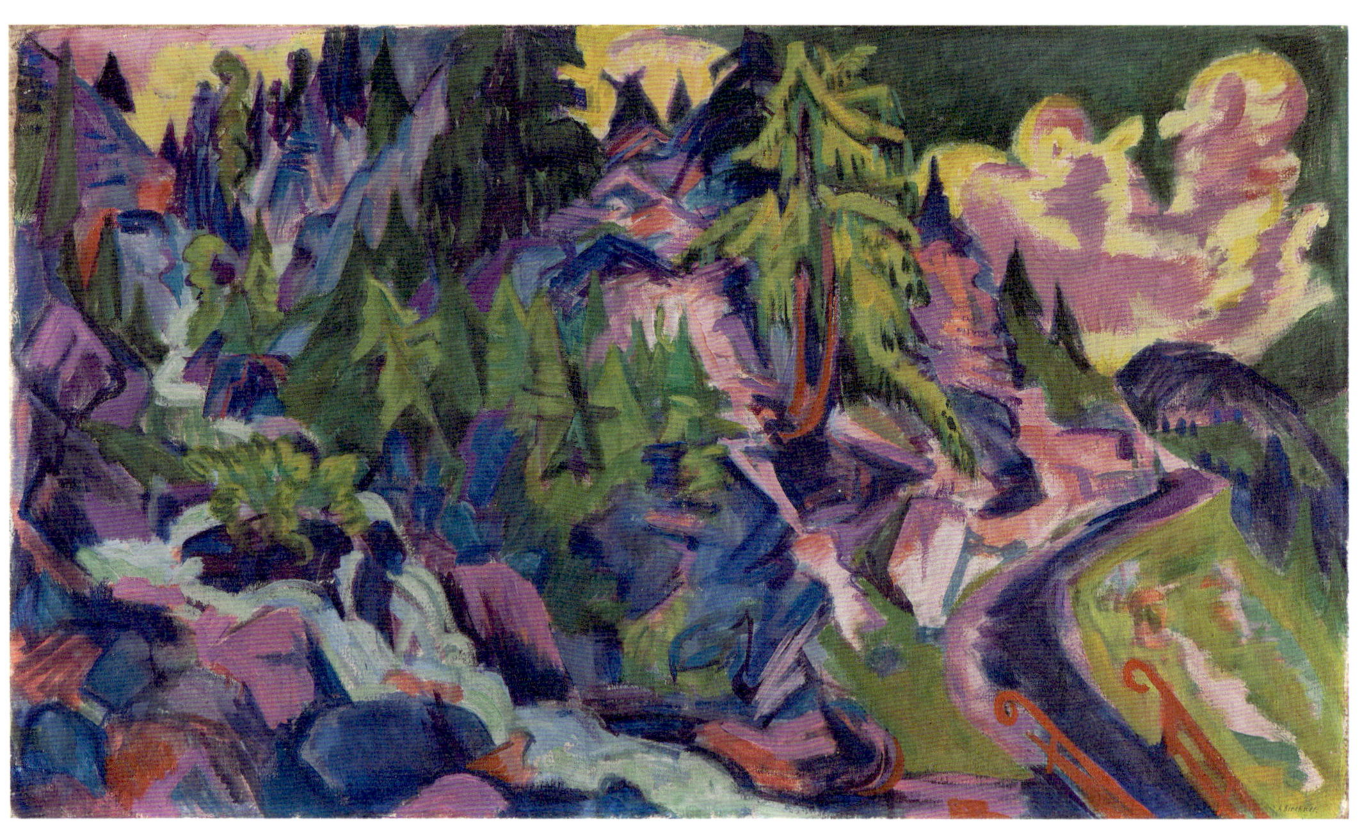

76 | **Ernst Ludwig Kirchner,** *Bergbach* / *Mountain Brook,* **1919/20,** Kunsthalle Mannheim

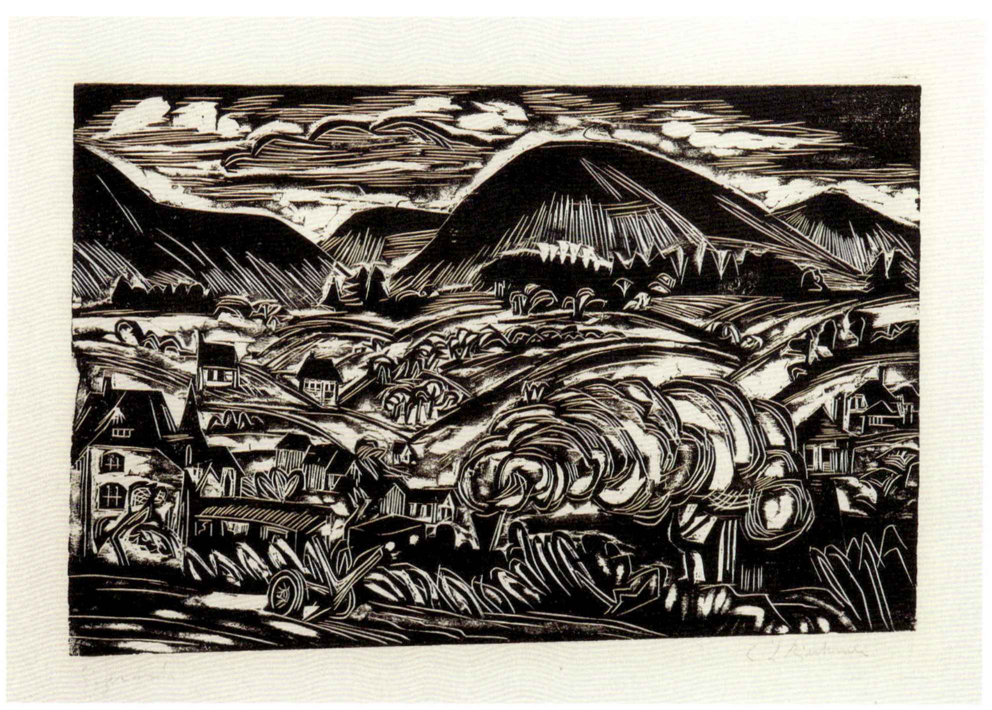

77 | **Ernst Ludwig Kirchner, *Taunuslandschaft* /**
Taunus Landscape, **1916,** Kunsthalle Mannheim

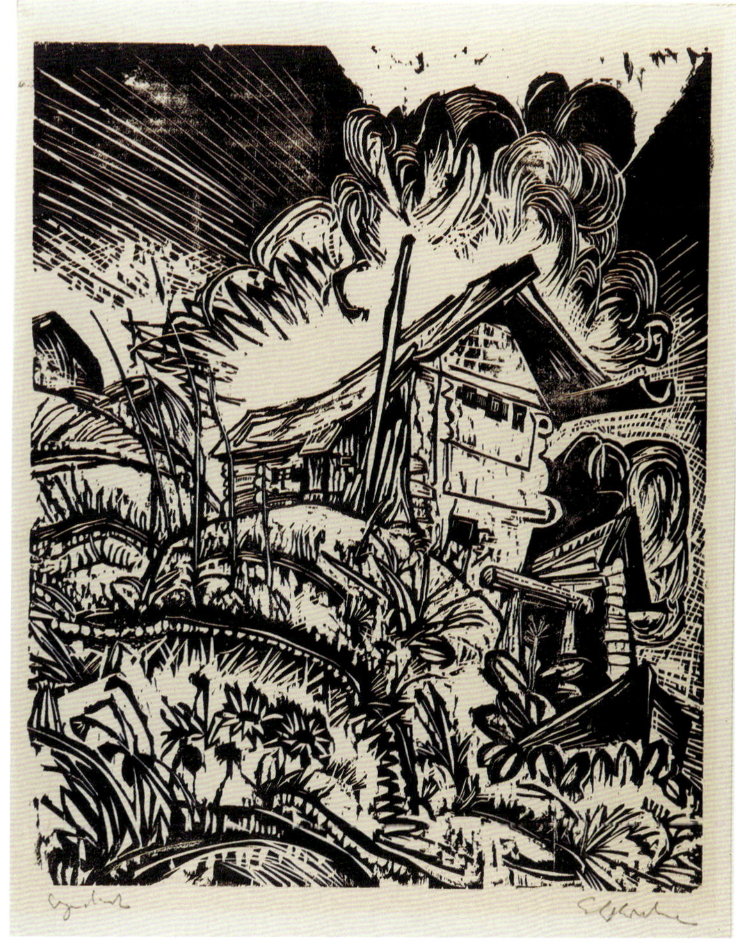

78 | **Ernst Ludwig Kirchner, *Berghaus mit Gewitterwolke* /** *Mountain Chalet with Storm Cloud,* **1917,** Kunsthalle Mannheim

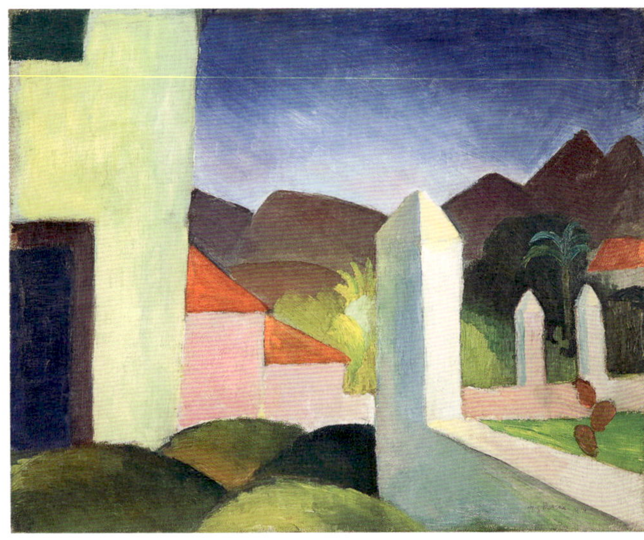

79 | **August Macke, *Afrikanische Landschaft*** / *African Landscape*, **1914,** Kunsthalle Mannheim

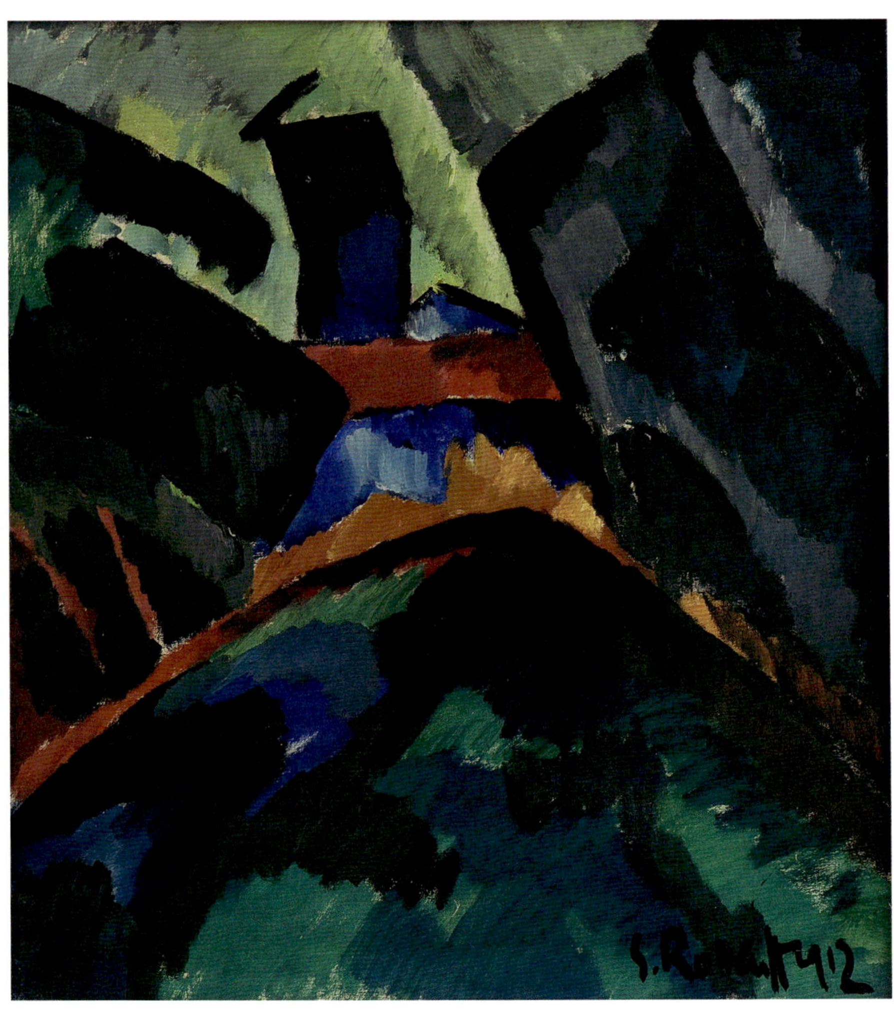

80 | **Karl Schmidt-Rottluff, *Villa mit Turm*** / *Villa with Tower*, **1912,** Kunsthalle Mannheim

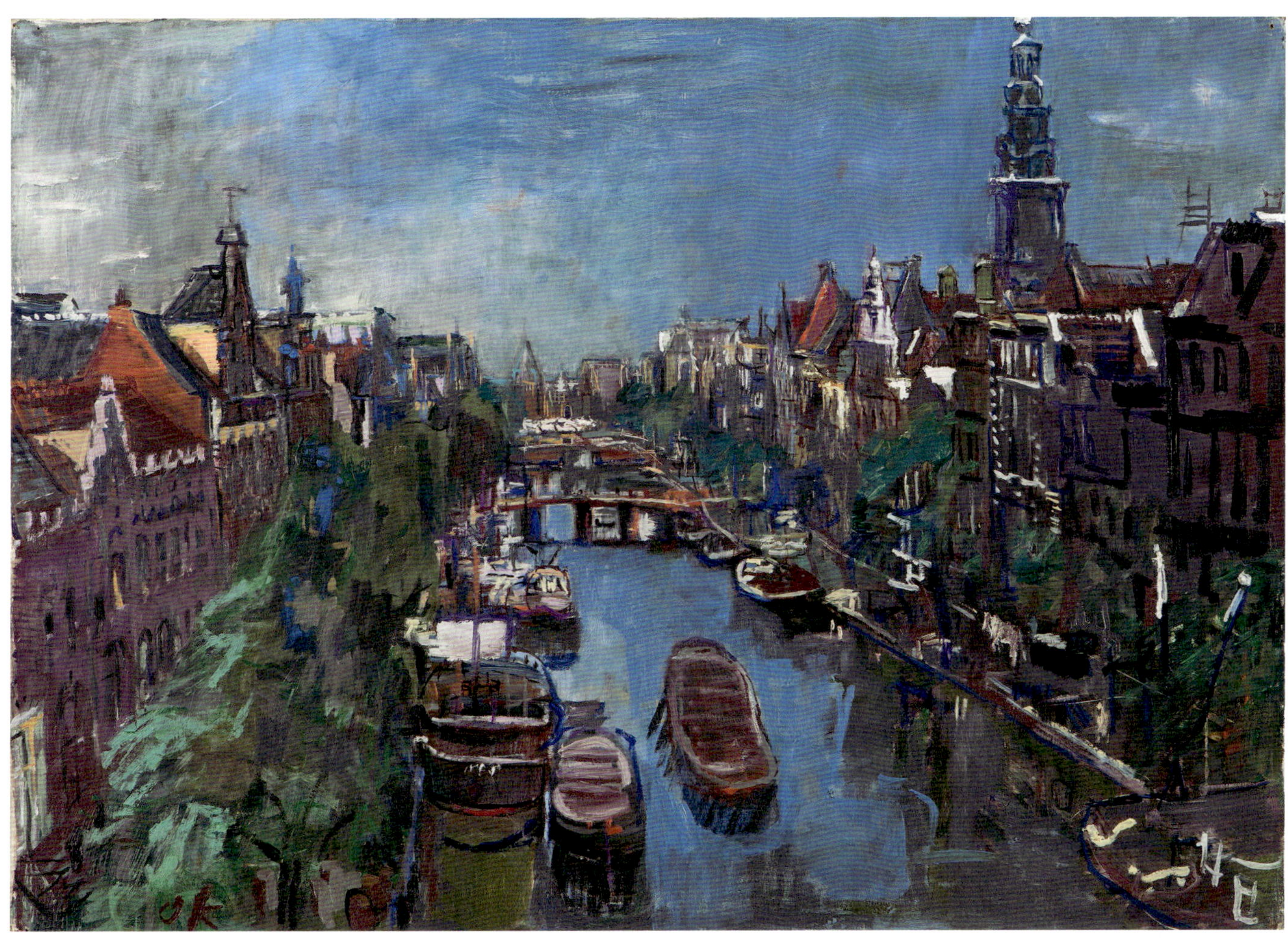

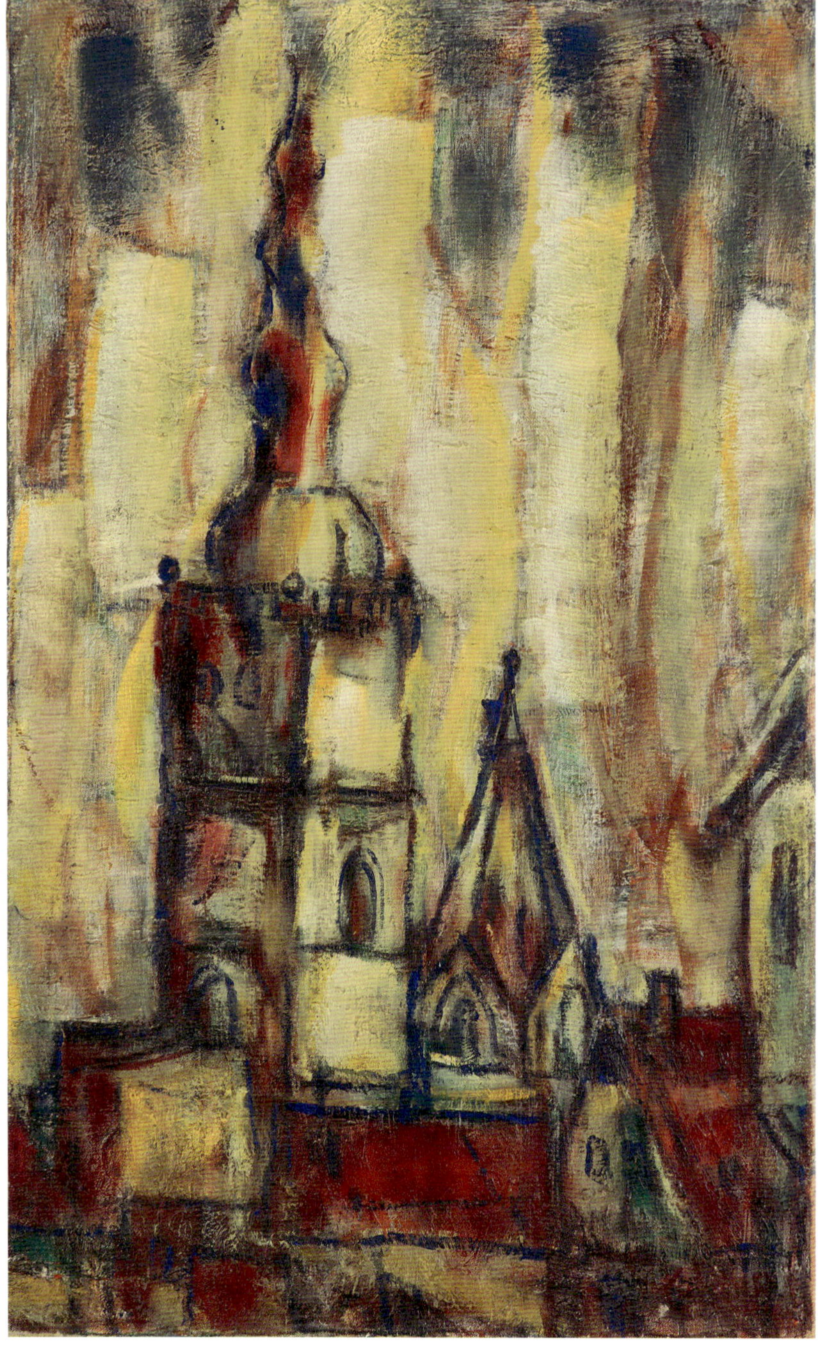

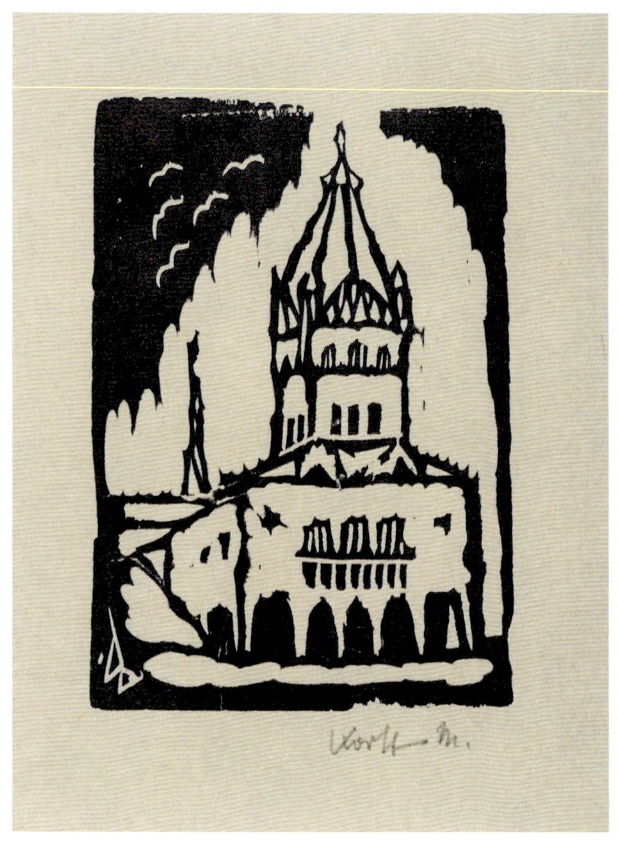

82 | **Christian Rohlfs, *Petriturm in Soest* /**
The Tower of St. Peter's Church in Soest, **1918,** Kunsthalle Mannheim

83 | **Wilhelm Morgner, *Patroklidom in Soest* /**
The Patroclus Cathedral in Soest, **1912,** Sammlung Geber / *Geber Collection*

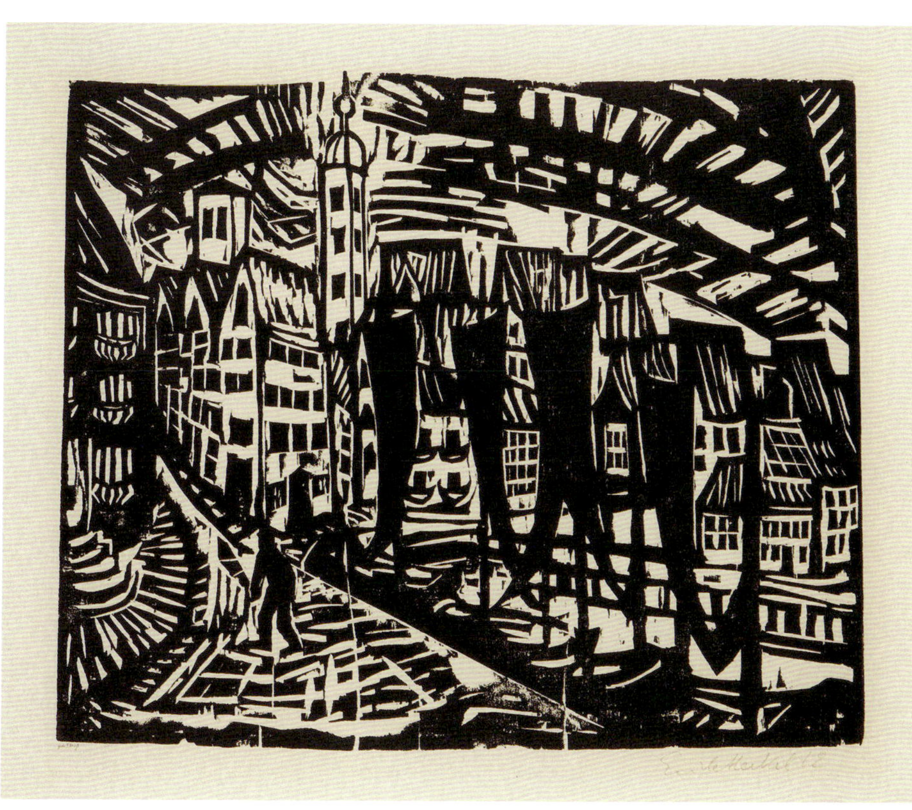

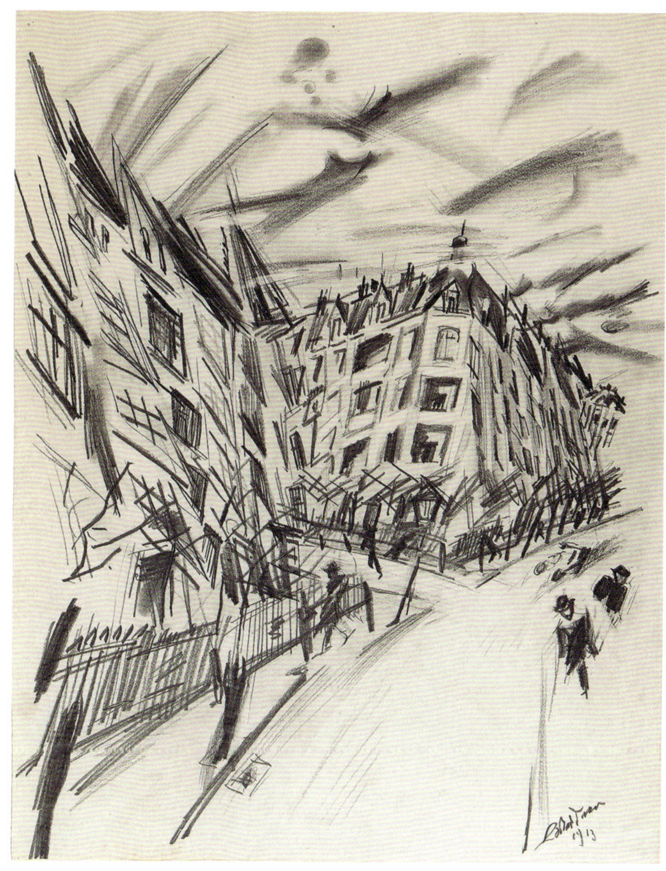

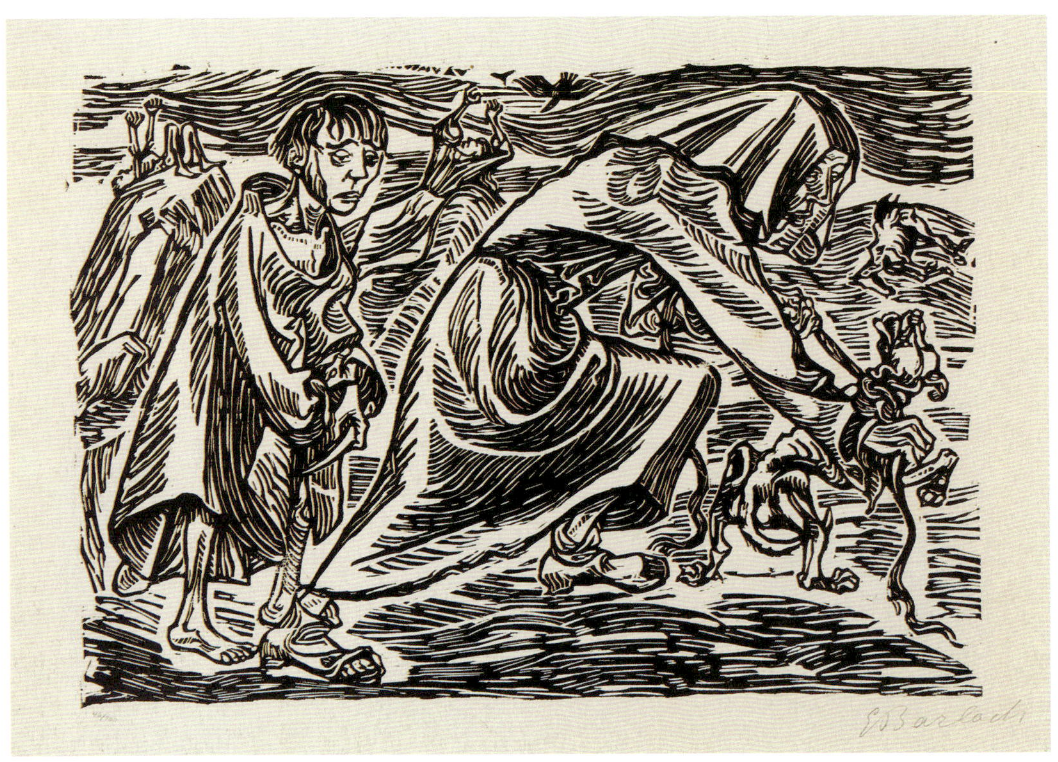

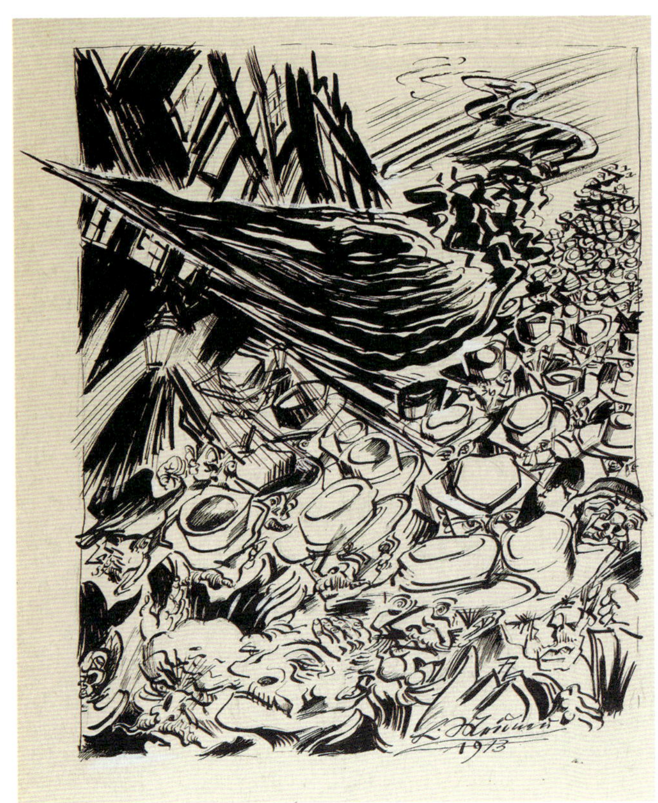

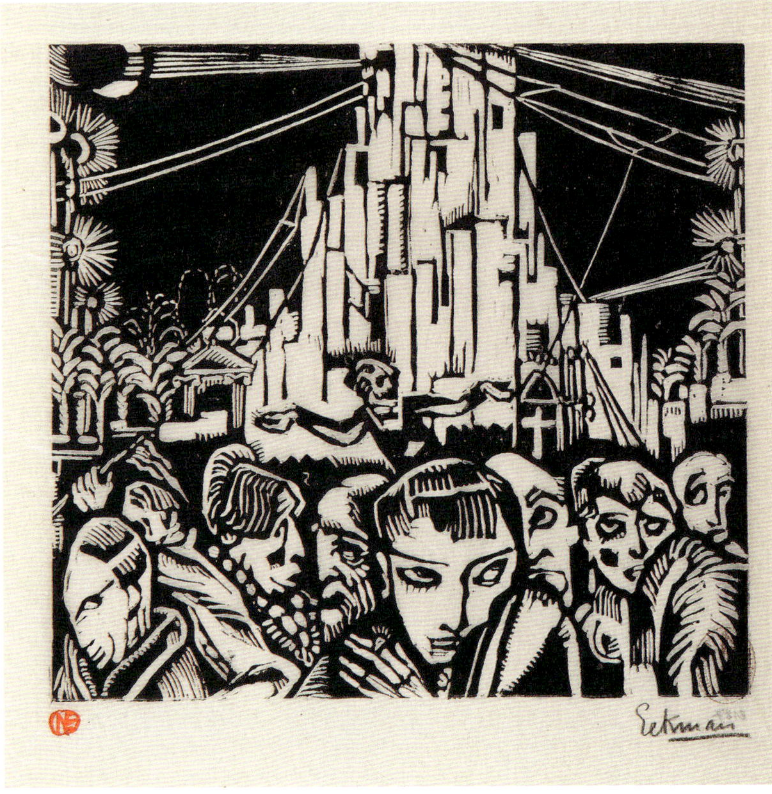

87 | **Ludwig Meidner,** *Demonstrationszug* /
Demonstration, **1913,** Kunsthalle Mannheim

88 | **Nicolas Mathieu Eekman,** *Hohe Stadt* /
High City, **um** / *ca.* **1925,** Kunsthalle Mannheim

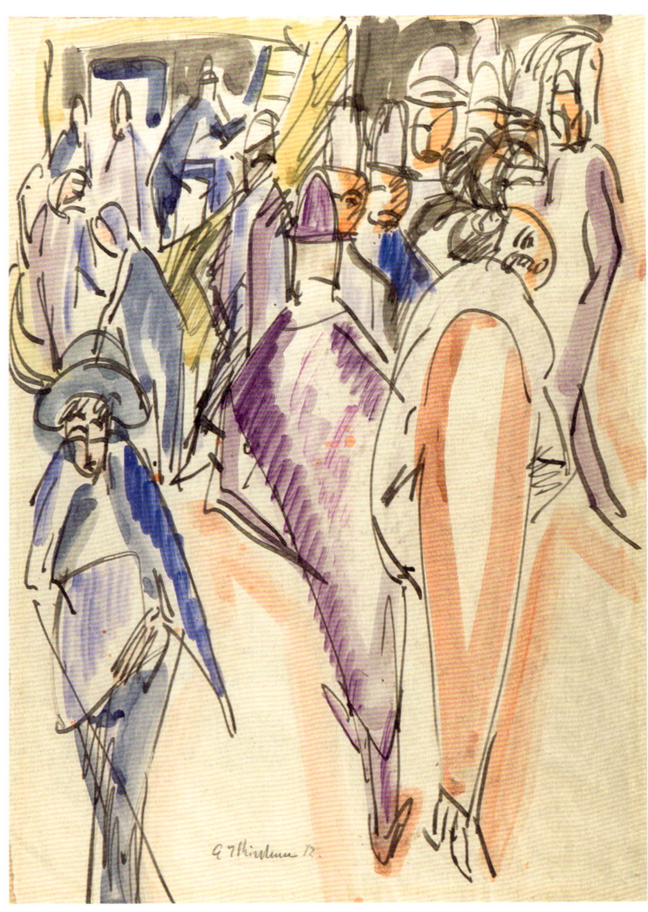

89 | **Ernst Ludwig Kirchner,** *Das elegante Paar* /
The Elegant Couple, **1912,** Kunsthalle Mannheim

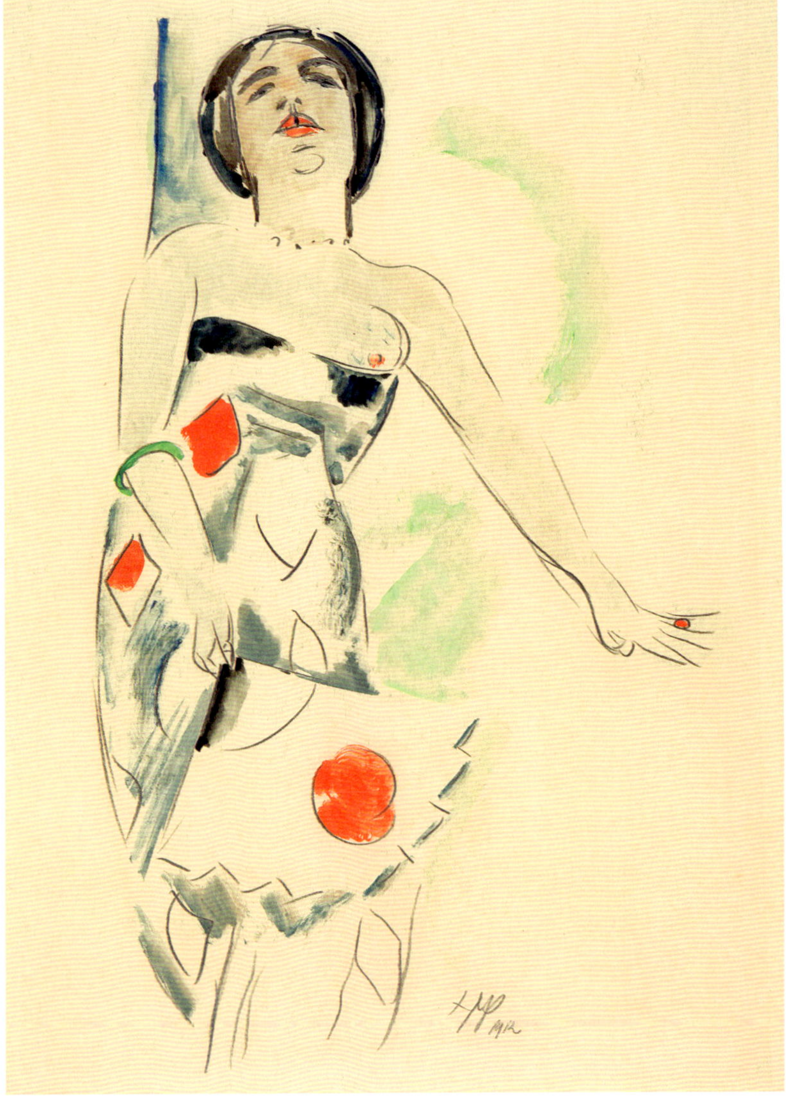

90 | **Max Pechstein,** *Stehende Frau mit Fächer* /
Standing Woman with Fan, **1912,** Kunsthalle Mannheim

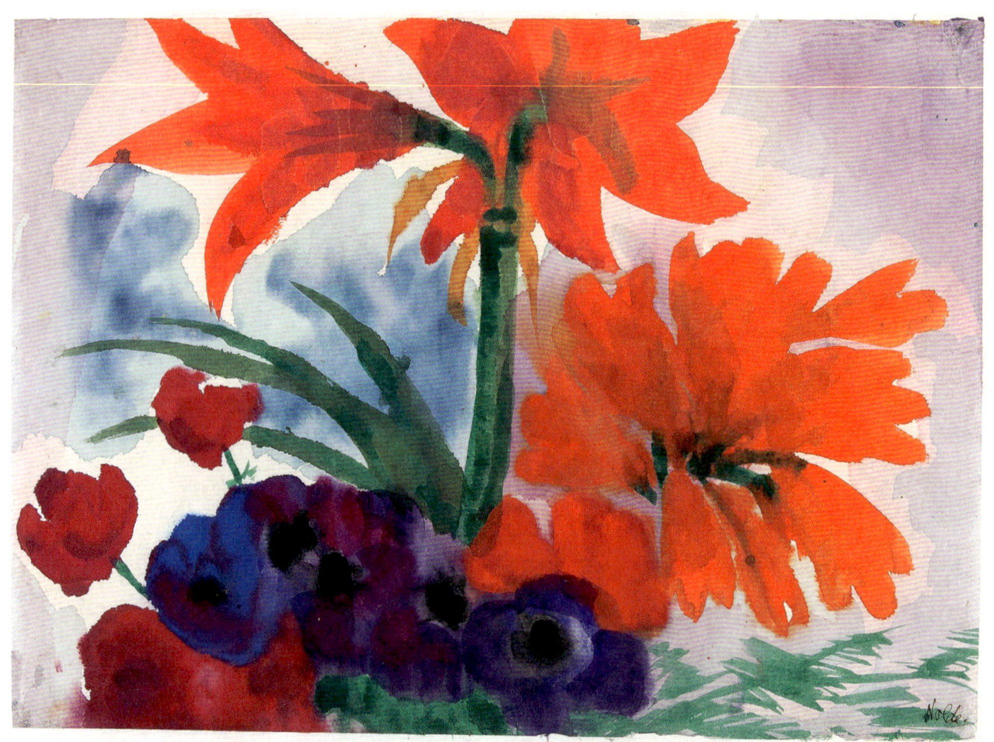

91 | **Emil Nolde,** *Blumen* / Flowers, **um** / ca. **1926,**
Kunsthalle Mannheim

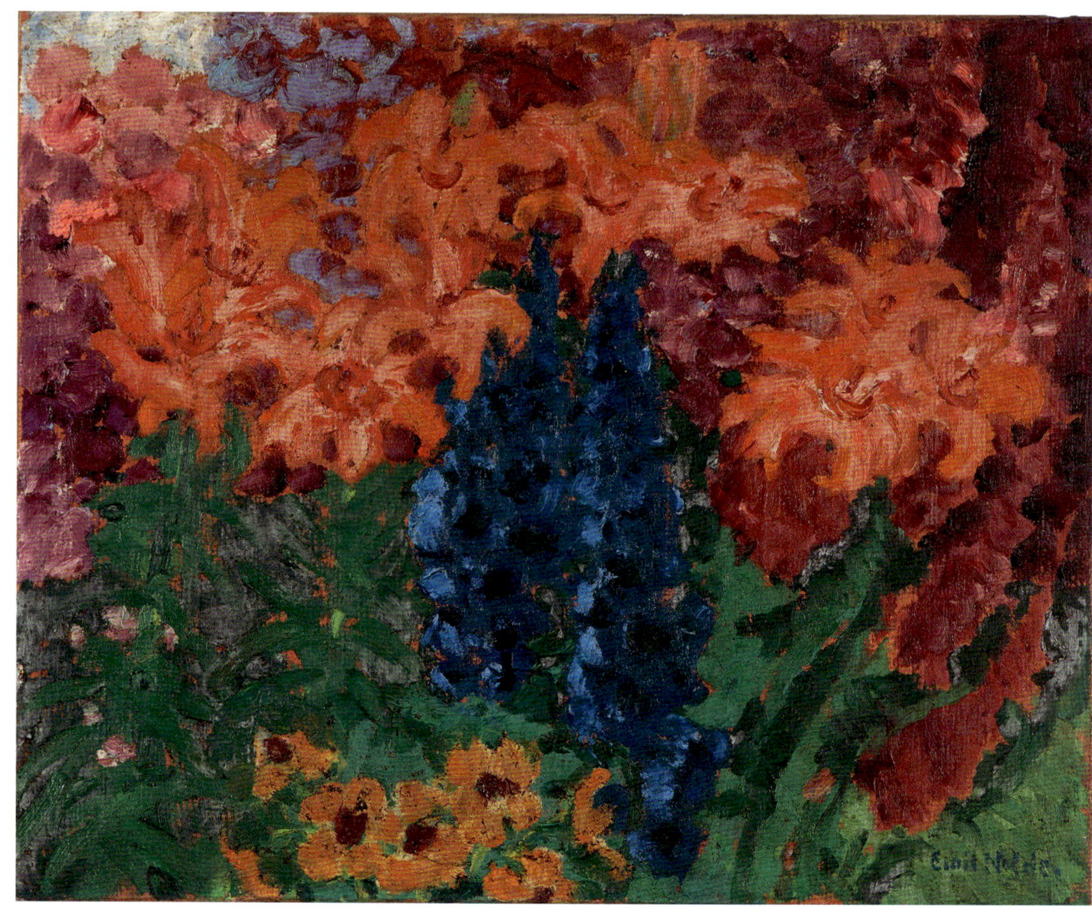

92 | **Emil Nolde,** *Feuerlilien und dunkler Rittersporn* / Tiger Lilies and Dark Larkspur, **1925,** Kunsthalle Mannheim

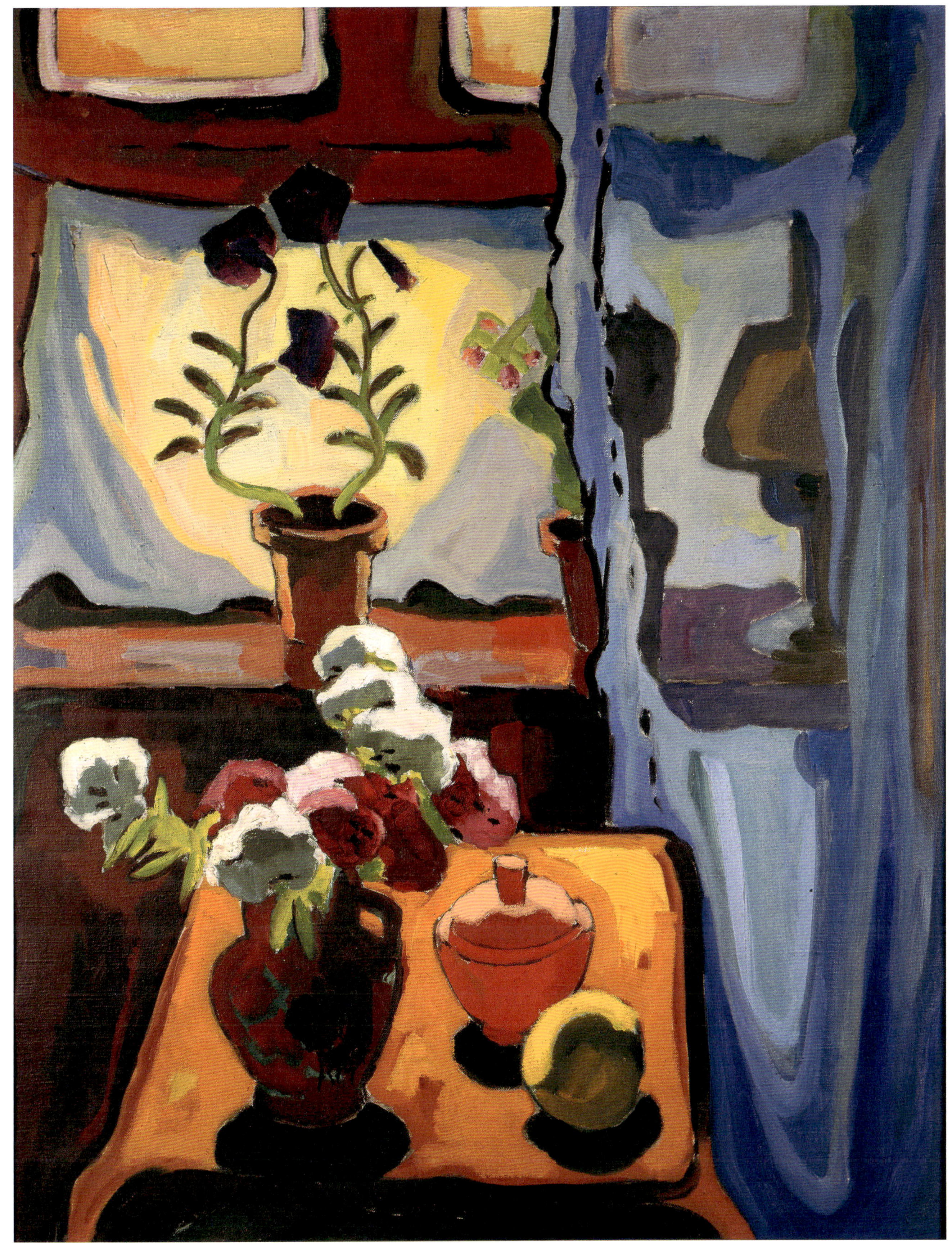

93 | **Karl Schmidt-Rottluff,** *Sommerliches Fenster* / *Window in Summer,* **1937,** Kunsthalle Mannheim

Expression and Alienation: The Portrait

Ursula Drahoss

Against the backdrop of research into the unconscious toward the end of the nineteenth century, Vincent van Gogh and Edvard Munch in particular influenced the portraiture of subsequent generations of artists. Form and color no longer served the Expressionists to reproduce the human face naturalistically and realistically but rather as an expressive means to convey subjective experience. For example, Oskar Kokoschka and the Brücke (Bridge) artists clung to figuration but abandoned the traditional type of portrait that aimed at representation in favor of expression and alienation; others, by contrast, such as the artists of the Blauer Reiter (Blue Rider), struck out on the path to abstraction.

Oskar Kokoschka became famous in Germany in 1910 for pen drawings published in Herwarth Walden's journal *Der Sturm* as illustrations for his own drama *Mörder, Hoffnung der Frauen* (Murderer, Hope of Women). The Kunsthalle Mannheim owns Kokoschka's important early portrait of the doctor and social reformer Auguste Forel from 1910 (cat. 94). Forel studied the connections between the brain and the mind and is considered the founder of Swiss psychiatry. Kokoschka concentrated entirely on the eloquent gestures of his hands, his hypnotic gaze, and his contemplative and cerebral-looking face. His monkish jacket rendered blotchily with open brushwork in shades of gray and brown, and the drawing-like scratching into the paint did not correspond at all to conventional portrait painting of his time— and hence probably also not with the taste of the client, who rejected the picture.[1] In 1913, Gustav Friedrich Hartlaub acquired it on the art market for the Kunsthalle Mannheim and showed it in the exhibition *Neue religiöse Kunst* (New Religious Art) in 1918. Kokoschka's works were also defamed as "degenerate" under the National Socialist regime in 1937 and banned from museums. The portrait of Auguste Forel was marked as "confiscated" on the corresponding lists but was apparently not removed from the Kunsthalle collection.[2]

The Expressionist self-portrait was characterized by subjectivity even more than other genres; artists turned their inner being outward and questioned themselves and their existence. This can be seen especially clearly in the woodcut. Because of the resistance of the material, the woodcut offered the ideal conditions for intensifying the expression of a (self-)portrait by means of a few hard lines reduced to the essential facial features and contrasting planes, thus lending it a monumental presence. In Erich Heckel's self-portrait (cat. 95), one is struck by the masklike gaze and the hard forms. The sharp-edged face of the thirty-four-year-old and the blocklike form of his head presumably reflect his character and state of mind. The potted plant in the background could also be seen as a metaphorical symbol for it. The woodcut from 1917 was published as a reprint in the journal *Der Anbruch*, which was first published in Vienna in 1919–20 and later in Berlin. Karl Friedrich Zähringer, too, occasionally placed motifs in the background of his paintings that referred to him. In his case, they are motifs from the landscape where he grew up to emphasize his origins in a language of simplified forms. The *Bauernköpfe* (Peasant Heads) series of seven woodcuts from 1920, to which the artist's self-portrait also belongs, includes in the background the mountainous landscape and the people and animals living there in order to show how this landscape influences the figures from his homeland shown in the foreground. His *Selbstporträt mit Holzstichel* (Self-Portrait with Wood Carving Knife) (cat. 96), which is the center of the series, is embedded in a mountain landscape with a shepherdess and edelweiss, its sharp peaks allude to his origins in the Black Forest and his profession as woodcarver. The large, brusque face

Ausdruck und Verfremdung: das Porträt

Ursula Drahoss

Vor dem Hintergrund der Erforschung des Unbewussten gegen Ende des 19. Jahrhunderts prägten vor allem Vincent van Gogh und Edvard Munch nachfolgende Generationen von Kunstschaffenden in der Porträtkunst. Form und Farbe dienten den Expressionist*innen nicht mehr der naturalistisch-realistischen Wiedergabe des menschlichen Antlitzes, sondern wurden zum Ausdrucksmittel für die Wiedergabe des subjektiven Erlebens. Dabei hielten zum Beispiel Oskar Kokoschka und die Künstler der Brücke an der figurativen Darstellungsweise fest, verließen aber den traditionellen, auf Repräsentation zielenden Porträttypus zugunsten von Expression und Verfremdung; andere hingegen, wie etwa die Künstler*innen des Blauen Reiter, suchten den Weg in die Abstraktion.

Oskar Kokoschka wurde in Deutschland 1910 mit Federzeichnungen bekannt, mit denen er sein eigenes Drama *Mörder, Hoffnung der Frauen* in Herwarth Waldens Zeitschrift *Der Sturm* illustrierte. Die Kunsthalle Mannheim besitzt Kokoschkas bedeutendes frühes Porträt des Arztes und Sozialreformers Auguste Forel von 1910 (Kat. 94). Forel erforschte die Zusammenhänge zwischen Gehirn und Seele und gilt als Begründer der Schweizer Psychiatrie.

Kokoschka konzentrierte sich ganz auf die beredte Gestik der Hände, den hypnotischen Blick und das nachdenkliche und vergeistigte Gesicht. Die mönchisch anmutende, in Grau- und Brauntönen fleckig und mit offenem Pinselstrich gemalte Jacke sowie die zeichenhaften Einritzungen in die Farbe entsprachen so gar nicht der konventionellen Porträtmalerei seiner Zeit – und damit wohl auch nicht dem Geschmack des Auftraggebers, der das Bild ablehnte.[1] 1913 erwarb es Gustav Friedrich Hartlaub über den Kunsthandel für die Kunsthalle Mannheim und zeigte es 1918 in der Ausstellung *Neue religiöse Kunst*. Auch Kokoschkas Werke wurden 1937 unter dem NS-Regime als „entartet" verfemt und aus den Museen verbannt. Das Porträt von Auguste Forel war zwar in den entsprechenden Listen als „beschlagnahmt" vermerkt, wurde aber offenbar nicht aus der Sammlung der Kunsthalle entfernt.[2]

Das Selbstbildnis im Expressionismus war noch stärker von Subjektivität geprägt als dies für die übrigen Genres galt; die Künstler*innen kehrten ihr inneres Wesen nach außen und hinterfragten sich selbst und ihr Dasein. Besonders deutlich ließ sich dies im Holzschnitt veranschaulichen. Der Holzschnitt bot durch die Widerständigkeit des Materials ideale Voraussetzungen, um mit wenigen, harten, auf wesentliche Gesichtszüge reduzierten Linien und kontrastierenden Flächen den Ausdruck eines (Selbst-)Porträts zu intensivieren und ihm eine monumentale Präsenz zu verleihen. In Erich Heckels Selbstbildnis von 1917 (Kat. 95) fallen der maskenhafte Blick und die harten Formen auf. Das scharfkantige Gesicht des damals 34-Jährigen und die blockhafte Gestaltung des Kopfes spiegeln wohl seinen Charakter und seine innere Verfassung wider. Auch die Topfpflanze im Hintergrund könnte als metaphorisches Symbol dafür gesehen werden. Der 1917 entstandene Holzschnitt erschien als Nachdruck in der Zeitschrift *Der Anbruch*, die 1919/20 zunächst in Wien, dann in Berlin erschien. Auch Karl Friedrich Zähringer versah seine Porträts gelegentlich mit Motiven im Hintergrund, die sich auf ihn selbst bezogen. Bei ihm sind es Motive aus der Landschaft, aus der er stammte und mit denen er in vereinfachter Formensprache seine Herkunft betonte. Die siebenteilige Holzschnittfolge *Bauernköpfe* von 1920, zu der auch das Selbstbildnis des Künstlers gehört, greift im Hintergrund die bergige Landschaft und die darin lebenden Menschen und Tiere auf und verdeutlicht so, wie diese Umgebung die im Vordergrund dargestellten Charakterköpfe prägt. Sein *Selbstporträt mit Holzstichel* (Kat. 96), das im Zentrum der Serie steht, ist in eine Berglandschaft mit Hirtin und

with deep furrows and dark eyes may express fear and illness:
the *Bauernköpfe* series was made when the artist had withdrawn
to the Todtmoos health resort in the southern Black Forest to
cure a lung ailment.[3]

Alexej von Jawlensky influenced twentieth-century portraiture
with his series of repeated variations on the same motif. The
oval face was the point of departure for his *Abstrakte Köpfe*
(Abstract Heads) series from the years 1918 to 1933, in which
curved nose lines and large, almond-shaped eyes are recur-
ring pictorial elements that point to the reduction of physical
presence.[4] The painting *Femina* of 1922 (cat. 62) shows an
abstracted woman's head in bright colors. It was made after
Jawlensky's exile in Switzerland, when he had returned to
Germany, divorced Marianne von Werefkin, and married Helene
Nesnakomoff.

1   Mathias Listl, "Oskar Kokoschka," in *Meisterwerke: Malerei und Skulptur,
    Kunsthalle Mannheim*, ed. Inge Herold, Ulrike Lorenz, and Stefanie Patruno
    (Cologne: Wienand, 2013), p. 176.
2   *(Re)Discovery: The Kunsthalle from 1933 to 1945 and the Aftermath*, ed.
    Mathias Listl and Ulrike Lorenz, exh. cat. (Mannheim: Kunsthalle Mannheim,
    2018), p. 38.
3   Günter Hoffmann, *Karl Friedrich Zähringer, 1886–1923: Ein vergessener
    Künstler vom Hochrhein* (Norderstedt: Books on Demand, 2016), pp. 13–15.
4   Clemens Weiler, *Jawlensky: Heads, Faces, Meditations*, trans. Edith Küstner
    and J. A. Underwood (London: Pal Mall, 1971). pp. 124–26.

Edelweiß eingebettet, deren spitze Gipfel auf seine Herkunft aus dem Schwarzwald und seinen Beruf als Holzschneider verweisen. Das große, schroffe Gesicht mit den tiefen Furchen und den dunklen Augen mag Angst und Krankheit ausdrücken: Die Serie der *Bauernköpfe* entstand, als sich der Künstler in den Luftkurort Todtmoos im Südschwarzwald zurückzog, um seine Lungenkrankheit auszukurieren.[3]

Alexej von Jawlensky prägte die Porträtkunst des 20. Jahrhunderts durch seine seriellen Darstellungen, bei denen er dasselbe Motiv wiederholt variierte. Das ovale Gesicht wurde zum Ausgangspunkt seiner Serie der *Abstrakten Köpfe*, die er in den Jahren 1918 bis 1933 schuf und in denen geschwungene Nasenlinien und große, mandelförmige Augen als wiederkehrende Bildelemente auf die Reduktion der körperlichen Präsenz verweisen.[4] Das Gemälde *Femina* von 1922 (Kat. 62) zeigt einen abstrahierten Frauenkopf in kräftigen Farben. Es entstand nach Jawlenskys Exil in der Schweiz, als er nach Deutschland zurückkehrte, sich von Marianne von Werefkin trennte und Helene Nesnakomoff heiratete.

1 Mathias Listl: Oskar Kokoschka, in: Inge Herold u. a. (Hrsg.): *Meisterwerke. Malerei und Skulptur, Kunsthalle Mannheim*, Köln 2013, S. 176.

2 Kat. Ausst. *(Wieder-)Entdecken. Die Kunsthalle Mannheim 1933 bis 1945 und die Folgen*, Kunsthalle Mannheim 2018, hrsg. v. Mathias Listl u. Ulrike Lorenz, Mannheim 2018, S. 38.

3 Günter Hoffmann: *Karl Friedrich Zähringer 1886–1923 ein vergessener Künstler vom Hochrhein*, Norderstedt 2016, S. 13–15.

4 Clemens Weiler: *Alexej Jawlensky. Köpfe, Gesichte, Meditationen*, Hanau 1970, S. 124–126.

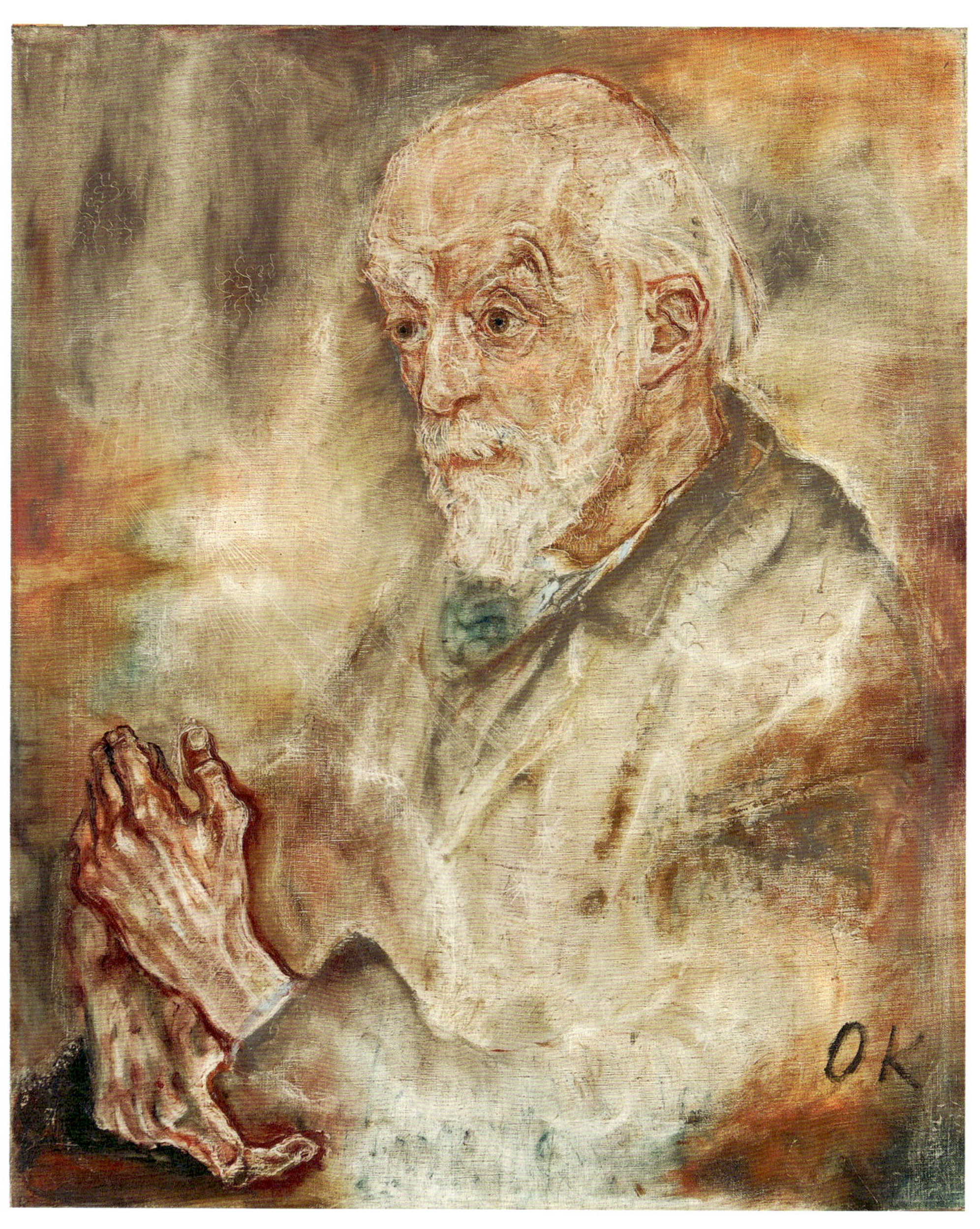

94 | **Oskar Kokoschka,** *Auguste Forel,* **1910,** Kunsthalle Mannheim

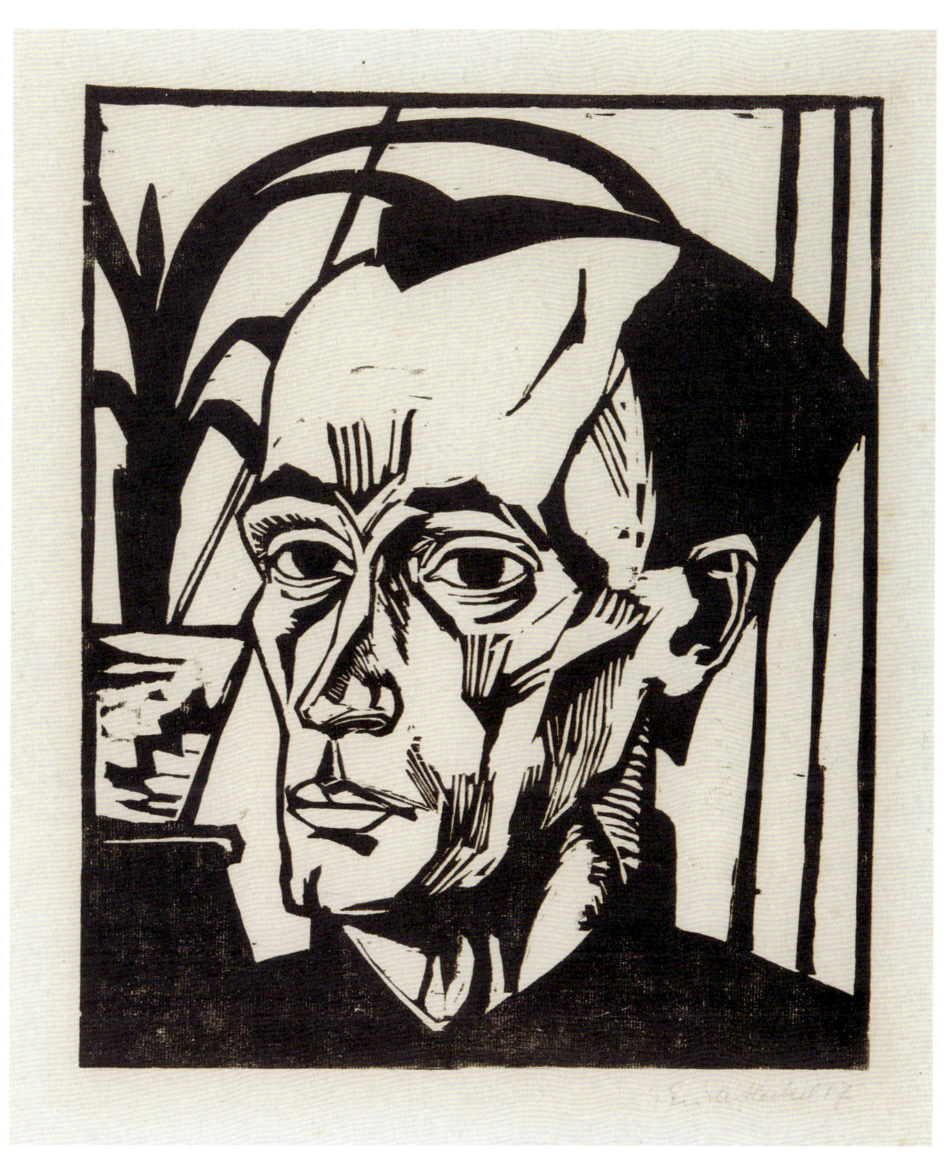

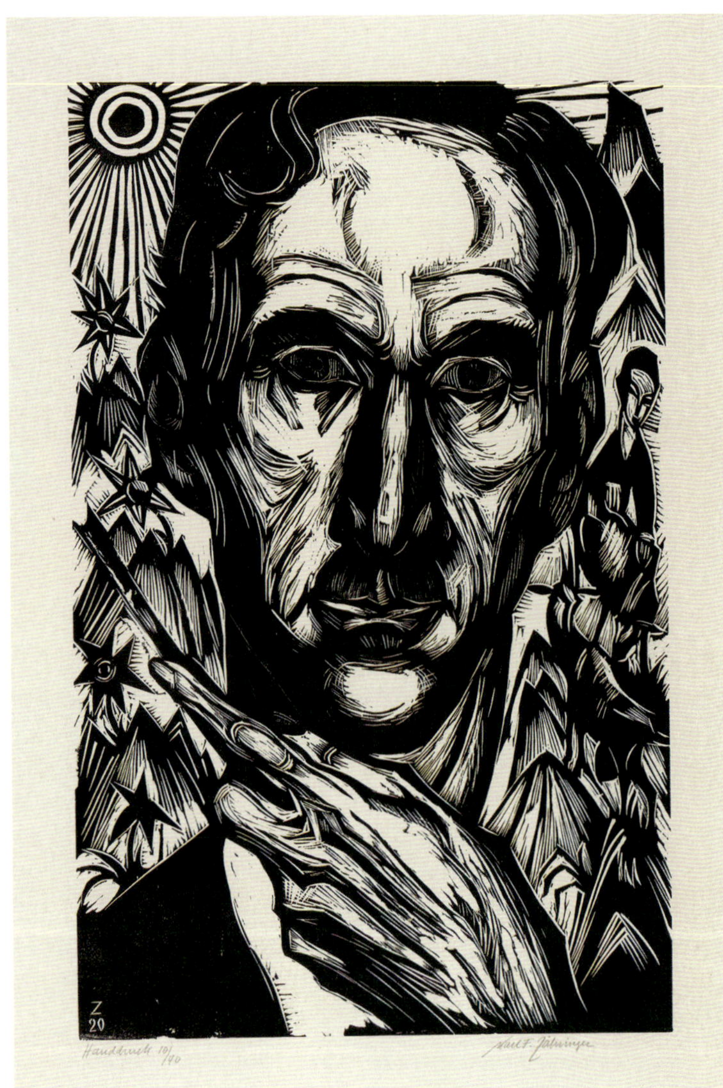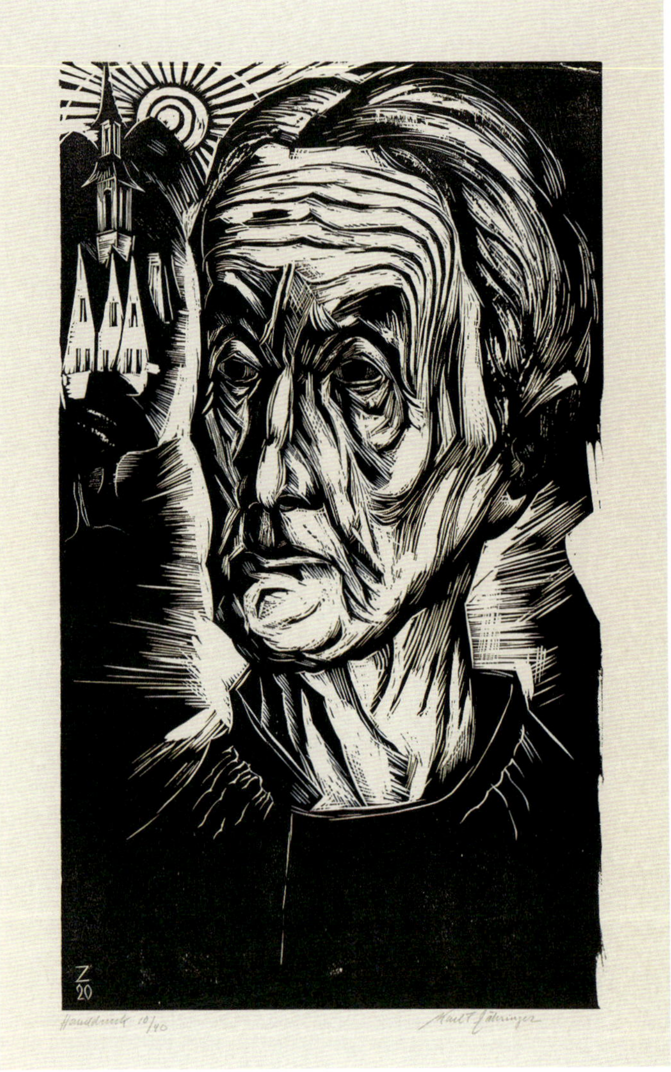

96 | **Karl Friedrich Zähringer,** *Selbstporträt mit Holzstichel*
aus der Serie *Bauernköpfe* **(Mappe mit sieben Holzschnitten)** /
Self-Portrait with Wood Carving Knife from the *Peasant Heads* series
(portfolio with seven woodcuts), **1920,** Kunsthalle Mannheim

97 | **Karl Friedrich Zähringer,**
Blatt aus der Serie *Bauernköpfe* **(Mappe mit sieben Holzschnitten** /
Sheet from the *Peasant Heads* series (portfolio with seven woodcuts), **1920,**
Kunsthalle Mannheim

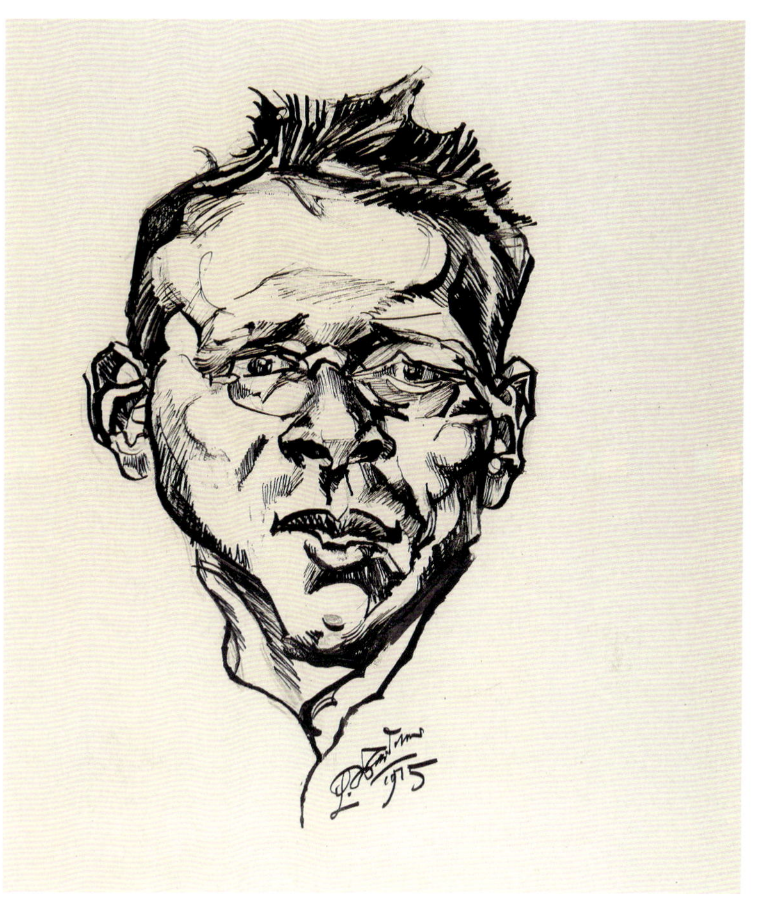

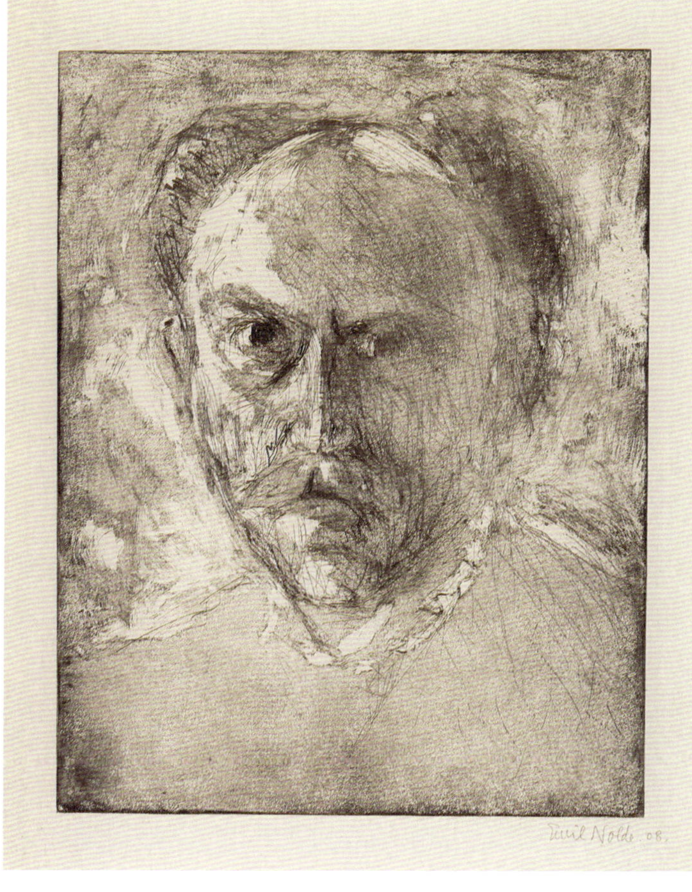

98 | **Emil Nolde,** *Selbstporträt /*
Self-Portrait, **1908,** Kunsthalle Mannheim

99 | **Ludwig Meidner,** *Bildnis eines Unbekannten /*
Portrait of an Unknown Man, **1915,** Kunsthalle Mannheim

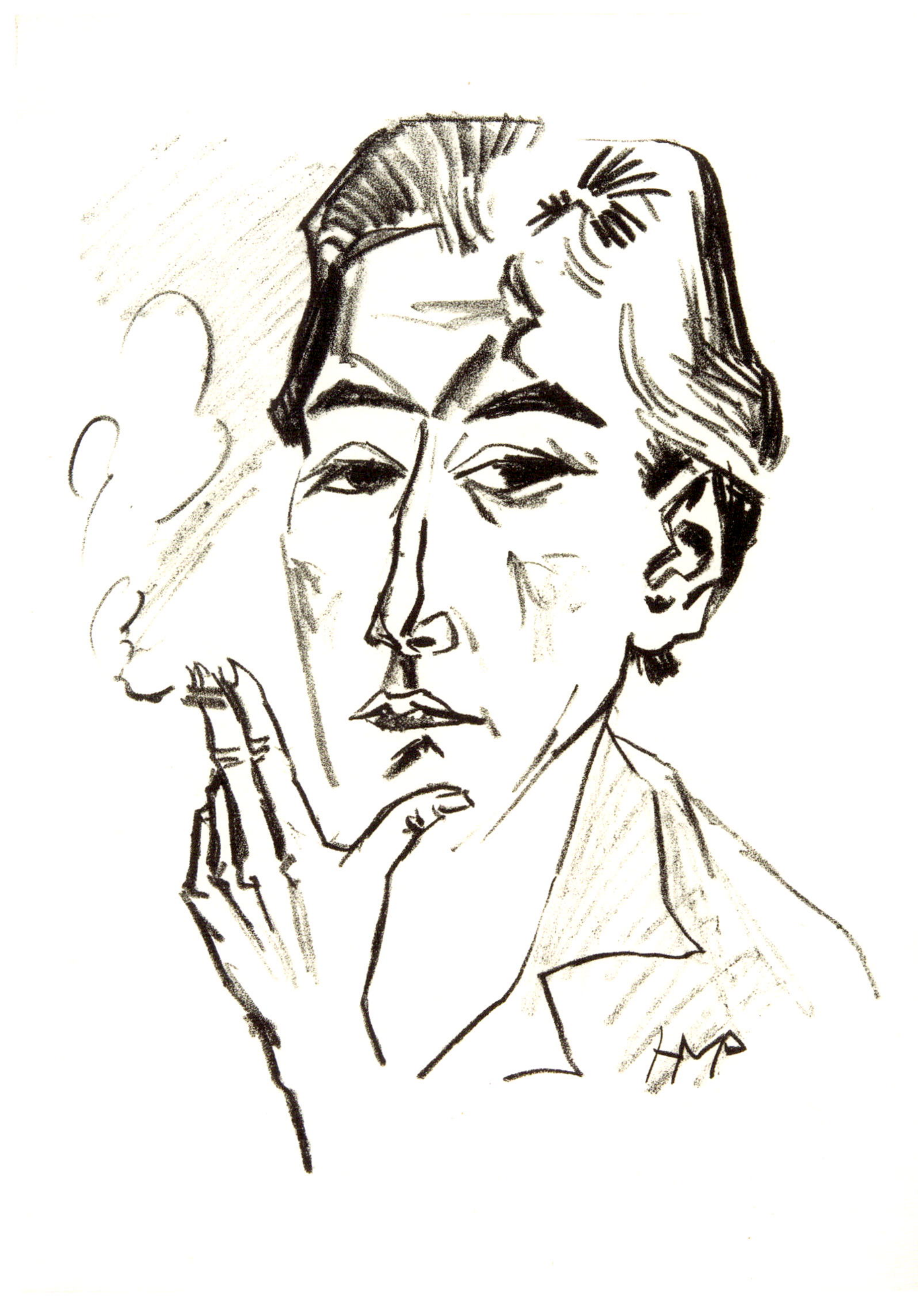

100 | **Max Pechstein**, *Rauchende* / *Woman Smoking*, **1918,** Kunsthalle Mannheim

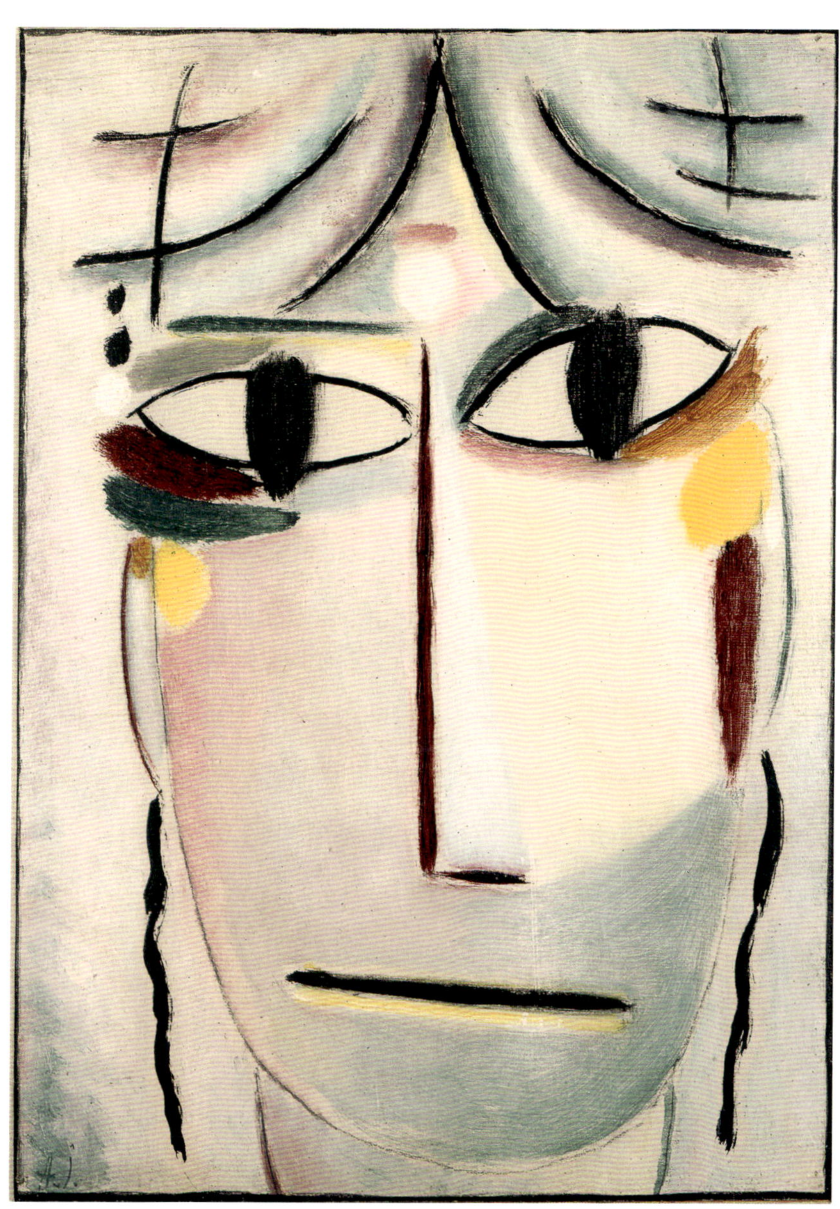

101 | **Alexej von Jawlensky,** *Heilandsgesicht: Wächter* / *Face of the Saviour: Guardian,* **1920,** Kunsthalle Mannheim

Defamation, Confiscation, Resale:
The Expressionism Collection of the Kunsthalle Mannheim under National Socialism

Luisa Heese

When the "Gesetz zur Wiederherstellung des Berufsbeamten-tums" (Law for the Restoration of the Professional Civil Service) was passed on April 7, 1933, Gustav Friedrich Hartlaub had already been affected: the director of the Kunsthalle Mannheim for many years had been "suspended" on March 20, making him one of the first museum directors in Germany to lose his post when the National Socialist regime took power. Several days before, on March 11, Lord Mayor Hermann Heimerich was arrested, and several Social Democratic city council members were taken into "protective custody." National Socialist city councilman Otto Gebele von Waldstein was placed in the Kunsthalle Mannheim as an advisory consultant to oversee the implementation of the rulings of the city council and municipal administration. As the leader of the local National Socialist group, he had repeatedly agitated against the progressive program of the Kunsthalle and its director and accused them of wasting public funds, privileging foreign artists, and supporting bad art. His mouthpiece for this purpose was the party's journal *Hakenkreuzbanner* (Swastika Banner), founded in 1931, in which Gebele von Waldstein published numerous articles agitating against Hartlaub. Almost as soon as he was in office,

Gebele von Waldstein prepared an exhibition intended to "prove the cultural bolshevist trend . . . and the squandering of public funds on the Jewish art trade."[1] The exhibition *Kulturbolsche-wistische Bilder* (Cultural Bolshevist Pictures), which opened at the Kunsthalle Mannheim on April 4, 1933, was thus the first defamatory exhibition and "in terms of its political object, ideological thrust, and propagandist presentation"[2] symbolized the sorry prelude to the exhibitions of "degenerate" art that would follow in numerous German cities in the coming years.

The focus of this first defamatory exhibition was on works of Expressionism and of those artists that Hartlaub had presented a few years earlier under the name *Neue Sachlichkeit* (New Objectivity). The fifty-five artists included Paula Modersohn-Becker; the Brücke painters Erich Heckel, Ernst Ludwig Kirchner, Emil Nolde, and Max Pechstein; as well as Franz Marc and Alexej von Jawlensky, who belonged to the Blauer Reiter (Blue Rider) group. A total of eighty-six paintings, sculptures, and graphic works were publicly defamed. The paintings were to be presented in as unfavorable a way as possible: for the exhibition, they were removed from their frames and hung closely together. In addition to the name of the artist and the title of the work, the signs indicated the year of acquisition and supposedly excessive price paid. In several cases, the "race" of the artist and art dealer responsible for the work was cited.[3] Moreover, these works were juxtaposed with works by artists from Mannheim in a so-called *Musterkabinett* (Cabinet of Models) as examples of the "German art" that was now supposed to point the way to the future.

The exhibition *Kulturbolschewistische Bilder*, which had had 20,141 attendees by June 5, 1933, took place at a time when there was a heated debate over Expressionism underway within the National Socialist Party, which had already started in the 1920s and early 1930s. Some voices in the party saw Expressionism as an authentic German alternative to French-influenced Impressionism; in particular, the "Northern Expressionism" of Emil Nolde, which was seen as having been inspired by the German Gothic, had prominent advocates in National Socialist circles.[4] Its opponents in turn saw it as a mockery of the German people with its not very naturalistic expression. This debate clearly shows the wavering attitudes in the "movement" and a lack of clarity about the aesthetic and ideological orientation of art. It would be a few years before the "Expressionism debate" in the National Socialist Party was decided in favor of the views of Adolf Hitler and his leading

Diffamierung, Beschlagnahmung, Verwertung: die Expressionismus-Sammlung der Kunsthalle Mannheim im Nationalsozialismus

Luisa Heese

Als das „Gesetz zur Wiederherstellung des Berufsbeamtentums"
am 7. April 1933 erlassen wurde, hatte es Gustav Friedrich Hartlaub schon getroffen: Der langjährige Direktor der Kunsthalle
Mannheim war bereits am 20. März „beurlaubt" worden und
somit einer der ersten Museumsdirektoren in Deutschland, die
ihren Posten nach der Machtübernahme durch das NS-Regime
verloren. Einige Tage zuvor, am 11. März, waren der Oberbürgermeister Hermann Heimerich inhaftiert und einige sozialdemo-
kratische Stadtverordnete in sogenannte Schutzhaft genommen
worden. In der Mannheimer Kunsthalle wurde der NSDAP-Stadt-
rat Otto Gebele von Waldstein als Hilfsreferent eingesetzt,
um den Vollzug der Beschlüsse von Stadträten und Verwaltung
zu überwachen. Als NSDAP-Ortsgruppenleiter hatte er zuvor
bereits wiederholt gegen das progressive Programm der Kunsthalle gehetzt und die Direktion der Verschwendung öffentlicher
Gelder, der Bevorzugung ausländischer Kunstschaffender sowie
der Förderung schlechter Kunst bezichtigt. Als Sprachrohr hierfür
diente ihm das 1931 gegründete Parteiblatt *Hakenkreuzbanner*,
in dem Gebele von Waldstein in zahlreichen Hetzartikeln gegen
Hartlaub Stimmung machte. Kaum im Amt, bereitete Gebele

von Waldstein eine Ausstellung vor, mit der „die kulturbolschewistische Tendenz" und „die Verschleuderung von öffentlichen
Geldern an den jüdischen Kunsthandel nachgewiesen werden"[1]
sollten. Die am 4. April 1933 in der Kunsthalle Mannheim eröffnete
Schau *Kulturbolschewistische Bilder* war somit die erste Feme-
Ausstellung, die „im Hinblick auf ihre politische Zielsetzung,
ideologische Stoßrichtung und propagandistische Inszenierung"[2]
den traurigen Auftakt der Ausstellungen „entarteter Kunst"
bildete, die in den kommenden Jahren in zahlreichen deutschen
Städten folgen sollten.

Der Schwerpunkt dieser ersten Feme-Ausstellung lag auf den
Werken des Expressionismus und jenen Künstlern, die Hartlaub
einige Jahre zuvor unter dem Begriff der Neuen Sachlichkeit
präsentiert hatte. Unter den 55 Künstler*innen waren auch Paula
Modersohn-Becker, die Brücke-Maler Erich Heckel, Ernst Ludwig
Kirchner, Emil Nolde und Max Pechstein, ebenso Franz Marc und
Alexej von Jawlensky, die der Gruppe Der Blaue Reiter ange-
hörten. Insgesamt wurden 86 Gemälde, Plastiken und Grafiken
öffentlich diffamiert. Die Gemälde sollten möglichst unvorteil-
haft erscheinen, sie wurden für die Ausstellung ausgerahmt
und in dichter Hängung präsentiert, die Objektschilder nannten
neben den Namen der Künstler*innen und den Werktiteln auch
das jeweilige Ankaufsjahr und den bezahlten, angeblich überteu-
erten Preis. In einigen Fällen wurde auch die „Rasse" des Künstlers
und des Kunsthändlers angeführt, von dem das Werk erstanden
wurde.[3] Zudem wurden diesen Werken in einem sogenannten
Musterkabinett Beispiele der nun als zukunftsweisend geltenden
„deutschen Kunst" von Mannheimer Künstlern gegenübergestellt.
Die Ausstellung *Kulturbolschewistische Bilder*, die bis zum 5. Juni
1933 von 20.141 Menschen besucht wurde, fand zu einem Zeitpunkt statt, als innerhalb der NSDAP eine erhitzte Debatte
um den Expressionismus im Gange war, die sich schon in den
1920er- und frühen 1930er-Jahren entwickelt hatte. So galt man-
chen Stimmen in der Partei der Expressionismus als authentische
deutsche Alternative zum französisch beeinflussten Impressionismus; insbesondere etwa der als von der deutschen Gotik
inspiriert verstandene „nordische Expressionismus" von Emil
Nolde hatte in nationalsozialistischen Kreisen prominente Für-
sprecher.[4] Die Gegner sahen in ihm wiederum eine Verhöhnung
des deutschen Volkes durch den wenig naturalistischen Ausdruck.
Diese Debatte zeigt deutlich die schwankenden Haltungen und
Unklarheiten bezüglich der ästhetisch-ideologischen Ausrichtung
der Kunst innerhalb der „Bewegung" auf. Es dauerte noch einige

ideologue, Alfred Rosenberg. Artists such as Nolde had hoped that their own work would be recognized by the Nazi state, but in fact it subjected art to increasingly rigorous restrictions.[5] In the summer of 1937, on the occasion of his seventieth birthday, an exhibition with works by Emil Nolde was still shown at the Kunsthaus Rudolf Probst in Mannheim, but it had to be closed after just a few days.

Under the leadership of Adolf Ziegler, president of the Reichskammer der bildenden Künste (Reich Chamber of the Fine Arts), on July 8 and August 28, 1937, the holdings of the Kunsthalle Mannheim—and at the same time around a hundred other German museums—were searched for "degenerate" art according to Nazi criteria. Numerous works were confiscated. The majority of the works from the collection in Mannheim that had previously been presented in 1933 as "manifestations of 'bolshevist' degeneration"[6] fell victim to these confiscations and remain lost to the Kunsthalle today: more than 570 works were placed on the lists and most were transported away. The Kunsthalle Mannheim was thus one of the hardest hit public collections in Germany. The majority of these works were destroyed; others were presented in exhibitions of "degenerate" art presented by the state and usually sold and "*verwertet*" (valorized), usually abroad, by art galleries and dealers.

As a result, works by Emil Nolde and many other Expressionist artists that once belonged to the collection of the Kunsthalle Mannheim are now in museums or private collections, which they reached in various ways. Thankfully, several of them could be obtained temporarily as loans on the occasion of the present exhibition *Kirchner, Lehmbruck, Nolde. Stories of Expressionism in Mannheim*: Emil Nolde's work *Figuren und Georginen* (Figures and Dahlias) of 1919 (cat. 104) was made available by the Statens Museum for Kunst, Denmark's national gallery. His work *Vorabend (Marschlandschaft)* (Twilight [Marsh Landscape]) of 1916 (cat. 106) has been in the collection of the Kunstmuseum Basel since 1939. The painting *Tulpen* (Tulips) of 1915 (cat. 103), which could be purchased directly from the artist for the collection in Mannheim in 1919 was brought to Berlin in 1937 and placed in storage in Schönhausen Palace along with other works of art for "resale internationally." Via various gallery commissions (the Galerie Gurlitt in Berlin und Böhmer in Güstrow, among others), the work ended up in a private collection and changed hands again several times after 1945 until it was donated to the Wallraff-Richartz-Museum in 1964; since 1976, it has been part of the collection

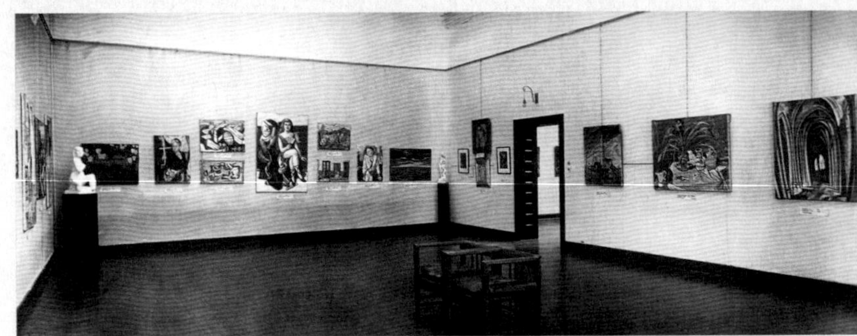

Abb./Fig. 37
Einblicke in die Ausstellung *Kulturbolschewistische Bilder I*
View of the exhibition Cultural Bolshevist Pictures, Kunsthalle Mannheim

of the Museum Ludwig in Cologne. *Drei Frauen* (Three Women) from 1921 by Erich Heckel (cat. 105) is now in the collection of the Brücke-Museum in Berlin, as a gift in 1977 from Rosemarie Baumgart-Möller, the daughter of the art dealer Ferdinand Möller, who had taken possession of the work in 1941 to sell it abroad on behalf of the German Reich. Instead, it remained in the family's possession until it was donated. Isolated exceptions among the mass of confiscated works now lost to the Kunsthalle Mannheim's collection include paintings such as *Sonnenblumen* (Sunflowers) by Erich Heckel (1913; cat. 121): although it had been included on the list of works to be confiscated, astonishingly it was never removed and remained in the collection of the Kunsthalle Mannheim. The painting *Drei Tiere (Hund, Fuchs und Katze)* (Three Animals [Dog, Fox, and Cat]) by Franz Marc (1912; cat. 102) was not sold in the auction organized by the Galerie Fischer in Lucerne, Switzerland, and was returned to the Kunsthalle already in 1940.[7] All of these works are now part of *Stories of Expressionism in Mannheim*.

1   Gebele von Waldstein quoted in Isgard Kracht, *Inszeniert und instrumentalisiert: Expressionismus im Nationalsozialismus; Ernst Barlach, Franz Marc, Emil Nolde* (Berlin and Boston: De Gruyter, 2023), p. 137.
2   Christoph Zuschlag, "Die Ausstellung 'Kulturbolschewistische Bilder' in Mannheim 1933: Inszenierung und Presseberichterstellung," in *Überbrückt: Ästhetische Moderne und Nationalsozialismus; Kunsthistoriker und Künstler, 1925–1937*, ed. Eugen Blume and Dieter Scholz (Cologne: Walther König, 1999), pp. 224–36, esp. p. 234.
3   See ibid., pp. 226–27.
4   See *Emil Nolde: The Artist during the Third Reich*, ed. Bernhard Fulda, Christian Ring, and Aya Soika, exh. cat., Neue Galerie im Hamburger Bahnhof—Museum für Gegenwart Berlin 2019 (Munich: Prestel, 2019), pp. 39–40.
5   See ibid., p. 45.
6   Zuschlag, "Die Ausstellung 'Kulturbolschewistische Bilder' in Mannheim" (see note 2), p. 226.
7   See Mathias Listl, "Mannheim's Modern Collection: Defamed, Confiscated, and Scattered throughout the World," in *(Re)Discovery: The Kunsthalle from 1933 to 1945 and the Aftermath*, ed. Mathias Listl and Ulrike Lorenz, exh. cat. (Mannheim: Kunsthalle Mannheim, 2018), pp. 21–61, esp. p. 30.

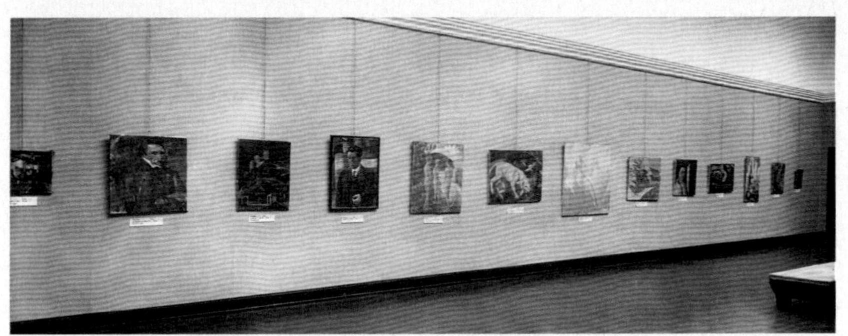

Abb./Fig. 38
Einblicke in die Ausstellung *Kulturbolschewistische Bilder I*
View of the exhibition Cultural Bolshevist Pictures, Kunsthalle Mannheim

Jahre, bis der „Expressionismusstreit" innerhalb der NSDAP zugunsten der Kunstauffassung Adolf Hitlers und seines führenden Ideologen Alfred Rosenberg entschieden war. Künstler wie Nolde hatten noch auf Anerkennung des eigenen Werkes im NS-Staat gehofft, der jedoch der Kunst immer rigorosere Beschränkungen auferlegte.[5] Im Sommer 1937 fand anlässlich seines 70. Geburtstages noch eine Ausstellung mit Werken von Emil Nolde im Kunsthaus Rudolf Probst in Mannheim statt, die jedoch nach wenigen Tagen geschlossen werden musste. Unter der Leitung von Adolf Ziegler, Präsident der Reichskammer der bildenden Künste, wurden schließlich am 8. Juli und 28. August 1937 in Mannheim und zeitgleich in rund 100 anderen deutschen Museen die Bestände nach laut NS-Kriterien „entarteter Kunst" durchsucht. Zahlreiche Werke wurden beschlagnahmt. Der Großteil der bereits 1933 als „bolschewistische' Degenerationserscheinungen"[6] präsentierten Werke der Mannheimer Sammlung fiel diesen Beschlagnahmungen zum Opfer, und bleibt bis heute für die Kunsthalle verloren: Insgesamt über 570 Werke wurden auf die Listen gesetzt und größtenteils abtransportiert. Damit zählt die Kunsthalle Mannheim zu den am stärksten betroffenen öffentlichen Sammlungen in Deutschland. Ein Großteil der Werke wurde zerstört, andere wurden in den staatlich organisierten Ausstellungen zur „entarteten Kunst" präsentiert sowie durch Galerien und Händler zumeist ins Ausland verkauft und „verwertet".

So finden sich Werke von Emil Nolde und zahlreichen weiteren expressionistischen Künstler*innen, die einst zur Sammlung der Kunsthalle Mannheim gehörten, heute in Privatsammlungen oder Museen, in die sie über verschiedene Wege gelangten. Einige von ihnen konnten anlässlich der jetzigen Ausstellung *Kirchner, Lehmbruck, Nolde. Geschichten des Expressionismus in Mannheim* dankenswerterweise als temporäre Leihgaben gewonnen werden: Emil Noldes Werk *Figuren und Georginen*

von 1919 (Kat. 104) stellt das Statens Museum for Kunst, die Nationalgalerie Dänemarks, zur Verfügung. Sein Werk *Vorabend (Marschlandschaft)* von 1916 (Kat. 106) befindet sich seit 1939 in der Sammlung des Kunstmuseums Basel. Das Gemälde *Tulpen* aus dem Jahr 1915 (Kat. 103), das 1919 direkt vom Künstler für die Mannheimer Sammlung erworben werden konnte, wurde 1937 nach Berlin verbracht und in das Depot im Schloss Schönhausen für „international verwertbare" Kunstwerke eingelagert. Über verschiedene Galerie-Kommissionen (unter anderem der Galerie Gurlitt in Berlin und Böhmer in Güstrow) gelangte das Werk in Privatbesitz und wechselte nach 1945 erneut mehrmals den Besitzer, bis es 1964 als Schenkung zunächst dem Wallraff-Richartz-Museum überlassen wurde, seit 1976 gehört es zur Sammlung des Museums Ludwig in Köln. Das 1921 entstandene Werk *Drei Frauen* von Erich Heckel (Kat. 105) befindet sich heute in der Sammlung des Brücke-Museums Berlin, wohin es 1977 als Schenkung von Rosemarie Baumgart-Möller gelangte: Tochter des Kunsthändlers Ferdinand Möller, der das Werk 1941 übernommen hatte, um es im Auftrag des Deutschen Reiches ins Ausland zu verkaufen. Stattdessen verblieb es bis zur Schenkung im Besitz der Familie. Einsame Ausnahmen in der Masse der beschlagnahmten und für die Sammlung der Kunsthalle Mannheim verlorenen Werke bilden Gemälde wie *Sonnenblumen* von Erich Heckel (1913; Kat. 121): War dieses zwar auf der Liste der zu beschlagnahmenden Werke vermerkt, wurde es jedoch erstaunlicherweise nicht abtransportiert und blieb der Sammlung der Kunsthalle Mannheim erhalten. Das Gemälde *Drei Tiere (Hund, Fuchs und Katze)* von Franz Marc (1912; Kat. 102) wiederum wurde auf der von der Galerie Fischer in Luzern organisierten Auktion nicht versteigert und bereits 1940 an die Kunsthalle zurückgegeben.[7] All diese Werke sind nun Teil der *Geschichten des Expressionismus in Mannheim.*

1 Gebele von Waldstein zitiert nach Isgard Kracht: *Inszeniert und instrumentalisiert. Expressionismus im Nationalsozialismus: Ernst Barlach, Franz Marc, Emil Nolde,* Berlin/Boston 2023, S. 137.
2 Christoph Zuschlag: Die Ausstellung „Kulturbolschewistische Bilder" in Mannheim 1933 – Inszenierung und Presseberichterstattung, in: Eugen Blume u. Dieter Scholz (Hrsg.): *Überbrückt. Ästhetische Moderne und Nationalsozialismus. Kunsthistoriker und Künstler 1925–1937,* Köln 1999, S. 224–236, S. 234.
3 Vgl. ebd., S. 226f.
4 Vgl. Kat. Ausst. *Emil Nolde. Eine deutsche Legende. Der Künstler im Nationalsozialismus,* Neue Galerie im Hamburger Bahnhof – Museum für Gegenwart Berlin 2019, hrsg. v. Bernhard Fulda, Christian Ring u. Aya Soika, München 2019, S. 39f.
5 Vgl. ebd., S. 45.
6 Zuschlag 1999 (wie Anm. 2), S. 226.
7 Vgl. Mathias Listl: Die Mannheimer Moderne-Sammlung: Diffamiert, beschlagnahmt und über die ganze Welt verstreut, in: Johan Holten (Hrsg.): *(Wieder-)Entdecken. Die Kunsthalle 1933 bis 1945 und die Folgen,* Kat. Ausst. Kunsthalle Mannheim 2018, 2. Aufl., Berlin 2020, S. 25–66, S. 30.

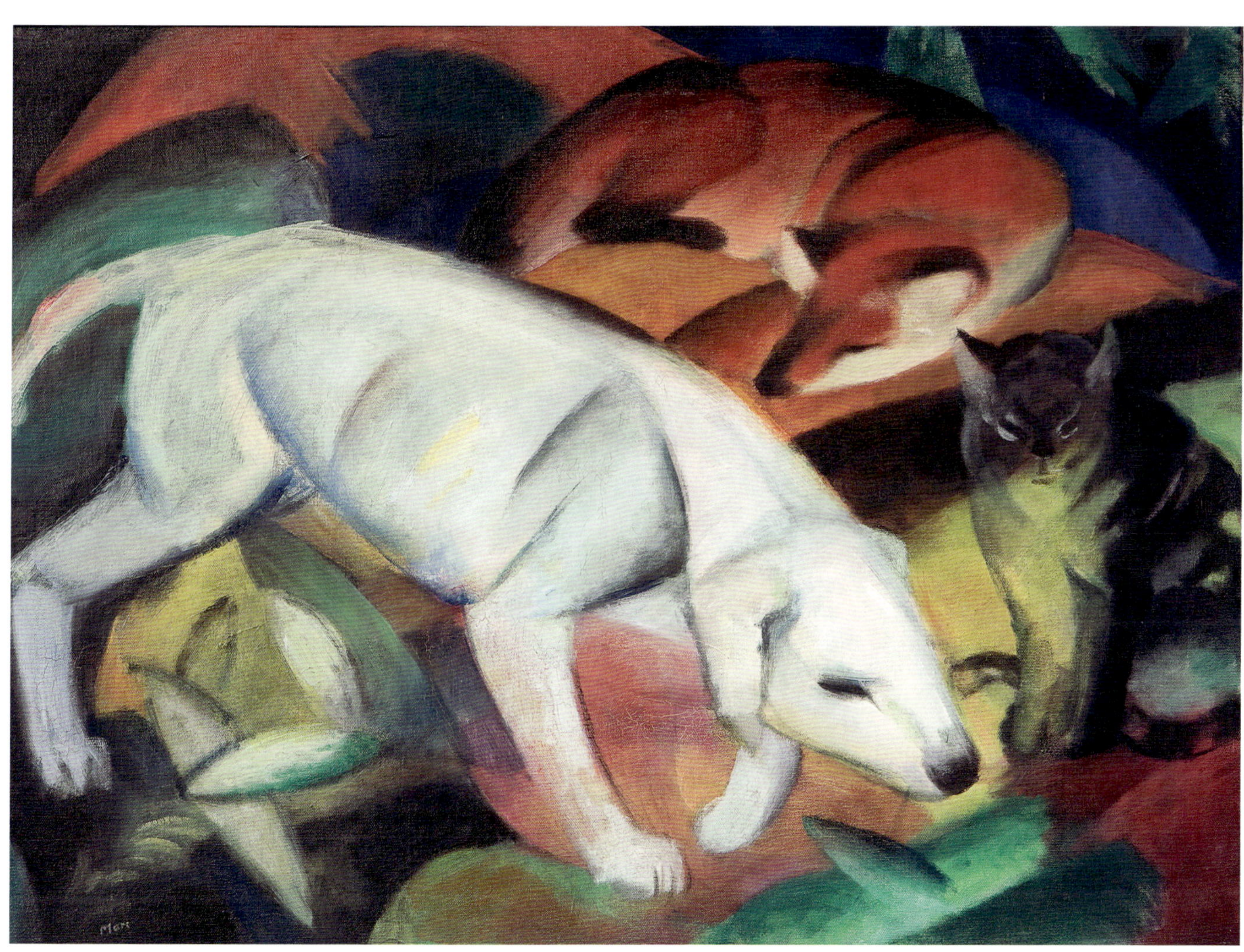

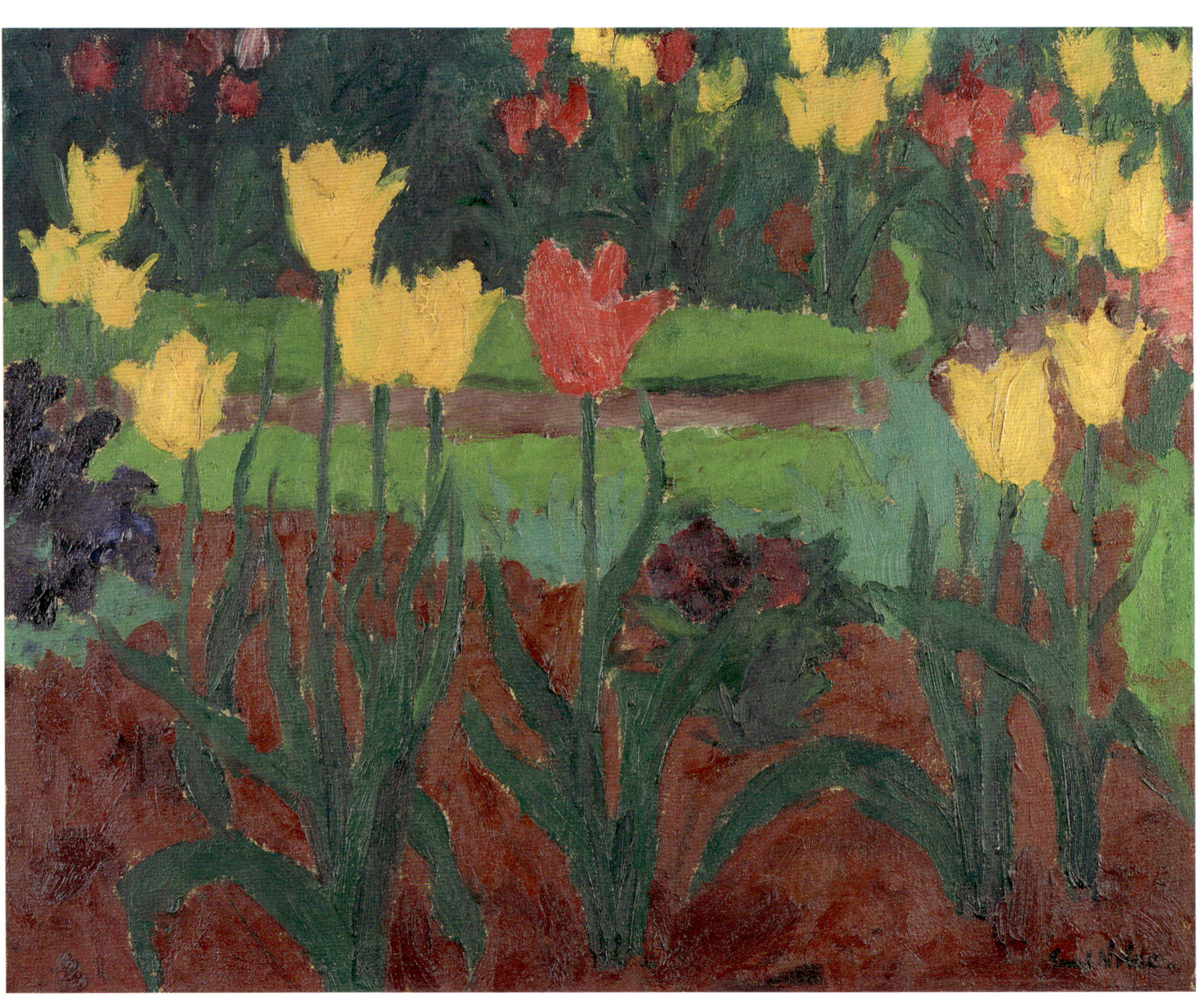

103 | **Emil Nolde,** *Tulpen* / *Tulips*, **1915,** Museum Ludwig, Köln

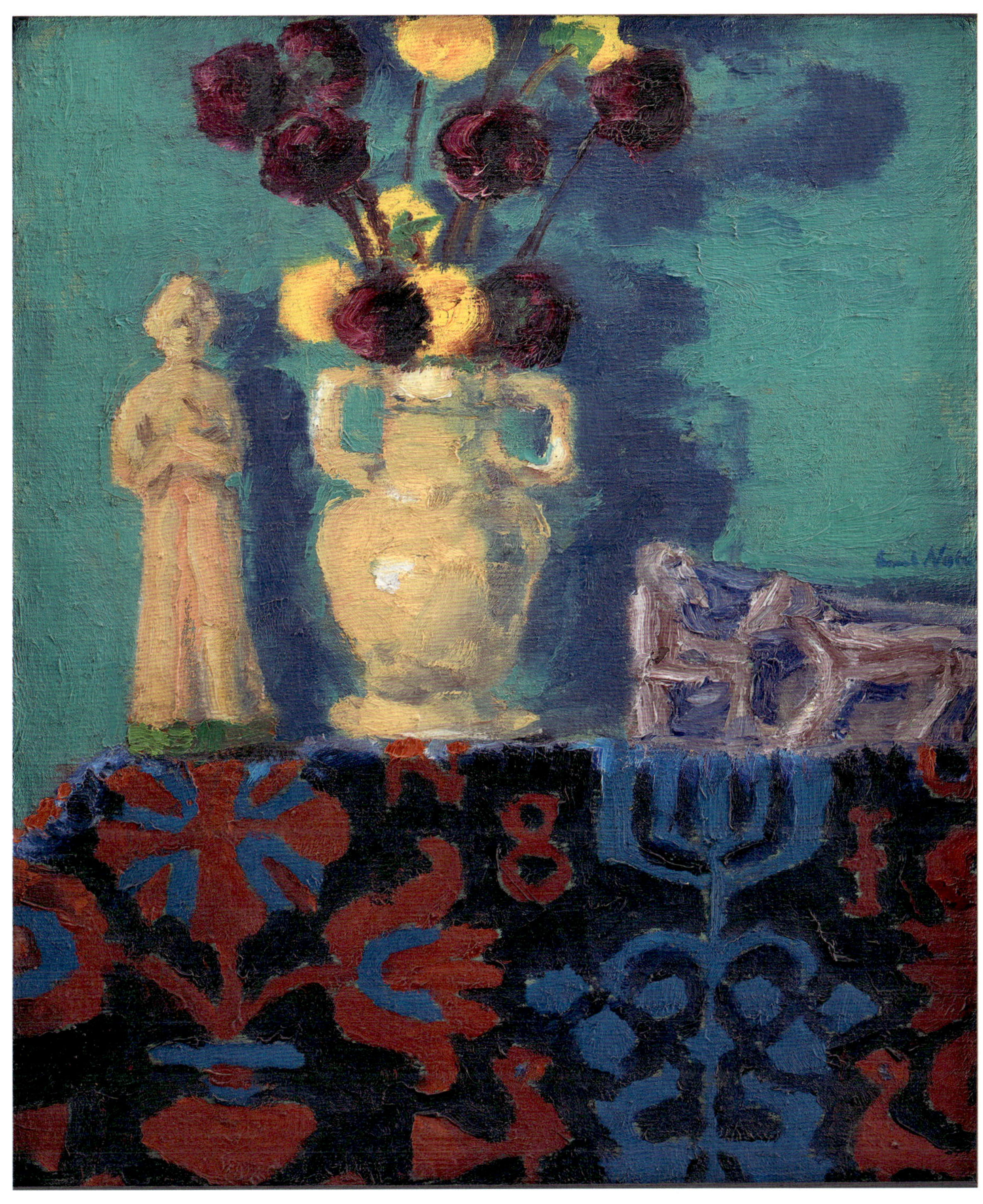

104 | **Emil Nolde, *Figuren und Georginen* / *Figures and Dahlias*, 1919,** Statens Museum for Kunst, *National Gallery of Denmark,* Kopenhagen / *Copenhagen*

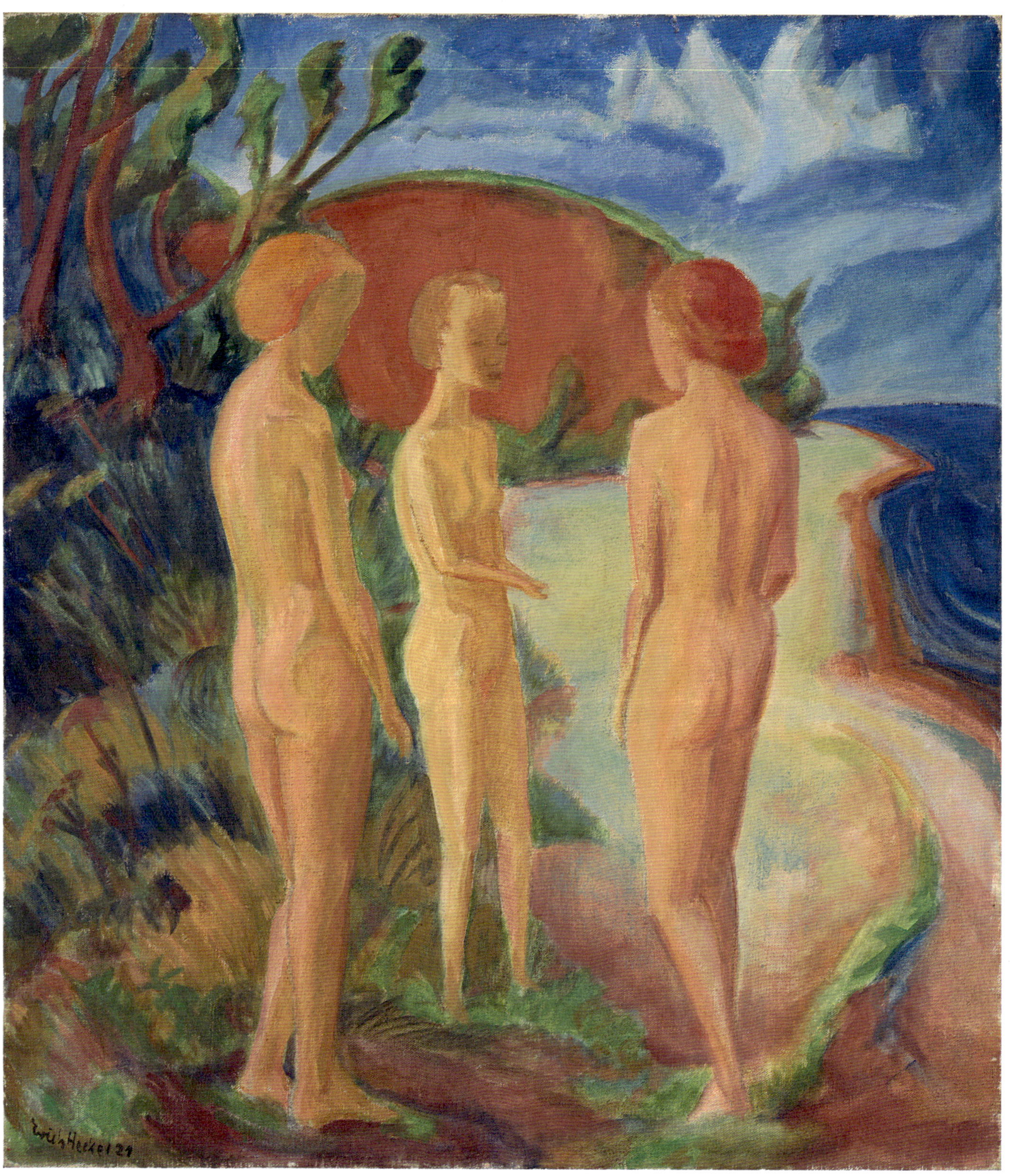

105 | **Erich Heckel,** *Drei Frauen* / Three Women, **1921,** Brücke-Museum Berlin

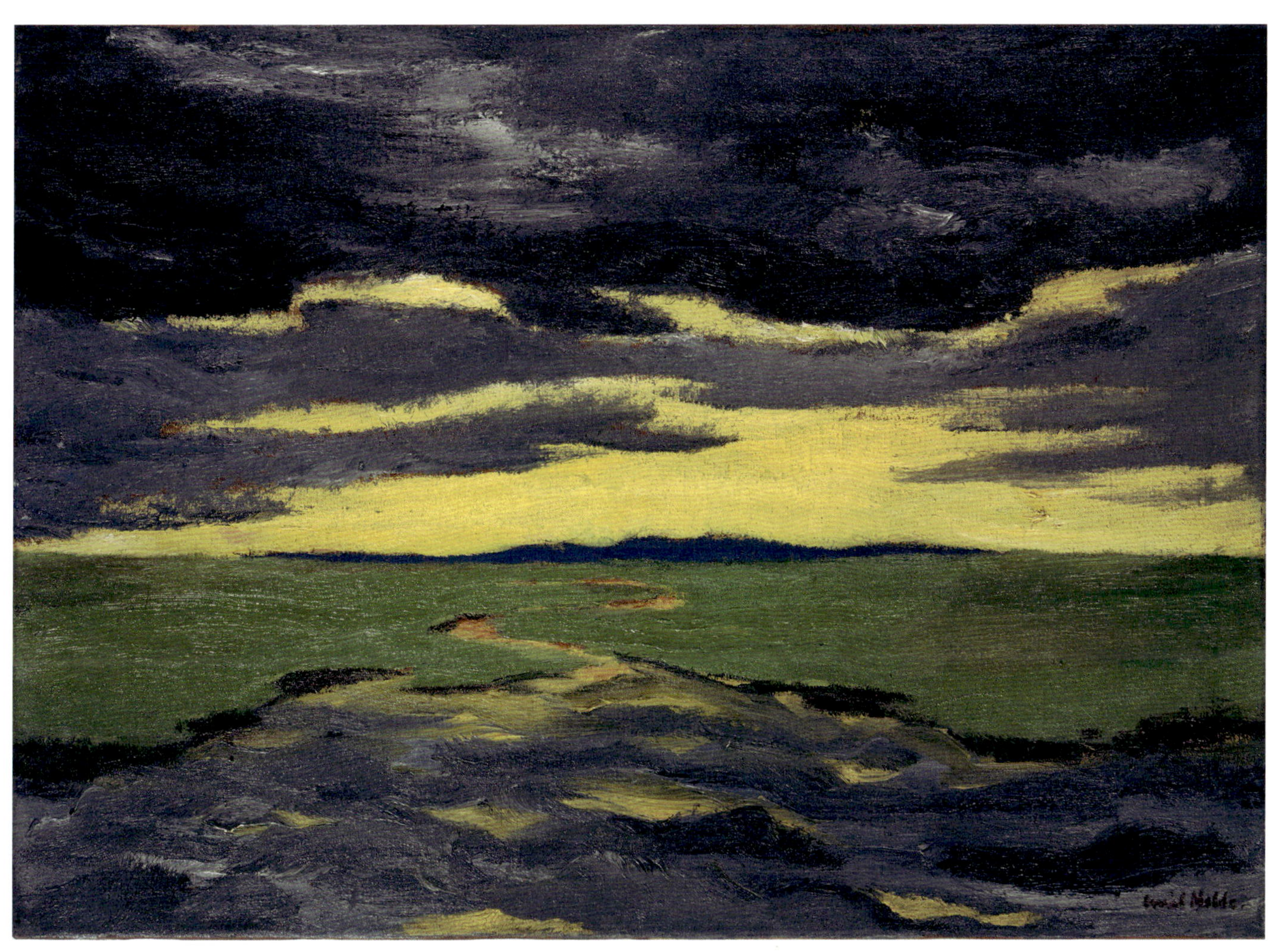

"Express your inner experience in the most concise form":[1] The Sculptor Milly Steger

Luisa Heese

For the sculptor Milly Steger (1881–1948), bringing emotional states to the surface[2] was the basis of her artistic urge. She is one of the few women artists who were able to establish themselves successfully in the field of sculpture already in the early decades of the twentieth century, when it was still dominated by men. For her artistic training, she had to take the detour of a school of the decorative arts. Until 1919, women were not permitted the public art academies, so she first attended the class for stuccoers and stone masons at the Kunstgewerbeschule in Elberfeld, near Wuppertal, and then took private lessons from 1901 to 1905 with the sculptor and academy professor Karl Janssen (one of Janssen's male master students at the Kunstakademie Düsseldorf was Wilhelm Lehmbruck). Steger then moved to Berlin and in the following years took numerous study trips on which she met artists such as Auguste Rodin, Aristide Maillol, and George Minne. In 1910, she accepted an invitation from the patron Karl Ernst Osthaus and moved to Hagen: there she first received several commissions for large architectural sculptures and around 1912 was named the city's official sculptor. For her home on the Stirnband in Hagen, she designed the façade relief

Karyatide (Caryatid) in 1917 (cat. 109). Her large-format architectural sculpture on the façade of the Theater Hagen caused a sensation that same year: the four female nudes prominently placed above the entrance touched off a scandal—and also increased the artist's fame.

In 1913, she participated in the exhibition of the Deutscher Künstlerbund (Association of German Artists) at the Kunsthalle Mannheim; in 1917, Steger returned to Berlin and took over Georg Kolbe's studio. The move went hand in hand with a change in her style: Steger was now pursuing a stark reduction to geometric forms and an intensification of expressive style. In the years that followed, she created Expressionist sculptures for which contemporary expressive dance served her as an important source of inspiration: she produced numerous portraits, figures, and dancers with androgynous, athletic bodies. This "subdued Expressionism"[3] also found expression in the work *Frauenbildnis* (Portrait of a Woman) of 1920 (cat. 107). It shows a woman's head turned upward and inclined slightly to one side, with a hand touching the chin, resulting in dynamic linework. The arched brows and nearly closed eyes in turn create a concentrated expression of pause. *Frauenbildnis* did not enter the collection of the Kunsthalle Mannheim during the artist's lifetime but rather in 1973 as a gift from the Jewish entrepreneur and art collector William Landmann. Landmann, who left his native city Mannheim in 1936 and emigrated with his family first to Nijmegen and then to Amsterdam, was able to get his considerable art collection housed in the Stedelijk Museum in 1939, shortly before the German occupation, and then continued to Toronto. After the war ended, it was returned to him and in the 1970s he decided to donate several works to the Kunsthalle Mannheim, including Steger's *Frauenbildnis*, Wilhelm Gerstel's bronze figure *Sinnende* (The Pensive Woman) (1903–1923), and Wladimir von Zabotin's painting *Sonntagmorgen in Danzig* (Sunday Morning in Danzig).[4]

In the 1920s, three drawings by Milly Steger were purchased for the Kunsthalle collection through Herbert Tannenbaum's Kunsthaus in Mannheim, but they were confiscated as "degenerate" in 1937 and destroyed.[5] Another sheet titled *Nordische Gotik (nach Bernd Notke)* (Nordic Gothic [after Bernd Notke]) (cat. 108), which the artist had donated in 1932 on the occasion of the Kunsthalle's twenty-fifth anniversary, remained in the collection. Milly Steger's role as an artist in the Third Reich was ambiguous. Steger's works were apparently not shown in the exhibitions of "degenerate" art

„Bringe dein inneres Erleben in knappster Form zum Ausdruck"[1]: die Bildhauerin Milly Steger

Luisa Heese

Seelische Zustände an die Oberfläche[2] zu bringen, war für die Bildhauerin Milly Steger (1881–1948) Grundlage ihres künstlerischen Antriebs. Sie zählt zu den wenigen Künstlerinnen, die sich bereits in den frühen Dekaden des 20. Jahrhunderts in dem damals männlich dominierten Feld der Bildhauerei erfolgreich durchsetzen konnten. Sie musste für ihre Ausbildung noch den Umweg über die Kunstgewerbeschule nehmen. Da Frauen der Zugang zu den öffentlichen Kunstakademien bis 1919 verwehrt blieb, besuchte sie zunächst die Klasse für Stuckateure und Steinmetze an der Kunstgewerbeschule in Elberfeld bei Wuppertal und nahm von 1901 bis 1905 Privatunterricht bei dem Bildhauer und Akademieprofessor Karl Janssen (zu Janssens männlichen Meisterschülern an der Akademie Düsseldorf gehörte auch Wilhelm Lehmbruck). Steger zog anschließend nach Berlin und unternahm in den folgenden Jahren zahlreiche Studienreisen, während denen sie Künstlern wie Auguste Rodin, Aristide Maillol und George Minne begegnete. 1910 nahm sie eine Einladung des Mäzens Karl Ernst Osthaus an und übersiedelte nach Hagen: Dort erhielt sie zunächst mehrere Aufträge für große Bauplastiken und wurde um 1912 zur offiziellen Stadtbildhauerin ernannt.

Für ihr Wohnhaus am Stirnband in Hagen entwarf sie 1917 das Fassadenrelief *Karyatide* (Kat. 109). Ihre großformatige Architekturplastik an der Fassade des Hagener Theaters führte im selben Jahr zum Eklat: Die vier Plastiken weiblicher Akte, die prominent über dem Eingang platziert waren, lösten in Hagen einen Skandal aus – und sorgten ebenso für breitere Bekanntheit der Künstlerin.

1913 nahm sie an der Ausstellung des Deutschen Künstlerbundes in der Kunsthalle Mannheim teil, 1917 kehrte Steger wieder nach Berlin zurück und übernahm dort das Atelier von Georg Kolbe. Der Umzug ging einher mit der Änderung ihres Stils: Steger verfolgte nun eine starke Reduktion auf geometrische Formen und die Intensivierung des expressiven Stils. In den darauffolgenden Jahren schuf sie expressionistische Plastiken, für die ihr der zeitgenössische Ausdruckstanz als wichtige Inspirationsquelle diente: Zahlreiche Porträts, Figuren, Tänzer*innen mit androgyn-athletischen Körpern entstanden. Dieser „beruhigte Expressionismus"[3] findet sich auch in dem Werk *Frauenbildnis* von 1920 (Kat. 107). Es zeigt einen nach oben gerichteten, leicht zur Seite geneigten Frauenkopf mit einer ans Kinn gelegten Hand, durch die sich eine dynamische Linienführung ergibt. Die hochgezogenen Brauen und fast geschlossenen Augen schaffen wiederum einen konzentrierten Ausdruck des Innehaltens. Das *Frauenbildnis* kam nicht zu Lebzeiten Stegers, sondern 1973 durch eine Schenkung des jüdischen Unternehmers und Kunstsammlers William Landmann in die Sammlung der Kunsthalle Mannheim. Landmann, der 1936 seine Heimatstadt Mannheim verließ und mit seiner Familie zunächst nach Nijmegen, dann nach Amsterdam emigrierte, konnte seine umfangreiche Kunstsammlung 1939, kurz vor der Besetzung durch die Deutschen, noch im Stedelijk Museum unterbringen und weiter nach Toronto emigrieren. Nach Kriegsende erhielt er sie wieder und entschied sich in den 1970er-Jahren, einige Werke an die Kunsthalle Mannheim zu stiften – darunter Stegers *Frauenbildnis,* Wilhelm Gerstels Bronzefigur *Sinnende* (1903–1923) und Wladimir von Zabotins Gemälde *Sonntagmorgen in Danzig.*[4]

In den 1920er-Jahren wurden für die Sammlung der Kunsthalle drei Zeichnungen von Milly Steger über das Kunsthaus von Herbert Tannenbaum in Mannheim angekauft, die jedoch 1937 als „entartet" beschlagnahmt und zerstört wurden.[5] Ein weiteres Blatt mit dem Titel *Nordische Gotik (nach Bernd Notke)* (Kat. 108), das die Künstlerin 1932 anlässlich des 25-jährigen Bestehens der Kunsthalle geschenkt hatte, verblieb in der Sammlung. Milly

in Munich and other cities. She was, however, represented in the first *Große Deutsche Kunstausstellung* (Great German Art Exhibition), which opened in Munich in July 1937, and in 1938 was awarded the Villa-Romana-Preis of the Deutscher Künstlerbund.[6] She was permitted to continue teaching her sculpture class at the Verein der Berliner Künstlerinnen (Association of Women Artists from Berlin) but received hardly any public commissions. A bombing raid in 1943 destroyed much of her work, which was in her studio in Berlin. After 1945, Steger moved into a new studio and participated in other exhibitions until her death in 1948.

1 Birgit Schulte with Erich Ranfft, eds., *Die Bildhauerin Milly Steger, 1881–1948: Die Grenzen des Frauseins aufheben* (Hagen: Neuer Folkwang-Verlag, 1998), pp. 51–52.
2 See Kai Artinger, "Milly Steger", in *Wie eine Nilbraut, die man in die Wellen wirft. Portraits expressionistischer Künstlerinnen und Schriftstellerinnen*, ed. Britta Jürgs (Grambin / Berlin: Aviva, 2002), pp. 250–267, esp. p. 262.
3 Arie Hartog, "Empty Pedestals: A Provisional History of Women Sculptors in Germany," in *Bildhauerinnen in Deutschland / Women Sculptors in Germany*, ed. Marc Gundel, Arie Hartog, and Frank Schmidt, exh. cat. Museen Böttcherstraße and Gerhard-Marcks-Haus Bremen, Kunsthalle Vogelmann Heilbronn (Cologne: Wienand, 2019), pp. 177–83, esp. p. 181.
4 For further discussion of William Landmann, see Mathias Listl, "The Kunsthalle and Its Jewish Patrons: The Fate of Five Families from Mannheim," in *(Re)Discovery: The Kunsthalle from 1933 to 1945 and the Aftermath*, ed. Mathias Listl and Ulrike Lorenz, exh. cat. (Mannheim: Kunsthalle Mannheim, 2018), pp. 63–85, esp. pp. 80ff.
5 Other works were confiscated at the same time from the Kronprinzenpalais in Berlin, the Museum für Kunst und Heimatgeschichte in Erfurt, the art collection of the Universität Göttingen, the Städelsches Kunstinstitut in Frankfurt am Main, and the Städtisches Museum in Hagen.
6 On this, see the research of the Zentrum für verfolgte Künste in Solingen: https://www.verfolgte-kuenste.com/kunstler-innen/milly-steger (accessed July 4, 2025).

Stegers Rolle als Künstlerin im Dritten Reich war ambivalent.
In den Feme-Ausstellungen zur „Entarteten Kunst" in München
und anderen Städten wurden die Werke Stegers offenbar nicht
gezeigt. In der *Ersten Großen Deutschen Kunstausstellung,* die
im Juli 1937 in München eröffnete, war sie wiederum vertreten
und gewann 1938 den Villa-Romana-Preis des Deutschen Künstlerbundes.[6] Die Bildhauerklasse des Vereins der Berliner Künstlerinnen konnte sie weiter unterrichten, erhielt jedoch kaum noch
öffentliche Aufträge. Ein Bombenangriff 1943 zerstörte einen
Großteil ihres Werkes, das sich in ihrem Berliner Atelier befand.
Nach 1945 bezog Steger ein neues Atelier und nahm bis zu ihrem
Tode 1948 an weiteren Ausstellungen teil.

1   Birgit Schulte (Hrsg.) u. Erich Ranfft (Mitarb.): *Die Bildhauerin Milly Steger
    1881–1948. Die Grenzen des Frauseins aufheben,* Oberhausen 1998, S. 51f.
2   Vgl. Kai Artinger: Milly Steger, in: Britta Jürgs (Hrsg.): *Wie eine Nilbraut, die
    man in die Wellen wirft. Portraits expressionistischer Künstlerinnen und
    Schriftstellerinnen.* Grambin / Berlin 2002, S. 250–267, S. 262.
3   Arie Hartog: Leere Sockel: eine vorläufige Geschichte der Bildhauerinnen
    in Deutschland, in: Kat. Ausst. *Bildhauerinnen in Deutschland,* Museen
    Böttcherstraße und Gerhard-Marcks-Haus Bremen, Kunsthalle Vogelmann
    Heilbronn, hrsg. v. Marc Gundel, Arie Hartog u. Frank Schmidt, Köln 2019,
    S. 168–176, S. 174.
4   Weitere Ausführungen zu William Landmann siehe: Mathias Listl: Die Kunst-
    halle und ihre jüdischen Mäzene: Schicksalswege fünf jüdischer Familien
    aus Mannheim, in: Kat. Ausst. *(Wieder-)Entdecken. Die Kunsthalle 1933 bis
    1945 und die Folgen,* Kunsthalle Mannheim 2018, hrsg. v. Mathias Listl u.
    Ulrike Lorenz, Mannheim 2018, S. 63–85, 80ff.
5   Weitere ihrer Werke wurden in diesem Zuge aus dem Berliner Kronprinzen-
    palais, dem Erfurter Museum für Kunst und Heimatgeschichte, der
    Kunstsammlung der Universität Göttingen, dem Städelschen Kunstinstitut
    Frankfurt am Main und dem Städtischen Museum Hagen beschlagnahmt.
6   Vgl. hierzu die Forschung des Zentrums für verfolgte Künste Solingen:
    https://www.verfolgte-kuenste.com/kunstler-innen/milly-steger [abgerufen
    am 04.07.2025].

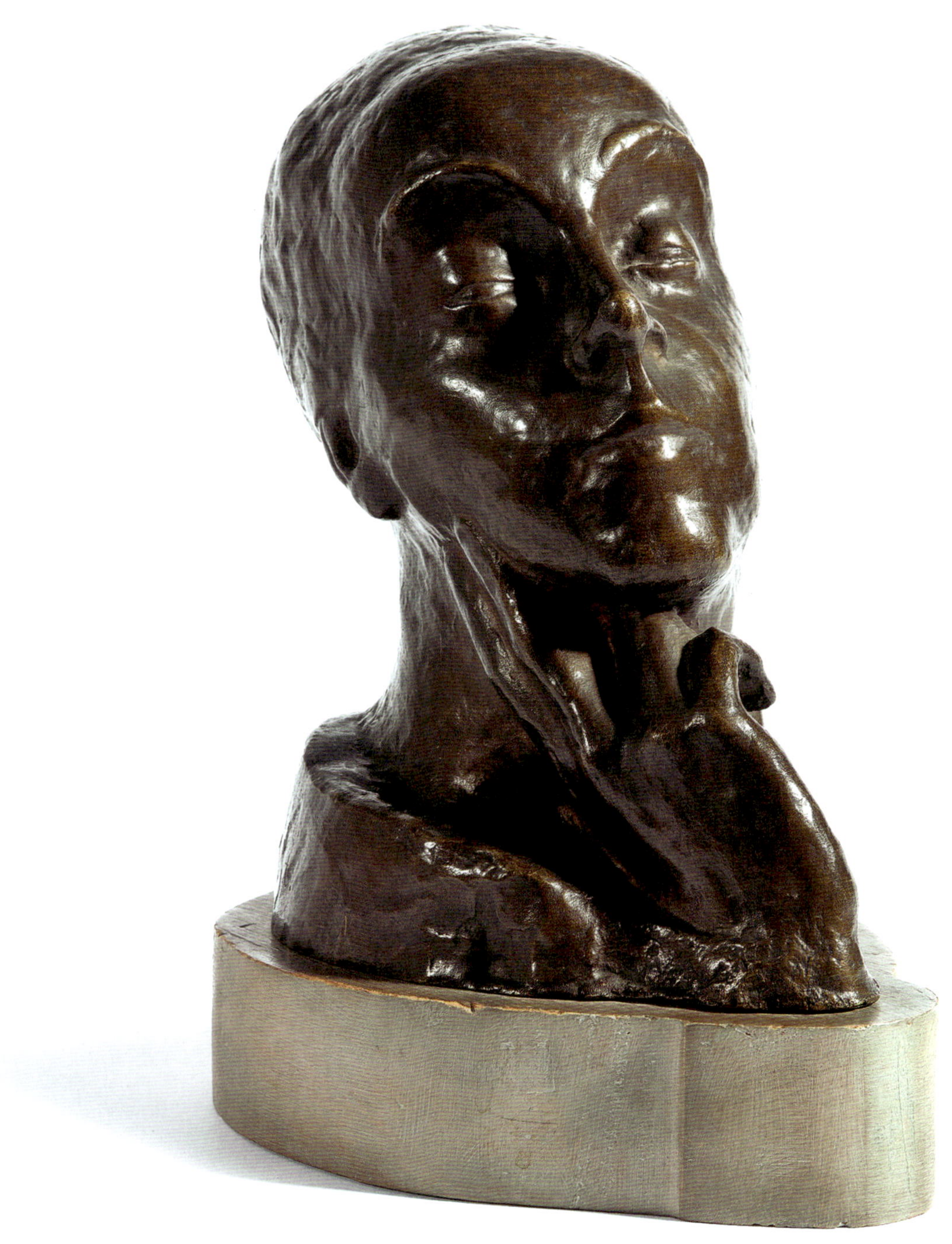

107 | **Milly Steger,** *Frauenbildnis* / *Portrait of a Woman,* **1920,** Kunsthalle Mannheim

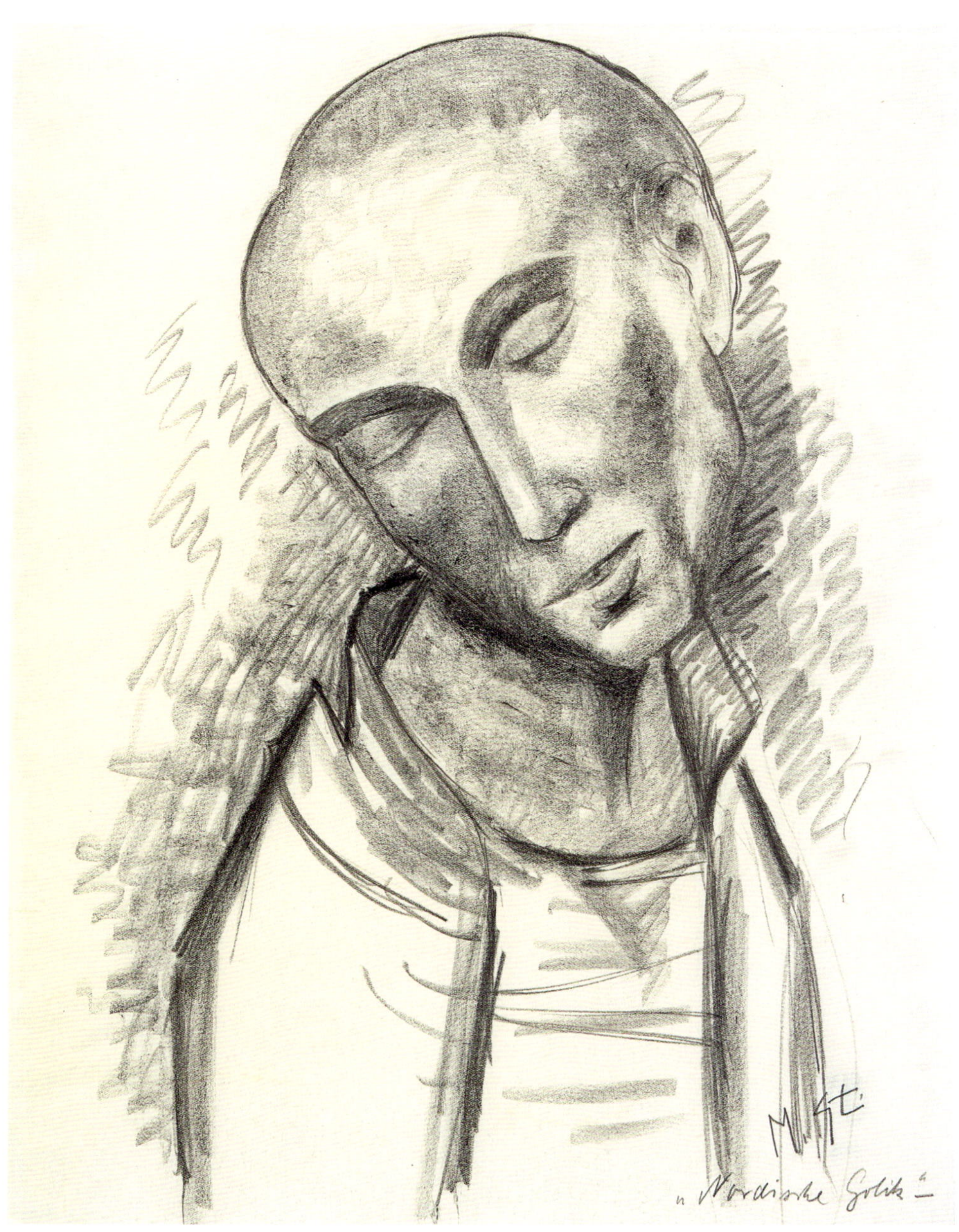

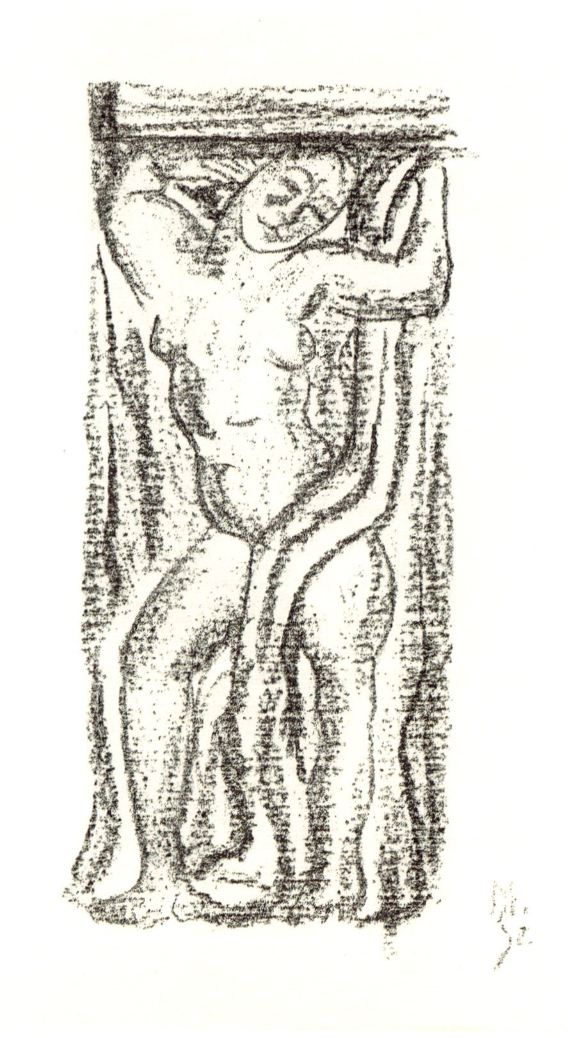

109 | **Milly Steger,** *Karyatide* / *Caryatid,* **1917,** Kunsthalle Mannheim

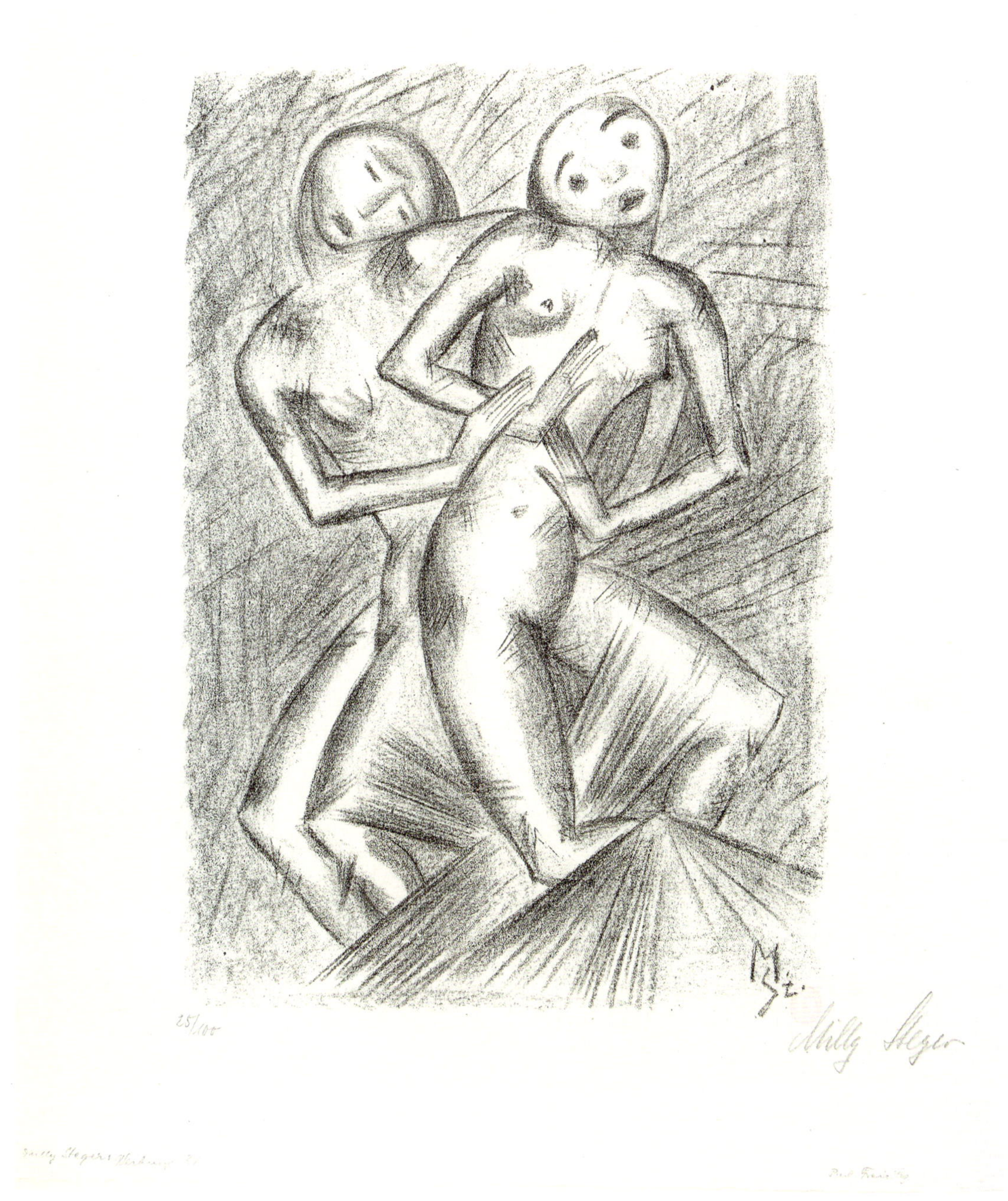

Depicting the Body: Nude and Child Models in Brücke Art

Dorotea Lorenz

The Brücke (Bridge) artists Ernst-Ludwig Kirchner, Erich Heckel, Karl Schmidt-Rottluff, and Max Pechstein in particular dedicated themselves to the nude in almost all media from painting and drawing to printmaking. This new interest derived from a view of art that sought to create a unity of art and life. The focus was not primarily on an idealizing or aesthetic depiction of the body; rather, these were distorted, raw, edgy, and dynamic nude studies that reveal a radical reinterpretation of the subject. Central locations for the nude study were, first, the artist's studio and, second, lakes, coasts, and the sea. In search of "free, natural life, of the harmony of human being and nature, of natural people in paradisical, original surroundings,"[1] the Brücke went to the Moritz-burg Lakes around Dresden, to the Baltic Sea islands Fehmarn and Hiddensee, and the spa towns Nidden and Osterholz between 1909 and 1914.

The *Viertelstundenakte* (quarter-hour nudes) became characteristic of the nude drawings of the Brücke artists: the models would change their position every fifteen minutes and thus force the artists to work quickly.[2] Ernst Ludwig Kirchner's *Tanzende Frauen im Wald* (Women Dancing in the Forest) of ca. 1925 (cat. 112) shows three figures captured in fleeting brushstrokes. Although it is not a realistic depiction of the three bodies, the expressive movement of the dance comes out clearly. The figures are embedded in the surrounding landscape. Their goal was to present not a staged pose but rather the natural movements of the body. Another example is Otto Mueller's *Kniender weiblicher Akt* (Kneeling Female Nude), a monotype from around 1912 (cat. 114): the crouching body of the woman bending forward, whose facial features are suggested only schematically, does not appear idealized at all. Instead, the focus is on capturing the organic, flowing pose. The work was purchased by the Kunsthalle Mannheim in 1913— a testimony to the progressive acquisition policy of its first director, Fritz Wichert, and his employee Gustav Friedrich Hartlaub.[3] The Kunsthalle Mannheim was already purchasing important works by the avant-garde Expressionist artists in the 1910s. Especially among the prints, numerous nudes illustrate their intense preoccupation with the theme of the human body outdoors.

The models of the Brücke artists were often young women and girls, whom they drew and painted in a deliberately turn away from the academic paradigm. The painter and model lived together in an unconstrained community that in some cases was also sexually permissive.[4] Indigenous peoples whom the artists saw as still living in harmony with supposedly unspoiled nature served as role models. One essential point of contact for this were so-called ethnological expositions.[5]

One of the most famous models of the Brücke artists' group is doubtless Lina Franziska Fehrmann (1900–1950), known as Fränzi, who appears in numerous works by Heckel and Kirchner in particular. Heckel's iconic color woodcut *Fränzi liegend* (Fränzi, Reclining) (cat. 111) from 1910 depicts in contrasting black, red, and white a slender, naked girl against a planar background. Fränzi was only eight when she first came into contact with the artists and from then on became their favorite model— along with the young Marzella Albertine Sprentzel. The artists believed that they could see their ideal of the primal and natural in the innocent and unspoiled bodies of child models.[6] For a long time, Fränzi's and Marzella's Identities remained unknown. In recent decades, however, intense research has made it possible to reconstruct at least in part the actual circumstances of their lives.[7]

Especially in the case of young or female bodies, however, the nude often becomes the arena of an ambivalent tension. From today's perspective, it is imperative to study the relationships

Körperdarstellungen: Akt- und Kindermodelle in der Brücke-Kunst

Dorotea Lorenz

Ein Hauptmotiv im Expressionismus ist die Darstellung des unbekleideten, bewegten oder badenden Körpers in der Natur. Insbesondere die Brücke-Künstler Ernst-Ludwig Kirchner, Erich Heckel, Karl Schmidt-Rottluff und Max Pechstein widmeten sich dem Akt in fast allen Medien von der Malerei und Zeichnung bis hin zur Druckgrafik. Dieses neue Interesse ging aus einer Kunstauffassung hervor, die eine Einheit zwischen Kunst und Leben zu schaffen versuchte. Dabei steht nicht eine idealisierende oder ästhetische Darstellung des Körpers im Vordergrund; vielmehr sind es verzerrte, rohe, kantige und dynamische Aktstudien, die eine radikale Neuinterpretation des Sujets offenbaren. Zentrale Orte für das Aktstudium waren zum einen die Ateliers der Künstler, zum anderen vor allem Seen, Küsten und das Meer. Auf der Suche „nach dem freien, natürlichen Leben, nach dem Einklang von Mensch und Natur, nach dem natürlichen Menschen in paradiesischer, ursprünglicher Umgebung"[1] begaben sich die Brücke-Künstler zwischen 1909 und 1914 an die Moritzburger Teiche um Dresden, auf die Ostseeinseln Fehmarn und Hiddensee sowie an die Badeorte Nidden und Osterholz.

Charakteristisch für die Aktzeichnung der Brücke-Künstler wurden die „Viertelstundenakte": Die Modelle wechselten alle 15 Minuten ihre Position und zwangen den Künstler so zur Schnelligkeit.[2] Die Zeichnung Ernst Ludwig Kirchners *Tanzende Frauen im Wald* um 1925 (Kat. 112) zeigt drei im flüchtigen Strich festgehaltene Figuren. Obwohl es sich nicht um eine wirklichkeitsgetreue Abbildung der drei Körper handelt, tritt der expressive Bewegungsablauf des Tanzes deutlich hervor. Die Figuren sind in die sie umgebende Landschaft eingebettet. Ziel war es nicht, eine inszenierte Pose darzustellen, sondern die natürlichen Bewegungen des Körpers. Hiervon zeugt beispielsweise auch Otto Muellers *Kniender weiblicher Akt*, eine Monotypie, die um 1912 entstanden ist (Kat. 114): Der hockende, nach vorn gebeugte Körper der Frau, deren Gesichtszüge nur schematisch angedeutet sind, wirkt keineswegs idealisiert. Vielmehr steht das Festhalten der organischen, fließenden Pose im Vordergrund. Das Werk wurde bereits im Jahr 1913 von der Kunsthalle Mannheim angekauft – ein Zeugnis der progressiven Ankaufspolitik des ersten Direktors Fritz Wichert und seines Mitarbeiters Gustav Friedrich Hartlaub.[3] Denn bereits in den 1910er-Jahren erwarb die Kunsthalle Mannheim bedeutende Werke der damals avantgardistischen expressionistischen Künstler. Darunter befinden sich vor allem im Bereich der Druckgrafik zahlreiche Aktdarstellungen, die die intensive Beschäftigung mit dem Thema des menschlichen Körpers im Freien veranschaulichen.

Die Modelle der Brücke-Künstler waren oft junge Frauen und Mädchen, die sie in bewusster Abkehr zum akademischen Vorbild zeichneten und malten. Maler und Modell lebten dabei in ungezwungener, teils auch sexuell freizügiger Gemeinschaft.[4] Als Vorbild fungierten indigene Völker, die in der Wahrnehmung der Künstler noch in Einklang mit der vermeintlich unverdorbenen Natur lebten. Ein wesentlicher Kontaktpunkt hierfür waren sogenannte Völkerschauen.[5]

Eines der bekanntesten Modelle der Künstlergruppe Brücke ist zweifellos Lina Franziska Fehrmann (1900–1950), genannt Fränzi, die vor allem in zahlreichen Werken Heckels und Kirchners auftaucht. Heckels ikonischer Farbholzschnitt *Fränzi liegend* (Kat. 111) aus dem Jahr 1910 zeigt in kontrastierendem Schwarz, Rot und Weiß ein nacktes, schmales Mädchen vor einem flächigen Hintergrund. Mit nur acht Jahren kam Fränzi in Kontakt mit der Künstlergruppe und wurde fortan – mit der ebenfalls jungen Marzella Sprentzel – zu deren Lieblingsmodell. Das Ideal der Ursprünglichkeit und Natürlichkeit glaubten die Künstler

these adult male artists had with their young, usually female models. In retrospect, this asymmetrical power structure raises questions. Although the child models are not shown explicitly in sexual activities, there are written statements by some of the artists in diaries and letters whose language and connotations at least suggest a sexual charge in their relationship to the model.[8] From the current state of the sources, however, it is no longer possible to establish with absolute certainly whether or not sexual abuse in fact occurred.[9] In order to examine the circumstances of these works' origin as discerningly as possible, one always has to ask who is being depicted, under what circumstances, and which perspectives may perhaps be left out. In the best case, one may assume that the still-developing bodies of children "served for the artists' imagination of the 'pure,' the 'authentic'" and ultimately "for the development of their aesthetic."[10]

1   Nicole Peterlein, "Die Sommeraufenthalte der 'Brücke'-Künstler von 1909 bis 1914," in *Die Badenden: Mensch und Natur im deutschen Expressionismus; Erich Heckel, Ernst Ludwig Kirchner, August Macke, Franz Marc, Otto Mueller, Emil Nolde, Max Pechstein, Karl Schmidt-Rottluff,* Kunsthalle Bielefeld 2000, ed. Jutta Hülsewig-Johnen and Thomas Kellein (Bielefeld: Kunsthalle, 2000), pp. 12–17, esp. p. 13.
2   Katharina Beisiegel, "Escapism and Fantasy Worlds: Ernst Ludwig Kirchner's Imaginary Travels," trans. Cynthia Hall, in *Ernst Ludwig Kirchner: Imaginary Travels,* ed. Katharina Beisiegel, exh. cat. Kirchner Museum Davos 2018 (Munich: Prestel, 2018), pp. 19–64, esp. p. 33.
3   Mathias Listl, "Otto Mueller, Kniender weiblicher Akt," https://www.ernst -von-siemens-kunststiftung.de/objekt/otto-mueller-kniender-weiblicher- akt.html (accessed May 19, 2025).
4   See Jutta Hülsewig-Johnen, "Der neue Mensch im Paradies?," in *Die Badenden: Mensch und Natur im deutschen Expressionismus: Erich Heckel, Ernst Ludwig Kirchner, August Macke, Franz Marc, Otto Mueller, Emil Nolde, Max Pechstein, Karl Schmidt-Rottluff,* ed. Jutta Hülsewig-Johnen and Thomas Kellein, exh. cat. (Bielefeld: Kunsthalle, 2000), pp. 64–79, esp. pp. 77–78.
5   See ibid., p. 78.
6   Laura Mang and Regina Klein, "Die Modelle der 'Brücke' und ihre Bedeutung," in *Fränzi und Marzella: Wer sie waren und wie sie sind; Auf Spurensuche im Brücke-Museum,* ed. Magdalena M. Moeller, exh. cat Brücke-Museum Berlin 2014 (Heidelberg: Kehrer, 2014), pp. 8–17, esp. p. 13.
7   Gerd Presler, "Fränzi und Marcella: Zwei Brücke-Modelle schreiben Kunstgeschichte," *Der Blick auf Fränzi und Marcella: Zwei Modelle der Brücke-Künstler Heckel, Kirchner und Pechstein,* ed. Norbert Nobis, exh. cat. Sprengel Museum Hannover 2010 (Bönen: Kettler, 2010), pp. 13–22.
8   See Irene Berkel, "Genealogische Verwirrungen," in *Der Blick auf Fränzi und Marcella: Zwei Modelle der Brücke-Künstler Heckel, Kirchner und Pechstein,* ed. Norbert Nobis, exh. cat. Sprengel Museum Hannover 2010 (Bönen: Kettler, 2010), pp. 123–29, p. 128.
9   As Beatrice von Bormann has rightly noted, we have no statements from the child models themselves, which would be indispensable in this context. See Beatrice von Bormann, "Ernst Ludwig Kirchner's Child Models," in *Kirchner and Nolde: Expressionism, Colonialism,* ed. Sophie Tates, exh. cat. Brücke-Museum, Berlin 2021 (Munich: Hirmer, 2021), pp. 238–40, esp. p. 239.
10 Ibid., p. 240.

im kindlichen, unschuldigen und unverdorbenen Körper der Kindermodelle zu erkennen.[6] Lange blieb Fränzis und Marzellas Identität unbekannt. Durch intensive Recherche konnten in den letzten Jahrzehnten ihre tatsächlichen Lebensumstände jedoch zumindest teilweise rekonstruiert werden.[7]

Gerade in Darstellungen junger oder weiblicher Körper wird der Akt jedoch häufig zum Schauplatz eines ambivalenten Spannungsfelds. Aus heutiger Perspektive ist es unerlässlich zu untersuchen, in welchem Verhältnis männliche, erwachsene Künstler mit meist weiblichen, jungen Modellen standen. Diese asymmetrische Machtstruktur wirft retrospektiv Fragen auf. Obwohl die Kindermodelle in den Darstellungen nicht explizit bei sexuellen Handlungen gezeigt werden, existieren dennoch schriftliche Äußerungen einzelner Künstler, etwa in Tagebüchern und Briefen, die durch ihre Sprache und Konnotationen eine sexuelle Aufladung der Beziehung zum Modell zumindest andeuten.[8] Aus dem heutigen Quellenstand lässt sich jedoch nicht mehr abschließend klären, ob es tatsächlich zu sexuellen Übergriffen kam oder nicht.[9] Um eine möglichst differenzierte Betrachtung der Entstehungsbedingungen zu ermöglichen, bleibt immer zu fragen, wer dargestellt wird, unter welchen Bedingungen, und welche Perspektiven dabei möglicherweise ausgeblendet bleiben. Im besten Fall kann man davon ausgehen, dass die sich noch entwickelnden Kinderkörper „Vorstellungen der Künstler vom ‚Reinen‘, vom ‚Ursprünglichen‘ [bedienten]" und letztendlich „für eine Weiterentwicklung ihrer Ästhetik benutzt [wurden]."[10]

1 Nicole Peterlein: Die Sommeraufenthalte der „Brücke"-Künstler von 1909 bis 1914, in: Kat. Ausst. *Die Badenden: Mensch und Natur im deutschen Expressionismus. Erich Heckel, Ernst Ludwig Kirchner, August Macke, Franz Marc, Otto Mueller, Emil Nolde, Max Pechstein, Karl Schmidt-Rottluff,* Kunsthalle Bielefeld 2000, hrsg. v. Jutta Hülsewig-Johnen u. Thomas Kellein, Bielefeld 2000, S. 12–17, S. 13.

2 Katharina Beisiegel: Weltflucht und Fantasiewelten. Ernst Ludwig Kirchners erträumte Reisen, in: Kat. Ausst. *Ernst Ludwig Kirchner – erträumte Reisen,* Kirchner Museum Davos 2018, hrsg. v. Katharina Beisiegel, München/London/New York 2018, S. 19–68, S. 33.

3 Mathias Listl: *Otto Mueller, Kniender weiblicher Akt,* https://www.ernst-von-siemens-kunststiftung.de/objekt/otto-mueller-kniender-weiblicher-akt.html [abgerufen am 19.05.2025].

4 Vgl. Jutta Hülsewig-Johnen: Der neue Mensch im Paradies?, in: Kat. Ausst. *Die Badenden: Mensch und Natur im deutschen Expressionismus. Erich Heckel, Ernst Ludwig Kirchner, August Macke, Franz Marc, Otto Mueller, Emil Nolde, Max Pechstein, Karl Schmidt-Rottluff,* Kunsthalle Bielefeld 2000, hrsg. v. Jutta Hülsewig-Johnen u. Thomas Kellein, Bielefeld 2000, S. 64–79, S. 77f.

5 Vgl. ebd., S. 78.

6 Laura Mang u. Regina Klein: Die Modelle der „Brücke" und ihre Bedeutung, in: Kat. Ausst. *Fränzi und Marzella. Wer sie waren und wie sie sind. Auf Spurensuche im Brücke-Museum,* Brücke-Museum Berlin 2014, hrsg. v. Magdalena M. Moeller, Heidelberg/Berlin 2014, S. 8–17, S. 13.

7 Gerd Presler: Fränzi und Marcella. Zwei Brücke-Modelle schreiben Kunstgeschichte, in: Kat. Ausst. *Der Blick auf Fränzi und Marcella. Zwei Modelle der Brücke-Künstler Heckel, Kirchner und Pechstein,* Sprengel Museum Hannover 2010, hrsg. v. Norbert Nobis, Bönen 2010, S. 13–22.

8 Vgl. Irene Berkel: Genealogische Verwirrungen, in: Kat. Ausst. *Der Blick auf Fränzi und Marcella. Zwei Modelle der Brücke-Künstler Heckel, Kirchner und Pechstein,* Sprengel Museum Hannover 2010, hrsg. v. Norbert Nobis, Bönen 2010, S. 123–129, S. 128.

9 Wie Beatrice von Bormann richtigerweise konstatiert, liegen uns keine Aussagen der Kindermodelle **selbst** vor, die in diesem Zusammenhang unerlässlich wären. Vgl. Beatrice von Bormann: Ernst Ludwig Kirchners Kindermodelle, in: Kat. Ausst. *Kirchner und Nolde. Expressionismus, Kolonialismus,* Brücke-Museum Berlin 2021, hrsg. v. Sophie Tates, München 2021, S. 238–240, S. 239.

10 Ebd., S. 240.

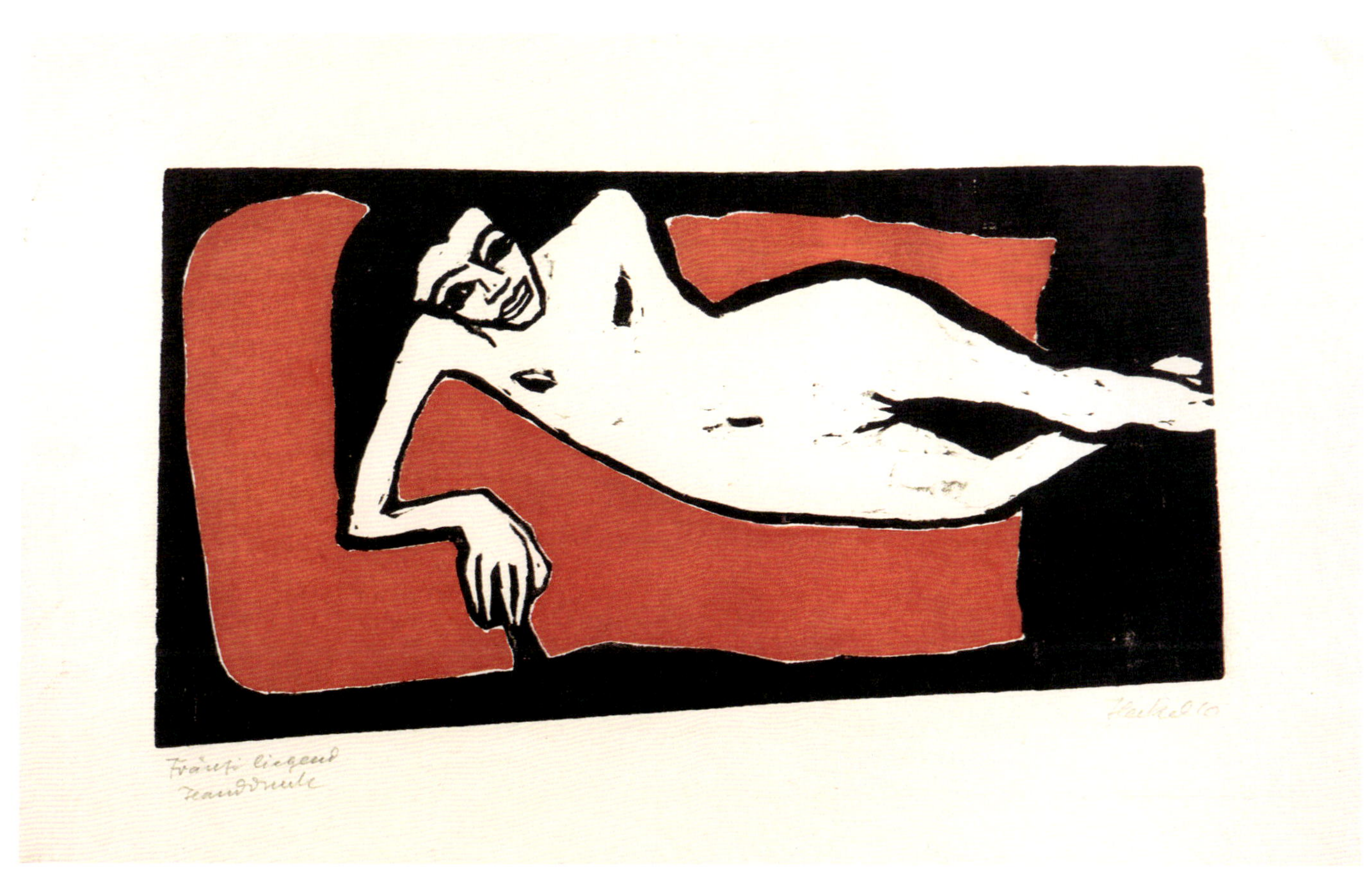

111 | **Erich Heckel,** ***Fränzi liegend*** / *Fränzi, Reclining,* **1910,** Kunsthalle Mannheim

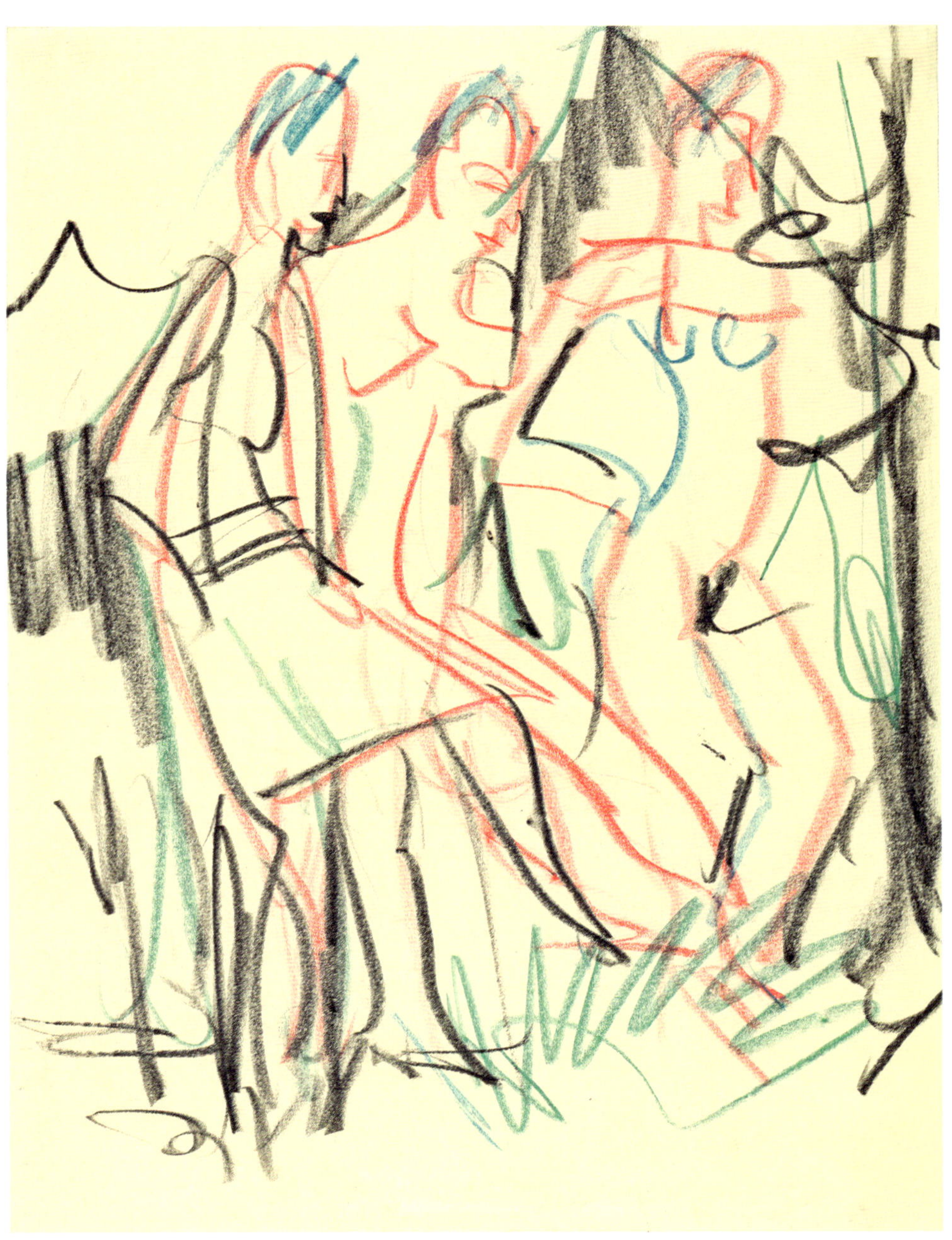

112 | **Ernst Ludwig Kirchner, *Tanzende Frauen im Wald*** / *Women Dancing in the Forest,* **um** / *ca.* **1925,** Privatsammlung Scherer / *Scherer private collection*

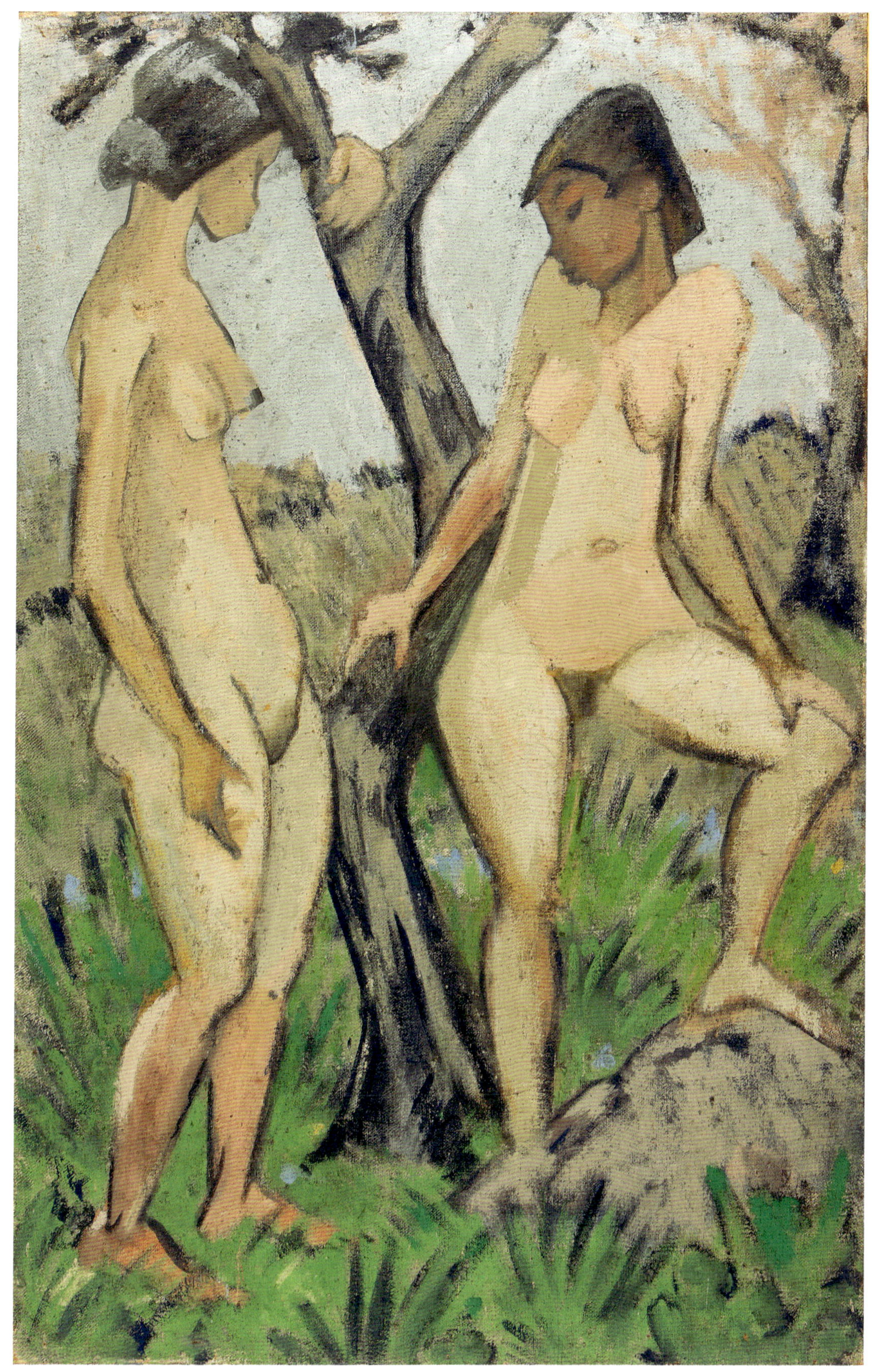

113 | **Otto Mueller**, **_Zwei weibliche Akte im Freien_** / _Two Nude Females in Nature_, **um** / _ca._ **1920**, Kunsthalle Mannheim

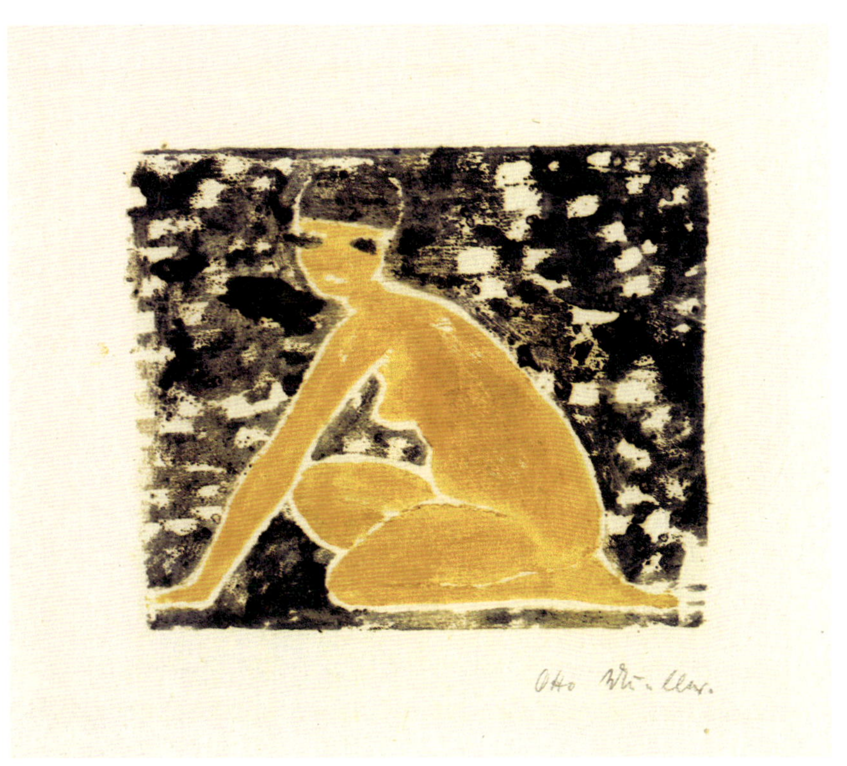

114 | **Otto Mueller,** *Kniender weiblicher Akt* /
Kneeling Female Nude, **um** / *ca.* **1912,** Kunsthalle Mannheim

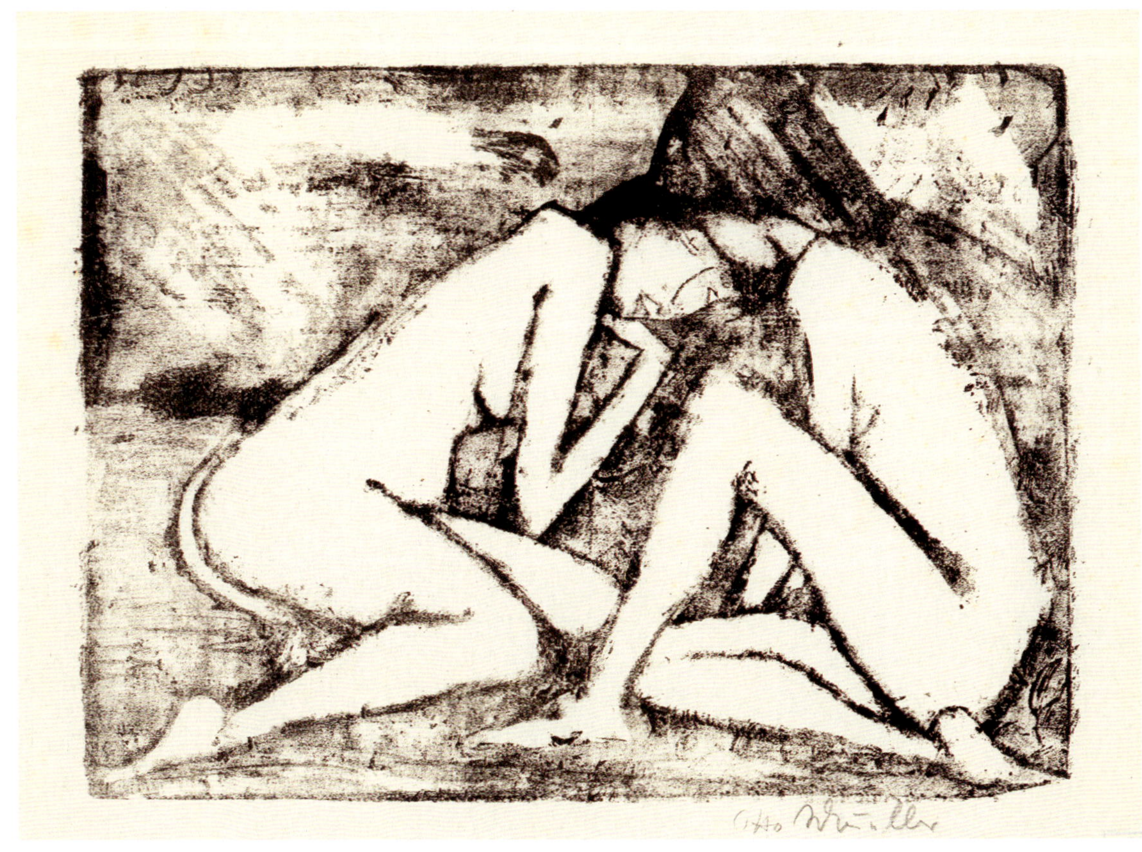

115 | **Otto Mueller,** *Zwei sitzende Mädchen II* / *Two Seated Girls II,* **1922,** Kunsthalle Mannheim

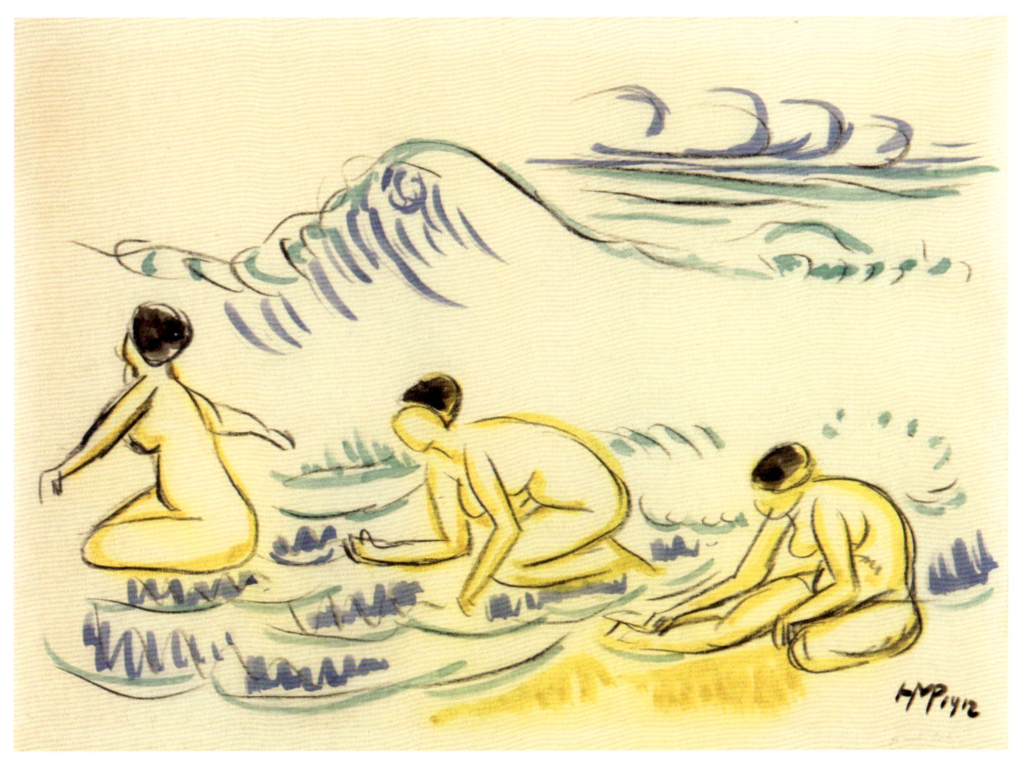

116 | **Max Pechstein, *Sitzende und kauernde nackte Frauen* /** *Seated and Crouching Naked Women*, **1912,** Kunsthalle Mannheim

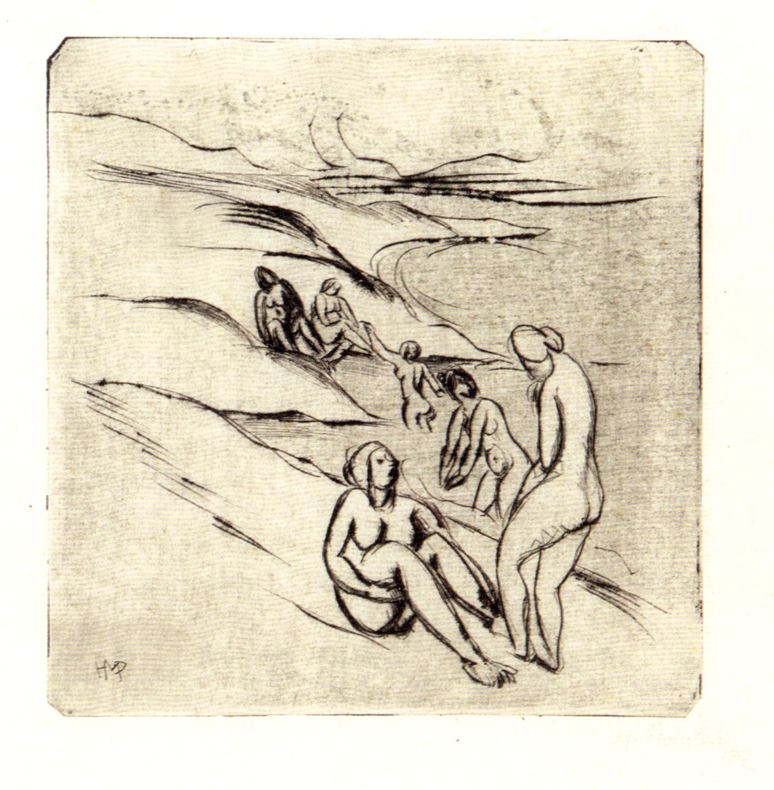

117 | **Max Pechstein, *Am Meer II* /** *By the Sea II*, **1912,** Kunsthalle Mannheim

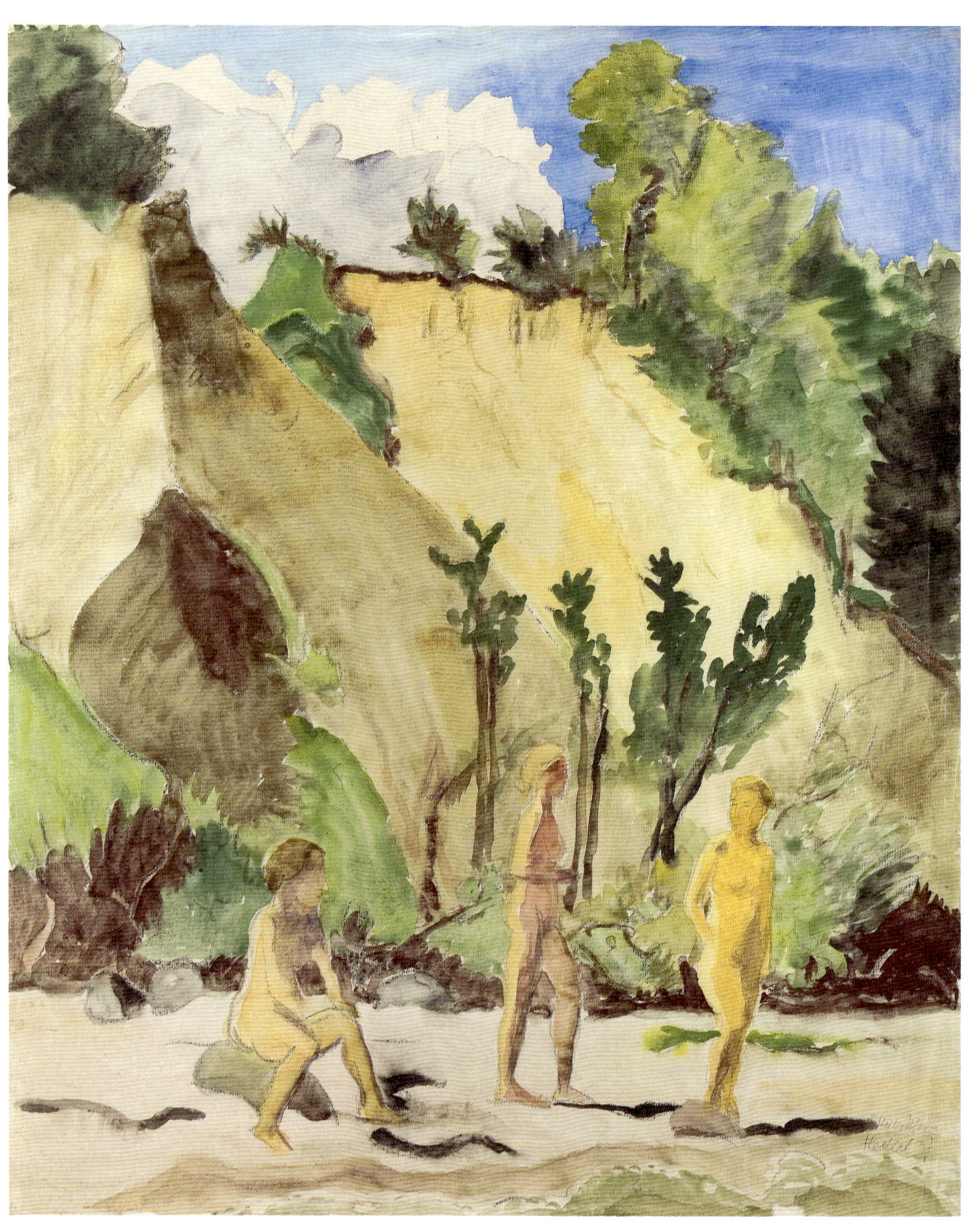

118 | **Erich Heckel,** *Steiles Ufer* / *Steep Bank,* **1937,** Kunsthalle Mannheim

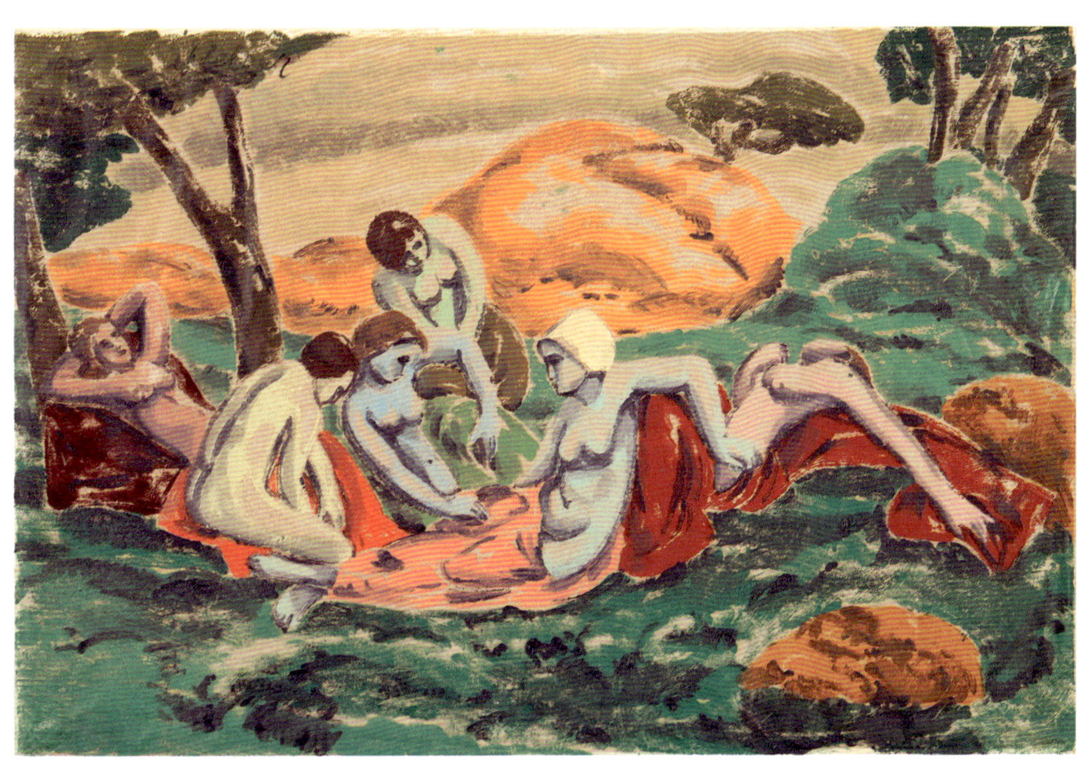

119 | **Moriz Melzer,** ***Frauen in Landschaft*** / *Women in the Landscape,* **1911/12,** Kunsthalle Mannheim

The Encounter with the "Foreign": Expressionist Artists between Fascination and Colonial Appropriation

Dorotea Lorenz

Expressionism belongs to an era in which the German Empire, which had existed since 1871, rose after 1900 to become an important colonial power, with colonies in Africa, the South Seas, and parts of China. In this historical context, many Expressionist artists began to expand their pictorial repertoire. They integrated motifs, forms, and styles of expression that they discovered in non-European, supposedly exotic cultures—whether from travels, visits to ethnological museums, or illustrations in books and journals. This turn to the "foreign" or "exotic" was, however, closely interwoven with the colonial power structures of the time, which made access to the objects possible in the first place.

At the beginning of the twentieth century, there was a conscious break with academic traditions and bourgeois norms. Many artists were searching for new forms of expression beyond the established view of art.[1] To that end, they also turned to the material culture of indigenous societies of Africa, Asia, Oceania, and America, whose products and artifacts were understood at the time as the epitome of the original and authentic and were categorized under the umbrella term of "primitive" art.[2]

From today's perspective, however, these very heterogeneous art forms have nothing in common other than "distance from academic art practice."[3] This engagement with non-European art moved within an area of tension between genuine interest, artistic yearning, and curiosity, on the one hand, and colonial appropriation, Eurocentric ideas of superiority, and stereotypical prejudices and racist practices, on the other.

The Brücke artists' group, founded in Dresden in 1905, united representatives of the Expressionist movement who became pioneers of high modernism. Two of the Brücke artists actually took trips outside of Europe. Emil Nolde traveled to what was then the colony German New Guinea with his wife, Ada, in 1913–14 as part of the *Medizinisch-demographische Deutsch-Neuguinea-Expedition* (Medical and Demographic German New Guinea Expedition).[4] Max Pechstein was drawn to the Palau Islands in 1914, attracted by an "idealized notion of a secluded life."[5] The artist who did not travel outside Europe themselves came into contact with the material culture of other regions of the world in ethnological museums, for example. At the beginning of the twentieth century, ethnological collections in Berlin, Dresden, Cologne, and Hamburg established themselves as among the most important museums of the kind in the world.[6] The objects they exhibited often came to Europe under dubious circumstances: as looted art or as products of colonial exploitation, conquest, and collecting practices.[7] In addition to ethnological museums and books,[8] so-called ethnological expositions[9] were central places to acquaint oneself with non-European ways of living.[10] These presentations served to "display supposed ethnic differences"[11] of people who were literally being exhibited and were intended to mark their "difference." When there were no trips abroad, numerous spa towns in the German Empire were declared paradisical places of yearning for Expressionist artists.[12] In Dangast, Nidden, Moritzburg, and Fehmarn, they tried to get closer to their idea of an unspoiled life.

Numerous paintings and prints in the current exhibition document engagement with and appropriation of non-European cultures and their production of art: many of these works had been acquired by the Kunsthalle Mannheim already in the 1910s and 1920s. Its early interest in "primitive" art is also noteworthy. In 1923, *Blicke in die Formenwelt der Primitiven* (Views into the Form World of the Primitives), organized by Gustav Friedrich Hartlaub, was held there. Works in the collection by artists who traveled to the South Seas, such as Emil Nolde and Max Pechstein, and those

Die Begegnung mit dem ‚Fremden': Künstler*innen des Expressionismus zwischen Faszination und kolonialer Aneignung

Dorotea Lorenz

Der Expressionismus fällt in eine Epoche, in der das Deutsche Kaiserreich, seit 1871 bestehend, ab 1900 zu einer bedeutenden Kolonialmacht aufstieg – mit Besitzungen in Afrika, der Südsee und Teilen Chinas. In diesem historischen Kontext begannen viele expressionistische Künstler*innen, ihr Bildrepertoire zu erweitern. Sie integrierten Motive, Formen und Ausdrucksweisen, die sie in nicht-europäischen, vermeintlich exotischen Kulturen entdeckten – sei es durch Reisen, durch den Besuch von Völkerkundemuseen oder durch Reproduktionen in Büchern und Zeitschriften. Diese Hinwendung zum ‚Fremden' oder ‚Exotischen' war jedoch eng mit den kolonialen Machtstrukturen der Zeit verflochten, die den Zugang zu den Objekten überhaupt erst ermöglichten.
Zu Beginn des 20. Jahrhunderts vollzog sich eine bewusste Abkehr von akademischen Traditionen und bürgerlichen Normen. Viele Künstler*innen suchten nach neuen Ausdrucksformen jenseits der etablierten Kunstauffassung.[1] Dafür wandten sie sich auch der materiellen Kultur indigener Gesellschaften aus Afrika, Asien, Ozeanien und Amerika zu, deren Erzeugnisse und Artefakte damals als Inbegriff des Ursprünglichen sowie Authentischen verstanden und unter dem Überbegriff der ‚primitiven' Kunst

zusammengefasst wurden.[2] Aus heutiger Sicht haben diese doch sehr heterogenen Kunstformen wohl nichts außer den „Abstand zur akademischen künstlerischen Praxis"[3] gemeinsam. Die Auseinandersetzung mit nicht-europäischer Kunst bewegte sich in einem Spannungsfeld: zwischen echtem Interesse, künstlerischer Sehnsucht und Neugier einerseits – und kolonialer Aneignung, eurozentrischem Überlegenheitsdenken, stereotypen Vorurteilen und rassistischen Praktiken andererseits.
Die in Dresden im Jahr 1905 gegründete Künstlergruppe Brücke vereinigte Vertreter der expressionistischen Bewegung, die zu Wegbereitern der klassischen Moderne wurden. Nur zwei der Brücke-Künstler unternahmen tatsächlich Reisen außerhalb Europas. Emil Nolde reiste in den Jahren 1913/14 mit seiner Frau Ada im Rahmen der *Medizinisch-demographischen Deutsch-Neuguinea-Expedition* in die damalige deutsche Kolonie Neuguinea.[4] Max Pechstein zog es 1914 zu den Palau-Inseln, getrieben von der „Idealvorstellung eines abgeschiedenen Lebens"[5]. Jene Künstler*innen, die selbst keine Reisen in nicht-europäische Gebiete unternahmen, kamen etwa in Völkerkundemuseen mit der materiellen Kultur anderer Weltregionen in Kontakt. Zu Beginn des 20. Jahrhunderts etablierten sich die ethnologischen Sammlungen in Berlin, Dresden, Köln und Hamburg zu den wichtigsten Museen weltweit.[6] Die dort ausgestellten Objekte gelangten oft unter fragwürdigen Umständen nach Europa – als Raubkunst oder als Produkt kolonialer Ausbeutung, Eroberung und Sammlungspraxis.[7] Neben Völkerkundemuseen sowie ethnologischen Büchern[8] waren auch sogenannte Völkerschauen[9] zentrale Orte, um nicht-europäische Lebensweisen kennenzulernen.[10] Diese Darbietungen dienten der „Zurschaustellung vermeintlicher ethnischer Unterschiede"[11] der regelrecht ausgestellten Menschen und sollten dabei deren ‚Andersartigkeit' markieren. Wo es zu keiner Auslandsreise kam, wurden zahlreiche Badeorte im Deutschen Reich von Künstler*innen des Expressionismus zu paradiesischen Sehnsuchtsorten erklärt.[12] In Dangast, Nidden, Moritzburg oder Fehmarn versuchten sie, der Vorstellung eines ursprünglichen Lebens nahezukommen.
Zahlreiche Gemälde und Grafiken in der aktuellen Ausstellung dokumentieren die Auseinandersetzung mit sowie die Aneignung von nicht-europäischen Kulturen und ihren Kunstproduktionen: Viele dieser Werke wurden bereits in den 1910er- und 1920er-Jahren von der Kunsthalle Mannheim erworben. Bemerkenswert ist außerdem das frühe Interesse für ‚primitive' Kunst. Im Jahr 1923 fand die von Gustav Friedrich Hartlaub zusammengestellte

of Karl Schmidt-Rottluff, Ernst Ludwig Kirchner, Otto Mueller, and Erich Heckel testify to an intense reception of non-European art. A first nucleus consists primarily of landscape motifs, such as Nolde's *Südseelandschaft II* (Landscape from the South Sea II) of 1915 (cat. 123) and numerous drawings he made at the Baltic Sea and on Fehmarn. Another frequently occurring motif is dancers and acrobats, as in Max Pechstein's *Akrobaten I* (Acrobats I) and *Akrobaten III* (Acrobats III) of 1912 (cat. 124, 125). A number of still lifes incorporating masks or statues also reveal a fascination with non-European art. Erich Heckel's *Sonnenblumen* (Sunflowers) of 1913 (cat. 121) and Max Pechstein's *Stilleben: Figur und Blumen* (Still Life: Figure and Flowers) of 1917 (cat. 120) are examples of this. It is striking that such objects are often integrated into the work without any context. Not only are the precise origin and the geographical location lost in the process, but their function is not explained in greater detail. In 1947, around three decades after his Expressionist period, Emil Nolde's *Ferne Mädchen* (Girls from Afar) (cat. 122)—presumably a memory of his trip to New Guinea in 1913–14. These are not individual portraits. The female figures remain anonymous and represent only a stylized representation of "afar."

It remains important to criticize the understanding of the appropriation of "foreign" art on which Expressionist art was based. Not least against the backdrop of current debates over issues of provenance and restitution, it seems all the more urgent to continue to explore and expose the close interlocking of artistic expression and colonial appropriation in Expressionism.

1   Tayfun Belgin, "Paradiesische Orte: Die Bildwelten Gauguins und der deutschen Expressionisten," in *Sehnsucht nach dem Paradies: Von Gauguin bis Nolde*, ed. Tayfun Belgin, exh. cat. (Krems: Kunsthalle Krems, 2004), pp. 7–18, esp. p. 12.

2   See Christoph Otterbeck, *Europa verlassen: Künstlerreisen am Beginn des 20. Jahrhunderts*, Studien zur Kunst 4 (Cologne: Böhlau, 2007), also PhD diss. (Philipps-Universität Marburg, 2004), p. 209; Klaus von Beyme, *Die Faszination des Exotischen: Exotismus, Rassismus und Sexismus in der Kunst* (Munich: Wilhelm Fink, 2008), pp. 133–34; Katharina Beisiegel, "Escapism and Fantasy Worlds: Ernst Ludwig Kirchner's Imaginary Travels," trans. Cynthia Hall, in *Ernst Ludwig Kirchner: Imaginary Travels*, ed. Katharina Beisiegel, exh. cat. Kirchner Museum Davos 2018 (Munich: Prestel, 2018), pp. 19–64, esp. p. 20.

3   Otterbeck, *Europa verlassen* (see note 2), p. 209.

4   Dorthe Aagesen and Beatrice von Bormann, "Expressionism and Colonialism: Introduction," in *Kirchner and Nolde: Expressionism, Colonialism*, ed. Sophie Tates, exh. cat. Brücke-Museum, Berlin 2021 (Munich: Hirmer, 2021), pp. 20–33, esp. p. 20.

5   Aya Soika, "Max Pechstein, ein 'Maler-Tourist': 'Allein, Allein, in einer noch nicht verfälschten Einheit von Mensch und Natur,'" in *Max Pechstein auf Reisen: Utopie und Wirklichkeit*, ed. Sebastian Möllers, exh. cat. Kunsthaus Stade 2012 (Munich: Hirmer, 2012), pp. 28–34, esp. p. 33.

6   See Aagesen and von Bormann, "Expressionism and Colonialism" (see note 4), p. 26.

7   H. Glenn Penny, "The Expressionists' Workshop? German Ethnographic Museums in the Age of Empire," in *Kirchner und Nolde* (see note 4), pp. 36–47, esp. p. 36.

8   Aagesen and von Bormann, "Expressionism and Colonialism" (see note 4), pp. 21–22.

9   In Mannheim, too, there was a so-called Völkerschau (ethnological exposition) as part of the anniversary of the city of Mannheim. See Arbeitskreis Kolonialgeschichte Mannheim, "Menschenzoos," https://kolonialgeschichtema.com/menschenzoos/ (accessed on May 19, 2025).

10 Otterbeck, *Europa verlassen* (see note 2), p. 59.

11 Aagesen and von Bormann, "Expressionism and Colonialism" (see note 4), p. 28 (translation modified).

12 Belgin, "Paradiesische Orte" (see note 1), p. 13.

Ausstellung *Blicke in die Formenwelt der Primitiven* statt. In der Sammlung zeugen neben Werken von Künstlern wie Emil Nolde und Max Pechstein, die selbst in die Südsee reisten, auch die Arbeiten von Karl Schmidt-Rottluff, Ernst Ludwig Kirchner, Otto Mueller und Erich Heckel von einer intensiven Rezeption nicht-europäischer Kunst. Einen ersten Nukleus bilden vor allem landschaftliche Motive, etwa Noldes *Südseelandschaft II* von 1915 (Kat. 123) oder zahlreiche Zeichnungen, die an der Ostsee und auf Fehmarn entstanden sind. Ein weiteres oft wiederkehrendes Motiv sind Tänzer*innen sowie Akrobat*innen, wie in Max Pechsteins *Akrobaten I* und *Akrobaten III* von 1912 (Kat. 124, 125). Zudem offenbaren eine Vielzahl an Stillleben, in denen Masken oder Statuen einbezogen werden, die Faszination für nicht-europäische Kunst. Erich Heckels *Sonnenblumen* von 1913 (Kat. 121) sowie Max Pechsteins *Stillleben: Figur und Blumen* von 1917 (Kat. 120) bilden Beispiele hierfür. Auffällig ist, dass die Objekte oft kontextlos in das Bild eingebaut werden. Nicht nur der genaue Ursprung und die geografische Zuordnung gehen hierbei verloren, auch deren Funktion wird nicht näher erläutert. Im Jahr 1947, rund drei Jahrzehnte nach der expressionistischen Periode, entstand Emil Noldes *Ferne Mädchen* (Kat. 122) – vermutlich eine Erinnerung an seine Neuguinea-Reise in den Jahren 1913/14. Es handelt sich hier nicht um individuelle Porträts, denn die anonym bleibenden Frauenfiguren bilden nur eine stilisierte Repräsentation des ‚Fernen‘.

Es bleibt, kritisch zu hinterfragen, welches Verständnis der Aneignung ‚fremder‘ Kunst den Künstler*innen des Expressionismus zugrunde lag. Nicht zuletzt vor dem Hintergrund aktueller Debatten um Provenienz- und Restitutionsfragen erscheint es umso dringlicher, die enge Verzahnung von künstlerischem Ausdruck und kolonialer Aneignung im Expressionismus weiter zu erforschen und offenzulegen.

1 Tayfun Belgin: Paradiesische Orte. Die Bildwelten Gauguins und der deutschen Expressionisten, in: Kat. Ausst. *Sehnsucht nach dem Paradies. Von Gauguin bis Nolde*, Kunsthalle Krems 2004, hrsg. v. Tayfun Belgin, Krems 2004, S. 7–18, S. 12.
2 Vgl. Christoph Otterbeck: *Europa verlassen. Künstlerreisen am Beginn des 20. Jahrhunderts*, Köln/Weimar/Wien 2007 (Studien zur Kunst, Bd. 4; zgl. Diss. Philipps-Universität Marburg, 2004), S. 209; Klaus von Beyme: *Die Faszination des Exotischen. Exotismus, Rassismus und Sexismus in der Kunst*, München 2008, S. 133f.; Katharina Beisiegel: Weltflucht und Fantasiewelten. Ernst Ludwig Kirchners erträumte Reisen, in: Kat. Ausst. *Ernst Ludwig Kirchner – erträumte Reisen*, Kirchner Museum Davos 2018, hrsg. v. Katharina Beisiegel, München/London/New York 2018, S. 19–68, S. 20.
3 Otterbeck 2007 (wie Anm. 2), S. 209.
4 Dorthe Aagesen u. Beatrice von Bormann: Expressionismus und Kolonialismus. Einführung der Kuratorinnen, in: Kat. Ausst. *Kirchner und Nolde. Expressionismus, Kolonialismus*, Brücke-Museum Berlin 2021, hrsg. v. Sophie Tates, München 2021, S. 20–33, S. 20.
5 Aya Soika: Max Pechstein, ein „Maler-Tourist“. „Allein, Allein, in einer noch nicht verfälschten Einheit von Mensch und Natur“, in: Kat. Ausst. *Max Pechstein auf Reisen. Utopie und Wirklichkeit*, Kunsthaus Stade 2012, hrsg. v. Sebastian Möllers, München 2012, S. 28–34, S. 33.
6 Vgl. Aagesen/von Bormann 2021 (wie Anm. 4), S. 26.
7 H. Glenn Penny: Die Werkstatt der Expressionisten? Deutsche Ethnologische Museen der Kaiserzeit, in: Kat. Ausst. *Kirchner und Nolde. Expressionismus, Kolonialismus*, Brücke-Museum Berlin 2021, hrsg. v. Sophie Tates, München 2021, S. 36–47, S. 36.
8 Aagesen/von Bormann 2021 (wie Anm. 4), S. 21f.
9 Auch in Mannheim fand im Jahr 1907 im Rahmen des Mannheimer Stadtjubiläums eine sogenannte Völkerschau statt. Vgl. Arbeitskreis Kolonialgeschichte Mannheim: *Menschenzoos*, https://kolonialgeschichtema.com/menschenzoos/ [abgerufen am 19.05.2025].
10 Otterbeck 2007 (wie Anm. 2), S. 59.
11 Aagesen/von Bormann 2021 (wie Anm. 4), S. 28.
12 Belgin 2004 (wie Anm. 1), S. 13.

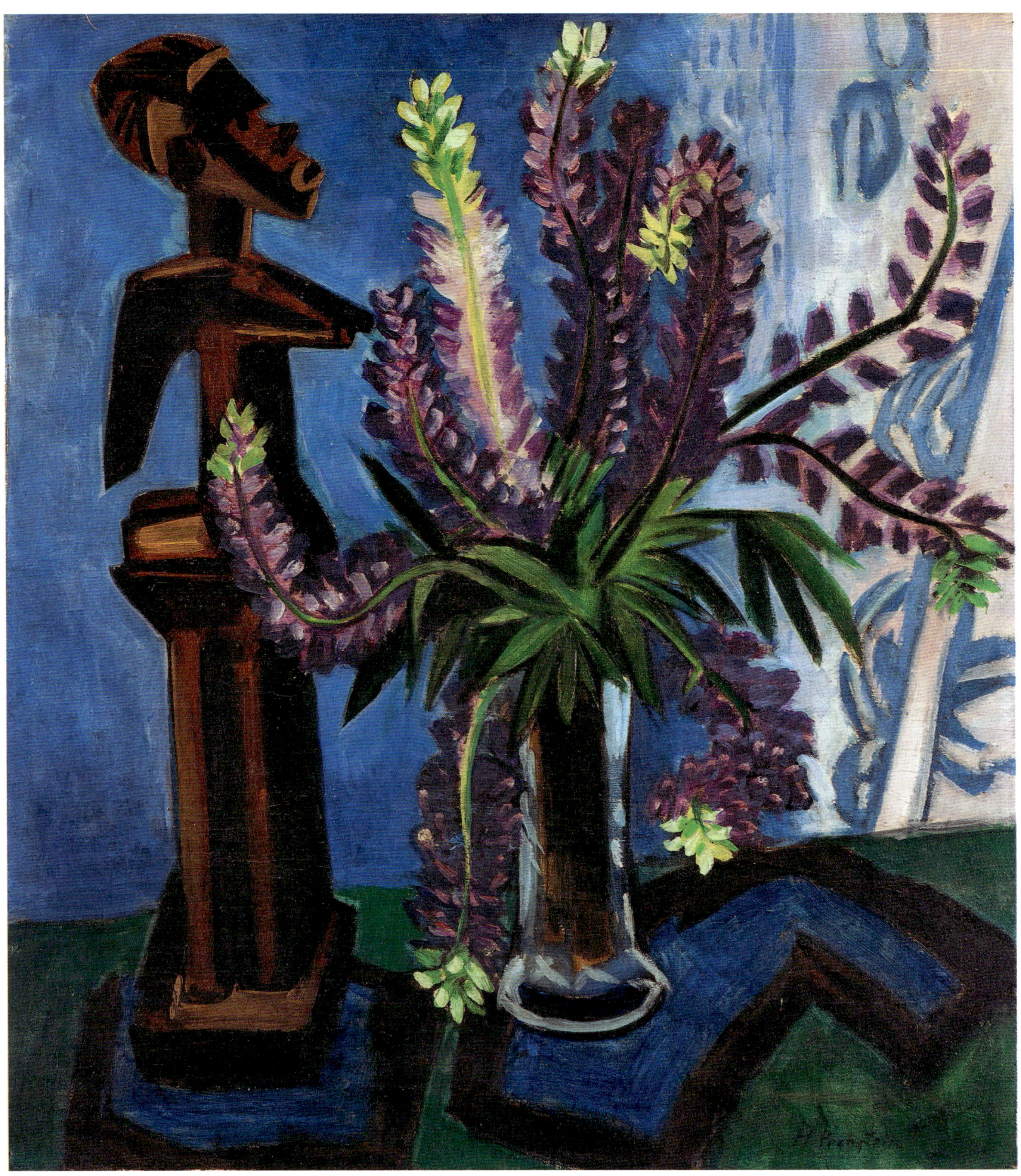

120 | **Max Pechstein,** *Stilleben: Figur und Blumen* / *Still Life: Figure and Flowers,* **1917,** Kunsthalle Mannheim

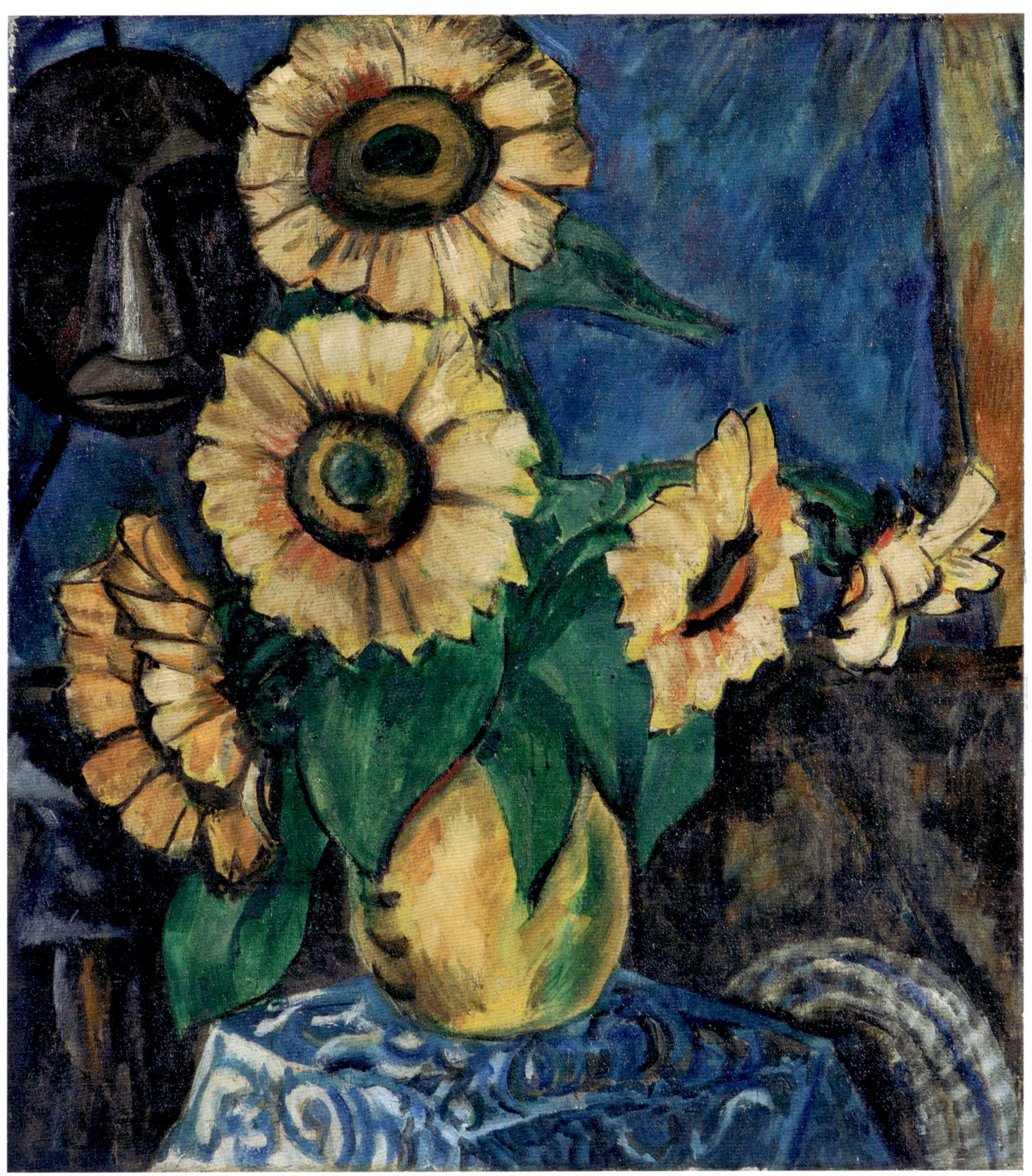

121 | **Erich Heckel,** ***Sonnenblumen*** */ Sunflowers,* **1913,** Kunsthalle Mannheim

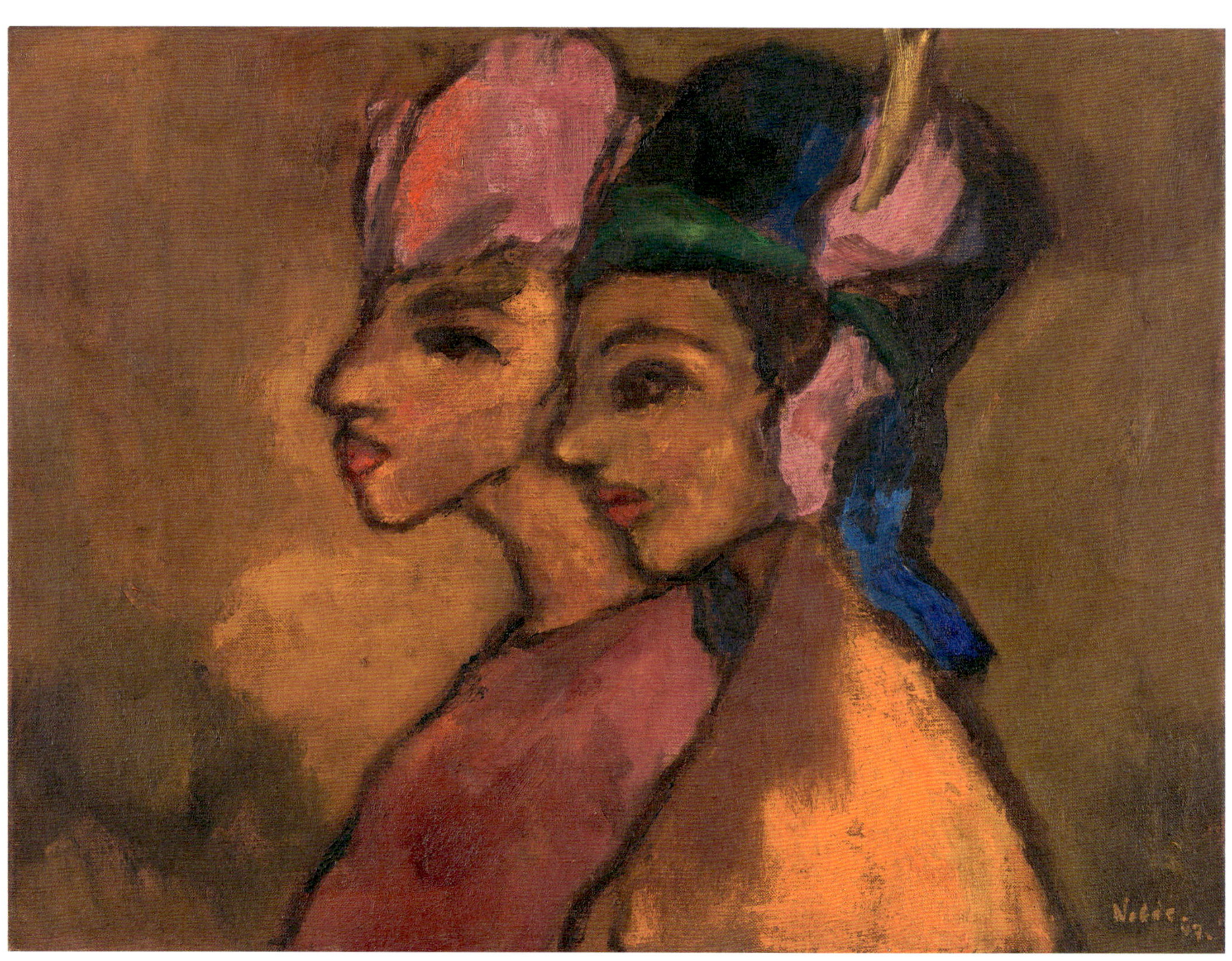

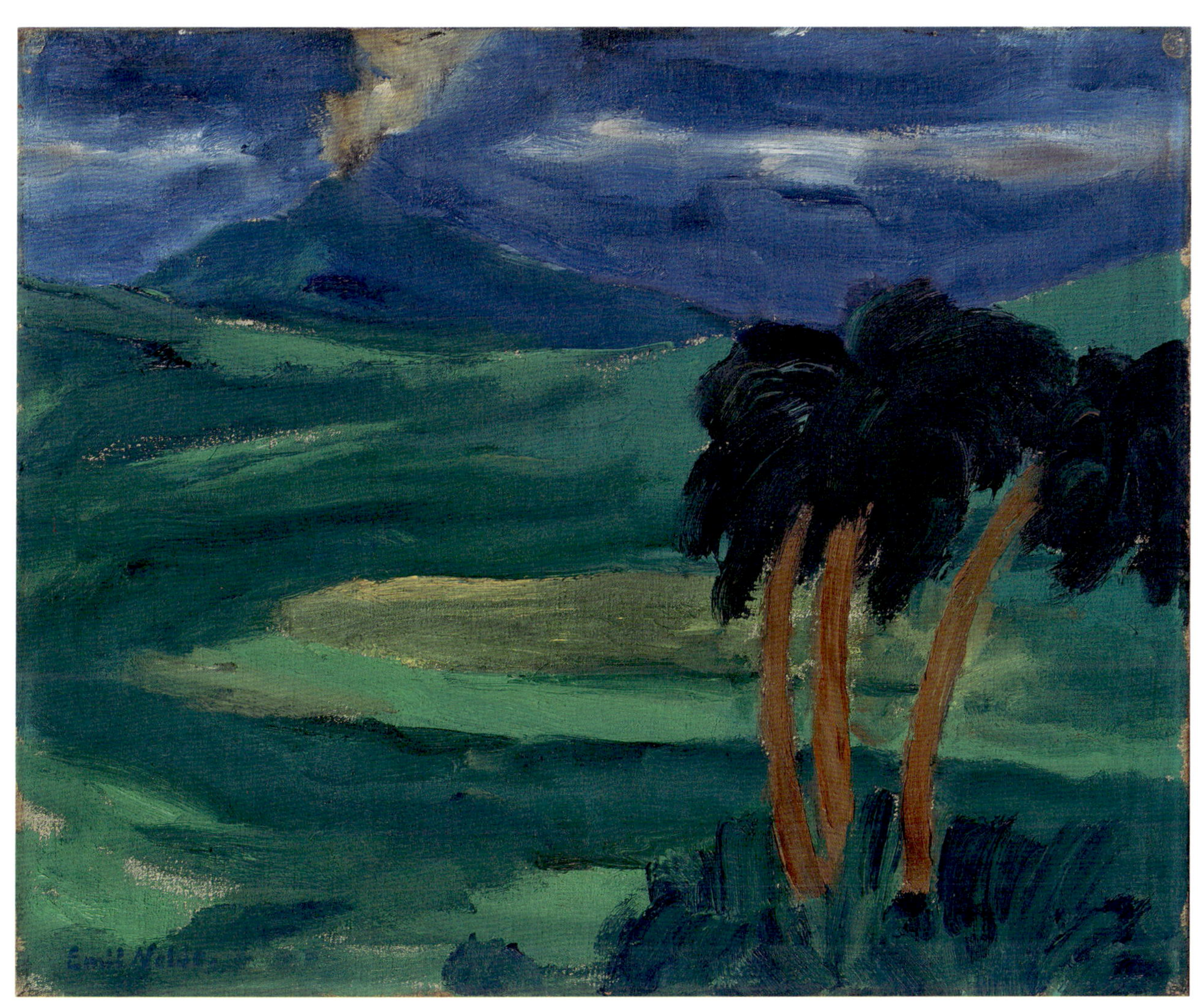

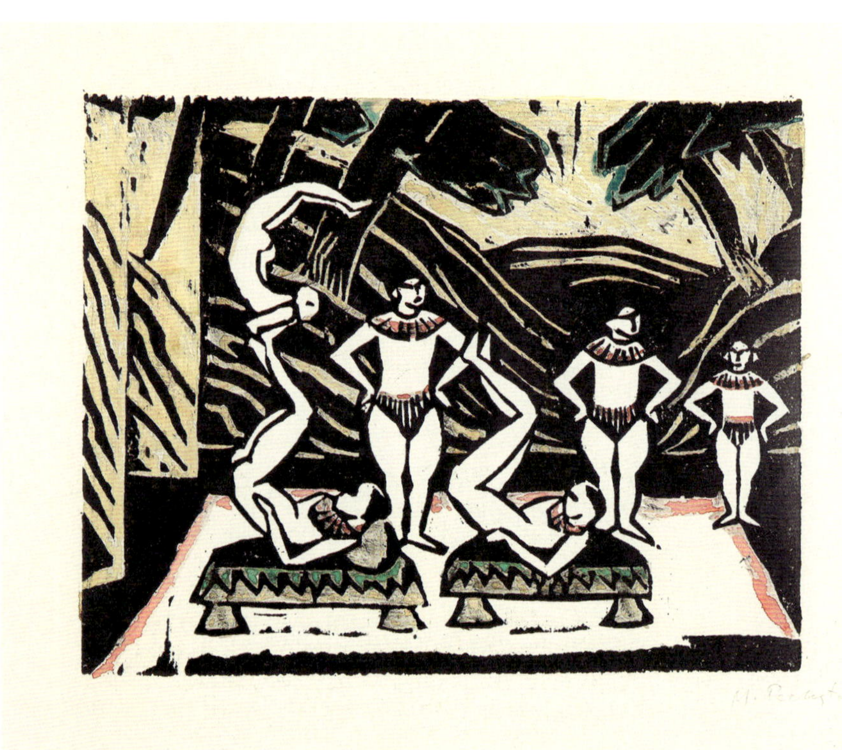

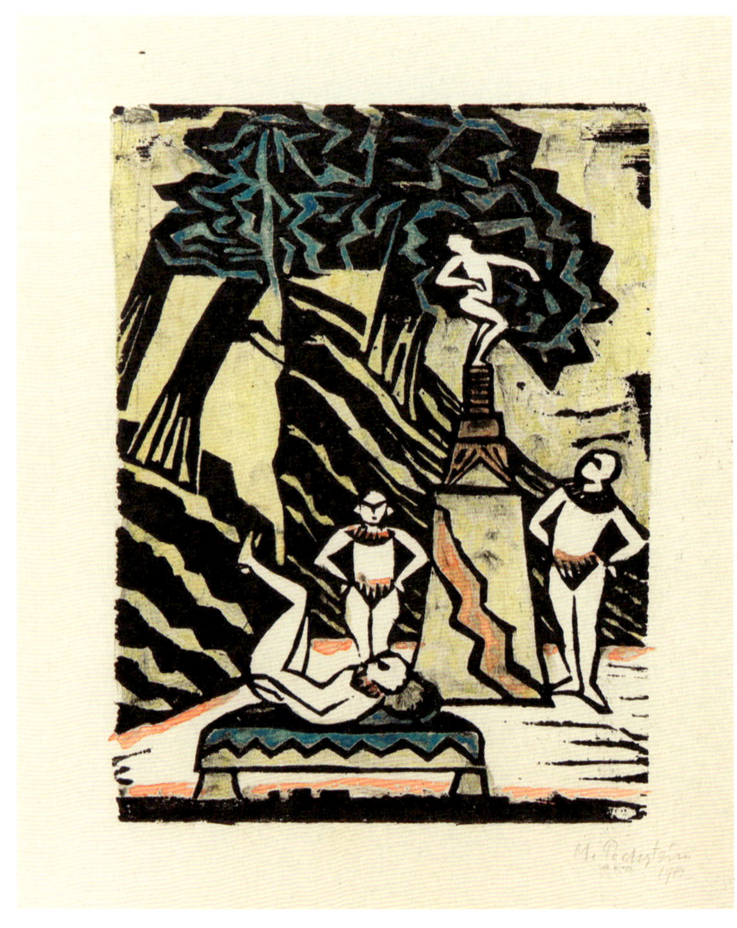

    124 | **Max Pechstein,** *Akrobaten III* / *Acrobats III,* **1912,** Kunsthalle Mannheim   125 | **Max Pechstein,** *Akrobaten I* / *Acrobats I,* **1912,** Kunsthalle Mannheim

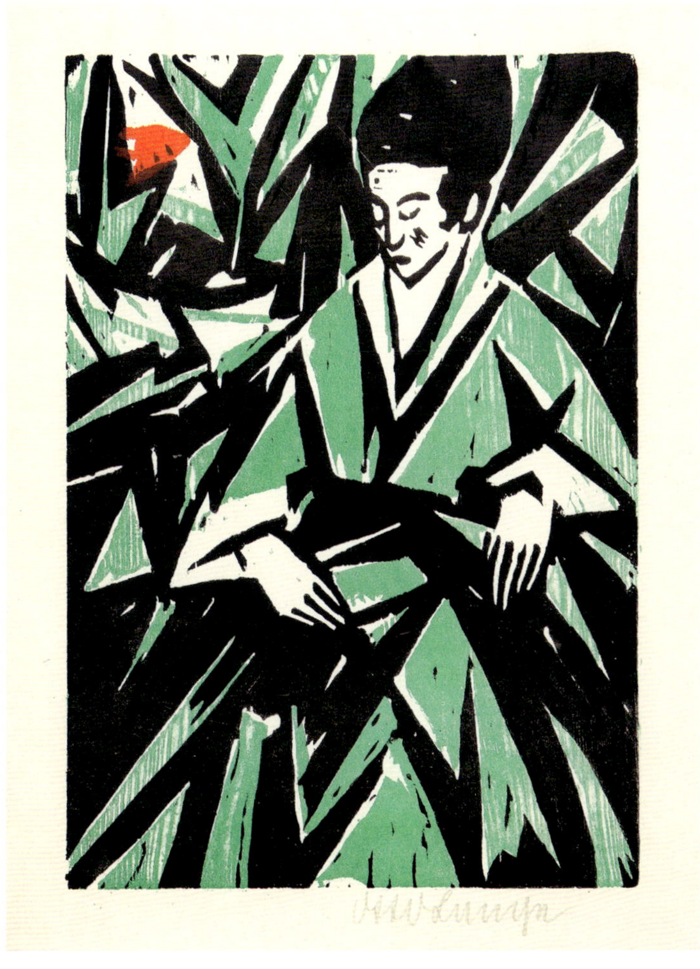 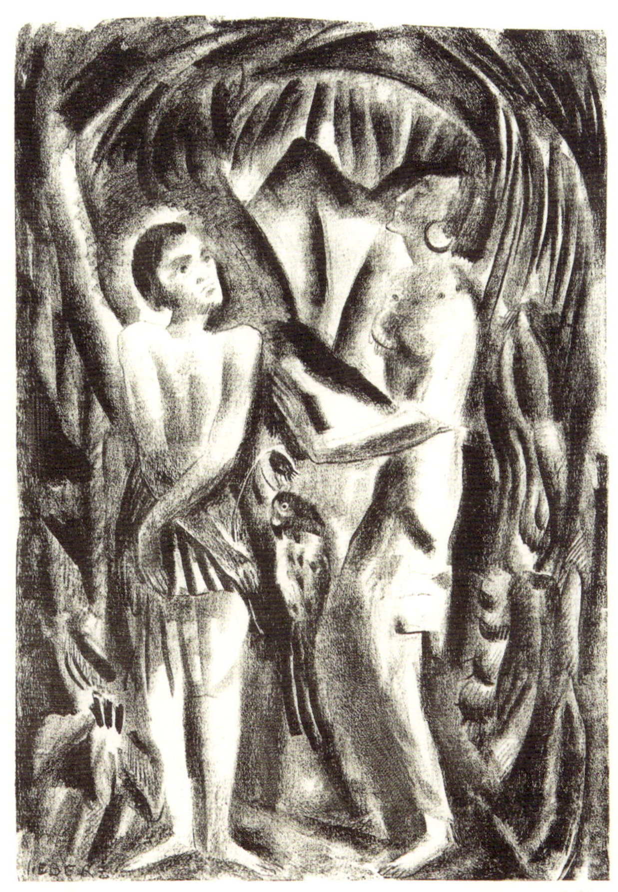

126 | **Otto Lange,** *Dame in Grün* / *Woman in Green Dress,* **1918/19,** Kunsthalle Mannheim   127 | **Josef Matthias Eberz,** *Paradies* / *Paradise,* **1919,** Kunsthalle Mannheim

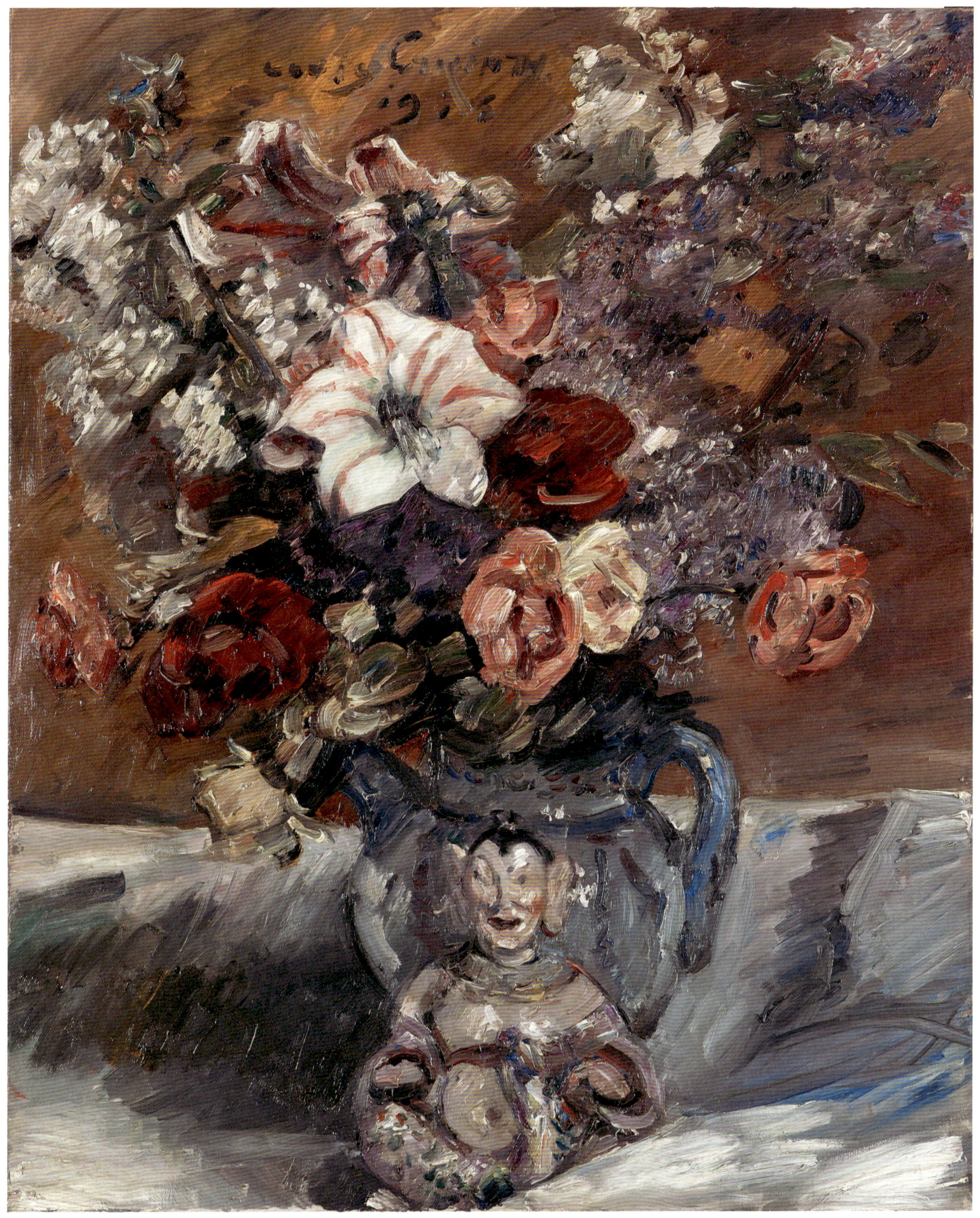

128 | **Lovis Corinth,** ***Blumen mit chinesischer Pagode*** */ Flowers with Chinese Pagoda,* **1916,** Kunsthalle Mannheim

"An immense gentleness and gravity radiate from her human and animal bodies":[1] The Artist Maria Uhden

Dorotea Lorenz

The graphic artist and painter Maria Uhden (1892–1918) is considered one of the most important female woodcarvers in the circle of the Berlin journal *Der Sturm* (The Storm), in which many of her works were published. Her death at just twenty-six ended her extraordinary production much too early. In just three years, she created an astonishing extensive oeuvre of oil paintings, watercolors, and gouaches in color, on the one hand, and black-and-white woodcuts and lithographs, on the other. In her works she developed a very individual choice of subjects and pictorial language.

Maria Uhden was raised in a middle-class family in Coburg, the eldest of five sisters, and began painting early on; at fifteen she was already drawing portraits of flowers in a postcard format.[2] In Wilhelmine Germany, women were not permitted to attend state academies, so she received private drawing lessons first from Julius Exter in Munich from 1911 onward and from 1914 at the Kunstgewerbemuseum (Museum of Decorative Arts) in Berlin. At the latter, she came into contact with Nell and Herwarth Walden, editors of the journal *Der Sturm*, which offered a platform to avant-garde artists. Uhden received recognition and support in the circle of the Waldens: "I am now hard at work again and will soon submit something. It is a very nice, secure feeling being understood and standing as a disciple under the protection of a revered master,"[3] she wrote to Walden in January 1916. In the November 1915 issue of *Der Sturm*, a first woodcut by her, *Vier Akte* (Four Nudes), was published as an original print.[4] The work already had features characteristic of her later work: in bold abstraction, four figures, two in the foreground, and two in the background of a square frame, adopted animated, interlocked poses. The practiced artist had already found her very own formal language at the age of twenty-four. Her confident line work expresses this evolution. At the Galerie *Der Sturm* that same year, Walden organized the first exhibition of Uhden's works along with works by other artists, including Jacoba van Heemskerck. Herwarth Walden introduced the painter Georg Schrimpf (1889–1938), one of the most important representatives of Neue Sachlichkeit (New Objectivity), to Uhden's work. Schrimpf and Uhden married in 1917 and moved to Munich. Shortly after the birth of their son in 1918, Uhden died. After her death, Walden continued to illustrate her works in *Der Sturm* and sent it on traveling exhibitions,[5] thus laying "the groundwork for the survival of her work and world of ideas."[6]

In the paintings and woodcuts of her brief creative life, Uhden illustrated a number of nocturnal, dreamy scenes: people wander silently and confidently in the darkness, guarded over by stars floating above them. They are accompanied and surrounded by animals: cows, horses, pigs, or dogs, united peacefully and safely in sleep. Some have seen this poetic harmony of creatures integrated into a dream world as the influence Franz Marc and Marc Chagall, whose works Uhden had encountered in the Waldens' extensive art collection.[7]

Another of these dreamlike scenes is the lithograph *Hirten* (Shepherds) (cat. 129) from 1917: a man and a woman with a child are wandering in a bucolic landscape, surrounded by sheep, trees, and a sun on the horizon. This lithograph is unusual because the other side of the sheet has a drawing by Georg Schrimpf: *Sitzendes Mädchen* (Seated Girl) of 1924, which the Kunsthalle Mannheim acquired that same year from the Neue Secession in Munich. Uhden's work on the verso long went unnoticed.[8] It was rediscovered in the context of the current exhibition and is now being presented to the public for the first time. It is reasonable to assume that Schrimpf made a drawing on a sheet that Uhden had already printed. Uhden's lithograph is mentioned in

„Eine ungeheure Sanftmut und Erdschwere strömt aus den Körpern von Mensch und Tier"[1]: die Künstlerin Maria Uhden

Dorotea Lorenz

Die Grafikerin und Malerin Maria Uhden (1892–1918) gilt als eine der bedeutendsten Holzschnitt-Künstlerinnen im Umfeld der Berliner Zeitschrift *Der Sturm,* in der zahlreiche ihrer Werke veröffentlicht wurden. Ihr Tod mit gerade einmal 26 Jahren beendete viel zu früh ihr außergewöhnliches Schaffen. In nur etwa drei Jahren schuf sie ein erstaunlich umfangreiches Œuvre aus farbigen Ölbildern, Aquarellen und Gouachen einerseits und schwarz-weißen Holzschnitten und Lithografien andererseits. In ihren Werken entwickelte sie eine sehr individuelle Sujetwahl und Bildsprache.

Maria Uhden wuchs als älteste von fünf Schwestern in Coburg in einer bürgerlichen Familie heran, begann früh mit dem Malen und zeichnete schon mit 15 Jahren Blumenporträts im Postkartenformat.[2] Ersten privaten Zeichenunterricht – Frauen war im wilhelminischen Deutschland der Besuch staatlicher Akademien verboten – erhielt sie ab 1911 in München bei Julius Exter, ab 1914 im Kunstgewerbemuseum in Berlin. Dort kam sie in Kontakt mit Nell und Herwarth Walden, Herausgeber der Zeitschrift *Der Sturm,* die Avantgarde-Künstler*innen eine Bühne bot. Im Kreis der Waldens erfuhr Uhden Anerkennung und Förderung: „Ich bin nun wieder tüchtig beim Arbeiten und werde bald etwas einsenden. Es ist ein zu schönes, geborgenes Gefühl, wenn man verstanden wird, und als Jünger im Schutze eines verehrten Meisters steht"[3], schrieb sie im Januar 1916 an Walden. In der Novemberausgabe 1915 des *Sturm* war ein erster Holzschnitt von ihr, *Vier Akte,* als Originalgrafik erschienen.[4] Das Werk zeigt bereits charakteristische Züge ihres weiteren Schaffens: In kühner Abstraktion drängen sich vier Figuren, je zwei im Vorder- und Hintergrund, in einem quadratischen Rahmen in lebhaften, untereinander verschränkten Haltungen. Die versierte Künstlerin hatte mit nur 24 Jahren eine ihr ganz eigene Formensprache gefunden. Ihre sichere, aufs Wesentliche konzentrierte Linienführung ist ein Ausdruck dieser Entwicklung. Im selben Jahr ermöglichte Walden in der *Sturm*-Galerie die erste Ausstellung mit Werken Uhdens und weiterer Künstler*innen, wie beispielsweise Jacoba van Heemskerck. Über Herwarth Walden lernte der Maler Georg Schrimpf (1889–1938) – einer der wichtigsten Vertreter der Neuen Sachlichkeit – das Werk Uhdens kennen. Schrimpf und Uhden heirateten im Jahr 1917 und übersiedelten nach München. Kurz nach der Geburt ihres ersten Sohnes im Jahr 1918 starb Uhden. Auch nach ihrem Tod bildete Walden ihre Werke weiterhin im *Sturm* ab, schickte sie auf Wanderausstellungen[5] und legte so „den Grundstein für das Weiterleben ihres Werkes und ihrer Gedankenwelt."[6]

In den Gemälden und Holzschnitten ihrer kurzen Schaffenszeit bildete Uhden mehrfach nächtliche, träumerische Szenen ab: Menschen wandern still und vertrauensvoll in der Dunkelheit, bewacht von Gestirnen, die über ihnen schweben. Begleitet und umgeben werden sie von Tieren: Kühe, Pferde, Schweine oder Hunde, friedlich und geborgen im Schlaf vereint. In dieser poetischen Harmonie der Kreaturen, eingebunden in eine Traumwelt, hat man den Einfluss Franz Marcs und Marc Chagalls erkennen wollen, deren Werke Uhden in der umfangreichen Kunstsammlung der Waldens kennenlernte.[7]

Zu diesen träumerischen Szenen gehört auch die Lithografie *Hirten* (Kat. 129) aus dem Jahr 1917: Ein Mann und eine Frau mit Kind wandern in einer bukolischen Landschaft, umgeben von Schafen, Bäumen und einer am Horizont stehenden Sonne. Die Besonderheit dieser Lithografie ist, dass sich auf der anderen Seite des Blattes die Zeichnung *Sitzendes Mädchen* von Georg Schrimpf aus dem Jahr 1924 befindet, welche die Kunsthalle Mannheim in ebendiesem Jahr von der Münchner Neuen Secession ankaufte. Das Werk Uhdens auf der Rückseite blieb

the catalogue raisonné of 1985,[9] but it has scarcely been noticed and appreciated. It therefore seems all the more urgent to bring to light once again this woman artist who has largely fallen into oblivion. For Maria Uhden's fate is no isolated case: the women artists of Expressionism long stood in the shadow of their male colleagues. Only recently has systematic review and reevaluation counteracted this marginalization.[10] Gabriele Münter (cat. 60), Marianne von Werefkin, and also Jacoba van Heemskerck (cat. 130) are just a few examples of women artists whose significance for Expressionism was recognized only after a long delay. Although Maria Uhden was only active for a brief time as a result of her early death and some of her oeuvre was confiscated and destroyed as part of National Socialist cultural policy,[11] she left behind an impressive artistic legacy: "Maria Uhden's entire oeuvre reveals her ability to counter the oppressive experiences of a world war with her own cosmos that bears witness to her creative energy and joie de vivre."[12]

1   Oskar Maria Graf, "Maria Uhden," *Der Cicerone* 13 (1921), pp. 73–82, esp. p. 73, https://doi.org/10.11588/diglit.27278#0093 (accessed May 19, 2025).

2   Christmut Präger, "Maria Uhden: Dream and the World," in *Sturm-Frauen: Künstlerinnen der Avantgarde in Berlin, 1910–1932*, ed. Ingrid Pfeiffer and Max Hollein, exh. cat. Schirn Kunsthalle, Frankfurt am Main 2015 (Cologne: Wienand, 2015), pp. 380–82, esp. p. 380.

3   See *Georg Schrimpf und Maria Uhden: Leben und Werk*, exh. cat., with a catalogue raisonné by Karl-Ludwig Hofmann and Christmut Präger, Haus am Waldsee Berlin 1985 (Berlin: Charlottenpresse; Frölich und Kaufmann), p. 62.

4   Präger, "Maria Uhden" (see note 2), p. 292.

5   See ibid., p. 292.

6   Ibid., p. 293.

7   Ibid., pp. 291–92.

8   This is noted in the historical inventory of the Kunsthalle Mannheim from 1924. There is no reference to the lithograph by Maria Uhden. See the mention of the purchase in 1924 in "Graphik-Inventar Nr. 1," p. 218, of the Graphic Arts Collection of the Kunsthalle Mannheim.

9   See *Georg Schrimpf und Maria Uhden* (see note 3), p. 246.

10 For example, in extensive exhibition projects such as *Sturm-Frauen* (see note 2).

11 "Datenbank zum Beschlagnahmeinventar der Aktion 'Entartete Kunst,'" Forschungsstelle 'Entartete Kunst,' Freie Universität Berlin, see Online-Datenbank (accessed May 19, 2025).

12 Präger, "Maria Uhden" (see note 2), p. 292.

lange unbemerkt.[8] Erst im Rahmen der jetzigen Ausstellung wiederentdeckt, wird es nun zum ersten Mal öffentlich präsentiert. Es kann vermutet werden, dass Schrimpf auf der Rückseite des von Uhden bereits bedruckten Blattes eine Zeichnung anfertigte, die die Kunsthalle Mannheim im Jahr 1924 ankaufte. Die Lithografie Uhdens ist im Werkverzeichnis von 1985 zwar erwähnt[9], ist aber darüber hinaus bis jetzt kaum wahrgenommen oder gewürdigt worden. Umso dringlicher erscheint es heute, diese weitgehend in Vergessenheit geratene Künstlerin wieder zum Vorschein zu bringen. Denn Maria Uhdens Schicksal ist kein Einzelfall: Künstlerinnen im Expressionismus standen lange im Schatten ihrer männlichen Kollegen. Erst in den letzten Jahren wurde dieser Marginalisierung durch systematische Aufarbeitung und Neubewertung entgegengewirkt.[10] Gabriele Münter (Kat. 60), Marianne von Werefkin und auch Jacoba van Heemskerck (Kat. 130) sind nur ein paar Beispiele für Künstlerinnen, deren Bedeutung für den Expressionismus erst mit großer zeitlicher Verzögerung anerkannt wurde.

Obwohl Maria Uhden durch ihren frühen Tod nur für eine kurze Zeit tätig war, zudem ein Teil ihres Werkes unter der NS-Kulturpolitik beschlagnahmt und zerstört wurde[11], hinterlässt sie ein eindrucksvolles künstlerisches Vermächtnis: „Im gesamten Werk Maria Uhdens tritt ihre Kraft zutage, den bedrückenden Erfahrungen eines Weltkriegs ihren eigenen Kosmos entgegenzustellen, der von Schaffenskraft und Lebensfreude kündet."[12]

1   Oskar Maria Graf: Maria Uhden, in: *Der Cicerone* 13 (1921), S. 73–82, https://doi.org/10.11588/diglit.27278#0093 [abgerufen am 19.05.2025], S. 73.
2   Christmut Präger: Maria Uhden. Traum und Welt, in: Kat. Ausst. *Sturm-Frauen. Künstlerinnen der Avantgarde in Berlin 1910–1932*, Schirn Kunsthalle Frankfurt am Main 2015, hrsg. v. Ingrid Pfeiffer u. Max Hollein, Köln 2015, S. 290–311, S. 290.
3   Kat. Ausst. *Georg Schrimpf und Maria Uhden. Leben und Werk*. Mit einem Werkverzeichnis von Karl-Ludwig Hofmann u. Christmut Präger, Haus am Waldsee Berlin 1985, hrsg. v. Wolfgang Storch, Berlin 1985, S. 62.
4   Präger 2015 (wie Anm. 2), S. 292.
5   Vgl. ebd., S. 292.
6   Ebd., S. 293.
7   Ebd., S. 291f.
8   So ist es im historischen Inventarbuch aus dem Jahr 1924 der Kunsthalle Mannheim vermerkt. Einen Verweis auf die Lithografie von Maria Uhden gibt es nicht. Vgl. im Graphik-Inventar Nr. 1, S. 218, der Graphischen Sammlung der Kunsthalle Mannheim den Ankauf im Jahr 1924.
9   Vgl.: Kat. Ausst. *Georg Schrimpf und Maria Uhden. Leben und Werk*. Mit einem Werkverzeichnis von Karl-Ludwig Hofmann u. Christmut Präger, Haus am Waldsee Berlin 1985, hrsg. v. Wolfgang Storch, Berlin 1985, S. 246.
10 Etwa durch umfangreiche Ausstellungsprojekte, z. B.: Kat. Ausst. *Sturm-Frauen. Künstlerinnen der Avantgarde in Berlin 1910–1932*, Schirn Kunsthalle Frankfurt am Main 2015, hrsg. v. Ingrid Pfeiffer u. Max Hollein, Köln 2015.
11 Datenbank zum Beschlagnahmeinventar der Aktion „Entartete Kunst", Forschungsstelle „Entartete Kunst", Freie Universität Berlin, vgl. Online-Datenbank [abgerufen am 19.05.2025].
12 Präger 2015 (wie Anm. 2), S. 292.

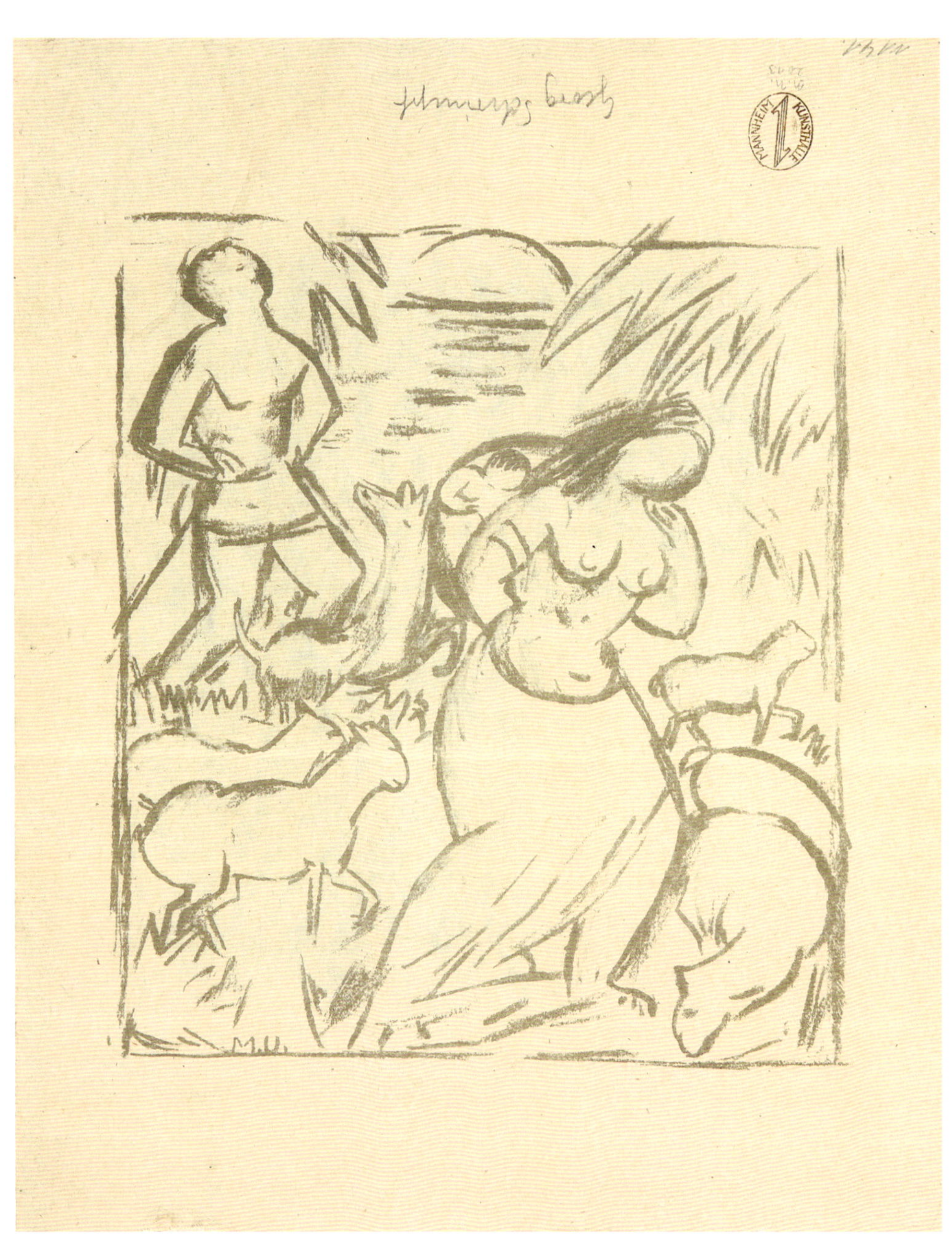

129 | **Maria Uhden,** *Hirten* / *Shepherds,* **1917,** Kunsthalle Mannheim

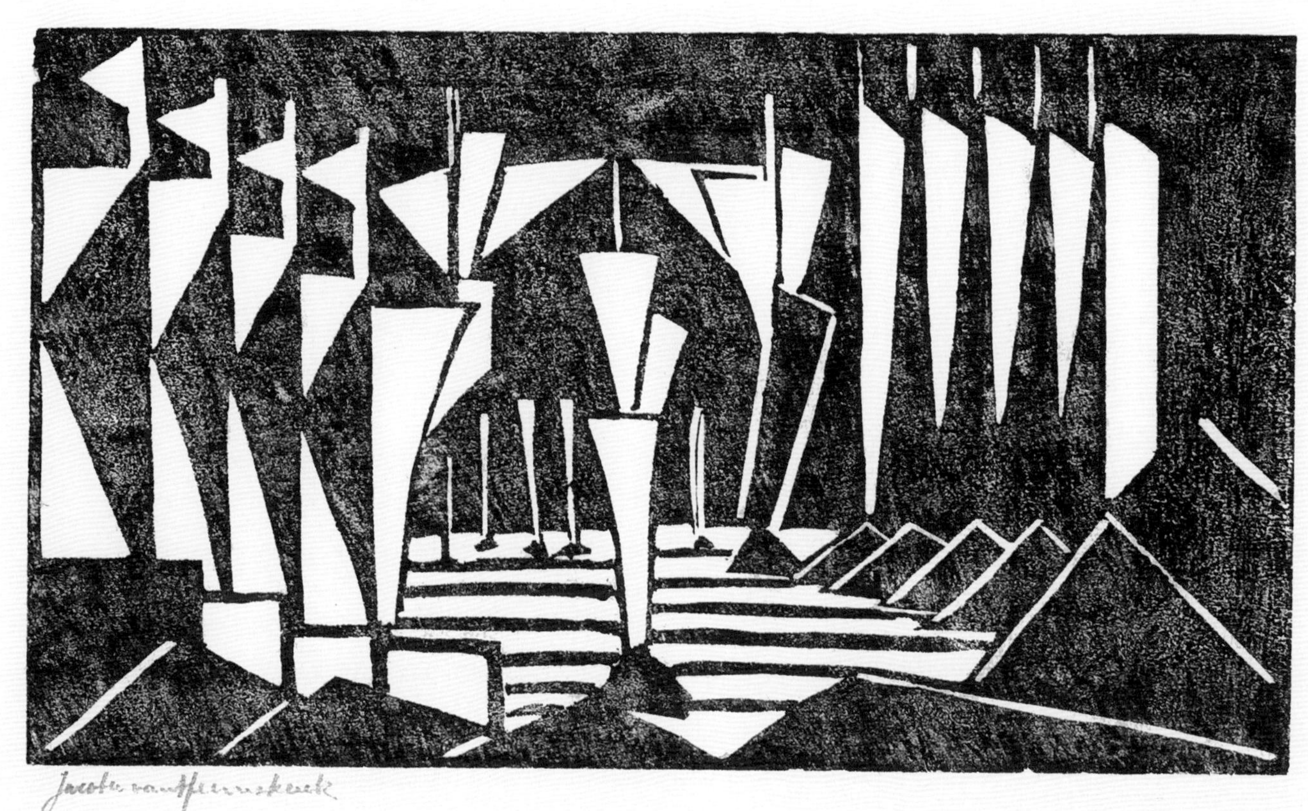

The Reception of Expressionism in Mannheim after 1945 up to the Present

Ursula Drahoss

When the National Socialist regime took power in 1933, most Expressionist artists found themselves subjected to open invective and defamation. But Expressionism was not completely rejected at first. Many artists were even hoping there could be a synthesis of Expressionism and the idea of a National Socialist–influenced "new German expressive art."[1] From 1933 onward, Nazi art propaganda was increasingly shaping the public's perception; that same year, the first exhibitions defaming modernism were held in Mannheim (*Kulturbolschewistische Bilder* [Cultural Bolshevist Pictures]) and Karlsruhe (*Regierungskunst, 1918–1933* [Government Art, 1918–1933]). Numerous museum directors and curators who had previously advocated for Expressionist works were dismissed, including Gustav Friedrich Hartlaub in Mannheim in 1933.

The final break with Expressionism then followed with the exhibition *Entartete Kunst* (Degenerate Art) in Munich and other German cities in 1937, which publicly disparaged this art movement. This was followed by a confiscation action of the same name, to which the holdings of many public collections fell victim. The Kunsthalle Mannheim, which, as one of the largest collections of Expressionist art at the time, suffered especially defamation, confiscation, and loss at the hands of the National Socialists.

After 1945, an intense process of reappropriating and reevaluating Expressionist art began. The acquisitions of works that had been confiscated was not only a decision on behalf of art but also a historical responsibility. Provenance research—the scholarly examination of the background of works of art—increasingly moved to the foreground not only because many works came from the illegal expropriation of Jewish private property by the National Socialist regime but also because many of the museums affected had an interest in the whereabouts of the treasures lost from their collections. Even today, addressing previous ownership raises ethical and legal questions. Many important works ended up on the international art market and from there found their way into other public collections, sometimes abroad. They are, even when they were once owned by the Kunsthalle Mannheim, usually irretrievably lost. Provenance research has, however, successfully located works that were once conserved at the Kunsthalle but of whose provenance scholars had meanwhile lost track. This is true, for example, of the woodcut *Tiger* by Franz Marc (cat. 133), which was brought from the Kunsthalle Mannheim to Munich in 1937 as part of the exhibition *Entartete Kunst* and afterward ended up in the art trade there. After the war, it was auctioned by the Kunstkabinett of Roman Norbert Ketterer in Stuttgart and in 1961 ended up back at the Kunsthalle Mannheim—then without knowledge of its history.

One important contribution to the rehabilitation of Expressionism in the public perception that the Kunsthalle Mannheim made after the war was a cycle of eight exhibitions titled *Deutsche Kunst des 20. Jahrhunderts* (German Art of the Twentieth Century), which began in 1946 with an exhibition of works by Wilhelm Lehmbruck, Ernst Barlach, Emil Nolde, Erich Heckel, and Christian Rohlfs, among others, followed by Franz Marc (1947), Lehmbruck again (1949), Heckel (1950), Karl Schmidt-Rottluff and Ernst Ludwig Kirchner (1951), and Nolde (1952). It made the Kunsthalle a central place for the rediscovery of Expressionism. In 1947, Gustav Friedrich Hartlaub, the former director of the Kunsthalle and an ardent supporter of the Expressionists, made an important contribution to the renewed recognition of the movement with his book on the graphic art of Expressionism, which was based on an earlier publication.[2] More recently, they were shown in Mannheim in connection with anniversaries: for

Die Rezeption des Expressionismus in Mannheim nach 1945 bis heute

Ursula Drahoss

Mit der Machtübernahme durch das NS-Regime im Jahr 1933 sahen sich die meisten expressionistischen Künstler*innen offener Schmähung und Diffamierung ausgesetzt. Eine völlige Ablehnung des Expressionismus blieb aber zunächst noch aus. Viele Kulturschaffende hofften sogar auf eine Synthese zwischen Expressionismus und der Idee einer nationalsozialistisch geprägten „neuen deutschen Ausdruckskunst".[1] Ab 1933 prägte die NS-Kunstpropaganda in immer größerem Maße die öffentliche Wahrnehmung, noch im selben Jahr fanden in Mannheim (*Kulturbolschewistische Bilder*) und Karlsruhe (*Regierungskunst 1918–1933*) bereits erste diffamierende Ausstellungen gegen die Moderne statt. In der Folge wurden zahlreiche Museumsdirektoren und Kuratoren entlassen, die sich zuvor für expressionistische Werke eingesetzt hatten, so auch 1933 Gustav Friedrich Hartlaub in Mannheim.

Der endgültige Bruch mit dem Expressionismus erfolgte dann 1937 mit der Ausstellung *Entartete Kunst* in München und anderen deutschen Städten, die diese Kunstrichtung öffentlich verunglimpfte und der die Bestände vieler öffentlicher Sammlungen zum Opfer fielen. Auch die Kunsthalle Mannheim hatte als eine der ehemals größten Sammlungen expressionistischer Kunst besonders unter der Diffamierung, Beschlagnahmung und dem damit verbundenen Verlust unter dem Nationalsozialismus zu leiden.

Nach 1945 setzte ein intensiver Prozess der Wiederaneignung und Neubewertung expressionistischer Kunst ein. Der Ankauf ehemals beschlagnahmter Werke war nicht nur eine Entscheidung für die Kunst, sondern auch eine historische Verantwortung. Die Provenienzforschung – die wissenschaftliche Erforschung der Herkunft von Kunstwerken – rückte zunehmend in den Vordergrund, denn viele Werke stammten nicht nur aus den unrechtmäßigen Enteignungen ehemals jüdischen Privateigentums durch das NS-Regime, sondern auch die von den Beschlagnahmungen betroffenen Museen hatten ein Interesse am Verbleib ihrer verlorenen Sammlungsschätze. Der Umgang mit den ehemaligen Besitzverhältnissen wirft bis heute ethische und rechtliche Fragen auf. Viele bedeutende Werke gelangten in den internationalen Kunsthandel und von dort in andere öffentliche, zum Teil internationale Sammlungen. Diese sind, auch wenn sie sich einst in Besitz der Kunsthalle Mannheim befanden, zumeist unwiederbringlich verloren. Der Provenienzforschung ist es aber auch schon mehrfach erfolgreich gelungen, Werke nachzuweisen, die sich einst in der Kunsthalle befanden, deren Provenienz aber aus dem Blick geraten war. Dies gilt beispielsweise für den Holzschnitt *Tiger* von Franz Marc (Kat. 133), der 1937 im Rahmen der Ausstellung *Entartete Kunst* aus der Kunsthalle Mannheim nach München verbracht wurde und anschließend dort in den Kunsthandel gelangte. In der Nachkriegszeit wurde das Blatt über das Stuttgarter Kunstkabinett von Roman Norbert Ketterer versteigert und gelangte 1961 – damals ohne Kenntnis seiner Herkunft – zurück in die Kunsthalle Mannheim.

Einen wichtigen Beitrag zur endgültigen Rehabilitierung des Expressionismus in der öffentlichen Wahrnehmung leistete die Kunsthalle Mannheim in der Nachkriegszeit mit dem achtteiligen Ausstellungszyklus *Deutsche Kunst des 20. Jahrhunderts,* deren Auftakt 1946 die Ausstellung mit Werken unter anderem von Wilhelm Lehmbruck, Ernst Barlach, Emil Nolde, Erich Heckel und Christian Rohlfs machte, gefolgt von Franz Marc (1947), erneut Lehmbruck (1949) und Heckel (1950), Karl Schmidt-Rottluff und Ernst Ludwig Kirchner (1951) sowie Nolde (1952). Damit wurde die Kunsthalle zu einem zentralen Ort der Wiederentdeckung des Expressionismus. 1947 trug der ehemalige Direktor der Kunsthalle und vehemente Förderer der Expressionist*innen, Gustav

example, Lehmbruck in 2001 for his 120th birthday, and Gabriele Münter's oeuvre of prints in 2002 for her 125th birthday In cooperation with the Ernst Ludwig Kirchner Archiv in Wichtrach, near Bern, and the Kirchner Museum Davos, the Kunsthalle Mannheim organized the exhibition *Der doppelte Kirchner: Die zwei Seiten der Leinwand* (The Double Kirchner: The Two Sides of the Canvas) in 2015, reevaluating the pictures painted on both sides and presenting both sides of the paintings. Questions of restitution were then addressed in the exhibitions *(Wieder-)Entdecken: Die Kunsthalle Mannheim 1933 bis 1945 und die Folgen* ([Re]Discovery: The Kunsthalle from 1933 to 1945 and the Aftermath) in 2018 and *Beschlagnahmt! Rückkehr der Meisterblätter* (Confiscated: The Return of the Master Sheets) in 2019. As a consequence of the joint efforts of provenance research, curators of the graphic arts collection and the administration of the Kunsthalle to get the graphic works back, the monotype *Kniender weiblicher Akt* (Kneeling Female Nude) (ca. 1912; cat. 114) by Otto Mueller, for example, could be "bought back" by the museum with financial support from the Ernst von Siemens Kunststiftung.

1 Christoph Otterbeck, "Expressionismus, Kunst und Politik nach 1933," in *Expressionismus im Rhein-Main-Gebiet: Künstler, Händler, Sammler*, exh. cat. Museum Giersch, Frankfurt am Main, 2011 (Petersberg: Michael Imhof, 2011), pp. 344–86, esp. pp. 345–47.
2 Gustav F. Hartlaub, *Die Graphik des Expressionismus in Deutschland* (Stuttgart and Calw: Hatje, 1947); Gustav F. Hartlaub, *Neue deutsche Graphik* (Berlin: Reiß, 1920).

Friedrich Hartlaub, mit seinem auf einer früheren Publikation
beruhenden wichtigen Buch über die Grafik des Expressionismus zur erneuten Anerkennung der Kunstrichtung bei.[2] In
jüngerer Zeit wurden die Künstler*innen in Mannheim etwa
in Zusammenhängen mit Jubiläen gezeigt – so etwa 2001
Lehmbruck zum 120. Geburtstag oder 2002 Gabriele Münters
druckgrafisches Werk zum 125. Geburtstag. In Kooperation mit
dem Ernst Ludwig Kirchner Archiv in Wichtrach/Bern und dem
Kirchner Museum Davos gestaltete die Kunsthalle Mannheim
im Jahr 2015 die Ausstellung *Der doppelte Kirchner. Die zwei
Seiten der Leinwand,* bei der die Rückseitenbilder neu bewer-
tet und die Gemälde doppelseitig präsentiert wurden. Eine
Auseinandersetzung mit Fragen der Restitution erfolgte zudem
in den Ausstellungen 2018 *(Wieder-)Entdecken. Die Kunsthalle
Mannheim 1933 bis 1945 und die Folgen* sowie 2019 *Beschlag-
nahmt! Rückkehr der Meisterblätter.* Als Folge der gemeinsamen
Bemühungen von Provenienzforschung, Kurator der grafischen
Sammlung und Leitung der Kunsthalle um die Rückholung
von Grafiken konnte zum Beispiel 2021 die Monotypie *Knien-
der weiblicher Akt* (um 1912; Kat. 114) von Otto Mueller vom
Museum mit finanzieller Unterstützung der Ernst von Siemens
Kunststiftung „zurückgekauft" werden.

1   Christoph Otterbeck: Expressionismus, Kunst und Politik nach 1933, in:
    Kat. Ausst. *Expressionismus im Rhein-Main-Gebiet. Künstler, Händler,
    Sammler,* Museum Giersch Frankfurt am Main 2011, hrsg. v. Museum
    Giersch, Frankfurt am Main 2011, S. S. 344–386, S. 345–347.
2   Gustav F. Hartlaub: *Die Graphik des Expressionismus in Deutschland,*
    Stuttgart/Calw 1947; Gustav F. Hartlaub: Neue deutsche Graphik, Berlin 1920.

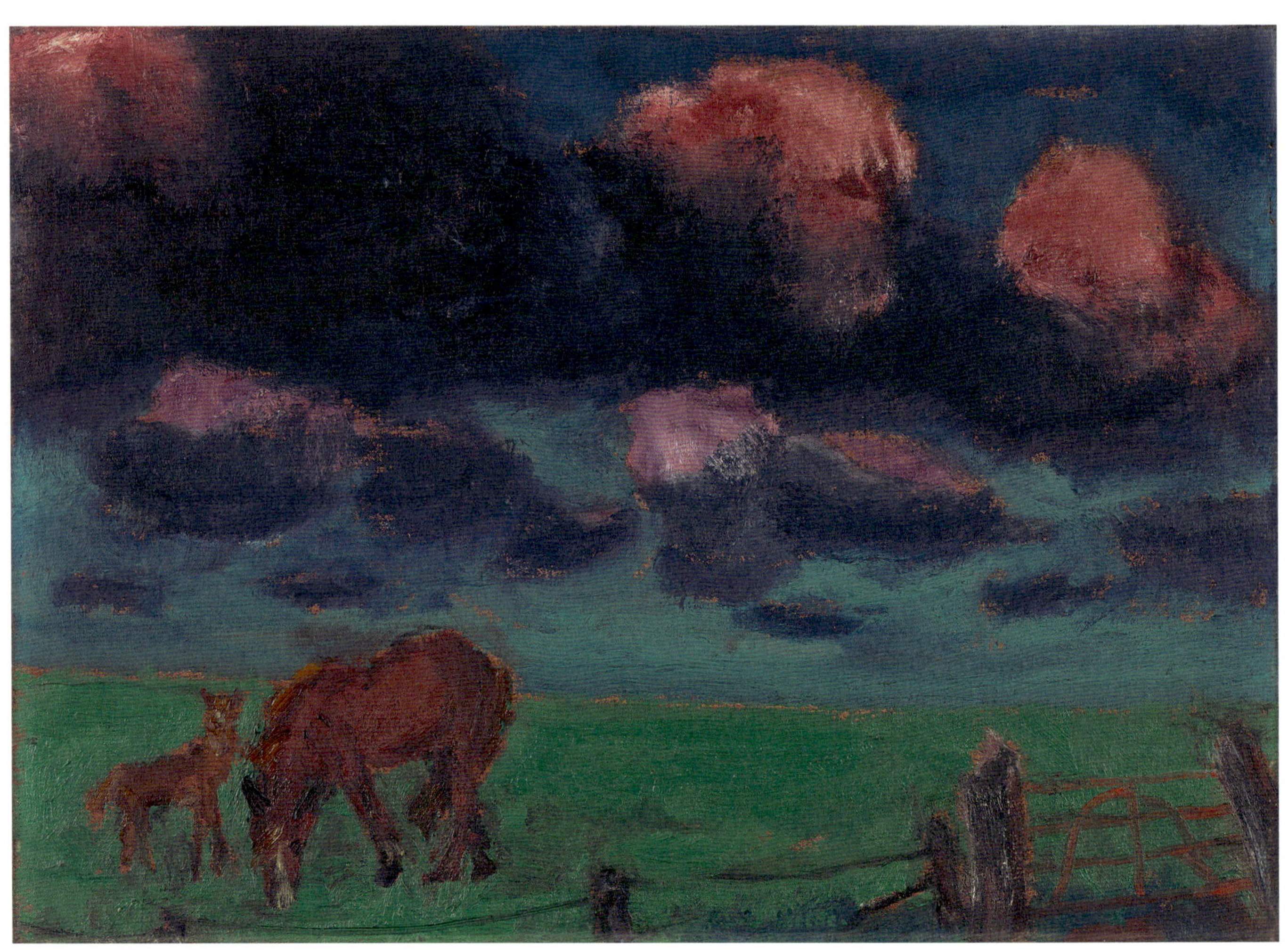

131 | **Emil Nolde**, *Pferd und Füllen* / Horse and Filly, **1915**, Kunsthalle Mannheim

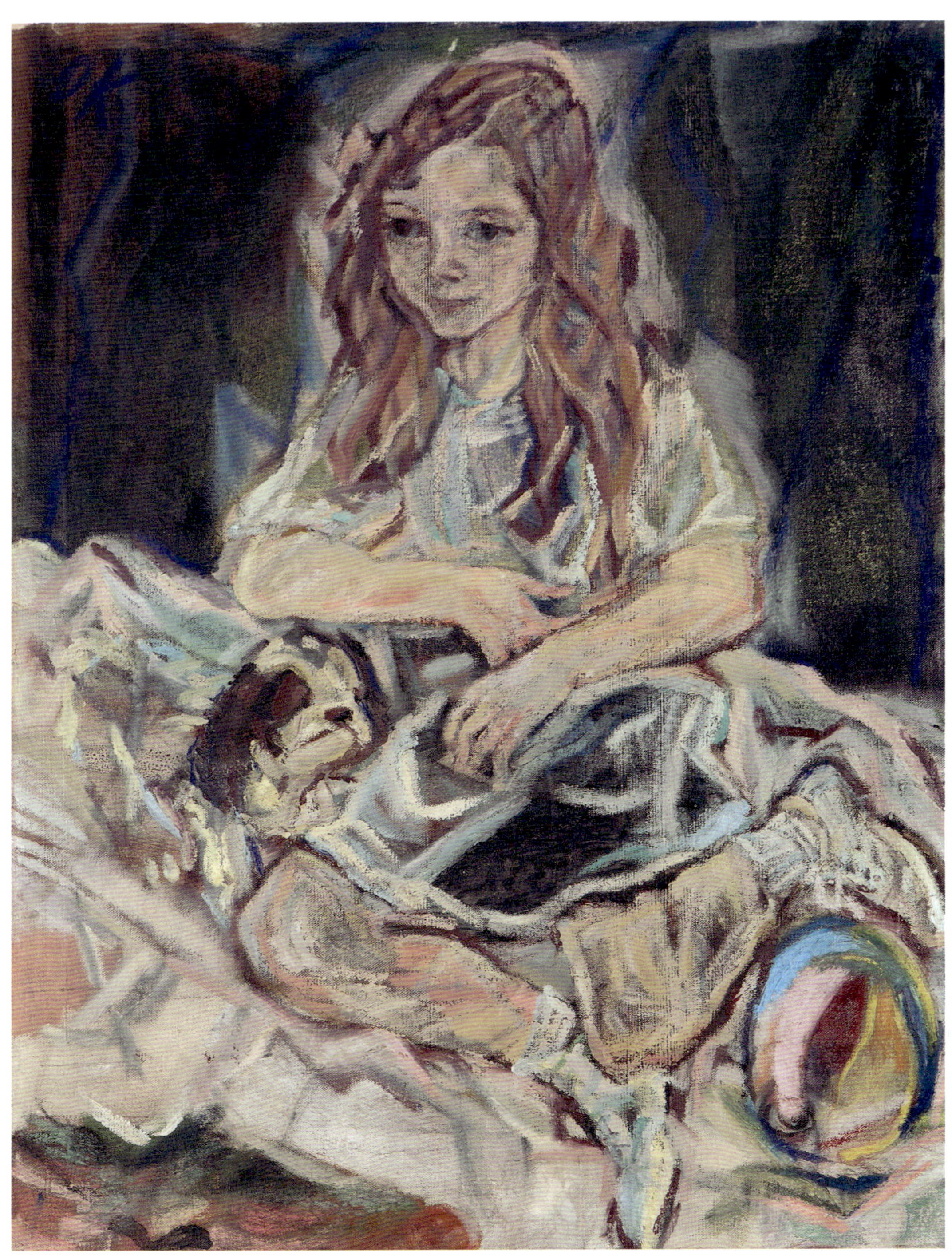

132 | **Oskar Kokoschka,** *Sonia Dungyersky II*, **1912,** Kunsthalle Mannheim

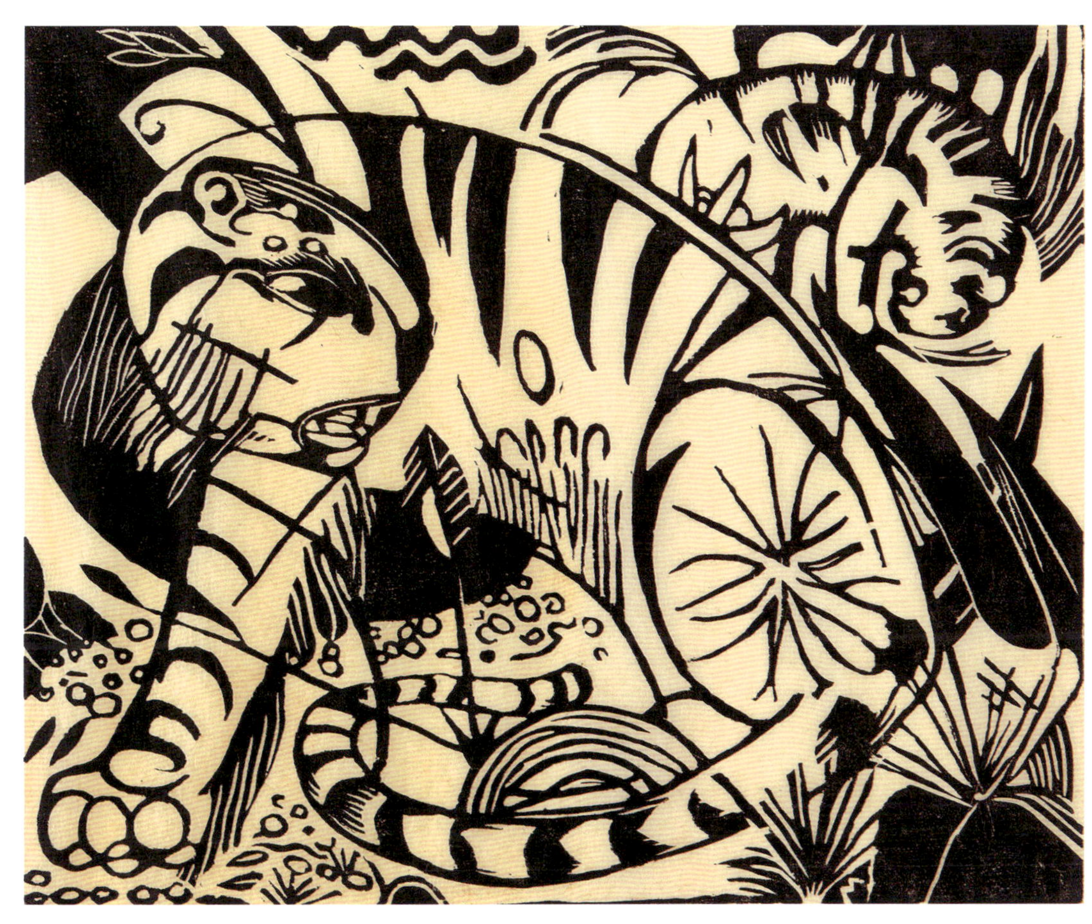

133 | **Franz Marc,** *Tiger,* **1912,** Kunsthalle Mannheim

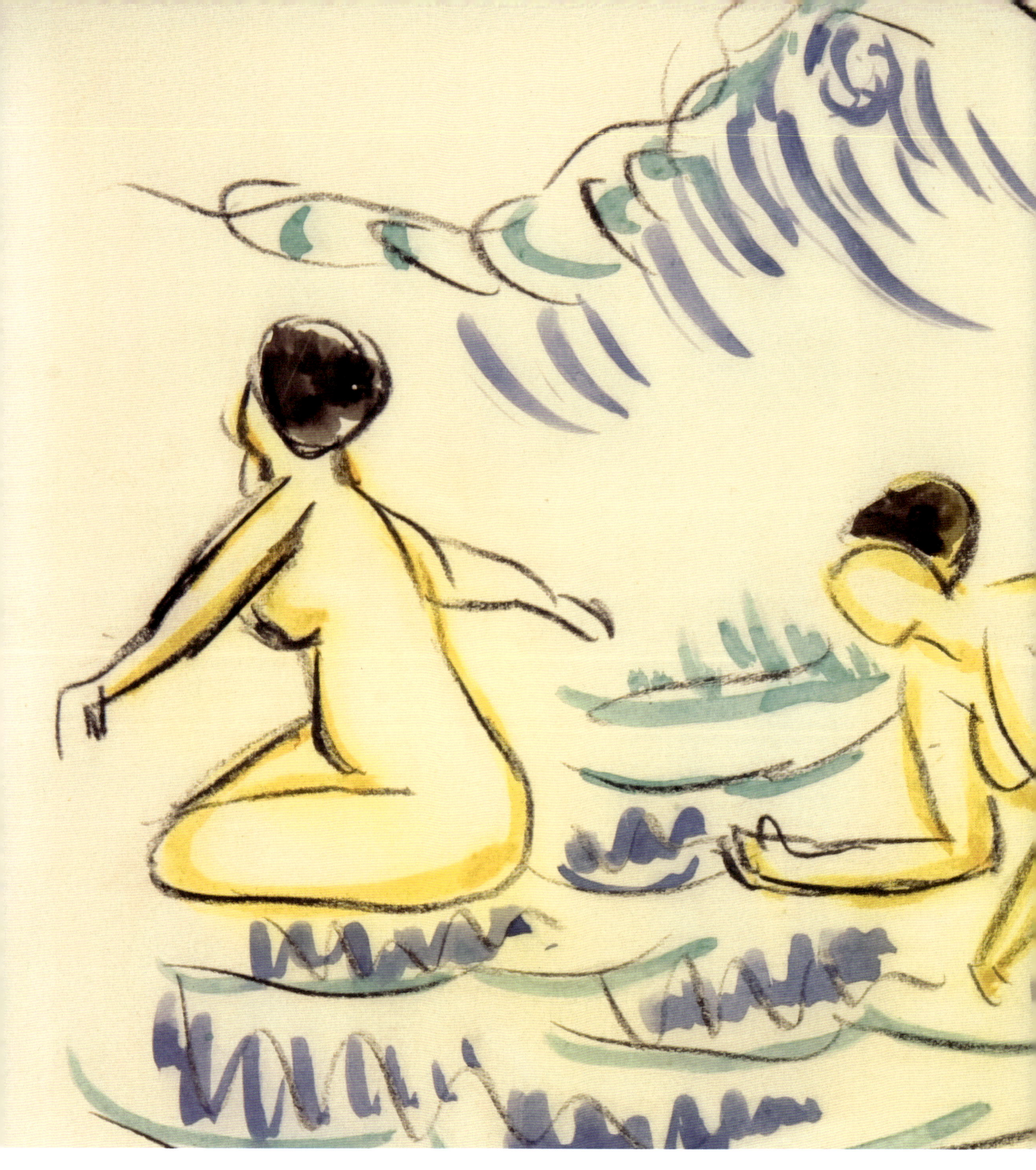

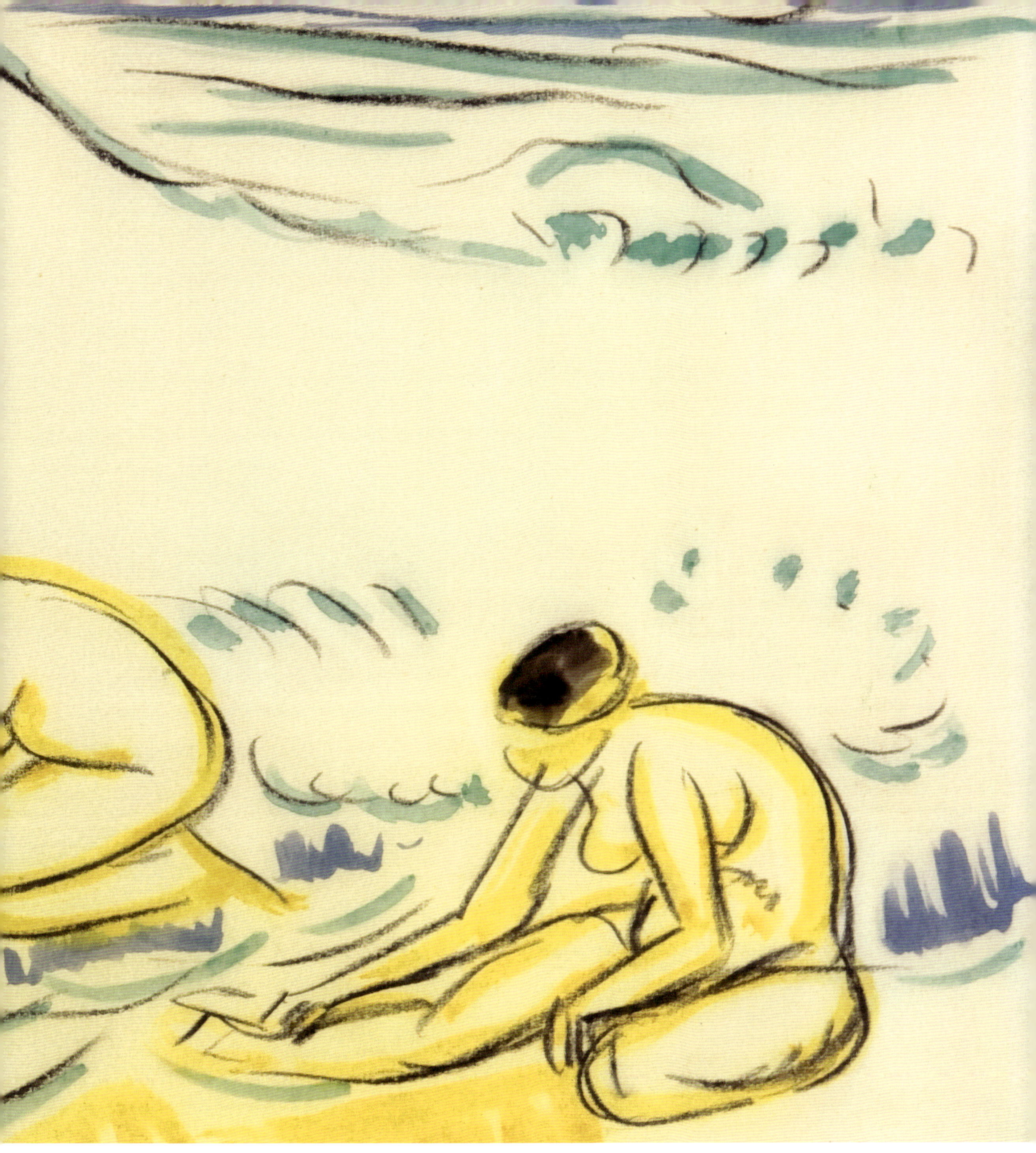

August Babberger 1885–1936
Am Pilatus/Near Mount Pilatus
um/*ca.* 1916
Aquarell/*Watercolor*
36,2 × 46,8 cm
Kunsthalle Mannheim

Ernst Barlach 1870–1938
Frost und Hunger/Frost and Hunger
1906/07
Kohle/*Charcoal*
45 × 57,9 cm
Kunsthalle Mannheim

Ernst Barlach 1870–1938
Hundefängerin/Dogcatcher
1919
Holzschnitt/*Woodcut*
36,6 × 45,2 cm
Kunsthalle Mannheim
Kat./*Cat.* 86 // S./*p.* 176

Ernst Barlach 1870–1938
Kindertod/Child's Grave
1919
Holzschnitt/*Woodcut*
36,3 × 44,7 cm
Kunsthalle Mannheim

Ernst Barlach 1870–1938
Die Kupplerin II/The Matchmaker II
1920
Bronze
46,2 × 21,5 × 21,3 cm
Kunsthalle Mannheim

Ernst Barlach 1870–1938
Der singende Mann/The Singing Man
1928
Bronze
49 × 52 × 33,5 cm
Kunsthalle Mannheim

Max Beckmann 1884–1950
Tannenbaum geht nach New York/
Tannenbaum Goes to New York
1947
Öl auf Leinwand/*Oil on canvas*
95,4 × 35,9 cm

Kunsthalle Mannheim, erworben 2004 mit Mitteln der Kulturstiftung der Länder, der Kulturstiftung der Bundesrepublik Deutschland, des Förderkreises für die Kunsthalle Mannheim e. V., der MVV Energie AG, der Landesbank Baden-Württemberg, der Wilhelm Müller-Stiftung, der Heinrich-Vetter-Stiftung, der Fuchs Petrolub AG, der Mannheimer Versicherungs AG, der Inter-Versicherung sowie zahlreicher privater Sponsoren/*Acquired in 2004 with funds from the Cultural Foundation of the German Federal States, the Cultural Foundation of the Federal Republic of Germany, the Friends of the Kunsthalle Mannheim, MVV Energie AG, the Landesbank Baden-Württemberg, the Wilhelm Müller Foundation, the Heinrich Vetter Foundation, Fuchs Petrolub AG, Mannheimer Versicherungs AG, Inter-Versicherung, and numerous private sponsors*
Kat./*Cat.* 38 //S./*p.* 121

Rudolf Belling 1886–1972
Dreiklang/Triad
1919
Bronze
89,7 × 67,7 × 73 cm
Kunsthalle Mannheim
Kat./*Cat.* 9 // S./*p.* 88

Rudolf Belling 1886–1972
Bildnis des Kunsthändlers Alfred Flechtheim/Portrait of the Art Dealer Alfred Flechtheim
1927
Bronze (evtl. Sandguss)/*Bronze (poss. cast sand)*
18,5 × 11,5 × 12,5 cm
Kunsthalle Mannheim
Kat./*Cat.* 36 // S./*p.* 119

Walther Bötticher 1885–1916
Sie sah den Baum und sie sah, daß es ein lustiger Baum war/She saw the tree and she saw that it was a good tree
1911
Holzschnitt/*Woodcut*
30,7 × 27 cm
Kunsthalle Mannheim

Walther Bötticher 1885–1916
Und sie gab ihm den Apfel und er aß/And she gave him the apple and he ate
1911
Holzschnitt/*Woodcut*
30,5 × 26,8 cm
Kunsthalle Mannheim

Lovis Corinth 1858–1925
Blumen mit chinesischer Pagode/Flowers with Chinese Pagoda
1916
Öl auf Leinwand/*Oil on canvas*

100 × 80 cm
Kunsthalle Mannheim
Kat./*Cat.* 128 // S./*p.* 231

Ernesto de Fiori 1884–1945
Jüngling (Der Leidende)/Youth (The Sufferer)
1911/12
Bronze
183 × 49,5 × 49,5 cm
Kunsthalle Mannheim, Stiftung Sally Falk 1921/*Gift of Sally Falk 1921*
(Kat./*Cat.* 1 // Abb./*Fig.* 30 // S./*p.* 72, 84)

Josef Matthias Eberz 1880–1942
Wandelnder Christus/Christ, Walking
1913
Farbige Kreide, Tusche, Bleistift/*Colored chalk, india ink, pencil*
18,8 × 23,8 cm
Kunsthalle Mannheim
Kat./*Cat.* 32 // S./*p.* 111

Josef Matthias Eberz 1880–1942
Paradies/Paradise
1919
Lithografie/*Lithograph*
50,8 × 36,4 cm
Kunsthalle Mannheim
Kat./*Cat.* 127 // S./*p.* 229

Nicolas Mathieu Eekman 1889–1973
Hohe Stadt/High City
um/*ca.* 1925
Holzschnitt/*Woodcut*
22,9 × 24,4 cm
Kunsthalle Mannheim
Kat./*Cat.* 88 // S./*p.* 176

Franz Emanuel Hecht 1877–nach/*after* 1964
Bergstadt/Mountain Town
um/*ca.* 1918
Holzschnitt/*Woodcut*
25,7 × 33 cm
Kunsthalle Mannheim

Franz Emanuel Hecht 1877–nach/*after* 1964
Kirche/Church
um/*ca.* 1918
Holzschnitt/*Woodcut*
33,1 × 26,1 cm
Kunsthalle Mannheim
Kat./*Cat.* 73 // S./*p.* 163

Franz Emanuel Hecht 1877–nach/*after* 1964
Versuchung des heiligen Antonius/The Temptation of Saint Anthony
um/*ca.* 1918
Holzschnitt/*Woodcut*
30,1 × 30,8 cm
Kunsthalle Mannheim

Erich Heckel 1883–1970
Bärtiger Mann/Bearded Man
1909
Ölkreide/*Oil crayon*
14 × 9 cm
Kunsthalle Mannheim
Kat./*Cat.* 49 // S./*p.* 133

Erich Heckel 1883–1970
Sitzendes Paar/Seated Couple
1909
Ölkreide/*Oil crayon*
9 × 14 cm
Kunsthalle Mannheim
Kat./*Cat.* 45 // S./*p.* 131

Erich Heckel 1883–1970
Fränzi liegend/Fränzi, Reclining
1910
Farbholzschnitt in Schwarz und Rot/*Color woodcut in black and red*
35,7 × 55,9 cm
Kunsthalle Mannheim
Kat./*Cat.* 111 // S./*p.* 213

Erich Heckel 1883–1970;
Ernst Ludwig Kirchner 1880–1938
Zwei Plastiken/Two Sculptures
1910
Tusche, Ölkreide/*India ink, oil crayon*
14 × 9 cm
Kunsthalle Mannheim
Kat./*Cat.* 47 // S./*p.* 132

Erich Heckel 1883–1970
Stralsund
1912
Holzschnitt/*Woodcut*
61 × 51 cm
Kunsthalle Mannheim
Kat./*Cat.* 84 // S./*p.* 175

Erich Heckel 1883–1970
Lesendes Mädchen/Girl Reading
1913
Öl auf Leinwand/*Oil on canvas*
86,5 × 69,5 cm
Sammlung Fuchs-Werle/*Fuchs-Werle Collection*
Kat./*Cat.* 63 // S./*p.* 152

Erich Heckel 1883–1970
Sonnenblumen/Sunflowers
1913
Öl auf Leinwand/*Oil on canvas*
80 × 70 cm
Kunsthalle Mannheim
Kat./*Cat.* 121 // S./*p.* 225

Erich Heckel 1883–1970
Gärtnerei/Nursery
um/*ca.* 1913
47,8 × 34,3 cm
Holzschnitt/*Woodcut*
Kunsthalle Mannheim

Erich Heckel 1883–1970
Kniende am Stein/Woman kneeling
near a rock
um/*ca.* 1913
Holzschnitt/*Woodcut*
61,5 × 51 cm
Kunsthalle Mannheim

Erich Heckel 1883–1970
Beim Vorlesen/Reading Aloud
1914
Holzschnitt/*Woodcut*
42,4 × 31,7 cm
Kunsthalle Mannheim
Kat./*Cat.* 68 // Abb./*fig.* 7 // S./*p.* 21, 161

Erich Heckel 1883–1970
Parksee/Park Lake
um/*ca.* 1914
Kaltnadel/*Drypoint*
35,2 × 30,9 cm
Kunsthalle Mannheim

Erich Heckel 1883–1970
Lärchenweg/Road with Larches
1914
Holzschnitt/*Woodcut*
35,6 × 43,9 cm
Kunsthalle Mannheim
Kat./*Cat.* 72 // S./*p.* 163

Erich Heckel 1883–1970
Bildnis E. H./Portrait of E. H.
1917
Holzschnitt/*Woodcut*
56,3 × 44,2 cm
Kunsthalle Mannheim
Kat./*Cat.* 95 // S./*p.* 185

Erich Heckel 1883–1970
Mädchen am Meer/Girl by the Sea
um / *ca.* 1918
Holzschnitt/*Woodcut*
60,8 × 44,4 cm
Kunsthalle Mannheim

Erich Heckel 1883–1970
Drei Frauen/Three Women
1921
Öl auf Leinwand/*Oil on canvas*
97 × 83 cm
Brücke-Museum Berlin
Kat./*Cat.* 105 // S./*p.* 198

Erich Heckel 1883–1970
Uferlandschaft/Waterside Landscape
1921
Aquarell, Bleistift/*Watercolor, pencil*
50,2 × 67,7 cm
Kunsthalle Mannheim

Erich Heckel 1883–1970
Blaue Berge/Blue Mountains
um/*ca.* 1922
Kreide, aquarelliert/*Chalk, watercolor*

38 × 45,3 cm
Kunsthalle Mannheim

Erich Heckel 1883–1970
Steiles Ufer/Steep Bank
1937
Aquarell, Kreide (schwarz)/*Watercolor,
chalk (black)*
69,5 × 56 cm
Kunsthalle Mannheim
Kat./*Cat.* 118 // S./*p.* 218

Jacoba van Heemskerck 1876–1923
*See mit Boot und Bäumen/
Lake with Boat and Trees*
1915
Holzschnitt, Japanpapier/*Woodcut,
Japan paper*
38 x 50,2 cm
Kunsthalle Mannheim

Jacoba van Heemskerck 1876–1923
See mit Segelbooten/Lake with Sailboats
1915
38,5 × 50,3 cm
Holzschnitt, Japanpapier/*Woodcut,
Japan paper*
Kunsthalle Mannheim
Kat./*Cat.* 130 // S./*p.* 237

Jacoba van Heemskerck 1876–1923
Berge mit See/Mountains and Lake
1916
Holzschnitt, Japanpapier/*Woodcut,
Japan paper*
20 x 27,7 cm
Kunsthalle Mannheim

Jacoba van Heemskerck 1876–1923
*Berg mit zwei Höhlen/
Mountain with Two Caves*
1916
Holzschnitt, Japanpapier/*Woodcut,
Japan paper*
38 × 50,4 cm
Kunsthalle Mannheim

Oswald Herzog 1881–*ca.* 1941
Verzückung/Rapture
1919
Holz, ölversilbert, gelüstert/*Wood, silver
plating, luster*
53 × 42 × 33 cm
Kunsthalle Mannheim, erworben mit
Mitteln der Wilhelm Müller-Stiftung,
Mannheim, 1993/*Acquired with funds
from the Willhelm Müller Foundation,
Mannheim, 1993*
Kat./*Cat.* 8 // S./*p.* 88

Karl Hofer 1878–1955
Javanische Tänzerin/Javanese Dancer
1921
Lithografie/*Lithograph*
44 × 28 cm

Sammlung Geber/*Geber Collection*
Kat./*Cat.* 66 // S./*p.* 155

Alexej von Jawlensky 1864–1941
Sommer in Murnau/Summer in Murnau
1908
Öl auf Karton/*Oil on cardboard*
54 × 65 cm
Sammlung Fuchs-Werle/*Fuchs-Werle
Collection*
Kat./*Cat.* 58 // S./*p.* 147

Alexej von Jawlensky 1864–1941
Küstenstadt/Coastal City
1914
Öl auf Karton/*Oil on cardboard*
49 × 53 cm
Sammlung Fuchs-Werle/*Fuchs-Werle
Collection*
Kat./*Cat.* 59 // S./*p.* 148

Alexej von Jawlensky 1864–1941
*Heilandsgesicht: Wächter/
Face of the Saviour: Guardian*
1920
Öl auf Karton/*Oil on cardboard*
37,5 × 26,5 cm
Kunsthalle Mannheim
Kat./*Cat.* 101 // S./*p.* 189

Alexej von Jawlensky 1864–1941
Femina
1922
Öl auf Karton/*Oil on cardboard*
40 × 31 cm
Sammlung Fuchs-Werle/*Fuchs-Werle
Collection*
Kat./*Cat.* 62 // S./*p.* 151

Ernst Ludwig Kirchner 1880–1938
*Zwei spielende Kinder (Rückseite von
Frauenkirch im Herbst)/
Two Children Playing (verso of Frauenkirch
in the Autumn)*
1909
Öl auf Leinwand/*Oil on canvas*
96 × 86,5 cm
Sammlung Fuchs-Werle/*Fuchs-Werle
Collection*
Kat./*Cat.* 52 // S./*p.* 141

Ernst Ludwig Kirchner 1880–1938
*Marokkaner (Rückseite von Gelbes
Engelufer, Berlin, 1913)/Moroccan Man
(verso of Yellow Engelufer, Berlin, 1913)*
um/*ca.* 1909/10
Öl auf Leinwand/*Oil on canvas*
71,5 × 80,5 cm
Kunsthalle Mannheim
Kat./*Cat.* 75 // Abb./*Fig.* 16 // S./*pp.* 36, 169

Ernst Ludwig Kirchner 1880–1938
*Landschaft: Hügel mit Feldern und
drei Häuser*/Landscape: Hill with Fields
and Three Houses

1911
Tusche, Kreide/*Ink, chalk*
9 × 14,2 cm
Kunsthalle Mannheim
Kat./*Cat.* 48 // S./*p.* 133

Ernst Ludwig Kirchner 1880–1938
*Das elegante Paar/
The Elegant Couple*
1912
Aquarell/*Watercolor*
54,4 × 39,2 cm
Kunsthalle Mannheim
Kat./*Cat.* 89 // S./*p.* 177

Ernst Ludwig Kirchner 1880–1938
*Gelbes Engelufer, Berlin/
Yellow Engelufer, Berlin*
1913
Öl auf Leinwand/*Oil on canvas*
71,5 × 80,5 cm
Kunsthalle Mannheim
Cover // Kat./*Cat.* 74 // S./*p.* 168

Ernst Ludwig Kirchner 1880–1938
*Roter Baum am Strand/
Red Tree at the Beach*
1913
Öl auf Leinwand/*Oil on canvas*
76 × 100 cm
Sammlung Fuchs-Werle/*Fuchs-Werle
Collection*
Kat./*Cat.* 50 // S./*pp.* 78/79, 139

Ernst Ludwig Kirchner 1880–1938
*Zwei Mädchenakte und Ofen/
Two Nude Girls and a Stove*
1914
Radierung/*Etching*
49 × 38,4 cm
Kunsthalle Mannheim

Ernst Ludwig Kirchner 1880–1938
*Segelboote bei Fehmarn/
Sailboats near Fehmarn*
1914
Holzschnitt/*Woodcut*
44,4 × 58,1 cm
Kunsthalle Mannheim
Kat./*Cat.* 71 // S./*p.* 162

Ernst Ludwig Kirchner 1880–1938
Taunuslandschaft/Taunus Landscape
1916
Holzschnitt/*Woodcut*
42,3 × 56,9 cm
Kunsthalle Mannheim
Kat./*Cat.* 77 // S./*p.* 171

Ernst Ludwig Kirchner 1880–1938
*Berghaus mit Gewitterwolke/
Mountain Chalet with Storm Cloud*
1917
Holzschnitt/*Woodcut*
59,1 × 43,2 cm

Kunsthalle Mannheim
Kat./*Cat.* 78 // S./*p.* 171

Ernst Ludwig Kirchner 1880–1938
Bergbach/*Mountain Brook*
1919/20
Öl auf Leinwand/*Oil on canvas*
91 × 152 cm
Kunsthalle Mannheim
Kat./*Cat.* 76 // S./*p.* 170

Ernst Ludwig Kirchner 1880–1938
Frauenkirch im Herbst/
Frauenkirch in the Autumn
1920
Öl auf Leinwand/*Oil on canvas*
96 × 86,5 cm
Sammlung Fuchs-Werle/*Fuchs-Werle*
Collection
Kat./*Cat.* 51 // S./*p.* 140

Ernst Ludwig Kirchner 1880–1938
Bildnis des Malers Albert Müller/
Portrait of the Painter Albert Müller
1924
Holzschnitt, Tonpapier (gelb)/
Woodcut, tone paper (yellow)
60,2 × 36 cm
Kunsthalle Mannheim

Ernst Ludwig Kirchner 1880–1938
Tanzende Frauen im Wald/
Women Dancing in the Forest
um/*ca.* 1925
Farbige Kreide auf gelbem Velinpapier/
Colored chalk on yellow vellum
46,5 × 36,5 cm
Privatsammlung Scherer/*Scherer private*
collection
Kat./*Cat.* 112 // S./*p.* 214

Oskar Kokoschka 1886–1980
Auguste Forel
1910
Öl auf Leinwand/*Oil on canvas*
70 × 58 cm
Kunsthalle Mannheim
Kat./*Cat.* 94 // S./*p.* 184

Oskar Kokoschka 1886–1980
Sonia Dungyersky II
1912
Öl auf Leinwand/*Oil on canvas*
94,6 × 72,5 cm
Kunsthalle Mannheim
Kat./*Cat.* 132 // S./*p.* 243

Oskar Kokoschka 1886–1980
Porträt Herwarth Walden/
Portrait of Herwarth Walden
1913
Faksimiledruck/*Facsimile print*
42,2 × 30,6 cm
Kunsthalle Mannheim

Oskar Kokoschka 1886–1980
Stockholm
1917
Öl auf Leinwand/*Oil on canvas*
95,5 × 125,5 cm
Sammlung Fuchs-Werle/*Fuchs-Werle*
Collection
Kat./*Cat.* 56 // S./*p.* 145

Oskar Kokoschka 1886–1980
Amsterdam, Kloveniersburgwal I
1925
Öl auf Leinwand/*Oil on canvas*
61 × 85 cm
Kunsthalle Mannheim
Kat./*Cat.* 81 // S./*p.* 173

Georg Kolbe 1877–1947
Chinese/*Chinese Man*
1911
Bronze, Sandguss/*Bronze, cast sand*
43,5 × 17,5 × 22 cm
Kunsthalle Mannheim

Georg Kolbe 1877–1947
Stehendes Mädchen/*Standing Girl*
1915
Bronze
181,5 × 52,7 × 40,2 cm
Kunsthalle Mannheim, Leihgabe aus
Privatbesitz seit 2004/*On loan from*
a private collection since 2004

Georg Kolbe 1877–1947
Sklavin/*Female Slave*
1916
Bronze
72,7 × 19,8 × 23,9 cm
Kunsthalle Mannheim, Stiftung Sally
Falk 1921/*Gift of Sally Falk 1921*
Kat./*Cat.* 2 // S./*p.* 85

Georg Kolbe 1877–1947
Porträt des Staatssekretärs
Richard von Kühlmann/
Portrait of State Secretary Richard von
Kühlmann
1917
Bronze, Marmorsockel/*Bronze, marble*
plinth
46,5 × 20,2 × 23,7 cm
Kunsthalle Mannheim

Georg Kolbe 1877–1947
Weibliches Köpfchen/*Female Head*
1918
Bronze auf Marmor- und Holzsockel/
Bronze on marble and wood plinth
28,3 × 14 × 16 cm
Kunsthalle Mannheim

Georg Kolbe 1877–1947
Emporsteigende/*Ascender*
1926
Bronze

158,5 × 51,5 × 39,2 cm
Kunsthalle Mannheim

Wilhelm Laage 1868–1930
Die Lärche/*The Larch*
1914
Holzschnitt/*Woodcut*
47,4 × 61,1 cm
Kunsthalle Mannheim

Otto Lange 1879–1944
Dame in Grün/*Woman in Green Dress*
1918/19
Farbholzschnitt/*Color woodcut*
41 × 31,2 cm
Kunsthalle Mannheim
Kat./*Cat.* 126 // S./*p.* 229

Wilhelm Lehmbruck 1881–1919
Frauenbüste (Büste Frau L.)/
Bust of Woman (Bust Mrs. L.)
1910
Bronze
80,5 × 52,5 × 27 cm
Kunsthalle Mannheim, Stiftung Sally
Falk 1921/*Gift of Sally Falk 1921*
Kat./*Cat.* 21 // S./*p.* 100

Wilhelm Lehmbruck 1881–1919
Große Stehende/*Tall Standing Woman*
1910
Steinguss/*Cast stone*
195 × 56 × 53 cm
Kunsthalle Mannheim
Kat./*Cat.* 17 // S./*p.* 98

Wilhelm Lehmbruck 1881–1919
Mutter und Kind/*Mother and Child*
1910
Radierung, Kaltnadel/*Etching, drypoint*
23,6 × 17,7 cm
Kunsthalle Mannheim

Wilhelm Lehmbruck 1881–1919
Stehender weiblicher Akt/
Standing Female Nude
1910
Rötel und blaue Kreide/*Red and blue*
chalk
60,2 × 42 cm
Kunsthalle Mannheim
Kat./*Cat.* 27 // S./*p.* 103

Wilhelm Lehmbruck 1881–1919
Hagener Torso/*Hagen Torso*
1910/11
Rötlich bemalter Gips/*Reddish-painted*
plaster
70 × 28 × 24 cm
Privatbesitz/*Private collection*, Mannheim
Kat./*Cat.* 7 // S./*p.* 87

Wilhelm Lehmbruck 1881–1919
Kleine Sinnende/
Small Contemplative Woman

1910/11
Terrakotta-Kunststein (Vollguss)/
Terracotta, cast stone (solid casting)
54,2 × 15,8 × 14,5 cm
Kunsthalle Mannheim, Stiftung Sally
Falk 1921/*Gift of Sally Falk 1921*
Kat./*Cat.* 19 // S./*p.* 99

Wilhelm Lehmbruck 1881–1919
Kleiner weiblicher Torso, sog.
*Hagener Torso/*Small Female Torso;
„Torso From Hagen"
1910/11
Bronze
68,6 × 26,2 × 22,7 cm
Kunsthalle Mannheim, Stiftung Sally
Falk 1921/*Gift of Sally Falk 1921*
Kat./*Cat.* 22 // S./*p.* 101

Wilhelm Lehmbruck 1881–1919
Büste der Knienden/
Bust of Kneeling Woman
1911
Rotbraun getönter Zementguss
(Lebzeitguss)/*Reddish-brown cast cement*
(cast during artist's lifetime)
49,8 × 47 × 30 cm
Privatbesitz/*Private collection*, Mannheim
Kat./*Cat.* 6 // S./*p.* 86

Wilhelm Lehmbruck 1881–1919
Badende/*Bathing Woman*
1912
Rötel/*Red chalk*
48,2 × 29,7 cm
Kunsthalle Mannheim

Wilhelm Lehmbruck 1881–1919
Brustbild eines weiblichen Aktes/
Head and Shoulders of a Female Nude
1912
Öl, Tempera und Kreide auf Leinwand/
Oil, tempera, and chalk on canvas
91,8 × 60 cm
Lehmbruck Museum, Duisburg
Kat./*Cat.* 16 // S./*p.* 97

Wilhelm Lehmbruck 1881–1919
Junges Mädchen (Martha)/
Young Girl (Martha)
1912
Öl auf Leinwand/*Oil on canvas*
95,4 × 61,5 cm
Lehmbruck Museum, Duisburg
Kat./*Cat.* 15 // S./*p.* 96

Wilhelm Lehmbruck 1881–1919
Kopf, groß/*Head, Large*
1912
Kaltnadel/*Drypoint*
50 × 32,7 cm
Kunsthalle Mannheim

Wilhelm Lehmbruck 1881–1919
Stehender Frauenakt/
Standing Nude Woman
1912
Blauer Farbstift/*Blue colored pencil*
47,9 × 31,1 cm
Kunsthalle Mannheim
Kat./*Cat.* 26 // S./*p.* 103

Wilhelm Lehmbruck 1881–1919
Badende/Bathing Woman
1913
Kunststein/*Artificial stone*
92 × 33 × 47,4 cm
Kunsthalle Mannheim, Stiftung Sally
Falk 1921/*Gift of Sally Falk 1921*
Kat./*Cat.* 20 // S./*p.* 99

Wilhelm Lehmbruck 1881–1919
Torso der Großen Sinnenden/
Torso of the Tall Contemplative Woman
1913/14
Rötlicher Steinguss auf grauem
Kunststeinsockel/*Reddish cast stone on*
gray cast stone base
125,7 × 46 × 34 cm
Kunsthalle Mannheim, Stiftung Sally
Falk 1921/*Gift of Sally Falk 1921*
Kat./*Cat.* 23 // S./*p.* 101

Wilhelm Lehmbruck 1881–1919
Der tote Mann/The Dead Man
1914
Kaltnadelradierung/*Drypoint*
23,8 × 18 cm
Kunsthalle Mannheim
Kat./*Cat.* 24 // S./*p.* 102

Wilhelm Lehmbruck 1881–1919
Rückblickende/Woman Looking Back
1914
Kunststein/*Cast stone*
92 × 25 × 30 cm
Kurpfälzisches Museum, Heidelberg
Kat./*Cat.* 18 // S./*p.* 98

Wilhelm Lehmbruck 1881–1919
Büste der Großen Sinnenden/
Bust of Large Contemplative Woman
nach/*after* 1914
Gelblicher Hartgips/*Yellowish plaster*
43,5 × 35 × 21,5 cm
Privatbesitz/*Private collection*, Mannheim
Kat./*Cat.* 5 // S./*p.* 86

Wilhelm Lehmbruck 1881–1919
Kopf der Schreitenden/
Head of Striding Woman
nach/*after* 1914
Terrakotta (mit Gips gefüllt)/
Terracotta (filled with plaster)
40 × 28 × 18 cm
Privatbesitz/*Private collection*, Mannheim
Kat./*Cat.* 4 // S./*p.* 86

Wilhelm Lehmbruck 1881–1919
Bildnisbüste Frau Adèle Falk/
Portrait Bust of Adèle Falk
1916
Gips/*Plaster*
66,4 × 50,6 × 29,3 cm
Kunsthalle Mannheim, Schenkung von
Maria Tannenbaum zur Erinnerung an
ihren Mann, Dr. Herbert Tannenbaum,
1960/*Gift of Maria Tannenbaum in mem-*
ory of her husband, Dr. Herbert Tannen-
baum, 1960
Kat./*Cat.* 12 // S./*p.* 94

Wilhelm Lehmbruck 1881–1919
Bildnisbüste Sally Falk/
Portrait Bust of Sally Falk
1916
Gips/*Plaster*
56 × 27 × 27 cm
Kunsthalle Mannheim, Schenkung von
Maria Tannenbaum zur Erinnerung an
ihren Mann, Dr. Herbert Tannenbaum,
1960/*Gift of Maria Tannenbaum in mem-*
ory of her husband, Dr. Herbert Tannen-
baum, 1960
Kat./*Cat.* 11 // S./*p.* 94

Wilhelm Lehmbruck 1881–1919
Frauenkopf/Head of a Woman
1916
Kohle/*Charcoal*
53,1 × 43 cm
Kunsthalle Mannheim
Kat./*Cat.* 25 // S./*p.* 102

Wilhelm Lehmbruck 1881–1919
Frauenkopf nach links/
Head of a Woman Facing Left
1916
Umdrucklithografie nach einer
Kreidezeichnung/*Transfer lithograph of*
a chalk drawing
48,3 × 31,9 cm
Kunsthalle Mannheim

Wilhelm Lehmbruck 1881–1919
Kopfmaske Sally Falk/
Head Mask of Sally Falk
1916
Gips, mit beiger Ölfarbe übermalt/*Plas-*
ter, beige oil paint
65,5 × 21,5 × 25,5 cm
Kunsthalle Mannheim

Wilhelm Lehmbruck 1881–1919
Porträt Sally Falk/Portrait of Sally Falk
1916
Kaltnadel/*Drypoint*
39 × 29,1 cm
Kunsthalle Mannheim
Kat./*Cat.* 13 // S./*p.* 95

Wilhelm Lehmbruck 1881–1919
Porträtkopf Frau F./
Portrait Head of Mrs. F.
1916
Kohle auf Papier/*Charcoal on paper*
33 × 21 cm
Staatsgalerie Stuttgart, Graphische
Sammlung, erworben 2017 aus Mit-
teln der Museumsstiftung Baden-
Württemberg und mit Unterstützung
der Kulturstiftung der Länder, restauriert
im Schauatelier Wüstenrot Stiftung/
Acquired in 2017 with funds from the
Museumsstiftung Baden-Württemberg and
with support from the Cultural Foundation
of the German Federal States, restored in
the studio of the Wüstenrot Foundation
Kat./*Cat.* 14 // S./*p.* 95

August Macke 1887–1914
Afrikanische Landschaft/
African Landscape
1914
Öl auf Leinwand/*Oil on canvas*
45 × 55 cm
Kunsthalle Mannheim
Kat./*Cat.* 79 // S./*p.* 172

Franz Marc 1880–1916
Drei Tiere (Hund, Fuchs und Katze)/
Three Animals (Dog, Fox, and Cat)
1912
Öl und Tempera auf Leinwand/*Oil and*
tempera on canvas
80 × 105 cm
Kunsthalle Mannheim
Kat./*Cat.* 102 // Abb./*Fig.* 29 // S./*pp.* 71, 195

Franz Marc 1880–1916
Tiger
1912
Holzschnitt/*Woodcut*
30,5 × 42,4 cm
Kunsthalle Mannheim
Kat./*Cat.* 133 // S./*p.* 245

Franz Marc 1880–1916
Reitschule nach Ridinger/
Riding School After Ridinger
1913
Holzschnitt/*Woodcut*
33,5 × 41,2 cm
Kunsthalle Mannheim

Ludwig Meidner 1884–1966
Demonstrationszug/Demonstration
1913
Tusche in Feder, laviert, Bleistift,
Deckweiß/*Pen and india ink, wash, pen-*
cil, opaque white
56,5 × 46,1 cm
Kunsthalle Mannheim
Kat./*Cat.* 87 // S./*p.* 176

Ludwig Meidner 1884–1966
Straße mit Menschen/
Street Scene with People
1913
Bleistift/*Pencil*
51,8 × 39,7 cm
Kunsthalle Mannheim
Kat./*Cat.* 85 // S./*p.* 175

Ludwig Meidner 1884–1966
Revolution
1913
Feder, Pinsel, schwarze Tusche, Bleistift,
Deckweiß/*Pen, brush, india ink, pencil,*
opaque white
46,1 × 52,1 cm
Kunsthalle Mannheim

Ludwig Meidner 1884–1966
Bildnis eines Unbekannten/
Portrait of an Unknown Man
1915
Feder in Tusche, Bleistift/*Pen and india*
ink, pencil
50,3 × 42,8 cm
Kunsthalle Mannheim
Kat./*Cat.* 99 // S./*p.* 187

Ludwig Meidner 1884–1966
Bildnis Ernst Cohn-Wiener/
Portrait of Ernst Cohn-Wiener
1916
Feder in Tusche, laviert, über Bleistift/
Pen and india ink, wash, on pencil
61,3 × 47,2 cm
Kunsthalle Mannheim

Moriz Melzer 1877–1966
Frauen in Landschaft/
Women in the Landscape
1911/12
Farbmonotypie (Öl, vom Stein gedruckt)/
Color monotype (oil, printed from stone)
34,2 × 49 cm
Kunsthalle Mannheim
Kat./*Cat.* 119 // S./*p.* 219

George Minne 1866–1941
L'agenouillé à la coquille
(Kniender Jüngling mit Muschel)/
Kneeling Youth with a Shell
1923
Bronze
70,4 × 25 × 47,1 cm
Kunsthalle Mannheim

George Minne 1866–1941
Adolescent à genoux, I.
(Kniender Jüngling I.)/Kneeling Youth I.
1925
Bronze
70,5 × 24,5 × 40 cm
Kunsthalle Mannheim
Kat./*Cat.* 3 // S./*p.* 85

Wilhelm Morgner 1891–1917
Patroklidom in Soest/
The Patroclus Cathedral in Soest
1912
Holzschnitt/*Woodcut*
32 × 23 cm
Sammlung Geber/*Geber Collection*
Kat./*Cat.* 83 // S./*p.* 174

Otto Mueller 1874–1930
Nacktes Mädchen auf Baum/
Naked Girl on Tree
1910
Leimfarbe auf Rupfen/*Distemper on
burlap*
120 × 90 cm
Sammlung Fuchs-Werle/*Fuchs-Werle
Collection*
Kat./*Cat.* 64 // S./*p.* 153

Otto Mueller 1874–1930
Kniender weiblicher Akt/
Kneeling Female Nude
um/*ca.* 1912
Monotypie, aquarelliert/*Monotype,
watercolor*
36 × 45,5 cm
Kunsthalle Mannheim, Miteigentum
der/*Co-owned by the* Ernst von Siemens
Kunststiftung
Kat./*Cat.* 114 // S./*p.* 216

Otto Mueller 1874–1930
Zwei weibliche Akte im Freien/
Two Nude Females in Nature
um/*ca.* 1920
Leimfarbe auf Leinwand/*Distemper
on canvas*
175,5 × 110,2 cm
Kunsthalle Mannheim
Kat./*Cat.* 113 // S./*p.* 215

Otto Mueller 1874–1930
Mädchenkopf/Girl's Head*
1922
Lithografie/*Lithograph*
38,8 × 29 cm
Kunsthalle Mannheim

Otto Mueller 1874–1930
Zwei sitzende Mädchen II/
Two Seated Girls II
1922
Lithografie/*Lithograph*
35,3 × 50,4 cm
Kunsthalle Mannheim
Kat./*Cat.* 115 // S./*p.* 216

Gabriele Münter 1877–1962
Gebirgslandschaft/
Mountain Landscape
1910
Öl auf Malkarton/*Oil on artist's board*
45,5 × 31,5 cm
Sammlung Fuchs-Werle/*Fuchs-Werle*

Collection
Kat./*Cat.* 60 // S./*p.* 149

Emil Nolde 1867–1956
Tingel-Tangel-Sängerin/
Tingel-Tangel Singer
1907
Farblithografie in Schwarz, Gelb und Braun/
Color lithograph in black, yellow and brown
56,4 × 43 cm
Kunsthalle Mannheim

Emil Nolde 1867–1956
Selbstporträt/Self-Portrait*
1908
Radierung, Kaltnadel, Aquatinta/
Etching, drypoint, aquatint
62 × 44,1 cm
Kunsthalle Mannheim
Kat./*Cat.* 98 // S./*p.* 187

Emil Nolde 1867–1956
Segelboot/Sailing Boat*
1910
Holzschnitt/*Woodcut*
36,1 × 47,5 cm
Kunsthalle Mannheim
Kat./*Cat.* 70 // S./*p.* 162

Emil Nolde 1867–1956
Aus dem chinesischen Gewässer/
From Chinese Waters
1913
Aquarell/*Watercolor*
28,6 × 33,4 cm
Kunsthalle Mannheim

Emil Nolde 1867–1956
Chinesischer Kahn/Chinese Rowing Boat*
1913
Aquarell/*Watercolor*
26,6 × 34,8 cm
Kunsthalle Mannheim

Emil Nolde 1867–1956
Chinesisches Segelboot/
Chinese Sailboat
1913
Aquarell/*Watercolor*
24,5 × 28,2 cm
Kunsthalle Mannheim

Emil Nolde 1867–1956
Madonna mit Blumen/
Virgin with Flowers
1915
Öl auf Leinwand/*Oil on canvas*
71,5 × 57,8 cm
Simu Stiftung/*Simu Foundation*
Kat./*Cat.* 39 // S./*p.* 122

Emil Nolde 1867–1956
Pferd und Füllen/Horse and Filly*
1915
Öl auf Leinwand/*Oil on canvas*

73,6 × 101 cm
Kunsthalle Mannheim
Kat./*Cat.* 131 // S./*p.* 242

Emil Nolde 1867–1956
Südseelandschaft II/
Landscape from the South Sea II
1915
Öl auf Leinwand/*Oil on canvas*
71,7 × 86,3 cm
Privatstiftung/*Private foundation*
Kat./*Cat.* 123 // S./*p.* 227

Emil Nolde 1867–1956
Tulpen/Tulips*
1915
Öl auf Leinwand/*Oil on canvas*
73 × 88 cm
Museum Ludwig, Schenkung Dr. Werner
Schulz, Köln/*Gift of Dr. Werner Schulz,
Cologne* 1964
Kat./*Cat.* 103 // S./*p.* 196

Emil Nolde 1867–1956
Vorabend (Marschlandschaft)/
Twilight (Marshy Landscape)
1916
Öl auf Leinwand/*Oil on canvas*
73,4 × 100,9 cm
Kunstmuseum Basel, Inv. 1751, mit einem
Sonderkredit der Basler Regierung
erworben 1939/*Acquired in 1939 with
a special loan from the government of
Basel*
Kat./*Cat.* 106 // S./*p.* 199

Emil Nolde 1867–1956
Hallighaus/Hallig House*
1916–1918
Aquarell/*Watercolor*
35,4 × 48,4 cm
Kunsthalle Mannheim

Emil Nolde 1867–1956
Figuren und Georginen/
Figures and Dahlias
1919
Öl auf Leinwand/*Oil on canvas*
88 × 73 cm
Statens Museum for Kunst, *National Gallery
of Denmark*, Kopenhagen/*Copenhagen*
Kat./*Cat.* 104 // S./*p.* 197

Emil Nolde 1867–1956
Kopfjäger und Georginen/
Headhunter and Dahlias
1920
Öl auf Leinwand/*Oil on canvas*
67 × 52 cm
Privatbesitz/*Private collection*
Kat./*Cat.* 40 // S./*p.* 123

Emil Nolde 1867–1956
Landschaft am Nachmittag/
Landscape in the Afternoon

1920
Öl auf Leinwand/*Oil on canvas*
73,5 × 100 cm
Sammlung Fuchs-Werle/*Fuchs-Werle
Collection*
Kat./*Cat.* 57 // S./*p.* 146

Emil Nolde 1867–1956
***Feuerlilien und dunkler Ritter-
sporn/***Tiger Lilies and Dark Larkspur*
1925
Öl auf Leinwand/*Oil on canvas*
73 × 88 cm
Kunsthalle Mannheim
Kat./*Cat.* 92 // S./*p.* 178

Emil Nolde 1867–1956
Blumen/Flowers*
um/*ca.* 1926
Aquarell/*Watercolor*
37,9 × 49,1 cm
Kunsthalle Mannheim
Kat./*Cat.* 91 // S./*p.* 178

Emil Nolde 1867–1956
Ferne Mädchen/Girls from Afar*
1947
Öl auf Leinwand/*Oil on canvas*
68,6 × 89,6 cm
Kunsthalle Mannheim
Kat./*Cat.* 122 // S./*p.* 226

Wilfried Otto 1901–1989
Madonna/Virgin*
1918
Holzschnitt, aquarelliert/*Woodcut,
watercolor*
27,8 × 22 cm
Kunsthalle Mannheim
Kat./*Cat.* 35 // S./*p.* 113

Max Pechstein 1881–1955
Im Restaurant/In the Restaurant*
1909
Tusche, Ölkreide/*India ink, oil crayon*
9 × 14 cm
Kunsthalle Mannheim
Kat./*Cat.* 46 // S./*p.* 132

Max Pechstein 1881–1955
Landschaft/Landscape*
1909
Ölkreide , Tusche/*Oil crayon, india ink*
17,6 × 26,3 cm
Kunsthalle Mannheim

Max Pechstein 1881–1955
Dame mit Hut/Lady with Hat*
1910
Tusche, laviert, Ölkreide/*India ink,
wash, oil crayon*
14 × 9 cm
Kunsthalle Mannheim
Kat./*Cat.* 42 // S./*p.* 130

Max Pechstein 1881–1955
Früher Morgen/Early Morning
1911
Öl auf Leinwand/*Oil on canvas*
75 × 100 cm
Sammlung Fuchs-Werle/*Fuchs-Werle
Collection*
Kat./*Cat.* 61 // S./*p.* 150

Max Pechstein 1881–1955
Abend/Evening
1912
Pinselzeichnung in Schwarz/*Brushwork
(black)*
35,1 × 44,7 cm
Kunsthalle Mannheim

Max Pechstein 1881–1955
Akrobaten I/Acrobats I
1912
Holzschnitt, aquarelliert/*Woodcut,
watercolor*
51,6 × 36,4 cm
Kunsthalle Mannheim
Kat./*Cat.* 125 // S./*p.* 228

Max Pechstein 1881–1955
Akrobaten III/Acrobats III
1912
Holzschnitt, aquarelliert/*Woodcut,
watercolor*
36,2 × 51,3 cm
Kunsthalle Mannheim
Kat./*Cat.* 124 // S./*p.* 228

Max Pechstein 1881–1955
Am Meer II/By the Sea II
1912
Kaltnadel/*Drypoint*
47,8 × 36,8 cm
Kunsthalle Mannheim
Kat./*Cat.* 117 // S./*p.* 217

Max Pechstein 1881–1955
*Betrunkene Fischer II/
Drunken Fishermen II*
1912
Kaltnadel/*Drypoint*
47,8 × 36,5 cm
Kunsthalle Mannheim

Max Pechstein 1881–1955
Fischer/Fishermen
1912
Holzschnitt, Aquarell, Gouache (in
Blau und Ocker)/*Woodcut, watercolor,
gouache (blue and ocher)*
38 × 58,2 cm
Kunsthalle Mannheim

Max Pechstein 1881–1955
*Segelschiffe mit Baum/
Sailboats with Tree*
1912

Bleistift, aquarelliert/*Pencil, watercolor*
36,5 × 26,9 cm
Kunsthalle Mannheim

Max Pechstein 1881–1955
*Sitzende und kauernde nackte Frauen/
Seated and Crouching Naked Women*
1912
Schwarze Kreide, Aquarell/*Chalk (black),
watercolor*
26,8 × 36,2 cm
Kunsthalle Mannheim
Kat./*Cat.* 116 // S./*pp.* 217, 246/247

Max Pechstein 1881–1955
*Stehende Frau mit Fächer/
Standing Woman with Fan*
1912
Bleistift, aquarelliert/*Pencil, watercolor*
69,5 × 49,2 cm
Kunsthalle Mannheim
Kat./*Cat.* 90 // S./*p.* 177

Max Pechstein 1881–1955
*Stilleben mit Fischen/
Still Life with Fish*
1912
Bleistift, aquarelliert/*Pencil, watercolour*
47 × 58 cm
Kunsthalle Mannheim

Max Pechstein 1881–1955
Tanzende Frauen/Dancing Women
1912
Tusche, laviert/*Indian ink, washed*
35,3 × 45,2 cm
Kunsthalle Mannheim

Max Pechstein 1881–1955
*Stillleben: Figur und Blumen/
Still Life: Figure and Flowers*
1917
Öl auf Leinwand/*Oil on canvas*
80,2 × 70,8 cm
Kunsthalle Mannheim
Kat./*Cat.* 120 // S./*p.* 224

Max Pechstein 1881–1955
Rauchende/Woman Smoking
1918
Kreidelithografie/*Chalk lithograph*
50,8 × 36,6 cm
Kunsthalle Mannheim
Kat./*Cat.* 100 // S./*p.* 188

Max Pechstein 1881–1955
Sitzender Akt/Seated Nude
1918
Holzschnitt/*Woodcut*
61,3 × 48,7 cm
Kunsthalle Mannheim
Kat./*Cat.* 69 // S./*p.* 161

Max Pechstein 1881–1955
Sommermorgen/Summer Morning

1919
Öl auf Leinwand/*Oil on canvas*
80 × 100 cm
Sammlung Fuchs-Werle/*Fuchs-Werle
Collection*
Kat./*Cat.* 55 // S./*p.* 144

Max Pechstein 1881–1955
Fischerkopf IX/Head of a Fisherman IX
1921
Holzschnitt/*Woodcut*
71 × 55,5 cm
Kunsthalle Mannheim

Max Pechstein 1881–1955
*Bauerngehöft – Spätsommer/
Farmstead–Late Summer*
o. J./*n. d.*
Öl auf Leinwand/*Oil on canvas*
70 × 80,4 cm
Privatbesitz/*Private collection*, Mannheim
Kat./*Cat.* 65 // S./*p.* 154

Christian Rohlfs 1849–1938
Bergpredigt/Sermon on the Mount
1916
Holzschnitt/*Woodcut*
44 × 41,8 cm
Kunsthalle Mannheim
Kat./*Cat.* 34 // S./*p.* 113

Christian Rohlfs 1849–1938
*Petriturm in Soest/
The Tower of St. Peter's Church in Soest*
1918
Öl und Tempera auf Leinwand/*Oil and
tempera on canvas*
100 × 61 cm
Kunsthalle Mannheim
Kat./*Cat.* 82 // S./*p.* 174

Hermann Scherer 1893–1927
Tanzende/Dancing Couple
1925
Arvenholz/*Swiss pinewood*
98,5 × 41,5 × 40 cm
Kunsthalle Mannheim, erworben mit
Mitteln des Museums-Shops 2001 /
*Acquired with funds from the Museum
Shop 2001*
Kat./*Cat.* 10 // S./*p.* 89

Hermann Scherer 1893–1927
*Männliches Bildnis (Selbstpor-
trät)/Portrait of a Man (Self-Portrait)*
um/*ca.* 1925
Holzschnitt/*Woodcut*
71 × 51,8 cm
Kunsthalle Mannheim

Hilde Schindler Lebensdaten unbekannt /
Life dates unknown
Der Krieg/The War
1915
Holzschnitt/*Woodcut*

39,4 × 31,3 cm
Kunsthalle Mannheim
Kat./*Cat.* 33 // S./*p.* 112

Karl Schmidt-Rottluff 1884–1976
Der rote Weg/The Red Road
1907
Öl auf Leinwand/*Oil on canvas*
77 × 77 cm
Sammlung Fuchs-Werle/*Fuchs-Werle
Collection*
Kat./*Cat.* 53 // S./*p.* 142

Karl Schmidt-Rottluff 1884–1976
*Bildnis (vermutlich Rosa Schapire)/
Portrait (presumably Rosa Schapire)*
1911
Ölpastellkreide, Bleistift/*Oil pastel
chalk, pencil*
14 × 9,2 cm
Kunsthalle Mannheim
Kat./*Cat.* 44 // S./*p.* 131

Karl Schmidt-Rottluff 1884–1976
Villa mit Turm/Villa with Tower
1912
Öl auf Leinwand/*Oil on canvas*
85 × 76,5 cm
Kunsthalle Mannheim, Leihgabe des
Landes Baden-Württemberg seit 1962/
*On loan from the State of Baden-
Württemberg since 1962*
Kat./*Cat.* 80 // S./*p.* 172

Karl Schmidt-Rottluff 1884–1976
Die Sonne/The Sun
1914
Holzschnitt/*Woodcut*
50 × 62,2 cm
Kunsthalle Mannheim

Karl Schmidt-Rottluff 1884–1976
Katzen II/Cats II
1914
Holzschnitt/*Woodcut*
57,4 × 68,2 cm
Kunsthalle Mannheim
Kat./*Cat.* 67 // S./*p.* 160

Karl Schmidt-Rottluff 1884–1976
*Bildnis R. S. (Rosa Schapire)/
Portrait of R. S. (Rosa Schapire)*
1915
Holzschnitt in Schwarz auf Velinpapier
(Druckstock: Fichte)/*Woodcut in black
ink on vellum (block: spruce)*
69,9 × 51,6 cm
Städel Museum, Frankfurt am Main
Kat./*Cat.* 41 // S./*p.* 129

Schmidt-Rottluff 1884–1976
Gang nach Emmaus/Road to Emmaus
1918
Holzschnitt/*Woodcut*
51 × 65,9 cm

Kunsthalle Mannheim
Kat./*Cat.* 30 // S./*p.* 110

Karl Schmidt-Rottluff 1884–1976
Kristus/Christ
1918
Holzschnitt/*Woodcut*
66,6 × 51,6 cm
Kunsthalle Mannheim
Kat./*Cat.* 29 // S./*p.* 109

Karl Schmidt-Rottluff 1884–1976
Kristus und die Ehebrecherin/
Christ and the Adulteress
1918
Holzschnitt/*Woodcut*
50,7 × 65,9 cm
Kunsthalle Mannheim

Karl Schmidt-Rottluff 1884–1976
Kuss in Liebe/Kiss in Love
1918
Holzschnitt/*Woodcut*
66,7 × 51,7 cm
Kunsthalle Mannheim

Karl Schmidt-Rottluff 1884–1976
Maria
1918
Holzschnitt/*Woodcut*
66,7 × 51,7 cm
Kunsthalle Mannheim

Karl Schmidt-Rottluff 1884–1976
Petri Fischzug/
Miraculous Catch of Fishes
1918
Holzschnitt/*Woodcut*
51 × 65,9 cm
Kunsthalle Mannheim
Kat./*Cat.* 31 // S./*p.* 110

Karl Schmidt-Rottluff 1884–1976
Landschaft mit früher Sonne/
Landscape with Early Sun
1919
Öl auf Leinwand/*Oil on canvas*
87 × 100 cm
Sammlung Fuchs-Werle/*Fuchs-Werle
Collection*
Kat./*Cat.* 54 // S./*p.* 143

Karl Schmidt-Rottluff 1884–1976
Drei am Meer/
Three Figures by the Sea
1920
Kreide/*Chalk*
10,3 × 15,6 cm
Kunsthalle Mannheim
Kat./*Cat.* 43 // S./*p.* 130

Karl Schmidt-Rottluff 1884–1976
Sommerliches Fenster/
Window in Summer
1937

Öl auf Leinwand/*Oil on canvas*
113 × 87,7 cm
Kunsthalle Mannheim
Kat./*Cat.* 93 // S./*p.* 179

Richard Seewald 1889–1976
Kanaan/Canaan
1915
Holzschnitt, koloriert/*Woodcut, colored*
31,6 × 24,5 cm
Kunsthalle Mannheim

Renée Sintenis 1888–1965
Porträt des Dichters Ernst Toller/
Portrait of the Poet Ernst Toller
1926
Stucco, Steinsockel/*Stucco, stone base*
42,5 × 20,7 × 19,2 cm
Kunsthalle Mannheim

Milly Steger 1881–1948
Karyatide/Caryatid
1917
Lithografie/*Lithograph*
28,2 × 21,5 cm
Kunsthalle Mannheim
Kat./*Cat.* 109 // S./*p.* 206

Milly Steger 1881–1948
Frauenbildnis/Portrait of a Woman
1920
Bronze, Holzsockel/*Bronze, wooden
plinth*
21,5 × 12,5 × 21,5 cm
Kunsthalle Mannheim, Schenkung von
William Landmann, Toronto, 1973/
Gift of William Landmann, Toronto, 1973
Kat./*Cat.* 107 // S./*p.* 204

Milly Steger 1881–1948
Weibung/Womanhood
1921
Kreidelithografie/*Chalk lithograph*
45,2 × 35,3 cm
Kunsthalle Mannheim
Kat./*Cat.* 110 // S./*p.* 207

Milly Steger 1881–1948
Nordische Gotik/Nordic Gothic
um/*ca.* 1932
Bleistift/*Pencil*
47,8 × 38,5 cm
Kunsthalle Mannheim
Kat./*Cat.* 108 // S./*p.* 205

Karl Thylmann 1888–1916
Ruhe auf der Flucht/Rest on the Flight
o. J./*n. d.*
Holzschnitt/*Woodcut*
32 × 25,5 cm
Kunsthalle Mannheim

Maria Uhden 1892–1918
Hirten/Shepherds
1917

Lithografie/*Lithograph*
33,2 × 24,8 cm
Kunsthalle Mannheim
Kat./*Cat.* 129 // S./*p.* 236

Christoph Voll 1897–1939
Kinder aus der Baracke/
Children from the Shack
um/*ca.* 1924
Holzschnitt/*Woodcut*
51 × 38,4 cm
Kunsthalle Mannheim

William Wauer 1866–1962
Lebendiges Eisen/Vivid Iron
1916
Gusseisen/*Cast iron*
24,5 × 9,5 × 9,8 cm
Kunsthalle Mannheim

Josef Weisz 1894–1969
Altarbild (Triptychon)/
Altarpiece (Triptych)
1915
Holzschnitt/*Woodcut*
31 × 42,5 cm
Kunsthalle Mannheim
Kat./*Cat.* 28 // S./*p.* 108

Wladimir von Zabotin 1884–1967
Porträt Maria und Herbert Tannenbaum/
Portrait of Maria and Herbert Tannenbaum
1920/21
Öl auf Leinwand/*Oil on canvas*
60 × 73,3 cm
Kunsthalle Mannheim, Geschenk von
Beatrice Newman, geb. Tannenbaum,
2001/*Gift of Beatrice Newman (née
Tannenbaum), 2001*
Kat./*Cat.* 37 // S./*p.* 120

Max Zachmann 1892–1917
Porträt eines bärtigen Mannes/
Portrait of a Bearded Man
vor/*before* 1915
Tusche, laviert/*India ink, wash*
36,6 × 31,6 cm
Kunsthalle Mannheim

Karl Friedrich Zähringer 1886–1923
Thalfahrt/Return from alpine pasture
1918
Holzschnitt/*Woodcut*
55,4 × 40,2 cm
Kunsthalle Mannheim

Karl Friedrich Zähringer 1886–1923
*Bauernköpfe (Mappe mit sieben
Holzschnitten)*/Peasant Heads series
(portfolio with seven woodcuts)
1920
Holzschnitt/*Woodcut*
7 Blätter, je/*7 sheets, each* 58 × 42 cm
Kunsthalle Mannheim
Kat./*Cat.* 97 // S./*p.* 186

Karl Friedrich Zähringer 1886–1923
*Selbstporträt mit Holzstichel, aus der
Serie Bauernköpfe (Mappe mit sieben
Holzschnitten)*/Self-Portrait with Wood
Carving Knife, from the Peasant Heads
series (portfolio with seven woodcuts)
1920
Holzschnitt/*Woodcut*
58 × 42 cm
Kunsthalle Mannheim
Kat./*Cat.* 96 // S./*p.* 186

Bildnachweis / Photo Credits

Die Bildvorlagen stammen, wenn nicht anders angegeben, von den Eigentümer*innen der Werke. / *Unless otherwise stated, the images were provided by the owners of the artworks.*

2025 © Photo Scala, Florence / Digital image, The Museum of Modern Art, New York/Scala, Florence / Credit Abby Aldrich Rockefeller Fund, Object number 268.1939 (Abb./*Fig.* 4 // S./p. 19)

bpk / Kunstmuseum Stuttgart, Sammlung Rudolf und Bertha Frank im Kunstmuseum Stuttgart (Abb./*Fig.* 14 // S./p. 32)

bpk / Privatsammlung/*Private collection* (Abb./*Fig.* 10 // S./p. 27)

bpk / Städel Museum (Kat./*Cat.* 41 // S./p. 129)

Brücke-Museum, Foto/*Photo:* Nick Ash (Kat./*Cat.* 105 // S./p. 198)

Courtesy National Gallery of Art, Washington / Credit Line Andrew W. Mellon Fund, Accession Number 1974.49.1 - https://www.nga.gov/ - Creative Commons CC0 (Abb./*Fig.* 5 // S./p. 19)

Courtesy Collection Walker Art Center, Minneapolis, Gift of the T.B. Walker Foundation, Gilbert M. Walker Fund, 1942 (Abb./*Fig.* 6 // S./p. 20)

Foto/*Photo:* Bernd Kirtz (Kat./*Cat.* 15 // S./p. 96) (Kat./*Cat.* 16 // S./p. 97)

Foto/*Photo:* Historisches Archiv der Stadt Köln mit Rheinischem Bildarchiv, Sabrina Walz, rba_d065211_01 (Kat./*Cat.* 103 // S./p. 196)

Foto/*Photo:* © Staatsgalerie Stuttgart (Kat./*Cat.* 14 // S./p. 95)

Kurpfälzisches Museum Heidelberg, Foto/*Photo:* K. Gattner (Kat./*Cat.* 18 // S./p. 98)

© Fotos/*Photos:* Thomas Henne, HENNE FOTODESIGN, Mannheim (Kat./*Cat.* 50 // S./p. 78/79, 139) (Kat./*Cat.* 51 // S./p. 140) (Kat./*Cat.* 52 // S./p. 141) (Kat./*Cat.* 53 // S./p. 142) (Kat./*Cat.* 54 // S./p. 143) (Kat./*Cat.* 55 // S./p. 144) (Kat./*Cat.* 56 // S./p. 145) (Kat./*Cat.* 57 // S./p. 146) (Kat./*Cat.* 58 // S./p. 147) (Kat./*Cat.* 59 // S./p. 148) (Kat./*Cat.* 60 // S./p. 149) (Kat./*Cat.* 61 // S./p. 150) (Kat./*Cat.* 62 // S./p. 151) (Kat./*Cat.* 63 // S./p. 152) (Kat./*Cat.* 64 // S./p. 153)

Fotostudio Bartsch, Karen Bartsch, Berlin (Kat./*Cat.* 39 // S./p. 122) (Kat./*Cat.* 123 // S./p. 227)

Grisebach GmbH (Kat./*Cat.* 40 // S./p. 123)

Kunsthalle Mannheim (Abb./*Fig.* 15 // S./p. 35) (Kat./*Cat.* 13 // S./p. 95) (Kat./*Cat.* 24–25 // S./p. 102) (Kat./*Cat.* 27 // S./p. 103) (Kat./*Cat.* 28 // S./p. 108) (Kat./*Cat.* 34 // S./p. 113) (Kat./*Cat.* 37 // S./p. 120) (Kat./*Cat.* 38 // S./p. 121) (Kat./*Cat.* 45 // S./p. 131) (Kat./*Cat.* 46 // S./p. 132) (Kat./*Cat.* 48 // S./p. 133) (Kat./*Cat.* 71 // S./p. 162) (Kat./*Cat.* 73 // S./p. 163) (Kat./*Cat.* 77 // S./p. 171) (Kat./*Cat.* 79 // S./p. 172) (Kat./*Cat.* 93 // S./p. 179) (Kat./*Cat.* 109 // S./p. 206) (Kat./*Cat.* 110 // S./p. 207) (Kat./*Cat.* 114 // S./p. 216) (Kat./*Cat.* 129 // S./p. 236)

Kunsthalle Mannheim, Bildarchiv/*Image archive* (S./p. 10) (Abb./*Fig.* 9 // S./p. 26) (Abb./*Fig.* 20 // S./p. 40 [Detail], 46) (Abb./*Fig.* 32 // S./p. 106) (Abb./*Fig.* 33 // S./p. 107) (Abb./*Fig.* 34 // S./p. 158) (Abb./*Fig.* 37 // S./p. 192) (Abb./*Fig.* 38 // S./p. 193)

Kunsthalle Mannheim / Foto/*Photo:* Cem Yücetas (Cover) (Abb./*Fig.* 1 // S./p. 14) (Abb./*Fig.* 7 // S./p. 21) (Abb./*Fig.* 16 // S./p. 36) (Abb./*Fig.* 29 // S./p. 71) (Kat./*Cat.* 1 // Abb./*Fig.* 30 // S./p. 72, 84) (Kat./*Cat.* 2–3 // S./p. 85) (Kat./*Cat.* 8–9 // S./p. 88) (Kat./*Cat.* 10 // S./p. 89) (Kat./*Cat.* 11–12 // S./p. 94) (Kat./*Cat.* 17 // S./p. 98) (Kat./*Cat.* 19–20 // S./p. 99) (Kat./*Cat.* 21 // S./p. 100) (Kat./*Cat.* 22–23 // S./p. 101) (Kat./*Cat.* 26 // S./p. 103) (Kat./*Cat.* 29 // S./p. 109) (Kat./*Cat.* 30–31 // S./p. 110) (Kat./*Cat.* 32 // S./p. 111) (Kat./*Cat.* 33 // S./p. 112) (Kat./*Cat.* 35 // S./p. 113) (Kat./*Cat.* 36 // S./p. 119) (Kat./*Cat.* 42–43 // S./p. 130) (Kat./*Cat.* 44 // S./p. 131) (Kat./*Cat.* 47 // S./p. 132) (Kat./*Cat.* 49 // S./p. 133) (Kat./*Cat.* 67 // S./p. 160) (Kat./*Cat.* 68–69 // S./p. 161) (Kat./*Cat.* 70 // S./p. 162) (Kat./*Cat.* 72 // S./p. 163) (Kat./*Cat.* 74 // S./p. 168) (Kat./*Cat.* 75 // Abb./*Fig.* 16 // S./p. 36, 169) (Kat./*Cat.* 76 // S./p. 170) (Kat./*Cat.* 78 // S./p. 171) (Kat./*Cat.* 81 // S./p. 173) (Kat./*Cat.* 82 // S./p. 174) (Kat./*Cat.* 84–85 // S./p. 175) (Kat./*Cat.* 86–88 // S./p. 176) (Kat./*Cat.* 89–90 // S./p. 177) (Kat./*Cat.* 91–92 // S./p. 178) (Kat./*Cat.* 94 // S./p. 184) (Kat./*Cat.* 95 // S./p. 185) (Kat./*Cat.* 98–99 // S./p. 187) (Kat./*Cat.* 100 // S./p. 188) (Kat./*Cat.* 101 // S./p. 189) (Kat./*Cat.* 102 // Abb./*Fig.* 29 // S./p. 71, 195) (Kat./*Cat.* 107 // S./p. 204) (Kat./*Cat.* 108 // S./p. 205) (Kat./*Cat.* 111 // S./p. 213) (Kat./*Cat.* 113 // S./p. 215) (Kat./*Cat.* 116 // S./p. 217, 246/247) (Kat./*Cat.* 117 // S./p. 217) (Kat./*Cat.* 118 // S./p. 218) (Kat./*Cat.* 119 // S./p. 219) (Kat./*Cat.* 120 // S./p. 224) (Kat./*Cat.* 121 // S./p. 225) (Kat./*Cat.* 124–125 // S./p. 228) (Kat./*Cat.* 126–127 // S./p. 229) (Kat./*Cat.* 128 // S./p. 231) (Kat./*Cat.* 130 // S./p. 237) (Kat./*Cat.* 132 // S./p. 243) (Kat./*Cat.* 133 // S./p. 245)

Kunsthalle Mannheim / Foto/*Photo:* Heiko Daniels (Kat./*Cat.* 83 // S./p. 174)

Kunsthalle Mannheim / Foto/*Photo:* Kathrin Schwab (Abb./*Fig.* 21 // S./p. 48) (Abb./*Fig.* 22 // S./p. 49) (Abb./*Fig.* 23–24 // S./p. 50) (Abb./*Fig.* 25 // S./p. 51) (Abb./*Fig.* 26–27 // S./p. 52) (Abb./*Fig.* 31 // S./p. 66 [Detail], 74) (Kat./*Cat.* 66 // S./p. 155) (Abb./*Fig.* 35–36 // S./p. 159) (Kat./*Cat.* 96–97 // S./p. 186) (Kat./*Cat.* 112 // S./p. 214) (Kat./*Cat.* 115 // S./p. 216) (Kat./*Cat.* 122 // S./p. 226) (Kat./*Cat.* 131 // S./p. 242)

Kunsthalle Mannheim, Foto/*Photo:* Kurt Schneyer (Abb./*Fig.* 17–19 // S./p. 43) (Abb./*Fig.* 28 // S./p. 54 [Detail])

Kunsthalle Mannheim / Foto/*Photo:* Margita Wickenhäuser (Kat./*Cat.* 80 // S./p. 172)

Kunstmuseum Basel, Martin P. Bühler (Kat./*Cat.* 106 // S./p. 199)

Nachlass Erich Heckel, Hemmenhofen (Abb./*Fig.* 2 // S./p. 16)

Public Domain: URL https://collections.lacma.org/node/205125 - *Gift of Richard Smooke, Michael Smooke, and Barry Smooke in honor of their parents, Marion and Nathan Smooke* (M.2003.90) (Abb./*Fig.* 12 // S./p. 28)

Rainer Diehl (Kat./*Cat.* 4–6 // S./p. 86) (Kat./*Cat.* 7 // S./p. 87) (Kat./*Cat.* 65 // S./p. 154)

Saint Louis Art Museum, Bequest of Curt Valentin, 185:1955 (Abb./*Fig.* 8 // S./p. 23)

SMK Photo/Jakob Skou-Hansen (Kat./*Cat.* 104 // S./p. 197)

E. L. Kirchner Archiv, Wichtrach/Bern (Abb./*Fig.* 11 // S./p. 27)

Aus:/*From:*
Karoline Hille: *Spuren der Moderne. Die Mannheimer Kunsthalle von 1918 bis 1933*, Kunst und Dokumentation 13, Städtische Kunsthalle Mannheim, (zgl. Diss. Freie Univ. Berlin), Berlin 1994, S. 34
Karoline Hille, *Spuren der Moderne: Die Mannheimer Kunsthalle von 1918 bis 1933*, Kunst und Dokumentation 13, Städtische Kunsthalle Mannheim (also PhD diss. Freie Univ. Berlin) (Berlin: Akademie, 1994), *p.* 34 (Abb./*Fig.* 3 // S./p. 18)

Kat. Ausst. *Für die Kunst! – Herbert Tannenbaum und sein Kunsthaus*, Reiss-Museum der Stadt Mannheim 1994, hrsg. von Karin von Welck, Mannheim 1994, S. 26
Für die Kunst! Herbert Tannenbaum und sein Kunsthaus, ed. Karin von Welck, exh. cat. Reiss-Museum der Stadt Mannheim 1994 (Mannheim: Vits & Kehrer, 1994), S. 26 (Abb./*Fig.* 13 // S./p. 31)

© VG Bild-Kunst, Bonn 2025, für die Werke von / *for the artworks by:*
Rudolf Belling
Nicolas Mathieu Eekman
Karl Hofer
Oskar Kokoschka
Gabriele Münter
Karl Schmidt-Rottluff
Die Geltendmachung der Ansprüche gem. § 60h UrhG für die Wiedergabe von Abbildungen der Exponate/Bestandswerke erfolgt durch die VG Bild-Kunst. / *The assertion of claims in accordance with § 60h UrhG for the reproduction of images of the exhibits/existing works is carried out by VG Bild-Kunst.*

© der Künstler*innen oder ihrer Nachlässe / *by the artists or their estates:*
Franz Emanuel Hecht © Rechte-Nachfolge/*Succession of rights*
Erich Heckel – © Nachlass Erich Heckel, Hemmenhofen
Ludwig Meidner – © Ludwig Meidner-Archiv, Jüdisches Museum der Stadt Frankfurt am Main
Moriz Melzer – © Renate Kneifel
Emil Nolde – © Nolde Stiftung Seebüll
Wilfried Otto © Rechte-Nachfolge/*Succession of rights*
Max Pechstein – 2025 © Pechstein Hamburg/Berlin
Hilde Schindler © Rechte-Nachfolge/*Succession of rights*
Josef Weisz © Rechte-Nachfolge/*Succession of rights*
Wladimir von Zabotin – © Sammlung Emma Zabotin

Wir danken allen Rechteinhaber*innen für die freundliche Genehmigung zum Abdruck. Dieser Nachweis wurde mit größter Sorgfalt erstellt. Sollten dennoch Namen, Referenzen oder Rechteinhaber*innen nicht genannt worden sein, so geschah dies ohne Absicht und wir bitten, sich gegebenenfalls mit dem Deutschen Kunstverlag oder der Kunsthalle Mannheim in Verbindung zu setzen. / *We thank all rights holders for their kind permission to reprint. This proof has been prepared with the greatest care. Should names, references or rights holders nevertheless not have been mentioned, this was done without intention and we kindly ask you to contact the Deutscher Kunstverlag or the Kunsthalle Mannheim if necessary.*

Diese Publikation erscheint anlässlich
der Ausstellung
Kirchner, Lehmbruck, Nolde.
Geschichten des Expressionismus in Mannheim
in der Kunsthalle Mannheim
vom 26. September 2025 bis 11. Januar 2026.

This catalogue is published on the occasion of
the exhibition
Kirchner, Lehmbruck, Nolde.
Stories of Expressionism in Mannheim
at the Kunsthalle Mannheim
from September 26, 2025 to January 11, 2026.

Herausgegeben von / *Edited by*
Luisa Heese und / *and* Johan Holten

Kunsthalle Mannheim
Friedrichsplatz 4
68165 Mannheim, Germany
T. +49(0)621 293-6423
www.kuma.art

AUSSTELLUNG / EXHIBITION
Kurator*innen / *Curators*
Ursula Drahoss, Luisa Heese, Johan Holten, Dorotea Lorenz

Sekretariat / *Management office*
Susanne Geffers

Leihverkehr / *Loans*
Selini Andres

Restaurierung / *Conservation support*
Petra Neff, Katrin Radermacher, Isabel Schulz,
Henrike Bierbrodt und / *and* Daniela Hedinger

Ausstellungstechnik / *Exhibition technology*
Filip Antonijevic, Lydia Kähny, David Maras und / *and*
Prisma Fine Art Services

Haustechnik, FM, Betriebsorganisation, IT, Sicherheit /
Building services, FM, organization, IT, security
Kevin Fröhlig, Reimund Haberstroh, Carsten Sattel,
Juan-Philipp Simo, Marcel Stefanski, Holger Vetter

Kaufmännische Leitung / *Director of administration*
Susanne Freising

Vergabe und Verträge / *Allocation and contracts*
Matthias Hummel

Finanzbuchhaltung und Controlling /
Finances and controlling
Nadine Bär, Arzu Esen, Eileen Nagler, Sylwia Obidowska

Fundraising
Theresa Krukies

Leitung Kommunikation und Vermittlung /
Head of communication and cultural education
Saskia Schallock

Kommunikation und Marketing, Presse und
Öffentlichkeitsarbeit /
Communication and marketing, press and public relations
Amber Holland-Cunz, Imke Koch, Nina Reinhardt,
Eva Wankelmuth (FSJ)

Kommunikationsdesign / *Communication design*
Miriam Pschorn

Bildrechte und Bibliothek / *Photo credits and library*
Claudia Dausch

Digitale Strategie und Sammlung Online /
Digital strategy and online collection
Heiko Daniels, Manuela Husemann

Kunstvermittlung / *Art education, visitor journey*
Hatice Korkmaz, Christiane Wichmann, Eva-Maria
Winter, Anna Quintus, Diellza Seferaj (FSJ)

Veranstaltungen, ProgrammPlus / *Events, ProgrammPlus*
Dörte Dennemann

KATALOG / CATALOGUE
Konzept und Redaktion / *Concept and editing*
Luisa Heese und / *and* Dorotea Lorenz

Projektmanagement Verlag / *Project management,*
publisher
Luzie Diekmann

Herstellungsmanagement Verlag /
Production management, publisher
Stefanie Kruszyk

Lektorat deutsch / *German copyediting*
Elke Thode

Übersetzung / *Translation*
Steven Lindberg

Lektorat englisch / *English copyediting*
Aaron Bogart

Gestaltung und Satz / *Design and typesetting*
Verena Gerlach

Druck und Bindung / *Printing and binding*
Gutenberg Beuys Feindruckerei GmbH

Verlag / Publisher
Deutscher Kunstverlag
Genthiner Straße 13
10785 Berlin
www.deutscherkunstverlag.de

Ein Verlag der Walter de Gruyter GmbH, Berlin/Boston
www.degruyterbrill.com

Fragen zur allgemeinen Produktsicherheit /
Questions on general product safety:
productsafety@degruyterbrill.com

Die Deutsche Nationalbibliothek verzeichnet diese
Publikation in der Deutschen Nationalbibliografie;
detaillierte bibliografische Daten sind im Internet über
http://dnb.dnb.de abrufbar. /
The German National Library lists this publication in the
German National Bibliography; detailed bibliographic
information is available on the Internet at http://dnb.d-nb.de.

Library of Congress Control Number:
2025944721

© 2025 Deutscher Kunstverlag
ISBN 978-3-422-80339-8

Die Ausstellung wird gefördert durch /
The exhibition is supported by

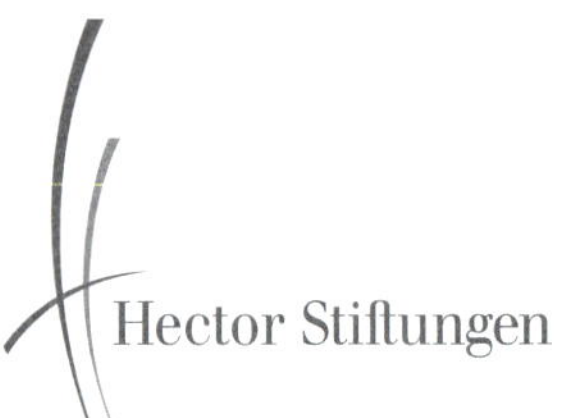

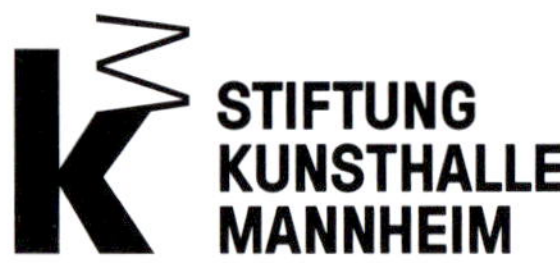

Ernst-Ludwig-Seibert-Stiftung

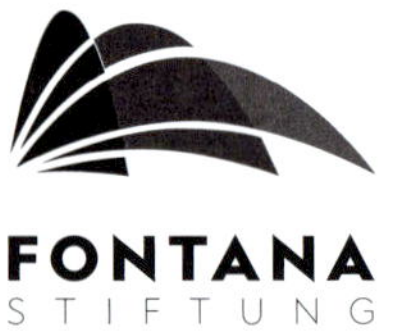

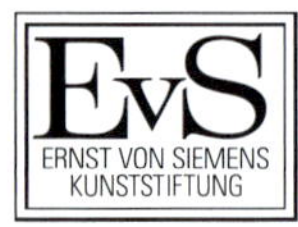

MANNHEIM[2]

franz dieter
und michaela kaldewei
kulturstiftung